W9-DFC-565

CAMBRIDGE TEXTS IN THE
HISTORY OF POLITICAL THOUGHT

HOBBES
Leviathan

CAMBRIDGE TEXTS IN THE HISTORY OF POLITICAL THOUGHT

Series editors
RAYMOND GEUSS
Lecturer in Philosophy, University of Cambridge

QUENTIN SKINNER
Regius Professor of Modern History in the University of Cambridge

Cambridge Texts in the History of Political Thought is now firmly established as the major student textbook series in political theory. It aims to make available to students all the most important texts in the history of western political thought, from ancient Greece to the early twentieth century. All the familiar classic texts will be included, but the series seeks at the same time to enlarge the conventional canon by incorporating an extensive range of less well-known works, many of them never before available in a modern English edition. Wherever possible, texts are published in complete and unabridged form, and translations are specially commissioned for the series. Each volume contains a critical introduction together with chronologies, biographical sketches, a guide to further reading and any necessary glossaries and textual apparatus. When completed the series will aim to offer an outline of the entire evolution of western political thought.

For a list of titles published in the series, please see end of book

THOMAS HOBBES

Leviathan

REVISED STUDENT EDITION

EDITED BY
RICHARD TUCK
Professor of Government, Harvard University

CAMBRIDGE
UNIVERSITY PRESS

PUBLISHED BY THE PRESS SYNDICATE OF THE UNIVERSITY OF CAMBRIDGE
The Pitt Building, Trumpington Street, Cambridge, United Kingdom

CAMBRIDGE UNIVERSITY PRESS
The Edinburgh Building, Cambridge CB2 2RU, UK
40 West 20th Street, New York, NY 10011–4211, USA
10 Stamford Road, Oakleigh, VIC 3166, Australia
Ruiz de Alarcón 13, 28014 Madrid, Spain
Dock House, The Waterfront, Cape Town 8001, South Africa

http://www.cambridge.org

© in the introduction and editorial matter
Cambridge University Press 1991, 1996

This book is in copyright. Subject to statutory exception
and to the provisions of relevant collective licensing agreements,
no reproduction of any part may take place without
the written permission of Cambridge University Press.

First published 1991 and reprinted several times
Revised student edition first published 1996
Reprinted 1997, 2000, 2001

Printed in the United Kingdom at the University Press, Cambridge

A catalogue record for this book is available from the British Library

Library of Congress Cataloguing in Publication data
Hobbes, Thomas, 1588–1679
Leviathan / edited by Richard Tuck. – Rev, student ed.
p. cm. – (Cambridge texts in the history of political
thought)
Includes bibliographical references (p.) and indexes.
ISBN 0 521 56099 3 (hardback). – ISBN 0 521 56797 1 (pbk.)
1. Political science – Early works to 1800. 2. State, The.
I. Tuck, Richard, 1949– . II. Title. III. Series.
JC153.H65 1996c
320.1–dc20 96–14525 CIP

First edition
ISBN 0 521 39492 9 hardback
ISBN 0 521 39641 7 paperback

This revised student edition
ISBN 0 521 56099 3 hardback
ISBN 0 521 56797 1 paperback

WV

Contents

Acknowledgements

As I explain in the note on the text, this edition is drawn from two sources: one is a special copy of *Leviathan* in the Cambridge University Library (where it is part of the Royal Library acquired from John Moore, the Bishop of Ely, and given to the University by George I in 1715), and the other is the manuscript of *Leviathan* in the British Library. I would like to thank the librarians in both institutions for their help and for giving permission to reproduce material in their charge; I owe a particular debt to Brian Jenkins, Under-Librarian in charge of the Rare Books Room at the University Library. I would also like to thank David McKitterick, Librarian of Trinity College, for help and advice about Moore's library; Peter Jones, Librarian of King's College, for letting me consult the college's remarkable collection of Hobbes's works (bequeathed to them by Lord Keynes) and for helping me in other ways; and Peter Day, Keeper of the Works of Art at Chatsworth, who helped to uncover the curious fact that there was apparently no copy of *Leviathan* at Hardwick or Chatsworth until the nineteenth century. Other scholars have given me a great deal of advice, especially Noel Malcolm, Quentin Skinner, Maurice Goldsmith, Ian Harris (see p. lxv) and Lucien Jaume.

vii

Introduction

I

Hobbes's *Leviathan* has always aroused strong feelings in its readers. Nowadays, it is generally reckoned to be the masterpiece of English political thought, and a work which more than any other defined the character of modern politics; from the late seventeenth century to the early twentieth century, all great writers on political theory have measured themselves against it. But when it first appeared in the bookshops of England, in late April or early May 1651,[1] it seemed to many of its readers to be deeply shocking and offensive, both in its unsentimental account of political power and in its extraordinarily heterodox vision of the role of religion in human society. Even people who had formerly admired Hobbes and his philosophical writings were affronted by the book; one of Hobbes's old acquaintances, the Anglican theologian Henry Hammond, described it later that same year as 'a farrago of Christian Atheism', a description which (as we shall see) was close to the mark.[2]

These old friends were particularly angered by the book because it seemed to them to be an act of treachery. They had known

[1] See the letter from Robert Payne to Gilbert Sheldon, 6 May 1651: 'I am advertised from Ox. that Mr Hobbes's book is printed and come thither: he calls it Leviathan. Much of his *de Cive* is translated into it: he seems to favour the present Government, and commends his book to be read in the Universities, despite all censures that may pass upon it. It is folio at 8s.6d. price, but I have not yet seen it.' [Anon], 'Illustrations of the State of the Church during the Great Rebellion', *The Theologian and Ecclesiastic* 6 (1848) p. 223.

[2] [Anon], 'Illustrations of the State of the Church during the Great Rebellion', *The Theologian and Ecclesiastic* 9 (1850) pp. 294–5.

Hobbes as an enthusiastic supporter of the royalist cause in the English Civil War between King and Parliament; indeed, he had been in exile at Paris since 1640 because of his adherence to that cause, and *Leviathan* was written in France. When the book appeared, however, it seemed to justify submission to the new republic introduced after the King's execution in January 1649, and the abandonment of the Church of England for which many of the royalists had fought. His friends' shock at this *volte face* coloured contemporary reactions to Hobbes, and has affected his reputation down to our own times; though they may have misinterpreted some of Hobbes's intentions in writing *Leviathan*.

The first task in assessing what those intentions were, and a basic question to raise about any text, is to ask when the book was written. Our first information about the composition of the work which later became *Leviathan* comes in a letter of May 1650. In it, one of these old royalist friends wrote to Hobbes with a request that he translate into English one of his earlier Latin works on politics, so that it could have an influence on the current English political scene. Hobbes apparently replied that 'he hath another trifle on hand, which is Politique in English, of which he hath finished thirty-seven chapters (intending about fifty in the whole,) which are translated into French by a learned Frenchman of good quality, as fast as he finishes them'. This 'trifle' was to be *Leviathan*, and when his friend learned what it contained he wrote 'again and again' to Hobbes pleading with him to moderate his views, though with no success.[3] *Leviathan* has forty-seven chapters rather than fifty, but Hobbes's programme of May 1650 was obviously fulfilled, though a French translation never appeared, and may not have been completed.

The fact that Hobbes wanted one tells us, incidentally, that he believed the book to be as relevant to the contemporary French political disturbances as to those of England. The years 1649–52 were the years when the 'Fronde', the confused uprising against the absolutist government of France, was at its height, and Paris itself had been seized by the rebels early in 1649: not only Englishmen needed instruction in the duties of subjects. We do not know how long Hobbes had taken to write the thirty-seven chapters which

---

[3] [Anon], 'Illustrations of the State of the Church during the Great Rebellion', *The Theologian and Ecclesiastic* 6 (1848) pp. 172–3.

he had finished by May 1650 (approximately 60% of the total work), but if he wrote them at the same speed as the last ten chapters he would have started to compose the book at the beginning of 1649 – interestingly, at the time at which King Charles I was being tried for his life.

It is true that there are a number of passages in *Leviathan* which speak of the Civil War as still in progress (notably one on p. 311), and that only right at the end (in a famous passage on the new ecclesiastical regime in England in the last chapter, and in the Review and Conclusion) does Hobbes talk as if there is a settled government in England once again. Since the Civil War is conventionally thought to have ended by 1649, it might be deduced that Hobbes must have written much of the book well before the execution. Similar passages in the Latin *Leviathan* of 1668 (see below), which are not always straightforward translations of the English text, have sometimes even been taken to imply that the Latin version is based on an earlier draft than the English version, though there is no good reason for thinking this.[4]

But we tend to forget that the execution of the King and the declaration of a republic in England were not seen by contemporaries as the end of the war, for there remained a strong army in Scotland which was opposed to the actions of the republicans in England. That army was conclusively defeated by Cromwell at Dunbar in September 1650, and the great historian of the Civil War Edward, Earl of Clarendon (himself a royalist) recorded that it was this victory which 'was looked upon, in all places, as the entire conquest of the whole kingdom'.[5] Though the royalists were still able to mount a resistance based in Scotland, which began in the spring of 1651 and ended ignominiously at the Battle of Worcester in September 1651, *Leviathan* was obviously completed in the political climate following Dunbar, when the war at last seemed to be over. It was at this time, in particular, that Hobbes penned the Review and Conclusion with its explicit call for submission to the

---

[4] For example, the Latin text at one point speaks of 'the war which is now being waged in England', whereas the English version has 'the late troubles' (p. 170). (*Leviathan*, trans. and ed. F. Tricaud (Paris 1971) pp. xxv–xxvi). But 'late' in seventeenth-century English does not necessarily mean 'now completed'; it can also mean 'recent'.

[5] Edward Hyde, Earl of Clarendon, *The History of the Rebellion and Civil Wars in England, . . . also his Life. . .* (Oxford 1843) p. 752.

new regime. The bulk of it had however been written during a time when the ultimate victor was not so clear, and when a Scottish army devoted to the King might still have enforced its wishes upon the two kingdoms. So when reading *Leviathan* we have to bear in mind Hobbes's uncertainty about the result of the civil wars in both England and France, and his hope that the arguments in the book might have some effect upon the outcome; in particular, we have to remember that Hobbes wrote it while still attending the court of the exiled King Charles II, and that he probably originally intended the King to be the dedicatee of the book (see the Note on the Text). It was in part a contribution to an argument among the exiles.[6]

II

The next question to ask is, what kind of life, both intellectual and practical, had Hobbes led by 1649?[7] He was already a thinker of some note, though less notoriety; indeed, many men of his time would have already ended their writing career at his age, for he was 61 in April 1649. He had survived a serious illness two years earlier which came close to killing him, but he had another thirty years to live – he died in December 1679. He had been born in Armada year, 1588, into a relatively poor family in Malmesbury (Wiltshire). His father was a low-grade clergyman (probably not even a university graduate) who became an alcoholic and then abandoned his family; Hobbes's education at the grammar school in Malmesbury and subsequently at a hall in Oxford (that is, a cheaper and less prestigious version of a college) was paid for by his uncle. Hobbes was clearly recognised as an extremely bright pupil, particularly at the central skill of the Renaissance curriculum, the study of languages. His facility at languages remained with him all his life, and he spent much time on the practice of translation: the first work published under his name (in 1629) was a translation of Thucydides, and one of the last (in 1674) was a translation of Homer. He

---

[6] While the first edition of the Cambridge *Leviathan* was in the press, Dr Glenn Burgess came independently to the same view, and has given a range of arguments in its favour. See his 'Contexts for the Writing and Publication of Hobbes's *Leviathan*', *History of Political Thought* 11 (1990) pp. 675–702.
[7] What follows is largely based on my *Hobbes* (Oxford 1989) and *Philosophy and Government 1572–1651* (Cambridge 1993).

was a fluent writer in Latin as well as English, and could also read Italian, French and Greek. These skills were allied to a sophistication of style, represented by his capacity to write poetry in two languages as well as elegant prose. As with all Renaissance writers, his education was first and foremost a *literary* one. Men with these skills were sought after in Renaissance Europe, for they could provide important assistance to anyone involved in public life. They could draft letters and speeches, reply to foreign correspondents, educate the older children of a household in the techniques of public life, and generally act rather like aides to modern Senators in the United States. This was indeed to be Hobbes's career throughout his life, for on graduating from Oxford in 1608 he was recommended to the post of secretary and tutor in the household of William Cavendish, soon to be the first Earl of Devonshire and one of the richest men in England. Thenceforward Hobbes (when in England) lived in the houses of the Earl, at Hardwick Hall in Derbyshire or Devonshire House in London, and he died at Hardwick still an honoured servant of the family, or 'domestic' as he once termed himself. He was not always employed directly by the Earls of Devonshire, for at various times there was no person in that family who was playing a part in public life; but at such times he would work for their neighbours in Derbyshire, and in particular for their cousins the Earls of Newcastle who lived at Welbeck. One of his duties was taking the heirs to the Earldoms on a Grand Tour of Europe, and between 1610 and 1640 he spent four years on the Continent. Because he was travelling with a young man of great social standing, he had access with his master to the most important political and intellectual figures of Europe, meeting (for example) the leaders of Venice in their struggle with the Papacy, Cardinals at Rome, senior figures in Geneva, and Galileo. His practical and personal knowledge of European politics was unrivalled by any English thinker of his generation (and arguably by only one on the Continent, the Dutchman Hugo Grotius).

Although careers of this kind (though not quite as international in character) would not have been uncommon anywhere in Western Europe since the beginnings of the Renaissance, the particular intellectual concerns which Hobbes seems to have had most at heart would have seemed unfamiliar to the men of the early Renaissance. In the eyes of the first humanists, the point of an education in the classics (particularly the Roman writers) was to equip a man for the kind of public service which their heroes such as Cicero had performed: the best way of life (they believed) was that of the active and engaged citizen, fighting for the liberty of his *respublica* or using his oratorical skills to persuade his fellow citizens to fight with him. 'Liberty' meant for them freedom both from external oppression by a foreign power, and from internal domination by a Caesar or any other figure who would reduce the republican citizens to mere subjects. Even Machiavelli, often associated by later ages with the techniques of princely domination, extolled these values in his *Discourses on the First Ten Books of Livy*, while *The Prince* itself does not completely eschew them; it contains, for example, notable pleas for the ruler to rely on the mass of the people, who will never let him down,[8] and to govern through a citizen army, the central institution of Renaissance republicanism.

But by the end of the sixteenth century, many European intellectuals had turned away from these values, though they retained a commitment to understanding their own time in terms of the ideas of antiquity, and a hostility to the kind of scholastic theories which had preceded the Rnenaissance. In place of Cicero, they read (and wrote like) Tacitus, the historian of the early Roman Empire; and in Tacitus' writings they found an account of politics as the domain of corruption and treachery, in which princes manipulated unstable and dangerous populations, and wise men either retreated from the public domain or were destroyed by it. Tacitus described in detail the techniques of manipulation which (he implied) all princes will use, and his Renaissance readers were equally fascinated by them; the study and analysis of these techniques gave rise to the remarkable literature of works on 'reason of state' which flooded the bookshops of Europe between 1590 and 1630. As the sixteenth century drew to its close, after decades of civil and religious war, and the corresponding construction of powerful monarchies to render the threat from civil war harmless, this political literature made extremely good sense of contemporary life.

Alongside this literature, and intersecting with it in various interesting ways, was another one, in which the themes of ancient Stoicism and Scepticism were explored in tandem. The advice of the

---

[8] See *The Prince*, ed. Quentin Skinner and Russell Price (Cambridge 1988) p. 37.

Stoic philosophers who were Tacitus' contemporaries had indeed been that the wise man should retreat from the forum and avoid emotionally committing himself to any principles which would lead him to hazard himself in the political struggle, and we find this advice reiterated by late sixteenth-century writers such as Justus Lipsius in the Netherlands and Michel de Montaigne in France, in the context (often) of an explicitly Tacitist account of politics. But it had seemed to many ancient authors who had debated these issues that mere emotional detachment was not enough: as the sceptics, the followers of Pyrrho and Carneades, urged, it was impossible to be fully detached if one continued to believe that the moral or political principles in question were *true*.[9] So the sceptics argued that the wise man would protect himself best by renouncing not just emotion, but also *belief*; reflection, particularly on the multiplicity of conflicting beliefs and practices to be found in the world, would quickly persuade him that his beliefs were indeed insufficiently founded. Since, in antiquity, ideas about the natural world were intimately bound up with ideas about human action and morality – for example, the Stoics believed that men were enmeshed in a world of deterministic physical causation, and could therefore not freely alter their situation – the sceptics also wanted to free the wise man from the burden of commitment to scientific theories. So they argued that all existing physical sciences were incoherent, and could not take account of such things as the prevalence of optical illusions; even pure mathematics were vitiated by (for example) the notorious difficulties involved in making sense of Euclid's fundamental definitions (a line without breadth, etc). Lipsius and Montaigne both sympathised with this extension of the original Stoic programme, and Montaigne in particular became famous for the richness and force of his sceptical arguments.[10]

Hobbes's duties in the Cavendish household included studying this new literature, and showing his pupils how to contribute to it. They were all particularly interested in the work of their contem-

---

[9] Pyrrho was the fourth-century BC founder of the Sceptical school; Carneades lived 150 years later, and developed the Sceptical tradition under the aegis of the 'New Academy' – whence his version of scepticism is conventionally termed 'Academic' as distinct from 'Pyrrhonian' Scepticism.

[10] For an account of this movement, see my *Philosophy and Government 1572–1651* (Cambridge 1993) pp. 31–64.

porary, an old friend of the Cavendish family, Sir Francis Bacon; in the 1650s it was still known that Hobbes highly regarded Bacon's works, and that he had even for a time acted as Bacon's amanuensis (he was probably loaned to Bacon by the Earl of Devonshire shortly before 1620).[11] Bacon was one of the first and most important figures in England to import this new kind of humanism: he wrote history in a Tacitist style himself, and also published the first volume of 'essays' to appear in English, modelled on the *essais* of Montaigne. But there was a degree of ambiguity in Bacon's approach, which in many ways remained a feature of Hobbes's outlook also. Bacon certainly believed that politics was in general an arena of princely manipulation, and that the sceptics were right to stress the inadequacy of conventional science; moreover, like the other philosophers in this *genre*, he believed in the necessity of psychological self-manipulation in order to fit oneself mentally for the modern world.[12] But he also still believed, like an early Renaissance man, that individual citizens ought to engage in public life, and that they should psychologically prepare themselves to do so. Moreover, Bacon argued (conspicuously against Montaigne) that the pursuit of the sciences was useful for active citizens, if the sciences could be properly put on a new foundation.

Hobbes was of course educating young men who were destined for political office, and he and his pupils seem to have found Bacon's blend of Tacitism and civic engagement rather appealing: together they wrote imitations of Bacon's essays and discourses, and Hobbes himself (it has recently been convincingly argued) composed his first long treatment of politics in the form of a discourse on the first four paragraphs of Tacitus' *Annals*, in which Tacitus gave a succinct account of the career of the Emperor Augustus.[13] It was

[11] For Hobbes's opinion of Bacon, see the letter to Hobbes from Du Verdus, August 1654, in Hobbes, *Correspondence* ed. Noel Malcolm (Oxford 1994) pp. 194, 196. For his association with Bacon, see *ibid.* pp. 628–9.

[12] See for example his long discussion of the appropriate techniques in his *The Advancement of Learning, Of the proficience and advancement of learning, divine and humane* (London 1605); *Works*, ed. James Spedding, Robert Leslie Ellis and Douglas Deron Heath V (London 1858) pp. 23–30.

[13] The technical statistical evidence for Hobbes's authorship of this discourse, together with a shorter piece, 'Of Lawes', and an interesting guide to contemporary Rome, is to be found in N.B. Reynolds and J.L. Hilton, 'Thomas Hobbes and Authorship of the *Horae Subsecivae*', *History of Political Thought* 14 (1993) pp. 361–80. The internal textual evidence, some of which I cite below, seems to me equally convincing, at least as far as the discourses on Tacitus and Rome go.

published together with some of his pupil's essays in an anonymous volume of 1620, by a publisher wanting to cash in on the craze for Baconian essays,[14] and it contains many themes familiar from *Leviathan*. These include the remark that a *'Popular state . . .* is to the Provinces not as one, but many tyrants'[15] (compare *Leviathan* p. 135) and the observation that all men are 'of this condition, that desire and hope of good more affecteth them than fruition: for this induceth satiety; but hope is a whetstone to mens desires, and will not suffer them to languish'[16] (*Leviathan* p. 46). It also reveals one of the roots of Hobbes's life-long concern with the idea of *liberty*; the first sentence of the *Annals* reads: 'In the beginning, kings ruled the city of Rome. Lucius Brutus founded freedom, and the consulate',[17] and it was often used in the Tacitist tradition as a peg upon which to hang a discussion of the true meaning of liberty. In his discourse, Hobbes remarked that Brutus had not really been justified in overthrowing the Roman monarchy, but that Tarquin's private crimes

> gave colour to his expulsion, & to the alteration of government. And this is by the author entitled, Liberty, not because bondage is always ioyned to Monarchy; but where Kings abuse their places, tyrannize over their Subiects [etc] . . . such usurpation over mens estates, and natures, many times breakes forth into attempts for liberty, and is hardly endured by mans nature, and passion, though reason and Religion teach us to beare the yoke. So that, it is not the government, but the abuse that makes the alteration be termed Liberty.[18]

Augustus, on the other hand, is praised throughout the discourse for his skill in manipulating his citizens, and in particular for con-

---

[14] The volume is entitled *Horae Subsecivae, Observations and Discourses* (London 1620). A full discussion of its complicated genesis is to be found in Noel Malcolm, 'Hobbes, Sandys and the Virginia Company', *Historical Journal* 24 (1981) pp. 297–321. The Hobbesian discourses are shortly to be published in a separate volume by Chicago University Press.

[15] *Horae Subsecivae* p. 269.

[16] *Ibid.* p. 291. Another example would be the fierce attack on ever buying-off political opponents – 'to heape benefits on the sullen, and averse, out of hope to win their affection, is unjust and prejudiciall' (*Horae Subsecivae* p. 266, compare *Leviathan* pp. 241–2).

[17] *Urbem Romam a principio reges habuere. Libertatem, & Consulatum L. Brutus instituit.*

[18] *Horae subsecivae* pp. 228–9. The term 'colour', incidentally, was a technical term of rhetoric much favoured by both Bacon and Hobbes.

cealing the true character of his rule.[19] And yet a certain nostalgia for the republic continually surfaces in the discourse, as it did in Tacitus himself: Hobbes agreed with contemporary Tacitists that free republics had to fall at the hands of manipulative princes, particularly (as he said p. 239) after a period of civil war, but he described the supercession of the old republican manners with some regret. The citizens

> now studie no more the Art of commanding, which had beene heretofore necessarie for any *Romane* Gentleman, when the rule of the whole might come to all of them in their turnes; but apply themselves wholly to the Arts of service, whereof *obsequiousnesse* is the chiefe, and is so long to bee accounted laudable, as it may bee distinguished from Flatterie, and profitable, whilest it turne not into tediousnesse.[20]

Hobbes followed up this discourse with the first work published under his name, a translation of the Greek historian Thucydides (1629), in which there is a somewhat similar ambivalence. Thucydides too depicted the fall of a republic, in terms remarkably similar to those Tacitus was to use, but at the same time put into the mouths of some of his characters a noble defence of republican and democratic values. Thucydides also argued that the true cause of the Peloponnesian war was the fear which the Spartans felt at the sheer growth in Athenian power; in a marginal note, Hobbes emphasised this point, something to which Bacon too had drawn attention while urging the English government to break its treaties and make war on Spain. The idea that fear in itself justified aggression was already a commonplace in the circles within which Hobbes moved.[21]

Eight years later Hobbes also published (anonymously) a radically altered version of Aristotle's *Rhetoric* in which the interest which

---

[19] E.g. 'it is not wisedome for one that is to convert a *free State* into a *Monarchy*, to take away all the shew of their libertie at one blowe, and on a suddaine make them feele servitude, without first introducing into their mindes some *previae dispositiones*, or preparatives whereby they may the better endure it' (p. 261).

[20] *Horae Subsecivae* p. 307.

[21] For his translation of Thucydides, see *Hobbes's Thucydides*, ed. Richard Schlatter (New Brunswick NJ 1975). The passage referred to is p. 42, and Hobbes's note is p. 577. Bacon's use of Thucydides is in *Considerations Touching a War with Spain* which he drafted for Prince Charles in 1624 as part of his campaign to reopen the war with Spain. *Works* ed. James Spedding *et al.*, XIV (London 1874) p. 474.

he had displayed already in the use of persuasion and rhetoric to gain power was given full rein. In particular, he advanced a startlingly simplified claim about the character of rhetoric. The ancient rhetoricians had usually supposed that there was no fundamental conflict between oratorical skill and the pursuit of truth, but Hobbes dismissed this: the principles of rhetoric

> are the *common Opinions* that men have concerning *Profitable*, and *UnProfitable*; *Just*, and *Unjust*; *Honourable*, and *Dishonourable* . . . For as in *Logick*, where certain and infallible knowledge is the scope of our proof, the *Principles* must be all *infallible Truths*: so in *Rhetorick* the *Principles* must be *common Opinions*, such as the Judge is already possessed with: because the end of *Rhetorick* is victory; which consists in having gotten *Belief*.[22]

The rhetorician, on Hobbes's account, employed some of the same techniques which the manipulative prince had used to secure victory over his people. The role of 'common Opinions' here is important: when Hobbes gave moral advice to his pupils, he was often concerned with making sure that their conduct fitted 'what the world calls' virtue.[23] As we shall see later, it remained characteristic of Hobbes's developed moral philosophy that he took as his starting-point a generally agreed description of some state of affairs.[24]

However, by the time he published his *A Briefe of the Art of Rhetorique* he had already begun to broaden his interests away from this humanist literature. In 1634 he had visited Paris with the son of the Earl of Devonshire, and had become aware of the critique of this kind of humanism which was being advanced particularly by writers connected with the French friar Marin Mersenne, including above all René Descartes. Under their influence he began to write philosophy proper for the first time, and he quickly produced the first of the great works which made his reputation. By 1641 he had drafted (in Latin) a long work entitled *The Elements of Philosophy* (*Elementa Philosophiae*), divided into three relatively freestanding

---

[22] *The English Works* VI, ed. W. Molesworth (London 1840) p. 426.
[23] See his remarkable letter to Charles Cavendish (August 1638) in *Correspondence*, ed. Malcolm pp. 52–53.
[24] For a perceptive account of the role of rhetoric, and hostility to the orator, in Hobbes's early work, see Quentin Skinner, "*Scientia civilis*' in Classical Rhetoric and in the Early Hobbes' in Nicholas Phillipson and Quentin Skinner, eds., *Political Discourse in Early Modern Britain* (Cambridge 1993) pp. 67–93.

'sections', of which the first was devoted to metaphysics and physics, the second was devoted to human action, sense perception and morality (understood as an account of human *mores* or manners and customs), and the last was devoted to politics.[25] It is an important fact about Hobbes that, having produced this draft very quickly, he spent almost twenty years fiddling with it, and that all through the period when he was writing *Leviathan* he was also rewriting and thinking about *The Elements of Philosophy*, which he believed to be his principal work.

He arranged for copies of the third section to be printed in 1642 at Paris, under the title *The Citizen* (*De Cive*), and distributed them among his friends, but he could not be persuaded to publish (in the proper sense) any of his philosophy until 1647, when the great Dutch firm of Elzevirs published a revised version of *De Cive* and Hobbes suddenly acquired a Europe-wide reputation. A version of the first section, entitled *Matter* (*De Corpore*), was finally sent to the printers in 1655, after Hobbes had returned to England, and the second section, *Man* (*De Homine*), in 1658. The three sections were finally published in their proper relationship and under their original title in 1668, as part of Hobbes's complete Latin works which appeared that year.[26] A Latin translation of *Leviathan* accompanied them, clear evidence that Hobbes continued to believe that *The Elements of Philosophy* and *Leviathan* were compatible and equally important accounts of his philosophy. At the same time as he was writing the first version of the Latin *Elements of Philosophy*, Hobbes also composed an English summary (and, one may conjecture, in some passages a translation) of the last two sections, which he called *Elements of Law, Natural and Politic*. He was circulating this extensively among his English friends by May 1640, and it remains the best short introduction to Hobbes's ideas, belonging as it does to the period when they were still newly minted.

III

Commentators on Hobbes have often argued among themselves about the relationship between his early humanist interests and his

---

[25] For the evidence for this claim, see my 'Hobbes and Descartes' in G.A.J. Rogers and Alan Ryan, eds., *Perspectives on Thomas Hobbes* (Oxford 1988) pp. 11–41, and *Correspondence*, ed. Malcolm pp. liii–lv.

[26] A proper edition of *The Elements* seems to have been projected in 1656; see Hobbes, *Correspondence*, ed. Malcolm p. 325.

later scientific and philosophical ones, and in particular over the question of whether the political ideas of *De Cive* and *Leviathan* are derived from his scientific theories; the position of *De Cive* in *The Elements of Philosophy*, after all, suggests that it was intended to be read as an extension of the theories presented in the first two sections. It was one of the great services of Leo Strauss to open up this question, and to urge that Hobbes's own account of the matter, in which his civil philosophy is consistently presented as growing out of his natural philosophy, may be misleading; Strauss believed that, in its essentials, Hobbes's political theory remained a humanist one, and was (if anything) distorted by its presentation in a deductive and scientific form.[27] But as I remarked earlier, a dichotomy of this kind between 'humanism' and 'science' is false: in the eyes of late sixteenth-century humanists, the status of the natural sciences was bound up with moral philosophy. The sceptics were hostile to the vain pursuit of scientific truths because they believed that they led people to epistemic and therefore moral commitments which would endanger them; while Bacon, on the other hand, welcomed at least a new kind of science precisely because it would enable people to lead a better life as active and effective citizens.

The same was true (though it is often overlooked) of Descartes; in his *Discourse on the Method* he carefully presented an image of himself as a typical humanist, 'brought up on letters' and leading an active and indeed military life, and he explained the point of his whole project in the following terms: 'I had always had an extreme desire to learn to distinguish true from false in order to see clearly into my own actions and proceed with confidence [*marcher avec assurance*] in this life'.[28] So it was a natural extension of all Hobbes's earlier concerns for him also to inquire into the foundations of the sciences, and it should not come as a surprise that the themes of his early humanism persisted into this new context. In particular, given Hobbes's earlier closeness to Bacon, it should not be surprising that he welcomed the possibility of what one might term a 'post-

---

[27] See Leo Strauss, *The Political Philosophy of Hobbes* (Oxford 1936). Strauss wanted to use *Horae Subsecivae* as evidence for Hobbes's early political beliefs, though he was deterred from doing so on learning that the essays were attributed to other authors; but we can now see that his instincts may have been right. There are some useful remarks on Strauss in J.W.N. Watkins, *Hobbes's System of Ideas* (London 1973) pp. 14–17.

[28] René Descartes, *The Philosophical Writings* I, trans. John Cottingham, Robert Stoothoff and Dugald Murdoch (Cambridge 1985) p. 115.

sceptical' science – that is, a natural science and a moral philosophy which in some fashion answered the sceptics' objections without denying the reasonableness of the sceptical arguments.

At the heart of the scientific project, for both Hobbes and Descartes, was the question of human sense perception. They both accepted the sceptics' argument that we can have no direct and truthful experience of the external world, and that all we can perceive is the internal activity of our own brain; this is the point of Chapter 1 of *Leviathan*, in which Hobbes makes (*inter alia*) the familiar sceptical points against the naïve realism of the Aristotelians. Descartes in a famous passage of his *Discourse on the Method* (June 1637; Hobbes was reading it already in October of that year)[29] had argued that this might imply that the external world did not exist, and that we might all be dreaming; this was the notorious 'hyperbolical doubt' which Descartes set himself to answer with his equally notorious *a priori* demonstration of God's existence, and the consequential claim that a benevolent God would not mislead his creation. Hobbes was clearly very impressed by the hyperbolical doubt, and a version of it appears in all the drafts of the *Elements of Philosophy*, in the form of a conjecture that the entire external universe may recently have been annihilated without us being conscious of its disappearance, since our inner mental life might simply continue as before.

In his early drafts, he apparently took the robust view that there is no entirely adequate criterion to distinguish between waking and dreaming, and that this does not matter, since in either case we can suppose that our mental life has been caused by some material forces outside us;[30] by the time he wrote *Leviathan*, he had modified this stance, and had come to believe that (as he says in Chapter 2) 'I am well satisfied, that being awake, I know I dreame not; though when I dreame, I think my selfe awake.' He had always given some rather low-level and imperfect reasons for distinguishing between dreams and waking thoughts, such as the greater incoherence of dreams, but the stress he now put on the capacity to distinguish between them was related to the prominence he gave in *Leviathan*

---

[29] *Ibid.* p. 109; Hobbes, *Correspondence*, ed. Malcolm p. 51.
[30] For a fuller account of why Hobbes thought this, see my 'Hobbes and Descartes' in G.A.J. Rogers and Alan Ryan, eds., *Perspectives on Thomas Hobbes* (Oxford 1988) pp. 11–41; his early view is represented by *Elements of Law* 1.3.8–10.

to the role of *ghosts* and other incorporeal beings in man's imaginative life, an issue which I deal with later. Hobbes had come to think by 1650 that a belief in ghosts was the consequence of a mistake about the status of dreams, and that to eliminate the belief required a clearer distinction between dreaming and waking than he had hitherto provided.[31]

But though Hobbes might be impressed by the hyperbolical doubt, he never sympathised with Descartes's answer to it. In all his works, Hobbes firmly denied the relevance of a conventional concept of a benevolent God to any philosophical enquiry. Reflection on the nature of the universe, he believed, would lead men to a concept of its creator – the being or event which started the mechanical processes which have persisted ever since. But no rational reflection could tell us anything about the *character* of this being. It was natural for human beings to honour and admire the power of whatever caused the universe, and that admiration could take the form of attributing to it desirable human properties such as benevolence; but we should understand that (as he put it in one of the best accounts of his religious beliefs) such attributions are more 'oblations' than 'propositions', that is, they are ways of honouring, comparable to prostrating oneself or making a sacrifice, but they do not have any genuine truth content.[32] God's benevolence could therefore not be used to solve any philosophical puzzle, and this determination to exclude a conventional notion of God from his philosophy persisted throughout all Hobbes's later works, including *Leviathan*.[33] The phenomenon of *religion*, however, remained of

---

[31] His critique of Thomas White (1643) already contains the claim that 'the ethnics' generated the idea of demons and other incorporeal substances out of their dreams, but adds cautiously that 'since it cannot be known by natural reason whether any substances are incorporeal, what has been revealed supernaturally by God must be true'. *Thomas White's* De Mundo *Examined*, trans. H.W. Jones (Bradford 1976) p. 54.

[32] This distinction comes from *Thomas White's* De Mundo *Examined* trans. Jones p. 434. The same work contains a remarkable application of this theory to the problem of evil: to describe God as all-powerful is to give him the highest honour, while to describe him as the author of evil would be to dishonour him. The two descriptions do not conflict, because neither is strictly speaking a proposition.

[33] For his explicit use of this point as an answer to Descartes, see his 'Objections to Descartes's *Meditations*', published along with Descartes's text in 1641, as the result of an invitation from Mersenne to contribute to the volume. Descartes, *The Philosophical Writings* II, trans. Cottingham, Stoothoff and Murdoch pp. 121–37 (see especially pp. 131–2).

major concern to him, and I shall discuss his views about it later.

Though Hobbes himself said in *Leviathan* that his own views about the relationship between perception and an external world were 'not very necessary to the businesse now in hand; and I have else-where written of the same at large' (p. 13),[34] he nevertheless still felt obliged to begin the work with a short summary of his theory. It is so short, unfortunately, that it has often misled readers. It is clear from his longer works on the foundation of the sciences that his distinctive theory was that our thoughts and mental life are constituted by *material* objects. Such things as mental images and other 'ideas', which for Descartes had been *immaterial* and which therefore had a problematic relationship to a possible material world, were for Hobbes simply part of that world. Since material objects cannot move themselves, our changing inner mental life must be the result of a chain of material causation stretching back an indefinite distance, and involving (we may presume) both internal bodily processes such as the circulation of the blood, and external events such as the impact of light on our eyes. We can, however, have confidence in the truth only of propositions which relate to the final perceptions, since we have direct acquaintance only with them; the rest of a natural science must remain hypothetical. There were two important implications of this for his moral and political theories.

The first was that the traditional notion of free will is absurd, since all intentions and actions must be caused by previous material processes. Hobbes wrote a great deal on this issue, and it is the subject of a striking passage in *Leviathan* (pp. 145–7); but it is important to understand what he meant by his denial of free will. He did not mean that we should not deliberate purposively about our actions and make choices, and, indeed, was particularly irritated when one of his opponents assumed this; as he responded, 'when it is determined, that one thing shall be chosen [by an agent] before another, it is determined also for what *cause* it shall so be chosen, which cause, for the most part, is *deliberation* or *consultation*, and therefore consultation is not in vain'.[35] Because, on this account, deliberation was not in vain, neither was deliberation about how to

---

[34] This last remark is an interesting indication that he was assuming that *The Elements of Philosophy* in some form would soon be available to his audience.

[35] See his remarks against Bramhall in *Of Liberty and Necessity* in *English Works* ed. Molesworth IV (1840) p. 255.

deliberate: Hobbes's moral philosophy presupposed the ability to perform complicated thinking about what kind of person we want to be and how we should live. We merely have to understand that this subjective sense of freedom to choose how to live is no more based on *real* freedom than our subjective sense of colour is based on *real* colour. Hobbes's confidence that deliberation and persuasion are *causally* efficacious was related to his long-standing humanist interest in rhetoric and political manipulation: the view of human agents in the Tacitean tradition was precisely that they were open to causal manipulation of a more or less reliable kind, and Hobbes's developed philosophy in this area (as in all the others) incorporated the insights of this tradition.

The second implication was that it was quite impossible to have a realist ethics. Again, it was a mistake to suppose that situations or agents outside our own minds had any moral qualities independently of our own judgement: descriptions such as 'good' or 'bad' were projections of our inner sensations onto an external world, just like 'red' or 'green'. As Hobbes said (p. 39), 'whatsoever is the object of any mans Appetite or Desire; that is it, which he for his part calleth *Good*: And the object of his Hate, and Aversion, *Evill*'. If human beings could be brought to recognise the inherently subjective character of these moral descriptions, there would of course be no disagreement among them about moral matters, any more than there is disagreement about avowedly subjective questions such as the taste of foods. Hobbes seems to have believed that a perspective on our moral language of this kind was possible for philosophers, and for all men when they had moments of quiet reflection;[36] but he also seems to have assumed that it could not be permanently maintained. Moral language, like colour language, constantly tempted its users to attribute to the external world a set of imaginary attributes, and as a consequence to dispute with one another about the world. Moreover, such disputation was not exclusively about what we would regard as 'moral' matters: men would equally dispute about questions of *interest* and *profit* (and, indeed, about matters ranging from the very definition of a man to quite trivial questions such as weights and measures).[37] The analysis

---

[36] See *De Cive* III.26.
[37] See in particular *Elements of Law* II.10.8, reproduced in (or based on) *De Cive* VI.9 and XVII.12.

of this conflict and an account of its resolution constitute Hobbes's mature civil philosophy.

It is important first to understand the point of philosophy, in Hobbes's eyes. Modern political philosophers have often assumed that their job is in some way to give a *rationale* of the actual political attitudes or practices of their society, and have treated Hobbes as an ally in this endeavour; his 'realistic' or 'pessimistic' assumptions about human nature apparently make him a plausible recruit. But Hobbes himself believed that the correct understanding and application of his philosophy would transform human life. From the beginning of his project he proclaimed the benefits which he was offering mankind: already in the *Elements of Law* he described his conclusions as 'of such nature, as, for want of them, government and peace have been nothing else to this day, but mutual fear' – a useful reminder of the fact that (contrary to many people's belief) Hobbes wished to *free* people from fear. He reiterated his hopes in *De Cive*: if moral philosophy could be as well founded as geometry, then

> I do not know what greater contribution human industry could have made to human happiness. For if the patterns of human action were known with the same certainty as the relations of magnitude in figures, then ambition and greed, whose power rests on the false opinions of the common people about right and wrong, would be disarmed, and the human race would enjoy such secure peace that (apart from conflicts over space as the population grew) it seems unlikely that it would ever have to fight again.
>
> (Epistle Dedicatory 6)

The same utopian ambition is manifest in *Leviathan* (e.g. p. 254), and indeed it is (as we shall see) even more extravagant there than in the earlier works.[38]

How, then, did Hobbes believe that philosophy could overcome the debilitating conflict which was hitherto inherent in human life, given the absence of any objective standards by which to measure what was right or wrong, or even what was beneficial or harmful to a human being? The first step was a recognition of the true

---

[38] It may be relevant to compare Hobbes's ambitions in this respect with the equally utopian ambitions of Bacon – who was, after all, the author of an avowedly utopian political work, the *New Atlantis*.

nature of the conflict, namely that it was indeed a conflict of *belief*. Again, it is tempting to suppose that Hobbes thought that the collisions of the state of nature were collisions between the differing interests of the people concerned, but, as he carefully explained in Chapter 6 of *Leviathan*, even the passions by which we appear to be moved have in most cases a vital *cognitive* component – so that, for example, *joy* arises from 'imagination of a mans own power and ability', while *grief* stems from 'opinion of want of power' (p. 42). The only desire which has no cognitive content is the fundamental desire to preserve oneself from death; all other passions and desires involve some belief about one's position in the world and the threats which one might be facing. If there were genuinely scarce resources of a basic kind, then there would be an irreducible conflict of interest; but Hobbes believed that in the world as presently constituted, there was no such shortage. The New World offered the prospect of a vast increase in production:

> The multitude of poor, and yet strong people still encreasing, they are to be transported into Countries not sufficiently habited: where neverthelesse, they are not to exterminate those they find there; but constrain them to inhabit closer together, and not range a great deal of ground, to snatch what they find; but to court each little Plot with art and labour, to give them their sustenance in due season. And when all the world is overcharged with Inhabitants, then the last remedy of all is Warre; which provideth for every man, by Victory, or Death.
>
> (p. 239)[39]

The wise man should therefore, on Hobbes's account, recognise that all conflict was at bottom a conflict of belief, and should also recognise that all beliefs which might be the material of conflict were inadequately founded.

To analyse this conflict and its resolution, Hobbes turned to what we should recognise as a rather surprising language, that of natural rights and natural laws. Neither the late humanism in which he grew up, nor the new philosophy of the Mersenne circle, was particularly sympathetic to this language, which was traditionally

---

[39] This is also the justification for the annexation of aboriginals' land provided by Locke: see J.H. Tully's 'Rediscovering America: The Two Treatises and Aboriginal Rights' in his *An Approach to Political Philosophy: Locke in Contexts* (Cambridge 1993) pp. 137–76.

associated with scholastic philosophy; and, indeed, many of Hobbes's central concerns continued to be discussed in France (by writers such as Pascal) without much use of these terms. But the language had recently been used by two authors to describe 'post-sceptical' moral theories. The more important of the two was the Dutchman Hugo Grotius, though Hobbes was probably also influenced by the other (who later became his friend), the Englishman John Selden. In his *De Iure Belli ac Pacis* of 1625, Grotius had argued (expressly against the sceptics) that a natural law theory was possible, provided it was based on a narrower set of moral principles than had been customary in the Aristotelian tradition. Grotius argued that the fundamental law of nature was the mutual recognition of the basic rights possessed by human beings, and in particular their rights to defend themselves against attack and to acquire the necessities of life. No society, argued Grotius, could ever be found or imagined which did not build into its laws and customs a respect for the right of self-preservation and a condemnation of wanton or unnecessary injury. Selden, in a couple of books written in the 1630s and partly directed at Grotius, agreed with the broad outlines of this theory, but argued that the implications of the right of self-preservation could be much more far-reaching than Grotius had assumed, and could (for example) include a very general right to make war on other people in pursuit of the agent's own goals.

Hobbes clearly recognised the compatibility between this kind of natural rights theory and his own moral philosophy, and he proceeded to interpret the fundamental conflicts of belief in terms of a 'state of nature' in which each individual made his own judgements about everything, including the desirable means to his own preservation, and in which he would be recognised by everyone else as having a 'right' to do so.[40] This mutual recognition of the right to self-preservation stemmed (on Hobbes's account) from each person understanding the salience in his own conduct of the desire for self-preservation, but it should be stressed that Hobbes's theory did not require us *always* to act on the basis of the principle of self-preservation. He was well aware that on occasion people could

---

[40] It is worth pointing out that the term 'state of nature' as used in this context seems to have been an invention of Hobbes – neither Grotius nor Selden use the term, though each of them clearly uses the concept.

sacrifice themselves for their parents, or for their religion.[41] But it would always seem *justifiable* to act on this basis: self-sacrifice could not be obligatory, and self-preservation was always understandable. Because anything might in principle appear necessary to the individual's preservation, this right in nature to use one's own judgement could also be viewed rather dramatically as a 'right to all things', though certain things (including pointless cruelty) were always seen by Hobbes as unlikely ever to be justifiable in terms of an agent's preservation.

A comparison between Grotius and Hobbes in this area is instructive. On the one hand, Hobbes accepted Grotius' argument that, in such a state, everyone would recognise that each individual was justified in preserving himself, so that there would be a basic agreement in the state of nature about the foundations of a moral theory; but on the other hand, he was quite unlike Grotius in observing that such a basic agreement was not enough in itself to generate a settled moral order, since there would still be radical disagreement about everything else, including most importantly the actual circumstances in which people might be justified in preserving themselves. As a consequence of this disagreement among people, the state of nature would inevitably be a state of war: I would defend myself against you in ways which you believe are unnecessary, since you believe that you are not in fact a danger to me, and so on. But it is important to stress that on Hobbes's account, if this secondary disagreement about the implementation of the right can be eliminated, then (just as in Grotius) there will be a secure basis for a moral consensus, since all men will accept the reasonableness of the proposition that each man has a fundamental right to preserve himself.

There has been much argument about whether Hobbes's state of nature was intended to be purely hypothetical, a kind of thought-experiment, or whether he supposed that it could be or had been a practical possibility. At different times in his works, Hobbes gave

---

[41] He is clearest about this in *De Cive*, where he observed (VI.13) that no man can be obliged by the sovereign 'to kill a parent, whether innocent or guilty and rightly condemned; since there are others who will do it, if ordered to do so, and a son may prefer to die rather than live in infamy and loathing', and where he urged Christians oppressed by their prince to 'go to Christ through Martyrdom' (XVIII.13).

examples of the state of nature: the regular ones were the international relations of states, and the condition of the aboriginal
peoples of North America and the primitive peoples of Europe. He
also added the example of Cain and Abel in the Latin *Leviathan*,
prompted (perhaps) by a discussion with a young French admirer
in the 1650s about just this issue. We do not have Hobbes's own
letters on the subject, but in 1657 the Frenchman acknowledged
receipt of a letter from Hobbes explaining what could count as
examples of the state of nature, and continued:

> I am very satisfied with your reply to my last queries ... The
> examples you give of soldiers who serve in different places and
> masons who work under different architects fail, in my view, to
> illustrate accurately enough the state of nature. For these are wars
> of each against each only successively and at different times;
> whereas the one I was discussing was at one and the same time.
>
> Having meditated a little on the subject, I found that, in my
> opinion, there is now and has always been a war of minds, so far
> as opinions and feelings are concerned, and that this war is exactly
> like the state of nature. For example: doesn't it often happen
> among the members of a single parliament that each man, having
> a different view and being convinced that he is right, obstinately
> maintains his view against each of his colleagues? So that there is
> a war of minds, waged by each against each. Similarly, in philos-
> ophy there are so many teachers of doctrines, and so many differ-
> ent sects. Each thinks he has found the truth, and imagines that
> each and every one of the others is wrong ...[42]

It is not clear precisely what Hobbes meant by the example of mer-
cenary soldiers or travelling masons, nor how he responded to the
extremely perceptive suggestions of his correspondent; but it is clear
that he envisaged the kind of conflict which constituted the state
of nature as something which could straightforwardly arise in practice, and which had frequently done so. Indeed, its heuristic power
was precisely that it represented a real threat, which civil society
was designed to pre-empt.

Men, on Hobbes's account, were to abandon the state of nature
by renouncing the right to all things – that is, in effect, renouncing
their own private right of judgement about what conduced to their

---

[42] Letter from François Peleau in Hobbes, *Correspondence*, ed. Malcolm p. 424. See
also Peleau's original query to Hobbes, *ibid.* p. 331.

preservation, except in such obvious and extreme cases that there could be no disagreement about the necessary means.[43] Hobbes's description of this process was that they were led to do so by their recognition of the force of the 'law' of nature, and the status of this law has proved to be perhaps the most puzzling aspect of Hobbes's whole theory. If it is true that there is radical disagreement about all moral matters, and no objective set of moral principles, how can men be persuaded to abandon their own moral and prudential judgement by reflection on an apparently objective law? During the middle years of this century, there was a popular theory (associated particularly with the name of Howard Warrender) which held that Hobbes's law of nature was indeed an objective principle which overrode the subjective disagreement represented by the right of nature, and which might best be understood (though Warrender was cautious on this point) as the law of God.[44] Such a view was particularly encouraged by the passage at the end of Chapter 15 of *Leviathan* in which Hobbes says that the laws of nature are but 'theorems', 'wheras Law, properly is the word of him, that by right hath command over others. But yet if we consider the same Theoremes, as delivered in the word of God, that by right commandeth all things; then are they properly called Lawes' (p. 111).

The easiest way to understand Hobbes's argument at this point is to go back to what I have argued is the non-juridical theory underlying his use of the language of rights and duties. The wise man will recognise the fragility of his own beliefs in any case where there is genuine disagreement with other people; he will also recognise that insisting on the truth of his beliefs in these situations will

---

[43] Hobbes's best discussion of this issue is in *De Cive* II.18, where he points out that nobody (not even a sovereign himself) will deny that someone who is under attack at the hands of the sovereign has the right to resist: 'a person bound by an agreement is normally trusted to perform (for trust is the only bond of agreements), but when people are being led out to punishment (whether capital or not), they are held in chains or escorted by guards; that is the clearest indication that they are not seen as sufficiently obligated by an agreement not to resist. . . Nor need the commonwealth itself require of anyone, as a condition of punishment, an agreement not to resist, but only that no one protect others.' See also *Leviathan* pp. 151–2 and 154.

[44] See Howard Warrender, *The Political Philosophy of Hobbes: His Theory of Obligation* (Oxford 1957), and, most helpfully, the articles by A.E. Taylor, S. Brown, J. Plamenatz and Warrender himself in *Hobbes Studies*, ed. K.C. Brown (Oxford 1965).

lead to conflict. The way to peace and tranquility therefore lies through the renunciation of those beliefs, just as the Renaissance sceptics (and, often, their Stoic allies) had taught. Our own profound commitment to self-preservation will teach us that using our own judgement about what conduces to preservation in debatable cases is self-defeating. This is only superficially paradoxical – it is analogous to Ulysses and the Sirens, or any of the other theories about how a higher-order set of wants prescribe the lower-order wants which one should try to induce oneself to have. If this is the structure which underpins Hobbes's juridical arguments, then there is no puzzle about the relationship between the right of nature and the law of nature: in our 'calmer moments' (as he said in *De Cive* III.26) we will see that we should deprive ourselves of the capacity to act on our independent and contentious judgement, as long as others do likewise, so that we can align our judgements with those of other men in order to form a civil society.

If this is right, then the force of the 'law' of nature does arise from considerations of self-interest, or at least from those of self-preservation. Why, then, does Hobbes describe it as a law, given that he has apparently earlier described self-preservation as a 'right', and (as he said), 'Law, and Right, differ as much, as Obligation, and Liberty; which in one and the same matter are inconsistent'? The answer to this question has two parts. The first is that, strictly speaking, Hobbes does not define the right of nature simply as a right to preserve oneself: in the words of *Leviathan*, it is 'the Liberty each man hath, *to use his own power, as he will himselfe*, for the preservation of his own Nature' (my italics).[45] In other words, it is the right to use one's own judgement about preservation which is in fact the right of nature, not the bare right of self-preservation. The right of nature rests on the recognition of the salience for everybody of their own survival, but like any right it is renounceable, and its renunciation is at the heart of Hobbes's theory. The second part is that, as the quotation about 'theorems' illustrates, Hobbes was indeed in two minds about describing the law of nature as a *law*; the 'word of God' in that quotation (as the

---

[45] Compare the formulations in his other works: 'It is therefore a *right of nature*: that every man may preserve his own life and limbs, with all the power he hath' (*Elements of Law* XIV.6); 'the first foundation of natural *Right* is that *each man protect his life and limbs as much as he can*' (*De Cive* I.7).

equivalent passage in *De Cive* III.33 amply illustrates) means Scripture, which does not of course have any power over natural men. His hesitation may well have stemmed from an awareness of the fact that (as we have seen) he elsewhere allowed that men were not *always* motivated by the desire for survival: the law of nature is indeed a 'theorem' which establishes the relationship between survival and the renunciation of the right of nature, but it does not affect people who have no desire to preserve themselves.

The way in which we renounce individual judgement, according to Hobbes, is that we enter into a *contractual* relationship with our fellow men and erect a sovereign whose judgements we will henceforward count as our own. It is fair to say that the contract in *Leviathan* has little independent moral force: we stick with our agreement to align our judgements because (as long as everyone else does so) there is no reason for us to defect from the arrangement. This has often puzzled readers of *Leviathan*, and Hobbes tried to answer their doubts (presumably, doubts originally expressed by readers of *De Cive*) in a notoriously baffling passage about 'the Foole' (pp. 101–2). Hobbes took the figure of 'the fool [who] hath said in his heart: There is no God' (*Psalm* 14.1) and depicted him as saying also that there is no justice,[46] and that if 'the kingdom of God' may be 'gotten by violence', it could not be wrong to seize it. (This startling image comes from Matthew's Gospel xi.12, 'from the days of John the Baptist until now the kingdom of heaven suffereth violence, and the violent take it by force', a passage whose interpretation is apparently still obscure.)

The important fact about this passage is that the fool is not concerned simply with increasing his own utility by (for example) burglary, but with vastly increasing his own power through the seizure of either an earthly or a heavenly kingdom. Hobbes, as we have seen, took the only generally accepted basis for rational conduct to be the securing of one's own preservation, and not any increase in personal utility, however slight (this is a vital difference between Hobbes and modern rational choice theorists, and renders any attempt to recast Hobbes's arguments into choice-theoretic terms highly misleading). So the only question Hobbes thought worth

---

[46] There may also be a reference here to a famous passage of ancient scepticism, in which Carneades argued that justice is foolishness.

asking was, suppose I could seize the sovereignty, would I not be better off in terms of my survival than if I remained an obedient citizen? And the answer he gave was then straightforward, which was that there is no benefit from being the sovereign rather than a citizen, and there is a greater risk of destruction if one embarks on treason rather than loyally obeying the laws. There is no advantage in being the sovereign rather than a citizen, because it does not matter (on Hobbes's theory) *who* makes the judgements about our preservation, as long as we all make the same judgements – I should not think that there is anything special about their being *my* judgements rather than someone else's, since all judgements (in contentious matters) are equally ill-founded.

IV

There is no doubt that the picture Hobbes drew of the relations between citizen and sovereign in civil society is a strange and disconcerting one. His ideal citizen would, like the wise man of much ancient philosophy, have become a man without belief and passion, accepting the laws of his sovereign as the only 'measure of Good and Evill actions' and treating them as 'the publique Conscience' which was entirely to supplant his own (p. 223). A natural response to this picture is to say (with Hume) that it is 'fitted only to promote tyranny', a response apparently confirmed by (for example) Hobbes's disdain for any distinction between the free republic of Lucca and the rule of the Sultan of Constantinople (p. 149). In *De Cive* he was even more blunt, declaring that to be a citizen is no more than to be a slave (*servus*) of the sovereign (Chapter VIII; see also *Leviathan* p. 142). This casualness about the difference between the free man and the slave is again reminiscent of a great deal of ancient philosophical writing about the life of wisdom, which (the Stoics for example argued) could be lived as well by a slave as by a master. But in Hobbes's case, it is not always clear that his theory points unequivocally in the direction of tyranny; it has often proved possible to read Hobbes as a surprisingly liberal author.[47]

---

[47] It is notable that many early nineteenth-century English liberals expressed great admiration for him – see for example the short essay on Hobbes in John Austin's *The Province of Jurisprudence Determined*, ed. H.L.A. Hart (London 1955) p. 276 n. 25 – p. 281.

The liberal interpretation of Hobbes begins from his theory of the sovereign as the *representative* of the citizens. Hobbes described the relationship in *Leviathan* as follows: the prospective citizens in the state of nature

> appoint one Man, or Assembly of men, to beare their Person; and every one to owne, and acknowledge himselfe to be Authour of whatsoever he that so beareth their Person, shall Act, or cause to be Acted, in those things, which concerne the Common Peace and Safetie; and therein to submit their Wills, every one to his Will, and their Judgements, to his Judgement. (p. 120)

In this passage, Hobbes deliberately used the language which was commonly used also by those theorists who wanted to limit the powers of sovereigns, or even introduce quasi-republican government. The idea that a sovereign 'bears the person' of the citizens was, for example, an allusion to a passage in Cicero's *De Officiis* (I.124) where Cicero, an enthusiast for the Roman republic and an opponent of Caesar, remarked that a magistrate should understand that he 'bears the person of the *civitas*' (a word Hobbes used in his Latin works as a synonym for 'commonwealth' in his English ones), and that the magistrate's office had been 'entrusted' to him (*ea fidei suae commissa*). The magistrates of the Roman republic had of course been elected by the people, and it was natural for republican theorists to describe the officials of a republic as 'representatives' or 'agents' of the people.

Moreover, in the *Elements of Law* and *De Cive*, Hobbes had gone to some lengths to depict the original sovereign created by the inhabitants of the state of nature as necessarily a democratic assembly, which could only transfer the rights of sovereignty to a single person or small group by a majority vote of its members: so Hobbes's theory was in its origins heavily involved with the forms of electoral politics.[48] (It is worth, again, comparing this with Grotius: Grotius too was famous among contemporaries for basing sovereignty upon a cession of power by individual citizens, but he never used the explicitly electoral model which Hobbes employed.) On the face of it, this is not true in *Leviathan*, and some scholars have made much of the difference; but it is not clear that the gulf

---

[48] See *Elements of Law* II.2.1–10; *De Cive* VII.5–16.

between the earlier works and *Leviathan* is as great as it might appear. Hobbes still presupposed that something like a majority vote among the inhabitants of the state of nature would be necessary to create any sovereign other than a democratic assembly.[49]

In a sense, in *Leviathan* Hobbes was working towards a theory rather like some later discussions of democracy and voting (for example, the theory in Rousseau – who was aware of some similarities between himself and Hobbes), in which he was trying to answer the puzzle about how someone can be said to be our 'representative', or how (in a direct democracy) we can be said to have 'consented' to the decision of our assembly, when we were outvoted and our apparent wishes were ignored. His answer, like Rousseau's and like most modern theorists', was that we have a prior and unanimous commitment to be bound by the result of the electoral process, and that it is this unanimity which renders legitimate the representative or the law in question.[50] In the absence of such a commitment, a people were (in Hobbes's terminology) merely a 'multitude', a disordered crowd with no legal personality. A theory of this kind was compatible with Hobbes's belief that individual citizens had few rights against their sovereign – as Hobbes was well aware, democracies can be extremely brutal towards their own citizens.

---

[49] See the beginning of Chapter 18: 'A *Common-wealth* is said to be *Instituted*, when a *Multitude* of men do Agree, and *Covenant*, *every one*, *with every one*, that to whatsoever *Man*, or *Assembly of Men*, shall be given by the major part, the *Right* to *Present* the Person of them all. (that is to say, to be their *Representative*;) every one, as well he that *Voted for it*, as he that *Voted against it*, shall *Authorise* all the Actions and Judgements, of that Man, or Assembly of men, in the same manner, as if they were his own. . .' (p. 121). Professor M.M. Goldsmith drew attention to this passage in his introduction to his edition of the *Elements of Law* (London 1969) p. xix, though he took it to be merely a relic of Hobbes's earlier position, and contrasted it with the passage from *Leviathan* p. 130 in which Hobbes said, 'It is manifest, that men who are in absolute liberty, may, if they please, give Authority to One man, to represent them every one; as well as give such Authority to any Assembly of men whatsoever; and consequently may subject themselves, if they think good, to a Monarch, as absolutely, as to any other Representative.' But there does not seem to me to be a significant divergence between these passages, since in the latter one Hobbes is not concerned to discuss the *actual mechanism* by which the men 'in absolute liberty . . . give Authority' to their chosen representative; majoritarianism may simply be implicit in this passage.

[50] The actual term 'representation' comes into Hobbes's works in the French translation of *De Cive*; what is new in *Leviathan* is simply the elaborate account of 'authorisation' which supplements the notion of representation.

Hobbes consistently endorsed another view which is fundamental to modern democratic politics, which is that it makes sense to say that sovereignty can lie with a people even when they do not directly exercise it. In all three of his works, he envisaged the possibility of a monarch elected for life but not empowered to nominate his successor, and observed that in this case, although the people had no practical part in government, '*sovereign power* (like *Ownership*) remained with the *people*; only its *use* or *exercise* was enjoyed by the time-limited *Monarch*, as a *usufuctuary*' (*De Cive* VII.16; see also *Leviathan* p. 136, *Elements of Law* II.2.9–10). During this period the people are, as he said, 'asleep'. The critical test which distinguished a regime of absolute monarchy from one of popular sovereignty was whether the electoral assembly of the people had reserved the right to meet on the monarch's death to determine a successor, and, correspondingly, whether the monarch had the legal right to appoint his own successor by will (*Leviathan* pp. 136–8, *De Cive* IX.11–19). This was an extremely hazardous test to use as the basis for a royalist theory, since the right of at least the King of England arbitrarily to define his own successor was far from clear. It had, for example, seriously been contemplated by Elizabeth's ministers that on the Queen's death a Parliament should gather to determine the succession, and possibly even decide to leave the throne temporarily vacant. Hobbes confidently asserted both that the King had such a right and (more plausibly) that no Parliament could meet without being summoned by the King, and that there was therefore no other candidate for the sovereign representative in England than the monarch;[51] but his fundamental theory was one which, later, radical democrats such as the Jacobins or the 'philosophic radicals' of early nineteenth-century England could easily turn to their own ends.

It should also be said that the representative character of the sovereign, strictly interpreted, entailed that the sovereign's powers

---

[51] It is, however, worth observing that in the *Elements of Law* Hobbes described the lower House of Parliament as 'a person civil . . . in the will whereof is included and involved the will of every one in particular' and which 'in this . . . sense . . . is all the commons, as long as they sit there with authority and right thereto'. The acceptance of the Commons as representative disappears from the later works, understandably enough. For Elizabeth's ministers, see Patrick Collinson, *Elizabethan Essays* (London 1994) pp. 31–57.

were not as far-reaching as might be thought. The sovereign's rights were purely those of any individual in the state of nature; and as we have seen, an individual on Hobbes's account had the right only to do those things which he sincerely believed conduced to his preservation (though virtually anything might turn out to qualify). Similarly, a sovereign in his capacity as their representative was strictly entitled only to enforce on his subjects those things which he believed necessary for their preservation. He might of course go beyond this limit, and subjects would have to accept his judgement; but he would in fact have had no natural right to do so, and he would be breaking the law of nature (as Hobbes made clear in his remarks on David and Uriah, p. 109). In such a situation the sovereign would act without right in ordering something on his subject, and the subject would act without right in resisting; while Hobbes was primarily concerned with the realm of rights and duties, his view of what might happen once that realm was left behind is contained in his melancholy observation at the end of Chapter 31 that the 'Negligent government of Princes' is punished with 'Rebellion; and Rebellion, with Slaughter' (p. 193). In addition, because a sovereign was the representative of his subjects, he had to take seriously the task of ensuring for them the necessities of life – Hobbes's sovereign had not only the right but also the duty to intervene in the economic system if its free workings threatened the survival of any of his citizens (pp. 128–9).

But in Hobbes's eyes the most important area of potential intervention by his sovereign was religion; it was the discussion of religion in the last two Parts of *Leviathan* which finally broke his links with his old royalist friends (though it must be observed that it may well have been welcomed by other royalists). This was where the argument of *Leviathan* differed most obviously from that of the *Elements of Law* or *De Cive*; in other areas, the differences can almost always be understood as an attempt by Hobbes to give greater clarity to his original ideas.[52] But on religion, he seems to

---

[52] David Johnston in *The Rhetoric of Leviathan* (Princeton 1986) and Quentin Skinner in '*Scientia civilis*' in Classical Rhetoric and in the Early Hobbes' (in Nicholas Phillipson and Quentin Skinner, eds., *Political Discourse in Early Modern Britain* (Cambridge 1993) pp. 67–93) have argued that another change between the earlier works and *Leviathan* was the greater value Hobbes now put on rhetoric: Skinner in particular has claimed that Hobbes 'in the sharpest volte face to be found at any point in the evolution of his civil philosophy' (p. 93) explicitly recanted 'his

have directly repudiated what he had argued in the earlier works, and in doing so he pushed *Leviathan* in a remarkably utopian direction. It is reasonable to say that it is Parts III and IV of *Leviathan* which constitute the prime purpose of the work.

In the *Elements of Law* and *De Cive*, Hobbes was careful to avoid a direct confrontation with the Anglican Church (among whose ministers he counted many friends). Whereas on most matters the sovereign had the right to determine his subjects' beliefs, both religion in general and Christianity in particular were special cases. These issues were explored most thoroughly in *De Cive*, where Hobbes argued that 'natural' religion is an inevitable feature of human psychology: it is a recognition of the existence of a first cause, and a feeling of awe and wonder at the power of such a cause to produce the universe (a close later parallel would be with Kant's sense of wonder at the starry heavens above). This natural religion does not straightforwardly result in conventional theism, as we know nothing of the nature of the first cause; but conventions in different societies about the expression of awe and wonder give rise to theological language, though such language is purely emotive in character and has no truth values. (A similar argument is found in Chapter 31 of *Leviathan*.) The sovereign is therefore the key figure in deciding how this awe should be expressed; all religion is thus in principle 'civil' religion, a claim contemporaries associated with Machiavelli, and deeply distrusted.

But in *De Cive* their distrust was forestalled by the special role which Hobbes accorded to Christianity. He argued there that if one had faith in the principles of Christianity (a faith which by its nature was not rational, philosophical or natural), then one would accept

earlier scepticism about the value of the rhetorical arts' in his remark in the Review and Conclusion that 'Reason, and Eloquence . . . may stand very well together'. I am not entirely persuaded by this: as we have seen, Hobbes was always aware of the power, and therefore the danger, of rhetoric, and there are still passages in *Leviathan* where he expresses anxiety about it. See for example his remarks about the Orators who are the 'Favourites of Soveraigne Assemblies' and have 'great power to hurt, [but] have little to save' (p. 132), and the similar remarks about the way orators fan the flames of men's passions in an assembly, p. 181. The salient difference between *Leviathan* and the earlier works in this area was that *Leviathan* was as much addressed to a ruler as to a citizen, and that (as Hobbes had observed more than thirty years before in his *Discourse upon the Beginnings of Tacitus*) an effective ruler might well use the techniques of rhetorical manipulation to govern his people.

the special character of the messages passed down from Christ himself through the apostolic succession of the priesthood. Even a sovereign (if Christian) must respect this, and 'interpret holy scripture . . . by means of duly ordained *Ecclesiastics*' (XVII.28). So in the vital area of religion, Hobbes's sovereign was obliged to endorse the orthodoxy of the apostolic church, and enforce its teachings upon his citizens; and there is nothing in the theology of Hobbes's early works which clearly contradicts this orthodoxy.[53] Though in each of them, for example, he described the soul as material (though of course not 'gross', i.e. not fully apprehendable by the senses), he was at pains to insist that it was nevertheless immortal.

In *Leviathan*, however, this qualification was tossed aside. Christianity was brought into line with the other religions of antiquity, and the sovereign could interpret Scripture or determine doctrine without paying any attention to ordained clergymen: this was the principal point of Part III, where Hobbes *inter alia* expressly denied any significance for the apostolic succession (pp. 297–300). Hobbes used Cardinal Bellarmine, the major spokesman of the papal theory of ecclesiastical power over temporal sovereigns, as his explicit target; but implicitly (as he signalled e.g. on pp. 341 and 388) his target was as much the claims by Presbyterians both in England and Scotland to a comparable power for their Church. (Bellarmine had been used as a stalking-horse for Presbyterians in a bitter controversy in both Holland and England a few years earlier, which Hobbes must have known about.)[54] Instead, the sovereign had to apply to the religion of his commonwealth the same set of considerations which governed his approach to its secular affairs.

Hobbes urged the sovereign to consider two things when promulgating doctrine. The first was the general question of social peace and the avoidance of sectarian conflict: and here he now argued that if a regime of toleration looked likely to do this job better than one of enforced uniformity, then the sovereign should implement such a regime. In a famous passage Hobbes eloquently welcomed the religious toleration brought about by the coming to power of the

---

[53] It should be noted, however, that in private even at this time Hobbes could be extremely critical of the political role which the clergy had played – see his letter to the Earl of Devonshire in July 1641, *Correspondence*, ed. Malcolm pp. 120–1.

[54] For this controversy, see David Nobbs, *Theocracy and Toleration: A Study of the Disputes in Dutch Calvinism from 1600 to 1650* (Cambridge 1938).

Independents in England (p. 385); this passage was, unsurprisingly, excised in the Latin *Leviathan*, but Hobbes continued to the end of his life to fight laws against heresy. The second thing he urged on the sovereign was, however, much more extraordinary, and most readers of *Leviathan* have shied away from its implications: it was that the sovereign should consider declaring the public doctrine of his country to be a radically reconstructed version of Christianity, based on a new interpretation of Scripture.

The salient feature of this new religion was its account of life after death. There were, it should also be said, some other remarkable features – for example, on pp. 338–41 Hobbes outlined the startling theory that the Trinity referred to the three great historical 'representations' or 'personations' of an unknown God – the first by Moses (God the Father), the second by Christ (God the Son) and the third by the Apostles (God the Holy Ghost).[55] He fended off some of the Unitarian implications of this theory by continuing to describe Christ as 'God and Man' (p. 340), but on the face of it he was moving well away from orthodox Trinitarian Christianity. However, it was Hobbes's account of heaven and hell which was most far-reaching, for he devoted prolonged exegetical labours to establishing the materiality of the soul, the terrestrial character of an afterlife, and the fact that there will be no eternal torments for the damned. In Hobbes's vision, faith in Christ (i.e. faith that he represented God) and obedience to the laws of nature were sufficient to guarantee one eternal life, while breach of faith or obedience condemned one to an eternal death (that is, a second death which was to follow the bodily resurrection of all men and their sentencing by God at the Day of Judgement) (pp. 315, 431–4).[56] He therefore urged the sovereign to teach the non-existence of Hell, and the minimal character of the acts necessary to gain admission to Heaven.

[55] It is worth asking whether it was this use of the notion of representation which attracted Hobbes's attention in the late 1640s, rather than its political possibilities.

[56] It should be noted that Hobbes on pp. 432–3 contemplated the possibility that after their resurrection the damned might live a normal life, produce children and then die (and though in the reprints of *Leviathan*, as I show in the Note on the Text, he or an editor cut out the starkest statement of this view, plenty of evidence for it remained). What seems to have mattered to Hobbes was establishing the proposition that the damned would suffer the normal human fate of mortality, and that he was willing to imagine that this mortality might follow other normal human activities.

Why does *Leviathan* suddenly take off into this fanciful direction? The costs to Hobbes were extremely high: he lost friends, money (for he had hoped for support from the exiled King, whose mathematical tutor he had briefly been in 1646–7) and a home (he was forced to return to England in 1652 as a result of the furore raised by the Anglicans in Paris over his book).[57] The theological speculations of *Leviathan* were not idle ones: there is a passion behind them which needs some explanation. Those historians who have asked themselves this question (notably J.G.A. Pocock) have on the whole replied that the theology of *Leviathan* was part of Hobbes's programme to ensure that the sovereign was the unquestioned moral and religious authority in the commonwealth. On this view, Hobbes was concerned to remove the possibility of a priesthood which could offer rewards or threaten punishments beyond the scope of a civil sovereign. But it is difficult to see in that case why Hobbes should have treated Heaven and Hell so differently: he did after all give the key of Heaven (effectively) to the sovereign, so why did he withhold from him the key of Hell? The claims of a priesthood to independent authority do not seem particularly relevant to this most salient feature of Hobbes's theology.

What Hobbes's theory *does* do, however, is *liberate men from unnecessary fear*. A great deal of Parts III and IV of *Leviathan*, and indeed almost the whole of Part IV, is devoted to establishing that we should not be frightened of entities such as ghosts or fairies, which do not exist, but which have filled men's imaginations down the ages. Hell is another of those entities: the idea of Hell has added a whole set of imaginary fears to men's lives, in addition to the natural and ineluctable fear of death. Hobbes's religion offered instead a new hope – of eternal life – and no new fear, for all that the damned were to suffer was what natural men would suffer

---

[57] Clarendon wrote to Nicholas on 27 January 1652, 'I had indeed some hand in the discountenancing my old friend Mr. Hobbes, nor was my Lord Lieutenant [the Marquis of Ormonde] at all slow in signifying the King's pleasure' (*Clarendon State Papers* III, ed. Thomas Monkhouse (Oxford 1786)) p. 45. *Mercurius Politicus* in January 1652 reported that Ormonde had refused to allow Hobbes to see the King when Hobbes turned up at court to receive (as he hoped) the King's thanks for a presentation copy of *Leviathan* – see below p. liii. See also Nicholas's letters to Clarendon, *Correspondence of Sir Edward Nicholas* I, ed. George F. Warner (Camden Society New Series XL 1886) pp. 284–6.

anyway. The religion could thus present itself as part of the grand Hobbesian enterprise of liberating men from terror, both of one another and of the unknown spiritual realm. At this point, the theory of *Leviathan* stands forth clearly as utopian, resembling very closely the utopias of the eighteenth or even the nineteenth century, in which a new religion was seen as a necessary part of reconstructing society.

If we take Hobbes's religion seriously in this way, we should at the same time remember that it was a proposal for a new *civil* religion – that is, Hobbes was suggesting that the sovereign should institute his religion because of its beneficial social and psychological effects, and because it was an extension of what the society already believed, and not because it was *true*. The accusation that Hobbes was an atheist, frequently made after 1660, centred on this point: for contemporaries not unreasonably supposed that if the sovereign could determine any religious dogmas, including those of Christianity itself, and if natural religion had so little of a personal God in it, then conventional theism itself had vanished from Hobbes's writings. Hammond's description of Hobbes's theology as 'Christian atheism' seems to me to be extremely acute.

On the face of it, the court of the exiled Prince of Wales at Paris in the late 1640s was an improbable place for speculations of this kind, which (if they resembled anything) looked most like the idiosyncratic theologies of some of the sectaries who were in the thick of the struggle against the Prince's father. But the royalists, both before their side's military defeat and after it, were always split over the question of the Church. Many of them (including particularly Hobbes's old friends such as Clarendon) fought for the King in order to preserve the Church of England; but others, especially the advisers round Queen Henrietta Maria, thought that the King should abandon his church in order to secure his political position (as the Queen's father, Henri IV of France, had done – 'Paris is worth a Mass'). If, as I suggested at the beginning, much of *Leviathan* was written while Hobbes was still in some sense a royalist (and some further evidence for this is given in the Note on the Text), its message was intelligible within this context; it would then resemble some of the royalist works produced at the end of the Civil War which called for a *rapprochement* between the King and the Independents, though it went much further and into much wilder territory than any of those works.[58] However, the last chapters and the Review and Conclusion illustrate that Hobbes had effectively abandoned both kinds of royalism by April 1651, perhaps because he recognised that it was among the victorious sectaries that he would now find more sympathetic readers. It might also be noted that the English Catholics in France who were natural supporters of the Queen included a number of people who were equally bold in their metaphysical speculations, and who constituted a group of Catholic sectaries not unlike the Protestant sectaries of their home country; at least one of them, Hobbes's old intellectual sparring-partner Thomas White, made the same choice as Hobbes in the 1650s and returned to England to live under the regime of the Independents.[59]

V

After he had published *Leviathan*, Hobbes learned very quickly that he would no longer be acceptable at an exiled court which had recently come under the sway of Clarendon again. He attempted to persuade Charles II of the merits of the book, but he was repudiated, largely at the instigation of Clarendon (see the discussion of the text, below). The ignominious failure of Charles's Scottish venture (which Henrietta Maria and her supporters had enthusiastically backed) left Hobbes with few influential friends at court. He returned to England in January or February 1652, and lived there for the rest of his life. He spent the 1650s working on his general philosophy, and in combat with Presbyterians or Anglicans who still hankered after a strong ecclesiastical discipline; but in the 1660s attempts to enforce religious orthodoxy upon the general population (in the shape of a series of Parliamentary Bills against Atheism and Heresy) led him to a flurry of work defending his ideas. He produced a series of manuscript treatises (including the well-known

---

[58] See e.g. Michael Hudson's *The Divine Right of Government* (London 1647), sigg. xiv ff for a discussion of toleration (though the book is very different from *Leviathan* in every other respect).

[59] For more details of this phenomenon, see my 'The Civil Religion of Thomas Hobbes' in Phillipson and Skinner, eds., *Political Discourse in Early Modern Britain* pp. 120–38.

Dialogue ... of the Common Laws of England) to substantiate his claim that there were no legal powers in England to act against heretical opinions, nor should there be; he also (as we have seen) translated *Leviathan* into Latin in 1668, with some interesting modifications and with an appendix rehearsing the same arguments about heresy.[60] Before the end of 1670 he wrote *Behemoth*, which is an interpretation of the Civil War as a struggle for ideological power over the English; the theme of heresy and its punishment was once again a marked feature of the book. His very last work on politics was a short essay dating from 1679 and dealing with the issue of Exclusion – the attempt by the Whigs (who included his patron's son) to have Charles II's brother excluded from the succession by an Act of Parliament. Hobbes, characteristically, gave ambiguous support to the Whigs, restating his fundamental constitutional principle that the sovereign could determine his own successor. His intellectual career thus covered almost the whole of the great seventeenth-century crisis; and *Leviathan* was the most considered and clear-headed response to that crisis produced by any observer. The states we inhabit were to a great extent formed by the conflicts of that period, and *Leviathan* is thus still one of the foundational texts of our politics.

---

[60] Tricaud's French translation of *Leviathan* (Paris 1971) is the only full study of the relationship between the Latin and English texts; he includes footnotes drawing attention to the salient differences, and translates the Latin appendix into French.

A note on the text[1]

I

The publishing history of *Leviathan* is extremely complicated, and its complexity is no doubt one reason why there has never been an accurate edition of the work. The first difficulty in establishing the text is that there are three separate editions all of which bear the imprint 'London, Printed for Andrew Crooke, at the Green Dragon in St. Pauls Church-yard, 1651'. (Crooke, incidentally, had been chosen as publisher by Hobbes because he had published Hobbes's last work to be printed in England, his *A Briefe of the Art of Rhetorique* of 1637.) These editions are differentiated by modern bibliographers on the basis of the different printers' ornaments which appear on their respective title-pages, and are thus known as the '*Head*', the '*Bear*' and the '*25 Ornaments*'. The *Bear* and the *25 Ornaments* appear to be effectively line-by-line reprints of the *Head*, though with a couple of interesting alterations; their later date is attested partly by the greater number of printers' errors corrected in them, but also by the fact that the spelling in each of them is significantly modernised – for example, such words as 'ecclesiasticall' in the *Head* frequently become 'ecclesiastical' in the *Bear* and *25 Ornaments*.

The famous engraved frontispiece is also much more worn in the *Bear* than the *Head*, and is actually partially re-engraved in the *25*

---

[1] I would particularly like to thank Professor M.M. Goldsmith for his comments on this section in the first edition. Partly as a result of his remarks, I have changed some of my views about the details of the printing of *Leviathan*.

Ornaments; it was this deterioration which led William Whewell to be the first modern scholar to observe (in 1842) that there were at least two editions bearing the same imprint.[2] Anthony Wood had however known in the late seventeenth century that there were two editions with the 1651 imprint, and that only one was authentic; he said (on what authority we do not know, but he was often accurate in these matters) that the other one had been printed at London in 1680. But it is clear that an attempt was made to produce an edition in London (apparently licensed by Crooke) in 1670, at a time when Hobbes was enjoying some (albeit surreptitious) government favour, and it may be that Wood was referring to this edition. Modern bibliographers have worked out from the ornaments that the *Bear* is likely to have been printed in Holland, so the London edition was presumably the *25 Ornaments*. The date of the *Bear* is unknown, but it is unlikely to be very distant from the *25 Ornaments*; it may also of course be that Wood was referring to the *Bear*, and was right about the date but wrong about the place of printing.[3]

The only substantial differences between the first (*Head*) edition and the two later ones occur in an area of Hobbes's theology: passages suggesting that after the Resurrection the wicked might lead a normal sexual life and propagate themselves eternally (p. 345) were eliminated. This brought the argument of the English *Leviathan* in this area closer to that of the Latin, which may imply that Hobbes had approved the change before his death; there is however no question of the *Bear* or *25 Ornaments* editions having been fully revised by Hobbes, for reasons which will appear below.

The principal modern editions (those of A.R. Waller in 1904, the Oxford University Press in 1909, Michael Oakeshott in 1946 and C.B. Macpherson in 1968) all based themselves, correctly, on the *Head* edition. So, it should be said, did John Campbell in his 1750 edition of Hobbes's English works, and Molesworth in his 1839 edition. It was also the *Head* (in the form of a copy in the British Library, B.L. 522.k.6) which was reproduced in facsimile by the Scolar Press in 1969. Waller in addition compared a copy of the *Head* systematically with a copy of one of the later editions, appar-

---

[2] William Whewell, *Lectures on the History of Moral Philosophy in England* (London 1842) p. 21.
[3] For all the details about these three editions, see H. Macdonald and M. Hargreaves, *Thomas Hobbes: A Bibliography* (London 1952) pp. 27–37.

ently the *25 Ornaments*. Unfortunately, the circumstances of the *Head*'s printing were such that one cannot simply reprint a conveniently available copy of the *Head* and assume that one has established a good text; to show this, I will briefly explain how the book was printed.[4]

Leviathan was printed in large sheets folded to make four pages of the final volume, in the customary manner of early modern printed books. Because early printers could not keep their small stocks of movable type set up in large numbers of sheets (or 'formes', as they were known), their procedure was necessarily to print all the copies of a sheet which they would need for the final edition, then break up the formes and set up new sheets in type, and so on until they had printed all the sheets of the entire edition. They might be able to keep half a dozen formes set up at any one time, but no more. Corrections could be made to the type at any point between its initial setting-up by the compositor, and the last sheet coming off the press; authorial corrections were generally made (if at all) quite late, after the in-house corrector had checked the type against the author's manuscript.

In the case of *Leviathan*, the printing house (or houses) faced an unusual problem. As we have already seen, Hobbes wrote the work in Paris, but he had it printed in London. Clarendon visited him in Paris in April 1651, and discovered that the book 'was then Printing in *England*, and that he receiv'd every week a Sheet to correct, of which he shewed me one or two Sheets'[5] – so Hobbes's English printers were sending proof sheets across to Paris for him to return with corrections. Hobbes had not yet sent the printer the dedicatory letter to Francis Godolphin, but it was common for dedications to be inserted at the end of the print run (and the dedication of *Leviathan* is printed in larger type than the rest of the work, implying that it was stretched to fit a space on the first sheet left by the printer).

There were two printing houses involved: the title-page of *Leviathan* records merely the publisher or bookseller's name, and

---

[4] For information about the printing of seventeenth-century books, see R.B. McKerrow, *An Introduction to Bibliography for Literary Students* (Oxford 1928) and P. Gaskell, *A New Introduction to Bibliography* (Oxford 1972).
[5] Edward Hyde, Earl of Clarendon, *A Brief View and Survey of . . . Leviathan* (Oxford 1676) p. 7.

Crooke usually employed other firms to print the works which he sold. It was common to use more than one firm to print large works, and Parts I and II of *Leviathan* were set up using a slightly different set of compositing conventions from those used in Parts III and IV (the gatherings of the former are signed on the first two leaves, and those of the latter on the first three). The decorations used in the two halves of the book are also different.[6] So Hobbes may have received a sheet from each firm every week. But even so, it was an extremely cumbersome and expensive way for a hand-printer to proceed: he would have all his type locked up in formes for the entire period during which the mails were taking the proof sheets to Paris and bringing them back, together with the period in which he was actually printing off copies (which could take several days). It would have been natural, therefore, if he had printed off quite a lot of copies before he received the author's corrections, and had incorporated those corrections only into a late stage of the print run; and there are indeed such striking variations between different surviving copies of the same sheet of text that this must have been the printer's practice.

In general, sheets were bound together to make the final volumes with little regard being paid to whether they were all equally corrected or not, so that we should speak not of correct copies of *Leviathan*, but only of correct sheets. However, our great good fortune is that there is one set of copies which we can be confident are fully corrected. *Leviathan*, it is clear, was intended to make a splash, and one sign of this is that it was accorded a privilege granted to major or expensive books, that of being issued in a large-paper edition (the normal page height of the book was 29–30 cm, but these special copies measured 35 cm, and were given hand-ruled red margin lines). A number of these large copies survive, and they all contain alterations to the text seldom or never found in standard-paper copies. It was usual, for obvious reasons, to print these special sheets at the end of the print-run of ordinary sheets, and we can therefore be reasonably confident that the text of a large-paper copy incorporates all the corrections which had been introduced on the press. Two further corrections came so late that the type for their sheets

---

[6] The two printing houses concerned are identified in the catalogue of the Carl H. Pforzheimer Library, *English Literature 1475–1700* (New York 1940) II p. 493 (I owe this reference to Quentin Skinner).

had already been broken up, and they had to be incorporated in the form of cancels – paper slips glued into place over the emended passages (pp. 88 and 108 of the original, 120 and 146 of this edition). The text of this edition is based primarily on a large-paper copy in the Cambridge University Library, *Syn*.3.65.1 (which I will refer to as *Syn*). All previous editions have been based on standard-paper copies, except (apparently) for the 1909 Oxford edition, though that failed to incorporate the cancels.[7]

I will give one example of how the large-paper copies can differ from standard-paper versions. On p. 108 of the original (p. 146 of this edition), where Hobbes was writing about the compatibility of liberty and necessity (and where he also had to have a cancel introduced – this page appears to have caused Hobbes a great deal of trouble), the manuscript refers to men's voluntary actions

> which, because they proceed from their will, proceeed from *liberty*; and yet, because every act of mans will, and every desire, and inclination proceeedeth from some cause, and that from another cause, which causes in a continuall chaine, (whose first link is in the hand of God the first of all causes) proceed from necessity.

It is clear that this passage is hard to understand: as it stands, the subject of the last verb 'proceed' is 'which causes', which leaves the sentence beginning 'because every act' without a final clause. In some standard-paper copies we find the manuscript reading simply reproduced; these copies include British Library c.175.n.3, and the copy in Toronto University Library (101397) which was the basis for Macpherson's edition. Campbell's 1750 edition also has this reading. In what was probably the first attempt to correct the passage, the sheets of some copies (including the one in B.L. 522.k.6) omit the words 'which causes', which makes the passage rather more

---

[7] Professor M.M. Goldsmith drew my attention to the fact that at least one large-paper copy does not include the cancels, despite including the most extensive corrections introduced to the sheets on the press (in particular the correction to the passage on p. 108, for which see below): this is a copy in the library of the University of Otago, also in New Zealand. It is interesting that the 1909 Oxford edition exhibits the same unusual combination of features – is this the copy from which it was made? The Otago copy lacks the ruled red lines, and was presumably not intended to be such a special presentation copy as *Syn*. Professor Goldsmith has also observed that some standard-paper copies include the cancels, though not all the corrections made on the press, including the copy in the library of his university, the Victoria University of Wellington, New Zealand.

grammatical, though still not easy to follow (the subject of 'proceed from necessity' is now men's actions, which also proceed from liberty). It is this text which was used by Molesworth, Waller and Oakeshott. In *Syn* the word 'they' is inserted before the word 'proceed', which makes full sense.

Most of the large-paper and some of the standard-paper copies also include the cancels, though their pasting-in may have been somewhat erratic; *Syn*, fortunately, contains them both. Only one is significant: on p. 88 of the original, Hobbes wrote (according to both the manuscript and *Syn*) that the sovereign 'hath the use of so much Power and Strength conferred on him, that by terror thereof, he is inabled to conforme the wills of them all, to Peace at home . . .'. In the copies as printed, 'performe' appears instead of 'conforme'. This obvious error was spotted by a corrector, and in the errata list which was inserted at the beginning of all copies, 'performe' was replaced by 'forme' – which just about makes sense, but is not as neat as the *Syn* reading. Later still, after the errata and the other preliminary material had been printed, Hobbes or the printer decided to run off a cancel which restored the proper reading. The Latin *Leviathan*, incidentally, also has *conformare*. The second cancel, on p. 108 of the original, merely corrects a peculiar piece of punctuation. None of these emendations are found in the *Bear* and the *25 Ornaments* versions, so it is clear, as I said, that they were not fully revised by Hobbes.

II

While *Syn* is the foundation for this edition, there is another text which had to be compared very closely with it, that of the manuscript. It has been publically known since 1813 that a manuscript copy of *Leviathan* exists, written out in scribal hands on vellum.[8] It had come into the possession of the great book-collector Lord Macartney (d. 1806), and was bought from his descendant by the British Museum in 1861. It is now British Library MS Egerton 1910. There seems no reason to doubt that it is the same copy mentioned by Clarendon in the preface to his *A Brief View and*

---

[8] See a note by William Henry Pratt in *The Gentleman's Magazine* 83 (1813) pp. 30–1.

Survey: Hobbes found 'when I return'd to the king [i.e. the exiled Charles II] to Paris, that I very much censur'd his Book, which he had presented, engross'd in Vellam in a marvellous fair hand, to the King' (p. 8). The MS lacks the dedication to Francis Godolphin, understandably enough if it was being presented to a King. It must have cost Hobbes a great deal of money to have it copied, suggesting that he hoped for great things from the King.

Though the MS has been known for so long, it has never been used as the basis of any edition, and has often been dismissed as identical to the printed copy; this is perhaps partly because, being written in poor-quality ink on vellum (which is non-absorbent), some of the text has been rubbed off and is now almost illegible. But though it is indeed substantially the same, there are many important minor variants; one dramatically transforms the sense of a major passage. Moreover its precise date and status have never been clarified. The one feature of the MS which has been studied is its frontispiece, which is a sketch for the later engraved frontispiece, with some interesting variations – in particular, the figures which comprise the person of the sovereign in the engraving, and which gaze up at the sovereign's head, are replaced in the sketch by faces looking out at the reader. Moreover the face of the sovereign may be a representation of Charles II. It is probable that the drawing is by Wenceslas Hollar, and that a revised version of it was sent to the engravers to be made into the plate which was used in the printed copy (though Hollar does not seem himself to have overseen the work of the engraver).[9]

In order to assess the status of the MS *vis-à-vis* the printed text, we need first to know when it was presented to Charles. We can give a plausible reply to this question, since in June 1650 Charles left Flanders (where he had been staying) for Scotland, and did not return to Paris until after the campaigning in Britain which culminated in the Battle of Worcester. He arrived in the city on 30 October 1651.[10] He was joined by Clarendon from Antwerp in mid-December, whose remarks in *A Brief View and Survey* quoted above seem to suggest that Hobbes had presented the King with the MS by then. By 11 January 1652 Hobbes had been banned from the

---

[9] See Keith Brown, 'The Artist of the *Leviathan* Title-page', *British Library Journal* 4 (1978) pp. 24–36.
[10] B.L. Add. MS 12186 f.303 (a despatch from Richard Browne).

royal court, largely as a result of Clarendon's reaction to *Leviathan*. Hobbes returned to England in February.[11] It was known already by 25 January in England that Hobbes had been banned: *Mercurius Politicus* for 8–15 January (Old Style, i.e. 18–25 on the Continent) reported that Hobbes 'sent one of his Books as a Present to the K. of *Scots*, which he accepted'. But the priests about the King then accused its author of atheism, and 'therefore when M. *Hobbs* came to make a tender of his service to him in person, he was rejected'.[12] It would seem therefore that Hobbes must have presented the MS to Charles in November or early December 1651.

However, internal evidence suggests that the text from which the scribal firm worked had been drafted by Hobbes at an earlier date than that of the copy from which Crooke and his printers in London worked. While the bulk of the MS is in scribal hands, there is also a significant number of emendations to the text in Hobbes's own hand. Some of these alterations correct the MS into readings identical to those of the printed text, but others correct it into new readings where it was already identical to the printed text. The clear implication is that Hobbes had already incorporated some of these emendations into the copy which he sent to Crooke, but that others occurred to him subsequently to correcting Crooke's sheets. Presumably he checked over the MS in November–December 1651, before sending it to Charles. One interesting alteration confirms that the MS dates from before the printed copy: on p. 315, the printed copy says, 'As for the distinction of Temporall, and Spirituall, let us consider . . .' The MS originally read, 'As for the distinction of Temporall, and Spirituall, I entend to examine it in another place, therefore passing it over for the present, let us consider . . .' Hobbes corrected it to read like the printed copy, presumably because the original reading was left over from an earlier draft when he had intended to discuss the distinction at a later point, something which he had abandoned by the time the copy was sent to the printers.

In a number of cases, the MS has readings which Hobbes allowed to stand, but which had been eliminated or altered in Crooke's copy; Hobbes had either forgotten that this was so, or now favoured them

---

[11] *Correspondence of Sir Edward Nicholas* I, ed. George F. Warren (Camden Society New Series XL 1886) pp. 284–6.
[12] *Mercurius Politicus* 84 (8–15 Jan. 1652) p. 1344.

once again in preference to the printed text. His checking of the MS was far from accurate, and a number of readings which he left are worse than readings in the printed text – for example, on p. 295 the printed copies say 'men that are once possessed of an opinion, that their obedience to the Sovereign Power, will bee more hurtfull to them, than their disobedience, will disobey the Laws ...' But the MS has '... they will disobey the Laws'. Here, the printed copy is clealy superior to the MS, as it is also in the passage about the compatibility of liberty and necessity quoted above. One group of passages which Hobbes eliminated from the printed copy but left in the MS has some historical interest, however: there are a couple of places (pp. 93, 122) where the MS refers in relatively uncomplimentary terms to the Independents, but the printed copies do not. The obvious implication is that Hobbes toned down the hostility displayed to both Presbyterians and Independents in the earlier part of the book in order to fit the support for Independency expressed in the later part, though in the King's MS he allowed the criticisms to stand.

If the scribal MS antedated Crooke's copy-text, it must belong to the autumn of 1650. Hobbes could not have sent copy to Crooke much after the beginning of 1651: it took about two days to compose one sheet of a book the size of *Leviathan*, so that even with (say) two compositors working simultaneously in each printers, it would have taken twenty-five working days to set up in type the fifty sheets of *Leviathan*. It also took a hand-printer about two days to print off all the copies of a sheet which he needed, so (with two printing houses each working two presses, a common number) it would have taken another twenty-five working days to print all the copies. The whole project could not reasonably have been concluded in less than ten weeks, and may have taken much more time. So Hobbes must have had his copy ready for Crooke by the end of 1650 (which incidentally confirms that the bulk of the work would have been written before the Battle of Dunbar in September 1650). The MS for Charles therefore dates from some time before that, though presumably still after Dunbar, as the MS too refers to the settled state of England in its last few pages – somewhat tactlessly in view of its proposed destination.

The relationship between the MS and the printed version, on this account, is almost identical to the relationship between the vellum manuscript of *De Cive* which Hobbes presented to the dedicatee of that work (the Earl of Devonshire) in 1641, and the subsequent printed edition.[13] It seems to have been Hobbes's habit at this stage of his life to have such lavish presentation manuscripts made independently of and prior to the printing of his works. We do not know for whom this dedicatory MS of *Leviathan* was intended initially; conceivably, Hobbes had always meant it for Charles, something suggested also by the passages at the ends of the Introduction and Part II which refer to a 'Soveraign' (p. 194) and 'he that is to govern a whole Nation' (p. 2). On this view, the dedication to Godolphin would be a late decision as well as a late composition, and might reflect Hobbes's scepticism that Charles would return from Britain; the presentation of the MS in November–December would then be an attempt on Hobbes's part to recover lost ground (which may account in part for his stony reception). The other view is that the MS was intended for Francis Godolphin and then switched to the King to gain favour. I myself favour the former theory, but there is now no hard evidence about Hobbes's intentions in the matter.

Given these facts about the MS, we can now assess what authority its readings enjoy over those of *Syn*. As I have said, in some cases Hobbes unequivocally signalled his choice of a new reading in his corrections to the MS; one of the most spectacular new readings in this edition is an example of this. The scribal MS and all the printed texts read on p. 128 of the original, p. 172 of this edition:

> For seeing the Soveraign, that is to say, the Common-wealth (whose Person he representeth,) is understood to do nothing but in order to the common Peace and Security, this Distribution of lands, is to be understood as done in order to the same: And consequently, whatsoever Distribution he shall make in prejudice thereof, is contrary to the will of every subject, that committed his Peace, and safety to his discretion, and conscience; and therefore by the will of every one of them, is to be reputed voyd.

But Hobbes corrected the MS by crossing out 'he' in the fifth line of this quotation, and substituting for it 'another' – thus radically altering, or perhaps clarifying, the sense of the whole passage. In cases such as this, we must obviously prefer Hobbes's emendations, and I have incorporated into my text Hobbes's alterations to the

[13] See *De Cive: The Latin Version*, ed. Howard Warrender (Oxford 1983) pp. 38–9.

MS, wherever the MS before alteration matched the printed copy. The altered passages will be found in the text between superscript numbers, and the original passages in the corresponding footnotes.

More difficult are the occasions where the printed copy is different from the MS, and Hobbes appears to have let the MS stand. As we have seen, in some instances the printed copy is clearly better, and in most cases the wording differs only slightly; there are only a few cases where the uncorrected MS has a reading obviously better than *Syn*. For these reasons, and because it was the printed copy which was read by contemporaries, I have preferred to follow *Syn*, and have not attempted to give a complete *variorum* edition of the text; that will be supplied by Noel Malcolm in his edition of *Leviathan* for the Oxford University Press's collected edition of Hobbes's works. The most important passages present in the MS but omitted in the printed copy will however be found in the footnotes (as will the few interesting alterations introduced into the fake first editions). For the same reasons, I have in general followed the spelling and punctuation of *Syn* rather than of the MS: they may to some extent be the product of the compositor rather than the author, but the same could no doubt be said of the scribes who worked on the MS. I have corrected obvious printers' errors, many of which are listed in the errata attached to the first edition or are confirmed as errors by the MS.

Equally, I have not given a detailed account of how the Latin *Leviathan* differs from the English. As I suggested in the introduction, the Latin *Leviathan* dates from a different period in Hobbes's life, with very different circumstances engaging his attention. Its basis appears to have been a large-paper copy, and not the MS. This is shown on the one hand by its use of *conformare* (above p. li), and on the other by a passage on p. 203 of the English text, where Hobbes referred (in both the printed and scribal copies) to '*Clement* the first (after St *Peter*) Bishop of *Rome*'. He crossed out the words in brackets when he revised the MS, but the Latin translation (p. 108) has '(post Petrum)'. Here too, Dr Malcolm's edition will give us a complete comparison of the texts.

Principal events in Hobbes's life

1588   *5 April*: born Malmesbury (Wilts.).
1602   Admitted to Magdalen Hall, Oxford.
1608   *February*: BA Oxford. Appointed tutor to William, the
       son of William Lord Cavendish, and joined his pupil in
       July at St John's College, Cambridge, incorporating as a
       BA.[1] Later that year settled with his pupil at the
       Cavendishes' houses, Hardwick Hall and Chatsworth in
       Derbyshire and Devonshire House in London.
1614   *Summer*: left England with his pupil to tour France and
       Italy. Probably met Paolo Sarpi in Venice.[2]
1615   *Summer*: returned to England.
1618   Lord Cavendish created first Earl of Devonshire.
1619   Hobbes in contact with Francis Bacon.[3] Between this year

---

[1] Hobbes, *Correspondence* ed. Noel Malcolm (Oxford 1994) p. 856.
[2] This differs from the chronology in the first edition, and from that usually found
in accounts of Hobbes's life. It is clear from the Hardwick account books that
Hobbes was in England 1611–14; he was given William's quarterly allowance in
February 1614. (I owe this fact to Quentin Skinner.) It is also clear that William
(and therefore Hobbes) was in Italy by September 1614, and that he had returned
by September 1615 (Noel Malcolm, 'Hobbes, Sandys and the Virginia Company',
Historical Journal 24 (1981) pp. 297–321; my *Philosophy and Government 1572–
1651* (Cambridge 1994) pp. 280–1). Traditionally, Hobbes is supposed to have left
for the trip in 1610; this date is based on the life of Hobbes by John Aubrey and
Richard Blackbourne (*Vitae Hobbianae Auctarium, Opera Latina* I, ed. Molesworth
(London 1839) p. xxiv), but that life, though quite authoritative, may have been
inaccurate on the details of Hobbes's early career. There is no suggestion either
in that life or in Hobbes's own autobiographical sketches (*Opera Latina* I pp. xiii–
xxi, .xxxi–xcix) that he made two visits to the Continent at this time.
[3] Hobbes, *Correspondence*, ed. Malcolm pp. 628–9.

and 1623 he acted as amanuensis to Bacon, on loan from the Cavendishes.

1620   Probably published a *Discourse upon the Beginnings of Tacitus* and a couple of other discourses, in a volume otherwise consisting of essays by William Cavendish, his former pupil, entitled *Horae Subsecivae*.[4]

1622   Became landowner in Virginia and associate of William Cavendish on the board of the Virginia Company, until its dissolution in 1624.

1626   *March*: first Earl of Devonshire died.

1628   *June*: second Earl of Devonshire died. Hobbes left service of Cavendishes.[5]

1629   Hobbes published translation of Thucydides, dedicated to third Earl of Devonshire (aged 11). He joined the household of Sir Gervase Clifton of Clifton (Notts.), and accompanied Clifton's son on a tour of France and Geneva.

1630   *Autumn*: returned to England and settled again with Cavendishes.[6] Probably began to associate with the Earl of Newcastle (cousin to the Earl of Devonshire) at Welbeck (Notts.).

1634   *Autumn*: took the Earl of Devonshire's son on a tour of France and Italy.

1635   Associated with Marin Mersenne, Gassendi and other French philosophers in Paris.

1636   *Spring*: visited Galileo in Florence.
         October: returned to England.

1637   Published *A Briefe of the Art of Rhetorique*.
         October: received Descartes's *Discourse on the Method* from Sir Kenelm Digby.

1640   *March*: suggestion that Hobbes should stand for Derby in the Short Parliament.
         May: finished manuscript of *Elements of Law* (published in two pirated parts in 1650, and completely in 1889).

---

[4] N.B. Reynolds and J.L. Hilton, 'Thomas Hobbes and Authorship of the *Horae Subsecivae*', *History of Political Thought* 14 (1993) pp. 361–80.

[5] Hobbes, *Correspondence*, ed. Malcolm p. 808.

[6] *Ibid.* p. 17; this seems to imply that he was 'home' earlier than Malcolm suggests at p. 808.

November: fled to Paris, anxious about being implicated in the Long Parliament's attack on Strafford.

1641 Contributed to the *Objections* to Descartes's *Meditations*.

1642 *March*: Civil War began in England.

April: Hobbes published *De Cive* at Paris.

1643 Drafted MS reply to Thomas White's *De Mundo* (published 1973).

1644 Contributed an essay on ballistics to Mersenne's *Ballistica*.

1646 Appointed reader in mathematics to the Prince of Wales in Paris. Controversy with John Bramhall over free will and determinism (published in 1654–5).

1647 *January*: published second edition of *De Cive*.

August: fell seriously ill.

1649 *January*: Charles I executed in London.

1651 *April*: Hobbes published *Leviathan*.

December: excluded from Charles's court.

1652 *February*: returned to England.

1655 Published *De Corpore*.

1658 Published *De Homine*.

1660 *May*: Charles II restored; Clarendon one of his chief ministers.

1666 *October*: Bill introduced into the House of Commons which would have rendered Hobbes liable to prosecution for atheism or heresy. Hobbes drafted MS *Dialogue . . . of the Common Laws* (published 1681).

1668 Drafted other MSS on heresy; published *Opera* at Amsterdam, including a Latin translation of *Leviathan*. Clarendon fell, to be replaced by the 'Cabal' Ministry, in which Hobbes found supporters.

1670 Composed MS of *Behemoth* (published in 1679).

1674 Cabal Ministry fell.

1675 Hobbes left London for the last time and settled finally at Hardwick and Chatsworth.

1679 Drafted a MS on the Exclusion Crisis for the third Earl's son, supporting the moderate Whig position.

3 December: died at Hardwick and was buried at Ault Hucknall.

Further reading

Other works by Hobbes

Oxford University Press is producing a modern edition of Hobbes's collected works, but so far only two works have appeared. The first was *De Cive* (1983), edited by Howard Warrender. (*The Latin Version* and *The English Version* are in separate volumes; but the English version is not (despite Warrender) in fact a translation by Hobbes himself, but by some rather inaccurate contemporary of his. A new and accurate translation by Michael Silverthorne will shortly appear in the Cambridge Texts in the History of Political Thought.) The second was an exemplary edition of Hobbes's *Correspondence*, edited by Noel Malcolm (1994). The standard collected edition is therefore still *The English Works of Thomas Hobbes*, edited by Sir William Molesworth (11 vols., London 1839–45), and *Thomae Hobbes . . . Opera Philosophica Quae Latina Scripsit Omnia*, also edited by Molesworth (5 vols., London 1839–45). There are useful editions of some other works: in particular, *The Elements of Law Natural and Politic*, edited by Ferdinand Toennies (London 1889), reprinted with new introductions by M.M. Goldsmith (London 1969) and J.C.A. Gaskin (Oxford 1994); *Thomas White's De Mundo Examined*, translated by H.W. Jones (Bradford 1976) – this is a translation of the Latin Text contained in *Critique du De Mundo* edited by Jean Jacquot and H.W. Jones (Paris 1973); *Behemoth*, edited by Ferdinand Toennies (London 1889), reprinted with new introductions by M.M. Goldsmith (London 1969) and Stephen Holmes (Chicago 1990); and *A Dialogue Between a Philosopher and a Student of the*

Common Law of England, edited by Joseph Cropsey (Chicago 1971). Part of *De Homine* is translated in *Man and Citizen*, edited by Bernard Gert (Humanities Press 1972).

Hobbes's biography

The most entertaining (and often the most perceptive) life of Hobbes is John Aubrey's in *Brief Lives*, of which there are many editions. Fuller accounts are in G.C. Robertson, *Hobbes* (London 1886) and my own *Hobbes* (Oxford 1989). A. Rogow, *Thomas Hobbes* (New York 1986) has a lot of information, but it must be used with caution. The biographical notes about Hobbes's correspondents appended to Malcolm's edition of the *Correspondence* constitute in effect the scaffolding for a biography, and are full of new and interesting information. Useful articles about Hobbes's life include J. Jacquot, 'Sir Charles Cavendish and his Learned Friends', *Annals of Science* 8 (1952); J.J. Hamilton, 'Hobbes's Study and the Hardwick Library', *Journal of the History of Philosophy* 16 (1978); N. Malcolm, 'Hobbes, Sandys and the Virginia Company', *Historical Journal* 24 (1981); Q.R.D. Skinner, 'Thomas Hobbes and his Disciples in France and England', *Comparative Studies in Society and History* 8 (1966) and Q.R.D. Skinner, 'Thomas Hobbes and the Nature of the Early Royal Society', *Historical Journal* 12 (1969); and my 'Hobbes and Descartes' in G.A.J. Rogers and Alan Ryan, eds., *Perspectives on Thomas Hobbes* (Oxford 1988) pp. 11–41. M.M. Goldsmith, 'Picturing Hobbes's Politics?', *Journal of the Warburg and Courtauld Institutes* 44 (1981) and Keith Brown, 'The Artist of the *Leviathan* Title-Page', *British Library Journal* 4 (1978), discuss the iconography of Hobbes's books. Important letters connected with Hobbes (of particular relevance to *Leviathan*) are to be found in [Anon], 'Illustrations of the State of the Church During the Great Rebellion', *The Theologian and Ecclesiastic* 6 (1848).

Introductions to Hobbes's ideas

The best general introductions are probably Richard Peters, *Hobbes* (Harmondsworth 1956); J.W.N. Watkins, *Hobbes's System of Ideas* (2nd edition, London 1973); Tom Sorell, *Hobbes* (London 1986); and my own *Hobbes* (Oxford 1989). Four useful collections of essays on various aspects of Hobbes's thought are K.C. Brown, ed., *Hobbes Studies* (Oxford 1965); M. Cranston and R. Peters, eds., *Hobbes and Rousseau: A Collection of Critical Essays* (New York 1972); G.A.J. Rogers and Alan Ryan, eds., *Perspectives on Thomas Hobbes* (Oxford 1988); and Tom Sorell, ed., *The Cambridge Companion to Hobbes* (Cambridge 1995).

Hobbes's scientific ideas

The principal works on Hobbes's science are F. Brandt, *Thomas Hobbes's Mechanical Conception of Nature* (Copenhagen 1928) and A. Pacchi, *Convenzione e ipotesi nella formazione della filosofia naturale di Thomas Hobbes* (Florence 1965). S. Shapin and S. Schaffer have discussed Hobbes's disputes with Boyle and Wallis in *Leviathan and the Air-Pump* (Princeton 1985), and A.E. Shapiro has given a careful account of Hobbes's optics in 'Kinematic Optics: A Study of the Wave Theory of Light in the Seventeenth Century', *Archive for the History of the Exact Sciences* 11 (1973). Terence Ball's 'Hobbes' Linguistic Turn', *Polity* 17 (1985), is a perceptive discussion of Hobbes's ideas on language, and Noel Malcolm's 'Hobbes and the Royal Society' in Rogers and Ryan (above) is the latest account of a notoriously vexed issue.

Hobbes's ethical and political ideas

The most distinctive and contentious modern accounts of Hobbes's ideas are those of C.B. Macpherson, in his edition of *Leviathan*, his essay 'Hobbes's Bourgeois Man' reprinted in Brown, *Hobbes Studies*, and his *The Political Theory of Possessive Individualism: Hobbes to Locke* (Oxford 1962); Leo Strauss, in his chapter on Hobbes in *Natural Right and History* (Chicago 1953), also reprinted in *Hobbes Studies*, and his earlier book on Hobbes, *The Political Philosophy of Hobbes: Its Basis and Genesis* (Oxford 1936); Michael Oakeshott, in *Hobbes on Civil Association* (Oxford 1975) – a collection of his earlier essays on Hobbes, including his famous introduction to *Leviathan*; and Howard Warrender in *The Political Philosophy of Hobbes: His Theory of Obligation* (Oxford 1957). Warrender also published a useful summary of his views in Brown's *Hobbes Studies*. The controversy about Warrender is best studied in that collection, with the addition of Thomas Nagel, 'Hobbes's Concept of Obligation', *Philosophical Review* 68 (1959) and Q.R.D. Skinner, 'Hobbes's *Leviathan*', *Historical Journal* 7 (1964).

More recent general accounts of Hobbes's ideas include M.M. Goldsmith, *Hobbes's Science of Politics* (New York 1966); D.D. Raphael, *Hobbes: Morals and Politics* (London 1977); Miriam M. Reik, *The Golden Lands of Thomas Hobbes* (Detroit 1977); Johann P. Sommerville, *Thomas Hobbes: Political Ideas in Historical Context* (London 1992); and Richard E. Flathman, *Thomas Hobbes: Skepticism, Individuality and Chastened Politics* (Newbury Park/London 1993).

Works which deal principally with Hobbes's ethical ideas include R.E. Ewin, *Virtues and Rights: The Moral Philosophy of Thomas Hobbes* (Boulder/Oxford 1991); S.A. Lloyd, *Ideals as Interests in Hobbes's Leviathan: The Power of Mind over Matter* (Cambridge 1992); and my own 'Hobbes's Moral Philosophy' in Sorell, ed., *The Cambridge Companion to Hobbes*.

There are a few distinguished works which consider Hobbes's theory in the light of modern accounts of rational self-interest; they include David Gauthier, *The Logic of Leviathan* (Oxford 1969); Jean Hampton, *Hobbes and the Social Contract Tradition* (Cambridge 1986); and Gregory S. Kavka, *Hobbesian Moral and Political Theory* (Princeton 1986).

Hobbes's account of the state and the concrete realities of government are dealt with in Deborah Baumgold, *Hobbes's Political Thought* (Cambridge 1988); Lucien Jaume, *Hobbes et l'état représentatif moderne* (Paris 1986); and Quentin Skinner, 'The State' in Terence Ball, James Farr and Russell L. Hanson, eds., *Political Innovation and Conceptual Change* (Cambridge 1989).

The connexion between Hobbes's ethical and political ideas and his view of rhetoric has attracted much recent attention. Good accounts are to be found in David Johnston, *The Rhetoric of Leviathan: Thomas Hobbes and the Politics of Cultural Transformation* (Princeton 1986); Tom Sorell, 'Hobbes's Persuasive Civil Science', *The Philosophical Quarterly* 40 (1990) and 'Hobbes's UnAristotelian Political Rhetoric', *Philosophy and Rhetoric* 23 (1990); Raia Prokhovnik, *Rhetoric and Philosophy in Hobbes's Leviathan* (New York 1991); and Quentin Skinner, "*Scientia civilis*' in Classical Rhetoric and in the Early Hobbes' in Nicholas Phillipson and Quentin Skinner, eds., *Political Discourse in Early Modern Britain* (Cambridge 1993).

Other useful articles on aspects of Hobbes's thought include R. Ashcraft, 'Hobbes's Natural Man', *Journal of Politics* 33 (1971); two related articles by Quentin Skinner, 'The Ideological Context of Hobbes's Political Thought', *Historical Journal* 9 (1966) and 'Conquest and Consent: Thomas Hobbes and the Engagement Controversy' in G.E. Aylmer, ed., *The Interregnum* (London 1972); the same author's 'Thomas Hobbes on the Proper Signification of Liberty', *Transactions of the Royal Historical Society* 5th Series 40 (1990); and Glenn Burgess, 'Contexts for the Writing and Publication of Hobbes's *Leviathan*', *History of Political Thought* 11 (1990).

Hobbes's religious ideas

There has been much interesting work recently in this area. The pioneer was J.G. A. Pocock, in 'Time, History and Eschatology in the Thought of Thomas Hobbes' in his *Politics, Language and Time* (London 1972); see also his 'Thomas Hobbes: Atheist or Enthusiast? His Place in a Restoration Debate', *History of Political Thought* 11 (1990). Subsequent contributions include R.J. Halliday, T. Kenyon and A. Reeve, 'Hobbes's Belief in God', *Political Studies* 31 (1983); Alan Ryan, 'Hobbes, Toleration, and the Inner Life' in D. Miller, ed., *The Nature of Political Theory* (Oxford 1983) and 'A More Tolerant Hobbes?' in Susan Mendus, ed., *Justifying Toleration* (Cambridge 1986); Edwin Curley, ''I Durst Not Write So Boldly': How to Read Hobbes's Theological-Political Treatise' in E. Giancotti, ed., *Proceedings of the Conference on Hobbes and Spinoza* (Urbino 1988); David Johnston, 'Hobbes and Mortalism', *History of Political Thought* 10 (1989); A.P. Martinich, *The Two Gods of Leviathan: Thomas Hobbes on Religion and Politics* (Cambridge 1992); and a couple of connected articles by myself, 'The Christian Atheism of Thomas Hobbes' in M. Hunter and D. Wootton, eds., *Atheism from the Reformation to the Enlightenment* (Oxford 1992) and 'The Civil Religion of Thomas Hobbes' in Nicholas Phillipson and Quentin Skinner, eds., *Political Discourse in Early Modern Britain* (Cambridge 1993).

Biographical notes and references

I am greatly indebted to Dr Ian Harris, of Jesus College Cambridge and Leicester University, for help with the entries relating to Scriptural characters (those marked with an asterisk), though I take full responsibility for any errors remaining in these notes.

*AARON. Elder brother of Moses and spiritual leader of the Jews under his rule. He also appears in the Bible as Moses' mouthpiece (Exodus VII.1), and Hobbes describes him as consecrated by Moses or subordinate to him.

*ABIATHAR. Son of the priest Ahimelech and with him priest at Nob near Jerusalem *c.* 1000 B.C. Later one of David's counsellors and priests (possibly the high priest). At the end of David's reign (*c.* 970 B.C.) he conspired against Solomon and was expelled from office.

*ABIMELECH. King of Gerar in Palestine at the time of Abraham, at whose court Abraham sought to pass Sarah (his wife) off as his sister.

*ABNER. Cousin of Saul, who made him 'captain of the host'. Initially he did not support David for the succession, but was won over; he offered to deliver Israel to David but was slain first.

*ABRAHAM. The ancestor of the Jews, who migrated *c.* 1900 B.C. from Ur to Canaan. He was the founder of the Jewish monotheistic religion and was supposed to have been granted special revelations by God in visions.

*ACHAN. A Judahite who violated a sacrificial ban on stealing in the assault on Jericho by Joshua, *c.* 1240 B.C. He and his family were stoned to death after the theft was discovered by the use of a lot.

*ADAM. The first man, later expelled from paradise after eating the fruit of the tree of knowledge.

ADRIAN, Pope. Pope Adrian IV, pope 1154–9, was born Nicholas Breakspear and was the only Englishman to become pope. He was Abbot of St Albans from 1137 to 1146 and Cardinal Bishop of Albano from 1146 to 1154. The incident Hobbes refers to on page 384 was in 1155, when the Emperor FREDERICK I, on his first visit to Rome, agreed (after an initial refusal) to act as the Pope's squire by holding his stirrup.

AEOLUS. Ruler of the winds in Greek and Roman mythology; his traditional home was Lipara, in the Lipari Islands.

*AGAG. The king of Amalek, who was spared by SAUL, contrary to God's command. SAMUEL then slew him, claiming God's warrant to do so; this was taken to be the moment at which Saul was rejected by God.

*AGAR. See HAGAR.

*AGUR. Known only as the son of Jakeh and author of part of the Book of Proverbs in the Old Testament.

*AHAB. Seventh king of Israel (874–853 B.C.) and husband of Jezebel. Jezebel encouraged false prophets and persecuted true religion.

*AHIJAH. A prophet from Shiloh, who protested against SOLOMON's idolatry and accurately prophesied the career of JEROBOAM.

ALEXANDER. Alexander the Great, king of Macedonia (356–323 B.C.). Son of King Philip of Macedon, he was educated by ARISTOTLE. He succeeded to the throne in 336 B.C. and as leader of a combined Greek army defeated the Persians in 334. He then swept through the Persian empire and established an astonishing empire of his own, stretching from Greece to the Punjab; but his sudden death after a banquet at Babylon led to his territories being divided among his generals.

*AMAZIAH. King of Judah (796–767 B.C.) who gained victory over Edom through following God, but was defeated when he worshipped idols.

AMBROSE, Saint (*c.* 339–97). Born at Trier, the son of the Prefect of Gaul; in 369 he was made Consular Prefect of Upper Italy. His success at handling the religious disputes in the province led to his being elected Bishop of Milan. While bishop, he excommunicated the Emperor THEODOSIUS for massacring the rebellious Thessalonians.

AMMIANUS MARCELLINUS (*c.* 330–90). Historian of Rome, born of Greek parents at Antioch. He wrote in Latin a history of the Roman empire, the surviving portion of which covers the years 353–78. Hobbes (p. 367) cites a passage of the History (XXVII.3.12–13) which recounts the struggle of DAMASUS and URSICINUS over a papal election in 366.

*AMOS. Author of one of the books of the Bible, probably in the eighth century B.C. It declares God's judgement on Judah and Samaria, to which God had called Amos to preach.

*ANANIAS. A follower of Jesus in Damascus, who befriended PAUL at his conversion and conveyed Christ's commission to him.

ANDROMEDA. Daughter of the king of Ethiopia in Greek myth, she was to be sacrificed to a sea monster but was rescued by the hero Perseus.

APOLLO. The Greek god who presided over both the arts and the realm of civil law.

ARISTIDES (died 468 B.C.). An Athenian politician, nicknamed 'the Just'. He was archon in 489 B.C., but (through the rivalry of another politician, Themistocles) suffered ostracism and banishment some time between 485 and 482. Recalled after the Battle of Salamis, he became a leading figure in Athenian politics.

ARISTOTLE (384–324 B.C.). One of the two principal Greek philosophers, he was the pupil of the other one, PLATO, and tutor to ALEXANDER the Great. His philosophy was based on an extensive critique of Plato and fell into some disfavour later in the ancient world; but when many of his works were rediscovered in Western Europe in the eleventh and twelfth centuries, they provided the basis for the most sophisticated medieval philosophy, known as 'scholasticism'. Hobbes was largely educated at Oxford on the works of Aristotle, but conceived a violent dislike for them, like many of his generation. He refers to the following works in *Leviathan*: to *De Anima* 432a ('sensible species' – though, as Hobbes acknowledges, the later medieval theory of vision was a considerable elaboration on passages such as this) (on page 14); to *Politics* 1254a13–1255a5 (slavery) (on page 107); to *Politics* 1253a6 (bees) (on page 119); to *Politics* 1317a40 (democracy and liberty) (on page 150); to *Politics*,

Ethics and *Metaphysics* (on page 461); to *Metaphysics* (on page 463); to *Physics* 255b14 (gravity) (on page 467); and to *Politics* 1284a35–1285b33 (tyranny) (on page 470).

AUGUSTINE, Saint (354–430). The greatest Latin father, a teacher of rhetoric until he became a Christian in 387. Bishop of Hippo from 395, he wrote extensively against Christian heresies. Hobbes cites (p. 434) his *Enarratio in Psalmum XXXVII* (J.P. Migne, *Patrologia Latina* xxxvi, col. 397).

AUGUSTUS (63 B.C.–A.D. 14). The first Roman emperor, he was the son of Julius CAESAR's niece. He rose to power in the course of the military struggle after the assassination of Caesar, who had made him his heir, in 44 B.C. In 42 he and his ally Antony defeated BRUTUS and Cassius at Philippi, and in 31 he defeated the fleet of Antony and Cleopatra, Queen of Egypt, at Actium. From 29 onwards he built up his position as *princeps* or emperor, relying on a continuous possession of the most important offices in the republic.

*AZARIAH. Hobbes calls by this name King Uzziah, an able and energetic ruler of Judah (*c.* 791–740 B.C.).

*BAAL. The general term for the master god worshipped by each pre-Israelite community in Canaan, and a constant challenge to the Hebrew religion.

*BALAAM. A prophet from Moab (Jordan), in the twelfth or eleventh century B.C., he prophesied the future greatness of Israel, but later sought to lure the Israelites into the cult of Baal and was slain by them.

*BARNABAS. Cognomen of Joseph, a leading early Christian missionary. He was particularly associated with PAUL. An apocryphal Epistle of Barnabas exists, dating probably from the second century.

BECKET, Thomas à (1118–70). In 1155 he became Chancellor to King HENRY II and in 1166 Archbishop of Canterbury. He became a severe critic of the royal attitude to the Church and was forced into a five-year exile from his see in 1165. Returning in 1170, he was assassinated by four knights in the cathedral at Canterbury in December, supposedly on the orders of Henry II. The king did public penance for the murder, and Becket was canonised in 1172.

BEDA. The Venerable Bede (*c.* 673–735) was born near Monkwearmouth in County Durham and lived in the ancient kingdom of Northumbria all his life, becoming a monk at the double monastery of

Jarrow–Monkwearmouth. He was the principal writer of Anglo-Saxon England, producing many biblical commentaries and other works, as well as his famous *Ecclesiastical History of the English People.* Hobbes refers (page 473) to his remarks on ghosts in the *History* V.12.

*BEELZEBUB. In the New Testament, the Pharisees accused Jesus of exorcising devils by 'Beelzebub, prince of devils'.

BELLARMINE, Robert (1542–1621). Born near Siena, he entered the Jesuit order in 1560 and enjoyed a distinguished academic career, culminating in the rectorship of the Collegio Romano in 1592. He was made a cardinal in 1599 and Archbishop of Capua in 1602. He devoted himself to the production of an encyclopaedic defence of the Catholic Church against the Protestants, the *Disputationes de Controversiis Christianae Fidei Adversus Huius Temporis Haereticos* (1581–92), and was also a leading propagandist against James I of England when the king introduced a loyalty oath discriminating against his Catholic subjects. He was Hobbes's principal target in Part III of *Leviathan* (pages 378 ff.), in which Hobbes attacked the third part of the *Disputationes, Tertia Controversia Generalis de Summo Pontifice (Disputationes* (Ingolstadt 1590 I coll. 582 ff.). In addition, there are the following references to him: (page 341) *Tertia Controversia (ibid.* I col. 596) and (page 434) *Sexta Controversia (ibid.* coll. 1779–85).

BERNARD, Saint (1090–1153). Born in Burgundy, he entered the Cistercian order in 1113 and became Abbot of Clairvaux in Champagne in 1115. He was a very influential writer and teacher, who reformed his branch of the Cistercians; he was canonised in 1174. Hobbes refers (page 473) to his views on ghosts, to be found in his *Sermones de Diversis* XLII and his *Sermones in Cantica* LXVI (J.P. Migne, *Patrologia Latina* clxxxiii coll. 663–4 and 1100).

BEZA, Theodore (1519–1605). Born in Burgundy, he was trained as a humanist and converted to Calvinism in 1549. In 1559 he became Professor of Theology at Geneva, and Calvin's principal associate. He translated the New Testament into Latin, with notes which Hobbes cited as follows: (page 427) *Annotationes Maiores in Novum Dn. Nostri Iesu Christi Testamentum* (1594) p. 199 [Mark 9.1] and (page 439) *Ibid.* p. 458 [Acts 2.24].

BRUTUS, Marcus Junius (*c.* 86–42 B.C.). Roman politician, who began as an opponent of CAESAR but then changed sides and supported him. However, he became one of Caesar's assassins and was subsequently defeated by AUGUSTUS at Philippi, where he committed suicide.

CADMUS, son of Agenor, king of Phoenicia. In Greek legend he was the founder and first king of Thebes, and was supposed to have invented the Greek alphabet (which was indeed based on the Phoenician alphabet).

CAESAR, Julius (102–44 B.C.). The man who was supposed to have destroyed the Roman republic, Caesar was its most successful general and a leading politician from 70 to 50 B.C.. His success prompted rivalry, particularly from POMPEY and led to a civil war which ended with Pompey's death in 45 B.C. Though Caesar refused a royal crown in 44, his immense personal power alarmed those loyal to the republic (including CICERO and BRUTUS), and led to his assassination on the ides (fifteenth day) of March 44.

*CAIAPHAS. Cognomen of Joseph, the high priest at the time of the trial of JESUS.

CALIGULA (12–41). The son of the nephew of the Emperor Tiberius, he replaced his father as heir-apparent to the emperor on his father's death in 19. He duly succeeded Tiberius on his death in 37, but seems to have gone mad within eight months of inheriting the throne. After four years of extraordinary and crazy excesses, he was murdered by his bodyguards.

CARACALLA (188–217). The son of the Emperor Septimius Severus, he and his brother succeeded their father as joint emperors in 211. Caracalla then had his brother and many other politicians murdered, but was himself murdered six years later by the head of the praetorian guard. He had, however, given to all free inhabitants of the empire the title and rights of Roman citizens.

CARNEADES (214–129 B.C.). A famous Greek philosopher, whose works are, however, substantially lost, he was the leading Sceptic of his generation and transformed the philosophical school founded by PLATO (the Academy) into a centre of Scepticism. In 155 he visited Rome on a diplomatic mission and gave a course of lectures there which included a demonstration that there was no adequate basis for any theory of justice; in protest, the Roman politician CATO had him ejected from the city.

CATILINE (Lucius Sergius Catilina, c. 109–62 B.C.). A Roman politician, he launched an insurrection in 63 after losing to CICERO in the consular election. Cicero led the drive to suppress the rising, with his famous Catilinarian orations, and Catiline was defeated and killed in a battle near Pistoia.

CATO, Marcus Porcius, 'the Elder' (232–147 B.C.).   Roman politician and general, who led the political and military struggle against Carthage. In 155 he protested at the lectures of CARNEADES and had him removed from Rome.

CERBERUS.   A multi-headed dog in Greek mythology who was supposed to guard the entrance to the underworld of Hades, at the landing-place where Charon deposited the shades of the dead after crossing the Styx.

CERES.   Roman goddess of corn and fertility.

CHARLEMAGNE (742–814).   The eldest son of King Pepin the Short of the Franks, he succeeded his father as king in 768. Thirty years of strenuous campaigning followed, in which he extended the bounds of Frankish power from the Ebro to the Elbe; on Christmas Day 800 he was crowned Emperor of the Romans by Pope Leo III in St Peter's Basilica.

CHARON.   The boatman who ferried the shades of the dead across the Styx in Greek mythology, being paid with an obol (the smallest coin) placed in the corpse's mouth before burial.

CHILPERIQUE.   An error by Hobbes for Childeric III, the last Merovingian king of Francia. Crowned in 743, he was deposed in 751 by his 'Mayor of the Palace' Pepin. Pepin addressed a famous question to Pope ZACHARIAS about whether such a step was permissible, and the pope gave a favourable judgement.

CICERO, Marcus Tullius (106–43 B.C.).   From 81 onwards Cicero was a leading figure in the Roman republic, acting as lawyer and politician, as well as philosopher. Consul in 63, he suppressed the Catilinarian conspiracy, and in the following years tried (in a somewhat ineffectual manner) to preserve the institutions of the republic against the development of 'Caesarism'. After CAESAR'S assassination he emerged as a leader of the republican party, but was proscribed and killed by the opposition under the command of AUGUSTUS and Antony. His writings have remained the most influential body of Latin literature down to our own time and acted as a canon for the correctness of the language. His *De Officiis* (a general moral treatise) was his most important work for the Middle Ages and the Renaissance, and Hobbes clearly knew it very well; but his citations from Cicero refer mainly to his orations. They are as follows: *De Oratore* II.102.5 (on page 112); *Pro Caecina* 73 and 70 (on page

Biographical notes

171); *Pro Caecina* 100 (on page 218); *De Divinatione* 119 (on page 461); and *Pro Milone* 32 (on page 474).

CLEMENT I. Usually reckoned today as the second or third successor to PETER as Bishop of Rome. He was supposed to have compiled a set of Apostolic Constitutions and Canons, but these are now thought to be spurious; one letter, dating from *c.* 95, is the only genuine product of his pen. The Constitutions and Canons to which Hobbes refers (pages 266 and 362) are to be found in J.P. Migne, *Patrologia Graeca* I coll. 557–1156 and II coll. 1605–12.

CLUVERIUS (Cluvier), Philip (1580–1623). Born in Danzig, he studied at Leiden University where he later became a professor. He also spent some time at Oxford in the second decade of the seventeenth century. He was a famous geographer; Hobbes refers (page 68) to his *Germaniae Antiquae Libri Tres* (Leiden 1616).

COKE, Sir Edward (1552–1634). English lawyer, who rose through the great legal offices under ELIZABETH and JAMES I to become Chief Justice of the King's Bench in 1613. He quarrelled with the king and was removed from his post in 1617; he remained broadly in opposition to the Crown (particularly in the Parliaments of the 1620s) until his death. His principal works were his *Reports*, published from 1600 to 1615, and his *Institutes* (four works published between 1628 and 1644), of which the first was his commentary on the late medieval textbook on tenures by Sir Thomas Littleton. Hobbes refers to this work by name in two places, and without naming it in one place, as follows: *The First Part of the Institutes of the Lawes of England* (2nd edn London 1629) p. 16r (I.1.8) (on page 102); *ibid.* p. 97v (II.6.138) (on page 187); and *ibid.* p. 373r (III.12.709) (on page 193).

CONSTANTINE (Flavius Constantinus, 274–337). Illegitimate son of the Emperor Constantius I, he was proclaimed emperor on his father's death by the troops at York. A complex struggle against other claimants ended in 312 with Constantine's victory at the Battle of the Milvian Bridge, nine miles north of Rome. Apparently as a consequence of a vision on the eve of the battle, he converted to Christianity and in 313 granted toleration to Christians in the empire; in 324 Christianity became the state religion. He presided over the Council of Nicaea in 325, in which an attempt was made to end the struggle between the Arian Christians (who denied the identity of Christ with God) and their opponents – whom Constantine sup-

lxxii

ported. It was thought in the Middle Ages that he was baptised by Pope SILVESTER in 326 and transferred power over Rome to the pope, but this was already questioned in the Renaissance and is now known to be quite untrue.

*CRISPUS. Crispus, Gaius and Stephanas were citizens of Corinth and among the Jews baptised by PAUL.

CYPRIAN, Saint (Thascius Caecilius Cyprianus, *c.* 200–58). Born in North Africa, he taught rhetoric and then became a Christian and a leading Latin writer on Church matters; he suffered martyrdom under the Emperor Valerian. Hobbes refers (page 393) to his views on the primacy of Rome, which are contained particularly in his letter to Cornelius (J.P. Migne, *Patrologia Latina* III coll. 818–19).

DAMASUS. Pope from 366 to 384, whose disputed election is recorded in AMMIANUS MARCELLINUS.

*DANIEL. The fourth of the greater prophets (605–535 B.C.), whose career is described in the Book of Daniel. Imprisoned by Nebuchadnezzar at Babylon, he gained repute as an interpreter of dreams. He prophesied the future triumph of Israel.

*DAVID. King of Israel 1010–970 B.C. As a boy he killed the giant Philistine Goliath and later overthrew SAUL, the existing king of Israel, without provoking God's wrath. He was thought to have been the author of the Psalms and the ancestor of Jesus. He contrived the death of Uriah the Hittite, one of his commanders, after committing adultery with his wife.

DIOCLESIAN (Gaius Aurelius Valerius Diocletianus, 245–313). A professional soldier, he was proclaimed emperor by his troops in 284. He reformed the government of the empire (including an abortive attempt to freeze all prices in 301); he also instituted a severe persecution of the Christians in 303. He abdicated in 305 and lived in his great palace at Split (Yugoslavia) until his death.

DOMITIAN (Titus Flavius Domitianus, 51–96). The younger son of the Emperor Vespasian, he succeeded his elder brother Titus in 81. A revolt by the soldiers of Upper Germany in 88–9 induced him to suppress all possible opposition to his rule in a most savage manner; he banished his cousin on suspicion of being a Christian, but in revenge was murdered in his bed by one of his cousin's freed slaves.

EGERIA. Nymph of a stream just outside Rome, she is said to have been the mistress of King NUMA and to have inspired his organisation of the Roman religion.

*ELEAZAR. Third son of AARON and like his father and brothers a priest. He assisted MOSES with a census and a land assessment.

*ELIJAH (also ELIAS and ELIAH). A ninth-century prophet of Israel and opponent of the worshippers of Baal, particularly Jezebel, the wife of AHAB. He was ultimately translated to heaven.

*ELISHA. A ninth-century prophet of Israel, to whom both the common people and the kings looked for advice (see NAAMAN).

ELIZABETH, Queen of England (1533–1603). The daughter of HENRY VIII and Anne Boleyn, she succeeded her sister Mary in 1558. On her accession she returned to Protestantism after Mary's Catholic reaction to their father's Reformation; her Church settlement was regarded in the seventeeth century as the foundation of the Episcopalian Church of England. In 1570 Pope Pius V excommunicated her and absolved her subjects of allegiance to her, and she found herself in a prolonged struggle both against Catholics at home and against the Spanish empire abroad (culminating in the famous Armada of 1588). In her later years she was also the object of hostility from Puritans in England who wished to introduce a more Calvinist form of Church government.

*ENOCH. Son of Jared, father of Methusaleh and great-grand-father of Noah, he was a member of the line from Seth (Adam's third son) through whom knowledge of God was preserved. Like Elijah, he was taken up into heaven without dying.

*EPHRAIM. Second son of Joseph (*c.* 1700 B.C.) and blessed by the sick Jacob with his right hand, to signify the future prosperity of Ephraim's descendants.

*ESDRAS or EZRA. Sent to Jerusalem by the king of Persia in 458 B.C. to enforce uniform observance of the Jewish law and make appointments to public offices. His mission is the subject of the Old Testament Book of Ezra.

*ESTHER. Wife of Xerxes, King of Persia (485–465 B.C.), she risked her life to serve the Jews within the Persian empire and suggested that they should massacre their enemies. Her story is told in the Book of Esther.

*EVE. The first woman, wife of ADAM, and the cause of the fall of man after picking the forbidden fruit.

*EZEKIEL. Prophet and supposed author of the Old Testament Book of Ezekiel, he was one of the heads of a priestly order and was deported to Babylon when that state dominated Israel (593–570 B.C.).

FREDERICK I 'Barbarossa' (*c.* 1123–90). Succeeded his father as Duke of Swabia in 1147 and his uncle as emperor in 1152. He subdued both the princes of Germany and the Italian city states and he led the third crusade against Saladin. A conflict with the papacy ended with agreements in 1183; but in 1155 he had reluctantly agreed to act as the pope's squire on his entry to Rome (see ADRIAN).

*GABRIEL. One of the two angels mentioned in the Bible (the other being MICHAEL). In the Old Testament he is an angel of punishment and the guardian of paradise, while in the New Testament he figures chiefly as a messenger.

*GIDEON. Son of Joash, he was the judge who delivered Israel from the Midianites (1169–1129 B.C.). He was summoned to do so by an angel of the Lord.

GODOLPHIN, Francis and Sidney. They were the sons of the owner of Godolphin in Cornwall. Sidney (1610–43) was a royalist M.P. in 1628 and 1640, and was also a poet of some note. He left the House in 1642 to join the king's army in Cornwall and was shot in a skirmish in Devon in February 1643. He left a bequest of £200 to Hobbes, who had been his friend before the war, and in his memory Hobbes dedicated *Leviathan* to his brother Francis (1605–67), who was the royalist governor of the Scilly Islands during the war until he surrendered them in 1646. He compounded for his estates and lived quietly in England until the Restoration, when he was created a Knight of the Bath.

GRACCHUS, Gaius and Tiberius. Tiberius (168–134 B.C.) was a Roman politician, tribune of the plebs in 133, who believed that the social problems of Rome could be solved by land reform and the splitting up of great estates. He passed a bill to this effect, but the measure was opposed by the aristocracy, and he was assassinated by a nobleman. His younger brother Gaius was elected tribune in 123 and 122, and tried to develop Tiberius' programme, but he, too, was opposed and committed suicide in 121 after a riot and massacre of his supporters.

GREGORY I, II and IX, popes. Gregory I (*c.* 540–604), 'the

Great', was born in Rome and became praetor, before resigning and entering a monastery. He was elected pope in 590 and thoroughly reorganised the Church (including sending Augustine on the mission to convert England). He wrote a number of theological works; Hobbes refers (page 473) to his views on ghosts, contained in his *Dialogorum Libri IV* IV.55 (J.P. Migne, *Patrologia Latina* lxxvii col. 421). Gregory II (669–731) was another Roman, elected pope in 715, who developed the power of the papacy in Italy at the expense of the Roman emperors, who were by then resident entirely in the East. Both Gregory I and Gregory II were emphatic in their public pronouncements that temporal power ought to be at the service of spiritual power, as manifested in the papacy. Gregory IX (1148–1241), pope from 1227, also asserted a high view of papal power against the Emperor Frederick II; he produced a collection of Decretals which Hobbes refers to on page 420, in a passage about INNOCENT III (*Decretales D. Gregorii Papae IX* V.7.13, e.g. in *Corpus Iuris Canonici* (Paris 1618) p. 686).

*HABAKKUK. The author of the Book of Habakkuk, about whom nothing is definitely known.

*HAGAR. Maidservant to Sarah, the wife of ABRAHAM.

*HAGGAI. Haggai and ZECHARIAH were the first two prophets after the return from exile in 537 B.C. Their prophecies dated from the time after the captivity, though Hobbes thought that they were produced during the exile.

*HASHABIAH. One of the Hebronites in the service of David.

HENRY II, king of England (1133–89). The son of the Count of Anjou, he succeeded to the throne of England in 1154 by virtue of his mother, the daughter of Henry I. He established effective government after the 'Anarchy' following his grandfather's death, and by his death ruled an empire on both sides of the Channel. He appointed BECKET to the See of Canterbury, but quarrelled with him and eventually had to do penance for his murder.

HENRY III, king of France (1551–89). Son of Henry II of France, he succeeded his brother Charles IX as king in 1575. His reign saw a prolonged civil war between the Catholics and the Protestants, in which the Catholics under the Duke of Guise formed a holy league to defend their cause. In 1588 Guise was assassinated; Henry joined the Protestant leader Henry of Navarre (later Henry IV, and father of Queen Henrietta Maria of England), and they marched on

Paris, but Henry III was himself stabbed to death by a Catholic in 1589.

HENRY VIII, king of England (1491–1547). Son of Henry VII, he succeeded to the throne in 1509. A glittering career as a young king was followed by the struggle with the papacy from 1527 onwards over his attempt to divorce his first wife, Catherine of Aragon, and marry Anne Boleyn. In 1534 he broke decisively with Rome, and Parliament passed a statute naming him supreme head of the Church of England; a series of other measures followed, including the dissolution of the monasteries. After Anne Boleyn was executed for treason, Henry continued to try to father a healthy male heir; he had married six times by his death, but had had only two girls (Mary and ELIZABETH) and one sickly boy (later Edward VI).

HERCULES. A hero in Greek mythology, famous for his great strength – exemplified in the story of the 'twelve labours' in which he conquered a variety of bizarre enemies.

HESIOD. An early Greek poet, who lived (probably) at the end of the eighth century B.C. in Boeotia. He was the author of a long poem on rural pursuits and of the *Theogony*, a poem systematising the legends of the gods.

*HEZEKIAH. One of the outstanding kings of Judah, who reigned in the late eighth century B.C. He reformed and purified the Jewish religion and led a successful rebellion against the Assyrians.

*HILKIAH. High priest in JOSIAH's reign (640–610 B.C.), who rediscovered the book of the law during repairs to the Temple. Subsequently he was part of a deputation to HULDAH, the prophetess, to discover what God wanted done with the book, and he also helped to put Josiah's reformation into action.

HOMER. Great Greek poet, living (probably) between 810 and 730 B.C. in western Asia Minor. He was supposed in later antiquity to have been blind. The *Iliad* and the *Odyssey* are attributed to him; both were translated into English by Hobbes in his old age.

*HOSEA. Author of one of the books of the Old Testament, centred on the death of his wife.

*HULDAH. A prophetess and wife of the Keeper of the Wardrobe under King JOSIAH, she was consulted about the authenticity of the book of the law discovered by HILKIAH. She accepted it as the divine word and also prophesied judgement against Jerusalem after Josiah's death.

HYPERBOLUS. An Athenian politician, who became unpopular

as a result of his attempt to have two leading generals ostracised during the Peloponnesian War. In retaliation, he was himself ostracised, and ARISTOTLE (*Politics* 1284a) says that this was thought to be such a debased use of the punishment that it was never employed again.

INNOCENT III, pope (1160–1216). Born at Agnagni, he was elected pope in 1198. He tried to enforce papal superiority over most of the rulers of Western Europe, including the emperor (he had Otto IV deposed) and the king of England (he excommunicated King John for refusing to recognise his nominee as Archbishop of Canterbury). He presided over the Fourth Lateran Council in 1215, the decisions of which about heresy Hobbes cites on page 420 from the Decretals of Gregory IX (see GREGORY IX).

*ISAAC. Son of ABRAHAM and Sarah, and an ancestor of the Israelites. He was born when his parents were very old and survived Abraham's proposed sacrifice of him as a child, thereby vindicating God's promise to Abraham. He was the father of Esau and JACOB.

*ISAIAH. A prophet, according to Jewish tradition of royal blood, who lived under kings Uzziah, Jotham, Ahaz and HEZEKIAH (second half of the eighth century B.C.). He was often very critical of the kings, and Hezekiah is said in the Book of Isaiah to have suffered misfortune after Isaiah has chastised him.

*JACOB. Son of ISAAC and ancestor of the Jews (*c.* 1800 B.C.). He attained the position of Isaac's heir by defrauding his brother Esau; fleeing from Esau's wrath, he had a vision of a ladder leading from heaven to earth with the God of his family standing above it – a confirmation of God's promise to ABRAHAM. He had many adventures in exile, in all of which he enjoyed God's favour. He eventually adopted the two sons of his youngest son Joseph, setting the younger over the elder. From these two descended the tribes of EPHRAIM and MANASSEH.

*JAKETH. Father of AGUR; the name means 'scrupulously pious'.

JAMES I, king of England (1566–1625). The son of Mary Queen of Scots, he succeeded to the Scottish throne on her abdication in 1569, as James VI. On the death of ELIZABETH in 1603 he became king of England. At the beginning of his reign he found himself in conflict with both Catholics (whom he obliged to take an oath of allegiance renouncing their loyalty to the pope) and Puritans (whose attack on Episcopal Church government he resisted). He wrote on theology and essays on various other polemical subjects.

*JAMES. Son of Zebedee, he was a Galilean fisherman called with his brother John to be one of the twelve apostles. Nicknamed 'sons of thunder' by Jesus, the brothers were rebuked by him for their impetuosity.

*JEHOSHAPHAT. The fourth king of Judah (*c.* 873–849 B.C.), he ended the traditional feud with Israel and allowed the apostate King AHAB of Israel to fight the Syrians. He was rebuked for doing so by the prophet JEHU.

*JEHU. (1) A prophet, son of Hanani, and critic of JEHOSHAPHAT. (2) Son of Jehoshaphat, the tenth king of Israel (*c.* 842–815 B.C.). ELISHA appointed a prophet to anoint Jehu king and commissioned him to extirpate the line of AHAB and Jezebel, the apostates.

*JEPHTHA. One of the judges of Israel *c.* 1100 B.C., who rose from lowly origins to command the Israelites during the invasion of the Ammonites. He triumphed by faith, promising to sacrifice to God the first person he saw after his decisive battle – who turned out to be his daughter.

*JEREMIAH. Old Testament prophet *c.* 630–590 B.C. He lived during the reign of the Babylonian king Nebuchadnezzar, at a time of great calamity for the Jews, and his name is a byword for grief.

*JEROBOAM. An Ephraimite who rebelled against REHOBOAM, son of SOLOMON, and became Israel's first king after the partition of Israel and Judah (930 B.C.). He may have been an idolater, but he won popular support by relieving the people of some of the oppressive policies of Solomon and Rehoboam.

JEROME, Saint (*c.* 342–420). A student of philosophy and rhetoric at Rome, he became a monk in 374 and an influential figure within the early Church (he was secretary to Pope DAMASUS). He is chiefly famous for producing the authoritative translation of the Bible into Latin, the Vulgate (which Hobbes seems to have used in his biblical quotations in *Leviathan*, translating them into English himself). Hobbes refers on pages 264 and 266 to Jerome's views on the canon of Scripture, which are to be found in his preface to the Book of Ezra in the Vulgate (J.P. Migne, *Patrologia Latina* xxviii col. 1403) or in his Epistola 53 (*ibid.* xxii coll. 545–6).

*JESUS CHRIST. In Christian doctrine, the son of God, sent to redeem the fall of ADAM by promising salvation to all who believe in him. His life and teachings are recorded in the New Testament and need no summary here. Hobbes's Christ is distinguished from the other 'representatives' of God, such as MOSES (e.g. page 267), by the fact that 'the Godhead . . . dwelleth bodily' in him (page 295).

*JETHRO.   Father-in-law of MOSES, who advised him to delegate the administration of justice.

*JOANNA.   One of several women healed by Jesus, who assisted in maintaining his company on its travels. Her husband Chuza was an official of Herod Antipas.

*JOASH.   King of Judah *c.* 837–800 B.C. He was rescued by his aunt Jehosheba, wife of Jehoiada, the high priest, when Athaliah, the queen mother, 'destroyed all the seed royal' in an attempt to keep power. After six years of Athaliah's rule, Jehoiada put Joash on the throne and put Athaliah to death.

*JOB.   His story is told in the Book of Job, and he is also mentioned in Ezekiel, XIV.14,20 and James V.11. As a result of divine permission Satan robbed him of wealth, health, children and wife, leaving him only the 'comfort' of three friends, about whose uselessness Job eloquently complained. Throwing himself on God's mercy, he learned how God's power justified all things – an appealing metaphor for Hobbes, who took the title of his book from a passage in Job XLI.1–34.

*JOEL.   A prophet and author of a book of the Old Testament some time between 800 and 200 B.C.

JOHN, king of England (1167–1216).   Son of HENRY II, he succeeded his brother Richard as king in 1199. In 1205 he began a long quarrel with the Church over the royal power to appoint bishops, and in 1208 INNOCENT III placed the country under an interdict. John submitted to the pope and agreed to hold England as a fief of the papacy in 1213. Domestic opposition to his policies from his barons forced him to issue the Magna Carta in 1215.

*JOHN the Apostle.   Traditionally supposed to have written the gospel and epistles under his name, he was the brother of BARNABAS and was closely associated with PETER.

*JOHN the Baptist.   Son of Zacharias, a priest, and Elizabeth, he received a prophetic call to make the people ready for the coming of Jesus, and in particular to institute the rite of baptism. Falling foul of Herod Antipas, he was imprisoned and executed. In the New Testament he is portrayed as the forerunner of Christ.

*JONAH. A prophet in the reign of Jeroboam II (eighth century B.C.). His book of the Bible is largely narrative, including the famous story of his being swallowed by a whale; its primary point was that God's mercy extends beyond the Jews to the whole human race.

*JONATHAN. (1) Son of Gershom and grandson of MOSES, he became a priest and the progenitor of a long line of priests. (2) Eldest son of SAUL, but a loyal friend of DAVID, his father's successor.

*JOSEPH. (1) The eleventh and favourite son of JACOB, who was sold into slavery in Egypt through the jealousy of his brothers. He prospered there, becoming the pharaoh's vizier (*c.* 1750 B.C.). From him were descended the tribes of EPHRAIM and MANASSEH. (2) Joseph, the husband of MARY, the mother of Jesus. According to MATTHEW's gospel, an angel appeared to Joseph in a dream to announce that Jesus had been conceived by the Holy Spirit.

JOSEPHUS, Flavius (37–*c.* 101). A Jewish historian and politician, who was appointed governor of Galilee by the Romans in 66. Despite siding with the Jewish rebels in 67, he remained influential at Rome and became a favourite of the Emperor Vespasian. He wrote (in Greek) a number of important works on Jewish history and religion; Hobbes refers (page 260) to his views on the canon of the Old Testament, which are to be found in his *Contra Apionem* 1.39–41.

*JOSHUA. Chosen by MOSES as an assistant, he distinguished himself as a soldier. He was formally consecrated as Moses' successor in the military leadership of the Jews, co-ordinate with the priesthood of ELEAZAR, though Hobbes (page 327) insisted that Eleazar was the sovereign. Hobbes observed (page 262) that Joshua did not write the Book under his name in the Old Testament, but he accepted it as historical.

*JOSIAH or JOSIAS. King of Judah *c.* 640–609 B.C. His reign was chiefly famous for the great religious reformation, the centrepiece of which was the rediscovery of the book of the law by HILKIAH. He was killed in battle by the Pharaoh Necho II, after refusing to accept the pharaoh's reasonable assurances that he meant only to march through Palestine to help the Assyrians against the Babylonians.

*JUDAS ISCARIOT. One of Jesus' first twelve disciples, he was their treasurer. He betrayed Jesus and later committed suicide; his place as an apostle was filled by MATTHIAS, after lots had been cast.

JULIAN, emperor (*c.* 331–63). The nephew of CONSTANTINE, he was proclaimed emperor in 361. He worked hard to restore the old religions of the empire, while tolerating Christianity and Judaism; in particular, he removed all privileges from the Church. He was killed in a campaign against the Persians.

JUPITER. The chief god in the Roman pantheon and special protector of the city; he was identified by the Romans with the Greek god Zeus.

JUVENTIUS. An inaccurate manuscript reading of the name now known to be Viventius Sciscianus, a Pannonian, prefect of Rome and praetorian prefect in Gaul, who retired in face of the violence at the papal election of Damasus (see AMMIANUS MARCELLINUS).

*KORAH. Korah, together with Dathan and Abiram, rebelled against MOSES and AARON on the grounds that they had set themselves above the other Israelites and had arrogated the priesthood to themselves. They were destroyed by the earth opening and by fire.

*LABAN. Uncle of JACOB and Esau, and later Jacob's father-in-law. He sought to trick Jacob but was outwitted by Jacob's superior cunning and by his support from God.

*LEMUEL. King of Massa in North Arabia, whose mother's advice on good government and self-discipline is recorded in the Book of Proverbs.

LEO III, pope (c. 750–816). Elected pope in 795, he sought the support of CHARLEMAGNE to establish his temporal power in Italy. In 800 he crowned Charlemagne emperor, and in return was formally granted temporal lordship over Rome and the Romagna, under imperial suzerainty.

*LEVI. Third son of JACOB, he was cursed for his treachery; but he was also the ancestor of the tribe of Levi, noted for their priest-like functions.

LIVY (Titus Livius, 59 B.C.–A.D. 17). Born at Padua, he spent most of his life at Rome. He wrote a history of Rome from 749 to 9 B.C., in 142 books, of which 35 survive, largely covering the period of the kings and the early republic. The history was popular throughout the Middle Ages and the Renaissance; Machiavelli's *Discorsi* are a commentary on the first ten books. Hobbes refers to two passages: on page 49 he refers to an incident in XLI.13.2, and on page 455 (the canonisation of Romulus after a report by Julius Proculus) to I.16.5–8.

*LOT. ABRAHAM's nephew, who selfishly chose to settle in the well-watered Jordan valley. This brought him into contact with the wicked men of Sodom, from whom he was rescued first by Abraham and then by two angels.

*LUKE. A Greek-speaking Gentile, who was a physician and follower of PAUL, he claimed thorough accuracy for his account of the life and teachings of Jesus. Tradition asserts that he survived Paul's martyrdom and died aged 84.

MAHOMET (570–632). Born at Mecca, he determined to reform the 'Abrahamic' religion of Judaism and Christianity, and became the prophet of a new version of the faith. From 622 onwards he established both military and spiritual authority over a wide area of Arabia. His prophecies are contained in the Koran, the Muslim Holy Book.

*MALACHI. The supposed author of the Book of Malachi in the Old Testament (though some authorities have thought it not a proper name but the common noun 'messenger' in Hebrew). The book was probably composed in the fifth century B.C.

*MANASSEH. The eldest son of JOSEPH, and brother of EPHRAIM. He lost the rights of the first-born when JOSEPH blessed EPHRAIM with his right hand and Manasseh with his left. His descendants, the tribe of Manasseh, were renowned for valour.

MARIUS, Gaius (157–86 B.C.). Roman general, who served as tribune of the plebs in 119 B.C. and became a leader of the popular party. He reformed the army and tried to introduce a degree of land reform into the state; but he was opposed by his great rival SULLA, and civil war ensued. It ended with a coup by Marius in 87, accompanied by a bloodbath in the city; but he died in the following year.

*MARK. The author of the second gospel, apparently a relative of BARNABAS. Not one of the original disciples, he travelled for some time with Barnabas and PAUL.

*MARTHA. The sister of the Mary who anointed Jesus shortly before his death and of Lazarus, whom Jesus raised from the dead. In Luke's narrative Martha is rebuked by Christ for her impatience with her sister and her excessive concern for the meal set before the assembled company.

*MARY. The mother of Jesus Christ.

*MARY MAGDALENE. Her name derives from the Galilean town of Magdala. She was amongst the women cured of evil spirits by Jesus and later witnessed his resurrection.

*MATTHEW. One of the twelve apostles, he had been a tax-gatherer. His gospel stresses the ethical teachings of Jesus and has generally been the most widely read of the four narratives.

*MATTHIAS. Matthias was chosen by lot as successor to JUDAS among the apostles. The basis of the lot-casting was apparently that God had already secretly chosen him. Nothing is known of his later career.

MEDEA. In Greek myth, the daughter of Aëetes, king of Colchis. She ran off with the hero Jason after he stole the Golden Fleece from her father, and to delay pursuit she cut up her younger brother and strewed the bits along the road. Later, she used her magical powers to persuade the daughters of Jason's uncle, King Pelias of Iolchus, that killing him and boiling up his dismembered body would bring him youth again (as Hobbes observes, page 234, it did not). After Jason left her to marry Glauce, she sent Glauce a poisoned robe which burned her to death; she then killed her own two children by Jason and fled to Athens.

MERCURY. The Roman god of the corn trade and commerce in general. He was usually identified with the Greek god Hermes, the messenger of the gods.

*MICAIAH or MICAH. The son of Imlah and a prophet in the days of AHAB. Nothing is known of him except for a single interview he had with Ahab.

*MICHAEL. One of the two angels (cf. GABRIEL) mentioned in the Bible. He was regarded as the patron and protector of Israel.

*MIRIAM. The daughter of Amram and Jochabed and the sister of AARON and MOSES. According to tradition she watched the infant Moses in the bullrushes. She and Aaron rebelled against Moses out of jealousy; divine judgement caused her to develop leprosy, but Moses interceded for her, and she was forgiven and cleansed.

*MOLOCH. A god worshipped by the Ammonites and associated with the sacrifice of children in fire. MOSES decreed the death of anyone who sacrificed to Moloch, and JOSIAH destroyed by fire Moloch's temples in Judah.

*MORDECAI. A Jewish exile who was a courtier of Xerxes, the

king of Persia 485–465 B.C. He frustrated a plot to kill the Jews in the Persian empire, and became Xerxes' grand vizier. The event was commemorated by a festival, the 'day of Mordecai'.

*MOSES (*c.* 1350–1230 B.C.). The great lawgiver through whom God brought the Hebrews out of Egypt, who made them into a nation and brought them within sight of the land promised to their ancestors. Saved from a pharaonic edict requiring the execution of male Hebrew children, he eventually gained some administrative position in Egypt. He slew an Egyptian who had been beating a Jew and fled into the wilderness. He remained there until recalled by a vision from God in the form of a burning bush that was not consumed. He persuaded the Egyptians to let the Jews leave by a variety of miracles and by the same means maintained his own sway over his people. He led the Jews out of Egypt to Sinai, where he received the Ten Commandments, standing alone on Mount Sinai. Jewish tradition regarded him as the author of the first five books of the Bible, the Pentateuch, though Hobbes was sceptical about this (page 262).

*NAAMAN. A Syrian army commander in the time of the prophet ELISHA. He was a leper who was cured after consulting Elisha; after recovering, he asked Elisha whether he could continue as a true believer while externally worshipping pagan idols. Elisha apparently gave him permission to do so.

*NAHUM. A prophet from Elkosh (in Judah?) who prophesied the sack of Nineveh by the Medes (612 B.C.) in the Old Testament Book of Nahum.

*NATHAN. A prophet at the time of DAVID who criticised the king's conduct towards Uriah.

*NEHEMIAH. The Jewish cupbearer of Artaxerxes I of Persia (465–424 B.C.). Learning of the desolate state of Jerusalem, he obtained permission to become its governor. He rebuilt its walls in fifty-two days. His account of this mission forms the bulk of the Old Testament Book of Nehemiah.

NEPTUNE. The Roman god of water, later identified with the Greek Poseidon, god of the sea.

NERO, emperor (37–68). The nephew of CALIGULA, he was educated by the philosopher Seneca and adopted by the Emperor Claudius, whom he succeeded in 54. He became notorious among contemporaries for his erratic conduct as emperor and among later generations for his persecution of the Christians. He committed suicide after a successful revolt by his army.

*NIMROD. A legendary warrior and huntsman whose kingdom included Babylon and Nineveh.

NOSTRADAMUS, Michael (1503–1566). Born in Provence, he became a famous doctor, astrologer and prophet. His predictions are contained in his *Centuries*, a poem of obscure, rhymed quatrains.

NUMA POMPILIUS. The second king of Rome, in the legendary history of the early kingdom. He is supposed to have been elected king in 714 B.C. and was chiefly famous for devising the public religion of the Roman state, under (allegedly) the inspiration of the nymph EGERIA. In the Renaissance, his system was often used as an example of a 'civil religion'.

*OBADIAH. A prophet who appears in the Old Testament Book of Obadiah. Nothing is known of him directly, but Hobbes (contrary to the Talmudic tradition) identified him with the Levite of that name who oversaw the rebuilding of the Temple under JOSIAH.

OBERON. A great magician, or king of the fairies, in Frankish and German folklore. He appears both in Shakespeare's *Midsummer Night's Dream*, and in Ben Jonson's masque *Oberon or the Fairy Prince*.

PAN. Greek god of flocks and herds, and responsible for inducing 'panic' in travellers.

*PAUL, Saint. Initially a persecutor of Christianity, Saul of Tarsus was miraculously converted by a vision·on the road to Damascus. Changing his name to Paul, he tirelessly preached the gospel in the eastern Mediterranean and Rome, where he was eventually martyred under Nero. His letters are the foundation of developed Christian theology.

PELEUS (for PELIAS). See MEDEA.

PERSEUS. See ANDROMEDA.

*PETER, Saint. One of the disciples, whose name stands first on the list. His particular significance is that he denied Christ but was forgiven, and he was proclaimed by Christ the 'rock' upon which a church was to be built (a pun upon his name in Greek). His missionary activity and martyrdom in Rome led to the tradition that he was the first bishop of Rome, and therefore the first pope.

*PHILIP. (1) The apostle, placed fifth in the New Testament lists, but not otherwise much mentioned. (2) One of the seven chosen as officials or 'deacons' in the Christian Church at Jerusalem. After the martyrdom of STEPHEN he acted as a missionary in Samaria.

PHILO (c. 15 B.C.–?). Jewish writer, born at Alexandria, who wrote extensively in Greek on both Greek philosophy and Judaism. In A.D. 40 he was part of a mission to protest to CALIGULA about a threatened desecration of the Temple in Jerusalem.

PHORMIO (Phormion). Athenian admiral who defeated the Peloponnesian fleet in 429 B.C..

PLATO (c. 427–c. 347 B.C.). One of the two great Greek philosophers, the other being his pupil ARISTOTLE. He was a pupil of Socrates, who founded a philosophical school in the Academy at Athens c. 387 B.C. He was also an adviser to the rulers of Syracuse in Sicily. His works survive more completely than those of any other Greek philosopher, and they have been studied and written about continually. His most famous work on politics was the *Republic*, to which Hobbes refers on page 254.

POMPEY (Gnaeus Pompeius Magnus, 106–48 B.C.). Roman general who fought with SULLA against the supporters of Marius. Consul in 70, he began to sympathise with the popular party at Rome and formed the first triumvirate with CAESAR and Crassus in 60. He quarrelled with Caesar and rejoined the aristocratic party, becoming sole consul in 52. In 49 a civil war broke out between his troops and those of Caesar, and Pompey was defeated at Pharsalus in 48. He was murdered while fleeing to Egypt.

PRIAPUS. In Greek mythology, the son of Dionysus and the god of fertility, represented as a phallus.

PROCULUS, Julius. A senator of the early kingdom of Rome (according to its legendary history), to whom the ghost of ROMULUS is supposed to have appeared. The story is recorded in LIVY.

PROMETHEUS. In Greek mythology, the son of a Titan, who stole fire from heaven for the good of mankind. Zeus punished him by chaining him to a mountain in the Caucasus, where an eagle ate his liver, which was renewed every day.

PTOLEMY II PHILADELPHUS. The second Greek ruler of Egypt after the division of ALEXANDER's empire, he reigned from 283 to 246 B.C.. He extended the famous library at Alexandria founded by Ptolemy I and organised the translation of the Hebrew Bible into Greek by seventy translators – the 'Septuagint'.

*REHOBOAM. The son of SOLOMON and king of Judah 930–913 B.C., he prospered while he followed God, but later permitted idolatry. As a punishment God sent Shishak, and pharaoh of Egypt, to harry Rehoboam's kingdom and capture Jerusalem.

ROMULUS. The legendary founder of Rome, in 753 B.C. He and his brother Remus were raised by a she-wolf (later the emblem of Rome); when Romulus built the first walls of the city, on the Palatine Hill, Remus ridiculed them, and Romulus killed him. Romulus was later carried up to heaven and was worshipped as the god Quirinus.

*SAMSON. One of the judges (c. 1070 B.C.), who was inspired by God to feats of great strength on behalf of Israel, but who was corrupted and betrayed to his Philistine enemies by his mistress Delilah. He committed suicide by pulling the temple down around himself and the leading Philistines.

*SAMUEL. The last and greatest of the judges and the first of the prophets, treated in the Old Testament as the greatest figure after MOSES. Possessed of divine revelations since boyhood, he took over the government of Israel after national disaster. With him the government by priests or judges on behalf of God ended: his sons were so wicked that their conduct caused discontent with the hierocracy and a demand for its replacement by a monarchy. God told Samuel to acquiesce (c. 1000 B.C.). The first king, SAUL, relied on Samuel's advice, even consulting a witch at Endor in a vain attempt to make contact with Samuel after his death. Samuel also anointed DAVID as Saul's destined successor.

SATURN. The Roman god of sowing and seed, who was supposed to have reigned over Italy in a golden age before recorded history. His festival at Rome, the Saturnalia, was the chief winter celebration.

SATURNINUS, Lucius. A Roman politician, he was tribune of the plebs in 103 B.C. and supported the reform programme of MARIUS. After a riot during Saturninus' third tribuneship, in 99, Marius reluctantly obeyed a senatorial order to arrest him, and Saturninus was killed in the resulting struggle.

*SAUL. The first king of Israel (c. 1000 B.C.). His reign began well with the defeat of the Ammonites at Jabesh-gilead. But he then arrogated the priestly power to himself and compounded what was seen as an error by sparing AGAG, King of the Ammonites, against God's instructions. After this, Samuel anointed DAVID to succeed

Saul. Saul turned against David, but David refused to kill him. After Samuel's death, Saul tried to speak to him through a witch at Endor; God is said to have used the witch to make known his displeasure to Saul. Saul shortly afterwards fell in battle against the Philistines.

SCIPIO AFRICANUS, Publius Cornelius (234–*c.* 183 B.C.). The principal general in the war of the Romans against the Carthaginians, he defeated Hannibal at Zama in Africa in 202. In his later years he was a leading politician, but retired after a bribery scandal in 184.

SELDEN, John (1584–1654). A leading English politician and political theorist, who served in the Parliaments of the 1620s and the Long Parliament. He was opposed to both extreme royalism and Presbyterianism, and wrote extensively on the history of the English constitution and on the law of nature. Of all his contemporaries, he was the closest intellectually to Hobbes (though they did not meet until after the publication of *Leviathan*, a presentation copy of which Hobbes sent to him). On page 69, Hobbes refers to Selden's *Titles of Honour* (1614), a study of the relationship between nobility and monarchy in all European states.

SILVESTER, I, Pope. Pope from 314 to 335, he was supposed (erroneously) to have baptised CONSTANTINE and to have received a grant of imperial power at Rome from him. He was the pope at the time of the Council of Nicaea (325).

SKANDERBEG (Iskander Bey, 1403–68). A Serbian who rose to power as a general of the Sultan of Constantinople, he renounced Islam and loyalty to the Turks in 1443 and created an independent Albania, which lasted until his death.

SOCRATES (469–399 B.C.). The principal philosophical influence on PLATO, who recorded his alleged views in his dialogues. He acted as a philosophical teacher in Athens, and in 404 was accused of impiety and corrupting the youth of the city. Condemned to death, he drank the hemlock poison prescribed by law in the spring of 399.

*SOLOMON. Third king of Israel (970–930 B.C.), after SAUL and DAVID, who was his father. Possessed of legendary wisdom, he reorganised his kingdom and built the Temple at Jerusalem, though he is criticised in the Old Testament for allowing foreign gods in Israel. Hobbes observed that he legislated (page 143), deposed Abiathar, the priest (page 329), performed acts of consecration (page 429) and had communications from God in a dream (page 294).

SOLON (*c.* 639–*c.* 559 B.C.). Political leader of Athens in its contest with Megara over Salamis and subsequently the archon of Athens (*c.* 595) with unlimited power. He remodelled the Athenian constitution, giving increased power to the popular assembly.

*STEPHEN, Saint. One of the seven chosen by the disciples after the resurrection to assist the widows of the Church, so that the apostles would be free to perform their peculiar mission of preaching the gospel. He quarrelled with some Jews and was stoned to death.

SUAREZ, Francisco de (1584–1617). Born at Granada (Spain), he became a Jesuit and taught theology at a number of Iberian universities and at Rome. He was the principal modern Aristotelian metaphysician, regarded as an authority by both Protestants and Catholics (though he wrote against the Protestants in a number of his more polemical works). In *Leviathan* (page 59) Hobbes ridicules a passage taken from Suarez's *De Concursu, Motione et Auxilio Dei* (II.1.6), in his *Varia Opuscula Theologica* (Madrid 1599) p. 20.

SULLA, Lucius Cornelius (138–78 B.C.). A successful Roman general who became the chief rival and opponent of MARIUS. In 82 he defeated the popular party and became dictator; thousands were killed in the proscription which he ordered of alleged enemies to the republic. He suddenly resigned in 79 and lived in retirement until his death.

*SUSANNA. See JOANNA.

SYLLA. See SULLA.

TARQUIN (Lucius Tarquinius Superbus). The legendary last king of Rome, who was supposed to have come to power in 534 B.C. He conquered some neighbouring cities, but in 510 B.C. his son (also called Tarquinius) raped Lucretia, the wife of his cousin Collatinus, and the entire family was expelled from Rome in a popular uprising, which also abolished the monarchy itself.

THEODOSIUS I (*c.* 346–395). A Roman general who became emperor in 379, he defeated the Goths and pacified the empire. He became a Trinitarian Christian in 380. In 390, after a massacre in Thessalonica in retribution for the murder of his governor there, he was excommunicated by AMBROSE and had to do eight months' penance. He was later reconciled with Ambrose, and is said to have died in his arms.

*THOMAS. One of the twelve apostles, who appears personally

only in JOHN's gospel, where his scepticism about Christ's resurrection was met by tactile proof. A Gospel of Thomas is one of the apocryphal books of the New Testament.

THOMAS (Thomas Aquinas, 1225–74). Born near Naples, he became a Dominican in 1243 and a pupil of the philosopher Albertus Magnus. From 1248 he began to publish commentaries on ARISTOTLE, and from 1252 to 1258 he taught at Paris (followed by time spent at a number of Italian universities). He was the most influential scholastic philosopher, particularly through his *Summa Theologiae*.

*URIAH. See DAVID.

URSICINUS. The defeated candidate in the papal election of 366, which was won by DAMASUS.

*UZZAH. He was a Levite who took hold of the Ark of the Covenant to stop it falling. This was an act of sacrilege, since it was forbidden to touch it, and he was struck dead by God.

VALENS. Roman emperor 374–8. He was elevated by his brother Valentinian I to rule the Eastern Empire, and was defeated and killed by the Visigoths at the battle of Adrianople. He was an ardent supporter of the Arians.

VARRO, Marcus Terentius (116–27 B.C.). An opponent of CAESAR in the civil war, he retired into private life under AUGUSTUS. He wrote extensively on Roman antiquities, including the history of the Latin language in *De Lingua Latina*. Fragments of his work on the religions of antiquity are preserved in later writers.

VENUS. The Roman goddess of fertility, later identified with the Greek Aphrodite.

VIRGIL (Publius Vergilius Maro, 70–19 B.C.). Born in Mantua, he became the most famous Latin poet, writing the *Eclogues*, the *Georgics* and the *Aeneid*. Hobbes quotes on page 312 from *Aeneid* VI 578–9.

WILLIAM I the Conqueror (1027–87). The bastard son of the Duke of Normandy, he succeeded his father as Duke in 1035. In 1051 he was promised the English succession by his cousin Edward the Confessor, a claim he made good in 1066 by his conquest of England. He organised England upon more systematically feudal lines than had been the case earlier, with all estates being held ultimately from the king.

WILLIAM II, Rufus (1066–1100). The second surviving son of WILLIAM the Conqueror, he inherited England on his father's death in 1087, while his elder brother Robert inherited Normandy. The Norman nobles in England supported Robert for the English kingship, but William granted them various privileges in return for their agreement to his accession. After years of conflict with both the Church and his brother, he was killed by an arrow while hunting in the New Forest.

*ZACCHAEUS. A chief tax-gatherer at Jericho who became a disciple of Jesus. He repaid Christ's forgiveness of his sins by giving half his goods to the poor and fourfold compensation to all those whom he had defrauded.

ZACHARY (Zacharias), pope 741–52. A Greek by background, born in Calabria, he recognised Pepin the Short as rightful king of the Franks in 751 (see CHILPERIQUE).

*ZADOK. He was a priest at DAVID's court along with ABIATHAR. He took part in the anointing of SOLOMON as David's successor, when Abiathar supported another candidate. Solomon rewarded him with Abiathar's job.

*ZECHARIAH (ZACHARIA, ZACHARIAS). A prophet, mentioned with HAGGAI in the Book of Esdras. The Book of Zechariah, probably by Zechariah, dates from 520–500 B.C.

*ZEDEKIAH. One of AHAB's four hundred court prophets and apparently their leader.

ZENO of Citium (355–263 B.C.). The founder of Stoic philosophy, who opened a school in the Stoa in the agora at Athens, after studying under various teachers including Cynics, Sophists and Platonists.

*ZEPHANIAH. He is mentioned as a prophet in the first verse of the Old Testament book which bears his name. It is largely concerned with God's judgement against the worshippers of BAAL. Modern scholars (unlike Hobbes) assign him to the reign of JOSIAH.

Fig. 1. T. Hobbes, *Leviathan* (London, 1651), title-page. 240×155 mm

LEVIATHAN,

OR

The Matter, Forme, & Power

OF A

COMMON-WEALTH

ECCLESIASTICALL

AND

CIVILL.

By THOMAS HOBBES *of* Malmesbury.

LONDON,

Printed for ANDREW CROOKE, at the Green Dragon
in St. Pauls Church-yard, 1651.

Fig. 2. T. Hobbes, *Leviathan* (1651), drawn title-page. Eg. 1910.
248×173 mm

TO
MY MOST HONOR'D FRIEND
Mr FRANCIS GODOLPHIN
of *Godolphin*.

Honor'd Sir,

Your most worthy Brother Mr *Sidney Godolphin*, when he lived, was pleas'd to think my studies something, and otherwise to oblige me, as you know, with reall testimonies of his good opinion, great in them-selves, and the greater for the worthinesse of his person. For there is not any vertue that disposeth a man, either to the service of God, or to the service of his Country, to Civill Society, or private Friendship, that did not manifestly appear in his conversation, not as acquired by necessity, or affected upon occasion, but inhaerent, and shining in a generous constitution of his nature. Therefore in honour and gratitude to him, and with devotion to your selfe, I humbly Dedicate unto you this my discourse of Common-wealth. I know not how the world will receive it, nor how it may reflect on those that shall seem to favour it. For in a way beset with those that contend, on one side for too great Liberty, and on the other side for too much Authority, 'tis hard to passe between the points of both unwounded. But yet, me thinks, the endeavour to advance the Civill Power, should not be by the Civill Power condemned; nor private men, by reprehending it, declare they think that Power too great. Besides, I speak not of the men, but (in the Abstract) of the Seat of Power, (like to those simple and unpartiall creatures in the Roman Capitol, that with their noyse defended those within it, not because they were they, but there,) offending none, I think, but those without, or such within (if there be any such) as favour them. That which perhaps may most offend, are certain Texts of Holy Scripture, alledged by me to other purpose than ordinarily they use to be by others. But I have done it with due submission, and also (in order to my Subject) necessarily; for they are the Outworks of the Enemy, from whence they impugne the Civill Power. If notwithstanding this, you find my labour generally decryed, you may be pleased to excuse your selfe, and say I am a man that love my own opinions, and think all true I say, that I honoured your

Brother, and honour you, and have presum'd on that, to assume the
Title (without your knowledge) of being, as I am,

SIR

Your most humble, and most
obedient servant,

Paris. *Aprill* $\frac{15}{25}$. 1651.   THO. HOBBES.

The Contents of the Chapters.

The first part,
Of MAN.

The Second Part,
Of COMMON-WEALTH.

The third Part.
Of A CHRISTIAN COMMON-WEALTH.

The fourth Part.
Of THE KINGDOME OF DARKNESSE.

THE
INTRODUCTION.

NATURE (the Art whereby God hath made and governes the World) is [1]
by the *Art* of man, as in many other things, so in this also imitated, that
it can make an Artificiall Animal. For seeing life is but a motion of
Limbs, the begining whereof is in some principall part within; why
may we not say, that all *Automata* (Engines that move themselves by
springs and wheeles as doth a watch) have an artificiall life? For what
is the *Heart*, but a *Spring*; and the *Nerves*, but so many *Strings*; and the
Joynts, but so many *Wheeles*, giving motion to the whole Body, such as
was intended by the Artificer? *Art* goes yet further, imitating that
Rationall and most excellent worke of Nature, *Man*. For by Art is
created that great LEVIATHAN called a COMMON-WEALTH, or
STATE, (in latine CIVITAS) which is but an Artificiall Man; though of
greater stature and strength than the Naturall, for whose protection
and defence it was intended; and in which, the *Soveraignty* is an
Artificiall *Soul*, as giving life and motion to the whole body; The
Magistrates, and other *Officers* of Judicature and Execution, artificiall
Joynts; *Reward* and *Punishment* (by which fastned to the seate of the
Soveraignty, every joynt and member is moved to performe his duty)
are the *Nerves*, that do the same in the Body Naturall; The *Wealth* and
Riches of all the particular members, are the *Strength*; *Salus Populi* (the
peoples safety) its *Businesse*; *Counsellors*, by whom all things needfull for
it to know, are suggested unto it, are the *Memory*; *Equity* and *Lawes*, an
artificiall *Reason* and *Will*; *Concord*, *Health*; *Sedition*, *Sicknesse*; and
Civill war, *Death*. Lastly, the *Pacts* and *Covenants*, by which the parts of
this Body Politique were at first made, set together, and united,

resemble that *Fiat*, or the *Let us make man*, pronounced by God in the Creation.

[2]   To describe the Nature of this Artificiall man, I will consider

First, the *Matter* thereof, and the *Artificer*, both which is *Man*.
Secondly, *How*, and by what *Covenants* it is made; what are the *Rights* and *just Power* or *Authority* of a *Soveraigne*; and what it is that *preserveth* and *dissolveth* it.
Thirdly, what is a *Christian Common-wealth*.
Lastly, what is the *Kingdome of Darkness*.

Concerning the first, there is a saying much usurped of late, That *Wisedome* is acquired, not by reading of *Books*, but of *Men*. Consequently whereunto, those persons, that for the most part can give no other proof of being wise, take great delight to shew what they think they have read in men, by uncharitable censures of one another behind their backs. But there is another saying not of late understood, by which they might learn truly to read one another, if they would take the pains; and that is, *Nosce teipsum*, *Read thy self*: which was not meant, as it is now used, to countenance, either the barbarous state of men in power, towards their inferiors; or to encourage men of low degree, to a sawcie behaviour towards their betters; But to teach us, that for the similitude of the thoughts, and Passions of one man, to the thoughts, and Passions of another, whosoever looketh into himself, and considereth what he doth, when he does *think, opine, reason, hope, feare*, &c, and upon what grounds; he shall thereby read and know, what are the thoughts, and Passions of all other men, upon the like occasions. I say the similitude of *Passions*, which are the same in all men, *desire, feare, hope*, &c; not the similitude of the *objects* of the Passions, which are the things *desired, feared, hoped*, &c: for these the constitution individuall, and particular education do so vary, and they are so easie to be kept from our knowledge, that the characters of mans heart, blotted and confounded as they are, with dissembling, lying, counterfeiting, and erroneous doctrines, are legible onely to him that searcheth hearts. And though by mens actions wee do discover their designe sometimes; yet to do it without comparing them with our own, and distinguishing all circumstances, by which the case may come to be altered, is to decypher without a key, and be for the most part deceived, by too much trust, or by too much diffidence; as he that reads, is himself a good or evil man.

But let one man read another by his actions never so perfectly, it serves him onely with his acquaintance, which are but few. He that is to govern a whole Nation, must read in himself, not this, or that particular man; but Man-kind: which though it be hard to do, harder than to learn any Language, or Science; yet, when I shall have set down my own reading orderly, and perspicuously, the pains left another, will be onely to consider, if he also find not the same in himself. For this kind of Doctrine, admitteth no other Demonstration.

PART 1.

OF MAN.

CHAP. I.
Of SENSE.

Concerning the Thoughts of man, I will consider them first *singly*, [3]
and afterwards in *Trayne*, or dependance upon one another. *Singly*,
they are every one a *Representation* or *Apparence*, of some quality, or
other Accident of a body without us; which is commonly called an
Object. Which Object worketh on the Eyes, Eares, and other parts of
mans body; and by diversity of working, produceth diversity of
Apparences.

The Originall of them all, is that which we call SENSE; (For there
is no conception in a mans mind, which hath not at first, totally, or by
parts, been begotten upon the organs of Sense.) The rest are derived
from that originall.

To know the naturall cause of Sense, is not very necessary to the
business now in hand; and I have else-where written of the same at
large. Nevertheless, to fill each part of my present method, I will
briefly deliver the same in this place.

The cause of Sense, is the Externall Body, or Object, which presseth the organ proper to each Sense, either immediately, as in the
Tast and Touch; or mediately, as in Seeing, Hearing, and Smelling:
which pressure, by the mediation of Nerves, and other strings, and
membranes of the body, continued inwards to the Brain, and Heart,
causeth there a resistance, or counter-pressure, or endeavour of the
heart, to deliver itself: which endeavour because *Outward*, seemeth to

be some matter without. And this *seeming*, or *fancy*, is that which men call *Sense*; and consisteth, as to the Eye, in a *Light*, or *Colour figured*; To the Eare, in a *Sound*; To the Nostrill, in an *Odour*; To the Tongue and Palat, in a *Savour*; And to the rest of the body, in *Heat, Cold, Hardnesse, Softnesse,* and such other qualities, as we discern by *Feeling*. All which qualities called *Sensible*, are in the object that causeth them, but so many several motions of the matter, by which it presseth our organs diversly. Neither in us that are pressed, are they any thing else, but divers motions; (for motion, produceth nothing but motion.) But their apparence to us is Fancy, the same waking, that dreaming. And as pressing, rubbing, or striking the Eye, makes us fancy a light; and pressing the Eare, produceth a dinne; so do the bodies also we see, or hear, produce the same by their strong, though unobserved action. For if those Colours, and Sounds, were in the Bodies, or Objects that cause them, they could not bee severed from them, as by glasses, and in Ecchoes by reflection, wee see they are; where we know the thing we see, is in one place; the apparence, in another. And though at some certain distance, the reall, and very object seem invested with the fancy it begets in us; Yet still the object is one thing, the image or fancy is another. So that Sense in all cases, is nothing els but originall fancy, caused (as I have said) by the pressure, that is, by the motion, of externall things upon our Eyes, Eares, and other organs thereunto ordained.

[4]

But the Philosophy-schooles, through all the Universities of Christendome, grounded upon certain Texts of *Aristotle*, teach another doctrine; and say, For the cause of *Vision*, that the thing seen, sendeth forth on every side a *visible species* (in English) a *visible shew*, *apparition*, or *aspect*, or *a being seen*; the receiving whereof into the Eye, is *Seeing*. And for the cause of *Hearing*, that the thing heard, sendeth forth an *Audible species*, that is, an *Audible aspect*, or *Audible being seen*; which entring at the Eare, maketh *Hearing*. Nay for the cause of *Understanding* also, they say the thing Understood sendeth forth *intelligible species*, that is, an *intelligible being seen*; which comming into the Understanding, makes us Understand. I say not this, as disapproving the use of Universities: but because I am to speak hereafter of their office in a Common-wealth, I must let you see on all occasions by the way, what things would be amended in them; amongst which the frequency of insignificant Speech is one.

CHAP. II.
Of IMAGINATION.

That when a thing lies still, unlesse somewhat els stirre it, it will lye
still for ever, is a truth that no man doubts of. But that when a thing is
in motion, it will eternally be in motion, unless somewhat els stay it,
though the reason be the same, (namely, that nothing can change it
selfe,) is not so easily assented to. For men measure, not onely other
men, but all other things, by themselves: and because they find themselves subject after motion to pain, and lassitude, think every thing els
growes weary of motion, and seeks repose of its own accord; little
considering, whether it be not some other motion, wherein that desire
of rest they find in themselves, consisteth. From hence it is, that the
Schooles say, Heavy bodies fall downwards, out of an appetite to rest,
and to conserve their nature in that place which is most proper for
them; ascribing appetite, and Knowledge of what is good for their
conservation, (which is more than man has) to things inanimate,
absurdly.

When a Body is once in motion, it moveth (unless something els
hinder it) eternally; and whatsoever hindreth it, cannot in an instant,
but in time, and by degrees quite extinguish it: And as wee see in the
water, though the wind cease, the waves give not over rowling for a
long time after; so also it happeneth in that motion, which is made in [5]
the internall parts of a man, then, when he Sees, Dreams, &c. For
after the object is removed, or the eye shut, wee still retain an image
of the thing seen, though more obscure than when we see it. And this
is it, the Latines call *Imagination*, from the image made in seeing; and
apply the same, though improperly, to all the other senses. But the
Greeks call it *Fancy*; which signifies *apparence*, and is as proper to one
sense, as to another. IMAGINATION therefore is nothing but *decaying
sense*; and is found in men, and many other living Creatures, aswell
sleeping, as waking.

The decay of Sense in men waking, is not the decay of the motion
made in sense; but an obscuring of it, in such manner, as the light of
the Sun obscureth the light of the Starres; which starrs do no less
exercise their vertue by which they are visible, in the day, than in the

night. But because amongst many stroaks, which our eyes, eares, and other organs receive from externall bodies, the predominant onely is sensible; therefore the light of the Sun being predominant, we are not affected with the action of the starrs. And any object being removed from our eyes, though the impression it made in us remain; yet other objects more present succeeding, and working on us, the Imagination of the past is obscured, and made weak; as the voyce of a man is in the noyse of the day. From whence it followeth, that the longer the time is, after the sight, or Sense of any object, the weaker is the Imagination. For the continuall change of mans body, destroyes in time the parts which in sense were moved: So that distance of time, and of place, hath one and the same effect in us. For as at a great distance of place, that which wee look at, appears dimme, and without distinction of the smaller parts; and as Voyces grow weak, and inarticulate: so also after great distance of time, our imagination of the Past is weak; and wee lose (for example) of Cities wee have seen, many particular Streets; and of Actions, many particular Circumstances. This *decaying sense*, when wee would express the thing it self, (I mean *fancy* it selfe,) wee call *Imagination*, as I said before: But when we would express the *decay*, and signifie that the Sense is fading, old, and past, it is called

Memory.   *Memory*. So that *Imagination* and *Memory*, are but one thing, which for divers considerations hath divers names.

Much memory, or memory of many things, is called *Experience*. Againe, Imagination being only of those things which have been formerly perceived by Sense, either all at once, or by parts at severall times; The former, (which is the imagining the whole object, as it was presented to the sense) is *simple Imagination*; as when one imagineth a man, or horse, which he hath seen before. The other is *Compounded*; as when from the sight of a man at one time, and of a horse at another, we conceive in our mind a Centaure. So when a man compoundeth the image of his own person, with the image of the actions of an other man; as when a man imagins himselfe a *Hercules*, or an *Alexander*, (which happeneth often to them that are much taken with reading of Romants) it is a compound imagination, and properly but a Fiction of

[6]   the mind. There be also other Imaginations that rise in men, (though waking) from the great impression made in sense: As from gazing upon the Sun, the impression leaves an image of the Sun before our eyes a long time after; and from being long and vehemently attent upon Geometricall Figures, a man shall in the dark, (though awake)

have the Images of Lines, and Angles before his eyes: which kind of
Fancy hath no particular name; as being a thing that doth not commonly fall into mens discourse.

The imaginations of them that sleep, are those we call *Dreams*. And   *Dreams.*
these also (as all other Imaginations) have been before, either totally,
or by parcells in the Sense. And because in sense, the Brain, and
Nerves, which are the necessary Organs of sense, are so benummed
in sleep, as not easily to be moved by the action of Externall Objects,
there can happen in sleep, no Imagination; and therefore no Dreame,
but what proceeds from the agitation of the inward parts of mans
body; which inward parts, for the connexion they have with the Brayn,
and other Organs, when they be distempered, do keep the same in
motion; whereby the Imaginations there formerly made, appeare as if
a man were waking; saving that the Organs of Sense being now
benummed, so as there is no new object, which can master and
obscure them with a more vigorous impression, a Dreame must needs
be more cleare, in this silence of sense, than are our waking thoughts.
And hence it cometh to passe, that it is a hard matter, and by many
thought impossible to distinguish exactly between Sense and Dreaming. For my part, when I consider, that in Dreames, I do not often,
nor constantly think of the same Persons, Places, Objects, and
Actions that I do waking; nor remember so long a trayne of coherent
thoughts, Dreaming, as at other times; And because waking I often
observe the absurdity of Dreames, but never dream of the absurdities
of my waking Thoughts; I am well satisfied, that being awake, I know
I dreame not; though when I dreame, I think my selfe awake.

And seeing dreames are caused by the distemper of some of the
inward parts of the Body; divers distempers must needs cause different Dreams. And hence it is, that lying cold breedeth Dreams of
Feare, and raiseth the thought and Image of some fearfull object (the
motion from the brain to the inner parts, and from the inner parts to
the Brain being reciprocall:) And that as Anger causeth heat in some
parts of the Body, when we are awake; so when we sleep, the over
heating of the same parts causeth Anger, and raiseth up in the brain
the Imagination of an Enemy. In the same manner; as naturall kindness, when we are awake causeth desire; and desire makes heat in
certain other parts of the body; so also, too much heat in those parts,
while wee sleep, raiseth in the brain an imagination of some kindness
shewn. In summe, our Dreams are the reverse of our waking

Imaginations; The motion when we are awake, beginning at one end; and when we Dream, at another.

Apparitions or Visions.
[7]
The most difficult discerning of a mans Dream, from his waking thoughts, is then, when by some accident we observe not that we have slept: which is easie to happen to a man full of fearfull thoughts; and whose conscience is much troubled; and that sleepeth, without the circumstances, of going to bed, or putting off his clothes, as one that noddeth in a chayre. For he that taketh pains, and industriously layes himself to sleep, in case any uncouth and exorbitant fancy come unto him, cannot easily think it other than a Dream. We read of *Marcus Brutus*, (one that had his life given him by *Julius Caesar*, and was also his favorite, and notwithstanding murthered him,) how at *Philippi*, the night before he gave battell to *Augustus Caesar*, hee saw a fearfull apparition, which is commonly related by Historians as a Vision: but considering the circumstances, one may easily judge to have been but a short Dream. For sitting in his tent, pensive and troubled with the horrour of his rash act, it was not hard for him, slumbering in the cold, to dream of that which most affrighted him; which feare, as by degrees it made him wake; so also it must needs make the Apparition by degrees to vanish: And having no assurance that he slept, he could have no cause to think it a Dream, or any thing but a Vision. And this is no very rare Accident: for even they that be perfectly awake, if they be timorous, and supperstitious, possessed with fearfull tales, and alone in the dark, are subject to the like fancies; and believe they see spirits and dead mens Ghosts walking in Church-yards; whereas it is either their Fancy onely, or els the knavery of such persons, as make use of such superstitious feare, to passe disguised in the night, to places they would not be known to haunt.

From this ignorance of how to distinguish Dreams, and other strong Fancies, from Vision and Sense, did arise the greatest part of the Religion of the Gentiles in time past, that worshipped Satyres, Fawnes, Nymphs, and the like; and now adayes the opinion that rude people have of Fayries, Ghosts, and Goblins; and of the power of Witches. For as for Witches, I think not that their witchcraft is any reall power; but yet that they are justly punished, for the false beliefe they have, that they can do such mischiefe, joyned with their purpose to do it if they can: their trade being neerer to a new Religion, than to a Craft or Science. And for Fayries, and walking Ghosts, the opinion of them has I think been on purpose, either taught, or not confuted, to keep in credit the use of Exorcisme, of Crosses, of holy Water, and other such inventions of Ghostly men. Neverthelesse, there is no doubt, but God can make unnaturall Apparitions: But that he does it so often, as men need to feare such things, more than they feare the stay, or change, of the course of Nature, which he also can stay, and change, is no point of Christian faith. But evill men under pretext that God can do anything, are so bold as to say any thing when it serves their turn, though they think it untrue; It is the part of a wise man, to believe them no further, than right reason makes that which they say, appear credible. If this superstitious fear of Spirits were taken away, and with it, Prognostiques from Dreams, false Prophecies, and many other things depending thereon, by which, crafty ambitious persons [8] abuse the simple people, men would be much more fitted than they are for civill Obedience.

And this ought to be the work of the Schooles: but they rather nourish such doctrine. For (not knowing what Imagination, or the Senses are), what they receive, they teach: some saying, that Imaginations rise of themselves, and have no cause: Others that they rise most commonly from the Will; and that Good thoughts are blown (inspired) into a man, by God; and Evill thoughts by the Divell: or that Good thoughts are powred (infused) into a man, by God, and Evill ones by the Divell. Some say the Senses receive the Species of things, and deliver them to the Common-sense; and the Common Sense delivers them over to the Fancy, and the Fancy to the Memory, and the Memory to the Judgement, like handing of things from one to another, with many words making nothing understood.

The Imagination that is raysed in man (or any other creature *Under-* indued with the faculty of imagining) by words, or other voluntary *standing.* signes, is that we generally call *Understanding*; and is common to Man and Beast. For a dogge by custome will understand the call, or the rating of his Master; and so will many other Beasts. That Understanding which is peculiar to man, is the Understanding not onely his will; but his conceptions and thoughts, by the sequell and contexture of the names of things into Affirmations, Negations, and other formes of Speech: And of this kinde of Understanding I shall speak hereafter.

CHAP. III.

Of the Consequence or TRAYNE *of Imaginations.*

By *Consequence,* or TRAYNE of Thoughts, I understand that succession of one Thought to another, which is called (to distinguish it from Discourse in words) *Mentall Discourse.*

When a man thinketh on any thing whatsoever, His next Thought after, is not altogether so casuall as it seems to be. Not every Thought to every Thought succeeds indifferently. But as wee have no Imagination, whereof we have not formerly had Sense, in whole, or in parts; so we have no Transition from one Imagination to another, whereof we never had the like before in our Senses. The reason whereof is this. All Fancies are Motions within us, reliques of those made in the Sense: And those motions that immediately succeeded one another in the sense, continue also together after Sense: In so much as the former comming again to take place, and be praedominant, the later followeth, by coherence of the matter moved, in such manner, as water upon a plain Table is drawn which way any one part of it is guided by the finger. But because in sense, to one and the same thing perceived, sometimes one thing, sometimes another succeedeth, it comes to passe in time, that in the Imagining of any thing, there is no certainty what we shall Imagine next; Onely this is certain, it shall be something that succeeded the same before, at one time or another.

[9]

This Trayne of Thoughts, or Mentall Discourse, is of two sorts.

Trayne of Thoughts unguided.

The first is *Unguided, without Designe,* and inconstant; Wherein there is no Passionate Thought, to govern and direct those that follow, to it self, as the end and scope of some desire, or other passion: In which case the thoughts are said to wander, and seem impertinent one to another, as in a Dream. Such are Commonly the thoughts of men, that are not onely without company, but also without care of any thing; though even then their Thoughts are as busie as at other times, but without harmony; as the sound which a Lute out of tune would yeeld to any man; or in tune, to one that could not play. And yet in this wild ranging of the mind, a man may oft-times perceive the way of it, and the dependance of one thought upon another. For in a Discourse of our present civill warre, what could seem more impertinent, than to ask (as one did) what was the value of a Roman Penny? Yet the Cohaerence to me was manifest enough. For the Thought of the warre, introduced the Thought of the delivering up the King to his Enemies; The Thought of that, brought in the Thought of the delivering up of Christ; and that again the Thought of the 30 pence, which was the price of that treason: and thence easily followed that malicious question; and all this in a moment of time; for Thought is quick.

The second is more constant; as being *regulated* by some desire, and designe. For the impression made by such things as wee desire, or feare, is strong and permanent, or, (if it cease for a time,) of quick return: so strong it is sometimes, as to hinder and break our sleep. From Desire, ariseth the Thought of some means we have seen produce the like of that which we ayme at; and from the thought of that, the thought of means to that mean; and so continually, till we come to some beginning within our own power. And because the End, by the greatnesse of the impression, comes often to mind, in case our thoughts begin to wander, they are quickly again reduced into the way: which observed by one of the seven wise men, made him give men this praecept, which is now worne out, *Respice finem*; that is to say, in all your actions, look often upon what you would have, as the thing that directs all your thoughts in the way to attain it. *Trayne of Thoughts regulated.*

The Trayne of regulated Thoughts is of two kinds; One, when of an effect imagined, wee seek the causes, or means that produce it: and this is common to Man and Beast. The other is, when imagining any thing whatsoever, wee seek all the possible effects, that can by it be produced; that is to say, we imagine what we can do with it, when wee have it. Of which I have not at any time seen any signe, but in man onely; for this is a curiosity hardly incident to the nature of any living creature that has no other Passion but sensuall, such as are hunger, thirst, lust, and anger. In summe, the Discourse of the Mind, when it is governed by designe, is nothing but *Seeking*, or the faculty of Invention, which the Latines call *Sagacitas*, and *Solertia*; a hunting out of the causes, of some effect, present or past; or of the effects, of some present or past cause. Sometimes a man seeks what he hath lost; and from that place, and time, wherein hee misses it, his mind runs back, from place to place, and time to time, to find where, and when he had [10]

21

it; that is to say, to find some certain, and limited time and place, in which to begin a method of seeking. Again, from thence, his thoughts run over the same places and times, to find what action, or other *Remem-* occasion might make him lose it. This we call *Remembrance,* or Calling *brance.* to mind: the Latines call it *Reminiscentia,* as it were a *Re-conning* of our former actions.

Sometimes a man knows a place determinate, within the compasse whereof he is to seek; and then his thoughts run over all the parts thereof, in the same manner, as one would sweep a room, to find a jewell; or as a Spaniel ranges the field, till he finds a sent; or as a man should run over the Alphabet, to start a rime.

Prudence. Sometime a man desires to know the event of an action; and then he thinketh of some like action past, and the events thereof one after another; supposing like events will follow like actions. As he that foresees what wil become of a Criminal, re-cons what he has seen follow on the like Crime before; having this order of thoughts, The Crime, the Officer, the Prison, the Judge, and the Gallowes. Which kind of thoughts, is called *Foresight,* and *Prudence,* or *Providence*; and sometimes *Wisdome*; though such conjecture, through the difficulty of observing all circumstances, be very fallacious. But this is certain; by how much one man has more experience of things past, than another; by so much also he is more Prudent, and his expectations the seldomer faile him. The *Present* onely has a being in Nature; things *Past* have a being in the Memory onely, but things *to come* have no being at all; the *Future* being but a fiction of the mind, applying the sequels of actions Past, to the actions that are Present; which with most certainty is done by him that has most Experience; but not with certainty enough. And though it be called Prudence, when the Event answereth our Expectation; yet in its own nature, it is but Presumption. For the foresight of things to come, which is Providence, belongs onely to him by whose will they are to come. From him onely, and supernaturally, proceeds Prophecy. The best Prophet naturally is the best guesser; and the best guesser, he that is most versed and studied in the matters he guesses at: for he hath most *Signes* to guesse by.

Signes. A *Signe,* is the Event Antecedent, of the Consequent; and contrarily, the Consequent of the Antecedent, when the like Consequences have been observed, before: And the oftner they have been observed, the lesse uncertain is the Signe. And therefore he that has most experience in any kind of businesse, has most Signes, whereby to guesse at the Future time; and consequently is the most prudent: And so much more prudent than he that is new in that kind of business, as not to be equalled by any advantage of naturall and extemporary wit: though perhaps many young men think the contrary.

Neverthelesse it is not Prudence that distinguisheth man from beast. There be beasts, that at a year old observe more, and pursue [11] that which is for their good, more prudently, than a child can do at ten.

As Prudence is a *Praesumtion* of the *Future*, contracted from the *Experience* of time *Past*: So there is a Praesumtion of things Past taken from other things (not future but) past also. For he that hath seen by what courses and degrees, a flourishing State hath first come into civil warre, and then to ruine; upon the sight of the ruines of any other State, will guesse, the like warre, and the like courses have been there also. But this conjecture, has the same incertainty almost with the conjecture of the Future; both being grounded onely upon Experience. *Conjecture of the time past.*

There is no other act of mans mind, that I can remember, naturally planted in him, so, as to need no other thing, to the exercise of it, but to be born a man, and live with the use of his five Senses. Those other Faculties, of which I shall speak by and by, and which seem proper to man onely, are acquired, and encreased by study and industry; and of most men learned by instruction, and discipline; and proceed all from the invention of Words, and Speech. For besides Sense, and Thoughts, and the Trayne of thoughts, the mind of man has no other motion; though by the help of Speech, and Method, the same Facultyes may be improved to such a height, as to distinguish men from all other living Creatures.

Whatsoever we imagine, is *Finite*. Therefore there is no Idea, or conception of any thing we call *Infinite*. No man can have in his mind an Image of infinite magnitude; nor conceive infinite swiftness, infinite time, or infinite force, or infinite power. When we say any thing is infinite, we signifie onely, that we are not able to conceive the ends, and bounds of the thing named; having no Conception of the thing, but of our own inability. And therefore the Name of *God* is used, not to make us conceive him; (for he is *Incomprehensible*; and his greatnesse, and power are unconceivable;) but that we may honour him. Also because whatsoever (as I said before,) we conceive, has been perceived first by sense, either all at once, or by parts; a man can have no thought, representing any thing, not subject to sense. No man therefore can conceive any thing, but he must conceive it in some place; and indued with some determinate magnitude; and which may be divided into parts; nor that any thing is all in this place, and all in another place at the same time; nor that two, or more things can be in one, and the same place at once: For none of these things ever have, or can be incident to Sense; but are absurd speeches, taken upon credit (without any signification at all,) from deceived Philosophers, and deceived, or deceiving Schoolemen.

CHAP. IV.
Of SPEECH.

Originall of Speech. The Invention of *Printing*, though ingenious, compared with the invention of *Letters*, is no great matter. But who was the first that found the use of Letters, is not known. He that first brought them into *Greece*, men say was *Cadmus*, the sonne of *Agenor*, King of Phaenicia. A profitable Invention for continuing the memory of time past, and the conjunction of mankind, dispersed into so many, and distant regions of the Earth; and with all difficult, as proceeding from a watchfull observation of the divers motions of the Tongue, Palat, Lips, and other organs of Speech; whereby to make as many differences of characters, to remember them. But the most noble and profitable invention of all other, was that of SPEECH, consisting of *Names* or *Appellations*, and their Connexion; whereby men register their Thoughts; recall them when they are past; and also declare them one to another for mutuall utility and conversation; without which, there had been amongst men, neither Common-wealth, nor Society, nor Contract, nor Peace, no more than amongst Lyons, Bears, and Wolves. The first author of Speech was *God* himself, that instructed *Adam* how to name such creatures as he presented to his sight; For the Scripture goeth no further in this matter. But this was sufficient to direct him to adde more names, as the experience and use of the creatures should give him occasion; and to joyn them in such manner by degrees, as to make himself understood; and so by succession of time, so much language might be gotten, as he had found use for;

though not so copious, as an Orator or Philosopher has need of. For I do not find any thing in the Scripture, out of which, directly or by consequence can be gathered, that *Adam* was taught the names of all Figures, Numbers, Measures, Colours, Sounds, Fancies, Relations; much less the names of Words and Speech, as *Generall*, *Speciall*, *Affirmative*, *Negative*, *Interrogative*, *Optative*, *Infinitive*, all which are usefull; and least of all, of *Entity*, *Intentionality*, *Quiddity*, and other insignificant words of the School.

But all this language gotten, and augmented by *Adam* and his posterity, was again lost at the tower of *Babel*, when by the hand of God, every man was stricken for his rebellion, with an oblivion of his former language. And being hereby forced to disperse themselves into severall parts of the world, it must needs be, that the diversity of Tongues that now is, proceeded by degrees from them, in such manner, as need (the mother of all inventions) taught them; and in tract of time grew every where more copious.

The generall use of Speech, is to transferre our Mentall Discourse, into Verbal; or the Trayne of our Thoughts, into a Trayne of Words; and that for two commodities; whereof one is, the Registring of the Consequences of our Thoughts; which being apt to slip out of our memory, and put us to a new labour, may again be recalled, by such words as they were marked by. So that the first use of names, is to serve for *Markes*, or *Notes* of remembrance. Another is, when many use the same words, to signifie (by their connexion and order,) one to another, what they conceive, or think of each matter; and also what they desire, feare, or have any other passion for. And for this use they are called *Signes*. Speciall uses of Speech are these; First, to Register, what by cogitation, wee find to be the cause of any thing, present or past; and what we find things present or past may produce, or effect: which in summe, is acquiring of Arts. Secondly, to shew to others that knowledge which we have attained; which is, to Counsell, and Teach one another. Thirdly, to make known to others our wills, and purposes, that we may have the mutuall help of one another. Fourthly, to please and delight our selves, and others, by playing with our words, for pleasure or ornament, innocently.

To these Uses, there are also foure correspondent Abuses. First, when men register their thoughts wrong, by the inconstancy of the signification of their words; by which they register for their conceptions, that which they never conceived; and so deceive themselves.

The use of Speech.

[13]

Abuses of Speech.

Secondly, when they use words metaphorically; that is, in other sense than that they are ordained for; and thereby deceive others. Thirdly, when by words they declare that to be their will, which is not. Fourthly, when they use them to grieve one another: for seeing nature hath armed living creatures, some with teeth, some with horns, and some with hands, to grieve an enemy, it is but an abuse of Speech, to grieve him with the tongue, unlesse it be one whom wee are obliged to govern; and then it is not to grieve, but to correct and amend.

The manner how Speech serveth to the remembrance of the consequence of causes and effects, consisteth in the imposing of *Names*, and the *Connexion* of them.

Names
Proper &
Common.

Of Names, some are *Proper*, and singular to one onely thing; as *Peter, John, This man, this Tree*: and some are *Common* to many things; as *Man, Horse, Tree*; every of which though but one Name, is nevertheless the name of divers particular things; in respect of all which

Universall.

together, it is called an *Universall*; there being nothing in the world Universall but Names; for the things named, are every one of them Individuall and Singular.

One Universall name is imposed on many things, for their similitude in some quality, or other accident: And wheras a Proper Name bringeth to mind one thing onely; Universals recall any one of those many.

And of Names Universall, some are of more, and some of lesse extent; the larger comprehending the lesse large: and some again of equall extent, comprehending each other reciprocally. As for example, the Name *Body* is of larger signification than the word *Man*, and comprehendeth it; and the names *Man* and *Rationall*, are of equall

[14]

extent, comprehending mutually one another. But here wee must take notice, that by a Name is not always understood, as in Grammar, one onely Word; but sometimes by circumlocution many words together. For all these words, *Hee that in his actions observeth the Lawes of his Country*, make but one Name, equivalent to this one word, *Just*.

By this imposition of Names, some of larger, some of stricter signification, we turn the reckoning of the consequences of things imagined in the mind, into a reckoning of the consequences of Appellations. For example, a man that hath no use of Speech at all, (such, as is born and remains perfectly deafe and dumb,) if he set before his eyes a triangle, and by it two right angles, (such as are the corners of a square figure,) he may by meditation compare and find, that the three angles of that triangle, are equall to those two right angles that stand by it. But if another triangle be shewn him different in shape from the former, he cannot know without a new labour, whether the three angles of that also be equall to the same. But he that hath the use of words, when he observes, that such equality was consequent, not to the length of the sides, nor to any other particular thing in his triangle; but onely to this, that the sides were straight, and the angles three; and that that was all, for which he named it a Triangle; will boldly conclude Universally, that such equality of angles is in all triangles whatsoever; and register his invention in these generall termes, *Every triangle hath its three angles equall to two right angles*. And thus the consequence found in one particular, comes to be registred and remembred, as an Universall rule; and discharges our mentall reckoning, of time and place; and delivers us from all labour of the mind, saving the first; and makes that which was found true *here*, and *now*, to be true in *all times* and *places*.

But the use of words in registring our thoughts, is in nothing so evident as in Numbring. A naturall foole that could never learn by heart the order of numerall words, as *one*, *two*, and *three*, may observe every stroak of the Clock, and nod to it, or say one, one, one; but can never know what houre it strikes. And it seems, there was a time when those names of number were not in use; and men were fayn to apply their fingers of one or both hands, to those things they desired to keep account of; and that thence it proceeded, that now our numerall words are but ten, in any Nation, and in some but five, and then they begin again. And he that can tell ten, if he recite them out of order, will lose himselfe, and not know when he has done: Much lesse will he be able to adde, and subtract, and performe all other operations of Arithmetique. So that without words, there is no possibility of reckoning of Numbers; much lesse of Magnitudes, of Swiftnesse, of Force, and other things, the reckonings whereof are necessary to the being, or well-being of man-kind.

When two Names are joyned together into a Consequence, or Affirmation; as thus, *A man is a living creature*; or thus, *if he be a man, he is a living creature*, If the later name *Living creature*, signifie all that the former name *Man* signifieth, then the affirmation, or consequence is *true*; otherwise false. For *True* and *False* are attributes of Speech, [15] not of Things. And where Speech is not, there is neither *Truth* nor *Falshood*. *Errour* there may be, as when wee expect that which shall not

27

be; or suspect what has not been: but in neither case can a man be charged with Untruth.

Seeing then that *truth* consisteth in the right ordering of names in our affirmations, a man that seeketh precise *truth*, had need to remember what every name he uses stands for; and to place it accordingly; or else he will find himselfe entangled in words, as a bird in lime-twiggs; the more he struggles, the more belimed. And therefore in Geometry, (which is the onely Science that it hath pleased God hitherto to bestow on mankind,) men begin at settling the significations of their words; which settling of significations, they call *Definitions*; and place them in the beginning of their reckoning.

By this it appears how necessary it is for any man that aspires to true Knowledge, to examine the Definitions of former Authors; and either to correct them, where they are negligently set down; or to make them himselfe. For the errours of Definitions multiply themselves, according as the reckoning proceeds; and lead men into absurdities, which at last they see, but cannot avoyd, without reckoning anew from the beginning; in which lyes the foundation of their errours. From whence it happens, that they which trust to books, do as they that cast up many little summs into a greater, without considering whether those little summes were rightly cast up or not; and at last finding the errour visible, and not mistrusting their first grounds, know not which way to cleere themselves; but spend time in fluttering over their bookes; as birds that entring by the chimney, and finding themselves inclosed in a chamber, flutter at the false light of a glasse window, for want of wit to consider which way they came in. So that in the right Definition of Names, lyes the first use of Speech; which is the Acquisition of Science: And in wrong, or no Definitions, lyes the first abuse; from which proceed all false and senslesse Tenets; which make those men that take their instruction from the authority of books, and not from their own meditation, to be as much below the condition of ignorant men, as men endued with true Science are above it. For between true Science, and erroneous Doctrines, Ignorance is in the middle. Naturall sense and imagination, are not subject to absurdity. Nature it selfe cannot erre: and as men abound in copiousnesse of language; so they become more wise, or more mad than ordinary. Nor is it possible without Letters for any man to become either excellently wise, or (unless his memory be hurt by disease, or ill constitution of organs) excellently foolish. For words

are wise mens counters, they do but reckon by them: but they are the
mony of fooles, that value them by the authority of an *Aristotle*, a
Cicero, or a *Thomas*, or any other Doctor whatsoever, if but a man.

Subject to Names, is whatsoever can enter into, or be considered in
an account; and be added one to another to make a summe; or
substracted one from another, and leave a remainder. The Latines
called Accounts of mony *Rationes*, and accounting, *Ratiocinatio*: and
that which we in bills or books of account call *Items*, they called
Nomina; that is, *Names*: and thence it seems to proceed, that they
extended the word *Ratio*, to the faculty of Reckoning in all other
things. The Greeks have but one word λόγος, for both *Speech* and
Reason; not that they thought there was no Speech without Reason;
but no Reasoning without Speech: And the act of reasoning they
called *Syllogisme*; which signifieth summing up of the consequences of
one saying to another. And because the same things may enter into
account for divers accidents; their names are (to shew that diversity)
diversly wrested, and diversified. This diversity of names may be
reduced to foure generall heads.

First, a thing may enter into account for *Matter*, or *Body*; as *living,
sensible, rationall, hot, cold, moved, quiet*; with all which names the word
Matter, or *Body* is understood; all such, being names of Matter.

Secondly, it may enter into account, or be considered, for some
accident or quality, which we conceive to be in it; as for *being moved*,
for *being so long*, for *being hot* &c; and then, of the name of the thing it
selfe, by a little change or wresting, wee make a name for that
accident, which we consider; and for *living* put into the account *life*;
for *moved, motion*; for *hot, heat*; for *long, length*, and the like: And all
such Names, are the names of the accidents and properties, by which
one Matter, and Body is distinguished from another. These are called
names Abstract; because severed (not from Matter, but) from the
account of Matter.

Thirdly, we bring into account, the Properties of our own bodies,
whereby we make such distinction: as when any thing is *Seen* by us, we
reckon not the thing it selfe; but the *sight*, the *Colour*, the *Idea* of it in
the fancy: and when any thing is *heard*, wee reckon it not; but the
hearing, or *sound* onely, which is our fancy or conception of it by the
Eare: and such are names of fancies.

Fourthly, we bring into account, consider, and give names, to
Names themselves, and to *Speeches*: For, *generall, universall, speciall*,

aequivocall, are names of Names. And *Affirmation, Interrogation, Commandement, Narration, Syllogisme, Sermon, Oration*, and many other such, are names of Speeches. And this is all the variety of Names *Positive*; which are put to mark somewhat which is in Nature, or may be feigned by the mind of man, as Bodies that are, or may be conceived to be; or of bodies, the Properties that are, or may be feigned to be; or Words and Speech.

Use of Names Positive.

There be also other Names, called *Negative*; which are notes to signifie that a word is not the name of the thing in question; as these words *Nothing, no man, infinite, indocible, three want foure*, and the like; which are nevertheless of use in reckoning, or in correcting of reckoning; and call to mind our past cogitations, though they be not names of any thing; because they make us refuse to admit of Names not rightly used.

Negative Names with their Uses.

All other Names, are but insignificant sounds; and those of two sorts. One, when they are new, and yet their meaning not explained by Definition; whereof there have been abundance coyned by Schoolemen, and pusled Philosophers.

Words insignificant.

[17]

Another, when men make a name of two Names, whose significations are contradictory and inconsistent; as this name, an *incorporeall body*, or (which is all one) an *incorporeall substance*, and a great number more. For whensoever any affirmation is false, the two names of which it is composed, put together and made one, signifie nothing at all. For example, if it be a false affirmation to say *a quadrangle is round*, the word *round quadrangle* signifies nothing; but is a meere sound. So likewise if it be false, to say that vertue can be powred, or blown up and down; the words *In-powred vertue, In-blown vertue*, are as absurd and insignificant, as a *round quadrangle*. And therefore you shall hardly meet with a senslesse and insignificant word, that is not made up of some Latin or Greek names. A Frenchman seldome hears our Saviour called by the name of *Parole*, but by the name of *Verbe* often; yet *Verbe* and *Parole* differ no more, but that one is Latin, the other French.

When a man upon the hearing of any Speech, hath those thoughts which the words of that Speech, and their connexion, were ordained and constituted to signifie; Then he is said to understand it: *Understanding* being nothing else, but conception caused by Speech. And therefore if Speech be peculiar to man (as for ought I know it is,) then is Understanding peculiar to him also. And therefore of absurd and

Understanding.

false affirmations, in case they be universall, there can be no Understanding; though many think they understand, then, when they do but
repeat the words softly, or con them in their mind.

What kinds of Speeches signifie the Appetites, Aversions, and
Passions of mans mind; and of their use and abuse, I shall speak when
I have spoken of the Passions.

The names of such things as affect us, that is, which please, and
displease us, because all men be not alike affected with the same
thing, nor the same man at all times, are in the common discourses of
men, of *inconstant* signification. For seeing all names are imposed to
signifie our conceptions; and all our affections are but conceptions;
when we conceive the same things differently, we can hardly avoyd
different naming of them. For though the nature of that we conceive,
be the same; yet the diversity of our reception of it, in respect of
different constitutions of body, and prejudices of opinion, gives every
thing a tincture of our different passions. And therefore in reasoning,
a man must take heed of words; which besides the signification of
what we imagine of their nature, have a signification also of the
nature, disposition, and interest of the speaker; such as are the names
of Vertues, and Vices; For one man calleth *Wisdome*, what another
calleth *feare*; and one *cruelty*, what another *justice*; one *prodigality*, what
another *magnanimity*; and one *gravity*, what another *stupidity*, &c. And
therefore such names can never be true grounds of any ratiocination.
No more can Metaphors, and Tropes of speech: but these are less
dangerous, because they profess their inconstancy; which the other do
not.

Inconstant names.

CHAP. V.

[18]

Of REASON, and SCIENCE.

When a man *Reasoneth*, hee does nothing else but conceive a summe
totall, from *Addition* of parcels; or conceive a Remainder, from
Substraction of one summe from another: which (if it be done by
Words,) is conceiving of the consequence* from*[1] the names of all
the parts, to the name of the whole; or from the names of the whole

Reason what it is.

[1] Syn.: of

31

and one part, to the name of the other part. And though in some things, (as in numbers,) besides *Adding* and *Substracting*, men name other operations, as *Multiplying* and *Dividing*; yet they are the same; for Multiplication, is but Adding together of things equall; and Division, but Substracting of one thing, as often as we can. These operations are not incident to Numbers onely, but to all manner of things that can be added together, and taken one out of another. For as Arithmeticians teach to adde and substract in *numbers*; so the Geometricians teach the same in *lines, figures* (solid and superficiall,) *angles, proportions, times*, degrees of *swiftnesse, force, power*, and the like; The Logicians teach the same in *Consequences of words*; adding together *two Names*, to make an *Affirmation*; and *two Affirmations*, to make a *Syllogisme*; and *many Syllogismes* to make a *Demonstration*; and from the *summe*, or *Conclusion* of a *Syllogisme*, they substract one *Proposition*, to finde the other. Writers of Politiques, adde together *Pactions*, to find mens *duties*; and Lawyers, *Lawes*, and *facts*, to find what is *right* and *wrong* in the actions of private men. In summe, in what matter soever there is place for *addition* and *substraction*, there also is place for *Reason*; and where these have no place, there *Reason* has nothing at all to do.

Reason defined.   Out of all which we may define, (that is to say determine,) what that is, which is meant by this word *Reason*, when wee reckon it amongst the Faculties of the mind. For REASON, in this sense, is nothing but *Reckoning* (that is, Adding and Substracting) of the Consequences of generall names agreed upon, for the *marking* and *signifying* of our thoughts; I say *marking* them, when we reckon by our selves; and *signifying*, when we demonstrate, or approve our reckonings to other men.

Right Reason where.   And as in Arithmetique, unpractised men must, and Professors themselves may often erre, and cast up false; so also in any other subject of Reasoning, the ablest, most attentive, and most practised men, may deceive themselves, and inferre false Conclusions; Not but that Reason it selfe is alwayes Right Reason, as well as Arithmetique is a certain and infallible Art: But no one mans Reason, nor the Reason of any one number of men, makes the certaintie; no more than an account is therefore well cast up, because a great many men have unanimously approved it. And therfore, as when there is a controversy in an account, the parties must by their own accord, set up for right Reason, the Reason of some Arbitrator, or Judge, to

[19]

32

whose sentence they will both stand, or their controversie must either
come to blowes, or be undecided, for want of a right Reason constituted by Nature; so is it also in all debates of what kind soever: And
when men that think themselves wiser than all others, clamor and
demand right Reason for judge; yet seek no more, but that things
should be determined, by no other mens reason but their own, it is as
intolerable in the society of men, as it is in play after trump is turned,
to use for trump on every occasion, that suite whereof they have most
in their hand. For they do nothing els, that will have every of their
passions, as it comes to bear sway in them, to be taken for right
Reason, and that in their own controversies: bewraying their want of
right Reason, by the claym they lay to it.

The Use and End of Reason, is not the finding of the summe, and
truth of one, or a few consequences, remote from the first definitions,
and settled significations of names; but to begin at these; and proceed
from one consequence to another. For there can be no certainty of the
last Conclusion, without a certainty of all those Affirmations and
Negations, on which it was grounded, and inferred. As when a master
of a family, in taking an account, casteth up the summs of all the bills
of expence, into one sum; and not regarding how each bill is summed
up, by those that give them in account; nor what it is he payes for; he
advantages himself no more, than if he allowed the account in grosse,
trusting to every of the accountants skill and honesty: so also in
Reasoning of all other things, he that takes up conclusions on the trust
of Authors, and doth not fetch them from the first Items in every
Reckoning, (which are the significations of names settled by definitions), loses his labour; and does not know any thing; but onely
beleeveth. *The use of Reason.*

When a man reckons without the use of words, which may be done
in particular things, (as when upon the sight of any one thing, wee
conjecture what was likely to have preceded, or is likely to follow upon
it;) if that which he thought likely to follow, followes not; or that which
he thought likely to have preceded it, hath not preceded it, this is
called ERROR; to which even the most prudent men are subject. But
when we Reason in Words of generall signification, and fall upon a
generall inference which is false; though it be commonly called *Error*,
it is indeed an ABSURDITY, or senslesse Speech. For Error is but a
deception, in presuming that somewhat is past, or to come; of which,
though it were not past, or not to come; yet there was no impossibility *Of Error and Absurdity.*

discoverable. But when we make a generall assertion, unlesse it be a true one, the possibility of it is unconceivable. And words whereby we conceive nothing but the sound, are those we call *Absurd, Insignificant,* and *Non-sense.* And therefore if a man should talk to me of a *round Quadrangle*; or *accidents of Bread in Cheese*; or *Immateriall Substances*; or of *A free Subject*; *A free-will*; or any *Free*, but free from being hindred by opposition, I should not say he were in an Errour, but that his words were without meaning; that is to say, Absurd.

[20] I have said before, (in the second chapter,) that a Man did excell all other Animals in this faculty, that when he conceived any thing what-soever, he was apt to enquire the consequences of it, and what effects he could do with it. And now I adde this other degree of the same excellence, that he can by words reduce the consequences he findes to generall Rules, called *Theoremes*, or *Aphorismes*; that is, he can Reason, or reckon, not onely in number; but in all other things, whereof one may be added unto, or substracted from another.

But this priviledge, is allayed by another; and that is, by the priviledge of Absurdity; to which no living creature is subject, but man onely. And of men, those are of all most subject to it, that professe Philosophy. For it is most true that *Cicero* sayth of them somewhere; that there can be nothing so absurd, but may be found in the books of Philosophers. And the reason is manifest. For there is not one of them that begins his ratiocination from the Definitions, or Explications of the names they are to use; which is a method that hath been used onely in Geometry; whose Conclusions have thereby been made indisputable.

Causes of absurditie.

1.

The first cause of Absurd conclusions I ascribe to the want of Method; in that they begin not their Ratiocination from Definitions; that is, from settled significations of their words: as if they could cast account, without knowing the value of the numerall words, *one*, *two*, and *three*.

And whereas all bodies enter into account upon divers considera-tions, (which I have mentioned in the precedent chapter;) these con-siderations being diversly named, divers absurdities proceed from the confusion, and unfit connexion of their names into assertions. And therefore

2.

The second cause of Absurd assertions, I ascribe to the giving of names of *bodies*, to *accidents*, or of *accidents*, to *bodies*; As they do, that say, *Faith is infused*, or *inspired*; when nothing can be *powred*, or *breathed* into any thing, but body; and that, *extension* is *body*; that *phantasmes* are *spirits*, &c.

The third I ascribe to the giving of the names of the *accidents* of 3. *bodies without us*, to the *accidents* of our *own bodies*; as they do that say, the *colour is in the body*; *the sound is in the ayre*, &c.

The fourth, to the giving of the names of *bodies*, to *names*, or 4. *speeches*; as they do that say, that *there be things universall*; that *a living creature is Genus*, or *a generall thing*, &c.

The fifth, to the giving of the names of *accidents*, to *names* and 5. *speeches*; as they do that say, *the nature of a thing is its definition*; *a mans command is his will*; and the like.

The sixth, to the use of Metaphors, Tropes, and other Rhetoricall 6. figures, in stead of words proper. For though it be lawfull to say, (for example) in common speech, *the way goeth, or leadeth hither, or thither, The Proverb sayes this or that* (whereas wayes cannot go, nor Proverbs speak;) yet in reckoning, and seeking of truth, such speeches are not to be admitted.

The seventh, to names that signifie nothing; but are taken up, and 7. learned by rote from the Schooles, as *hypostatical, transubstantiate,* [21] *consubstantiate, eternal-Now*, and the like canting of Schoole-men.

To him that can avoyd these things, it is not easie to fall into any absurdity, unlesse it be by the length of an account; wherein he may perhaps forget what went before. For all men by nature reason alike, and well, when they have good principles. For who is so stupid, as both to mistake in Geometry, and also to persist in it, when another detects his error to him?

By this it appears that Reason is not as Sense, and Memory, borne   *Science.* with us; nor gotten by Experience onely, as Prudence is; but attayned by Industry; first in apt imposing of Names; and secondly by getting a good and orderly Method in proceeding from the Elements, which are Names, to Assertions made by Connexion of one of them to another; and so to Syllogismes, which are the Connexions of one Assertion to another, till we come to a knowledge of all the Conse-quences of names appertaining to the subject in hand; and that is it, men call S CIENCE. And whereas Sense and Memory are but know-ledge of Fact, which is a thing past, and irrevocable; *Science* is the knowledge of Consequences, and dependance of one fact upon another: by which, out of that we can presently do, we know how to do something else when we will, or the like, another time: Because when we see how any thing comes about, upon what causes, and by what manner; when the like causes come into our power, wee see how to make it produce the like effects.

Children therefore are not endued with Reason at all, till they have attained the use of Speech: but are called Reasonable Creatures, for the possibility apparent of having the use of Reason in time to come. And the most part of men, though they have the use of Reasoning a little way, as in numbring to some degree; yet it serves them to little use in common life; in which they govern themselves, some better, some worse, according to their differences of experience, quicknesse of memory, and inclinations to severall ends; but specially according to good or evill fortune, and the errors of one another. For as for *Science*, or certain rules of their actions, they are so farre from it, that they know not what it is. Geometry they have thought Conjuring: But for other Sciences, they who have not been taught the beginnings, and some progresse in them, that they may see how they be acquired and generated, are in this point like children, that having no thought of generation, are made believe by the women, that their brothers and sisters are not born, but found in the garden.

But yet they that have no *Science*, are in better, and nobler condition with their naturall Prudence; than men, that by mis-reasoning, or by trusting them that reason wrong, fall upon false and absurd generall rules. For ignorance of causes, and of rules, does not set men so farre out of their way, as relying on false rules, and taking for causes of what they aspire to, those that are not so, but rather causes of the contrary.

[22] To conclude, The Light of humane minds is Perspicuous Words, but by exact definitions first snuffed, and purged from ambiguity; *Reason* is the *pace*; Encrease of *Science*, the *way*; and the Benefit of man-kind, the *end*. And on the contrary, Metaphors, and senslesse and ambiguous words, are like *ignes fatui*; and reasoning upon them, is wandering amongst innumerable absurdities; and their end, contention, and sedition, or contempt.

Prudence &
Sapience,
with their
difference.

As, much Experience, is *Prudence*; so, is much Science, *Sapience*. For though wee usually have one name of Wisedome for them both; yet the Latines did alwayes distinguish between *Prudentia* and *Sapientia*; ascribing the former to Experience, the later to Science. But to make their difference appeare more cleerly, let us suppose one man endued with an excellent naturall use, and dexterity in handling his armes; and another to have added to that dexterity, an acquired

Science, of where he can offend, or be offended by his adversarie, in every possible posture, or guard: The ability of the former, would be to the ability of the later, as Prudence to Sapience; both usefull; but the later infallible. But they that trusting onely to the authority of books, follow the blind blindly, are like him that trusting to the false rules of a master of Fence, ventures praesumptuously upon an adversary, that either kills, or disgraces him.

The signes of Science, are some, certain and infallible; some, uncertain. Certain, when he that pretendeth the Science of any thing, can teach the same; that is to say, demonstrate the truth thereof perspicuously to another: Uncertain, when onely some particular events answer to his pretence, and upon many occasions prove so as he sayes they must. Signes of prudence are all uncertain; because to observe by experience, and remember all circumstances that may alter the successe, is impossible. But in any businesse, whereof a man has not infallible Science to proceed by; to forsake his own naturall judgement, and be guided by generall sentences read in Authors, and subject to many exceptions, is a signe of folly, and generally scorned by the name of Pedantry. And even of those men themselves, that in Councells of the Common-wealth, love to shew their reading of Politiques and History, very few do it in their domestique affaires, where their particular interest is concerned; having Prudence enough for their private affaires: but in publique they study more the reputation of their owne wit, than the successe of anothers businesse. *Signes of Science.*

CHAP. VI.   [23]

Of the Interiour Beginnings of Voluntary Motions; commonly called the PASSIONS. *And the Speeches by which they are expressed.*

There be in Animals, two sorts of *Motions* peculiar to them: One called *Vitall*; begun in generation, and continued without interruption through their whole life; such as are the *course* of the *Bloud*, the *Pulse*, *Motion Vitall and Animal.*

the *Breathing*, the *Concoction*, *Nutrition*, *Excretion*, &c; to which Motions there needs no help of Imagination: The other is *Animall motion*, otherwise called *Voluntary motion*; as to *go*, to *speak*, to *move* any of our limbes, in such manner as is first fancied in our minds. That Sense, is Motion in the organs and interiour parts of mans body, caused by the action of the things we See, Heare, &c; And that Fancy is but the Reliques of the same Motion, remaining after Sense, has been already sayd in the first and second Chapters. And because *going*, *speaking*, and the like Voluntary motions, depend always upon a precedent thought of *whither*, *which way*, and *what*; it is evident, that the Imagination is the first internall beginning of all Voluntary Motion. And although unstudied men, doe not conceive any motion at all to be there, where the thing moved is invisible; or the space it is moved in, is (for the shortnesse of it) insensible; yet that doth not hinder, but that such Motions are. For let a space be never so little, that which is moved over a greater space, whereof that little one is part, must first be moved over that. These small beginnings of Motion, within the body of Man, before they appear in walking, speaking, striking, and other

Endeavour.   visible actions, are commonly called ENDEAVOUR.

     This Endeavour, when it is toward something which causes it, is

Appetite.
Desire.   called APPETITE, or DESIRE; the later, being the generall name; and the other, often-times restrayned to signifie the Desire of Food,

Hunger.
Thirst.
Aversion.   namely *Hunger* and *Thirst*. And when the Endeavour is fromward something, it is generally called AVERSION. These words *Appetite*, and *Aversion* we have from the *Latines*; and they both of them signifie the motions, one of approaching, the other of retiring. So also do the Greek words for the same, which are ὁρμὴ, and ἀφορμὴ. For Nature it selfe does often presse upon men those truths, which afterwards, when they look for somewhat beyond Nature, they stumble at. For the Schooles find in meere Appetite to go, or move, no actuall Motion at all: but because some Motion they must acknowledge, they call it Metaphoricall Motion; which is but an absurd speech: for though Words may be called metaphoricall; Bodies, and Motions cannot.

Love.
Hate.   That which men Desire, they are also sayd to LOVE: and to HATE those things, for which they have Aversion. So that Desire, and Love,

[24]   are the same thing; save that by Desire, we always signifie the Absence of the Object; by Love, most commonly the Presence of the same. So also by Aversion, we signifie the Absence; and by Hate, the Presence of the Object.

Of Appetites, and Aversions, some are born with men; as Appetite of food, Appetite of excretion, and exoneration, (which may also and more properly be called Aversions, from somewhat they feele in their Bodies,) and some other Appetites, not many. The rest, which are Appetites of particular things, proceed from Experience, and triall of their effects upon themselves, or other men. For of things wee know not at all, or believe not to be, we can have no further Desire, than to tast and try. But Aversion wee have for things, not onely which we know have hurt us; but also that we do not know whether they will hurt us, or not.

Those things which we neither Desire, nor Hate, we are said to *Contemne*: CONTEMPT being nothing else but an immobility, or con- *Contempt.* tumacy of the Heart, in resisting the action of certain things; and proceeding from that the Heart is already moved otherwise, by other more potent objects; or from want of experience of them.

And because the constitution of a mans Body, is in continuall mutation; it is impossible that all the same things should alwayes cause in him the same Appetites, and Aversions: much lesse can all men consent, in the Desire of almost any one and the same Object.

But whatsoever is the object of any mans Appetite or Desire; that is it, which he for his part calleth *Good*: And the object of his Hate, and *Good.* Aversion, *Evill*; And of his Contempt, *Vile* and *Inconsiderable*. For *Evill.* these words of Good, Evill, and Contemptible, are ever used with relation to the person that useth them: There being nothing simply and absolutely so; nor any common Rule of Good and Evill, to be taken from the nature of the objects themselves; but from the Person of the man (where there is no Common-wealth;) or, (in a Common-wealth,) from the Person that representeth it; or from an Arbitrator or Judge, whom men disagreeing shall by consent set up, and make his sentence the Rule thereof.

The Latine Tongue has two words, whose significations approach to those of Good and Evill; but are not precisely the same; And those are *Pulchrum* and *Turpe*. Whereof the former signifies that, which by *Pulchrum.* some apparent signes promiseth Good; and the later, that, which *Turpe.* promiseth Evil. But in our Tongue we have not so generall names to express them by. But for *Pulchrum* we say in some things, *Fayre*; in others *Beautifull*, or *Handsome*, or *Gallant*, or *Honourable*, or *Comely*, or *Amiable*; and for *Turpe*, *Foul*, *Deformed*, *Ugly*, *Base*, *Nauseous*, and the like, as the subject shall require; All which words, in their proper places signifie nothing els, but the *Mine*, or Countenance, that promiseth Good and Evil *or the lustre and glosse of some ability to Good [...]*¹. So that of Good there be three kinds; Good in the Promise, that is *Pulchrum*; Good in Effect, as the end desired, which *Delightfull.* is called *Jucundum, Delightfull*; and Good as the Means, which is *Profitable.* called *Vtile, Profitable*; and as many of Evil: For *Evill*, in Promise, is [25] that they call *Turpe*; Evil in Effect, and End, is *Molestum, Unpleasant, Unpleasant.* *Troublesome*; and Evill in the Means, *Inutile, Unprofitable, Hurtfull.* *Unprofitable.*

As, in Sense, that which is really within us, is (as I have sayd before) onely Motion, caused by the action of externall objects, but in apparence; to the Sight, Light and Colour; to the Eare, Sound; to the Nostrill, Odour, &c: so, when the action of the same object is continued from the Eyes, Eares, and other organs to the Heart; the reall effect there is nothing but Motion, or Endeavour; which consisteth in Appetite, or Aversion, to, or from the object moving. But the *Delight.* apparence, or sense of that motion, is that wee either call DELIGHT, or *Displeasure.* TROUBLE OF MIND.

This Motion, which is called Appetite, and for the apparence of it *Pleasure.* *Delight*, and *Pleasure*, seemeth to be, a corroboration of Vitall motion, and a help thereunto; and therefore such things as caused Delight, were not improperly called *Jucunda*, (*à Juvando*,) from helping or *Offence.* fortifying; and the contrary, *Molesta, Offensive*, from hindering, and troubling the motion vitall.

Pleasure therefore, (or *Delight*,) is the apparence, or sense of Good; and *Molestation* or *Displeasure*, the apparence, or sense of Evill. And consequently all Appetite, Desire, and Love, is accompanied with some Delight more or lesse; and all Hatred, and Aversion, with more or lesse Displeasure and Offence.

Of Pleasures, or Delights, some arise from the sense of an object *Pleasures of* Present; And those may be called *Pleasures of Sense*, (The word *sensu-* *Sense.* *all*, as it is used by those onely that condemn them, having no place till there be Lawes.) Of this kind are all Onerations and Exonerations of the body; as also all that is pleasant, in the *Sight, Hearing, Smell, Tast, or Touch*; Others arise from the Expectation, that proceeds from foresight of the End, or Consequence of things; whether those things *Pleasures of* in the Sense Please or Displease: And these are *Pleasures of the Mind* *the Mind.* of him that draweth those consequences; and are generally called *Joy.* JOY. In the like manner, Displeasures, are some in the Sense, and

---

¹ Inserted by T.H. (rest of insertion now illegible).

called PAYNE; others, in the Expectation of consequences, and are called GRIEFE.

These simple Passions called *Appetite*, *Desire*, *Love*, *Aversion*, *Hate*, *Joy*, and *Griefe*, have their names for divers considerations diversified. As first, when they one succeed another, they are diversly called from the opinion men have of the likelihood of attaining what they desire. Secondly, from the object loved or hated. Thirdly, from the consideration of many of them together. Fourthly, from the Alteration or succession it selfe.

For *Appetite* with an opinion of attaining, is called HOPE.

The same, without such opinion, DESPAIRE.

Aversion, with opinion of *Hurt* from the object, FEARE.

The same, with hope of avoyding that Hurt by resistence, COURAGE.

Sudden *courage*, ANGER.

Constant *Hope*, CONFIDENCE of our selves.

Constant *Despayre*, DIFFIDENCE of our selves.

Anger for great hurt done to another, when we conceive the same to be done by Injury, INDIGNATION.

Desire of good to another, BENEVOLENCE, GOOD WILL, CHARITY. If to man generally, GOOD NATURE.

Desire of Riches, COVETOUSNESSE: a name used alwayes in signification of blame; because men contending for them, are displeased with one anothers attaining them; though the desire in it selfe, be to be blamed, or allowed, according to the means by which those Riches are sought.

Desire of Office, or precedence, AMBITION: a name used also in the worse sense, for the reason before mentioned.

Desire of things that conduce but a little to our ends; And fear of things that are but of little hindrance, PUSILLANIMITY.

Contempt of little helps, and hindrances, MAGNANIMITY.

Magnanimity, in danger of Death, or Wounds, VALOUR, FORTITUDE.

Magnanimity, in the use of Riches, LIBERALITY.

Pusillanimity, in the same WRETCHEDNESSE, MISERABLENESSE; or PARSIMONY; as it is liked, or disliked.

Love of Persons for society, KINDNESSE.

Love of Persons for Pleasing the sense only, NATURALL LUST.

Payne.

Griefe.

Hope.

Despaire.

Feare.

Courage.

Anger.

Confidence.

Diffidence.

[26]

Indignation.

Benevolence.

Good Nature.

Covetousnesse.

Ambition.

Pusillanimity.

Magnanimity.

Valour.

Liberality.

Miserablenesse.

Kindnesse.

Naturall Lust.

Luxury.

Love of the same, acquired from Rumination, that is, Imagination of Pleasure past, LUXURY.

The passion of Love. Jealousie.

Love of one singularly, with desire to be singularly beloved, THE PASSION OF LOVE. The same, with fear that the love is not mutuall, JEALOUSIE.

Revengeful-nesse.

Desire, by doing hurt to another, to make him condemn some fact of his own, REVENGEFULNESSE.

Curiosity.

Desire, to know why, and how, CURIOSITY; such as is in no living creature but *Man*: so that Man is distinguished, not onely by his Reason; but also by this singular Passion from other *Animals*; in whom the appetite of food, and other pleasures of Sense, by praedominance, take away the care of knowing causes; which is a Lust of the mind, that by a perseverance of delight in the continuall and indefatigable generation of Knowledge, exceedeth the short vehemence of any carnall Pleasure.

Religion. Superstition. True Religion. Panique. Terrour.

Feare of power invisible, feigned by the mind, or imagined from tales publiquely allowed, RELIGION; not allowed, SUPERSTITION. And when the power imagined, is truly such as we imagine, TRUE RELIGION.

Feare, without the apprehension of why, or what, PANIQUE TERROR; called so from the Fables, that make *Pan* the author of them; whereas in truth, there is alwayes in him that so feareth, first, some apprehension of the cause, though the rest run away by Example; every one supposing his fellow to know why. And therefore this Passion happens to none but in a throng, or multitude of people.

Admiration.

Joy, from apprehension of novelty, ADMIRATION; proper to Man, because it excites the appetite of knowing the cause.

[27]

Glory.

Joy, arising from imagination of a mans own power and ability, is that exultation of the mind which is called GLORYING: which if grounded upon the experience of his own former actions, is the same with *Confidence*: but if grounded on the flattery of others; or onely supposed by himself, for delight in the consequences of it, is called

Vain-glory.

VAINE-GLORY: which name is properly given; because a well grounded *Confidence* begetteth Attempt; whereas the supposing of power does not, and is therefore rightly called *Vaine*.

Dejection.

Griefe, from opinion of want of power, is called DEJECTION of mind.

The *vain-glory* which consisteth in the feigning or supposing of abilities in our selves, which we know are not, is most incident to young men, and nourished by the Histories, or Fictions of Gallant Persons; and is corrected oftentimes by Age, and Employment.

Sudden Glory, is the passion which maketh those *Grimaces* called L A U G H T E R; and is caused either by some sudden act of their own, that pleaseth them; or by the apprehension of some deformed thing in another, by comparison whereof they suddenly applaud themselves. And it is incident most to them, that are conscious of the fewest abilities in themselves; who are forced to keep themselves in their own favour, by observing the imperfections of other men. And therefore much Laughter at the defects of others, is a signe of Pusillanimity. For of great minds, one of the proper workes is, to help and free others from scorn; and compare themselves onely with the most able. *Sudden Glory. Laughter.*

On the contrary, *Sudden Dejection*, is the passion that causeth W E E P I N G; and is caused by such accidents, as suddenly take away some vehement hope, or some prop of their power: And they are most subject to it, that rely principally on helps externall, such as are Women, and Children. Therefore some Weep for the losse of Friends; Others for their unkindnesse; others for the sudden stop made to their thoughts of revenge, by Reconciliation. But in all cases, both Laughter, and Weeping, are sudden motions; Custome taking them both away. For no man Laughs at old jests; or Weeps for an old calamity. *Sudden Dejection. Weeping.*

Griefe, for the discovery of some defect of ability, is S H A M E, or the passion that discovereth it selfe in B L U S H I N G; and consisteth in the apprehension of some thing dishonourable; and in young men, is a signe of the love of good reputation; and commendable: In old men it is a signe of the same; but because it comes too late, not commendable. *Shame. Blushing.*

The *Contempt* of good Reputation is called I M P U D E N C E. *Impudence.*

Griefe, for the Calamity of another, is P I T T Y; and ariseth from the imagination that the like calamity may befall himselfe; and therefore is called also C O M P A S S I O N, and in the phrase of this present time a F E L L O W - F E E L I N G: And therefore for Calamity arriving from great wickedness, the best men have the least Pitty; and for the same Calamity, those have least Pitty, that think themselves least obnoxious to the same. *Pitty.*

Contempt, or little sense of the calamity of others, is that which men

28

Cruelty.

call CRUELTY; proceeding from Security of their own fortune. For, that any man should take pleasure in other mens great harmes, without other end of his own, I do not conceive it possible.

Griefe, for the successe of a Competitor in wealth, honour, or other good, if it be joyned with Endeavour to enforce our own abilities to equall or exceed him, is called EMULATION: But joyned with Endeavour to supplant, or hinder a Competitor, ENVIE.

Emulation.
Envy.

When in the mind of man, Appetites, and Aversions, Hopes, and Feares, concerning one and the same thing, arise alternately; and divers good and evill consequences of the doing, or omitting the thing propounded, come successively into our thoughts; so that sometimes we have an Appetite to it; sometimes an Aversion from it; sometimes Hope to be able to do it; sometimes Despaire, or Feare to attempt it; the whole summe of Desires, Aversions, Hopes and Fears, continued till the thing be either done, or thought impossible, is that we call DELIBERATION.

Deliberation.

Therefore of things past, there is no *Deliberation*; because manifestly impossible to be changed: nor of things known to be impossible, or thought so; because men know, or think such Deliberation vain. But of things impossible, which we think possible, we may Deliberate; not knowing it is in vain. And it is called *Deliberation*; because it is a putting an end to the *Liberty* we had of doing, or omitting, according to our own Appetite, or Aversion.

This alternate Succession of Appetites, Aversions, Hopes and Fears, is no lesse in other living Creatures then in Man: and therefore Beasts also Deliberate.

Every *Deliberation* is then sayd to *End*, when that whereof they Deliberate, is either done, or thought impossible; because till then wee retain the liberty of doing, or omitting, according to our Appetite, or Aversion.

The Will.

In Deliberation, the last Appetite, or Aversion, immediately adhaering to the action, or to the omission thereof, is that wee call the WILL; the Act, (not the faculty,) of *Willing.* And Beasts that have *Deliberation*, must necessarily also have *Will.* The Definition of the *Will*, given commonly by the Schooles, that it is a *Rationall Appetite*, is not good. For if it were, then could there be no Voluntary Act against Reason. For a *Voluntary Act* is that, which proceedeth from the *Will*, and no other. But if in stead of a Rationall Appetite, we shall say an

44

Appetite resulting from a precedent Deliberation, then the Definition is the same that I have given here. *Will* therefore *is the last Appetite in Deliberating.* And though we say in common Discourse, a man had a Will once to do a thing, that neverthelesse he forbore to do; yet that is properly but an Inclination, which makes no Action Voluntary; because the action depends not of it, but of the last Inclination, or Appetite. For if the intervenient Appetites, make any action Voluntary; then by the same Reason all intervenient Aversions, should make the same action Involuntary; and so one and the same action, should be both Voluntary & Involuntary.

By this it is manifest, that not onely actions that have their begin- [29] ning from Covetousnesse, Ambition, Lust, or other Appetites to the thing propounded; but also those that have their beginning from Aversion, or Feare of those consequences that follow the omission, are *voluntary actions.*

The formes of Speech by which the Passions are expressed, are partly the same, and partly different from those, by which wee expresse our Thoughts. And first, generally all Passions may be expressed *Indicatively*; as *I love, I feare, I joy, I deliberate, I will, I command*: but some of them have particular expressions by themselves, which neverthelesse are not affirmations, unlesse it be when they serve to make other inferences, besides that of the Passion they proceed from. Deliberation is expressed *Subjunctively*; which is a speech proper to signifie suppositions, with their consequences; as, *If this be done, then this will follow*; and differs not from the language of Reasoning, save that Reasoning is in generall words; but Deliberation for the most part is of Particulars. The language of Desire, and Aversion, is *Imperative*; as *Do this, forbeare that*; which when the party is obliged to do, or forbeare, is *Command*; otherwise *Prayer*; or els *Counsell*. The language of Vain-Glory, of Indignation, Pitty and Revengefulness, *Optative*: But of the Desire to know, there is a peculiar expression, called *Interrogative*; as, *What is it, when shall it, how is it done*, and *why so?* other language of the Passions I find none: For Cursing, Swearing, Reviling, and the like, do not signifie as Speech; but as the actions of a tongue accustomed.

These formes of Speech, I say, are expressions, or voluntary significations of our Passions: but certain signes they be not; because they may be used arbitrarily, whether they that use them, have such

Formes of Speech in Passion.

45

Passions or not. The best signes of Passions present, are *in*[1] the countenance, motions of the body, actions, and ends, or aimes, which we otherwise know the man to have.

And because in Deliberation, the Appetites, and Aversions are raised by foresight of the good and evill consequences, and sequels of the action whereof we Deliberate; the good or evill effect thereof dependeth on the foresight of a long chain of consequences, of which very seldome any man is able to see to the end. But for so farre as a man seeth, if the Good in those consequences, be greater than the Evill, the whole chaine is that which Writers call *Apparent*, or *Seeming Good*. And contrarily, when the Evill exceedeth the Good, the whole is *Apparent*, or *Seeming Evill*: so that he who hath by Experience, or Reason, the greatest and surest prospect of Consequences, Deliberates best himselfe; and is able when he will, to give the best counsell unto others.

Good and Evill apparent.

Continuall successe in obtaining those things which a man from time to time desireth, that is to say, continuall prospering, is that men call F E L I C I T Y; I mean the Felicity of this life. For there is no such thing as perpetuall Tranquillity of mind, while we live here; because Life it selfe is but Motion, and can never be without Desire, nor without Feare, no more than without Sense. What kind of Felicity God hath ordained to them that devoutly honour him, a man shall no sooner know, than enjoy; being joyes, that now are as incomprehensible, as the word of Schoole-men *Beatificall Vision* is unintelligible.

Felicity.

[30]

The forme of Speech whereby men signifie their opinion of the Goodnesse of any thing, is P R A I S E. That whereby they signifie the power and greatnesse of any thing, is M A G N I F Y I N G. And that whereby they signifie the opinion they have of a mans Felicity, is by the Greeks called μακαρισμός, for which wee have no name in our tongue. And thus much is sufficient for the present purpose, to have been said of the P A S S I O N S.

Praise.

Magnifi-cation.

μακαρισμός.

[1] *Syn.*: either in

46

CHAP. VII.
Of the Ends, *or* Resolutions of DISCOURSE.

Of all *Discourse*, governed by desire of Knowledge, there is at last an *End*, either by attaining, or by giving over. And in the chain of Discourse, wheresoever it be interrupted, there is an End for that time.

If the Discourse be meerly Mentall, it consisteth of thoughts that the thing will be, and will not be; or that it has been, and has not been, alternately. So that wheresoever you break off the chayn of a mans Discourse, you leave him in a Praesumption of *it will be*, or, *it will not be*; or *it has been*, or, *has not been*; All which is *Opinion*. And that which is alternate Appetite, in Deliberating concerning Good and Evil; the same is alternate Opinion, in the Enquiry of the truth of *Past*, and *Future*. And as the last Appetite in Deliberation, is called the *Will*; so the last Opinion in search of the truth of Past, and Future, is called the J U D G E M E N T, or *Resolute* and *Finall Sentence* of him that discour- *Judgement,* seth. And as the whole chain of Appetites alternate, in the question of *or Sentence* Good, or Bad, is called *Deliberation*; so the whole chain of Opinions *final.* alternate, in the question of True, or False, is called D O U B T. *Doubt.*

No Discourse whatsoever, can End in absolute knowledge of Fact, past, or to come. For, as for the knowledge of Fact, it is originally, Sense; and ever after, Memory. And for the knowledge of Consequence, which I have said before is called Science, it is not Absolute, but Conditionall. No man can know by Discourse, that this, or that, is, has been, or will be; which is to know absolutely: but onely, that if This be, That is; if This has been, That has been; if This shall be, That shall be: which is to know conditionally; and that not the consequence of one thing to another; but of one name of a thing, to another name of the same thing.

And therefore, when the Discourse is put into Speech, and begins with the Definitions of Words, and proceeds by Connexion of the same into generall Affirmations, and of these again into Syllogismes; the End or last summe is called the Conclusion; and the thought of [31] the mind by it signified, is that conditionall Knowledge, or Knowledge of the consequence of words, which is commonly called

Science. SCIENCE. But if the first ground of such Discourse, be not Definitions; or if the Definitions be not rightly joyned together into Syllogismes, then the End or Conclusion, is again OPINION, namely of
Opinion. the truth of somewhat said, though sometimes in absurd and senselesse words, without possibility of being understood. When two, or more men, know of one and the same fact, they are said to be
Conscience. CONSCIOUS of it one to another; which is as much as to know it together. And because such are fittest witnesses of the facts of one another, or of a third; it was, and ever will be reputed a very Evill act, for any man to speak against his *Conscience*; or to corrupt, or force another so to do: Insomuch that the plea of Conscience, has been always hearkened unto very diligently in all times. Afterwards, men made use of the same word metaphorically, for the knowledge of their own secret facts, and secret thoughts; and therefore it is Rhetorically said, that the Conscience is a thousand witnesses. And last of all, men, vehemently in love with their own new opinions, (though never so absurd,) and obstinately bent to maintain them, gave those their opinions also that reverenced name of Conscience, as if they would have it seem unlawfull, to change or speak against them; and so pretend to know they are true, when they know at most, but that they think so.

When a mans Discourse beginneth not at Definitions, it beginneth either at some other contemplation of his own, and then it is still called Opinion; Or it beginneth at some saying of another, of whose ability to know the truth, and of whose honesty in not deceiving, he doubteth not; and then the Discourse is not so much concerning the
Beliefe. Thing, as the Person; and the Resolution is called BELEEFE, and
Faith. FAITH: *Faith, in* the man; *Beleefe,* both *of* the man, and *of* the truth of what he sayes. So that in Beleefe are two opinions; one of the saying of the man; the other of his vertue. To *have faith in,* or *trust to,* or *beleeve a man,* signifie the same thing; namely, an opinion of the veracity of the man: But to *beleeve what is said,* signifieth onely an opinion of the truth of the saying. But wee are to observe that this Phrase, *I beleeve in*; as also the Latine, *Credo in*; and the Greek, πιστέυω ἔις are never used but in the writings of Divines. In stead of them, in other writings are put, *I beleeve him*; *I trust him*; *I have faith in him*; *I rely on him*: and in Latin, *Credo illi*; *fido illi*: and in Greek, πιστέυω αὐτῷ: and that this singularity of the Ecclesiastique use

of the word hath raised many disputes about the right object of the Christian Faith.

But by *Beleeving in*, as it is in the Creed, is meant, not trust in the Person; but Confession and acknowledgement of the Doctrine. For not onely Christians, but all manner of men do so believe in God, as to hold all for truth they heare him say, whether they understand it, or not; which is all the Faith and trust can possibly be had in any person whatsoever: But they do not all believe the Doctrine of the Creed.

From whence we may inferre, that when wee believe any saying [32] whatsoever it be, to be true, from arguments taken, not from the thing it selfe, or from the principles of naturall Reason, but from the Authority, and good opinion wee have, of him that hath sayd it; then is the speaker, or person we believe in, or trust in, and whose word we take, the object of our Faith; and the Honour done in Believing, is done to him only. And consequently, when wee Believe that the Scriptures are the word of God, having no immediate revelation from God himselfe, our Beleefe, Faith, and Trust is in the Church; whose word we take, and acquiesce therein. And they that believe that which a Prophet relates unto them in the name of God, take the word of the Prophet, do honour to him, and in him trust, and believe, touching the truth of what he relateth, whether he be a true, or a false Prophet. And so it is also with all other History. For if I should not believe all that is written by Historians, of the glorious acts of *Alexander*, or *Caesar*, I do not think the Ghost of *Alexander*, or *Caesar*, had any just cause to be offended; or any body else, but the Historian. If *Livy* say the Gods made once a Cow speak, and we believe it not; wee distrust not God therein, but *Livy*. So that it is evident, that whatsoever we believe, upon no other reason, then what is drawn from authority of men onely, and their writings; whether they be sent from God or not, is Faith in men onely.

CHAP. VIII.

Of the VERTUES *commonly called* INTELLECTUALL; *and their contrary* DEFECTS.

Vertue generally, in all sorts of subjects, is somewhat that is valued for eminence; and consisteth in comparison. For if all things were equally in all men, nothing would be prized. And by *Vertues* INTELLECTUALL, are alwayes understood such abilityes of the mind, as men praise, value, and desire should be in themselves; and go commonly under the name of a *good wit*; though the same word WIT, be used also, to distinguish one certain ability from the rest.

Intellectuall Vertue defined.

These *Vertues* are of two sorts; *Naturall*, and *Acquired*. By Naturall, I mean not, that which a man hath from his Birth: for that is nothing else but Sense; wherein men differ so little one from another, and from brute Beasts, as it is not to be reckoned amongst Vertues. But I mean, that *Wit*, which is gotten by Use onely, and Experience; without Method, Culture, or Instruction. This NATURALL WIT, consisteth principally in two things; *Celerity of Imagining*, (that is, swift succession of one thought to another;) and *steddy direction* to some approved end. On the Contrary a slow Imagination, maketh that Defect, or fault of the mind, which is commonly called DULNESSE, *Stupidity*, and sometimes by other names that signifie slownesse of motion, or difficulty to be moved.

Wit, Naturall, or Acquired.

Natural Wit.

[33]

And this difference of quicknesse, is caused by the difference of mens passions; that love and dislike, some one thing, some another: and therefore some mens thoughts run one way, some another; and are held to, and observe differently the things that passe through their imagination. And whereas in this succession of mens thoughts, there is nothing to observe in the things they think on, but either in what they be *like one another,* or in what they be *unlike,* or *what they serve for,* or *how they serve to such a purpose;* Those that observe their similitudes, in case they be such as are but rarely observed by others, are sayd to have a *Good Wit*; by which, in this occasion, is meant a *Good Fancy.*

Good Wit, or Fancy.

But they that observe their differences, and dissimilitudes; which is called *Distinguishing*, and *Discerning*, and *Judging* between thing and thing; in case, such discerning be not easie, are said to have a *good Judgement*: and particularly in matter of conversation and businesse; wherein, times, places, and persons are to be discerned, this Vertue is called DISCRETION. The former, that is, Fancy, without the help of Judgement, is not commended as a Vertue: but the later which is Judgement, and Discretion, is commended for it selfe, without the help of Fancy. Besides the Discretion of times, places, and persons, necessary to a good Fancy, there is required also an often application of his thoughts to their End; that is to say, to some use to be made of them. This done; he that hath this Vertue, will be easily fitted with similitudes, that will please, not onely by illustration of his discourse, and adorning it with new and apt metaphors; but also, by the rarity of their invention. But without Stedinesse, and Direction to some End, a great Fancy is one kind of Madnesse; such as they have, that entring into any discourse, are snatched from their purpose, by every thing that comes in their thought, into so many, and so long digressions, and Parentheses, that they utterly lose themselves: Which kind of folly, I know no particular name for: but the cause of it is, sometimes want of experience; whereby that seemeth to a man new and rare, which doth not so to others: sometimes Pusillanimity; by which that seems great to him, which other men think a trifle: and whatsoever is new, or great, and therefore thought fit to be told, withdrawes a man by degrees from the intended way of his discourse.

In a good Poem, whether it be *Epique*, or *Dramatique*; as also in *Sonnets*, *Epigrams*, and other Pieces, both Judgement and Fancy are required: But the Fancy must be more eminent; because they please for the Extravagancy; but ought not to displease by Indiscretion.

In a good History, the Judgement must be eminent; because the goodnesse consisteth, in the Method, in the Truth, and in the Choyse of the actions that are most profitable to be known. Fancy has no place, but onely in adorning the stile.

In Orations of Prayse, and in Invectives, the Fancy is praedominant; because the designe is not truth, but to Honour or Dishonour; which is done by noble, or by vile comparisons. The Judgement does but suggest what circumstances make an action laudable, or culpable.

In Hortatives, and Pleadings, as Truth, or Disguise serveth best to

Good Judgement.

Discretion.

[34]

the Designe in hand; so is the Judgement, or the Fancy most required.

In Demonstration, in Councell, and all rigourous search of Truth, Judgement does all; except sometimes the understanding have need to be opened by some apt similitude; and then there is so much use of Fancy. But for Metaphors, they are in this case utterly excluded. For seeing they openly professe deceipt; to admit them into Councell, or Reasoning, were manifest folly.

And in any Discourse whatsoever, if the defect of Discretion be apparent; how extravagant soever the Fancy be, the whole discourse will be taken for a signe of want of wit; and so will it never when the Discretion is manifest, though the Fancy be never so ordinary.

The secret thoughts of a man run over all things, holy, prophane, clean, obscene, grave, and light, without shame, or blame; which verball discourse cannot do, farther than the Judgement shall approve of the Time, Place, and Persons. An Anatomist, or a Physitian may speak, or write his judgement of unclean things; because it is not to please, but profit: but for another man to write his extravagant, and pleasant fancies of the same, is as if a man, from being tumbled into the dirt, should come and present himselfe before good company. And 'tis the want of Discretion that makes the difference. Again, in profest remissnesse of mind, and familiar company, a man may play with the sounds, and aequivocall significations of words; and that many times with encounters of extraordinary Fancy: but in a Sermon, or in publique, or before persons unknown, or whom we ought to reverence, there is no Gingling of words that will not be accounted folly: and the difference is onely in the want of Discretion. So that where Wit is wanting, it is not Fancy that is wanting, but Discretion. Judgement therefore without Fancy is Wit, but Fancy without Judgement not.

Prudence. When the thoughts of a man, that has a designe in hand, running over a multitude of things, observes how they conduce to that designe; or what designe they may conduce unto; if his observations be such as are not easie, or usuall, This wit of his is called PRUDENCE; and dependeth on much Experience, and Memory of the like things, and their consequences heretofore. In which there is not so much difference of Men, as there is in their Fancies and Judgements; Because the Experience of men equall in age, is not much unequall, as to the quantity; but lyes in different occasions; every one having his private designes. To govern well a family, and a kingdome, are not different degrees of Prudence; but different sorts of businesse; no more than to draw a picture in little, or as great, or greater then the life, are different degrees of Art. A plain husband-man is more Prudent in affaires of his own house, then a Privy Counseller in the affaires of another man.

To Prudence, if you adde the use of unjust, or dishonest means, such as usually are prompted to men by Feare, or Want; you have that Crooked Wisdome, which is called C R A F T; which is a signe of Pusil- *Craft.* lanimity. For Magnanimity is contempt of unjust, or dishonest helps. [35] And that which the Latines call *Versutia*, (translated into English, *Shifting*,) and is a putting off of a present danger or incommodity, by engaging into a greater, as when a man robbs one to pay another, is but a shorter sighted Craft, called *Versutia*, from *Versura*, which signi-fies taking mony at usurie, for the present payment of interest.

As for *acquired Wit*, (I mean acquired by method and instruction,) *Acquired* there is none but Reason; which is grounded on the right use of *Wit.* Speech; and produceth the Sciences. But of Reason and Science, I have already spoken in the fifth and sixth Chapters.

The causes of this difference of Witts, are in the Passions: and the difference of Passions, proceedeth partly from the different Constitu-tion of the body, and partly from different Education. For if the difference proceeded from the temper of the brain, and the organs of Sense, either exterior or interior, there would be no lesse difference of men in their Sight, Hearing, or other Senses, than in their Fancies, and Discretions. It proceeds therefore from the Passions; which are different, not onely from the difference of mens complexions; but also from their difference of customes, and education.

The Passions that most of all cause the differences of Wit, are principally, the more or lesse Desire of Power, of Riches, of Know-ledge, and of Honour. All which may be reduced to the first, that is Desire of Power. For Riches, Knowledge and Honour are but severall sorts of Power.

And therefore, a man who has no great Passion for any of these things; but is as men terme it indifferent; though he may be so farre a good man, as to be free from giving offence; yet he cannot possibly have either a great Fancy, or much Judgement. For the Thoughts, are to the Desires, as Scouts, and Spies, to range abroad, and find the way to the things Desired: All Stedinesse of the minds motion, and all quicknesse of the same, proceeding from thence. For as to have no Desire, is to be Dead: so to have weak Passions, is Dulnesse; and to have Passions indifferently for every thing, GIDDINESSE, and *Distraction*; and to have stronger, and more vehement Passions for any thing, than is ordinarily seen in others, is that which men call MADNESSE.

Giddinesse.

Madnesse.

Whereof there be almost as many kinds, as of the Passions themselves. Sometimes the extraordinary and extravagant Passion, proceedeth from the evill constitution of the organs of the Body, or harme done them; and sometimes the hurt, and indisposition of the Organs, is caused by the vehemence, or long continuance of the Passion. But in both cases the Madnesse is of one and the same nature.

The Passion, whose violence, or continuance maketh Madnesse, is either great *vaine-Glory*; which is commonly called *Pride*, and *self-conceipt*; or great *Dejection* of mind.

Pride, subjecteth a man to Anger, the excesse whereof, is the Madnesse called RAGE, and FURY. And thus it comes to passe that excessive desire of Revenge, when it becomes habituall, hurteth the organs, and becomes Rage: That excessive love, with jealousie, becomes also Rage: Excessive opinion of a mans own selfe, for divine inspiration, for wisdome, learning, forme, and the like, becomes Distraction, and Giddinesse: The same, joyned with Envy, Rage: Vehement opinion of the truth of any thing, contradicted by others, Rage.

Rage.

[36]

Dejection, subjects a man to causelesse fears; which is a Madnesse commonly called MELANCHOLY, apparent also in divers manners; as in haunting of solitudes, and graves; in superstitious behaviour; and in fearing some one, some another particular thing. In summe, all Passions that produce strange and unusual behaviour, are called by the generall name of Madnesse. But of the severall kinds of Madnesse, he that would take the paines, might enrowle a legion. And if the Excesses be madnesse, there is no doubt but the Passions themselves, when they tend to Evill, are degrees of the same.

Melancholy.

(For example,) Though the effect of folly, in them that are possessed of an opinion of being inspired, be not visible alwayes in one man, by any very extravagant action, that proceedeth from such Passion; yet when many of them conspire together, the Rage of the whole multitude is visible enough. For what argument of Madnesse can there be greater, than to clamour, strike, and throw stones at our best friends? Yet this is somewhat lesse than such a multitude will do. For they will clamour, fight against, and destroy those, by whom all their life-time before, they have been protected, and secured from injury. And if this be Madnesse in the multitude, it is the same in every particular man. For as in the middest of the sea, though a man perceive no sound of that part of the water next him; yet he is well assured, that part contributes as much, to the Roaring of the Sea, as any other part, of the same quantity: so also, though wee perceive no great unquietnesse, in one, or two men; yet we may be well assured, that their singular Passions, are parts of the Seditious roaring of a troubled Nation. And if there were nothing else that bewrayed their madnesse; yet that very arrogating such inspiration to themselves, is argument enough. If some man in Bedlam should entertaine you with sober discourse; and you desire in taking leave, to know what he were, that you might another time requite his civility; and he should tell you, he were God the Father; I think you need expect no extravagant action for argument of his Madnesse.

This opinion of Inspiration, called commonly, Private Spirit, begins very often, from some lucky finding of an Errour generally held by others; and not knowing, or not remembring, by what conduct of reason, they came to so singular a truth, (as they think it, though it be many times an untruth they light on,) they presently admire themselves; as being in the speciall grace of God Almighty, who hath revealed the same to them supernaturally, by his Spirit.

Again, that Madnesse is nothing else, but too much appearing Passion, may be gathered out of the effects of Wine, which are the same with those of the evill disposition of the organs. For the variety of behaviour in men that have drunk too much, is the same with that [37] of Mad-men: some of them Raging, others Loving, others Laughing, all extravagantly, but according to their severall domineering Passions: For the effect of the wine, does but remove Dissimulation; and take from them the sight of the deformity of their Passions. For, (I believe) the most sober men, when they walk alone without care and employment of the mind, would be unwilling the vanity and Extravagance of their thoughts at that time should be publiquely seen: which is a confession, that Passions unguided, are for the most part meere Madnesse.

The opinions of the world, both in antient and later ages, concerning the cause of madnesse, have been two. Some, deriving them from the Passions; some, from Daemons, or Spirits, either good, or bad, which they thought might enter into a man, possesse him, and move his organs in such strange, and uncouth manner, as mad-men use to do. The former sort, therefore, called such men, Mad-men: but the Later, called them sometimes *Daemoniacks*, (that is, possessed with spirits;) sometimes *Energumeni*, (that is, agitated, or moved with spirits;) and now in *Italy* they are called not onely *Pazzi*, Madmen; but also *Spiritati*, men possest.

There was once a great conflux of people in *Abdera*, a City of the Greeks, at the acting of the Tragedy of *Andromeda*, upon an extream hot day: whereupon, a great many of the spectators falling into Fevers, had this accident from the heat, and from the Tragedy together, that they did nothing but pronounce Iambiques, with the names of *Perseus* and *Andromeda*; which together with the Fever, was cured, by the comming on of Winter: And this madnesse was thought to proceed from the Passion imprinted by the Tragedy. Likewise there raigned a fit of madnesse in another Graecian City, which seized onely the young Maidens; and caused many of them to hang themselves. This was by most then thought an act of the Divel. But one that suspected, that contempt of life in them, might proceed from some Passion of the mind, and supposing they did not contemne also their honour, gave counsell to the Magistrates, to strip such as so hang'd themselves, and let them hang out naked. This the story says cured that madnesse. But on the other side, the same Graecians, did often ascribe madnesse, to the operation of the Eumenides, or Furyes; and sometimes of *Ceres*, *Phoebus*, and other Gods: so much did men attribute to Phantasmes, as to think them aëreal living bodies; and generally to call them Spirits. And as the Romans in this, held the same opinion with the Greeks: so also did the Jewes; For they called mad-men Prophets, or (according as they thought the spirits good or bad) Daemoniacks; and some of them called both Prophets, and Daemoniacks, mad-men; and some called the same man both Daemoniack, and mad-man. But for the Gentiles, 'tis no wonder; because Diseases, and Health; Vices, and Vertues; and many naturall accidents, were with them termed, and worshipped as Daemons. So that a man was to understand by Daemon, as well (sometimes) an Ague, as a Divell. But for the Jewes to have such opinion, is somewhat strange. For neither *Moses*, nor

[38]

56

Abraham pretended to Prophecy by possession of a Spirit; but from the voyce of God; or by a Vision or Dream: Nor is there any thing in his Law, Morall or Ceremoniall, by which they were taught, there was any such Enthusiasme; or any Possession. When God is sayd, *Numb.*11.25. to take from the Spirit that was in *Moses*, and give to the 70. Elders, the Spirit of God (taking it for the substance of God) is not divided. The Scriptures by the Spirit of God in man, mean a mans spirit, enclined to Godlinesse. And where it is said *Exod.*28.3. *Whom I have filled with the spirit of wisdome to make garments for Aaron*, is not meant a spirit put into them, that can make garments; but the wisdome of their own spirits in that kind of work. In the like sense, the spirit of man, when it produceth unclean actions, is ordinarily called an unclean spirit; and so other spirits, though not alwayes, yet as often as the vertue or vice so stiled, is extraordinary, and Eminent. Neither did the other Prophets of the old Testament pretend Enthusiasme; or, that God spake in them; but to them by Voyce, Vision, or Dream; and the *Burthen of the Lord* was not Possession, but Command. How then could the Jewes fall into this opinion of possession? I can imagine no reason, but that which is common to all men; namely, the want of curiosity to search naturall causes; and their placing Felicity, in the acquisition of the grosse pleasures of the Senses, and the things that most immediately conduce thereto. For they that see any strange, and unusual ability, or defect in a mans mind; unlesse they see withall, from what cause it may probably proceed, can hardly think it naturall; and if not naturall, they must needs thinke it supernaturall; and then what can it be, but that either God, or the Divell is in him? And hence it came to passe, when our Saviour (*Mark* 3.21.) was compassed about with the multitude, those of the house doubted he was mad, and went out to hold him: but the Scribes said he had *Belzebub*, and that was it, by which he cast out divels; as if the greater mad-man had awed the lesser. And that (*John* 10.20) some said, *He hath a Divell, and is mad*; whereas others holding him for a Prophet, sayd, *These are not the words of one that hath a Divell*. So in the old Testament he that came to anoynt *Jehu*, 2 *Kings* 9.11. was a Prophet; but some of the company asked *Jehu*, *What came that mad-man for?* So that in summe, it is manifest, that whosoever behaved himselfe in extraordinory manner, was thought by the Jewes to be possessed either with a good, or evill spirit; except by the Sadduces, who erred so farre on the other hand, as not to believe there were at all any spirits, (which is very neere to direct Atheisme;) and thereby perhaps the more provoked others, to terme such men Daemoniacks, rather than mad-men.

But why then does our Saviour proceed in the curing of them, as if they were possest; and not as if they were mad? To which I can give no other kind of answer, but that which is given to those that urge the Scripture in like manner against the opinion of the motion of the Earth. The Scripture was written to shew unto men the kingdome of God, and to prepare their mindes to become his obedient subjects; leaving the world, and the Philosophy thereof, to the disputation of men, for the exercising of their naturall Reason. Whether the Earths, or Suns motion make the day, and night; or whether the Exorbitant actions of men, proceed from Passion, or from the Divell, (so we worship him not) it is all one, as to our obedience, and subjection to God Almighty; which is the thing for which the Scripture was written. As for that our Saviour speaketh to the disease, as to a person; it is the usuall phrase of all that cure by words onely, as Christ did, (and Inchanters pretend to do, whether they speak to a Divel or not.) For is not Christ also said (*Math.*8.26) to have rebuked the winds? *but because you may say, winds are spirits, is*[1] not he said also (*Luk.*4.39) to rebuke a Fever? Yet this does not argue that a Fever is a Divel. And whereas many of those Divels are said to confesse Christ; it is not necessary to interpret those places otherwise, than that those mad-men confessed him. And whereas our Saviour (*Math.*12.43.) speaketh of an unclean Spirit, that having gone out of a man, wandreth through dry places, seeking rest, and finding none; and returning into the same man, with seven other spirits worse than himselfe; It is manifestly a Parable, alluding to a man, that after a little endeavour to quit his lusts, is vanquished by the strength of them; and becomes seven times worse than he was. So that I see nothing at all in the Scripture, that requireth a beliefe, that Daemoniacks were any other thing but Mad-men.

There is yet another fault in the Discourses of some men; which may also be numbred amongst the sorts of Madnesse; namely, that abuse of words, whereof I have spoken before in the fifth chapter, by the Name of Absurdity. And that is, when men speak such words, as

Insignificant Speech.

[39]

---

[1] *Syn.*: Is

put together, have in them no signification at all; but are fallen upon by some, through misunderstanding of the words they have received, and repeat by rote; by others, from intention to deceive by obscurity. And this is incident to none but those, that converse in questions of matters incomprehensible, as the Schoole-men; or in questions of abstruse Philosophy. The common sort of men seldome speak Insignificantly, and are therefore, by those other Egregious persons counted Idiots. But to be assured their words are without any thing correspondent to them in the mind, there would need some Examples; which if any man require, let him take a Schoole-man into his hands, and see if he can translate any one chapter concerning any difficult point; as the Trinity; the Deity; the nature of Christ; Transubstantiation; Free-will, *&c.* into any of the moderne tongues, so as to make the same intelligible; or into any tolerable Latine, such as they were acquainted withall, that lived when the Latine tongue was Vulgar. What is the meaning of these words. *The first cause does not necessarily inflow any thing into the second, by force of the Essentiall subordination of the second causes, by Which it may help it to worke?* They are the Translation of the Title of the sixth chapter of *Suarez* first Booke, *Of the Concourse, Motion, and Help of God.* When men write whole volumes of such stuffe, are they not Mad, or intend to make others so? And particularly, in the question of Transubstantiation; [40] where after certain words spoken, they that say, the White*nesse,* Round*nesse,* Magni*tude,* Quali*ty,* Corruptibili*ty,* all which are incorporeall, *&c.* go out of the Wafer, into the Body of our blessed Saviour, do they not make those *Nesses, Tudes,* and *Ties,* to be so many spirits possessing his body? For by Spirits, they mean alwayes things, that being incorporeall, are neverthelesse moveable from one place to another. So that this kind of Absurdity, may rightly be numbred amongst the many sorts of Madnesse; and all the time that guided by clear Thoughts of their worldly lust, they forbear disputing, or writing thus, but Lucide Intervals. And thus much of the Vertues and Defects Intellectuall.

59

CHAP. IX.
Of the Severall SUBJECTS *of* KNOWLEDGE.

There are of KNOWLEDGE two kinds; whereof one is *Knowledge of Fact*: the other *Knowledge of the Consequence of one Affirmation to another.* The former is nothing else, but Sense and Memory, and is *Absolute Knowledge*; as when we see a Fact doing, or remember it done: And this is the Knowledge required in a Witnesse. The later is called *Science*; and is *Conditionall*; as when we know, that, *If the figure showne be a circle, then any straight line throught the Center shall divide it into two equall parts.* And this is the Knowledge required in a Philosopher; that is to say, of him that pretends to Reasoning.

The Register of *Knowledge of Fact* is called *History.* Whereof there be two sorts: one called *Natural History*; which is the History of such Facts, or Effects of Nature, as have no Dependance on Mans *Will*; Such as are the Histories of *Metalls*, *Plants*, *Animals*, *Regions*, and the like. The other, is *Civill History*; which is the History of the Voluntary Actions of men in Common-wealths.

The Registers of Science, are such *Books* as contain the *Demonstrations* of Consequences of one Affirmation, to another; and are commonly called *Books of Philosophy*; whereof the sorts are many, according to the diversity of the Matter; And may be divided in such manner as I have divided them in the following Table.

SCIENCE, that is, knowledge of Consequences; which is called also PHILOSOPHY.

- Consequences from the Accidents of Bodies Naturall, which is called NATURAL PHILOSOPHY.
  - Consequences from the Accidents common to all Bodies Naturall; which are *Quantity*, and *Motion*.
    - Consequences from *Quantity*, and *Motion indeterminate*; which being the Principles, or first foundation of Philosophy, is called *Philosophia Prima* → **PHILOSOPHIA PRIMA**
    - Consequences from *Motion*, and *Quantity determined*.
      - Consequences from *Quantity*, and *Motion determined*. — *Mathematiques*,
        - In *Figure* → **GEOMETRY**
        - In *Number* → **ARITHMETIQUE**
      - Consequences from the *Motion*, and *Quantity of Bodies in Speciall*.
        - Consequences from the *Motion*, and *Quantity* of the great parts of the World, as the *Earth* and *Starres*. — *Cosmography*;
          - **ASTRONOMY**
          - **GEOGRAPHY**
        - Consequences from the *Motion* of *Speciall kinds*, and Figures of Body. — *Mechaniques*, Doctrine of *Weight*.
          - **Science of ENGINEERS**
          - **ARCHITECTURE**
          - **NAVIGATION**
  - PHYSIQUES, or Consequences from *Qualities*.
    - Consequences from the Qualities of Bodies *Transient*, such as sometimes appear, sometimes vanish. → **METEOROLOGY**
    - Consequences from the Qualities of Bodies *Permanent*.
      - Consequences from the Qualities of the *Starres*.
        - Consequences from the *Light* of the *Starres*. Out of this, and the Motion of the Sunne, is made the Science of .... → **SCIOGRAPHY**
        - Consequences from the *Influence* of the *Starres*. → **ASTROLOGY**
      - Consequences from the Qualities of Bodies *Terrestrial*.
        - Consequences from the parts of the Earth, that are *without sense*.
          - Consequences of the Qualities from *Liquid* Bodies that fill the space between the Starres; such as are the *Ayre*, or substance aethereall.
          - Consequences from the Qualities of *Minerals*, such as *Stones*, *Metalls*, &c.
          - Consequences from the Qualities of *Vegetables*.
        - Consequences from the Qualities of *Animals*.
          - Consequences from the Qualities of *Animals in generall*.
            - Consequences from *Vision*, → **OPTIQUES**
            - Consequences from *Sounds*, → **MUSIQUE**
            - Consequences from the rest of the Senses.
          - Consequences from the Qualities of *Men in Speciall*.
            - Consequences from the Passions of Men, → **ETHIQUES**
            - Consequences from *Speech*, in
              - In *Magnifying*, *Vilifying*, &c. → **POETRY**
              - In *Persuading*, → **RHETORIQUE**
              - In *Reasoning*, → **LOGIQUE**
              - In *Contracting*. → The Science of **JUST** and **UNJUST**
- Consequences from the Accidents of *Politique* Bodies; which is called POLITIQUES, and CIVIL PHILOSOPHY.
  - 1 Of Consequences from the *Institution* of COMMON-WEALTHS, to the *Rights*, and *Duties* of the *Body Politique*, or Sovereign.
  - 2 Of Consequences from the same, to the *Duty* and *Right* of the Subjects.

CHAP. X.

Of POWER, WORTH, DIGNITY, HONOUR, *and* WORTHINESSE.

The POWER *of a Man*, (to take it Universally,) is his present means, to obtain some future apparent Good. And is either *Originall*, or *Instrumentall*.

Naturall Power, is the eminence of the Faculties of Body, or Mind: as extraordinary Strength, Forme, Prudence, Arts, Eloquence, Liberality, Nobility. *Instrumentall* are those Powers, which acquired by these, or by fortune, are means and Instruments to acquire more: as Riches, Reputation, Friends, and the secret working of God, which men call Good Luck. For the nature of Power, is in this point, like to Fame, increasing as it proceeds; or like the motion of heavy bodies, which the further they go, make still the more hast.

The Greatest of humane Powers, is that which is compounded of the Powers of most men, united by consent, in one person, Naturall, or Civill, that has the use of all their Powers depending on his will; such as is the Power of a Common-wealth: Or depending on the wills of each particular; such as is the Power of a Faction, or of divers factions leagued. Therefore to have servants, is Power; To have friends, is Power: for they are strengths united.

Also Riches joyned with liberality, is Power; because it procureth friends, and servants: Without liberality, not so; because in this case they defend not; but expose men to Envy, as a Prey.

Reputation of power, is Power; because it draweth with it the adhaerence of those that need protection.

So is Reputation of love of a mans Country, (called Popularity,) for the same Reason.

Also, what quality soever maketh a man beloved, or feared of many; or the reputation of such quality, is Power; because it is a means to have the assistance, and service of many.

Good successe is Power; because it maketh reputation of Wisdome, or good fortune; which makes men either feare him, or rely on him.

Affability of men already in power, is encrease of Power; because it gaineth love.

Reputation of Prudence in the conduct of Peace or War, is Power; because to prudent men, we commit the government of our selves, more willingly than to others.

Nobility is Power, not in all places, but onely in those Commonwealths, where it has Priviledges: for in such priviledges consisteth their Power.

Eloquence is power; because it is seeming Prudence.

Forme is Power; because being a promise of Good, it recommendeth men to the favour of women and strangers.   [42]

The Sciences, are small Power; because not eminent; and therefore, not acknowledged in any man; nor are at all, but in a few; and in them, but of a few things. For Science is of that nature, as none can understand it to be, but such as in a good measure have attayned it.

Arts of publique use, as Fortification, making of Engines, and other Instruments of War; because they conferre to Defence, and Victory, are Power: And though the true Mother of them, be Science, namely the Mathematiques; yet, because they are brought into the Light, by the hand of the Artificer, they be esteemed (the Midwife passing with the vulgar for the Mother,) as his issue.

The *Value*, or WORTH of a man, is as of all other things, his Price; *Worth.* that is to say, so much as would be given for the use of his Power: and therefore is not absolute; but a thing dependant on the need and judgement of another. An able conductor of Souldiers, is of great Price in time of War present, or imminent; but in Peace not so. A learned and uncorrupt Judge, is much Worth in time of Peace; but not so much in War. And as in other things, so in men, not the seller, but the buyer determines the Price. For let a man (as most men do,) rate themselves at the highest Value they can; yet their true Value is no more than it is esteemed by others.

The manifestation of the Value we set on one another, is that which is commonly called Honouring, and Dishonouring. To Value a man at a high rate, is to *Honour* him; at a low rate, is to *Dishonour* him. But high, and low, in this case, is to be understood by comparison to the rate that each man setteth on himselfe.

The publique worth of a man, which is the Value set on him by the Common-wealth, is that which men commonly call DIGNITY. And *Dignity.*

63

this Value of him by the Common-wealth, is understood, by offices of Command, Judicature, publike Employment; or by Names and Titles, introduced for distinction of such Value.

To pray to another, for ayde of any kind, is *to* H O N O U R; because a signe we have an opinion he has power to help; and the more difficult the ayde is, the more is the Honour.

To obey, is to Honour; because no man obeyes them, whom they think have no power to help, or hurt them. And consequently to disobey, is to *Dishonour.*

To give great gifts to a man, is to Honour him; because 'tis buying of Protection, and acknowledging of Power. To give little gifts, is to Dishonour; because it is but Almes, and signifies an opinion of the need of small helps.

To be sedulous in promoting anothers good; also to flatter, is to Honour; as a signe we seek his protection or ayde. To neglect, is to Dishonour.

To give way, or place to another, in any Commodity, is to Honour; being a confession of greater power. To arrogate, is to Dishonour.

[43]

To shew any signe of love, or feare of another, is to Honour; for both to love, and to feare, is to value. To contemne, or lesse to love or feare, then he expects, is to Dishonour; for 'tis undervaluing.

To praise, magnifie, or call happy, is to Honour; because nothing but goodnesse, power, and felicity is valued. To revile, mock, or pitty, is to Dishonour.

To speak to another with consideration, to appear before him with decency, and humility, is to Honour him; as signes of fear to offend. To speak to him rashly, to do any thing before him obscenely, slovenly, impudently, is to Dishonour.

To believe, to trust, to rely on another, is to Honour him; signe of opinion of his vertue and power. To distrust, or not believe, is to Dishonour.

To hearken to a mans counsell, or discourse of what kind soever, is to Honour; as a signe we think him wise, or eloquent, or witty. To sleep, or go forth, or talk the while is to Dishonour.

To do those things to another, which he takes for signes of Honour, or which the Law or Custome makes so, is to Honour; because in approving the Honour done by others, he acknowledgeth the power which others acknowledge. To refuse to do them, is to Dishonour.

To agree with in opinion, is to Honour; as being a signe of approving his judgement, and wisdome. To dissent, is Dishonour, and an upbraiding of errour; and (if the dissent be in many things) of folly.

To imitate, is to Honour; for it is vehemently to approve. To imitate ones Enemy, is to Dishonour.

To honour those another honours, is to Honour him; as a signe of approbation of his judgement. To honour his Enemies, is to Dishonour him.

To employ in counsell, or in actions of difficulty, is to Honour; as a signe of opinion of his wisdome, or other power. To deny employment in the same cases, to those that seek it, is to Dishonour.

All these wayes of Honouring, are naturall; and as well within, as without Common-wealths. But in Common-wealths, where he, or they that have the supreme Authority, can make whatsoever they please, to stand for signes of Honour, there be other Honours.

A Soveraigne doth Honour a Subject, with whatsoever Title, or Office, or Employment, or Action, that he himselfe will have taken for a signe of his will to Honour him.

The King of *Persia*, Honoured *Mordecay*, when he appointed he should be conducted through the streets in the Kings Garment, upon one of the Kings Horses, with a Crown on his head, and a Prince before him, proclayming, *Thus shall it be done to him that the King will honour.* And yet another King of *Persia*, or the same another time, to one that demanded for some great service, to weare one of the Kings robes, gave him leave so to do; but with this addition, that he should weare it as the Kings foole; and then it was Dishonour. So that of Civill Honour, the Fountain is in the person of the Common-wealth, and dependeth on the Will of the Soveraigne; and is therefore temporary, and called *Civill Honour*; such as are Magistracy, Offices, [44] Titles; and in some places Coats, and Scutchions painted: and men Honour such as have them, as having so many signes of favour in the Common-wealth; which favour is Power.

Honourable is whatsoever possession, action, or quality, is an argument and signe of Power.   *Honourable.*

And therefore To be Honoured, loved, or feared of many, is Honourable; as arguments of Power. To be Honoured of few or none, *Dishonourable.*   *Dishonourable.*

Dominion, and victory is Honourable; because acquired by Power; and Servitude, for need, or feare, is Dishonourable.

Good fortune (if lasting,) Honourable; as a signe of the favour of God. Ill fortune, and losses, Dishonourable. Riches, are Honourable; for they are Power. Poverty, Dishonourable. Magnanimity, Liberality, Hope, Courage, Confidence, are Honourable; for they proceed from the conscience of Power. Pusillanimity, Parsimony, Fear, Diffidence, are Dishonourable.

Timely Resolution, or determination of what a man is to do, is Honourable; as being the contempt of small difficulties, and dangers. And Irresolution, Dishonourable; as a signe of too much valuing of little impediments, and little advantages: For when a man has weighed things as long as the time permits, and resolves not, the difference of weight is but little; and therefore if he resolve not, he overvalues little things, which is Pusillanimity.

All Actions, and Speeches, that proceed, or seem to proceed from much Experience, Science, Discretion, or Wit, are Honourable; For all these are Powers. Actions, or Words that proceed from Errour, Ignorance, or Folly, Dishonourable.

Gravity, as farre forth as it seems to proceed from a mind employed on some thing else, is Honourable; because employment is a signe of Power. But if it seem to proceed from a purpose to appear grave, it is Dishonourable. For the gravity of the former, is like the steddinesse of a Ship laden with Merchandise; but of the later, like the steddinesse of a Ship ballasted with Sand, and other trash.

To be Conspicuous, that is to say, to be known, for Wealth, Office, great Actions, or any eminent Good, is Honourable; as a signe of the power for which he is conspicuous. On the contrary, Obscurity, is Dishonourable.

To be descended from conspicuous Parents, is Honourable; because they the more easily attain the aydes, and friends of their Ancestors. On the contrary, to be descended from obscure Parentage, is Dishonourable.

Actions proceeding from Equity, joyned with losse, are Honourable; as signes of Magnanimity: for Magnanimity is a signe of Power. On the contrary, Craft, Shifting, neglect of Equity, is Dishonourable.

Covetousnesse of great Riches, and ambition of great Honours, are Honourable; as signes of power to obtain them. Covetousnesse, and ambition, of little gaines, or preferments, is Dishonourable.

Nor does it alter the case of Honour, whether an action (so it be great and difficult, and consequently a signe of much power,) be just or unjust: for Honour consisteth onely in the opinion of Power.

[45]

Therefore the ancient Heathen did not thinke they Dishonoured, but greatly Honoured the Gods, when they introduced them in their Poems, committing Rapes, Thefts, and other great, but unjust, or unclean acts: In so much as nothing is so much celebrated in *Jupiter*, as his Adulteries; nor in *Mercury*, as his Frauds, and Thefts: of whose praises, in a hymne of *Homer*, the greatest is this, that being born in the morning, he had invented Musique at noon, and before night, stolne away the Cattell of *Apollo*, from his Herdsmen.

Also amongst men, till there were constituted great Common-wealths, it was thought no dishonour to be a Pyrate, or a High-way Theefe; but rather a lawfull Trade, not onely amongst the Greeks, but also amongst all other Nations; as is manifest by the Histories of antient time. And at this day, in this part of the world, private Duels are, and alwayes will be Honourable, though unlawfull, till such time as there shall be Honour ordained for them that refuse, and Ignominy for them that make the Challenge. For Duels also are many times effects of Courage; and the ground of Courage is always Strength or Skill, which are Power; though for the most part they be effects of rash speaking, and of the fear of Dishonour, in one, or both the Combatants; who engaged by rashnesse, are driven into the Lists to avoyd disgrace.

Scutchions, and Coats of Armes haereditary, where they have any eminent Priviledges, are Honourable; otherwise not: for their Power consisteth either in such Priviledges, or in Riches, or some such thing as is equally honoured in other men. This kind of Honour, commonly called Gentry, has been derived from the Antient Germans. For there never was any such thing known, where the German Customes were unknown. Nor is it now any where in use, where the Germans have not inhabited. The antient Greek Commanders, when they went to war, had their Shields painted with such Devises as they pleased; insomuch as an unpainted Buckler was a signe of Poverty, and of a common Souldier: but they transmitted not the Inheritance of them. The Romans transmitted the Marks of their Families: but they were the Images, not the Devises of their Ancestors. Amongst the people of *Asia*, *Afrique*, and *America*, there is not, nor was ever, any such thing. The Germans onely had that custome; from whom it has been derived into *England*, *France*, *Spain* and *Italy*, when in great numbers they either ayded the Romans, or made their own Conquests in these Westerne parts of the world.

For *Germany*, being antiently, as all other Countries, in their begin-

Coats of Armes.

nings, divided amongst an infinite number of little Lords, or Masters of Families, that continually had wars one with another; those Masters or Lords, principally to the end they might, when they were Covered with Arms, be known by their followers; and partly for ornament, both painted their Armor, or their Scutchion, or Coat, with the picture of some Beast, or other thing; and also put some eminent and visible mark upon the Crest of their Helmets. And this ornament both of the Armes, and Crest, descended by inheritance to their Children; to the eldest pure, and to the rest with some note of diversity, such as the Old master, that is to say in Dutch, the *Here-alt* thought fit. But when many such Families, joyned together, made a greater Monarchy, this duty of the Herealt, to distinguish Scutchions, was made a private Office a part. And the issue of these Lords, is the great and antient Gentry; which for the most part bear living creatures, noted for courage, and rapine; or Castles, Battlements, Belts, Weapons, Bars, Palisadoes, and other notes of War; nothing being then in honour, but vertue military. Afterwards, not onely Kings, but popular Common-wealths, gave divers manners of Scutchions, to such as went forth to the War, or returned from it, for encouragement, or recompence to their service. *All which, by an observing Reader, may be found in such antient Histories, Greek and Latine, as make mention of the German Nation, and Manners, in their times.*[1]

Titles of Honour. Titles of *Honour*, such as are Duke, Count, Marquis, and Baron, are Honourable; as signifying the value set upon them by the Soveraigne Power of the Common-wealth: Which Titles, were in old times titles of Office, and Command, derived some from the Romans, some from the Germans, and French. Dukes, in Latine *Duces*, being Generalls in War: Counts, *Comites*, such as bare the Generall company out of friendship; and were left to govern and defend places conquered, and pacified: Marquises, *Marchiones*, were Counts that governed the Marches, or bounds of the Empire. Which titles of Duke, Count, and Marquis, came into the Empire, about the time of *Constantine* the Great, from the customes of the German *Militia*. But Baron, seems to have been a Title of the Gaules, and signifies a Great man; such as were the Kings, or Princes men, whom they employed in war about their persons; and seems to be derived from *Vir*, to *Ber* and

---

[1] Scribal MS reads: The places of antient History out of wch this that I have sayd may be gathered are at large collected by Philip Cluverius in his *Germania antiqua*.

Bar, that signified the same in the Language of the Gaules, that *Vir* in Latine; and thence to *Bero*, and *Baro*: so that such men were called *Berones*, and after *Barones*; and (in Spanish) *Varones*. But he that would know more particularly the originall of Titles of Honour, may find it, as I have done this, in Mr. *Seldens* most excellent Treatise of that subject. In processe of time these offices of Honour, by occasion of trouble, and for reasons of good and peaceable government, were turned into meer Titles; serving for the most part, to distinguish the precedence, place, and order of subjects in the Common-wealth: and men were made Dukes, Counts, Marquises, and Barons of Places, wherein they had neither possession, nor command: and other Titles also, were devised to the same end.

WORTHINESSE, is a thing different from the worth, or value of a man; and also from his merit, or desert; and consisteth in a particular power, or ability for that, whereof he is said to be worthy: which particular ability, is usually named FITNESSE, or *Aptitude*. *Fitnesse.*

For he is Worthiest to be a Commander, to be a Judge, or to have any other charge, that is best fitted, with the qualities required to the well discharging of it; and Worthiest of Riches, that has the qualities [47] most requisite for the well using of them: any of which qualities being absent, one may neverthelesse be a Worthy man, and valuable for some thing else. Again, a man may be Worthy of Riches, Office, and Employment, that neverthelesse, can plead no right to have it before another; and therefore cannot be said to merit or deserve it. For Merit, praesupposeth a right, and that the thing deserved is due by promise: Of which I shall say more hereafter, when I shall speak of Contracts.

Worthinesse.

CHAP. XI.
Of the difference of MANNERS.

By MANNERS, I mean not here, Decency of behaviour; as how one man should salute another, or how a man should wash his mouth, or pick his teeth before company, and such other points of the *Small Moralls*; But those qualities of man-kind, that concern their living together in Peace, and Unity. To which end we are to consider, that

What is here meant by Manners.

the Felicity of this life, consisteth not in the repose of a mind satisfied. For there is no such *Finis ultimus*, (utmost ayme,) nor *Summum Bonum*, (greatest Good,) as is spoken of in the Books of the old Morall Philosophers. Nor can a man any more live, whose Desires are at an end, than he, whose Senses and Imaginations are at a stand. Felicity is a continuall progresse of the desire, from one object to another; the attaining of the former, being still but the way to the later. The cause whereof is, That the object of mans desire, is not to enjoy once onely, and for one instant of time; but to assure for ever, the way of his future desire. And therefore the voluntary actions, and inclinations of all men, tend, not onely to the procuring, but also to the assuring of a contented life; and differ onely in the way: which ariseth partly from the diversity of passions, in divers men; and partly from the difference of the knowledge, or opinion each one has of the causes, which produce the effect desired.

A restlesse desire of Power, in all men.
So that in the first place, I put for a generall inclination of all mankind, a perpetuall and restlesse desire of Power after power, that ceaseth onely in Death. And the cause of this, is not alwayes that a man hopes for a more intensive delight, than he has already attained to; or that he cannot be content with a moderate power: but because he cannot assure the power and means to live well, which he hath present, without the acquisition of more. And from hence it is, that Kings, whose power is greatest, turn their endeavours to the assuring it at home by Lawes, or abroad by Wars: and when that is done, there succeedeth a new desire; in some, of Fame from new Conquest; in others, of ease and sensuall pleasure; in others, of admiration, or being flattered for excellence in some art, or other ability of the mind.

[48]
Love of Contention from Competition.
Competition of Riches, Honour, Command, or other power enclineth to Contention, Enmity, and War: Because the way of one Competitor, to the attaining of his desire, is to kill, subdue, supplant, or repell the other. Particularly, competition of praise, enclineth to a reverence of Antiquity. For men contend with the living, not with the dead; to these ascribing more than due, that they may obscure the glory of the other.

Civil obedience from love of Ease. From feare of Death, or Wounds.
Desire of Ease, and sensuall Delight, disposeth men to obey a common Power: Because by such Desires, a man doth abandon the protection might be hoped for from his own Industry, and labour. Fear of Death, and Wounds, disposeth to the same; and for the same reason. On the contrary, needy men, and hardy, not contented with

their present condition; as also, all men that are ambitious of Military command, are enclined to continue the causes of warre; and to stirre up trouble and sedition: for there is no honour Military but by warre; nor any such hope to mend an ill game, as by causing a new shuffle.

Desire of Knowledge, and Arts of Peace, enclineth men to obey a common Power: For such Desire, containeth a desire of leasure; and consequently protection from some other Power than their own.

And from love of Arts.

Desire of Praise, disposeth to laudable actions, such as please them whose judgement they value; for of those men whom we contemn, we contemn also the Praises. Desire of Fame after death does the same. And though after death, there be no sense of the praise given us on Earth, as being joyes, that are either swallowed up in the unspeakable joyes of Heaven, or extinguished in the extreme torments of Hell: yet is not such Fame vain; because men have a present delight therein, from the foresight of it, and of the benefit that may redound thereby to their posterity: which though they now see not, yet they imagine; and any thing that is pleasure in the sense, the same also is pleasure in the imagination.

Love of Vertue from love of Praise.

To have received from one, to whom we think our selves equall, greater benefits than there is hope to Requite, disposeth to counter-feit love; but really secret hatred; and puts a man into the estate of a desperate debtor, that in declining the sight of his creditor, tacitely wishes him there, where he might never see him more. For benefits oblige; and obligation is thraldome; and unrequitable obligation, perpetuall thraldome; which is to ones equall, hatefull. But to have received benefits from one, whom we acknowledge for superiour, enclines to love; because the obligation is no new depression: and cheerfull acceptation, (which men call *Gratitude*,) is such an honour done to the obliger, as is taken generally for retribution. Also to receive benefits, though from an equall, or inferiour, as long as there is hope of requitall, disposeth to love: for in the intention of the receiver, the obligation is of ayd, and service mutuall; from whence proceedeth an Emulation of who shall exceed in benefiting; the most noble and profitable contention possible; wherein the victor is pleased with his victory, and the other revenged by confessing it.

Hate, from difficulty of Requiting great Benefits.

To have done more hurt to a man, than he can, or is willing to expiate, enclineth the doer to hate the sufferer. For he must expect revenge, or forgivenesse; both which are hatefull.

And from Conscience of deserving to be hated.

[49]

Feare of oppression, disposeth a man to anticipate, or to seek ayd

Promptnesse to hurt, from Fear.

71

by society: for there is no other way by which a man can secure his life and liberty.

And from distrust of their own wit.

Men that distrust their own subtilty, are in tumult, and sedition, better disposed for victory, than they that suppose themselves wise, or crafty. For these love to consult, the other (fearing to be circumvented,) to strike first. And in sedition, men being alwayes in the procincts of battell, to hold together, and use all advantages of force, is a better stratagem, than any that can proceed from subtilty of Wit.

Vain undertaking from Vain-glory.

Vain-glorious men, such as without being conscious to themselves of great sufficiency, delight in supposing themselves gallant men, are enclined onely to ostentation; but not to attempt: Because when danger or difficulty appears, they look for nothing but to have their insufficiency discovered.

Vain-glorious men, such as estimate their sufficiency by the flattery of other men, or the fortune of some precedent action, without assured ground of hope from the true knowledge of themselves, are enclined to rash engaging; and in the approach of danger, or difficulty, to retire if they can: because not seeing the way of safety, they will rather hazard their honour, which may be salved with an excuse; than their lives, for which no salve is sufficient.

Ambition, from opinion of sufficiency.

Men that have a strong opinion of their own wisdome in matter of government, are disposed to Ambition. Because without publique Employment in counsell or magistracy, the honour of their wisdome is lost. And therefore Eloquent speakers are enclined to Ambition; for Eloquence seemeth wisedome, both to themselves and others.

Irresolution, from too great valuing of small matters.

Pusillanimity disposeth men to Irresolution, and consequently to lose the occasions, and fittest opportunities of action. For after men have been in deliberation till the time of action approach, if it be not then manifest what is best to be done, 'tis a signe, the difference of Motives, the one way and the other, are not great: Therefore not to resolve then, is to lose the occasion by weighing of trifles; which is Pusillanimity.

Frugality, (though in poor men a Vertue,) maketh a man unapt to atchieve such actions, as require the strength of many men at once: For it weakeneth their Endeavour, which is to be nourished and kept in vigor by Reward.

Confidence in others from Ignorance of the marks of

Eloquence, with flattery, disposeth men to confide in them that have it; because the former is seeming Wisdome, the later seeming Kindnesse. Adde to them Military reputation, and it disposeth men to adhaere, and subject themselves to those men that have them. The *Wisdome and* two former, having given them caution against danger from him; the *Kindnesse.* later gives them caution against danger from others.

Want of Science, that is, Ignorance of causes, disposeth, or rather *And from* constraineth a man to rely on the advise, and authority of others. For *Ignorance of* all men whom the truth concernes, if they rely not on their own, must *causes.* rely on the opinion of some other, whom they think wiser than themselves, and see not why he should deceive them.

Ignorance of the signification of words; which is, want of under- [50] standing, disposeth men to take on trust, not onely the truth they *And from* know not; but also the errors; and which is more, the non-sense of *want of* them they trust: For neither Error, nor non-sense, can without a *Under-* perfect understanding of words, be detected. *standing.*

From the same it proceedeth, that men give different names, to one and the same thing, from the difference of their own passions: As they that approve a private opinion, call it Opinion; but they that mislike it, Haeresie: and yet haeresie signifies no more than private opinion; but has onely a greater tincture of choler.

From the same also it proceedeth, that men cannot distinguish, without study and great understanding, between one action of many men, and many actions of one multitude; as for example, between the one action of all the Senators of *Rome* in killing *Castiline*, and the many actions of a number of Senators in killing *Caesar*; and therefore are disposed to take for the action of the people, that which is a multitude of actions done by a multitude of men, led perhaps by the perswasion of one.

Ignorance of the causes, and originall constitution of Right, Equity, *Adhaerence* Law, and Justice, disposeth a man to make Custome and Example the *to Custome,* rule of his actions; in such manner, as to think that Unjust which it *from* hath been the custome to punish; and that Just, of the impunity and *Ignorance of* approbation whereof they can produce an Example, or (as the *the nature of* Lawyers which only use this false measure of Justice barbarously call *Right and* it) a Precedent; like little children, that have no other rule of good and *Wrong.* evill manners, but the correction they receive from their Parents, and Masters; save that children are constant to their rule, whereas men are not so; because grown strong, and stubborn, they appeale from custome to reason, and from reason to custome, as it serves their turn; receding from custome when their interest requires it, and setting themselves against reason, as oft as reason is against them: Which is the cause, that the doctrine of Right and Wrong, is perpetually disputed, both by the Pen and the Sword: Whereas the doctrine of Lines, and Figures, is not so; because men care not, in that subject what be truth, as a thing that crosses no mans ambition, profit, or lust. For I doubt not, but if it had been a thing contrary to any mans right of dominion, or to the interest of men that have dominion, *That the three Angles of a Triangle, should be equall to two Angles of a Square*; that doctrine should have been, if not disputed, yet by the burning of all books of Geometry, suppressed, as farre as he whom it concerned was able.

Adhaerence to private men, From ignorance of the Causes of Peace.

Ignorance of remote causes, disposeth men to attribute all events, to the causes immediate, and Instrumentall: For these are all the causes they perceive. And hence it comes to passe, that in all places, men that are grieved with payments to the Publique, discharge their anger upon the Publicans, that is to say, Farmers, Collectors, and other Officers of the publique Revenue; and adhaere to such as find fault with the publike Government; and thereby, when they have engaged themselves beyond hope of justification, fall also upon the Supreme Authority, for feare of punishment, or shame of receiving pardon.

[51]

Credulity from Ignorance of nature.

Ignorance of naturall causes disposeth a man to Credulity, so as to believe many times impossibilities: For such know nothing to the contrary, but that they may be true; being unable to detect the Impossibility. And Credulity, because men love to be hearkened unto in company, disposeth them to lying: so that Ignorance it selfe without Malice, is able to make a man both to believe lyes, and tell them; and sometimes also to invent them.

Curiosity to know, from Care of future time. Naturall Religion, from the same.

Anxiety for the future time, disposeth men to enquire into the causes of things: because the knowledge of them, maketh men the better able to order the present to their best advantage.

Curiosity, or love of the knowledge of causes, draws a man from consideration of the effect, to seek the cause; and again, the cause of that cause; till of necessity he must come to this thought at last, that there is some cause, whereof there is no former cause, but is eternall; which is it men call God. So that it is impossible to make any profound enquiry into naturall causes, without being enclined thereby to believe there is one God Eternall; though they cannot have any Idea of him in their mind, answerable to his nature. For as a man that is born blind, hearing men talk of warming themselves by the fire, and

74

being brought to warm himself by the same, may easily conceive, and assure himselfe, there is somewhat there, which men call *Fire*, and is the cause of the heat he feeles; but cannot imagine what it is like; nor have an Idea of it in his mind, such as they have that see it: so also, by the visible things of this world, and their admirable order, a man may conceive there is a cause of them, which men call God; and yet not have an Idea, or Image of him in his mind.

And they that make little, or no enquiry into the naturall causes of things, yet from the feare that proceeds from the ignorance it selfe, of what it is that hath the power to do them much good or harm, are enclined to suppose, and feign unto themselves, severall kinds of Powers Invisible; and to stand in awe of their own imaginations; and in time of distresse to invoke them; as also in the time of *unexpec-ted*[1] good successe, to give them thanks; making the creatures of their own fancy, their Gods. By which means it hath come to passe, that from the innumerable variety of Fancy, men have created in the world innumerable sorts of Gods. And this Feare of things invisible, is the naturall Seed of that, which every one in himself calleth Religion; and in them that worship, or feare that Power otherwise than they do, Superstition.

And this seed of Religion, having been observed by many; some of those that have observed it, have been enclined thereby to nourish, dresse, and forme it into Lawes; and to adde to it of their own invention, any opinion of the causes of future events, by which they thought they should best be able to govern others, and make unto themselves the greatest use of their Powers.

CHAP. XII.
Of Religion.

[52]

Seeing there are no signes, nor fruit of *Religion*, but in Man onely; there is no cause to doubt, but that the seed of *Religion*, is also onely in Man; and consisteth in some peculiar quality, or at least in some eminent degree thereof, not to be found in other Living creatures.

Religion, in Man onely.

[1] *Syn.*: an expected.

75

*First, from
his desire of
knowing
Causes.*

And first, it is peculiar to the nature of Man, to be inquisitive into the Causes of the Events they see, some more, some lesse; but all men so much, as to be curious in the search of the causes of their own good and evill fortune.

*From the
consideration
of the
Begining of
things.
From his
observation of
the Sequell of
things.*

Secondly, upon the sight of any thing that hath a Beginning, to think also it had a cause, which determined the same to begin, then when it did, rather than sooner or later.

Thirdly, whereas there is no other Felicity of Beasts, but the enjoying of their quotidian Food, Ease, and Lusts; as having little, or no foresight of the time to come, for want of observation, and memory of the order, consequence, and dependance of the things they see; Man observeth how one Event hath been produced by another; and remembreth in them Antecedence and Consequence; And when he cannot assure himselfe of the true causes of things, (for the causes of good and evill fortune for the most part are invisible,) he supposes causes of them, either such as his own fancy suggesteth; or trusteth to the Authority of other men, such as he thinks to be his friends, and wiser than himselfe.

*The naturall
Cause of
Religion, the
Anxiety of
the time to
come.*

The two first, make Anxiety. For being assured that there be causes of all things that have arrived hitherto, or shall arrive hereafter; it is impossible for a man, who continually endeavoureth to secure himselfe against the evill he feares, and procure the good he desireth, not to be in a perpetuall solicitude of the time to come; So that every man, especially those that are over provident, are in an estate like to that of *Prometheus*. For as *Prometheus*, (which interpreted, is, *The prudent man*,) was bound to the hill *Caucasus*, a place of large prospect, where, an Eagle feeding on his liver, devoured in the day, as much as was repayred in the night: So that man, which looks too far before him, in the care of future time, hath his heart all the day long, gnawed on by feare of death, poverty, or other calamity; and has no repose, nor pause of his anxiety, but in sleep.

*Which makes
them fear the
Power of
Invisible
things.*

This perpetuall feare, always accompanying mankind in the ignorance of causes, as it were in the Dark, must needs have for object something. And therefore when there is nothing to be seen, there is nothing to accuse, either of their good, or evil fortune, but some *Power*, or Agent *Invisible*: In which sense perhaps it was, that some of the old Poets said, that the Gods were at first created by humane Feare: which spoken of the Gods, (that is to say, of the many

Gods of the Gentiles) is very true. But the acknowledging of one God [53]
Eternall, Infinite, and Omnipotent, may more easily be derived, from
the desire men have to know the causes of naturall bodies, and their
severall vertues, and operations; than from the feare of what was to
befall them in time to come. For he that from any effect hee seeth
come to passe, should reason to the next and immediate cause
thereof, and from thence to the cause of that cause, and plonge
himselfe profoundly *into*[1] the pursuit of causes; shall at last come to
this, that there must be (as even the Heathen Philosophers confessed)
one First Mover; that is, a First, and an Eternall cause of all things;
which is that which men mean by the name of God: And all this
without thought of their fortune; the solicitude whereof, both enclines
to fear, and hinders them from the search of the causes of other
things; and thereby gives occasion of feigning of as many Gods, as
there be men that feigne them.

And for the matter, or substance of the Invisible Agents, so   *And suppose*
fancyed; they could not by naturall cognition, fall upon any other   *them*
conceipt, but that it was the same with that of the Soule of man; and   *Incorporeall.*
that the Soule of man, was of the same substance, with that which
appeareth in a Dream, to one that sleepeth; or in a Looking-glasse, to
one that is awake; which, men not knowing that such apparitions are
nothing else but creatures of the Fancy, think to be reall, and externall
Substances; and therefore call them Ghosts; as the Latines called
them *Imagines*, and *Umbrae*; and thought them Spirits, that is, thin
aëreall bodies; and those Invisible Agents, which they feared, to bee
like them; save that they appear, and vanish when they please. But the
opinion that such Spirits were Incorporeall, or Immateriall, could
never enter into the mind of any man by nature; because, though men
may put together words of contradictory signification, as *Spirit*, and
Incorporeall; yet they can never have the imagination of any thing
answering to them: And therefore, men that by their own meditation,
arrive to the acknowledgement of one Infinite, Omnipotent, and
Eternall God, choose rather to confesse he is Incomprehensible, and
above their understanding; than to define his Nature by *Spirit
Incorporeall*, and then confesse their definition to be unintelligible: or
if they give him such a title, it is not *Dogmatically*, with intention to

---

[1] *Syn.*: in

make the Divine Nature understood; but *Piously*, to honour him with attributes, of significations, as remote as they can from the grossenesse of Bodies Visible.

But know not the way how they effect anything. Then, for the way by which they think these Invisible Agents wrought their effects; that is to say, what immediate causes they used, in bringing things to passe, men that know not what it is that we call *causing*, (that is, almost all men) have no other rule to guesse by, but by observing, and remembring what they have seen to precede the like effect at some other time, or times before, without seeing between the antecedent and subsequent Event, any dependance or connexion at all: And therefore from the like things past, they expect the like things to come; and hope for good or evill luck, superstitiously, from things that have no part at all in the causing of it: As the Athenians did for their war at *Lepanto*, demand another *Phormio*; The Pompeian faction for their warre in *Afrique*, another *Scipio*; and others have done in divers other occasions since. In like manner they attribute their fortune to a stander by, to a lucky or unlucky place, to words spoken, especially if the name of God be amongst them; as Charming, and Conjuring (the Leiturgy of Witches;) insomuch as to believe, they have power to turn a stone into bread, bread into a man, or any thing, into any thing.

[54]

But honour them as they honour men. Thirdly, for the worship which naturally men exhibite to Powers invisible, it can be no other, but such expressions of their reverence, as they would use towards men; Gifts, Petitions, Thanks, Submission of Body, Considerate Addresses, sober Behaviour, premeditated Words, Swearing (that is, assuring one another of their promises,) by invoking them. Beyond that reason suggesteth nothing; but leaves them either to rest there; or for further ceremonies, to rely on those they believe to be wiser than themselves.

And attribute to them all extraordinary events. Lastly, concerning how these Invisible Powers declare to men the things which shall hereafter come to passe, especially concerning their good or evill fortune in generall, or good or ill successe in any particular undertaking, men are naturally at a stand; save that using to conjecture of the time to come, by the time past, they are very apt, not onely to take casuall things, after one or two encounters, for Prognostiques of the like encounter ever after, but also to believe the like Prognostiques from other men, of whom they have once conceived a good opinion.

And in these foure things, Opinion of Ghosts, Ignorance of second causes, Devotion towards what men fear, and Taking of things Casuall for Prognostiques, consisteth the Naturall seed of *Religion*; which by reason of the different Fancies, Judgements, and Passions of severall men, hath grown up into ceremonies so different, that those which are used by one man, are for the most part ridiculous to another. *Foure things, Naturall seeds of Religion.*

For these seeds have received culture from two sorts of men. One sort have been they, that have nourished, and ordered them, according to their own invention. The other, have done it, by Gods commandement, and direction: but both sorts have done it, with a purpose to make those men that relyed on them, the more apt to Obedience, Lawes, Peace, Charity, and civill Society. So that the Religion of the former sort, is a part of humane Politiques; and teacheth part of the duty which Earthly Kings require of their Subjects. And the Religion of the later sort is Divine Politiques; and containeth Precepts to those that have yeelded themselves subjects in the Kingdome of God. Of the former sort, were all the founders of Common-wealths, and the Law-givers of the Gentiles: Of the later sort, were *Abraham*, *Moses*, and our *Blessed Saviour*; by whom have been derived unto us the Lawes of the Kingdome of God. *Made different by Culture.*

And for that part of Religion, which consisteth in opinions concerning the nature of Powers Invisible, there is almost nothing that has a name, that has not been esteemed amongst the Gentiles, in one place or another, a God, or Divell; or by their Poets feigned to be inanimated, inhabited, or possessed by some Spirit or other. *The absurd opinion of Gentilisme.*

[55]

The unformed matter of the World, was a God, by the name of *Chaos*.

The Heaven, the Ocean, the Planets, the Fire, the Earth, the Winds, were so many Gods.

Men, Women, a Bird, a Crocodile, a Calf, a Dogge, a Snake, an Onion, a Leeke, Deified. Besides, that they filled almost all places, with spirits called *Daemons*: the plains, with *Pan*, and *Panises*, or Satyres; the Woods, with Fawnes, and Nymphs; the Sea, with Tritons, and other Nymphs; every River, and Fountayn, with a Ghost of his name, and with Nymphs; every house, with its *Lares*, or Familiars; every man, with his *Genius*; Hell, with Ghosts, and spirituall Officers, as *Charon*, *Cerberus*, and the *Furies*; and in the night time, all places with *Larvae, Lemures*, Ghosts of men deceased, and a whole kingdome of Fayries, and Bugbears. They have also ascribed Divinity, and built Temples to meer Accidents, and Qualities; such as are Time, Night, Day, Peace, Concord, Love, Contention, Vertue, Honour, Health, Rust, Fever, and the like; which when they prayed for, or against, they prayed to, as if there were Ghosts of those names hanging over their heads, and letting fall, or withholding that Good, or Evill, for, or against which they prayed. They invoked also their own Wit, by the name of *Muses*; their own Ignorance, by the name of *Fortune*; their own Lust, by the name of *Cupid*; their own Rage, by the name *Furies*; their own privy members by the name of *Priapus*; and attributed their pollutions, to *Incubi*, and *Succubae*: insomuch as there was nothing, which a Poet could introduce as a person in his Poem, which they did not make either a *God*, or a *Divel*.

The same authors of the Religion of the Gentiles, observing the second ground for Religion, which is mens Ignorance of causes; and thereby their aptnesse to attribute their fortune to causes, on which there was no dependance at all apparent, took occasion to obtrude on their ignorance, in stead of second causes, a kind of second and ministeriall Gods; ascribing the cause of Foecundity, to *Venus*; the cause of Arts, to *Apollo*; of Subtilty and Craft, to *Mercury*; of Tempests and stormes, to *Aelous*; and of other effects, to other Gods: insomuch as there was amongst the Heathen almost as great variety of Gods, as of businesse.

And to the Worship, which naturally men conceived fit to bee used towards their Gods, namely Oblations, Prayers, Thanks, and the rest formerly named; the same Legislators of the Gentiles have added their Images, both in Picture, and Sculpture; that the more ignorant sort, (that is to say, the most part, or generality of the people,) thinking the Gods for whose representation they were made, were really included, and as it were housed within them, might so much the more stand in feare of them: And endowed them with lands, and houses, and officers, and revenues, set apart from all other humane uses; that is, consecrated, and made holy to those their Idols; as Caverns, Groves, Woods, Mountains, and whole Ilands; and have attributed to them, not onely the shapes, some of Men, some of Beasts, some of Monsters; but also the Faculties, and Passions of men and beasts; as Sense, Speech, Sex, Lust, Generation, (and this not onely by mixing one with another, to propagate the kind of Gods; but also by mixing

[56]

with men, and women, to beget mongrill Gods, and but inmates of Heaven, as *Bacchus, Hercules*, and others;) besides, Anger, Revenge, and other passions of living creatures, and the actions proceeding from them, as Fraud, Theft, Adultery, Sodomie, and any vice that may be taken for an effect of Power, or a cause of Pleasure; and all such Vices, as amongst men are taken to be against Law, rather than against Honour.

Lastly, to the Prognostiques of time to come; which are naturally, but Conjectures upon the Experience of time past; and supernaturally, divine Revelation; the same authors of the Religion of the Gentiles, partly upon pretended Experience, partly upon pretended Revelation, have added innumerable other superstitious wayes of Divination; and made men believe they should find their fortunes, sometimes in the ambiguous or senslesse answers of the Priests at *Delphi, Delos, Ammon*, and other famous Oracles; which answers, were made ambiguous by designe, to own the event both wayes; or absurd, by the intoxicating vapour of the place, which is very frequent in sulphurous Cavernes: Sometimes in the leaves of the Sibills; of whose Prophecyes (like those perhaps of *Nostradamus*; for the fragments now extant seem to be the invention of later times) there were some books in reputation in the time of the Roman Republique: Sometimes in the insignificant Speeches of Mad-men, supposed to be possessed with a divine Spirit; which Possession they called Enthusiasme; and these kinds of foretelling events, were accounted Theomancy, or Prophecy: Sometimes in the aspect of the Starres at their Nativity; which was called Horoscopy, and esteemed a part of judiciary Astrology: Sometimes in their own hopes and feares, called Thumomancy, or Presage: Sometimes in the Prediction of Witches, that pretended conference with the dead; which is called Necromancy, Conjuring, and Witchcraft; and is but juggling and confederate knavery: Sometimes in the Casuall flight, or feeding of birds; called Augury: Sometimes in the Entrayles of a sacrificed beast; which was *Aruspicina*: Sometimes in Dreams: Sometimes in Croaking of Ravens, or chattering of Birds: Sometimes in the Lineaments of the face; which was called Metoposcopy; or by Palmistry in the lines of the hand; *Sometimes in*[1] casuall words, called *Omina*: Sometimes in Monsters, or unusuall accidents; as Ecclipses, Comets,

---

[1] *Syn.*: in

rare Meteors, Earthquakes, Inundations, uncouth Births, and the like, which they called *Portenta*, and *Ostenta*, because they thought them to portend, or foreshew some great Calamity to come: Somtimes, in meer Lottery, as Crosse and Pile; counting holes in a sive; dipping of Verses in *Homer*, and *Virgil*; and innumerable other such vaine conceipts. So easie are men to be drawn to believe any thing, from such men as have gotten credit with them; and can with gentlenesse, and dexterity, take hold of their fear, and ignorance.

[57]
*The designes
of the
Authors of
the Religion
of the
Heathen.*

And therefore the first Founders, and Legislators of Commonwealths amongst the Gentiles, whose ends were only to keep the people in obedience, and peace, have in all places taken care; First, to imprint in their minds a beliefe, that those precepts which they gave concerning Religion, might not be thought to proceed from their own device, but from the dictates of some God, or other Spirit; or else that they themselves were of a higher nature than mere mortalls, that their Lawes might the more easily be received: So *Numa Pompilius* pretended to receive the Ceremonies he instituted amongst the Romans, from the Nymph *Egeria*: and the first King and founder of the Kingdome of *Peru*, pretended himselfe and his wife to be the children of the Sunne: and *Mahomet*, to set up his new Religion, pretended to have conferences with the Holy Ghost, in forme of a Dove. Secondly, they have had a care, to make it believed, that the same things were displeasing to the Gods, which were forbidden by the Lawes. Thirdly, to prescribe Ceremonies, Supplications, Sacrifices, and Festivalls, by which they were to believe, the anger of the Gods might be appeased; and that ill success in War, great contagions of Sicknesse, Earthquakes, and each mans private Misery, came from the Anger of the Gods; and their Anger from the Neglect of their Worship, or the forgetting, or mistaking some point of the Ceremonies required. And though amongst the antient Romans, men were not forbidden to deny, that which in the Poets is written of the paines, and pleasures after this life; *and which*[1] divers of great authority, and gravity in that state, have in their *Harangues* openly derided; yet that beliefe was alwaies more cherished, than the contrary.

And by these, and such other Institutions, they obtayned in order to their end, (which was the peace of the Commonwealth,) that the

---

[1] *Syn.:* which

common people in their misfortunes, laying the fault on neglect, or errour in their Ceremonies, or on their own disobedience to the lawes, were the lesse apt to mutiny against their Governors. And being entertained with the pomp, and pastime of Festivalls, and publike Games, made in honour of the Gods, needed nothing else but bread, to keep them from discontent, murmuring, and commotion against the State. And therefore the Romans, that had conquered the greatest part of the then known World, made no scruple of tollerating any Religion whatsoever in the City of *Rome* it selfe; unlesse it had somthing in it, that could not consist with their Civill Government; nor do we read, that any Religion was there forbidden, but that of the Jewes; who (being the peculiar Kingdome of God) thought it unlawfull to acknowledge subjection to any mortall King or State whatsoever. And thus you see how the Religion of the Gentiles was a part of their Policy.

But where God himselfe, by supernaturall Revelation, planted Religion; there he also made to himselfe a peculiar Kingdome; and gave Lawes, not only of behaviour towards himselfe; but also towards one another; and thereby in the Kingdome of God, the Policy, and lawes Civill, are a part of Religion; and *the*[1] distinction of Temporall, and Spirituall Domination, hath there no place. It is true, that God is King of all the Earth: Yet may he be King of a peculiar, and chosen Nation. For there is no more incongruity therein, than that he that hath the generall command of the whole Army, should have withall a peculiar Regiment, or Company of his own. God is King of all the Earth by his Power: but of his chosen people, he is King by Covenant. But to speake more largly of the Kingdome of God, both by Nature, and Covenant, I have in the following discourse assigned an other place.

The true Religion, and the lawes of Gods kingdome the same.

[58]

From the propagation of Religion, it is not hard to understand the causes of the resolution of the same into its first seeds, or principles; which are only an opinion of a Deity, and *of Powers*[2] invisible, and supernaturall; that can never be so abolished out of humane nature, but that new Religions may againe be made to spring out of them, by the culture of such men, as for such purpose are in reputation.

Chap. 35. The causes of Change in Religion.

For seeing all formed Religion, is founded at first, upon the faith which a multitude hath in some one person, whom they believe not

---

[1] *Syn.*: therefore the   [2] *Syn.*: Powers

only to be a wise man, and to labour to procure their happiness, but also to be a holy man, to whom God himselfe vouchsafeth to declare his will supernaturally; It followeth necessarily, when they that have the Government of Religion, shall come to have either the wisedome of those men, their sincerity, or their love suspected; or that they shall be unable to shew any probable token of Divine Revelation; that the Religion which they desire to uphold, must be suspected likewise; and (without the feare of the Civill Sword) contradicted and rejected.

Injoyning beleefe of Impossibilities.

That which taketh away the reputation of Wisedome, in him that formeth a Religion, or addeth to it when it is allready formed, is the enjoyning of a beliefe of contradictories: For both parts of a contradiction cannot possibly be true: and therefore to enjoyne the beliefe of them, is an argument of ignorance; which detects the Author in that; and discredits him in all things else he shall propound as from relevation supernaturall: which revelation a man may indeed have of many things above, but of nothing against naturall reason.

Doing contrary to the Religion they establish.

That which taketh away the reputation of Sincerity, is the doing, or saying of such things, as appeare to be signes, that what they require other men to believe, is not believed by themselves; all which doings, or sayings are therefore called Scandalous, because they be stumbling blocks, that make men to fall in the way of Religion: as Injustice, Cruelty, Prophanesse, Avarice, and Luxury. For who can believe, that he that doth ordinarily such actions, as proceed from any of these rootes, believeth there is any such Invisible Power to be feared, as he affrighteth other men withall, for lesser faults?

That which taketh away the reputation of Love, is the being detected of private ends: as when the beliefe they require of others, conduceth or seemeth to conduce to the acquiring of Dominion, Riches, Dignity, or secure Pleasure, to themselves onely, or specially. For that which men reap benefit by to themselves, they are thought to do for their own sakes, and not for love of others.

[59]

Want of the testimony of Miracles.

Lastly, the testimony that men can render of divine Calling, can be no other, than the operation of Miracles; or true Prophecy, (which also is a Miracle;) or extraordinary Felicity. And therefore, to those points of Religion, which have been received from them that did such Miracles; those that are added by such, as approve not their Calling by some Miracle, obtain no greater beliefe, than what the Custome, and Lawes of the places, in which they be educated, have wrought into them. For as in nautrall things, men of judgement require naturall signes, and arguments; so in supernaturall things, they require signes supernaturall, (which are Miracles,) before they consent inwardly, and from their hearts.

All which causes of the weakening of mens faith, do manifestly appear in the Examples following. First, we have the Example of the children of Israel; who when *Moses*, that had approved his Calling to them by Miracles, and by the happy conduct of them out of *Egypt*, was absent but but 40. dayes, revolted from the worship of the true God, recommended to them by him; and setting up ⋆ a Golden Calfe for ⋆ *Exod. 32.* their God, relapsed into the Idolatry of the Egyptians; from whom *1,2.* they had been so lately delivered. And again, after *Moses*, *Aaron*, *Joshua*, and that generation which had seen the great works of God in Israel, ⋆ were dead; another generation arose, and served *Baal*. So ⋆ *Judges* that Miracles fayling, Faith also failed. *2.11.*

Again, when the sons of *Samuel*, ⋆ being constituted by their father ⋆ *1 Sam.* Judges in *Bersabee*, received bribes, and judged unjustly, the people of *8.3.* Israel refused any more to have God to be their King, in other manner than he was King of other people; and therefore cryed out to *Samuel*, to choose them a King after the manner of the Nations. So that Justice fayling, Faith also fayled: Insomuch, as they deposed their God, from reigning over them.

And whereas in the planting of Christian Religion, the Oracles ceased in all parts of the Roman Empire, and the number of Christians encreased wonderfully every day, and in every place, by the preaching of the Apostles, and Evangelists; a great part of that successe, may reasonably be attributed, to the contempt, into which the Priests of the Gentiles of that time, had brought themselves, by their uncleannesse, avarice, and jugling between Princes. Also the Religion of the Church of *Rome*, was partly, for the same cause abolished in *England*, and many other parts of Christendome; insomuch, as the fayling of Vertue in the Pastors, maketh Faith faile in the People: and partly from bringing of the Philosophy, and doctrine of *Aristotle* into Religion, by the Schoole-men; from whence there arose so many contradictions, and absurdities, as brought the Clergy into a reputation both of Ignorance, and of Fraudulent intention; and enclined people to revolt from them, either against the will of their own Princes, as in *France*, and *Holland*; or with their will, as in *England*.

Lastly, amongst the points by the Church of *Rome* declared necess- [60] ary for Salvation, there be so many, manifestly to the advantage of the

Pope, and of his spirituall subjects, residing in the territories of other Christian Princes, that were it not for the mutuall emulation of those Princes, they might without warre, or trouble, exclude all foraign Authority, as easily as it has been excluded in *England.* For who is there that does not see, to whose benefit it conduceth, to have it believed, that a King hath not his Authority from Christ, unlesse a Bishop crown him? That a King, if he be a Priest, cannot Marry? That whether a Prince be born in lawfull Marriage, or not, must be judged by Authority from *Rome*? That Subjects may be freed from their Alleageance, if by the Court of *Rome*, the King be judged an Heretique? That a King (as *Chilperique* of *France*) may be deposed by a Pope (as Pope *Zachary,*) for no cause; and his Kingdome given to one of his Subjects? That the Clergy, and Regulars, in what Country soever, shall be exempt from the Jurisdiction of their King, in cases criminall? Or who does not see, to whose profit redound the Fees of private Masses, and *the veyles*[1] of Purgatory; with other signes of private interest, enough to mortifie the most lively Faith, if (as I sayd) the civill Magistrate, and Custome did not more sustain it, than any opinion they have of the Sanctity, Wisdome, or Probity of their Teachers? So that I may attribute all the changes of Religion in the world, to one and the same cause; and that is, unpleasing Priests; and those not onely amongst Catholiques, but even in that Church that hath presumed most of Reformation.[2]

CHAP. XIII.

Of the NATURALL CONDITION *of Mankind, as concerning their Felicity, and Misery.*

Men by nature Equall.

Nature hath made men so equall, in the faculties of body, and mind; as that though there bee found one man sometimes manifestly

[1] *Syn.*: Vales
[2] Scribal MS reads: On whom men by common frailty are carried to execute their anger. They beare downe not onely Religion wch they reduce to Private fancy but also the Civil government that would uphold it reducing it to the naturall Condition of Private force.

stronger in body, or of quicker mind then another; yet when all is reckoned together, the difference between man, and man, is not so considerable, as that one man can thereupon claim to himselfe any benefit, to which another may not pretend, as well as he. For as to the strength of body, the weakest has strength enough to kill the strongest, either by secret machination, or by confederacy with others, that are in the same danger with himselfe.

And as to the faculties of the mind, (setting aside the arts grounded upon words, and especially that skill of proceeding upon generall, and infallible rules, called Science; which very few have, and but in few things; as being not a native faculty, born with us; nor attained, (as Prudence,) while we look after somewhat els,) I find yet a greater equality amongst men, than that of strength. For Prudence, is but Experience; which equall time, equally bestowes on all men, in those [61] things they equally apply themselves unto. That which may perhaps make such equality incredible, is but a vain conceipt of ones owne wisdome, which almost all men think they have in a greater degree, than the Vulgar; that is, than all men but themselves, and a few others, whom by Fame, or for concurring with themselves, they approve. For such is the nature of men, that howsoever they may acknowledge many others to be more witty, or more eloquent, or more learned; Yet they will hardly believe there be many so wise as themselves: For they see their own wit at hand, and other mens at a distance. But this proveth rather that men are in that point equall, than unequall. For there is not ordinarily a greater signe of the equall distribution of any thing, than that every man is contented with his share.

From this equality of ability, ariseth equality of hope in the attaining of our Ends. And therefore if any two men desire the same thing, *From Equality proceeds Diffidence.* which neverthelesse they cannot both enjoy, they become enemies; and in the way to their End, (which is principally their owne conservation, and sometimes their delectation only,) endeavour to destroy, or subdue one an other. And from hence it comes to passe, that where an Invader hath no more to feare, than an other mans single power; if one plant, sow, build, or possesse a convenient Seat, others may probably be expected to come prepared with forces united, to dispossesse, and deprive him, not only of the fruit of his labour, but also of his life, or liberty. And the Invader again is in the like danger of another.

And from this diffidence of one another, there is no way for any *From Diffidence Warre.* man to secure himselfe, so reasonable, as Anticipation; that is, by force, or wiles, to master the persons of all men he can, so long, till he see no other power great enough to endanger him: And this is no more than his own conservation requireth, and is generally allowed. Also because there be some, that taking pleasure in contemplating their own power in the acts of conquest, which they pursue farther than their security requires; if others, that otherwise would be glad to be at ease within modest bounds, should not by invasion increase their power, they would not be able, long time, by standing only on their defence, to subsist. And by consequence, such augmentation of dominion over men, being necessary to a mans conservation, it ought to be allowed him.

Againe, men have no pleasure, (but on the contrary a great deale of griefe) in keeping company, where there is no power able to over-awe them all. For every man looketh that his companion should value him, at the same rate he sets upon himselfe: And upon all signes of contempt, or undervaluing, naturally endeavours, as far as he dares (which amongst them that have no common power to keep them in quiet, is far enough to make them destroy each other,) to extort a greater value from his contemners, by dommage; and from others, by the example.

So that in the nature of man, we find three principall causes of quarrell. First, Competition; Secondly, Diffidence; Thirdly, Glory.

[62]

The first, maketh men invade for Gain; the second, for Safety; and the third, for Reputation. The first use Violence, to make themselves Masters of other mens persons, wives, children, and cattell; the second, to defend them; the third, for trifles, as a word, a smile, a different opinion, and any other signe of undervalue, either direct in their Persons, or by reflexion in their Kindred, their Friends, their Nation, their Profession, or their Name.

Out of Civil States, there is alwayes Warre of every one against every one.

Hereby it is manifest, that during the time men live without a common Power to keep them all in awe, they are in that condition which is called Warre; and such a warre, as is of every man, against every man. For WARRE, consisteth not in Battell onely, or the act of fighting; but in a tract of time, wherein the Will to contend by Battell is sufficiently known: and therefore the notion of *Time*, is to be considered in the nature of Warre; as it is in the nature of Weather. For as the nature of Foule weather, lyeth not in a showre or two of rain; but in an inclination thereto of many dayes together: So the nature of War, consisteth not in actuall fighting; but in the known

88

disposition thereto, during all the time there is no assurance to the contrary. All other time is PEACE.

Whatsoever therefore is consequent to a time of Warre, where every man is Enemy to every man; the same is consequent to the time, wherein men live without other security, than what their own strength, and their own invention shall furnish them withall. In such condition, there is no place for Industry; because the fruit thereof is uncertain: and consequently no Culture of the Earth; no Navigation, nor use of the commodities that may be imported by Sea; no commodious Building; no Instruments of moving, and removing such things as require much force; no Knowledge of the face of the Earth; no account of Time; no Arts; no Letters; no Society; and which is worst of all, continuall feare, and danger of violent death; And the life of man, solitary, poore, nasty, brutish, and short. *The Incommodities of such a War.*

It may seem strange to some man, that has not well weighed these things; that Nature should thus dissociate, and render men apt to invade, and destroy one another: and he may therefore, not trusting to this Inference, made from the Passions, desire perhaps to have the same confirmed by Experience. Let him therefore consider with himselfe, when taking a journey, he armes himselfe, and seeks to go well accompanied; when going to sleep, he locks his dores; when even in his house he locks his chests; and this when he knowes there bee Lawes, and publike Officers, armed, to revenge all injuries shall bee done him; what opinion he has of his fellow subjects, when he rides armed; of his fellow Citizens, when he locks his dores; and of his children, and servants, when he locks his chests. Does he not there as much accuse mankind by his actions, as I do by my words? But neither of us accuse mans nature in it. The Desires, and other Passions of man, are in themselves no Sin. No more are the Actions, that proceed from those Passions, till they know a Law that forbids them: which till Lawes be made they cannot know: nor can any Law be made, till they have agreed upon the Person that shall make it.

It may peradventure be thought, there was never such a time, nor condition of warre as this; and I believe it was never generally so, over all the world: but there are many places, where they live so now. For the savage people in many places of *America*, except the government of small Families, the concord whereof dependeth on naturall lust, have no government at all; and live at this day in that brutish manner, as I said before. Howsoever, it may be perceived what manner of life [63] there would be, where there were no common Power to feare; by the manner of life, which men that have formerly lived under a peacefull government, use to degenerate into, in a civill Warre.

But though there had never been any time, wherein particular men were in a condition of warre one against another; yet in all times, Kings, and Persons of Soveraigne authority, because of their Independency, are in continuall jealousies, and in the state and posture of Gladiators; having their weapons pointing, and their eyes fixed on one another; that is, their Forts, Garrisons, and Guns upon the Frontiers of their Kingdomes; and continuall Spyes upon their neighbours, which is a posture of War. But because they uphold thereby, the Industry of their Subjects; there does not follow from it, that misery, which accompanies the Liberty of particular men.

In such a Warre, nothing is Unjust. To this warre of every man against every man, this also is consequent; that nothing can be Unjust. The notions of Right and Wrong, Justice and Injustice have there no place. Where there is no common Power, there is no Law: where no Law, no Injustice. Force, and Fraud, are in warre the two Cardinall vertues. Justice, and Injustice are none of the Faculties neither of the Body, nor Mind. If they were, they might be in a man that were alone in the world, as well as his Senses, and Passions. They are Qualities, that relate to men in Society, not in Solitude. It is consequent also to the same condition, that there be no Propriety, no Dominion, no *Mine* and *Thine* distinct; but onely that to be every mans, that he can get; and for so long, as he can keep it. And thus much for the ill condition, which man by meer Nature is actually placed in; though with a possibility to come out of it, consisting partly in the Passions, partly in his Reason.

The Passions that incline men to Peace. The Passions that encline men to Peace, are Feare of Death; Desire of such things as are necessary to commodious living; and a Hope by their Industry to obtain them. And Reason suggesteth convenient Articles of Peace, upon which men may be drawn to agreement. These Articles, are they, which otherwise are called the Lawes of Nature: whereof I shall speak more particularly, in the two following Chapters.

CHAP. XIV.   [64]

Of the first and second NATURALL LAWES, *and of* CONTRACTS.

The RIGHT OF NATURE, which Writers commonly call *Jus Naturale*, is the Liberty each man hath, to use his own power, as he will himselfe, for the preservation of his own Nature; that is to say, of his own Life; and consequently, of doing any thing, which in his own Judgement, and Reason, hee shall conceive to be the aptest means thereunto.

Right of Nature what.

By LIBERTY, is understood, according to the proper signification of the word, the absence of externall Impediments: which Impediments, may oft take away part of a mans power to do what hee would; but cannot hinder him from using the power left him, according as his judgement, and reason shall dictate to him.

Liberty what.

A LAW OF NATURE, (*Lex Naturalis*,) is a Precept, or generall Rule, found out by Reason, by which a man is forbidden to do, that, which is destructive of his life, or taketh away the means of preserving the same; and to omit, that, by which he thinketh it may be best preserved. For though they that speak of this subject, use to confound *Jus*, and *Lex*, *Right* and *Law*; yet they ought to be distinguished; because RIGHT, consisteth in liberty to do, or to forbeare; Whereas LAW, determineth, and bindeth to one of them: so that Law, and Right, differ as much, as Obligation, and Liberty; which in one and the same matter are inconsistent.

A Law of Nature what.

Difference of Right and Law.

And because the condition of Man, (as hath been declared in the precedent Chapter) is a condition of Warre of every one against every one; in which case every one is governed by his own Reason; and there is nothing he can make use of, that may not be a help unto him, in preserving his life against his enemyes; It followeth, that in such a condition, every man has a Right to every thing; even to one anothers body. And therefore, as long as this naturall Right of every man to every thing endureth, there can be no security to any man, (how strong or wise soever he be,) of living out the time, which Nature ordinarily alloweth men to live. And consequently it is a precept, or

Naturally every man has Right to every thing.

The Funda-
mentall Law
of *Nature.
To seek
peace*[1]

generall rule of Reason, *That every man, ought to endeavour Peace, as farre as he has hope of obtaining it; and when he cannot obtain it, that he may seek, and use, all helps, and advantages of Warre.* The first branch of which Rule, containeth the first, and Fundamentall Law of Nature; which is, *to seek Peace, and follow it.* The Second, the summe of the Right of Nature; which is, *By all means we can, to defend our selves.*

The second
Law of
*Nature.
Contract in
way of
peace*[2]

[65]

From this Fundamentall Law of Nature, by which men are commanded to endeavour Peace, is derived this second Law; *That a man be willing, when others are so too, as farre-forth, as for Peace, and defence of himselfe he shall think it necessary, to lay down this right to all things; and be contented with so much liberty against other men, as he would allow other men against himselfe.* For as long as every man holdeth this Right, of doing any thing he liketh; so long are all men in the condition of Warre. But if other men will not lay down their Right, as well as he; then there is no Reason for any one, to devest himselfe of his: For that were to expose himselfe to Prey, (which no man is bound to) rather than to dispose himselfe to Peace. This is that Law of the Gospell; *Whatsoever you require that others should do to you, that do ye to them.* And that Law of all men, *Quod tibi fieri non vis, alteri ne feceris.*

What it is to
lay down a
Right.

To *lay downe* a mans *Right* to any thing, is to *devest* himselfe of the *Liberty*, of hindring another of the benefit of his own Right to the same. For he that renounceth, or passeth away his Right, giveth not to any other man a Right which he had not before; because there is nothing to which every man had not Right by Nature: but onely standeth out of his way, that he may enjoy his own originall Right, without hindrance from him; not without hindrance from another. So that the effect which redoundeth to one man, by another mans defect of Right, is but so much diminution of impediments to the use of his own Right originall.

Renouncing a
Right what it
is.
Transferring
Right what.

Obligation.

Right is layd aside, either by simply Renouncing it; or by Transferring it to another. By *Simply* RENOUNCING; when he cares not to whom the benefit thereof redoundeth. By TRANSFERRING; when he intendeth the benefit thereof to some certain person, or persons. And when a man hath in either manner abandoned, or granted away his Right; then is he said to be OBLIGED, or BOUND, not to hinder those, to whom such Right is granted, or abandoned, from the benefit

---

[1] *Syn.*: Nature.   [2] *Syn.*: Nature.

of it: and that he *Ought*, and it is his DUTY, not to make voyd that   *Duty.*
voluntary act of his own: and that such hindrance is INJUSTICE, and   *Injustice.*
INJURY, as being *Sine Jure*; the Right being before renounced, or
transferred. So that *Injury*, or *Injustice*, in the controversies of the
world, is somewhat like to that, which in the disputations of Scholers
is called *Absurdity*. For as it is there called an Absurdity, to contradict
what one maintained in the Beginning: so in the world, it is called
Injustice, and Injury, voluntarily to undo that, which from the beginning he had voluntarily done. The way by which a man either simply
Renounceth, or Transferreth his Right, is a Declaration, or Signification, by some voluntary and sufficient signe, or signes, that he doth so
Renounce, or Transferre; or hath so Renounced, or Transferred the
same, to him that accepteth it. And these Signes are either Words
onely, or Actions onely; or (as it happeneth most often) both Words,
and Actions. And the same are the BONDS, by which men are bound,
and obliged: Bonds, that have their strength, not from their own
Nature, (for nothing is more easily broken than a mans word,) but
from Feare of some evill consequence upon the rupture.

Whensoever a man Transferreth his Right, or Renounceth it; it is
either in consideration of some Right reciprocally transferred to him-   [66]
selfe; or for some other good he hopeth for thereby. For it is a
voluntary act: and of the voluntary acts of every man, the object is
some *Good to himselfe*. And therefore there be some Rights, which no   *Not all*
man can be understood by any words, or other signes, to have   *Rights are*
abandoned, or transferred. As first a man cannot lay down the right of   *alienable.*
resisting them, that assault him by force, to take away his life; because
he cannot be understood to ayme thereby, at any Good to himself.
The same may be sayd of Wounds, and Chayns, and Imprisonment;
both because there is no benefit consequent to such patience; as there
is to the patience of suffering another to be wounded, or imprisoned:
as also because a man cannot tell, when he seeth men proceed against
him by violence, whether they intend his death or not. And lastly the
motive, and end for which this renouncing and transferring of Right is
introduced, is nothing else but the security of a mans person, in his
life, and in the means of so preserving life, as not to be weary of it.
And therefore if a man by words, or other signes, seem to despoyle
himselfe of the End, for which those signes were intended; he is not
to be understood as if he meant it, or that it was his will; but that he

was ignorant of how such words and actions were to be interpreted.

The mutuall transferring of Right, is that which men call CONTRACT.

There is difference, between transferring of Right to the Thing; and transferring, or tradition, that is, delivery of the Thing it selfe. For the Thing may be delivered together with the Translation of the Right; as in buying and selling with ready mony; or exchange of goods, or lands: and it may be delivered some time after.

Again, one of the Contractors, may deliver the Thing contracted for on his part, and leave the other to perform his part at some determinate time after, and in the mean time be trusted; and then the Contract on his part, is called PACT, or COVENANT: Or both parts may contract now, to performe hereafter: in which cases, he that is to performe in time to come, being trusted, his performance is called *Keeping of Promise*, or Faith; and the fayling of performance (if it be voluntary) *Violation of Faith*.

When the transferring of Right, is not mutuall; but one of the parties transferreth, in hope to gain thereby friendship, or service from another, or from his friends; or in hope to gain the reputation of Charity, or Magnanimity; or to deliver his mind from the pain of compassion; or in hope of reward in heaven; This is not Contract, but GIFT, FREE-GIFT, GRACE: which words signifie one and the same thing.

Signes of Contract, are either *Expresse*, or *by Inference*. Expresse, are words spoken with understanding of what they signifie: And such words are either of the time *Present*, or *Past*; as, *I Give, I Grant, I have Given, I have Granted, I will that this be yours*: Or of the future; as, *I will Give, I will Grant*: which words of the future are called PROMISE.

Signes by Inference, are sometimes the consequence of Words; sometimes the consequence of Silence; sometimes the consequence of Actions; somtimes the consequence of Forbearing an Action: and generally a signe by Inference, of any Contract, is whatsoever sufficiently argues the will of the Contractor.

Words alone, if they be of the time to come, and contain a bare promise, are an insufficient signe of a Free-gift and therefore not obligatory. For if they be of the time to Come, as, *To morrow I will Give*, they are a signe I have not given yet, and consequently that my right is not transferred, but remaineth till I transferre it by some other Act. But if the words be of the time Present, or Past, as, *I have given, or do give to be delivered to morrow*, then is my to morrows Right given away to day; and that by the vertue of the words, though there were no other argument of my will. And there is a great difference in the signification of these words, *Volo hoc tuum esse cras*, and *Cras dabo*; that is, between *I will that this be thine to morrow*, and, *I will give it thee to morrow*: For the word *I will*, in the former manner of speech, signifies an act of the will Present; but in the later, it signifies a promise of an act of the will to Come: and therefore the former words, being of the Present, transferre a future right; the later, that be of the Future, transferre nothing. But if there be other signes of the Will to transferre a Right, besides Words; then, though the gift be Free, yet may the Right be understood to passe by words of the future: as if a man propound a Prize to him that comes first to the end of a race, The gift is Free; and though the words be of the Future, yet the Right passeth: for if he would not have his words *so*[1] understood, he should not have let them runne.

In Contracts, the right passeth, not onely where the words are of the time Present, or Past; but also where they are of the Future: because all Contract is mutuall translation, or change of Right; and therefore he that promiseth onely, because he hath already received the benefit for which he promiseth, is to be understood as if he intended the Right should passe: for unlesse he had been content to have his words so understood, the other would not have performed his part first. And for that cause, in buying, and selling, and other acts of Contract, a Promise is equivalent to a Covenant; and therefore obligatory. *Signes of Contract are words both of the Past, Present, and Future.*

He that performeth first in the case of a Contract, is said to M E R I T *Merit what.* that which he is to receive by the performance of the other; and he hath it as *Due*. Also when a Prize is propounded to many, which is to be given to him onely that winneth; or mony is thrown amongst many, to be enjoyed by them that catch it; though this be a Free gift; yet so to Win, or so to Catch, is to *Merit*, and to have it as D U E. For the Right is transferred in the Propounding of the Prize, and in throwing down the mony; though it be not determined to whom, but by the Event of the contention. But there is between these two sorts of Merit, this difference, that In Contract, I Merit by vertue of my own power, and the Contractors need; but in this case of Free gift, I am enabled to

---

[1] *Syn.*: so be

Merit onely by the benignity of the Giver: In Contract, I merit at the Contractors hand that hee should depart with his right; In this case of Gift, I Merit not that the giver should part with his right; but that when he has parted with it, it should be mine, rather than anothers. And this I think to be the meaning of that distinction of the Schooles, between *Meritum congrui*, and *Meritum condigni.* For God Almighty, having promised Paradise to those men (hoodwinkt with carnall desires,) that can walk through this world according to the Precepts, and Limits prescribed by him; they say, he that shall so walk, shall Merit Paradise *Ex congruo.* But because no man can demand a right to it, by his own Righteousnesse, or any other power in himselfe, but by the Free Grace of God onely; they say, no man can Merit Paradise *ex condigno.* This I say, I think is the meaning of that distinction; but because Disputers do not agree upon the signification of their own termes of Art, longer than it serves their turn; I will not affirme any thing of their meaning: onely this I say; when a gift is given indefinitely, as a prize to be contended for, he that winneth Meriteth, and may claime the Prize as Due.

Covenants of Mutuall trust, when Invalid. If a Covenant be made, wherein neither of the parties performe presently, but trust one another; in the condition of meer Nature, (which is a condition of Warre of every man against every man,) upon any reasonable suspition, it is Voyd: But if there be a common Power set over them both, with right and force sufficient to compell performance; it is not Voyd. For he that performeth first, has no assurance the other will performe after; because the bonds of words are too weak to bridle mens ambition, avarice, anger, and other Passions, without the feare of some coërcive Power; which in the condition of meer Nature, where all men are equall, and judges of the justnesse of their own fears, cannot possibly be supposed. And therfore he which performeth first, does but betray himselfe to his enemy; contrary to the Right (he can never abandon) of defending his life, and means of living.

But in a civill estate, where there is a Power set up to constrain those that would otherwise violate their faith, that feare is no more reasonable; and for that cause, he which by the Covenant is to perform first, is obliged so to do.

The cause of feare, which maketh such a Covenant invalid, must be alwayes something arising after the Covenant made; as some new fact, or other signe of the Will not to performe: else it cannot make the

Covenant voyd. For that which could not hinder a man from promising, ought not to be admitted as a hindrance of performing.

He that transferreth any Right, transferreth the Means of enjoying it, as farre as lyeth in his power. As he that selleth Land, is understood to transferre the Herbage, and whatsoever growes upon it; Nor can he that sells a Mill turn away the Stream that drives it. And they that give to a man the Right of government in Soveraignty, are understood to give him the right of levying mony to maintain Souldiers; and of appointing Magistrates for the administration of Justice.   *Right to the End, Containeth Right to the Means.*

To make Covenants with bruit Beasts, is impossible; because not understanding our speech, they understand not, nor accept of any translation of Right; nor can translate any Right to another: and without mutuall acceptation, there is no Covenant.   *No Covenant with Beasts.* [69]

To make Covenant with God, is impossible, but by Mediation of such as God speaketh to, either by Revelation supernaturall, or by his Lieutenants that govern under him, and in his Name: For otherwise we know not whether our Covenants be accepted, or not. And therefore they that Vow any thing contrary to any law of Nature, Vow in vain; as being a thing unjust to pay such Vow. And if it be a thing commanded by the Law of Nature, it is not the Vow, but the Law that binds them.   *Nor with God without speciall Revelation.*

The matter, or subject of a Covenant, is always something that falleth under deliberation; (For to Covenant, is an act of the Will; that is to say an act, and the last act, of deliberation;) and is therefore always understood to be something to come; and which is judged Possible for him that Covenanteth, to performe.   *No Covenant, but of Possible and Future.*

And therefore, to promise that which is known to be Impossible, is no Covenant. But if that prove impossible afterwards, which before was thought possible, the Covenant is valid, and bindeth, (though not to the thing it selfe,) yet to the value; or, if that also be impossible, to the unfeigned endeavour of performing as much as is possible: for to more no man can be obliged.

Men are freed of their Covenants two wayes; by Performing; or by being Forgiven. For Performance, is the naturall end of obligation; and Forgivenesse, the restitution of liberty; as being a re-transferring of that Right, in which the obligation consisted.   *Covenants, how made voyd.*

Covenants entred into by fear, in the condition of meer Nature, are obligatory. For example, if I Covenant to pay a ransome, or service for my life, to an enemy; I am bound by it. For it is a Contract, wherein   *Covenants extorted by feare are valide.*

97

one receiveth the benefit of life; the other is to receive mony, or service for it; and consequently, where no other Law (as in the condition, of meer Nature) forbiddeth the performance, the Covenant is valid. Therefore Prisoners of warre, if trusted with the payment of their Ransome, are obliged to pay it: And if a weaker Prince, make a disadvantageous peace with a stronger, for feare; he is bound to keep it; unlesse (as hath been sayd before) there ariseth some new, and just cause of feare, to renew the war. And even in Common-wealths, if I be forced to redeem my selfe from a Theefe by promising him money, I am bound to pay it, till the Civill Law discharge me. For whatsoever I may lawfully do without Obligation, the same I may lawfully Covenant to do through feare: and what I lawfully Covenant, I cannot lawfully break.

The former Covenant to one, makes voyd the later to another.

A former Covenant, makes voyd a later. For a man that hath passed away his Right to one man to day, hath it not to passe to morrow to another: and therefore the later promise passeth no Right, but is null.

A mans Covenant not to defend himselfe, is voyd.

A Covenant not to defend my selfe from force, by force, is always voyd. For (as I have shewed before) no man can transferre, or lay down his Right to save himselfe from Death, Wounds, and Imprisonment, (the avoyding whereof is the onely End of laying down any Right,) and therefore the promise of not resisting force, in no Covenant transferreth any right; nor is obliging. For though a man may Covenant thus, *Unlesse I do so, or so, kill me*; he cannot Covenant thus, *Unlesse I do so, or so, I will not resist you, when you come to kill me.* For man by nature chooseth the lesser evill, which is danger of death in resisting; rather than the greater, which is certain and present death in not resisting. And this is granted to be true by all men, in that they lead Criminals to Execution, and Prison, with armed men, notwithstanding that such Criminals have consented to the Law, by which they are condemned.

[70]

No man obliged to accuse himself.

A Covenant to accuse ones selfe, without assurance of pardon, is likewise invalid. For in the condition of Nature, where every man is Judge, there is no place for Accusation: and in the Civill State, the Accusation is followed with Punishment; which being Force, a man is not obliged not to resist. The same is also true, of the Accusation of those, by whose Condemnation a man falls into misery; as of a Father, Wife, or Benefactor. For the Testimony of such an Accuser, if it be not willingly given, is praesumed to be corrupted by Nature; and therefore not to be received: and where a mans Testimony is not to be credited, he is not bound to give it. Also Accusations upon Torture, are not to be reputed as Testimonies. For Torture is to be used but as means of conjecture, and light, in the further examination, and search of truth: and what is in that case confessed, tendeth to the ease of him that is Tortured; not to the informing of the Torturers: and therefore ought not to have the credit of a sufficient Testimony: for whether he deliver himselfe by true, or false Accusation, he does it by the Right of preserving his own life.

The force of Words, being (as I have formerly noted) too weak to *The End of* hold men to the performance of their Covenants; there are in mans *an Oath.* nature, but two imaginable helps to strengthen it. And those are either a Feare of the consequence of breaking their word; or a Glory, or Pride in appearing not to need to breake it. This later is a Generosity too rarely found to be presumed on, especially in the pursuers of Wealth, Command, or sensuall Pleasure; which are the greatest part of Mankind. The Passion to be reckoned upon, is Fear; whereof there be two very generall Objects: one, The Power of Spirits Invisible; the other, The Power of those men they shall therein Offend. Of these two, though the former be the greater Power, yet the feare of the later is commonly the greater Feare. The Feare of the former is in every man, his own Religion: which hath place in the nature of man before Civill Society. The later hath not so; at least not place enough, to keep men to their promises; because in the condition of meer Nature, the inequality of Power is not discerned, but by the event of Battell. So that before the time of Civill Society, or in the interruption thereof by Warre, there is nothing can strengthen a Covenant of Peace agreed on, against the temptations of Avarice, Ambition, Lust, or other strong desire, but the feare of that Invisible Power, which they every one Worship as God; and Feare as a Revenger of their perfidy. All [71] therefore that can be done between two men not subject to Civill Power, is to put one another to swear by the God he feareth: Which *Swearing*, or O A T H, is a *Forme of Speech, added to a Promise; by which he* *The forme of* *that promiseth, signifieth, that unless he performe, he renounceth the mercy* *an Oath.* *of his God, or calleth to him for vengeance on himselfe.* Such was the Heathen Forme, *Let* Jupiter *kill me else, as I kill this Beast.* So is our Forme, *I shall do thus, and thus, so help me God.* And this, with the Rites and Ceremonies, which every one useth in his own Religion, that the feare of breaking faith might be the greater. *No Oath, but*

By this it appears, that an Oath taken according to any other *by God.*

99

Forme, or Rite, then his, that sweareth, is in vain; and no Oath: And that there is no Swearing by any thing which the Swearer thinks not God. For though men have sometimes used to swear by their Kings, for feare, or flattery; yet they would have it thereby understood, they attributed to them Divine honour. And that Swearing unnecessarily by God, is but prophaning of his name: and Swearing by other things, as men do in common discourse, is not Swearing, but an impious Custome, gotten by two much vehemence of talking.

An Oath addes nothing to the Obligation.

It appears also, that the Oath addes nothing to the Obligation. For a Covenant, if lawfull, binds in the sight of God, without the Oath, as much as with it: if unlawfull, bindeth not at all; though it be confirmed with an Oath.

CHAP. XV.
Of other Lawes of Nature.

The third Law of Nature, Justice.

From that law of Nature, by which we are obliged to transferre to another, such Rights, as being retained, hinder the peace of Mankind, there followeth a Third; which is this, *That men performe their Covenants made*: without which, Covenants are in vain, and but Empty words; and the Right of all men to all things remaining, wee are still in the condition of Warre.

Justice and Injustice what.

And in this law of Nature, consisteth the Fountain and Originall of JUSTICE. For where no Covenant hath preceded, there hath no Right been transferred, and every man has right to every thing; and consequently, no action can be Unjust. But when a Covenant is made, then to break it is *Unjust*: And the definition of INJUSTICE, is no other than *the not Performance of Covenant*. And whatsoever is not Unjust, is *Just*.

Justice and Propriety begin with the Constitution of Common-wealth.

But because Covenants of mutuall trust, where there is a feare of not performance on either part, (as hath been said in the former Chapter,) are invalid; though the Originall of Justice be the making of Covenants; yet Injustice actually there can be none, till the cause of such feare be taken away; which while men are in the naturall condition of Warre, cannot be done. Therefore before the names of Just, and Unjust can have place, there must be some coërcive Power, to compell men equally to the performance of their Covenants, by the terrour of some punishment, greater than the benefit they expect by [72] the breach of their Covenant; and to make good that Propriety, which by mutuall Contract men acquire, in recompence of the universal Right they abandon: and such power there is none before the erection of a Common-wealth. And this is also to be gathered out of the ordinary definition of Justice in the Schooles: For they say, that *Justice is the constant Will of giving to every man his own.* And therefore where there is no *Own*, that is, no Propriety, there is no Injustice; and where there is no coërceive Power erected, that is, where there is no Common-wealth, there is no Propriety; all men having Right to all things: Therefore where there is no Common-wealth, there nothing is Unjust. So that the nature of Justice, consisteth in keeping of valid Covenants: but the Validity of Covenants begins not but with the Constitution of a Civill Power, sufficient to compell men to keep them: And then it is also that Propriety begins.

The Foole hath sayd in his heart, there is no such thing as Justice; *Justice not* and sometimes also with his tongue; seriously alleaging, that every *Contrary to* mans conservation, and contentment, being committed to his own *Reason.* care, there could be no reason, why every man might not do what he thought conduced thereunto: and therefore also to make, or not make; keep, or not keep Covenants, was not against Reason, when it conduced to ones benefit. He does not therein deny, that there be Covenants; and that they are sometimes broken, sometimes kept; and that such breach of them may be called Injustice, and the observance of them Justice: but he questioneth, whether Injustice, taking away the feare of God, (for the same Foole hath said in his heart there is no God,) may not sometimes stand with that Reason, which dictateth to every man his own good; and particularly then, when it conduceth to such a benefit, as shall put a man in a condition, to neglect not onely the dispraise, and revilings, but also the power of other men. The Kingdome of God is gotten by violence: but what if it could be gotten by unjust violence? were it against Reason so to get it, when it is impossible to receive hurt by it? and if it be not against Reason, it is not against Justice: or else Justice is not to be approved for good. From such reasoning as this, Successfull wickednesse hath obtained the name of Vertue: and some that in all other things have disallowed the violation of Faith; yet have allowed it, when it is for the getting of a Kingdome. And the Heathen that believed, that *Saturn* was deposed by his son *Jupiter*, believed neverthelesse the same *Jupiter* to be the avenger of Injustice: Somewhat like to a piece of Law in *Cokes* Commentaries on *Litleton*; where he sayes, If the right Heire of the Crown be attainted of Treason; yet the Crown shall descend to him, and *eo instante* the Atteynder be voyd: From which instances a man will be very prone to inferre; that when the Heire apparent of a Kingdome, shall kill him that is in possession, though his father; you may call it Injustice, or by what other name you will; yet it can never be against Reason, seeing all the voluntary actions of men tend to the benefit of themselves; and those actions are most Reasonable, that conduce most to their ends. This specious reasoning is neverthelesse false.

[73]　　For the question is not of promises mutuall, where there is no security of performance on either side; as when there is no Civill Power erected over the parties promising; for such promises are no Covenants: But either where one of the parties has performed already; or where there is a Power to make him performe; there is the question whether it be against reason, that is, against the benefit of the other to performe, or not. And I say it is not against reason. For the manifestation whereof, we are to consider; First, that when a man doth a thing, which notwithstanding any thing can be foreseen, and reckoned on, tendeth to his own destruction, howsoever some accident which he could not expect, arriving, may turne it to his benefit; yet such events do not make it reasonably or wisely done. Secondly, that in a condition of Warre, wherein every man to every man, for want of a common Power to keep them all in awe, is an Enemy, there is no man can hope by his own strength, or wit, to defend himselfe from destruction, without the help of Confederates; where every one expects the same defence by the Confederation, that any one else does: and therefore he which declares he thinks it reason to deceive those that help him, can in reason expect no other means of safety, than what can be had from his own single Power. He therefore that breaketh his Covenant, and consequently declareth that he thinks he may with reason do so, cannot be received into any Society, that unite themselves for Peace and Defence, but by the errour of them that receive him; nor when he is received, be retayned in it, without seeing the danger of their errour; which errours a man cannot reasonably reckon upon as the means of his security: and therefore if he be left, or cast out of Society, he perisheth; and if he live in Society, it is by the errours of other men, which he could not foresee, nor reckon

upon; and consequently against the reason of his preservation; and so, as all men that contribute not to his destruction, forbear him onely out of ignorance of what is good for themselves.

As for the Instance of gaining the secure and perpetuall felicity of Heaven, by any way; it is frivolous: there being but one way imaginable; and that is not breaking, but keeping of Covenant.

And for the other Instance of attaining Soveraignty by Rebellion; it is manifest, that though the event follow, yet because it cannot reasonably be expected, but rather the contrary; and because by gaining it so, others are taught to gain the same in like manner, the attempt thereof is against reason. Justice therefore, that is to say, Keeping of Covenant, is a Rule of Reason, by which we are forbidden to do any thing destructive to our life; and consequently a Law of Nature.

There be some that proceed further; and will not have the Law of Nature, to be those Rules which conduce to the preservation of mans life on earth; but to the attaining of an eternall felicity after death; to which they think the breach of Covenant may conduce; and consequently be just and reasonable; (such are they that think it a work of merit to kill, or depose, or rebell against, the Soveraigne Power [74] constituted over them by their own consent.) But because there is no naturall knowledge of mans estate after death; much lesse of the reward that is then to be given to breach of Faith; but onely a beliefe grounded upon other mens saying, that they know it supernaturally, or that they know those, that knew them, that knew others, that knew it supernaturally; Breach of Faith cannot be called a Precept of Reason, or Nature.

Others, that allow for a Law of Nature, the keeping of Faith, do neverthelesse make exception of certain persons; as Heretiques, and such as use not to performe their Covenant to others: And this also is against reason. For if any fault of a man, be sufficient to discharge our Covenant made; the same ought in reason to have been sufficient to have hindred the making of it. *Covenants not discharged by the Vice of the Person to whom they are made.*

The names of Just, and Injust, when they are attributed to Men, signifie one thing; and when they are attributed to Actions, another. When they are attributed to Men, they signifie Conformity, or Inconformity of Manners, to Reason. But when they are attributed to Actions, they signifie the Conformity, or Inconformity to Reason, not of Manners, or manner of life, but of particular Actions. A Just man *Justice of Men, & Justice of Actions what.*

therefore, is he that taketh all the care he can, that his Actions may be all Just: and an Unjust man, is he that neglecteth it. And such men are more often in our Language stiled by the names of Righteous, and Unrighteous; then Just, and Unjust; though the meaning be the same. Therefore a Righteous man, does not lose that Title, by one, or a few unjust Actions, that proceed from sudden Passion, or mistake of Things, or Persons: nor does an Unrighteous man, lose his character, for such Actions, as he does, or forbeares to do, for feare: because his Will is not framed by the Justice, but by the apparent benefit of what he is to do. That which gives to humane Actions the relish of Justice, is a certain Noblenesse or Gallantnesse of courage, (rarely found,) by which a man scorns to be beholding for the contentment of his life, to fraud, or breach of promise. This Justice of the Manners, is that which is meant, where Justice is called a Vertue; and Injustice a Vice.

But the Justice of Actions denominates men, not Just, but *Guiltlesse*: and the Injustice of the same, (which is also called Injury,) gives them *the*[1] name of *Guilty*.

Justice of Manners, and Justice of Actions.

Again, the Injustice of Manners, is the disposition, or aptitude to do Injurie; and is Injustice before it proceed to Act; and without supposing any individuall person injured. But the Injustice of an Action, (that is to say Injury,) supposeth an individuall person Injured; namely him to whom the Covenant was made: And therefore many times the injury is received by one man, when the dammage redoundeth to another. As when the Master commandeth his servant to give mony to a stranger; if it be not done, the Injury is done to the Master, whom he had before Covenanted to obey; but the dammage redoundeth to the stranger, to whom he had no Obligation; and therefore could not Injure him. And so also in Common-wealths, private men may remit to one another their debts; but not robberies or other violences, whereby they are endammaged; because the detaining of Debt, is an Injury to themselves; but Robbery and Violence, are Injuries to the Person of the Common-wealth.

[75]

Nothing done to a man, by his own consent can be Injury.

Whatsoever is done to a man, conformable to his own Will signified to the doer, is no Injury to him. For if he that doeth it, hath not passed away his originall right to do what he please, by some Antecedent Covenant, there is no breach of Covenant; and therefore no Injury done him. And if he have; then his Will to have it done being signi-

[1] *Syn.*: but the

fied, is a release of that Covenant: and so again there is no Injury done him.

Justice of Actions, is by Writers divided into *Commutative*, and *Distributive*: and the former they say consisteth in proportion Arithmeticall; the later in proportion Geometricall. Commutative therefore, they place in the equality of value of the things contracted for; And Distributive, in the distribution of equall benefit, to men of equall merit. As if it were Injustice to sell dearer than we buy; or to give more to a man than he merits. The value of all things contracted for, is measured by the Appetite of the Contractors: and therefore the just value, is that which they be contented to give. And Merit (besides that which is by Covenant, where the performance on one part, meriteth the performance of the other part, and falls under Justice Commutative, not Distributive,) is not due by Justice; but is rewarded of Grace onely. And therefore this distinction, in the sense wherein it useth to be expounded, is not right. To speak properly, Commutative Justice, is the Justice of a Contractor; that is, a Performance of Covenant, in Buying, and Selling; Hiring, and Letting to Hire; Lending, and Borrowing; Exchanging, Bartering, and other acts of Contract.

And Distributive Justice, the Justice of an Arbitrator; that is to say, the act of defining what is Just. Wherein, (being trusted by them that make him Arbitrator,) if he performe his Trust, he is said to distribute to every man his own: and this is indeed Just Distribution, and may be called (though improperly) Distributive Justice; but more properly Equity; which also is a Law of Nature, as shall be shewn in due place.

Justice Commutative, and Distributive.

As Justice dependeth on Antecedent Covenant; so does GRATITUDE depend on Antecedent Grace; that is to say, Antecedent Free-gift: and is the fourth Law of Nature; which may be conceived in this Forme, *That a man which receiveth Benefit from another of meer Grace, Endeavour that he which giveth it, have no reasonable cause to repent him of his good will.* For no man giveth, but with intention of Good to himselfe; because Gift is Voluntary; and of all Voluntary Acts, the Object is to every man his own Good; of which if men see they shall be frustrated, there will be no beginning of benevolence, or trust; nor consequently of mutuall help; nor of reconciliation of one man to another; and therefore they are to remain still in the condition of *War*, which is contrary to the first and Fundamentall Law of Nature, which commandeth men to *Seek Peace*. The breach of this Law, is called

The fourth Law of Nature, Gratitude.

[76] *Ingratitude*; and hath the same relation to Grace, that Injustice hath to Obligation by Covenant.

The fifth, Mutuall accommodation, or Compleasance. A fifth Law of Nature, is COMPLEASANCE; that is to say, *That every man strive to accommodate himselfe to the rest.* For the understanding whereof, we may consider, that there is in mens aptnesse to Society, a diversity of Nature, rising from their diversity of Affections; not unlike to that we see in stones brought together for building of an Aedifice. For as that stone which by the asperity, and irregularity of Figure, takes more room from others, than it selfe fills; and for the hardnesse, cannot be easily made plain, and thereby hindereth the building, is by the builders cast away as unprofitable, and troublesome: so also, a man that by asperity of Nature, will strive to retain those things which to himself are superfluous, and to others necessary; and for the stubbornness of his Passions, cannot be corrected, is to be left, or cast out of Society, as combersome thereunto. For seeing every man, not onely by Right, but also by necessity of Nature, is supposed to endeavour all he can, to obtain that which is necessary for his conservation; He that shall oppose himselfe against it, for things superfluous, is guilty of the warre that thereupon is to follow; and therefore doth that, which is contrary to the fundamentall Law of Nature, which commandeth *to seek Peace.* The observers of this Law, may be called SOCIABLE, (the Latines call them *Commodi*;) The contrary, *Stubborn, Insociable, Froward, Intractable.*

The sixth, Facility to Pardon. A sixth Law of Nature, is this, *That upon caution of the Future time, a man ought to pardon the offences past of them that repenting, desire it.* For PARDON, is nothing but granting of Peace; which though granted to them that persevere in their hostility, be not Peace, but Feare; yet not granted to them that give caution of the Future time, is signe of an aversion to Peace; and therefore contrary to the Law of Nature.

The seventh, that in Revenges, men respect onely the future good. A seventh is, *That in Revenges,* (that is, retribution of Evil for Evil,) *Men look not at the greatnesse of the evill past, but the greatnesse of the good to follow.* Whereby we are forbidden to inflict punishment with any other designe, than for correction of the offender, or direction of others. For this Law is consequent to the next before it, that commandeth Pardon, upon security of the Future time. Besides, Revenge without respect to the Example, and profit to come, is a triumph, or glorying in the hurt of another, tending to no end; (for the End is always somewhat to Come;) and glorying to no end, is vain-glory, and contrary to reason; and to hurt without reason, tendeth to the introduction of Warre; which is against the Law of Nature; and is commonly stiled by the name of *Cruelty*.

And because all signes of hatred, or contempt, provoke to fight; insomuch as most men choose rather to hazard their life, than not to be revenged; we may in the eighth place, for a Law of Nature, set down this Precept, *That no man by deed, word, countenance, or gesture, declare Hatred, or Contempt of another*. The breach of which Law, is commonly called *Contumely*.

The eighth, against Contumely.

The question who is the better man, has no place in the condition of meer Nature; where, (as has been shewn before,) all men are equall. The inequallity that now is, has bin introduced by the Lawes civill. I know that *Aristotle* in the first booke of his Politiques, for a foundation of his doctrine, maketh men by Nature, some more worthy to Command, meaning the wiser sort (such as he thought himselfe to be for his Philosophy;) others to Serve, (meaning those that had strong bodies, but were not Philosophers as he;) as if Master and Servant were not introduced by consent of men, but by difference of Wit: which is not only against reason; but also against experience. For there are very few so foolish, that had not rather governe themselves, than be governed by others: Nor when the wise in their own conceit, contend by force, with them who distrust their owne wisdome, do they alwaies, or often, or almost at any time, get the Victory. If Nature therefore have made men equall; that equalitie is to be acknowledged: or if Nature have made men unequall; yet because men that think themselves equall, will not enter into conditions of Peace, but upon Equall termes, such equalitie must be admitted. And therefore for the ninth law of Nature, I put this, *That every man acknowledge other for his Equall by Nature*. The breach of this Precept is *Pride*.

The ninth, against Pride.

[77]

On this law, dependeth another, *That at the entrance into conditions of Peace, no man require to reserve to himselfe any Right, which he is not content should be reserved to every one of the rest.* As it is necessary for all men that seek peace, to lay down certaine Rights of Nature; that is to say, not to have libertie to do all they list: so it is necessarie for mans life, to retaine some; as right to governe their owne bodies; enjoy aire, water, motion, waies to go from place to place; and all things else, without which a man cannot live, or not live well. If in this case, at the making of Peace, men require for themselves, that which they would not have to be granted to others, they do contrary to the precedent law, that commandeth the acknowledgment of naturall equalitie, and

The tenth, against Arrogance.

therefore also against the law of Nature. The observers of this law, are those we call *Modest*, and the breakers *Arrogant* men. The Greeks call the violation of this law πλεονεξία; that is, a desire of more than their share.

The eleventh Equity.

Also, if *a man be trusted to judge between man and man*, it is a precept of the Law of Nature, *that he deale Equally between them*. For without that, the Controversies of men cannot be determined but by Warre. He therefore that is partiall in judgment, doth what in him lies, to deterre men from the use of Judges, and Arbitrators; and consequently, (against the fundamentall Lawe of Nature) is the cause of Warre.

The observance of this law, from the equall distribution to each man, of that which in reason belongeth to him, is called EQUITY, and (as I have sayd before) distributive Justice: the violation, *Acception of persons*, προσωποληψία.

The twelfth, Equall use of things Common.

And from this followeth another law, *That such things as cannot be divided, be enjoyed in Common, if it can be; and if the quantity of the thing permit, without Stint; otherwise Proportionably to the number of them that have Right*. For otherwise the distribution is Unequall, and contrary to Equitie.

[78]

The thirteenth, of Lot.

But some things there be, that can neither be divided, nor enjoyed in common. Then, The Law of Nature, which prescribeth Equity, requireth, *That the Entire Right; or else, (making the use alternate,) the First Possession, be determined by Lot*. For equall distribution, is of the Law of Nature; and other means of equall distribution cannot be imagined.

The fourteenth, of Primogeniture, and First seising.

Of *Lots* there be two sorts, *Arbitrary*, and *Naturall*. Arbitrary, is that which is agreed on by the Competitors: Naturall, is either *Primogeniture*, (which the Greek calls Κληρονομία, which signifies, *Given by Lot;*) or *First Seisure*.

And therefore those things which cannot be enjoyed in common, nor divided, ought to be adjudged to the First Possessor; and in some cases to the First-Borne, as acquired by Lot.

The fifteenth, of Mediators.

It is also a Law of Nature, *That all men that mediate Peace, be allowed safe Conduct*. For the Law that commandeth Peace, as the *End*, commandeth Intercession, as the *Means*; and to Intercession the Means is safe Conduct.

The sixteenth, of

And because, though men be never so willing to observe these Lawes, there may neverthelesse arise questions concerning a mans

action; First, whether it were done, or not done; Secondly (if done) *Submission*
whether against the Law, or not against the Law; the former whereof, *to*
is called a question *Of Fact*; the later a question *Of Right*; therefore *Arbitrement.*
unlesse the parties to the question, Covenant mutually to stand to the
sentence of another, they are as farre from Peace as ever. This other,
to whose Sentence they submit, is called an ARBITRATOR. And therefore it is of the Law of Nature, *That they that are at controversie, submit
their Right to the judgement of an Arbitrator.*

And seeing every man is presumed to do all things in order to his *The*
own benefit, no man is a fit Arbitrator in his own cause: and if he were *seventeenth,*
never so fit; yet Equity allowing to each party equall benefit, if one be *No man is his own*
admitted to be Judge, the other is to be admitted also; & so the *Judge.*
controversie, that is, the cause of War, remains, against the Law of
Nature.

For the same reason no man in any Cause ought to be received for *The*
Arbitrator, to whom greater profit, or honour, or pleasure apparently *eighteenth,*
ariseth out of the victory of one party, than of the other: for hee hath *no man to be Judge, that*
taken (though an unavoydable bribe, yet) a bribe; and no man can be *has in him a*
obliged to trust him. And thus also the controversie, and the condition *natural cause*
of War remaineth, contrary to the Law of Nature. *of Partiality.*

And in a controversie of *Fact*, the Judge being to give no more *The*
credit to one, than to the other, (if there be no other Arguments) must *nineteenth, of*
give credit to a third; or to a third and fourth; or more: For else the *Witnesses.*
question is undecided, and left to force, contrary to the Law of
Nature.

These are the Lawes of Nature, dictating Peace, for a means of the
conservation of men in multitudes; and which onely concern the
doctrine of Civill Society. There be other things tending to the
destruction of particular men; as Drunkenness, and all other parts of
Intemperance; which may therefore also be reckoned amongst those
things which the Law of Nature hath forbidden; but are not necessary
to be mentioned, nor are pertinent enough to this place. [79]

And though this may seem too subtile a deduction of the Lawes of *A Rule by*
Nature, to be taken notice of by all men; whereof the most part are too *which the Laws of*
busie in getting food, and the rest too negligent to understand; yet to *Nature may*
leave all men unexcusable, they have been contracted into one easie *easily be*
sum, intelligible, even to the meanest capacity; and that is, *Do not that* *examined.*
to another, which thou wouldest not have done to thy selfe; which sheweth
him, that he has no more to do in learning the Lawes of Nature, but,

109

when weighing the actions of other men with his own, they seem too heavy, to put them into the other part of the ballance, and his own into their place, that his own passions, and selfe-love, may adde nothing to the weight; and then there is none of these Lawes of Nature that will not appear unto him very reasonable.

The Lawes of Nature oblige in Conscience alwayes, but in Effect then onely where there is Security.

The Lawes of Nature oblige *in foro interno*; that is to say, they bind to a desire they should take place: but *in foro externo*; that is, to the putting them in act, not alwayes. For he that should be modest, and tractable, and performe all he promises, in such time, and place, where no man els should do so, should but make himselfe a prey to others, and procure his own certain ruine, contrary to the ground of all Lawes of Nature, which tend to Natures preservation. And again, he that having sufficient Security, that others shall observe the same Lawes towards him, observes them not himselfe, seeketh not Peace, but War; & consequently the destruction of his Nature by Violence.

And whatsoever Lawes bind *in foro interno*, may be broken, not onely by a fact contrary to the Law, but also by a fact according to it, in case a man think it contrary. For though his Action in this case, be according to the Law; yet his Purpose was against the Law; which where the Obligation is *in foro interno*, is a breach.

The Laws of Nature are Eternal;

The Lawes of Nature are Immutable and Eternall; For Injustice, Ingratitude, Arrogance, Pride, Iniquity, Acception of persons, and the rest, can never be made lawfull. For it can never be that Warre shall preserve life, and Peace destroy it.

And yet Easie.

The sames Lawes, because they oblige onely to a desire, and endeavour, I mean an unfeigned and constant endeavour, are easie to be observed. For in that they require nothing but endeavour; he that endeavoureth their performance, fulfilleth them; and he that fulfilleth the Law, is Just.

The Science of these Lawes, is the true Morall Philosophy.

And the Science of them, is the true and onely Moral Philosophy. For Morall Philosophy is nothing else but the Science of what is *Good*, and *Evill*, in the conversation, and Society of man-kind. *Good*, and *Evill*, are names that signifie our Appetites, and Aversions; which in different tempers, customes, and doctrines of men, are different: And divers men, differ not onely in their Judgement, on the senses of what is pleasant, and unpleasant to the tast, smell, hearing, touch, and sight; but also of what is conformable, or disagreeable to Reason, in the actions of common life. Nay, the same man, in divers times, differs from himselfe; and one time praiseth, that is, calleth Good, what another time he dispraiseth, and calleth Evil: From whence arise [80] Disputes, Controversies, and at last War. And therefore so long a man is in the condition of meer Nature, (which is a condition of War,) as private Appetite is the measure of Good, and Evill: And consequently all men agree on this, that Peace is Good, and therefore also the way, or means of Peace, which (as I have shewed before) are *Justice, Gratitude, Modesty, Equity, Mercy,* & the rest of the Laws of Nature, are good; that is to say, *Morall Vertues*; and their contrarie *Vices,* Evill. Now the science of Vertue and Vice, is Morall Philosophie; and therefore the true Doctrine of the Lawes of Nature, is the true Morall Philosophie. But the Writers of Morall Philosophie, though they acknowledge the same Vertues and Vices; Yet not seeing wherein consisted their Goodnesse; nor that they come to be praised, as the meanes of peaceable, sociable, and comfortable living; place them in a mediocrity of passions: as if not the Cause, but the Degree of daring, made Fortitude; or not the Cause, but the Quantity of a gift, made Liberality.

These dictates of Reason, men use to call by the name of Lawes, but improperly: for they are but Conclusions, or Theoremes concerning what conduceth to the conservation and defence of themselves; wheras Law, properly is the word of him, that by right hath command over others. But yet if we consider the same Theoremes, as delivered in the word of God, that by right commandeth all things; then are they properly called Lawes.

CHAP. XVI.

Of PERSONS, AUTHORS, *and things Personated.*

A PERSON, is he, *whose words or actions are considered, either as his own,*   *A Person* *or as representing the words or actions of an other man, or of any other thing*   *what.* *to whom they are attributed, whether Truly or by Fiction.*

When they are considered as his owne, then is he called a *Naturall*   *Person* *Person:* And when they are considered as representing the words and   *Naturall,* actions of an other, then is he a *Feigned* or *Artificiall person.*   *and*   *Artificiall.*

The word Person is latine: insteed whereof the Greeks have πϱόσωπον, which signifies the *Face*, as *Persona* in latine signifies the *disguise*, or *outward appearance* of a man, counterfeited on the Stage; and sometimes more particularly that part of it, which disguiseth the face, as a Mask or Visard: And from the Stage, hath been translated to any Representer of speech and action, as well in Tribunalls, as Theaters. So that a *Person*, is the same that an *Actor* is, both on the Stage and in common Conversation; and to *Personate*, is to *Act*, or *Represent* himselfe, or an other; and he that acteth another, is said to beare his Person, or act in his name; (in which sence *Cicero* useth it where he saies, *Unus sustineo tres Personas*; *Mei, Adversarii, & Judicis*, I beare three Persons; my own, my Adversaries, and the Judges;) and is called in diverse occasions, diversly; as a *Representer*, or *Representative*, a *Lieutenant*, a *Vicar*, an *Attorney*, a *Deputy*, a *Procurator*, an *Actor*, and the like.

[81]

Actor, Author.

Of Persons Artificiall, some have their words and actions *Owned* by those whom they represent. And then the Person is the *Actor*; and he that owneth his words and actions, is the AUTHOR: In which case the Actor acteth by Authority. For that which in speaking of goods and possessions, is called an *Owner*, and in latine *Dominus*, in Greeke κύϱιος, speaking of Actions, is called *an Author.*[1] And as the Right of possession, is called Dominion; so the Right of doing any Action, is called *AUTHORITY and sometimes *warrant*.*[2] So that by Authority, is always understood a Right of doing any act: and *done by Authority*, done by Commission, or Licence from him whose right it is.

Authority.

Covenants by Authority, bind the Author.

From hence it followeth, that when the Actor maketh a Covenant by Authority, he bindeth thereby the Author, no lesse than if he had made it himselfe; and no lesse subjecteth him to all the consequences of the same. And therfore all that hath been said formerly, (*Chap.* 14.) of the nature of Covenants between man and man in their naturall capacity, is true also when they are made by their Actors, Representers, or Procurators, that have authority from them, so far-forth as is in their Commission, but no farther.

And therefore he that maketh a Covenant with the Actor, or Representer, not knowing the Authority he hath, doth it at his own perill. For no man is obliged by a Covenant, whereof he is not Author;

[1] *Syn.*: Author   [2] *Syn.*: AUTHORITY

nor consequently by a Covenant made against, or beside the Authority he gave.

When the Actor doth any thing against the Law of Nature by command of the Author, if he be obliged by former Covenant to obey him, not he, but the Author breaketh the Law of Nature: for though the Action be against the Law of Nature; yet it is not his: but contrarily, to refuse to do it, is against the Law of Nature, that forbiddeth breach of Covenant. *But not the Actor.*

And he that maketh a Covenant with the Author, by mediation of the Actor, not knowing what Authority he hath, but onely takes his word; in case such Authority be not made manifest unto him upon demand, is no longer obliged: For the Covenant made with the Author, is not valid, without his Counter-assurance. But if he that so Covenanteth, knew before hand he was to expect no other assurance, than the Actors word; then is the Covenant valid; because the Actor in this case maketh himselfe the Author. And therefore, as when the Authority is evident, the Covenant obligeth the Author, not the Actor; so when the Authority is feigned, it obligeth the Actor onely; there being no Author but himselfe. *The Authority is to be shewne.*

There are few things, that are uncapable of being represented by Fiction. Inanimate things, as a Church, an Hospital, a Bridge, may be Personated by a Rector, Master, or Overseer. But things Inanimate, cannot be Authors, nor therefore give Authority to their Actors: Yet the Actors may have Authority to procure their maintenance, given them by those that are Owners, or Governours of those things. And therefore, such things cannot be Personated, before there be some state of Civill Government. *Things, personated, Inanimate.* [82]

Likewise Children, Fooles, and Mad-men that have no use of Reason, may be Personated by Guardians, or Curators; but can be no Authors (during that time) of any action done by them, longer then (when they shall recover the use of Reason) they shall judge the same reasonable. Yet during the Folly, he that hath right of governing them, may give Authority to the Guardian. But this again has no place but in a State Civill, because before such estate, there is no Dominion of Persons. *Irrational;*

An Idol, or meer Figment of the brain, may be Personated; as were the Gods of the Heathen; which by such Officers as the State appointed, were Personated, and held Possessions, and other Goods, and Rights, which men from time to time dedicated, and consecrated unto *False Gods;*

them. But Idols cannot be Authors: for an Idol is nothing. The Authority proceeded from the State: and therefore before introduction of Civill Government, the Gods of the Heathen could not be Personated.

The true God.

The true God may be Personated. As he was; first, by *Moses*; who governed the Israelites, (that were not his, but Gods people,) not in his own name, with *Hoc dicit Moses*; but in Gods Name, with *Hoc dicit Dominus*. Secondly, by the Son of man, his own Son, our Blessed Saviour *Jesus Christ*, that came to reduce the Jewes, and induce all Nations into the Kingdome of his Father; not as of himselfe, but as sent from his Father. And thirdly, by the Holy Ghost, or Comforter, speaking, and working in the Apostles: which Holy Ghost, was a Comforter that came not of himselfe; but was sent, and proceeded from them *both on the day of Pentecost.*[1]

A Multitude of men, how one Person.

A Multitude of men, are made *One* Person, when they are by one man, or one Person, Represented; so that it be done with the consent of every one of that Multitude in particular. For it is the *Unity* of the Representer, not the *Unity* of the Represented, that maketh the Person *One*. And it is the Representer that beareth the Person, and but one Person: And *Unity*, cannot otherwise be understood in Multitude.

Every one is Author.

And because the Multitude naturally is not *One*, but *Many*; they cannot be understood for one; but many Authors, of every thing their Representative saith, or doth in their name; Every man giving their common Representer, Authority from himselfe in particular; and owning all the actions the Representer doth, in case they give him Authority without stint: Otherwise, when they limit him in what, and how farre he shall represent them, none of them owneth more, than they gave him commission to Act.

An Actor may be Many men made One by Plurality of Voyces.

And if the Representative consist of many men, the voyce of the greater number, must be considered as the voyce of them all. For if the lesser number pronounce (for example) in the Affirmative, and the greater in the Negative, there will be Negatives more than enough to destroy the Affirmatives; and thereby the excesse of Negatives, standing uncontradicted, are the onely voyce the Representative hath.

[83]

Representatives, when the number is even, unprofitable.

And a Representative of even number, especially when the number is not great, whereby the contradictory voyces are oftentimes equall, is therefore oftentimes mute, and uncapable of Action. Yet in some

[1] *Syn.*: both.

114

cases contradictory voyces equall in number, may determine a question; as in condemning, or absolving, equality of votes, even in that they condemne not, do absolve; but not on the contrary condemne, in that they absolve not. For when a Cause is heard; not to condemne, is to absolve: but on the contrary, to say that not absolving, is condemning, is not true. The like it is in a deliberation of executing presently, or deferring till another time: For when the voyces are equall, the not decreeing Execution, is a decree of Dilation.

Or if the number be odde, as three, or more, (men, or assemblies;) whereof every one has by a Negative Voice, authority to take away the effect of all the Affirmative Voices of the rest, This number is no Representative; because by the diversity of Opinions, and Interests of men, it becomes oftentimes, and in cases of the greatest consequence, a mute Person, and unapt, as for many things else, so for the government of a Multitude, especially in time of Warre. *Negative voyce.*

Of Authors there be two sorts. The first simply so called; which I have before defined to be him, that owneth the Action of another simply. The second is he, that owneth an Action, or Covenant of another conditionally; that is to say, he undertaketh to do it, if the other doth it not, at, or before a certain time. And these Authors conditionall, are generally called SURETYES, in Latine *Fidejussores*, and *Sponsores*; and particularly for Debt, *Praedes*; and for Appearance before a Judge, or Magistrate, *Vades*.

PART 2

OF COMMON-WEALTH.

CHAP. XVII.

Of the Causes, Generation, and Definition of a COMMON-WEALTH.

The finall Cause, End, or Designe of men, (who naturally love Liberty, and Dominion over others,) in the introduction of that restraint upon themselves, (in which wee see them live in Common-wealths,) is the foresight of their own preservation, and of a more contented life thereby; that is to say, of getting themselves out from that miserable condition of Warre, which is necessarily consequent (as hath been shewn) to the naturall Passions of men, when there is no visible Power to keep them in awe, and tye them by feare of punishment to the performance of their Covenants, and observation of those Lawes of Nature set down in the fourteenth and fifteenth Chapters.

    For the Lawes of Nature (as *Justice, Equity, Modesty, Mercy,* and (in summe) *doing to others, as wee would be done to,*) of themselves, without the terrour of some Power, to cause them to be observed, are contrary to our naturall Passions, that carry us to Partiality, Pride, Revenge, and the like. And Covenants, without the Sword, are but Words, and of no strength to secure a man at all. Therefore notwithstanding the Lawes of Nature, (which every one hath then kept, when he has the

The End of Common-wealth, particular Security:

Chap. 13.

Which is not to be had from the Law of Nature:

117

will to keep them, when he can do it safely,) if there be no Power erected, or not great enough for our security; every man will, and may lawfully rely on his own strength and art, for caution against all other men. And in all places, where men have lived by small Families, to robbe and spoyle one another, has been a Trade, and so farre from being reputed against the Law of Nature, that the greater spoyles they gained, the greater was their honour; and men observed no other Lawes therein, but the Lawes of Honour; that is, to abstain from cruelty, leaving to men their lives, and instruments of husbandry. And as small Familyes did then; so now do Cities and Kingdomes which are but greater Families (for their own security) enlarge their Dominions, upon all pretences of danger, and fear of Invasion, or assistance that may be given to Invaders, endeavour as much as they can, to subdue, or weaken their neighbours, by open force, and secret arts, for want of other Caution, justly; and are remembred for it in after ages with honour.

Nor from the conjunction of a few men or familyes:

[86]

Nor is it the joyning together of a finall number of men, that gives them this security; because in small numbers, small additions on the one side or the other, make the advantage of strength so great, as is sufficient to carry the Victory; and therefore gives encouragement to an Invasion. The Multitude sufficient to confide in for our Security, is not determined by any certain number, but by comparison with the Enemy we feare; and is then sufficient, when the odds of the Enemy is not of so visible and conspicuous moment, to determine the event of warre, as to move him to attempt.

Nor from a great Multitude, unlesse directed by one judgement.

And be there never so great a Multitude; yet if their actions be directed according to their particular judgements, and particular appetites, they can expect thereby no defence, nor protection, neither against a Common enemy, nor against the injuries of one another. For being distracted in opinions concerning the best use and application of their strength, they do not help, but hinder one another; and reduce their strength by mutuall opposition to nothing: whereby they are easily, not onely subdued by a very few that agree together; but also when there is no common enemy, they make warre upon each other, for their particular interests. For if we could suppose a great Multitude of men to consent in the observation of Justice, and other Lawes of Nature, without a common Power to keep them all in awe; we might as well suppose all Man-kind to do the same; and then there

neither would be, nor need to be any Civill Government, or Common-wealth at all; because there would be Peace without subjection.

Nor is it enough for the security, which men desire should last all *And that* the time of their life, that they be governed, and directed by one *continually.* judgement, for a limited time; as in one Battell, or one Warre. For though they obtain a Victory by their unanimous endeavour against a forraign enemy; yet afterwards, when either they have no common enemy, or he that by one part is held for an enemy, is by another part held for a friend, they must needs by the difference of their interests dissolve, and fall again into a Warre amongst themselves.

It is true, that certain living creatures, as Bees, and Ants, live *Why certain* sociably one with another, (which are therefore by *Aristotle* numbred *creatures* amongst Politicall creatures;) and yet have no other direction, than *without reason, or* their particular judgements and appetites; nor speech, whereby one of *speech, do* them can signifie to another, what he thinks expedient for the com- *neverthelesse* mon benefit: and therefore some man may perhaps desire to know, *Society,* why Man-kind cannot do the same. To which I answer, *without any*

First, that men are continually in competition for Honour and *coërcive* Dignity, which these creatures are not; and consequently amongst *Power.* men there ariseth on that ground, Envy and Hatred, and finally Warre; but amongst these not so.

Secondly, that amongst these creatures, the Common good dif-
fereth not from the Private; and being by nature enclined to their private, they procure thereby the common benefit. But man, whose Joy consisteth in comparing himselfe with other men, can relish nothing but what is eminent.

Thirdly, that these creatures, having not (as man) the use of reason, do not see, nor think they see any fault, in the administration of their common businesse: whereas amongst men, there are very many, that [87] thinke themselves wiser, and abler to govern the Publique, better than the rest; and these strive to reforme and innovate, one this way, another that way; and thereby bring it into Distraction and Civill warre.

Fourthly, that these creatures, though they have some use of voice, in making knowne to one another their desires, and other affections; yet they want that art of words, by which some men can represent to others, that which is Good, in the likenesse of Evill; and Evill, in the likenesse of Good; and augment, or diminish the apparent greatnesse of Good and Evill; discontenting men, and troubling their Peace at their pleasure.

Fiftly, irrationall creatures cannot distinguish betweene *Injury*, and *Dammage*; and therefore as long as they be at ease, they are not offended with their fellowes: whereas Man is then most troublesome, when he is most at ease: for then it is that he loves to shew his Wisdome, and controule the Actions of them that governe the Common-wealth.

Lastly, the agreement of these creatures is Naturall; that of men, is by Covenant only, which is Artificiall: and therefore it is no wonder if there be somwhat else required (besides Covenant) to make their Agreement constant and lasting; which is a Common Power, to keep them in awe, and to direct their actions to the Common Benefit.

The Generation of a Common-wealth. The only way to erect such a Common Power, as may be able to defend them from the invasion of Forraigners, and the injuries of one another, and thereby to secure them in such sort, as that by their owne industrie, and by the fruites of the Earth, they may nourish themselves and live contentedly; is, to conferre all their power and strength upon one Man, or upon one Assembly of men, that may reduce all their Wills, by plurality of voices, unto one Will: which is as much as to say, to appoint one Man, or Assembly of men, to beare their Person; and every one to owne, and acknowledge himselfe to be Author of whatsoever he that so beareth their Person, shall Act, or cause to be Acted, in those things which concerne the Common Peace and Safetie; and therein to submit their Wills, every one to his Will, and their Judgements, to his Judgment. This is more than Consent, or Concord; it is a reall Unitie of them all, in one and the same Person, made by Covenant of every man with every man, in such manner, as if every man should say to every man, *I Authorise and give up my Right of Governing my selfe, to this Man, or to this Assembly of men, on this condition, that thou give up thy Right to him, and Authorise all his Actions in like manner.* This done, the Multitude so united in one Person, is called a COMMON-WEALTH, in latine CIVITAS. This is the Generation of that great LEVIATHAN, or rather (to speake more reverently) of that *Mortall God*, to which wee owe under the *Immortal God*, our peace and defence. For by this Authoritie, given him by every particular man in the Common-Wealth, he hath the use of so much Power and Strength conferred on him, that by terror thereof, he is inabled to *con*¹forme the wills of them all, to Peace at home, and mutuall ayd

[88]

¹ This is a cancel (see p. xxx) replacing 'per'.

against their enemies abroad. And in him consisteth the Essence of the Commonwealth; which (to define it,) is *One Person, of whose Acts a great Multitude, by mutuall Covenants one with another, have made themselves every one the Author, to the end he may use the strength and means of them all, as he shall think expedient, for their Peace and Common Defence.*

The Definition of a Commonwealth.

And he that carryeth this Person, is called S O V E R A I G N E, and said to have *Soveraigne Power*; and every one besides, his S U B J E C T.

Soveraigne, and Subject, what.

The attaining to this Soveraigne Power, is by two wayes. One, by Naturall force; as when a man maketh his children, to submit themselves, and their children to his government, as being able to destroy them if they refuse; or by Warre subdueth his enemies to his will, giving them their lives on that condition. The other, is when men agree amongst themselves, to submit to some Man, or Assembly of men, voluntarily, on confidence to be protected by him against all others. This later, may be called a Politicall Common-wealth, or Common-wealth by *Institution*; and the former, a Common-wealth by *Acquisition*. And first, I shall speak of a Common-wealth by Institution.

CHAP. XVIII.
Of the R I G H T S *of Soveraignes by Institution.*

A *Common-wealth* is said to be *Instituted*, when a *Multitude* of men do Agree, and *Covenant, every one, with every one*, that to whatsoever *Man*, or *Assembly of Men*, shall be given by the major part, the *Right* to *Present* the Person of them all, (that is to say, to be their *Representative*;) every one, as well he that *Voted for it*, as he that *Voted against it*, shall *Authorise* all the Actions and Judgements, of that Man, or Assembly of men, in the same manner, as if they were his own, to the end, to live peaceably amongst themselves, and be protected against other men.

The act of Instituting a Commonwealth, what.

From this Institution of a Common-wealth are derived all the *Rights*, and *Facultyes* of him, or them, on whom the Soveraigne Power is conferred by the consent of the People assembled.

The Consequences to such Institution, are 1. The Subjects cannot change the forme of government.

First, because they Covenant, it is to be understood, they are not obliged by former Covenant to any thing repugnant hereunto. And Consequently they that have already Instituted a Common-wealth, being thereby bound by Covenant, to own the Actions, and Judgements of one, cannot lawfully make a new Covenant, amongst themselves, to be obedient to any other, in any thing whatsoever, without his permission. And therefore, they that are subjects to a Monarch, cannot without his leave cast off Monarchy, and return to the confusion of a disunited Multitude; nor transferre their Person from him that beareth it, to another Man, or other Assembly of men: for they [89] are bound, every man to every man, to Own, and be reputed Author of all, that he that already is their Soveraigne, shall do, and judge fit to be done: so that any one man dissenting, all the rest should break their Covenant made to that man, which is injustice: and they have also every man given the Soveraignty to him that beareth their Person; and therefore if they depose him, they take from him that which is his own, and so again it is injustice. Besides, if he that attempteth to depose his Soveraign, be killed, or punished by him for such attempt, he is author of his own punishment, as being by the Institution, Author of all his Sovereign shall do: And because it is injustice for a man to do any thing, for which he may be punished by his own authority, he is also upon that title, unjust. And whereas some men have pretended for their disobedience to their Soveraign, a new Covenant, made, not with men, but with God; this also is unjust: for there is no Covenant with God, but by mediation of some body that representeth Gods Person; which none doth but Gods Lieutenant, who hath the Soveraignty under God. But this pretence of Covenant with God, is so evident a lye, even in the pretenders own consciences, that it is not onely an act of an unjust, but also of a vile, and unmanly disposition.

2. *Soveraigne Power cannot be forfeited.* Secondly, Because the Right of bearing the Person of them all, is given to him they make Soveraigne, by Covenant onely of one to another, and not of him to any of them; there can happen no breach of Covenant on the part of the Soveraigne; and consequently none of his Subjects, by any pretence of forfeiture, can be freed from his Subjection. That he which is made Soveraigne maketh no Covenant with his Subjects before-hand, is manifest; because either he must make it with the whole multitude, as one party to the Covenant; or he must make a severall Covenant with every man. With the whole, as one party, it is impossible; because as yet they are not one Person: and if

he make so many severall Covenants as there be men, those
Covenants after he hath the Soveraignty are voyd, because what act
soever can be pretended by any one of them for breach thereof, is the
act both of himselfe, and of all the rest, because done in the Person,
and by the Right of every one of them in particular. Besides, if any
one, or more of them, pretend a breach of the Covenant made by the
Soveraigne at his Institution; and others, or one other of his Subjects,
or himselfe alone, pretend there was no such breach, there is in this
case, no Judge to decide the controversie: it returns therefore to the
Sword again; and every man recovereth the right of Protecting himselfe by his own strength, contrary to the designe they had in the
Institution. It is therefore in vain to grant Soveraignty by way of
precedent Covenant. The opinion that any Monarch receiveth his
Power by Covenant, that is to say on Condition, proceedeth from
want of understanding this easie truth, that Covenants being but
words, and breath, have no force to oblige, contain, constrain, or
protect any man, but what it has from the publique Sword; that is,
from the untyed hands of that Man, or Assembly of men that hath the
Soveraignty, and whose actions are avouched by them all, and performed by the strength of them all, in him united. But when an [90]
Assembly of men is made Soveraigne; then no man imagineth any
such Covenant to have past in the Institution; for no man is so dull as
to say, for example, the People of *Rome*, made a Covenant with the
Romans, to hold the Soveraignty on such or such conditions; which
not performed, the Romans might lawfully depose the Roman People.
That men see not the reason to be alike in a Monarchy, and in a
Popular Government, proceedeth from the ambition of some, that are
kinder to the government of an Assembly, whereof they may hope to
participate, than of Monarchy, which they despair to enjoy.

Thirdly, because the major part hath by consenting voices declared
a Soveraigne; he that dissented must now consent with the rest; that
is, be contented to avow all the actions he shall do, or else justly be
destroyed by the rest. For if he voluntarily entered into the Congregation of them that were assembled, he sufficiently declared thereby his
will (and therefore tacitely covenanted) to stand to what the major part
should ordayne: and therefore if he refuse to stand thereto, or make
Protestation against any of their Decrees, he does contrary to his
Covenant, and therfore unjustly. And whether he be of the Congregation, or not; and whether his consent be asked, or not, he must either

*3. No man
can without
injustice
protest
against the
Institution of
the
Soveraigne
declared by
the major
part.*

submit to their decrees, or be left in the condition of warre he was in before; wherein he might without injustice be destroyed by any man whatsoever.

4. The Soveraigns Actions cannot be justly accused by the Subject.

Fourthly, because every Subject is by this Institution Author of all the Actions, and Judgments of the Soveraigne Instituted; it followes, that whatsoever he doth, it can be no injury to any of his Subjects; nor ought he to be by any of them accused of Injustice. For he that doth any thing by authority from another, doth therein no injury to him by whose authority he acteth: But by this Institution of a Common-wealth, every particular man is Author of all the Soveraigne doth; and consequently he that complaineth of injury from his Soveraigne, complaineth of that whereof he himselfe is Author; and therefore ought not to accuse any man but himselfe; no nor himselfe of injury; because to do injury to ones selfe, is impossible. It is true that they that have Soveraigne power, may commit Iniquity; but not Injustice, or Injury in the proper signification.

5. What soever the Soveraigne doth, is unpunishable by the Subject.

Fiftly, and consequently to that which was sayd last, no man that hath Soveraigne power can justly be put to death, or otherwise in any manner by his Subjects punished. For seeing every Subject is Author of the actions of his Soveraigne; he punisheth another, for the actions committed by himselfe.

6. The Soveraigne is judge of what is necessary for the Peace and Defence of his Subjects.

And because the End of this Institution, is the Peace and Defence of them all; and whosoever has right to the End, has right to the Means; it belongeth of Right, to whatsoever Man, or Assembly that hath the Soveraignty, to be Judge both of the meanes of Peace and Defence; and also of the hindrances, and disturbances of the same; and to do whatsoever he shall think necessary to be done, both before hand, for the preserving of Peace and Security, by prevention of Discord at home, and Hostility from abroad; and, when Peace and Security are lost, for the recovery of the same. And therefore,

[91]

And Judge of what Doctrines are fit to be taught them.

Sixtly, it is annexed to the Soveraignty, to be Judge of what Opinions and Doctrines are averse, and what conducing to Peace; and consequently, on what occasions, how farre, and what, men are to be trusted withall, in speaking to Multitudes of people; and who shall examine the Doctrines of all bookes before they be published. For the Actions of men proceed from their Opinions; and in the wel governing of Opinions, consisteth the well governing of mens Actions, in order to their Peace, and Concord. And though in matter of Doctrine, nothing ought to be regarded but the Truth; yet this is not repugnant to regulating of the same by Peace. For Doctrine repugnant to Peace, can no more be True, than Peace and Concord can be against the Law of Nature. It is true, that in a Common-wealth, where by the negligence, or unskilfullnesse of Governours, and Teachers, false Doctrines are by time generally received; the contrary Truths may be generally offensive: Yet the most sudden, and rough busling in of a new Truth, that can be, does never breake the Peace, but only somtimes awake the Warre. For those men that are so remissely governed, that they dare take up Armes, to defend, or introduce an Opinion, are still in Warre; and their condition not Peace, but only a Cessation of Armes for feare of one another; and they live as it were, in the procincts of battaile continually. It belongeth therefore to him that hath the Soveraign Power, to be Judge, or constitute all Judges of Opinions and Doctrines, as a thing necessary to Peace; therby to prevent Discord and Civill Warre.

Seventhly, is annexed to the Soveraigntie, the whole power of prescribing the Rules, whereby every man may know, what Goods he may enjoy, and what Actions he may doe, without being molested by any of his fellow Subjects: And this is it men call *Propriety*. For before constitution of Soveraign Power (as hath already been shewn) all men had right to all things; which necessarily causeth Warre: and therefore this Proprietie, being necessary to Peace, and depending on Soveraign Power, is the Act of that Power, in order to the publique peace. These Rules of Propriety (or *Meum* and *Tuum*) and of *Good*, *Evill*, *Lawfull*, and *Unlawfull* in the actions of Subjects, are the Civill Lawes; that is to say, the Lawes of each Common-wealth in particular; though the name of Civill Law be now restrained to the antient Civill Lawes of the City of *Rome*; which being the head of a great part of the World, her Lawes at that time were in these parts the Civill Law.

7. The Right of making Rules, whereby the Subjects may every man know what is so his owne, as no other Subject can without injustice take it from him.

Eightly, is annexed to the Soveraigntie, the Right of Judicature; that is to say, of hearing and deciding all Controversies, which may arise concerning Law, either Civill, or Naturall, or concerning Fact. For without the decision of Controversies, there is no protection of one Subject, against the injuries of another; the Lawes concerning *Meum* and *Tuum* are in vaine; and to every man remaineth, from the naturall and necessary appetite of his own conservation, the right of protecting himselfe by his private strength, which is the condition of Warre; and contrary to the end for which every Common-wealth is instituted.

8. To him also belongeth the Right of all Judicature and decision of Controversie:

[92]

125

9. And of making War, and Peace, as he shall think best:

Ninthly, is annexed to the Soveraignty, the Right of making Warre, and Peace with other Nations, and Common-wealths; that is to say, of Judging when it is for the publique good, and how great forces are to be assembled, armed, and payd for that end; and to levy mony upon the Subjects, to defray the expences thereof. For the Power by which the people are to be defended, consisteth in their Armies; and the strength of an Army, in the union of their strength under one Command; which Command the Soveraign Instituted, therefore hath; because the command of the *Militia*, without other Institution, maketh him that hath it Soveraign. And therefore whosoever is made Generall of an Army, he that hath the Soveraign Power is alwayes Generallissimo.

10. And of choosing all Counsellours, and Ministers, both of Peace, and Warre:

Tenthly, is annexed to the Soveraignty, the choosing of all Counsellours, Ministers, Magistrates, and Officers, both in Peace, and War. For seeing the Soveraign is charged with the End, which is the common Peace and Defence; he is understood to have Power to use such Means, as he shall think most fit for his discharge.

11. And of Rewarding, Punishing, and that (where no former Law hath determined the measure of it) arbitrary:

Eleventhly, to the Soveraign is committed the Power of Rewarding with riches, or honour; and of Punishing with corporall, or pecuniary punishment, or with ignominy every Subject according to the Law he hath formerly made; or if there be no Law made, according as he shall judge most to conduce to the encouraging of men to serve the Common-wealth, or deterring of them from doing dis-service to the same.

12. And of Honour and Order.

Lastly, considering what values men are naturally apt to set upon themselves; what respect they look for from others; and how little they value other men; from whence continually arise amongst them, Emulation, Quarrells, Factions, and at last Warre, to the destroying of one another, and diminution of their strength against a Common Enemy; It is necessary that there be Lawes of Honour, and a publique rate of the worth of such men as have deserved, or are able to deserve well of the Common-wealth; and that there be force in the hands of some or other, to put those Lawes in execution. But it hath already been shewn, that not onely the whole *Militia*, or forces of the Common-wealth; but also the Judicature of all Controversies, is annexed to the Soveraignty. To the Soveraign therefore it belongeth also to give titles of Honour; and to appoint what Order of place, and dignity, each man shall hold; and what signes of respect, in publique or private meetings, they shall give to one another.

These are the Rights, which make the Essence of Soveraignty; and which are the markes, whereby a man may discern in what Man, or Assembly of men, the Soveraign Power is placed, and resideth. For these are incommunicable, and inseparable. The Power to coyn Mony; to dispose of the estate and persons of Infant heires; to have praeemption in Markets; and all other Statute Praerogatives, may be transferred by the Soveraign; and yet the Power to protect his Subjects be retained. But if he transferre the *Militia*, he retains the Judicature in vain, for want of execution of the Lawes: Or if he grant away the Power of raising Mony; the *Militia* is in vain: or if he give away the government of Doctrines, men will be frighted into rebellion with the feare of Spirits. And so if we consider any one of the said Rights, we shall presently see, that the holding of all the rest, will produce no effect, in the conservation of Peace and Justice, the end for which all Common-wealths are Instituted. And this division is it, whereof it is said, *a Kingdome divided in it selfe cannot stand*: For unless this division precede, division into opposite Armies can never happen. If there had not first been an opinion received of the greatest part of *England*, that these Powers were divided between the King, and the Lords, and the House of Commons, the people had never been divided, and fallen into this Civill Warre; first between *those that disagreed in Politiques; and after between the Dissenters about the liberty of Religion*[1]; which have so instructed men in this point of Soveraign Right, that there be few now (in *England*,) that do not see, that these Rights are inseparable, and will be so generally acknowledged, at the next return of Peace; and so continue, till their miseries are forgotten; and no longer, except the vulgar be better taught than they have hetherto been.

These Rights are indivisible.

[93]

And because they are essentiall and inseparable Rights, it follows necessarily, that in whatsoever words any of them seem to be granted away, yet if the Soveraign Power it selfe be not in direct termes renounced, and the name of Soveraign no more given by the Grantees to him that Grants them, the Grant is voyd: for when he has granted all he can, if we grant back the Soveraignty, all is restored, as inseparably annexed thereunto.

And can by no Grant passe away without direct renouncing of the Soveraign Power.

[1] Scribal MS reads: the temporall factions of parlamentarians and royalists, by the name of Roundheads and Cavaliers, and since between the doctrinall factions of presbyterians and Independents

*The Power
and Honour
of Subjects
vanisheth in
the presence
of the Power
Soveraign.*

This great Authority being Indivisible, and inseparably annexed to the Soveraignty, there is little ground for the opinion of them, that say of Soveraign Kings, though they be *singulis majores*, of greater Power than every one of their Subjects, yet they be *Universis minores*, of lesse power than them all together. For if by *all together*, they mean not the collective body as one person, then *all together*, and *every one*, signifie the same; and the speech is absurd. But if by *all together*, they understand them as one Person (which person the Soveraign bears,) then the power of all together, is the same with the Soveraigns power; and so again the speech is absurd: which absurdity they see well enough, when the Soveraignty is in an Assembly of the people; but in a Monarch they see it not; and yet the power of Soveraignty is the same in whomsoever it be placed.

And as the Power, so also the Honour of the Soveraign, ought to be greater, than that of any, or all the Subjects. For in the Soveraignty is the fountain of Honour. The dignities of Lord, Earle, Duke, and Prince are his Creatures. As in the presence of the Master, the Servants are equall, and without any honour at all; So are the Subjects, in the presence of the Soveraign. And though they shine some more, some lesse, when they are out of his sight; yet in his presence, they shine no more than the Starres in presence of the Sun.

[94]
*Soveraigne
Power not so
hurtfull as
the want of
it, and the
hurt proceeds
for the
greatest part
from not
submitting
readily, to a
lesse.*

But a man may here object, that the Condition of Subjects is very miserable; as being obnoxious to the lusts, and other irregular passions of him, or them that have so unlimited a Power in their hands. And commonly they that live under a Monarch, think it the fault of Monarchy; and they that live under the government of Democracy, or other Soveraign Assembly, attribute all the inconvenience to that forme of Common-wealth; whereas the Power in all formes, if they be perfect enough to protect them, is the same; not considering that the estate of Man can never be without some incommodity or other; and that the greatest, that in any forme of Government can possibly happen to the people in generall, is scarce sensible, in respect of the miseries, and horrible calamities, that accompany a Civill Warre; or that dissolute condition of masterlesse men, without subjection to Lawes, and a coërcive Power to tye their hands from rapine, and revenge: nor considering that the greatest pressure of Soveraign Governours, proceedeth not from any delight, or profit they can expect in the dammage, or weakening of their Subjects, in whose vigor, consisteth their own strength and glory; but in the restiveness of them-selves, that unwillingly contributing to their own defence, make it necessary for their Governours to draw from them what they can in time of Peace, that they may have means on any emergent occasion, or sudden need, to resist, or take advantage of their Enemies. For all men are by nature provided of notable multiplying glasses, (that is their Passions and Selfe-love,) through which, every little payment appeareth a great grievance; but are destitute of those prospective glasses, (namely Morall and Civill Science,) to see a farre off the miseries that hang over them, and cannot without such payments be avoyded.

CHAP. XIX.

Of the severall Kinds of COMMON-WEALTH *by Institution, and of Succession to the Soveraigne Power.*

The difference of Common-wealths, consisteth in the difference of the Soveraign, or the Person representative of all and every one of the Multitude. And because the Soveraignty is either in one Man, or in an Assembly of more than one; and into that Assembly either Every man hath right to enter, or not every one, but Certain men distinguished from the rest; it is manifest, there can be but Three kinds of Com-mon-wealth. For the Representative must needs be One man, or More: and if more, then it is the Assembly of All, or but of a Part. When the Representative is One man, then is the Common-wealth a MONARCHY: when an Assembly of All that will come together, then it is a DEMOCRACY, or Popular Common-wealth: when an Assembly of a Part onely, then it is called an ARISTOCRACY. Other kind of Com-mon-wealth there can be none: for either One, or More, or All, must have the Soveraign Power (which I have shewn to be indivisible) entire.

The different Formes of Common-wealths but three.

There be other names of Government, in the Histories, and books [95]

Tyranny and Oligarchy, but different names of Monarchy, and Aristocracy.

of Policy; as *Tyranny*, and *Oligarchy*: But they are not the names of other Formes of Government, but of the same Formes misliked. For they that are discontented under *Monarchy*, call it *Tyranny*; and they that are displeased with *Aristocracy*, called it *Oligarchy*: So also, they which find themselves grieved under a *Democracy*, call it *Anarchy*, (which signifies want of Government;) and yet I think no man believes, that want of Government, is any new kind of Government: nor by the same reason ought they to believe, that the Government is of one kind, when they like it, and another, when they mislike it, or are oppressed by the Governours.

Subordinate Represen-tatives dangerous.

It is manifest, that men who are in absolute liberty, may, if they please, give Authority to One man, to represent them every one; as well as give such Authority to any Assembly of men whatsoever; and consequently may subject themselves, if they think good, to a Monarch, as absolutely, as to any other Representative. Therefore, where there is already erected a Soveraign Power, there can be no other Representative of the same people, but onely to certain particular ends, by the Soveraign limited. For that were to erect two Soveraigns; and every man to have his person represented by two Actors, that by opposing one another, must needs divide that Power, which (if men will live in Peace) is indivisible; and thereby reduce the Multitude into the condition of Warre, contrary to the end for which all Soveraignty is instituted. And therefore as it is absurd, to think that a Soveraign Assembly, inviting the People of their Dominion, to send up their Deputies, with power to make known their Advise, or Desires, should therefore hold such Deputies, rather than themselves, for the absolute Representative of the people: so it is absurd also, to think the same in a Monarchy. And I know not how this so manifest a truth, should of late be so little observed; that in a Monarchy, he that had the Soveraignty from a descent of 600 years, was alone called Soveraign, had the title of Majesty from every one of his Subjects, and was unquestionably taken by them for their King, was notwithstanding never considered as their Representative; that name without contradiction passing for the title of those men, which at his command were sent up by the people to carry their Petitions, and give him (if he permitted it) their advise. Which may serve as an admonition, for those that are the true, and absolute Representative of a People, to instruct men in the nature of that Office, and to take heed how they admit of any other generall Representation upon any occasion whatsoever, if they mean to discharge the trust committed to them.

The difference between these three kindes of Common-wealth, consisteth not in the difference of Power; but in the difference of Convenience, or Aptitude to produce the Peace, and Security of the people; for which end they were instituted. And to compare Monarchy with the other two, we may observe; First, that whosoever beareth the Person of the people, or is one of that Assembly that bears it, beareth also his own naturall Person. And though he be carefull in his politique Person to procure the common interest; yet he is more, or no lesse carefull to procure the private good of himselfe, his family, kindred and friends; and for the most part, if the publique interest chance to crosse the private, he preferrs the private: for the Passions of men, are commonly more potent than their Reason. From whence it follows, that where the publique and private interest are most closely united, there is the publique most advanced. Now in Monarchy, the private interest is the same with the publique. The riches, power, and honour of a Monarch arise onely from the riches, strength and reputation of his Subjects. For no King can be rich, nor glorious, nor secure; whose Subjects are either poore, or contemptible, or too weak through want, or dissention, to maintain a war against their enemies: Whereas in a Democracy, or Aristocracy, the publique prosperity conferres not so much to the private fortune of one that is corrupt, or ambitious, as doth many times a perfidious advice, a treacherous action, or a Civill warre.

Secondly, that a Monarch receiveth counsell of whom, when, and where he pleaseth; and consequently may heare the opinion of men versed in the matter about which he deliberates, of what rank or quality soever, and as long before the time of action, and with as much secrecy, as he will. But when a Soveraigne Assembly has need of Counsell, none are admitted but such as have a Right thereto from the beginning; which for the most part are of those who have beene versed more in the acquisition of Wealth than of Knowledge; and are to give their advice in long discourses, which may, and do commonly excite men to action, but not governe them in it. For the *Understanding* is by the flame of the Passions, never enlightened, but dazled: Nor is there any place, or time, wherein an Assemblie can receive Counsell with secrecie, because of their owne Multitude.

Thirdly, that the Resolutions of a Monarch, are subject to no other

Comparison of Monarchy, with Soveraign Assemblyes.

[96]

Inconstancy, than that of Humane Nature; but in Assemblies, besides that of Nature, there ariseth an Inconstancy from the Number. For the absence of a few, that would have the Resolution once taken, continue firme, (which may happen by security, negligence, or private impediments,) or the diligent appearance of a few of the contrary opinion, undoes to day, all that was concluded yesterday.

Fourthly, that a Monarch cannot disagree with himselfe, out of envy, or interest; but an Assembly may; and that to such a height, as may produce a Civill Warre.

Fifthly, that in Monarchy there is this inconvenience; that any Subject, by the power of one man, for the enriching of a favourite or flatterer, may be deprived of all he possesseth; which I confesse is a great and inevitable inconvenience. But the same may as well happen, where the Soveraigne Power is in an Assembly: For their power is the same; and they are as subject to evill Counsell, and to be seduced by Orators, as a Monarch by Flatterers; and becoming one an others Flatterers, serve one anothers Covetousnesse and Ambition by turnes. And whereas the Favorites of Monarchs, are few, and they have none els to advance but their owne Kindred; the Favorites of an Assembly, are many; and the Kindred much more numerous, than of any Monarch. Besides, there is no Favourite of a Monarch, which cannot as well succour his friends, as hurt his enemies: But Orators, that is to say, Favourites of Soveraigne Assemblies, though they have great power to hurt, have little to save. For to accuse, requires lesse Eloquence (such is mans Nature) than to excuse; and condemnation, than absolution more resembles Justice.

Sixtly, that it is an inconvenience in Monarchie, that the Soveraigntie may descend upon an Infant, or one that cannot discerne between Good and Evill: and consisteth in this, that the use of his Power, must be in the hand of another Man, or of some Assembly of men, which are to governe by his right, and in his name; as Curators, and Protectors of his Person, and Authority. But to say there is inconvenience, in putting the use of the Soveraign Power, into the hand of a Man, or an Assembly of men; is to say that all Government is more Inconvenient, than Confusion, and Civill Warre. And therefore all the danger that can be pretended, must arise from the Contention of those, that for an office of so great honour, and profit, may become Competitors. To make it appear, that this inconvenience, proceedeth not from that forme of Government we call Monarchy, we are to consider, that the precedent Monarch, hath appointed who shall have the Tuition of his Infant Successor, either expressely by Testament, or tacitly, by not controlling the Custome in that case received: And then such inconvenience (if it happen) is to be attributed, not to the Monarchy, but to the Ambition, and Injustice of the Subjects; which in all kinds of Government, where the people are not well instructed in their Duty, and the Rights of Soveraignty, is the same. Or else the precedent Monarch, hath not at all taken order for such Tuition; And then the Law of Nature hath provided this sufficient rule, That the Tuition shall be in him, that hath by Nature most interest in the preservation of the Authority of the Infant, and to whom least benefit can accrue by his death, or diminution. For seeing every man by nature seeketh his own benefit, and promotion; to put an Infant into the power of those, that can promote themselves by his destruction, or dammage, is not Tuition, but Trechery. So that sufficient provision being taken, against all just quarrell, about the Government under a Child, if any contention arise to the disturbance of the publique Peace, it is not to be attributed to the forme of Monarchy, but to the ambition of Subjects, and ignorance of their Duty. On the other side, there is no great Common-wealth, the Soveraignty whereof is in a great Assembly, which is not, as to consultations of Peace, and Warre, and making of Lawes, in the same condition, as if the Government were in a Child. For as a Child wants the judgement to dissent from counsell given him, and is thereby necessitated to take the advice of them, or him, to whom he is committed: So an Assembly wanteth the liberty, to dissent from the counsell of the major part, be it good, or bad. And as a Child has need of a Tutor, or Protector, to preserve his Person, and Authority: So also (in great Common-wealths,) the Soveraign Assembly, in all great dangers and troubles, have need of *Custodes libertatis*; that is of Dictators, or Protectors of their Authoritie; which are as much as Temporary Monarchs; to whom for a time, they may commit the entire exercise of their Power; and have (at the end of that time) been oftner deprived thereof, than Infant Kings, by their Protectors, Regents, or any other Tutors. [98]

Though the Kinds of Soveraigntie be, as I have now shewn, but three; that is to say, Monarchie, where One Man has it; or Democracie, where the generall Assembly of Subjects hath it; or Aristocracie, where it is in an Assembly of certain persons nominated, or otherwise distinguished from the rest: Yet he that shall consider the particular Common-wealthes that have been, and are in the world, will not perhaps easily reduce them to three, and may thereby be inclined to think there be other Formes, arising from these mingled together. As for example, Elective Kingdomes; where Kings have the Soveraigne Power put into their hands for a time; or Kingdomes, wherein the King hath a power limited: which Governments, are nevertheless by most Writers called Monarchie. Likewise if a Popular, or Aristocraticall Common-wealth, subdue an Enemies Countrie, and govern the same, by a President, Procurator, or other Magistrate; this may seeme perhaps at first sight, to be a Democraticall, or Aristocraticall Government. But it is not so. For Elective Kings, are not Soveraignes, but Ministers of the Soveraigne; not limited Kings, Soveraignes, but Ministers of them that have the Soveraigne Power: Nor are those Provinces which are in subjection to a Democracie, or Aristocracie of another Common-wealth, Democratically, or Aristocratically governed, but Monarchically.

And first, concerning an Elective King, whose power is limited to his life, as it is in many places of Christendome at this day; or to certaine Yeares or Moneths, as the Dictators power amongst the Romans; If he have Right to appoint his Successor, he is no more Elective but Hereditary. But if he have no Power to elect his Successor, then there is some other Man, or Assembly known, which after his decease may elect a new, or else the Common-wealth dieth, and dissolveth with him, and returneth to the condition of Warre. If it be known who have the power to give the Soveraigntie after his death, it is known also that the Soveraigntie was in them before: For none have right to give that which they have not right to possesse, and keep to themselves, if they think good. But if there be none that can give the Soveraigntie, after the decease of him that was first elected; then has he power, nay he is obliged by the Law of Nature, to provide, by establishing his Successor, to keep those that had trusted him with the Government, from relapsing into the miserable condition of Civill warre. And consequently he was, when elected, a Soveraign absolute.

Secondly, that King whose power is limited, is not superiour to him, or them that have the power to limit it; and he that is not superiour, is not supreme; that is to say not Soveraign. The Soveraignty therefore was alwaies in that Assembly which had the Right to Limit him; and by consequence the government not

[99]

134

Monarchy, but either Democracy, or Aristocracy; as of old time in *Sparta*; where the Kings had a priviledge to lead their Armies; but the Soveraignty was in the *Ephori*.

Thirdly, whereas heretofore the Roman People, governed the land of *Judea* (for example) by a President; yet was not *Judea* therefore a Democracy; because they were not governed by any Assembly, into the which, any of them, had right to enter; nor by an Aristocracy; because they were not governed by any Assembly, into which, any man could enter by their Election: but they were governed by one Person, which though as to the people of *Rome* was an Assembly of the people, or Democracy; yet as to people of *Judea*, which had no right at all of participating in the government, was a Monarch. For though where the people are governed by an Assembly, chosen by themselves out of their own number, the government is called a Democracy, or Aristocracy; yet when they are governed by an Assembly, not of their own choosing, 'tis a Monarchy; not of *One* man, over another man; but of one people, over another people.

Of all these Formes of Government, the matter being mortall, so that not onely Monarchs, but also whole Assemblies dy, it is necessary for the conservation of the peace of men, that as there was order taken for an Artificiall Man, so there be order also taken, for an Artificiall Eternity of life; without which, men that are governed by an Assembly, should return into the condition of Warre in every age; and they that are governed by One man, assoon as their Governour dyeth. This Artificiall Eternity, is that which men call the Right of *Succession*. *Of the Right of Succession.*

There is no perfect forme of Government, where the disposing of the Succession is not in the present Soveraign. For if it be in any other particular Man, or private Assembly, it is in a person subject, and may be assumed by the Soveraign at his pleasure; and consequently the Right is in himselfe. And if it be in no particular man, but left to a new choyce; then is the Common-wealth dissolved; and the Right is in him that can get it; contrary to the intention of them that did Institute the Common-wealth, for their perpetuall, and not temporary security.

In a Democracy, the whole Assembly cannot faile, unlesse the Multitude that are to be governed faile. And therefore questions of the right of Succession, have in that forme of Government no place at all.

In an Aristocracy, when any of the Assembly dyeth, the election of

The present Monarch hath Right to dispose of the Succession.

another into his room belongeth to the Assembly, as the Soveraign, to whom belongeth the choosing of all Counsellours, and Officers. For that which the Representative doth, as Actor, every one of the Subjects doth, as Author. And though the Soveraign Assembly, may give Power to others, to elect new men, for supply of their Court; yet it is still by their Authority, that the Election is made; and by the same it may (when the publique shall require it) be recalled.

[100]

The greatest difficultie about the right of Succession, is in Monarchy: And the difficulty ariseth from this, that at first sight, it is not manifest who is to appoint the Successor; nor many times, who it is whom he hath appointed. For in both these cases, there is required a more exact ratiocination, than every man is accustomed to use. As to the question, who shall appoint the Successor, of a Monarch that hath the Soveraign Authority; that is to say, who shall determine of the right of Inheritance, (for Elective Kings and Princes have not the Soveraign Power in propriety, but in use only,) we are to consider, that either he that is in possession, has right to dispose of the Succession, or else that right is again in the dissolved Multitude. For the death of him that hath the Soveraign power in propriety, leaves the Multitude without any Soveraign at all; that is, without any Representative in whom they should be united, and be capable of doing any one action at all: And therefore they are incapable of Election of any new Monarch; every man having equall right to submit himselfe to such as he thinks best able to protect him; or if he can, protect himselfe by his owne sword; which is a returne to Confusion, and to the condition of a War of every man against every man, contrary to the end for which Monarchy had its first Institution. Therefore it is manifest, that by the Institution of Monarchy, the disposing of the Successor, is alwaies left to the Judgment and Will of the present Possessor.

And for the question (which may arise sometimes) who it is that the Monarch in possession, hath designed to the succession and inheritance of his power; it is determined by his expresse Words, and Testament; or by other tacite signes sufficient.

Succession passeth by expresse Words;

By expresse Words, or Testament, which it is declared by him in his life time, *viva voce,* or by Writing; as the first Emperours of *Rome* declared who should be their Heires. For the word Heire does not of it selfe imply the Children, or nearest Kindred of a man; but whomsoever a man shall any way declare, he would have to succeed him in his Estate. If therefore a Monarch declare expresly, that such a man shall be his Heire, either by Word or Writing, then is that man immediately after the decease of his Predecessor, Invested in the right of being Monarch.

But where Testament, and expresse Words are wanting, other naturall signes of the Will are to be allowed: whereof the one is Custome. And therefore where the Custome is, that the next of Kindred absolutely succeedeth, there also the next of Kindred hath right to the Succession; for that, if the will of him that was in posession had been otherwise, he might easily have declared the same in his life time. And likewise where the Custome is, that the next of the Male Kindred succeedeth, there also the right of Succession is in the next of the Kindred Male, for the same reason. And so it is if the Custome were to advance the Female. For whatsoever Custome a man may by a word controule, and does not, it is a naturall signe he would have that Custome stand. *Or, by not controlling a Custome;*

But where neither Custome, nor Testament hath preceded, there it is to be understood, First, that a Monarchs will is, that the government remain Monarchicall; because he hath approved that government in himselfe. Secondly, that a Child of his own, Male, or Female, be preferred before any other; because men are presumed to be more enclined by nature, to advance their own children, than the children of other men; and of their own, rather a Male than a Female; because men, are naturally fitter than women, for actions of labour and danger. Thirdly, where his own Issue faileth, rather a Brother than a stranger; and so still the neerer in bloud, rather than the more remote; because it is always presumed that the neerer of kin, is the neerer in affection; and 'tis evident that a man receives alwayes, by reflexion, the most honour from the greatnesse of his neerest kindred. [101] *Or, by presumption of naturall affection.*

But if it be lawfull for a Monarch to dispose of the Succession by words of Contract, or Testament, men may perhaps object a great inconvenience: for he may sell, or give his Right of governing to a stranger; which, because strangers (that is, men not used to live under the same government, nor speaking the same language) do commonly undervalue one another, may turn to the oppression of his Subjects; which is indeed a great inconvenience: but it proceedeth not necessarily from the subjection to a strangers government, but from the unskilfulnesse of the Governours, ignorant of the true rules of Politiques. And therefore the Romans when they had subdued many Nations, to make their Government digestible, were wont to take *To dispose of the Succession, though to a King of another Nation, not unlawfull.*

away that grievance, as much as they thought necessary, by giving sometimes to whole Nations, and sometimes to Principall men of every Nation they conquered, not onely the Privileges, but also the Name of Romans; and took many of them into the Senate, and Offices of charge, *in*[1] the Roman City. And this was it our most wise *King*[2] *James*, aymed at, in endeavouring the Union of his two Realms of *England* and *Scotland*. Which if he could have obtained, had in all likelihood prevented the Civill warres, which make both those Kingdomes, at this present, miserable. It is not therefore any injury to the people, for a Monarch to dispose of the Succession by Will; though by the fault of many Princes, it hath been sometimes found inconvenient. Of the lawfulnesse of it, this also is an argument, that whatsoever inconvenience can arrive by giving a Kingdome to a stranger, may arrive also by so marrying with strangers, as the Right of Succession may descend upon them: yet this by all men is accounted lawfull.

CHAP. XX.
Of Dominion PATERNALL, *and* DESPOTICALL.

A Common-wealth by Acquisition.

[102]

A *Common-wealth by Acquisition*, is that, where the Soveraign Power is acquired by Force; And it is acquired by force, when men singly, or many together by plurality of voyces, for fear of death, or bonds, do authorise all the actions of that Man, or Assembly, that hath their lives and liberty in his Power.

Wherein different from a Common-wealth by Institution.

And this kind of Dominion, or Soveraignty, differeth from Soveraignty by Institution, onely in this, That men who choose their Soveraign, do it for fear of one another, and not of him whom they Institute: But in this case, they subject themselves, to him they are afraid of. In both cases they do it for fear: which is to be noted by them, that hold all such Covenants, as proceed from fear of death, or violence, voyd: which if it were true, no man, in any kind of Common-

---

[1] *Syn.*: even in   [2] *Syn.*: King, King

wealth, could be obliged to Obedience. It is true, that in a Common-wealth once Instituted, or acquired, Promises proceeding from fear of death, or violence, are no Covenants, nor obliging, when the thing promised is contrary to the Lawes; But the reason is not, because it was made upon fear, but because he that promiseth, hath no right in the thing promised. Also, when he may lawfully performe, and doth not, it is not the Invalidity of the Covenant, that absolveth him, but the Sentence of the Soveraign. Otherwise, whensoever a man lawfully promiseth, he unlawfully breaketh: But when the Soveraign, who is the Actor, acquitteth him, then he is acquitted by him that extorted the promise, as by the Author of such absolution.

But the Rights, and Consequences of Soveraignty, are the same in both. His Power cannot, without his consent, be Transferred to another: He cannot Forfeit it: He cannot be Accused by any of his Subjects, of Injury: He cannot be Punished by them: He is Judge of what is necessary for Peace; and Judge of Doctrines: He is Sole Legislator; and Supreme Judge of Controversies; and of the Times, and Occasions of Warre and Peace: to him it belongeth to choose Magistrates, Counsellours, Commanders, and all other Officers, and Ministers; and to determine of Rewards, and Punishments, Honour, and Order. The reasons whereof, are the same which are alledged in the precedent Chapter, for the same Rights, and Consequences of Soveraignty by Institution. *The Rights of Soveraignty the same in both.*

Dominion is acquired two wayes; By Generation, and by Conquest. The right of Dominion by Generation, is that, which the Parent hath over his Children; and is called PATERNALL. And is not so derived from the Generation, as if therefore the Parent had Dominion over his Child because he begat him; but from the Childs Consent, either expresse, or by other sufficient arguments declared. For as to the Generation, God hath ordained to man a helper; and there be alwayes two that are equally Parents: the Dominion therefore over the Child, should belong equally to both; and he be equally subject to both, which is impossible; for no man can obey two Masters. And whereas some have attributed the Dominion to the Man onely, as being of the more excellent Sex; they misreckon in it. For there is not alwayes that difference of strength, or prudence between the man and the woman, as that the right can be determined without War. In Common-wealths, this controversie is decided by the Civill Law: and for the most part, (but not alwayes) the sentence is in favour of the Father; *Dominion Paternall how attained. Not by Generation, but by Contract;*

because for the most part Common-wealths have been erected by the
Fathers, not by the Mothers of families. But the question lyeth now in
the state of meer Nature; where there are supposed no lawes of
Matrimony; no lawes for the Education of Children; but the Law of
Nature, and the naturall inclination of the Sexes one to another, and
to their children. In this condition of meer Nature, either the Parents
between themselves dispose of the dominion over the Child by Contract; or do not dispose thereof at all. If they dispose thereof, the right
passeth according to the Contract. We find in History that the
Amazons Contracted with the Men of the neighbouring Countries, to
whom they had recourse for issue, that the issue Male should be sent
back, but the Female remain with themselves: so that the dominion of
the Females was in the Mother.

Or Education;

If there be no Contract, the Dominion is in the Mother. For in the
condition of meer Nature, where there are no Matrimoniall lawes, it
cannot be known who is the Father, unlesse it be declared by the
Mother: and therefore the right of Dominion over the Child
dependeth on her will, and is consequently hers. Again, seeing the
Infant is first in the power of the Mother, so as she may either
nourish, or expose it; if she nourish it, it oweth its life to the Mother;
and is therefore obliged to obey her, rather than any other; and by
consequence the Dominion over it is hers. But if she expose it, and
another find, and nourish it, the Dominion is in him that nourisheth
it. For it ought to obey him by whom it is preserved; because
preservation of life being the end, for which one man becomes subject
to another, every man is supposed to promise obedience, to him, in
whose power it is to save, or destroy him.

Or Preced[ent] subjection one of the Parents to the other.

If the Mother be the Fathers subject, the Child, is in the Fathers
power: and if the Father be the Mothers subject, (as when a
Soveraign Queen marrieth one of her subjects,) the Child is subject to
the Mother; because the Father also is her subject.

If a man and a woman, Monarches of two severall Kingdomes, have
a Child, and contract concerning who shall have the Dominion of
him, the Right of the Dominion passeth by the Contract. If they
contract not, the Dominion followeth the Dominion of the place of his
residence. For the Soveraign of each Country hath Dominion over all
that reside therein.

He that hath the Dominion over the Child, hath Dominion also
over the Children of the Child; and over their Childrens Children.

For he that hath Dominion over the person of a man, hath Dominion over all that is his; without which, Dominion were but a Title, without the effect.

The Right of Succession to Paternall Dominion, proceedeth in the same manner, as doth the Right of Succession to Monarchy; of which I have already sufficiently spoken in the precedent chapter. *The Right of Succession followeth the Rules of the Right of Possession.*

Dominion acquired by Conquest, or Victory in war, is that which some Writers call D E S P O T I C A L L, from *Δεσπότης*, which signifieth a Lord, or *Master*; and is the Dominion of the Master over his Servant. And this Dominion is then acquired to the Victor, when the Vanquished, to avoyd the present stroke of death, covenanteth either in expresse words, or by other sufficient signes of the Will, that so long as his life, and the liberty of his body is allowed him, the Victor shall have the use thereof, at his pleasure. And after such Covenant made, the Vanquished is a S E R V A N T, and not before: for by the word *Servant* (whether it be derived from *Servire*, to Serve, or from *Servare*, to Save, which I leave to Grammarians to dispute) is not meant a Captive, which is kept in prison, or bonds, till the owner of him that took him, or bought him of one that did, shall consider what to do with him: (for such men, (commonly called Slaves,) have no obligation at all; but may break their bonds, or the prison; and kill, or carry away captive their Master, justly:) but one, that being taken, hath corporall liberty allowed him; and upon promise not to run away, nor to do violence to his Master, is trusted by him. *Despoticall Dominion how attained.* [104]

It is not therefore the Victory, that giveth the right of Dominion over the Vanquished, but his own Covenant. Nor is he obliged because he is Conquered; that is to say, beaten, and taken, or put to flight; but because he commeth in, and Submitteth to the Victor; Nor is the Victor obliged by an enemies rendring himselfe, (without promise of life,) to spare him for this his yeelding to discretion; which obliges not the Victor longer, than in his own discretion hee shall think fit. *Not by the Victory, but by the Consent of the Vanquished.*

And that which men do, when they demand (as it is now called) *Quarter*, (which the Greeks called *Ζωγρία, taking alive*,) is to evade the present fury of the Victor, by Submission, and to compound for their life, with Ransome, or Service: and therefore he that hath Quarter, hath not his life given, but deferred till farther deliberation; For it is not an yeelding on condition of life, but to discretion. And then onely is his life in security, and his service due, when the Victor

141

hath trusted him with his corporall liberty. For Slaves that work in Prisons, or Fetters, do it not of duty, but to avoyd the cruelty of their task-masters.

The Master of the Servant, is Master also of all he hath; and may exact the use thereof; that is to say, of his goods, of his labour, of his servants, and of his children, as often as he shall think fit. For he holdeth his life of his Master, by the convenant of obedience; that is, of owning, and authorising whatsoever the Master shall do. And in case the Master, if he refuse, kill him, or cast him into bonds, or otherwise punish him for his disobedience, he is himselfe the author of the same; and cannot accuse him of injury.

In summe, the Rights and Consequences of both *Paternall* and *Despoticall* Dominion, are the very same with those of a Soveraign by Institution; and for the same reasons: which reasons are set down in the precedent chapter. So that for a man that is Monarch of divers Nations, whereof he hath, in one the Soveraignty by Institution of the people assembled, and in another by Conquest, that is by the Submission of each particular, to avoyd death or bonds; to demand of one Nation more than of the other, from the title of Conquest, *or as*[1] being a Conquered Nation, is an act of ignorance of the Rights of Soveraignty. For the Soveraign is absolute over both alike; or else there is no Soveraignty at all; and so every man may Lawfully protect himselfe, if he can, with his own sword, which is the condition of war.

Difference between a Family and a Kingdom.

By this it appears, that a great Family if it be not part of some Common-wealth, is of it self, as to the Rights of Soveraignty, a little Monarchy; whether that Family consist of a man and his children; or of a man and his servants; or of a man, and his children, and servants together: wherein the Father or Master is the Soveraign. But yet a Family is not properly a Common-wealth; unlesse it be of that power by its own number, or by other opportunities, as not to be subdued without the hazard of war. For where a number of men are manifestly too weak to defend themselves united, every one may use his own reason in time of danger, to save his own life, either by flight, or by submission to the enemy, as hee shall think best; in the same manner as a very small company of souldiers, surprised by an army, may cast down their armes, and demand quarter, or run away, rather than be put to the sword. And thus much shall suffice; concerning what I find by speculation, and deduction, of Soveraign Rights, from the nature,

[105]

---

[1] *Syn.*: as

need, and designes of men, in erecting of Common-wealths, and putting themselves under Monarchs, or Assemblies, entrusted with power enough for their protection.

Let us now consider what the Scripture teacheth in the same point. To *Moses*, the children of *Israel* say thus. ★ *Speak thou to us, and we will heare thee; but let not God speak to us, lest we dye.* ★ This is absolute obedience to *Moses*. Concerning the Right of Kings, God himself by the mouth of *Samuel*, saith, ★ *This shall be the Right of the King you will have to reigne over you. He shall take your sons, and set them to drive his Chariots, and to be his horsemen, and to run before his chariots; and gather in his harvest; and to make his engines of War, and Instruments of his chariots; and shall take your daughters to make perfumes, to be his Cookes, and Bakers. He shall take your fields, your vine-yards, and your olive-yards, and give them to his servants. He shall take the tyth of your corne and wine, and give it to the men of his chamber, and to his other servants. He shall take your man-servants, and your maid-servants, and the choice of your youth, and employ them in his businesse. He shall take the tyth of your flocks; and you shall be his servants.* This is absolute power, and summed up in the last words, *you shall be his servants.* Againe, when the people heard what power their King was to have, yet they consented thereto, and say thus, ★ *We will be as all other nations, and our King shall judge our causes, and goe before us, to conduct our wars.* Here is confirmed the Right that Soveraigns have, both to the *Militia*, and to all *Judicature*; in which is conteined as absolute power, as one man can possibly transferre to another. Again, the prayer of King *Salomon* to God, was this. ★ *Give to thy servant understanding, to judge thy people, and to discerne between Good and Evill.* It belongeth therefore to the Soveraigne to bee *Judge*, and to praescribe the Rules of *discerning Good and Evill*: which Rules are Lawes; and therefore in him is the Legislative Power. *Saul* sought the life of *David*; yet when it was in his power to slay *Saul*, and his Servants would have done it, *David* forbad them saying, ★ *God forbid I should do such an act against my Lord, the annoynted of God.* For obedience of servants St. *Paul* saith, ★ *Servants obey your masters in All things*; and, ★ *Children obey your Parents in All things.* There is simple obedience in those that are subject to Paternall, or Despoticall Dominion. Again, ★ *The Scribes and Pharisees sit in Moses chayre, and therefore All that they shall bid you observe, that observe and do.* There again is simple obedience. And St *Paul*, ★ *Warn them that they subject themselves to Princes, and to those that are in Authority, & obey them.* This obedience is also simple. Lastly, our

The Rights of Monarchy from Scripture.
★ *Exod.* 20.19.
★ 1 *Sam.* 8.11, 12, &c.

★ *Verse.* 19, &c.

★ 1 *Kings* 3.9.
[106]

★ 1 *Sam.* 24.9.
★ *Coll.* 3.20.
★ *Verse* 22.

★ *Math.* 23.2, 3.

★ *Tit.*3.2.

Saviour himselfe acknowledges, that men ought to pay such taxes as are by Kings imposed, where he sayes, *Give to Caesar that which is Caesars*; and payed such taxes himselfe. And that the Kings word, is sufficient to take any thing from any Subject, when there is need; and that the King is Judge of that need: For he himselfe, as King of the Jewes, commanded his Disciples to take the Asse, and Asses Colt to carry him into *Jerusalem*, saying ★ *Go into the Village over against you, and you shall find a shee Asse tyed, and her Colt with her, unty them, and bring them to me. And if any man ask you, what you mean by it, Say the Lord hath need of them: And they will let them go.* They will not ask whether his necessity be a sufficient title; nor whether he be judge of that necessity; but acquiesce in the will of the Lord.

To these places may be added also that of *Genesis*, ★ *You shall be as Gods*, knowing Good and Evill. And verse 11. *Who told thee that thou wast naked? hast thou eaten of the tree, of which I commanded thee thou shouldest not eat?* For the Cognisance or Judicature of *Good* and *Evill*, being forbidden by the name of the fruit of the tree of Knowledge, as a triall of *Adams* obedience; The Divel to enflame the Ambition of the woman, to whom that fruit already seemed beautifull, told her that by tasting it, they should be as Gods, knowing *Good* and *Evill*. Whereupon having both eaten, they did indeed take upon them Gods office, which is Judicature of Good and Evill; but acquired no new ability to distinguish between them aright. And whereas it is sayd, that having eaten, they saw they were naked; no man hath so interpreted that place, as if they had been formerly blind, and saw not their own skins: the meaning is plain, that it was then they first judged their nakednesse (wherein it was Gods will to create them) to be uncomely; and by being ashamed, did tacitely censure God himselfe. And thereupon God saith, *Hast thou eaten, &c.* as if he should say, doest thou that owest me obedience, take upon thee to judge of my Commandements? Whereby it is cleerly, (though Allegorically,) signified, that the Commands of them that have the right to command, are not by their Subjects to be censured, nor disputed.

So that it appeareth plainly, to my understanding, both from Reason, and Scripture, that the Soveraign Power, whether placed in One Man, as in Monarchy, or in one Assembly of men, as in Popular, and Aristocraticall Common-wealths, is as great, as possibly men can be imagined to make it. And though of so unlimited a Power, men may fancy many evill consequences, yet the consequences of the want of it, which is perpetuall warre of every man against his neighbour, are *wealths to be* much worse. The condition of man in this life shall never be without *absolute.* Inconveniences; but there happeneth in no Common-wealth any great Inconvenience, but what proceeds from the Subjects disobedience, and breach of those Covenants, from which the Commonwealth hath its being. And whosoever thinking Soveraign Power too great, will seek to make it lesse; must subject himselfe, to the Power, that can limit it; that is to say, to a greater.

The greatest objection is, that of the Practise; when men ask, where, and when, such Power has by Subjects been acknowledged. But one may ask them again, when, or where has there been a Kingdome long free from Sedition and Civill Warre. In those Nations, whose Common-wealths have been long-lived, and not been destroyed, but by forraign warre, the Subjects never did dispute of the Soveraign Power. But howsoever, an argument from the Practise of men, that have not sifted to the bottom, and with exact reason weighed the causes, and nature of Common-wealths, and suffer daily those miseries, that proceed from the ignorance thereof, is invalid. For though in all places of the world, men should lay the foundation of their houses on the sand, it could not thence be inferred, that so it ought to be. The skill of making, and maintaining Common-wealths, consisteth in certain Rules, as doth Arithmetique and Geometry; not (as Tennis-play) on Practise onely: which Rules, neither poor men have the leisure, nor men that have had the leisure, have hitherto had the curiosity, or the method to find out.

CHAP. XXI.
Of the LIBERTY of Subjects.

LIBERTY, or FREEDOME, signifieth (properly) the absence of *Liberty what.* Opposition; (by Opposition, I mean externall Impediments of motion;) and may be applyed no lesse to Irrationall, and Inanimate creatures, than to Rationall. For whatsoever is so tyed, or environed, as it cannot move, but within a certain space, which space is determined by the opposition of some externall body, we say it hath not Liberty to go further. And so of all living creatures, whilest they are imprisoned, or restrained, with walls, or chayns; and of the water whilest it is kept in by banks, or vessels, that otherwise would spread it selfe into a larger space, we use to say, they are not at Liberty, to move in such manner, as without those externall impediments they would. But when the impediment of motion, is the constitution of the thing it selfe, we use not to say, it wants the Liberty; but the Power to move; as when a stone lyeth still, or a man is fastned to his bed by sicknesse.

[108]

What it is to be Free.

And according to this proper, and generally received meaning of the word, *A* F R E E - M A N, *is he, that in those things, which by his strength and wit he is able to do, is not hindred to doe what he has a will to.* But when the words *Free*, and *Liberty*, are applyed to any thing but *Bodies*, they are abused; for that which is not subject to Motion, is not subject to Impediment: And therefore, when 'tis said (for example) The way is *Free*, no Liberty of the way is signified, but of those that walk in it without stop. And when we say a *Guift* is *Free*, there is not meant any Liberty of the *Guift*, but of the Giver, that was not bound by any law, or Covenant to give it. So when we *speak Freely*, it is not the Liberty of voice, or pronunciation, but of the man, whom no law hath obliged to speak otherwise than he did. Lastly, from the use of the word *Free-will*, no Liberty can be inferred of the will, desire, or inclination, but the Liberty of the man; which consisteth in this, that he finds no stop, in doing what he has the will, desire, or inclination to doe.

Feare and Liberty consistent.

Feare, and Liberty are consistent; as when a man throweth his goods into the Sea for *feare* the ship should sink, he doth it never-thelesse very willingly, and may refuse to doe it if he will: It is therefore the action, of one that was *free*: so a man sometimes pays his debt, only for *feare* of Imprisonment, which because no body hindred him from detaining, was the action of a man at *liberty*. And generally all actions which men doe in Common-wealths, for *feare* of the law, are actions, which the doers had *liberty* to omit.

Liberty and Necessity consistent.

Liberty, and *Necessity* are consistent*; as*[1] in the water, that hath not only *liberty*, but a *necessity* of descending by the Channel; so likewise in the Actions which men voluntarily doe: which, because they proceed from their will, proceed from *liberty*; and yet, because every act of mans will, and every desire, and inclination proceedeth from some cause, and that from another cause, in a continuall chaine, (whose first link is in the hand of God the first of all causes,) they proceed

[1] This is a cancel (see my Introduction p. xxx); it replaced: ':As'.

from *necessity*. So that to him that could see the connexion of those causes, the *necessity* of all mens voluntary actions, would appeare manifest. And therefore God, that seeth, and disposeth all things, seeth also that the *liberty* of man in doing what he will, is accompanied with the *necessity* of doing that which God will, & no more, nor lesse. For though men may do many things, which God does not command, nor is therefore Author of them; yet they can have no passion, nor appetite to any thing, of which appetite Gods will is not the cause. And did not his will assure the *necessity* of mans will, and consequently of all that on mans will dependeth, the *liberty* of men would be a contradiction, *and an*[2] impediment to the omnipotence and *liberty* of God. And this shall suffice, (as to the matter in hand) of that naturall *liberty*, which only is properly called *liberty*.

But as men, for the atteyning of peace, and conservation of themselves thereby, have made an Artificiall Man, which we call a Common-wealth; so also have they made Artificiall Chains, called *Civill Lawes*, which they themselves, by mutuall covenants, have fastned at one end, to the lips of that Man, or Assembly, to whom they have given the Soveraigne Power; and at the other end to their own Ears. These Bonds in their own nature but weak, may neverthelesse be made to hold, by the danger, though not by the difficulty of breaking them. *Artificiall Bonds, or Covenants.* [109]

In relation to these Bonds only it is, that I am to speak now, of the *Liberty* of *Subjects*. For seeing there is no Common-wealth in the world, wherein there be Rules enough set down, for the regulating of all the actions, and words of men, (as being a thing impossible:) it followeth necessarily, that in all kinds of actions, by the laws praetermitted, men have the Liberty, of doing what their own reasons shall suggest, for the most profitable to themselves. For if wee take Liberty in the proper sense, for corporall Liberty; that is to say, freedome from chains, and prison, it were very absurd for men to clamor as they doe, for the Liberty they so manifestly enjoy. Againe, if we take Liberty, for an exemption from Lawes, it is no lesse absurd, for men to demand as they doe, that Liberty, by which all other men may be masters of their lives. And yet as absurd as it is, this is it they demand; not knowing that the Lawes are of no power to protect them, without a Sword in the hands of a man, or men, to cause those laws to *Liberty of Subjects consisteth in Liberty from covenants.*

[2] *Syn.*: and

147

be put in execution. The Liberty of a Subject, lyeth therefore only in those things, which in regulating their actions, the Soveraign hath praetermitted: such as is the Liberty to buy, and sell, and otherwise contract with one another; to choose their own aboad, their own diet, their own trade of life, and institute their children as they themselves think fit; & the like.

Liberty of the Subject consistent with the unlimited power of the Soveraign.

Neverthelesse we are not to understand, that by such Liberty, the Soveraign Power of life, and death, is either abolished, or limited. For it has been already shewn, that nothing the Soveraign Representative can doe to a Subject, on what pretence soever, can properly be called Injustice, or Injury; because every Subject is Author of every act the Soveraign doth; so that he never wanteth Right to any thing, otherwise, than as he himself is the Subject of God, and bound thereby to observe the laws of Nature. And therefore it may, and doth often happen in Common-wealths, that a Subject may be put to death, by the command of the Soveraign Power; and yet neither doe the other wrong: As when *Jeptha* caused his daughter to be sacrificed: In which, and the like cases, he that so dieth, had Liberty to doe the action, for which he is neverthelesse, without Injury put to death. And the same holdeth also in a Soveraign Prince, that putteth to death an Innocent Subject. For though the action be against the law of Nature, as being contrary to Equitie, (as was the killing of *Uriah*, by *David*;) yet it was not an Injurie to *Uriah*; but to God. Not to *Uriah*, because the right to doe what he pleased, was given him by *Uriah* himself: And yet to *God*, because *David* was *Gods* Subject; and prohibited all Iniquitie by the law of Nature. Which distinction, *David* himself, when he repented the fact, evidently confirmed, saying, *To thee only have I sinned.* In the same manner, the people of *Athens*, when they banished the most potent of their Common-wealth for ten years, thought they committed no Injustice; and yet they never questioned what crime he had done; but what hurt he would doe: Nay they commanded the banishment of they knew not whom; and every Citizen bringing his Oystershell into the market place, written with the name of him he desired should be banished, without actuall accusing him, sometimes banished an *Aristides*, for his reputation of Justice; And sometimes a scurrilous Jester, as *Hyperbolus*, to make a Jest of it. And yet a man cannot say, the Soveraign People of *Athens* wanted right to banish them; or an *Athenian* the Libertie to Jest, or to be Just.

The Libertie, whereof there is so frequent, and honourable mention, in the Histories, and Philosophy of the Antient Greeks, and
Romans, and in the writings, and discourse of those that from them
have received all their learning in the Politiques, is not the Libertie of
Particular men; but the Libertie of the Common-wealth: which is the
same with that, which every man then should have, if there were no
Civil Laws, nor Common-wealth at all. And the effects of it also be
the same. For as amongst masterlesse men, there is perpetuall war, of
every man against his neighbour; no inheritance, to transmit to the
Son, nor to expect from the Father; no propriety of Goods, or Lands;
no security; but a full and absolute Libertie in every Particular man:
So in States, and Common-wealths not dependent on one another,
every Common-wealth, (not every man) has an absolute Libertie, to
doe what it shall judge (that is to say, what that Man, or Assemblie
that representeth it, shall judge) most conducing to their benefit. But
withall, they live in the condition of a perpetuall war, and upon the
confines of battel, with their frontiers armed, and canons planted
against their neighbours round about. The *Athenians*, and *Romanes*
were free; that is, free Common-wealths: not that any particular man
had the Libertie to resist their own Representative; but that their
Representative had the Libertie to resist, or invade other people.
There is written on the Turrets of the city of *Luca* in great characters
at this day, the word *LIBERTAS*; yet no man can thence inferre,
that a particular man has more Libertie, or Immunitie from the
service of the Commonwealth there, than in *Constantinople*. Whether
a Common-wealth be Monarchicall, or Popular, the Freedome is still
the same.

But it is an easy thing, for men to be deceived, by the specious
name of Libertie; and for want of Judgement to distinguish, mistake
that for their Private Inheritance, and Birth right, which is the right of
the Publique only. And when the same errour is confirmed by the
authority of men in reputation for their writings in this subject, it is no
wonder if it produce sedition, and change of Government. In these
westerne parts of the world, we are made to receive our opinions
concerning the Institution, and Rights of Common-wealths, from
Aristotle, *Cicero*, and other men, Greeks and Romanes, that living
under Popular States, derived those Rights, not from the Principles of
Nature, but transcribed them into their books, out of the Practise of

*The Liberty
which writers
praise, is the
Liberty of
Soveraigns;
not of
Private men.*

[111]   their own Common-wealths, which were Popular; as the Grammarians describe the Rules of Language, out of the Practise of the
time; or the Rules of Poetry, out of the Poems of *Homer* and *Virgil*.
And because the Athenians were taught, (to keep them from desire of
changing their Government,) that they were Free-men, and all that
lived under Monarchy were slaves; therefore *Aristotle* puts it down in
his *Politiques*, (*lib.6.cap.2.*) *In democracy*, Liberty *is to be supposed: for 'tis
commonly held, that no man is* Free *in any other Government.* And as
Aristotle; so *Cicero*, and other Writers have grounded their Civill doctrine, on the opinions of the Romans, who were taught to hate
Monarchy, at first, by them that having deposed their Soveraign,
shared amongst them the Soveraignty of *Rome*; and afterwards by
their Successors. And by reading of these Greek, and Latine Authors,
men from their childhood have gotten a habit (under a falseshew of
Liberty,) of favouring tumults, and of licentious controlling the
actions of their Soveraigns; and again of controlling those controllers,
with the effusion of so much blood; as I think I may truly say, there
was never any thing so deerly bought, as these Western parts have
bought the learning of the Greek and Latine tongues.

Liberty of   To come now to the particulars of the true Liberty of a Subject;
Subjects how that is to say, what are the things, which though commanded by the
to be   Soveraign, he may neverthelesse, without Injustice, refuse to do; we
measured. are to consider, what Rights we passe away, when we make a Common-wealth; or (which is all one,) what Liberty we deny our selves, by
owning all the Actions (without exception) of the Man, or Assembly
we make our Soveraign. For in the act of our *Submission*, consisteth
both our *Obligation*, and our *Liberty*; which must therefore be inferred
by arguments taken from thence; there being no Obligation on any
man, which ariseth not from some Act of his own; for all men equally,
are by Nature Free. And because such arguments, must either be
drawn from the expresse words, *I Authorise all his Actions*, or from the
Intention of him that submitteth himselfe to his Power, (which Intention is to be understood by the End for which he so submitteth;) The
Obligation, and Liberty of the Subject, is to be derived, either from
those Words, (or others equivalent;) or else from the End of the
Institution of Soveraignty; namely, the Peace of the Subjects within
themselves, and their Defence against a common Enemy.

Subjects have   First therefore, seeing Soveraignty by Institution, is by Covenant of
Liberty to   every one to every one; and Soveraignty by Acquisition, by Covenants

of the Vanquished to the Victor, or Child to the Parent; It is manifest, *defend their*
that every Subject has Liberty in all those things, the right whereof *own bodies,*
cannot by Covenant be transferred. I have shewn before in the *even against*
14.Chapter, that Covenants, not to defend a mans own body, are *them that*
voyd. Therefore, *lawfully*
invade them;

If the Soveraign command a man (though justly condemned,) to *Are not*
kill, wound, or mayme himselfe; or not to resist those that assault him; *bound to*
or to abstain from the use of food, ayre, medicine, or any other thing, *hurt*
without which he cannot live; yet hath that man the Liberty to *themselves;*
disobey. *[112]*

If a man be interrogated by the Soveraign, or his Authority, concerning a crime done by himselfe, he is not bound (without assurance
of Pardon) to confesse it; because no man (as I have shewn in the
same Chapter) can be obliged by Covenant to accuse himselfe.

Again, the Consent of a Subject to Soveraign Power, is contained
in these words, *I Authorise, or take upon me, all his actions*; in which
there is no restriction at all, of his own former naturall Liberty: For by
allowing him to *kill me*, I am not bound to kill my selfe when he
commands me. 'Tis one thing to say, *Kill me, or my fellow, if you please*;
another thing to say, *I will kill my selfe, or my fellow*. It followeth
therefore, that

No man is bound by the words themselves, either to kill himselfe,
or any other man; And consequently, that the Obligation a man may
sometimes have, upon the Command of the Soveraign to execute any
dangerous, or dishonourable Office, dependeth not on the Words of
our Submission; but on the Intention; which is to be understood by
the End thereof. When therefore our refusall to obey, frustrates the
End for which the Soveraignty was ordained; then there is no Liberty
to refuse: otherwise there is.

Upon this ground, a man that is commanded as a Souldier to fight *Nor to*
against the enemy, though his Soveraign have Right enough to punish *warfare,*
his refusall with death, may neverthelesse in many cases refuse, *unlesse they*
without Injustice; as when he substituteth a sufficient Souldier in his *voluntarily*
place: for in this case he deserteth not the service of the Common- *undertake it.*
wealth. And there is allowance to be made for naturall timorousnesse,
not onely to women, (of whom no such dangerous duty is expected,)
but also to men of feminine courage. When Armies fight, there is on
one side, or both, a running away; yet when they do it not out of
trechery, but fear, they are not esteemed to do it unjustly, but dis-

honourably. For the same reason, to avoyd battell, is not Injustice, but Cowardice. But he that inrowleth himselfe a Souldier, or taketh imprest mony, taketh away the excuse of a timorous nature; and is obliged, not onely to go to the battell, but also not to run from it, without his Captaines leave. And when the Defence of the Common-wealth, requireth at once the help of all that are able to bear Arms, every one is obliged; because otherwise the Institution of the Com-mon-wealth, which they have not the purpose, or courage to preserve, was in vain.

To resist the Sword of the Common-wealth, in defence of another man, guilty, or innocent, no man hath Liberty; because such Liberty, takes away from the Soveraign, the means of Protecting us; and is therefore destructive of the very essence of Government. But in case a great many men together, have already resisted the Soveraign Power unjustly, or committed some Capitall crime, for which every one of them expecteth death, whether have they not the Liberty then to joyn together, and assist, and defend one another? Certainly they have: For they but defend their lives, which the Guilty man may as well do, as the Innocent. There was indeed injustice in the first breach of their duty; Their bearing of Arms subsequent to it, though it be to maintain what they have done, is no new unjust act. And if it be onely to defend their persons, it is not unjust at all. But the offer of pardon taketh from them, to whom it is offered, the plea of self-defence, and maketh their perseverance in assisting, or defending the rest, unlawfull.

[113]

The Greatest Liberty of Subjects, dependeth on the Silence of the Law.

As for other Lyberties, they depend on the Silence of the Law. In cases where the Soveraign has prescribed no rule, there the Subject hath the Liberty to do, or forbeare, according to his own discretion. And therefore such Liberty is in some places more, and in some lesse; and in some times more, in other times lesse, according as they that have the Soveraignty shall think most convenient. As for Example, there was a time, when in *England* a man might enter in to his own Land, (and dispossesse such as wrongfully possessed it,) by force. But in after-times, that Liberty of Forcible Entry, was taken away by a Statute made (by the King) in Parliament. And in some places of the world, men have the Liberty of many wives: in other places, such Liberty is not allowed.

If a Subject have a controversie with his Soveraigne, of debt, or of right of possession of lands or goods, or concerning any service required at his hands, or concerning any penalty, corporall, or pecuniary, grounded on a precedent Law; he hath the same Liberty to sue for his right, as if it were against a Subject; and before such Judges, as are appointed by the Soveraign. For seeing the Soveraign demandeth by force of a former Law, and not by vertue of his Power; he declareth thereby, that he requireth no more, than shall appear to be due by that Law. The sute therefore is not contrary to the will of the Soveraign; and consequently the Subject hath the Liberty to demand the hearing of his Cause; and sentence, according to that Law. But if he demand, or take any thing by pretence of his Power; there lyeth, in that case, no action of Law: for all that is done by him in Vertue of his Power, is done by the Authority of every Subject, and consequently, he that brings an action against the Soveraign, brings it against himselfe.

If a Monarch, or Soveraign Assembly, grant a Liberty to all, or any of his Subjects, which Grant standing, he is disabled to provide for their safety, the Grant is voyd; unlesse he directly renounce, or transferre the Soveraignty to another. For in that he might openly, (if it had been his will,) and in plain terms, have renounced, or trans-ferred it, and did not; it is to be understood it was not his will; but that the Grant proceeded from ignorance of the repugnancy between such a Liberty and the Soveraign Power: and therefore the Soveraignty is still retayned; and consequently all those Powers, which are necessary to the exercising thereof; such as are the Power of Warre, and Peace, of Judicature, of appointing Officers, and Councellours, of levying Mony, and the rest named in the 18th Chapter.

The Obligation of Subjects to the Soveraign, is understood to last as long, and no longer, than the power lasteth, by which he is able to protect them. For the right men have by Nature to protect themselves, when none else can protect them, can by no Covenant be relinquished. The Soveraignty is the Soule of the Common-wealth; which once departed from the Body, the members doe no more receive their motion from it. The end of Obedience is Protection; which, wheresoever a man seeth it, either in his own, or in anothers sword, Nature applyeth his obedience to it, and his endeavour to maintaine it. And though Soveraignty, in the intention of them that make it, be immortall; yet is it in its own nature, not only subject to violent death, by forreign war; but also through the ignorance, and passions of men, it hath in it, from the very institution, many seeds of a naturall mortality, by Intestine Discord.

[114]
In what Cases Subjects are absolved of their obedience to their Soveraign.

In case of
Captivity.

If a Subject be taken prisoner in war; or his person, or his means of life be within the Guards of the enemy, and hath his life and corporall Libertie given him, on condition to be Subject to the Victor, he hath Libertie to accept the condition; and having accepted it, is the subject of him that took him; because he had no other way to preserve himself. The case is the same, if he be deteined on the same termes, in a forreign country. But if a man be held in prison, or bonds, or is not trusted with the libertie of his bodie; he cannot be understood to be bound by Covenant to subjection; and therefore may, if he can, make his escape by any means whatsoever.

In case the
Soveraign
cast off the
government
from himself
and his
Heyrs.

If a Monarch shall relinquish the Soveraignty, both for himself, and his heires; His Subjects returne to the absolute Libertie of Nature; because, though Nature may declare who are his Sons, and who are the nerest of his Kin; yet it dependeth on his own will, (as hath been said in the precedent chapter,) who shall be his Heyr. If therefore he will have no Heyre, there is no Soveraignty, nor Subjection. The case is the same, if he dye without known Kindred, and without declaration of his Heyre. For then there can no Heire be known, and consequently no Subjection be due.

In case of
Banishment.

If the Soveraign Banish his Subject; during the Banishment, he is not Subject. But he that is sent on a message, or hath leave to travell, is still Subject; but it is, by Contract between Soveraigns, not by vertue of the covenant of Subjection. For whosoever entreth into anothers dominion, is Subject to all the Laws thereof; unlesse he have a privilege by the amity of the Soveraigns, or by speciall licence.

In case the
Soveraign
render
himself
Subject to
another.

If a Monarch subdued by war, render himself Subject to the Victor; his Subjects are delivered from their former obligation, and become obliged to the Victor. But if he be held prisoner, or have not the liberty of his own Body; he is not understood to have given away the Right of Soveraigntie; and therefore his Subjects are obliged to yield obedience to the Magistrates formerly placed, governing not in their own name, but in his. For, his Right remaining, the question is only of the Administration; that is to say, of the Magistrates and Officers; which, if he have not means to name, he is supposed to approve those, which he himself had formerly appointed.

[115]

154

CHAP. XXII.

Of SYSTEMES *Subject, Politicall, and Private.*

Having spoken of the Generation, Forme, and Power of a Common-wealth, I am in order to speak next of the parts thereof. And first of Systemes, which resemble the similar parts, or Muscles of a Body naturall. By SYSTEMES; I understand any numbers of men joyned in one Interest, or one Businesse. Of which, some are *Regular*, and some *Irregular*. *Regular* are those, where one Man, or Assembly of men, is constituted Representative of the whole number. All other are *Irregular*. *The divers sorts of Systemes of People.*

Of Regular, some are *Absolute*, and *Independent*, subject to none but their own Representative: such are only Common-wealths; Of which I have spoken already in the 5. last precedent chapters. Others are Dependent; that is to say, Subordinate to some Soveraign Power, to which every one, as also their Representative is *Subject*.

Of Systemes subordinate, some are *Politicall*, and some *Private*. *Politicall* (otherwise Called *Bodies Politique*, and *Persons in Law*,) are those, which are made by authority from the Soveraign Power of the Common-wealth. *Private*, are those, which are constituted by Subjects amongst themselves, or by authoritie from a stranger. For no authority derived from forraign power, within the Dominion of another, is Publique there, but Private.

And of Private Systemes, some are *Lawfull*; some *Unlawfull*: *Lawfull*, are those which are allowed by the Common-wealth: all other are *Unlawfull*. *Irregular* Systemes, are those which having no Representative, consist only in concourse of People; which if not forbidden by the Common-wealth, nor made on evill designe, (such as are conflux of People to markets, or shews, or any other harmelesse end,) are Lawfull. But when the Intention is evill, or (if the number be considerable) unknown, they are Unlawfull. *In all Bodies Politique the power of the Representative is Limited.*

In Bodies Politique, the power of the Representative is alwaies Limited: And that which prescribeth the Limits thereof, is the Power Soveraign. For Power Unlimited, is absolute Soveraignty. And the

Soveraign, in every Commonwealth, is the absolute Representative of all the subjects; and therefore no other, can be Representative of any part of them, but so far forth, as he shall give leave: And to give leave to a Body Politique of Subjects, to have an absolute Representative to all intents and purposes, were to abandon the government of so much of the Commonwealth, and to divide the Dominion, contrary to their Peace and Defence, which the Soveraign cannot be understood to doe, by any Grant, that does not plainly, and directly discharge them of their subjection. For consequences of words, are not the signes of his will, when other consequences are signes of the contrary; but rather signes of errour, and misreckonning; to which all mankind is too prone.

[116]

The bounds of that Power, which is given to the Representative of a Bodie Politique, are to be taken notice of, from two things. One is their Writt, or Letters from the Soveraign: the other is the Law of the Common-wealth.

By Letters Patents:

For though in the Institution or Acquisition of a Common-wealth, which is independent, there needs no Writing, because the Power of the Representative has there no other bounds, but such as are set out by the unwritten Law of Nature; yet in subordinate bodies, there are such diversities of Limitation necessary, concerning their businesses, times, and places, as can neither be remembred without Letters, nor taken notice of, unlesse such Letters be Patent, that they may be read to them, and withall sealed, or testified, with the Seales, or other permanent signes of the Authority Soveraign.

And the Lawes.

And because such Limitation is not alwaies easie, or perhaps possible to be described in writing; the ordinary Lawes, common to all Subjects, must determine, what the Representative may lawfully do, in all Cases, where the Letters themselves are silent. And therefore

When the Representative is one man, his unwarranted Acts are his own onely.

In a Body Politique, if the Representative be one man, whatsoever he does in the Person of the Body, which is not warranted in his Letters, nor by the Lawes, is his own act, and not the act of the Body, nor of any other Member thereof besides himselfe: Because further than his Letters, or the Lawes limit, he representeth no mans person, but his own. But what he does according to these, is the act of every one: For of the Act of the Soveraign every one is Author, because he is their Representative unlimited; and the act of him that recedes not from the Letters of the Soveraign, is the act of the Soveraign, and therefore every member of the Body is Author of it.

156

But if the Representative be an Assembly; whatsoever that Assembly shall Decree, not warranted by their Letters, or the Lawes, is the act of the Assembly, or Body Politique, and the act of every one by whose Vote the Decree was made; but not the act of any man that being present Voted to the contrary; nor of any man absent, unlesse he Voted it by procuration. It is the act of the Assembly, because Voted by the major part; and if it be a crime, the Assembly may be punished, as farre-forth as it is capable, as by dissolution, or forfeiture of their Letters, (which is to such artificiall, and fictitious Bodies, capitall,) or (if the Assembly have a Common stock, wherein none of the Innocent Members have propriety,) by pecuniary Mulct. For from corporall penalties Nature hath exempted all Bodies Politique. But they that gave not their Vote, are therefore Innocent, because the Assembly cannot Represent any man in things unwarranted by their Letters, and consequently are not involved in their Votes.

When it is an Assembly, it is the act of them that assented onely.

If the person of the Body Politique being in one man, borrow mony of a stranger, that is, of one that is not of the same Body, (for no Letters need limit borrowing, seeing it is left to mens own inclinations to limit lending) the debt is the Representatives. For if he should have Authority from his Letters, to make the members pay what he borroweth, he should have by consequence the Soveraignty of them; and therefore the grant were either voyd, as proceeding from Errour, commonly incident to humane Nature, and an unsufficient signe of the will of the Granter; or if it be avowed by him, then is the Representer Soveraign, and falleth not under the present question, which is onely of Bodies subordinate. No member therefore is obliged to pay the debt so borrowed, but the Representative himselfe: because he that lendeth it, being a stranger to the Letters, and to the qualification of the Body, understandeth those onely for his debtors, that are engaged; and seeing the Representer can ingage himselfe, and none else, has him onely for Debtor; who must therefore pay him, out of the common stock (if there be any,) or (if there be none) out of his own estate.

[117]
When the Representative is one man, if he borrow mony, or owe it, by Contract; he is lyable onely, the members not.

If he come into debt by Contract, or Mulct, the case is the same.

But when the Representative is an Assembly, and the debt to a stranger; all they, and onely they are responsible for the debt, that gave their votes to the borrowing of it, or to the Contract that made it due, or to the fact for which the Mulct was imposed; because every one of those in voting did engage himselfe for the payment: For he

When it is an Assembly, they onely are liable that have assented.

that is author of the borrowing, is obliged to the payment, even of the whole debt, though when payd by any one, he be discharged.

If the debt be to one of the Assembly, the Body onely is obliged.

But if the debt be to one of the Assembly, the Assembly onely is obliged to the payment, out of their common stock (if they have any:) For having liberty of Vote, if he Vote the Mony, shall be borrowed, he Votes it shall be payd; If he Vote if shall not be borrowed, or be absent, yet because in lending, he voteth the borrowing, he contradicteth his former Vote, and is obliged by the later, and becomes both borrower and lender, and consequently cannot demand payment from any particular man, but from the common Treasure onely; which fayling he hath no remedy, nor complaint, but against himselfe, that being privy to the acts of the Assembly, and to their means to pay, and not being enforced, did neverthelesse through his own folly lend his mony.

Protestation against the Decrees of Bodies Politique sometimes lawful; but against Soveraign Power never.

It is manifest by this, that in Bodies Politique subordinate, and subject to a Soveraign Power, it is sometimes not onely lawfull, but expedient, for a particular man to make open protestation against the decrees of the Representative Assembly, and cause their dissent to be Registred, or to take witnesse of it; because otherwise they may be obliged to pay debts contracted, and be responsible for crimes committed by other men: But in a Soveraign Assembly, that liberty is taken away, both because he that protesteth there, denies their Soveraignty; and also because whatsoever is commanded by the Soveraign Power, is as to the Subject (though not so always in the sight of God) justified by the Command; for of such command every Subject is the Author.

[118]

Bodies Politique for Government of a Province, Colony, or Town.

The variety of Bodies Politique, is almost infinite: for they are not onely distinguished by the severall affaires, for which they are constituted, wherein there is an unspeakable diversitie; but also by the times, places, and numbers, subject to many limitations. And as to their affaires, some are ordained for Government; As first, the Government of a Province may be committed to an Assembly of men, wherein all resolutions shall depend on the Votes of the major part; and then this Assembly is a Body Politique, and their power limited by Commission. This word Province signifies a charge, or care of businesse, which he whose businesse it is, committeth to another man, to be administred for, and under him; and therefore when in one Common-wealth there be divers Countries, that have their Lawes distinct one from another, or are farre distant in place, the Administration of the Government being committed to divers persons, those Countries where the Soveraign is not resident, but governs by Commission, are called Provinces. But of the government of a Province, by an Assembly residing in the Province it selfe, there be few examples. The Romans who had the Soveraignty of many Provinces; yet governed them alwaies by Presidents, and Praetors; and not by Assemblies, as they governed the City of *Rome*, and Territories adjacent. In like manner, when there were Colonies sent from *England*, to Plant *Virginia*, and *Sommer-Ilands*; though the government of them here, were committed to Assemblies in *London*, yet did those Assemblies never commit the Government under them to any Assembly there; but did to each Plantation send one Governour; For though every man, where he can be present by Nature, desires to participate of government; yet where they cannot be present, they are by Nature also enclined, to commit the Government of their common Interest rather to a Monarchicall, then a Popular form of Government: which is also evident in those men that have great private estates; who when they are unwilling to take the paines of administring the businesse that belongs to them, choose rather to trust one Servant, then an Assembly either of their friends or servants. But howsoever it be in fact, yet we may suppose the Government of a Province, or Colony committed to an Assembly: and when it *is so,*[1] that which in this place I have to say, is this; that whatsoever debt is by that Assembly contracted; or whatsoever unlawfull Act is decreed, is the Act onely of those that assented, and not of any that dissented, or were absent, for the reasons before alledged. Also that an Assembly residing out of the bounds of that Colony whereof they have the government, cannot execute any power over the persons, or goods of any of the Colonie, to seize on them for debt, or other duty, in any place without the Colony it selfe, as having no Jurisdiction, nor Authoritie elsewhere, but are left to the remedie, which the Law of the place alloweth them. And though the Assembly have right, to impose a Mulct upon any of their members, that shall break the Lawes they make; yet out of the Colonie it selfe, they have no right to execute the same. And that which is said here, of the Rights of an Assembly, for the government of a

---

[1] *Syn.:* is,

Province, or a Colony, is appliable also to an Assembly for the Government of a Town, an University, or a College, or a Church, or for any other Government over the persons of men.

And generally, in all Bodies Politique, if any particular member conceive himself Injuried by the Body it self, the Cognisance of his cause belongeth to the Soveraign, and those the Soveraign hath ordained for Judges in such causes, or shall ordaine for that particular cause; and not to the Body it self. For the whole Body is in this case his fellow subject, which in a Soveraign Assembly, is otherwise: for there, if the Soveraign be not Judge, though in his own cause, there can be no Judge at all.

Bodies Politique for ordering of Trade. In a Bodie Politique, for the well ordering of forraigne Traffique, the most commodious Representative is an Assembly of all the members; that is to say, such a one, as every one that adventureth his mony, may be present at all the Deliberations, and Resolutions of the Body, if they will themselves. For proof whereof, we are to consider the end, for which men that are Merchants, and may buy and sell, export, and import their Merchandise, according to their own discretions, doe neverthelesse bind themselves up in one Corporation. It is true, there be few Merchants, that with the Merchandise they buy at home, can fraight a Ship, to export it; or with that they buy abroad, to bring it home; and have therefore need to joyn together in one Society; where every man may either participate of the gaine, according to the proportion of his adventure; or take his own, and sell what he transports, or imports, at such prices as he thinks fit. But this is no Body Politique, there being no Common Representative to oblige them to any other Law, than that which is common to all other subjects. The End of their Incorporating, is to make their gaine the greater; which is done two wayes; by sole buying, and sole selling, both at home, and abroad. So that to grant to a Company of Merchants to be a Corporation, or Body Politique, is to grant them a double Monopoly, whereof one is to be sole buyers; another to be sole sellers. For when there is a Company incorporate for any particular forraign Country, they only export the Commodities vendible in that Country; which is sole buying at home, and sole selling abroad. For at home there is but one buyer, and abroad but one that selleth: both which is gainfull to the Merchant, because thereby they buy at home at lower, and sell abroad at higher rates: And abroad there is but one buyer of forraign Merchandise, and but one that sels them at home; both which againe are gainfull to the adventurers.

Of this double Monopoly one part is disadvantageous to the people at home, the other to forraigners. For at home by their sole exportation they set what price they please on the husbandry, and handyworks of the people; and by the sole importation, what price they please on all forraign commodities the people have need of; both which are ill for the people. On the contrary, by the sole selling of the native commodities abroad, and sole buying the forraign commodities upon the place, they raise the price of those, and abate the price of these, to the disadvantage of the forraigner: For where but one selleth, the Merchandise is the dearer; and where but one buyeth the [120] cheaper: Such Corporations therefore are no other then Monopolies; though they would be very profitable for a Common-wealth, if being bound up into one body in forraigne Markets they were at liberty at home, every man to buy, and sell at what price he could.

The end then of these Bodies of Merchants, being not a Common benefit to the whole Body, (which have in this case no common stock, but what is deducted out of the particular adventures, for building, buying, victualling and manning of Ships,) but the particular gaine of every adventurer, it is reason that every one be acquainted with the employment of his own; that is, that every one be of the Assembly, that shall have the power to order the same; and be acquainted with their accounts. And therefore the Representative of such a Body must be an Assembly, where every member of the Body may be present at the consultations, if he will.

If a Body Politique of Merchants, contract a debt to a stranger by the act of their Representative Assembly, every Member is lyable by himself for the whole. For a stranger can take no notice of their private Lawes, but considereth them as so many particular men, obliged every one to the whole payment, till payment made by one dischargeth all the rest: But if the debt be to one of the Company, the creditor is debter for the whole to himself, and cannot therefore demand his debt, but only from the common stock, if there be any.

If the Common-wealth impose a Tax upon the Body, it is understood to be layd upon every Member proportionably to his particular adventure in the Company. For there is in this case no other common stock, but what is made of their particular adventures.

If a Mulct be layd upon the Body for some unlawfull act, they only are lyable by whose votes the act was decreed, or by whose assistance it was executed; for in none of the rest is there any other crime but being of the Body; which if a crime, (because the Body was ordeyned by the authority of the Common-wealth,) is not his.

If one of the Members be indebted to the Body, he may be sued by the Body; but his goods cannot be taken, nor his person imprisoned by the authority of the Body; but only by Authority of the Common-wealth: for if they can doe it by their own Authority, they can by their own Authority give judgement that the debt is due, which is as much as to be Judge in their own Cause.

A Bodie Politique for Counsel to be given to the Soveraign. These Bodies made for the government of Men, or of Traffique, be either perpetuall, or for a time prescribed by writing. But there be Bodies also whose times are limited, and that only by the nature of their businesse. For example, if a Soveraign Monarch, or a Soveraign Assembly, shall think fit to give command to the towns, and other severall parts of their territory, to send to him their Deputies, to enforme him of the condition, and necessities of the Subjects, or to advise with him for the making of good Lawes, or for any other cause, as with one Person representing the whole Country, such Deputies, having a place and time of meeting assigned them, are there, and at that time, a Body Politique, representing every Subject of that Dominion; but it is onely for such matters as shall be propounded unto them by that Man, or Assembly, that by the Soveraign Authority sent for them; and when it shall be declared that nothing more shall be propounded, nor debated by them, the Body is dissolved. For if they were the absolute Representative of the people, then were it the Soveraign Assembly; and so there would be two Soveraign Assemblies, or two Soveraigns, over the same people; which cannot consist with their Peace. And therefore where there is once a Soveraignty, there can be no absolute Representation of the people, but by it. And for the limits of how farre such a Body shall represent the whole People, they are set forth in the Writing by which they were sent for. For the People cannot choose their Deputies to other intent, than is in the Writing directed to them from their Soveraign expressed.

[121]

A Regular Private Body, Lawfull, as a Family. Private Bodies Regular, and Lawfull, are those that are constituted without Letters, or other written Authority, saving the Lawes common to all other Subjects. And because they be united in one Person Representative, they are held for Regular; such as are all Families, in which the Father, or Master ordereth the whole Family. For he obligeth his Children, and Servants, as farre as the Law permitteth, though not further, because none of them are bound to obedience in those actions, which the Law hath forbidden to be done. In all other actions, during the time they are under domestique government, they are subject to their Fathers, and Masters, as to their immediate Soveraigns. For the Father, and Master being before the Institution of Common-wealth, absolute Soveraigns in their own Families, they lose afterward no more of their Authority, than the Law of the Common-wealth taketh from them.

Private Bodies Regular, but Unlawfull, are those that unite themselves into one person Representative, without any publique Authority at all; such as are the Corporations of Beggars, Theeves and Gipsies, the better to order their trade of begging, and stealing; and the Corporations of men, that by Authority from any forraign Person, unite themselves in anothers Dominion, for the easier propagation of Doctrines, and for making a party, against the Power of the Common-wealth. *Private Bodies Regular, but Unlawfull.*

Irregular Systemes, in their nature, but Leagues, or sometimes meer concourse of people, without union to any particular designe, *by*[1] obligation of one to another, but proceeding onely from a similitude of wills and inclinations, become Lawfull, or Unlawfull, according to the lawfulnesse, or unlawfulnesse of every particular mans designe therein: And his designe is to be understood by the occasion. *Systemes Irregular, such as are Private Leagues.*

The League of Subjects, (because Leagues are commonly made for mutuall defence,) are in a Common-wealth (which is no more than a League of all the Subjects together) for the most part unnecessary, and savour of unlawfull designe; and are for that cause Unlawfull, and go commonly by the name of Factions, or Conspiracies. For a League being a connexion of men by Covenants, if there be no power given to any one Man, or Assembly (as in the condition of meer Nature) to compell them to performance, is so long onely valid, as there ariseth no just cause of distrust: and therefore Leagues between Common-wealths, over whom there is no humane Power established, to keep them all in awe, are not onely lawfull, but also profitable for the time they last. But Leagues of the Subjects of one [122]

---

[1] *Syn.*: not by

and the same Common-wealth, where every one may obtain his right by means of the Soveraign Power, are unnecessary to the maintaining of Peace and Justice, and (in case the designe of them be evill, or Unknown to the Common-wealth) unlawfull. For all uniting of strength by private men, is, if for evill intent, unjust; if for intent unknown, dangerous to the Publique, and unjustly concealed.

Secret Cabals. If the Soveraign Power be in a great Assembly, and a number of men, part of the Assembly, without authority, consult a part, to contrive the guidance of the rest; This is a Faction, or Conspiracy unlawfull, as being a fraudulent seducing of the Assembly for their particular interest. But if he, whose private interest is to be debated, and judged in the Assembly, make as many friends as he can; in him it is no Injustice; because in this case he is no part of the Assembly. And though he hire such friends with mony, (unlesse there be an expresse Law against it,) yet it is not Injustice. For sometimes, (as mens manners are,) Justice cannot be had without mony; and every man may think his own cause just, till it be heard, and judged.

Feuds of private Families. In all Common-wealths, if a private man entertain more servants, than the government of his estate, and lawfull employment he has for them requires, it is Faction, and unlawfull. For having the protection of the Common-wealth, he needeth not the defence of private force. And whereas in Nations not throughly civilized, severall numerous Families have lived in continuall hostility, and invaded one another with private force; yet it is evident enough, that they have done unjustly; or else that they had no Common-wealth.

Factions for Government. And as Factions for Kindred, so also Factions for Government of Religion, as of Papists, Protestants, *&c.*[1] or of State, as Patricians, and Plebeians of old time in *Rome*, and of Aristocraticalls and Democraticalls of old time in *Greece*, are unjust, as being contrary to the peace and safety of the people, and a taking of the Sword out of the hand of the Soveraign.

Concourse of people, is an Irregular Systeme, the lawfulnesse, or unlawfulnesse, whereof dependeth on the occasion, and on the number of them that are assembled. If the occasion be lawfull, and manifest, the Concourse is lawfull; as the usuall meeting of men at Church, or at a publique Shew, in usuall numbers: for if the numbers

---

[1] Scribal MS reads: Independents,

be extraordinarily great, the occasion is not evident; and consequently he that cannot render a particular and good account of his being amongst them, is to be judged conscious of an unlawfull and tumultuous designe. It may be lawfull for a thousand men, to joyn in a Petition to be delivered to a Judge, or Magistrate; yet if a thousand men come to present it, it is a tumultuous Assembly; because there [123] needs but one or two for that purpose. But in such cases as these, it is not a set number that makes the Assembly Unlawfull, but such a number, as the present Officers are not able to suppresse, and bring to Justice.

When an unusuall number of men, assemble against a man whom they accuse; the Assembly is an Unlawfull tumult; because they may deliver their accusation to the Magistrate by a few, or by one man. Such was the case of St. *Paul* at *Ephesus*; where *Demetrius*, and a great number of other men, brought two of *Pauls* companions before the Magistrate, saying with one Voyce, *Great is Diana of the Ephesians*; which was their way of demanding Justice against them for teaching the people such doctrine, as was against their Religion, and Trade. The occasion here, considering the Lawes of that People, was just; yet was their Assembly Judged Unlawfull, and the Magistrate repre-hended them for it, in these words, * *If Demetrius and the other work-*   * *Acts* *men can accuse any man, of any thing, there be Pleas, and Deputies, let them*   19.40. *accuse one another. And if you have any other thing to demand, your case may be judged in an Assembly Lawfully called. For we are in danger to be accused for this dayes sedition, because, there is no cause by which any man can render any reason of this Concourse of People.* Where he calleth an Assembly, whereof men can give no just account, a Sedition, and such as they could not answer for. And this is all I shall say concerning *Systemes*, and Assemblyes of People, which may be compared (as I said,) to the Similar parts of mans Body; such as be Lawfull, to the Muscles; such as are Unlawfull, to Wens, Biles, and Apostemes, engendred by the unnaturall conflux of evill humours.

CHAP. XXIII.

Of the Publique Ministers *of Soveraign Power.*

In the last Chapter I have spoken of the Similar parts of a Common-wealth: In this I shall speak of the parts Organicall, which are Publique Ministers.

Publique Minister Who.

A Publique Minister, is he, that by the Soveraign, (whether a Monarch, or an Assembly,) is employed in any affaires, with Authority to represent in that employment, the Person of the Common-wealth. And whereas every man, or assembly that hath Soveraignty, represen-teth two Persons, or (as the more common phrase is) has two Capaci-ties, one Naturall, and another Politique, (as a Monarch, hath the person not onely of the Common-wealth, but also of a man; and a Soveraign Assembly hath the Person not onely of the Common-wealth, but also of the Assembly); they that be servants to them in their naturall Capacity, are not Publique Ministers; but those onely

[124]

that serve them in the Administration of the Publique businesse. And therefore neither Ushers, nor Sergeants, nor other Officers that waite on the Assembly, for no other purpose, but for the commodity of the men assembled, in an Aristocracy, or Democracy; nor Stewards, Chamberlains, Cofferers, or any other Officers of the houshold of a Monarch, are Publique Ministers in a Monarchy.

Ministers for the generall Adminis-tration.

Of Publique Ministers, some have charge committed to them of a generall Administration, either of the whole Dominion, or of a part thereof. Of the whole, as to a Protector, or Regent, may bee commit-ted by the Predecessor of an Infant King, during his minority, the whole Administration of his Kingdome. In which case, every Subject is so far obliged to obedience, as the Ordinances he shall make, and the commands he shall give be in the Kings name, and not incon-sistent with his Soveraigne Power. Of a part, or Province; as when either a Monarch, or a Soveraign Assembly, shall give the generall charge thereof to a Governour, Lieutenant, Praefect or Vice-Roy: And in this case also, every one of that Province, is obliged to all he

shall doe in the name of the Soveraign, and *that is*[1] not incompat-
ible with the Soveraigns Right. For such Protectors, Vice-Roys, and
Governors, have no other right, but what depends on the Soveraigns
Will; and no Commission that can be given them, can be interpreted
for a Declaration of the will to transferre the Soveraignty, without
expresse and perspicuous words to that purpose. And this kind of
Publique Ministers resembleth the Nerves, and Tendons that move
the severall limbs of a body naturall.

Others have speciall Administration; that is to say, charges of some *For speciall Adminis-tration, as for Oeconomy.*
speciall businesse, either at home, or abroad: As at home, First, for
the Oeconomy of a Common-wealth, They that have Authority concerning the *Treasure*, as Tributes, Impositions, Rents, Fines, or whatsoever publique revenue, to collect, receive, issue, or take the
Accounts thereof, are Publique Ministers: Ministers, because they
serve the Person Representative, and can doe nothing against his
Command, nor without his Authority: Publique, because they serve
him in his Politicall Capacity.

Secondly, they that have Authority concerning the *Militia*; to have
the custody of Armes, Forts, Ports; to Levy, Pay, or Conduct
Souldiers; or to provide for any necessary thing for the use of war,
either by Land or Sea, are publique Ministers. But a Souldier without
Command, though he fight for the Common-wealth, does not therefore represent the Person of it; because there is none to represent it
to. For every one that hath command, represents it to them only
whom he commandeth.

They also that have authority to teach, or to enable others to teach *For instruction of the People.*
the people their duty to the Soveraign Power, and instruct them in the
knowledge of what is just, and unjust, thereby to render them more
apt to live in godlinesse, and in peace amongst themselves, and resist
the publique enemy, are Publique Ministers: Ministers, in that they
doe it not by their own Authority, but by anothers; and Publique,
because they doe it (or should doe it) by no Authority, but that of the [125]
Soveraign. The Monarch, or the Soveraign Assembly only hath
immediate Authority from God, to teach and instruct the people; and
no man but the Soveraign, receiveth his power *Dei gratiâ* simply; that
is to say, from the favour of none but God: All other, receive theirs

---

[1] *Syn.*: that

from the favour and providence of God, and their Soveraigns; as in a Monarchy *Dei gratiâ & Regis*; or *Dei providentiâ & voluntate Regis.*

They also to whom Jurisdiction is given, are Publique Ministers. For in their Seats of Justice they represent the person of the Soveraign; and their Sentence, is his Sentence; For (as hath been before declared) all Judicature is essentially annexed to the Soveraignty; and therefore all other Judges are but Ministers of him, or them that have the Soveraign Power. And as Controversies are of two sorts, namely of *Fact*, and of *Law*; so are Judgements, some of Fact, some of Law: And consequently in the same controversie, there may be two Judges, one of Fact, another of Law.

And in both these controversies, there may arise a controversie between the party Judged, and the Judge; which because they be both Subjects to the Soveraign, ought in Equity to be Judged by men agreed on by consent of both; for no man can be Judge in his own cause. But the Soveraign is already agreed on for Judge by them both, and is therefore either to heare the Cause, and determine it himself, or appoint for Judge such as they shall both agree on. And this agreement is then understood to be made between them divers wayes; as first, if the Defendant be allowed to except against such of his Judges, whose interest maketh him suspect them, (for as to the Complaynant he hath already chosen his own Judge,) those which he excepteth not against, are Judges he himself agrees on. Secondly, if he appeale to any other Judge, he can appeale no further; for his appeale is his choice. Thirdly, if he appeale to the Soveraign himself, and he by himself, or by Delegates which the parties shall agree on, give Sentence; that Sentence is finall: for the Defendant is Judged by his own Judges, that is to say, by himself.

These properties of just and rationall Judicature considered, I cannot forbeare to observe the excellent constitution of the Courts of Justice, established both for Common, and also for Publique Pleas in *England*. By Common Pleas, I meane those, where both the Complaynant and Defendant are Subjects: and by Publique, (which are also called Pleas of the Crown) those, where the Complaynant is the Soveraign. For whereas there were two orders of men, whereof one was Lords, the other Commons; The Lords had this Priviledge, to have for *Judges if the plea were publique*[1] in all Capitall crimes,

---

[1] *Syn.:* Judges

none but Lords; and of them, as many as would be present; which being ever acknowledged as a Priviledge of favour, their Judges were none but such as they had themselves desired. And in all controversies, every Subject (as also in civill controversies the Lords) had for Judges, men of the Country where the matter in controversie lay; against which he might make his exceptions, till at last Twelve men without exception being agreed on, they were Judged by those twelve. [126] So that having his own Judges, there could be nothing alledged by the party, why the sentence should not be finall. These publique persons, with Authority from the Soveraign Power, either to Instruct, or Judge the people, are such members of the Common-wealth, as may fitly be compared to the organs of Voice in a Body naturall.

Publique Ministers are also all those, that have Authority from the Soveraign, to procure the Execution of Judgements given; to publish the Soveraigns Commands; to suppresse Tumults; to apprehend, and imprison Malefactors; and other acts tending to the conservation of the Peace. For every act they doe by such Authority, is the act of the Common-wealth; and their service, answerable to that of the Hands in a Bodie naturall. *For Execution.*

Publique Ministers abroad, are those that represent the Person of their own Soveraign, to forraign States. Such are Ambassadors, Messengers, Agents, and Heralds, sent by publique Authoritie, and on publique Businesse.

But such as are sent by Authoritie only of some private partie of a troubled State, though they be received, are neither Publique, nor Private Ministers of the Common-wealth; because none of their actions have the Common-wealth for Author. Likewise, an Ambassador sent from a Prince, to congratulate, condole, or to assist at a solemnity, though the Authority be Publique; yet because the businesse is Private, and belonging to him in his naturall capacity; is a Private person. Also if a man be sent into another Country, secretly to explore their counsels, and strength; though both the Authority, and the Businesse be Publique; yet because there is none to take notice of any Person in him, but his own; he is but a Private Minister; but yet a Minister of the Common-wealth; and may be compared to an Eye in the Body naturall. And those that are appointed to receive the Petitions or other informations of the People, and are as it were the publique Eare, are Publique Ministers, and represent their Soveraign in that office.

Counsellers without other employment then to Advise are not Publique Ministers.

Neither a Counsellor (nor a Councell of State, if we consider it with no Authority of Judicature or Command, but only of giving Advice to the Soveraign when it is required, or of offering it when it is not required,) is a Publique Person. For the Advice is addressed to the Soveraign only, whose person cannot in his own presence, be represented to him, by another. But a Body of Counsellors, are never without some other Authority, either of Judicature, or of immediate Administration: As in a Monarchy, they represent the Monarch, in delivering his Commands to the Publique Ministers: In a Democracy, the Councell, or Senate propounds the Result of their deliberations to the people, as a Councell; but when they appoint Judges, or heare Causes, or give Audience to Ambassadors, it is in the quality of a Minister of the People: And in an Aristocracy the Councell of State is the Soveraign Assembly it self; and gives counsell to none but themselves.

[127]

CHAP. XXIV.
Of the NUTRITION, *and* PROCREATION *of a Common-wealth.*

The Nourishment of a Common-wealth consisteth in the Commodities of Sea and Land:

The NUTRITION of a Common-wealth consisteth, in the *Plenty*, and *Distribution* of *Materials* conducing to Life: In *Concoction*, or *Preparation*; and (when concocted) in the *Conveyance* of it, by convenient conduits, to the Publique use.

As for the Plenty of Matter, it is a thing limited by Nature, to those commodities, which from (the two breasts of our common Mother) Land, and Sea, God usually either freely giveth, or for labour selleth to man-kind.

For the Matter of this Nutriment, consisting in Animals, Vegetals, and Minerals, God hath freely layd them before us, in or neer to the face of the Earth; so as there needeth no more but the labour, and industry of receiving them. Insomuch as Plenty dependeth (next to Gods favour) meerly on the labour and industry of men.

This Matter, commonly called Commodities, is partly *Native*, and partly *Forraign*: *Native*, that which is to be had within the Territory of the Common-wealth: *Forraign*, that which is imported from without. And because there is no Territory under the Dominion of one Common-wealth, (except it be of very vast extent,) that produceth all things needfull for the maintenance, and motion of the whole Body; and few that produce not something more than necessary; the superfluous commodities to be had within, become no more superfluous, but supply these wants at home, by importation of that which may be had abroad, either by Exchange, or by just Warre, or by Labour: for a mans Labour also, is a commodity exchangeable for benefit, as well as any other thing: And there have been Common-wealths that having no more Territory, than hath served them for habitation, have neverthelesse, not onely maintained, but also encreased their Power, partly by the labour of trading from one place to another, and partly by selling the Manifactures, whereof the Materials were brought in from other places.

The Distribution of the Materials of this Nourishment, is the constitution of *Mine*, and *Thine*, and *His*; that is to say, in one word *Propriety*; and belongeth in all kinds of Common-wealth to the Soveraign Power. For where there is no Common-wealth, there is (as hath been already shewn) a perpetuall warre of every man against his neighbour; And therefore every thing is his that getteth it, and keepeth it by force; which is neither *Propriety*, nor *Community*; but *Uncertainty*. Which is so evident, that even *Cicero*, (a passionate defender of Liberty,) in a publique pleading, attributeth all Propriety to the Law Civil, *Let the Civill Law*, saith he, *be once abandoned, or but negligently guarded, (not to say oppressed,) and there is nothing, that any man can be sure to receive from his Ancestor, or leave to his Children.* And again; *Take away the Civill Law, and no man knows what is his own, and what another mans.* Seeing therefore the Introduction of *Propriety* is an effect of Common-wealth; which can do nothing but by the Person that Represents it, it is the act onely of the Soveraign; and consisteth in the Lawes, which none can make that have not the Soveraign Power. And this they well knew of old, who called that Νόμος, (that is to say, *Distribution*,) which we call Law; and defined Justice, by *distributing* to every man *his own*.

In this Distribution, the First Law, is for Division of the Land it selfe: wherein the Soveraign assigneth to every man a portion, according as he, and not according as any Subject, or any number of them, shall judge agreeable to Equity, and the Common Good. The

And the right Distribution of them.

[128]

All private Estates of land proceed originally from the Arbitrary Distribution of the Soveraign.

Children of Israel, were a Common-wealth in the Wildernesse; but wanted the commodities of the Earth, till they were masters of the Land of Promise; which afterward was divided amongst them, not by their own discretion, but by the discretion of *Eleazar* the Priest, and *Joshua* their Generall: who when there were twelve Tribes, making them thirteen by subdivision of the Tribe of *Joseph*; made neverthelesse but twelve portions of the Land; and ordained for the Tribe of *Levi* no land; but assigned them the Tenth part of the whole fruits; which division was therefore Arbitrary. And though a People comming into possession of a Land by warre, do not alwaies exterminate the antient Inhabitants, (as did the Jewes,) but leave to many, or most, or all of them their Estates; yet it is manifest they hold them afterwards, as of the Victors distribution; as the people of *England* held all theirs of *William* the *Conquerour*.

Propriety of a Subject excludes not the Dominion of the Soveraign, but onely of another Subject. From whence we may collect, that the Propriety which a subject hath in his lands, consisteth in a right to exclude all other subjects from the use of them; and not to exclude their Soveraign, be it an Assembly, or a Monarch. For seeing the Soveraign, that is to say, the Common-wealth (whose Person he representeth,) is understood to do nothing but in order to the common Peace and Security, this Distribution of lands, is to be understood as done in order to the same: And consequently, whatsoever Distribution *another*[1] shall make in prejudice thereof, is contrary to the will of every subject, that committed his Peace, and safety to his discretion, and conscience; and therefore by the will of every one of them, is to be reputed voyd. It is true, that a Soveraign Monarch, or the greater part of a Soveraign Assembly, may ordain the doing of many things in pursuit of their Passions, contrary to their own consciences, which is a breach of trust, and of the Law of Nature; but this is not enough to authorise any subject, either to make warre upon, or so much as to accuse of Injustice, or any way to speak evill of their Soveraign; because they have authorised all his actions, and in bestowing the Soveraign Power, made them their own. But in what cases the Commands of Soveraigns are contrary to Equity, and the Law of Nature, is to be considered hereafter in another place.

The Publique is not to be dieted.

[129]

In the Distribution of land, the Common-wealth it selfe, may be conceived to have a portion, and possesse, and improve the same by

---

[1] *Syn.*: there

172

their Representative; and that such portion may be made sufficient, to susteine the whole expence to the common Peace, and defence necessarily required: Which were very true, if there could be any Representative conceived free from humane passions, and infirmities. But the nature of men being as it is, the setting forth of Publique Land, or of any certaine Revenue for the Common-wealth, is in vaine; and tendeth to the dissolution of Government, and to the condition of meere Nature, and War, assoon as ever the Soveraign Power falleth into the hands of a Monarch, or of an Assembly, that are either too negligent of mony, or too hazardous in engaging the publique stock, into a long, or costly war. Common-wealths can endure no Diet: For seeing their expence is not limited by their own appetite, but by externall Accidents, and the appetites of their neighbours, the Publique Riches cannot be limited by other limits, than those which the emergent occasions shall require. And whereas in *England*, there were by the Conquerour, divers Lands reserved to his own use, (besides Forrests, and Chases, either for his recreation, or for preservation of Woods,) and divers services reserved on the Land he gave his Subjects; yet it seems they were not reserved for his Maintenance *as in*[1] his Publique, but *as in*[2] his Naturall capacity: For he, and his Successors did for all that, lay Arbitrary Taxes on all Subjects Land, when they judged it necessary. Or if those publique Lands, and Services, were ordained as a sufficient maintenance of the Common-wealth, it was contrary to the scope of the Institution; being (as it appeared by those ensuing Taxes) insufficient, and (as it appeares by the late small Revenue of the Crown) Subject to Alienation, and Diminution. It is therefore in vaine, to assign a portion to the Common-wealth; which may sell, or give it away; and does sell, and give it away when tis done by their Representative.

As the Distribution of Lands at home; so also to assigne in what places, and for what commodities, the Subject shall traffique abroad, belongeth to the Soveraign. For if it did belong to private persons to use their own discretion therein, some of them would bee drawn for gaine, both to furnish the enemy with means to hurt the Common-wealth, and hurt it themselves, by importing such things, as pleasing mens appetites, be neverthelesse noxious, or at least unprofitable to them. And therefore it belongeth to the Common-wealth, (that is, to

The Places and matter of Traffique depend, as their Distribution, on the Soveraign.

[1] *Syn.*: in   [2] *Syn.*: in

the Soveraign only,) to approve, or disapprove both of the places, and matter of forraign Traffique.

The Laws of transferring propriety belong also to the Soveraign.

Further, seeing it is not enough to the Sustentation of a Commonwealth, that every man have a propriety in a portion of Land, or in some few commodities, or a naturall property in some usefull art, and *that there**[1] is no art in the world, but is necessary either for the being, or well being almost of every particular man; it is necessary, that men distribute that which they can spare, and transferre their propriety therein, mutually one to another, by exchange, and mutuall

[130]

contract. And therefore it belongeth to the Common-wealth, (that is to say, to the Soveraign,) to appoint in what manner, all kinds of contract between Subjects, (as buying, selling, exchanging, borrowing, lending, letting, and taking to hire,) are to bee made; and by what words, and signes they shall be understood for valid. And for the Matter, and Distribution of the Nourishment, to the severall Members of the Common-wealth, thus much (considering the modell of the whole worke) is sufficient.

Mony the Bloud of a Common-wealth.

By Concoction, I understand the reducing of all commodities, which are not presently consumed, but reserved for Nourishment in time to come, to some thing of equall value, and withall so portable, as not to hinder the motion of men from place to place; to the end a man may have in what place soever, such Nourishment as the place affordeth. And this is nothing else but Gold, and Silver, and Mony. For Gold and Silver, being (as it happens) almost in all Countries of the world highly valued, is a commodious measure of the value of all things else between Nations; and Mony (of what matter soever coyned by the Soveraign of a Common-wealth,) is a sufficient measure of the value of all things else, between the Subjects of that Common-wealth. By the means of which measures, all commodities, Moveable, and Immoveable, are made to accompany a man, to all places of his resort, within and without the place of his ordinary residence; and the same passeth from Man to Man, within the Common-wealth; and goes round about, Nourishing (as it passeth) every part thereof; In so much as this Concoction, is as it were the Sanguification of the Common-wealth: For naturall Bloud is in like manner made of the fruits of the Earth; and circulating, nourisheth by the way, every Member of the Body of Man.

[1] *Syn.*: there

And because Silver and Gold, have their value from the matter it self; they have first this priviledge, that the value of them cannot be altered by the power of one, nor of a few Common-wealths; as being a common measure of the commodities of all places. But base Mony, may easily be enhansed, or abased. Secondly, they have the priviledge to make Common-wealths move, and stretch out their armes, when need is, into forraign Countries; and supply, not only private Subjects that travell, but also whole Armies with Provision. But that Coyne, which is not considerable for the Matter, but for the Stamp of the place, being unable to endure change of ayr, hath its effect at home only; where also it is subject to the change of Laws, and thereby to have the value diminished, to the prejudice many times of those that have it.

The Conduits, and Wayes by which it is conveyed to the Publique use, are of two sorts; One, that Conveyeth it to the Publique Coffers; The other, that Issueth the same out againe for publique payments. Of the first sort, are Collectors, Receivers, and Treasurers; of the second are the Treasurers againe, and the Officers appointed for payment of severall publique or private Ministers. And in this also, the Artificiall Man maintains his resemblance with the Naturall; whose Veins receiving the Bloud from the severall Parts of the Body, carry it to the Heart; where being made Vitall, the Heart by the Arteries sends it out again, to enliven, and enable for motion all the Members of the same. *The Conduits and Way of mony to the Publique use.* [131]

The Procreation, or Children of a Common-wealth, are those we call *Plantations*, or *Colonies*; which are numbers of men sent out from the Common-wealth, under a Conductor, or Governour, to inhabit a Forraign Country, either formerly voyd of Inhabitants, or made voyd then, by warre. And when a Colony is setled, they are either a Common-wealth of themselves, discharged of their subjection to their Soveraign that sent them, (as hath been done by many Common-wealths of antient time,) in which case the Common-wealth from which they went was called their Metropolis, or Mother, and requires no more of them, then Fathers require of the Children, whom they emancipate, and make free from their domestique government, which is Honour, and Friendship; or else they remain united to their Metropolis, as were the Colonies of the people of *Rome*; and then they are no Common-wealths themselves, but Provinces, and parts of the Common-wealth that sent them. So that the Right of Colonies (saving *The Children of a Common-wealth Colonies.*

Honour, and League with their Metropolis,) dependeth wholly on their Licence, or Letters, by which their Soveraign authorised them to Plant.

CHAP. XXV.
Of COUNSELL.

Counsell what.

How fallacious it is to judge of the nature of things, by the ordinary and inconstant use of words, appeareth in nothing more, than in the confusion of Counsels, and Commands, arising from the Imperative manner of speaking in them both, and in many other occasions besides. For the words *Doe this*, are the words not onely of him that Commandeth; but also of him that giveth Counsell; and of him that Exhorteth; and yet there are but few, that see not, that these are very different things; or that cannot distinguish between them, when they perceive who it is that speaketh, and to whom the Speech is directed, and upon what occasion. But finding those phrases in mens writings, and being not able, or not willing to enter into a consideration of the circumstances, they mistake sometimes the Precepts of Counsellours, for the Precepts of them that Command; and sometimes the contrary; according as it best agreeth with the conclusions they would inferre, or the actions they approve. To avoyd which mistakes, and render to those termes of Commanding, Counselling, and Exhorting, their proper and distinct significations, I define them thus.

Differences between Command, and Counsell.
[132]

COMMAND is, where a man saith, *Doe this*, or *Doe not this*, without expecting other reason than the Will of him that sayes it. From this it followeth manifestly, that he that Commandeth, pretendeth thereby his own Benefit: For the reason of his Command is his own Will onely, and the proper object of every mans Will, is some Good to himselfe.

COUNSELL, is where a man saith, *Doe*, or *Doe not this*, and deduceth his reasons from the benefit that arriveth by it to him to whom he saith it. And from this it is evident, that he that giveth Counsell, pretendeth onely (whatsoever he intendeth) the good of him, to whom he giveth it.

Therefore between Counsell and Command, one great difference is, that Command is directed to a mans own benefit; and Counsell to the benefit of another man. And from this ariseth another difference, that a man may be obliged to do what he is Commanded; as when he hath covenanted to obey: But he cannot be obliged to do as he is Counselled, because the hurt of not following it, is his own; or if he should covenant to follow it, then is the Counsell turned into the nature of a Command. A third difference between them is, that no man can pretend a right to be of another mans Counsell; because he is not to pretend benefit by it to himselfe: but to demand right to Counsell another, argues a will to know his designes, or to gain some other Good to himselfe; which (as I said before) is of every mans will the proper object.

This also is incident to the nature of Counsell; that whatsoever it be, he that asketh it, cannot in equity accuse, or punish it: For to ask Counsell of another, is to permit him to give such Counsell as he shall think best; And consequently, he that giveth counsell to his Soveraign, (whether a Monarch, or an Assembly) when he asketh it, cannot in equity be punished for it, whether the same be conformable to the opinion of the most, or not, so it be to the Proposition in debate. For if the sense of the Assembly can be taken notice of, before the Debate be ended, they should neither ask, nor take any further Counsell; For the Sense of the Assembly, is the Resolution of the Debate, and End of all Deliberation. And generally he that demandeth Counsell, is Author of it; and therefore cannot punish it; and what the Soveraign cannot, no man else can. But if one Subject giveth Counsell to another, to do any thing contrary to the Lawes, whether that Counsell proceed from evill intention, or from ignorance onely, it is punishable by the Common-wealth; because ignorance of the Law, is no good excuse, where every man is bound to take notice of the Lawes to which he is subject.

EXHORTATION, and DEHORTATION, is Counsell, accompanied with signes in him that giveth it, of vehement desire to have it followed; or to say it more briefly, *Counsell vehemently pressed.* For he that Exhorteth, doth not deduce the consequences of what he adviseth to be done, and tye himselfe therein to the rigour of true reasoning; but encourages him he Counselleth, to Action: As he that Dehorteth, deterreth him from it. And therefore they have in their speeches, a regard to the common Passions, and opinions of men, in deducing their reasons; and make use of Similitudes, Metaphors, Examples,

Exhortation and Dehortation what.

and other tooles of Oratory, to perswade their Hearers of the Utility, Honour, or Justice of following their advise.

From whence may be inferred, First, that Exhortation and Dehortation, is directed to the Good of him that giveth the Counsell, not of him that asketh it, which is contrary to the duty of a Counsellour; who (by the definition of Counsell) ought to regard, not his own benefit, but his whom he adviseth. And that he directeth his Counsell to his own benefit, is manifest enough, by the long and vehement urging, or by the artificiall giving thereof; which being not required of him, and consequently proceeding from his own occasions, is directed principally to his own benefit, and but accidentarily to the good of him that is Counselled, or not at all.

Secondly, that the use of Exhortation and Dehortation lyeth onely, where a man is to speak to a Multitude; because when the Speech is addressed to one, he may interrupt him, and examine his reasons more rigorously, than can be done in a Multitude; which are too many to enter into Dispute, and Dialogue with him that speaketh indifferently to them all at once.

Thirdly, that they that Exhort and Dehort, where they are required to give Counsell, are corrupt Counsellours, and as it were bribed by their own interest. For though the Counsell they give be never so good; yet he that gives it, is no more a good Counsellour, than he that giveth a Just Sentence for a reward, is a Just Judge. But where a man may lawfully Command, as a Father in his Family, or a Leader in an Army, his Exhortations and Dehortations, are not onely lawfull, but also necessary, and laudable: But then they are no more Counsells, but Commands; which when they are for Execution of soure labour; sometimes necessity, and alwayes humanity requireth to be sweetned in the delivery, by encouragement, and in the tune and phrase of Counsell, rather then in harsher language of Command.

Examples of the difference between Command and Counsell, we may take from the formes of Speech that expresse them in Holy Scripture. *Have no other Gods but me; Make to thy selfe no graven Image; Take not Gods name in vain; Sanctifie the Sabbath; Honour thy Parents; Kill not; Steale not*, &c. are Commands; because the reason for which we are to obey them, is drawn from the will of God our King, whom we are obliged to obey. But these words, *Sell all thou hast; give it to the poore; and follow me*, are Counsell; because the reason for which we are to do so, is drawn from our own benefit; which is this, that we shall have *Treasure in heaven*. These words, *Go into the Village over against you, and you shall find an Asse tyed, and her Colt; loose her, and bring her to me*, are a Command: for the reason of their fact is drawn from the will of their Master: but these words, *Repent, and be Baptized in the Name of Jesus*, are Counsell; because the reason why we should so do, tendeth not to any benefit of God Almighty, who shall still be King in what manner soever we rebell; but of our selves, who have no other means of avoyding the punishment hanging over us for our *sins past.*[1]

As the difference of Counsell from Command, hath been now deduced from the nature of Counsell, consisting in a deducing of the benefit, or hurt that may arise to him that is to be Counselled, by the necessary or probable consequences of the action he propoundeth; so may also the differences between *apt*, and *inept* Counsellours be derived from the same. For Experience, being but Memory of the consequences of like actions formerly observed, and Counsell but the Speech whereby that experience is made known to another; the Vertues, and Defects of Counsell, are the same with the Vertues, and Defects Intellectuall: And to the Person of a Common-wealth, his Counsellours serve him in the place of Memory, and Mentall Discourse. But with this resemblance of the Common-wealth, to a naturall man, there is one dissimilitude joyned, of great importance; which is, that a naturall man receiveth his experience, from the naturall objects of sense, which work upon him without passion, or interest of their own; whereas they that give Counsell to the Representative person of a Common-wealth, may have, and have often their particular ends, and passions, that render their Counsells alwayes suspected, and many times unfaithfull. And therefore we may set down for the first condition of a good Counsellour, *That his Ends, and Interest, be not inconsistent with the Ends and Interest of him he Counselleth.*

Secondly, Because the office of a Counsellour, when an action comes into deliberation, is to make manifest the consequences of it, in such manner, as he that is Counselled may be truly and evidently informed; he ought to propound his advise, in such forme of speech, as may make the truth most evidently appear; that is to say, with as firme ratiocination, as significant and proper language, and as briefly,

Differences of fit and unfit Counsellours.
[134]

---

[1] *Syn.*: sins.

as the evidence will permit. And therefore *rash, and unevident Inferences*; (such as are fetched onely from Examples, or authority of Books, and are not arguments of what is good, or evill, but witnesses of fact, or of opinion;) *obscure, confused, and ambiguous Expressions, also all metaphoricall Speeches, tending to the stirring up of Passion,* (because such reasoning, and such expressions, are usefull onely to deceive, or to lead him we Counsell towards other ends than his own) *are repugnant to the Office of a Counsellour.*

Thirdly, Because the Ability of Counselling proceedeth from Experience, and long study; and no man is presumed to have experience in all those things that to the Administration of a great Common-wealth are necessary to be known, *No man is presumed to be a good Counsellour, but in such Businesse, as he hath not onely been much versed in, but hath also much meditated on, and considered.* For seeing the businesse of a Common-wealth is this, to preserve the people in Peace at home, and defend them against forraign Invasion, we shall find, it requires great knowledge of the disposition of Man-kind, of the Rights of Government, and of the nature of Equity, Law, Justice, and Honour, not to be attained without study; And of the Strength, Commodities, Places, both of their own Country, and their Neighbours; as also of the inclinations, and designes of all Nations that may any way annoy them. And this is not attained to, without much experience. Of which things, not onely the whole summe, but every one of the particulars requires the age, and observation of a man in years, and of more than ordinary study. The wit required for Counsel, as I have said before (Chap. 8.) is Judgement. And the differences of men in that point come from different education, of some to one kind of study, or businesse, and of others to another. When for the doing of any thing, there be Infallible rules, (as in Engines, and Edifices, the rules of Geometry,) all the experience of the world cannot equall his Counsell, that has learnt, or found out the Rule. And when there is no such Rule, he that hath most experience in that particular kind of businesse, has therein the best Judgement, and is the best Counsellour.

Fourthly, to be able to give Counsell to a Common-wealth, in a businesse that hath reference to another Common-wealth, *It is necessary to be acquainted with the Intelligences, and Letters that come from thence, and with all the records of Treaties, and other transactions of State* between them; which none can doe, but such as the Representative

[135]

shall think fit. By which we may see, that they who are not called to Counsell, can have no good Counsell in such cases to obtrude.

Fifthly, Supposing the number of Counsellors equall, a man is better Counselled by hearing them apart, then in an Assembly; and that for many causes. First, in hearing them apart, you have the advice of every man; but in an Assembly many of them deliver their advise with *I*, or *No*, or with their hands, or feet, not moved by their own sense, but by the eloquence of another, or for feare of displeasing some that have spoken, or the whole Assembly, by contradiction; or for feare of appearing duller in apprehension, than those that have applauded the contrary opinion. Secondly, in an Assembly of many, there cannot choose but be some whose interests are contrary to that of the Publique; and these their Interests make passionate, and Passion eloquent, and Eloquence drawes others into the same advice. For the Passions of men, which asunder are moderate, as the heat of one brand; in Assembly are like many brands, that enflame one another, (especially when they blow one another with Orations) to the setting of the Common-wealth on fire, under pretence of Counselling it. Thirdly, in hearing every man apart, one may examine (when there is need) the truth, or probability of his reasons, and of the grounds of the advise he gives, by frequent interruptions, and objections; which cannot be done in an Assembly, where (in every difficult question) a man is rather astonied, and dazled with the variety of discourse upon it, than informed of the course he ought to take. Besides, there cannot be an Assembly of many, called together for advice, wherein there be not some, that have the ambition to be thought eloquent, and also learned in the Politiques; and give not their advice with care of the businesse propounded, but of the applause of their motly orations, made of the divers colored threds, or shreds of Authors; which is an Impertinence at least, that takes away the time of serious Consultation, and in the secret way of Counselling apart, is easily avoided. [136] Fourthly, in Deliberations that ought to be kept secret, (whereof there be many occasions in Publique Businesse,) the Counsells of many, and especially in Assemblies, are dangerous; And therefore great Assemblies are necessitated to commit such affaires to lesser numbers, and of such persons as are most *versed in them,*[1] and in whose fidelity they have most confidence.

[1] Syn.: versed

To conclude, who is there that so far approves the taking of Coun-sell from a great Assembly of Counsellours, that wisheth for, or would accept of their pains, when there is a question of marrying his Chil-dren, disposing of his Lands, governing his Household, or managing his private Estate, especially if there be amongst them such as wish not his prosperity? A man that doth his businesse by the help of many and prudent Counsellours, with every one consulting apart in his proper element, does it best, as he that useth able Seconds at Tennis play, placed in their proper stations. He does next best, that useth his own Judgement only; as he that has no Second at all. But he that is carried up and down to his businesse in a framed Counsell, which cannot move but by the plurality of consenting opinions, the execution whereof is commonly (out of envy, or interest) retarded by the part dissenting, does it worst of all, *and is*[2] like one that is carried to the ball, though by good Players, yet in a Wheele-barrough, or other frame, heavy of it self, and retarded also by the inconcurrent judge-ments, and endeavours of them that drive it; and so much the more, as they be more that set their hands to it; and most of all, when there is one, or more amongst them, that desire to have him lose. And though it be true, that many eys see more then one; yet it is not to be understood of many Counsellours; but then only, when the finall Resolution is in one man. Otherwise, because many eyes see the same thing in divers lines, and are apt to look asquint towards their private benefit; they that desire not to misse their marke, though they look about with two eyes, yet they never ayme but with one; And therefore no great Popular Common-wealth was ever kept up; but either by a forraign Enemy that united them; or by the reputation of some one eminent Man amongst them; or by the secret Counsell of a few; or by the mutuall feare of equall factions; and not by the open Consul-tations of the Assembly. And as for very little Common-wealths, be they Popular, or Monarchicall, there is no humane wisdome can uphold them, longer than the Jealousy lasteth of their potent Neighbours.

[2] *Syn.*: and

CHAP. XXVI.
Of Civill Lawes.

By Civill Lawes, I understand the Lawes, that men are therefore   *Civill Law*
bound to observe, because they are Members, not of this, or that   *what.*
Common-wealth in particular, but of a Common-wealth. For the
knowledge of particular Lawes belongeth to them, that professe the   [137]
study of the Lawes of their severall Countries; but the knowledge of
Civill Law in generall, to any man. The antient Law of *Rome* was
called their *Civil Law*, from the word *Civitas*, which signifies a Common-wealth: And those Countries, which having been under the
Roman Empire, and governed by that Law, retaine still such part
thereof as they think fit, *and call*¹ that part the Civill Law, to
distinguish it from the rest of their own Civill Lawes. But that is not it
I intend to speak of here; my designe being not to shew what is Law
here, and there; but what is Law; as *Plato, Aristotle, Cicero*, and divers
others have done, without taking upon them the profession of the
study of the Law.

And first it is manifest, that Law in generall, is not Counsell, but
Command; nor a Command of any man to any man; but only of him,
whose Command is addressed to one formerly obliged to obey him.
And as for Civill Law, it addeth only the name of the person Com-
manding, which is *Persona Civitatis*, the Person of the
Common-wealth.

Which considered, I define Civill Law in this manner. CIVILL
LAW, *Is to every Subject, those Rules, which the Common-wealth hath
Commanded him, by Word, Writing, or other sufficient Sign of the Will, to
make use of, for the Distinction of Right, and Wrong; that is to say, of what
is contrary, and what is not contrary to the Rule.*

In which definition, there is nothing that is not at first sight evident.
For every man seeth, that some Lawes are addressed to all the Subjects in generall; some to particular Provinces; some to particular
Vocations; and some to particular Men; and are therefore Lawes, to
every of those to whom the Command is directed; and to none else.

---

¹ *Syn.*: call [but this may be a better reading].

183

As also, that Lawes are the Rules of Just, and Unjust; nothing being reputed Unjust, that is not contrary to some Law. Likewise, that none can make Lawes but the Common-wealth; because our Subjection is to the Common-wealth only: and that Commands, are to be signified by sufficient Signs; because a man knows not otherwise how to obey them. And therefore, whatsoever can from this definition by necessary consequence be deduced, ought to be acknowledged for truth. Now I deduce from it this that followeth.

The Soveraign is Legislator:

1. The Legislator in all Common-wealths, is only the Soveraign, be he one Man, as in a Monarchy, or one Assembly of men, as in a Democracy, or Aristocracy. For the Legislator, is he that maketh the Law. And the Common-wealth only, praescribes, and commandeth the observation of those rules, which we call Law: Therefore the Common-wealth is the Legislator. But the Common-wealth is no Person, nor has capacity to doe any thing, but by the Representative, (that is, the Soveraign;) and therefore the Soveraign is the sole Legislator. For the same reason, none can abrogate a Law made, but the Soveraign; because a Law is not abrogated, but by another Law, that forbiddeth it to be put in execution.

And not Subject to Civill Law.

[138]

2. The Soveraign of a Common-wealth, be it an Assembly, or one Man, is not Subject to the Civill Lawes. For having power to make, and repeale Lawes, he may when he pleaseth, free himselfe from that subjection, by repealing those Lawes that trouble him, and making of new; and consequently he was free before. For he is free, that can be free when he will: Nor is it possible for any person to be bound to himselfe; because he that can bind, can release; and therefore he that is bound to himselfe onely, is not bound.

Use, a Law not by vertue of Time, but of the Soveraigns consent.

3. When long Use obtaineth the authority of a Law, it is not the Length of Time that maketh the Authority, but the Will of the Soveraign signified by his silence, (for Silence is sometimes an argument of Consent;) and it is no longer Law, then the Soveraign shall be silent therein. And therefore if the Soveraign shall have a question of Right grounded, not upon his present Will, but upon the Lawes formerly made; the Length of Time shal bring no prejudice to his Right; but the question shal be judged by Equity. For many unjust Actions, and unjust Sentences, go uncontrolled a longer time, than any man can remember. And our Lawyers account no Customes Law, but such as are reasonable, and that evill Customes are to be abolished: But the Judgement of what is reasonable, and of what is to

be abolished, belongeth to him that maketh the Law, which is the Soveraign Assembly, or Monarch.

4. The Law of Nature, and the Civill Law, contain each other, and are of equall extent. For the Lawes of Nature, which consist in Equity, Justice, Gratitude, and other morall Vertues on these depending, in the condition of meer Nature (as I have said before in the end of the 15th Chapter,) are not properly Lawes, but qualities that dispose men to peace, and to obedience. When a Common-wealth is once settled, then are they actually Lawes, and not before; as being then the commands of the Common-wealth; and therefore also Civill Lawes: For it is the Soveraign Power that obliges men to obey them. For in the differences of private men, to declare, what is Equity, what is Justice, and what is morall Vertue, and to make them binding, there is need of the Ordinances of Soveraign Power, and Punishments to be ordained for such as shall break them; which Ordinances are therefore part of the Civill Law. The Law of Nature therefore is a part of the Civill Law in all Common-wealths of the world. Reciprocally also, the Civill Law is a part of the Dictates of Nature. For Justice, that is to say, Performance of Covenant, and giving to every man his own, is a Dictate of the Law of Nature. But every subject in a Common-wealth, hath covenanted to obey the Civill Law, (either one with another, as when they assemble to make a common Representative, or with the Representative it selfe one by one, when subdued by the Sword they promise obedience, that they may receive life;) And therefore Obedience to the Civill Law is part also of the Law of Nature. Civill, and Naturall Law are not different kinds, but different parts of Law; whereof one part being written, is called Civill, the other unwritten, Naturall. But the Right of Nature, that is, the naturall Liberty of man, may by the Civill Law be abridged, and restrained: nay, the end of making Lawes, is no other, but such Restraint; without the which there cannot possibly be any Peace. And Law was brought into the world for nothing else, but to limit the naturall liberty of particular men, in such manner, as they might not hurt, but assist one another, and joyn together against a common Enemy.

5. If the Soveraign of one Common-wealth, subdue a People that have lived under other written Lawes, and afterwards govern them by the same Lawes, by which they were governed before; yet those Lawes are the Civill Lawes of the Victor, and not of the Vanquished Common-wealth. For the Legislator is he, not by whose authority the

The Law of Nature, and the Civill Law contain each other.

[139]

Provinciall Lawes are not made by Custome, but by the Soveraign Power.

Lawes were first made, but by whose authority they now continue to be Lawes. And therefore where there be divers Provinces, within the Dominion of a Common-wealth, and in those Provinces diversity of Lawes, which commonly are called the Customes of each severall Province, we are not to understand that such Customes have their force, onely from Length of Time; but that they were antiently Lawes written, or otherwise made known, for the Constitutions, and Statutes of their Soveraigns; and are now Lawes, not by vertue of the Praescription of time, but by the Constitutions of their present Soveraigns. But if an unwritten Law, in all the Provinces of a Dominion, shall be generally observed, and no iniquity appear in the use thereof; that Law can be no other but a Law of Nature, equally obliging all man-kind.

Some foolish opinions of Lawyers concerning the making of Lawes. 6. Seeing then all Lawes, written, and unwritten, have their Authority, and force, from the Will of the Common-wealth; that is to say, from the Will of the Representative; which in a Monarchy is the Monarch, and in other Common-wealths the Soveraign Assembly; a man may wonder from whence proceed such opinions, as are found in the Books of Lawyers of eminence in severall Common-wealths, directly, or by consequence making the Legislative Power depend on private men, or subordinate Judges. As for example, *That the Common Law, hath no Controuler but the Parlament*; which is true onely where a Parlament has the Soveraign Power, and cannot be assembled, nor dissolved, but by their own discretion. For if there be a right in any else to dissolve them, there is a right also to controule them, and consequently to controule their controulings. And if there be no such right, then the Controuler of Lawes is not *Parlamentum*, but *Rex in Parlamento*. And where a Parlament is Soveraign, if it should assemble never so many, or so wise men, from the Countries subject to them, for whatsoever cause; yet there is no man will believe, that such an Assembly hath thereby acquired to themselves a Legislative Power. *Item*, that the two arms of a Common-wealth, are *Force, and Justice; the first whereof is in the King; the other deposited in the hands of the Parlament*. As if a Common-wealth could consist, where the Force were in any hand, which Justice had not the Authority to command and govern.

7. That Law can never be against Reason, our Lawyers are agreed; and that not the Letter, (that is, every construction of it,) but that

which is according to the Intention of the Legislator, is the Law. And it is true: but the doubt is, of whose Reason it is, that shall be received for Law. It is not meant of any private Reason; for then there would be as much contradiction in the Lawes, as there is in the Schooles; nor yet, (as Sr. *Ed. Coke* makes it,) an *Artificiall perfection of Reason, gotten by long study, observation, and experience,* (as his was.) For it is possible long study may encrease, and confirm erroneous Sentences: and where men build on false grounds, the more they build, the greater is the ruine: and of those that study, and observe with equall time, and diligence, the reasons and resolutions are, and must remain discordant: and therefore it is not that *Juris prudentia,* or wisedome of subordinate Judges; but the Reason of this our Artificiall Man the Common-wealth, and his Command, that maketh Law: And the Common-wealth being in their Representative but one Person, there cannot easily arise any contradiction in the Lawes; and when there doth, the same Reason is able, by interpretation, or alteration, to take it away. In all Courts of Justice, the Soveraign (which is the Person of the Common-wealth,) is he that Judgeth: The subordinate Judge, ought to have regard to the reason, which moved his Soveraign to make such Law, that his Sentence may be according thereunto; which then is his Soveraigns Sentence; otherwise it is his own, and an unjust one.

[140]

Sir Edw. Coke upon Littleton, Lib.2. Ch.6. fol.97.b.

8. From this, that the Law is a Command, and a Command consisteth in declaration, or manifestation of the will of him that commandeth, by voyce, writing, or some other sufficient argument of the same, we may understand, that the Command of the Common-wealth, is Law onely to those, that have means to take notice of it. Over naturall fooles, children, or mad-men there is no Law, no more than over brute beasts; nor are they capable of the title of just, or unjust; because they had never power to make any covenant, or to understand the consequences thereof; and consequently never took upon them to authorise the actions of any Soveraign, as they must do that make to themselves a Common-wealth. And as those from whom Nature, or Accident hath taken away the notice of all Lawes in generall; so also every man, from whom any accident, nor proceeding from his own default, hath taken away the means to take notice of any particular Law, is excused, if he observe it not; And to speak properly, that Law is no Law to him. It is therefore necessary, to consider in

Law made, if not also made known, is no Law.

this place, what arguments, and signes be sufficient for the knowledge of what is the Law; that is to say, what is the will of the Soveraign, as well in Monarchies, as in other formes of government.

Unwritten Lawes are all of them Lawes of Nature.
And first, if it be a Law that obliges all the Subjects without exception, and is not written, nor otherwise published in such places as they may take notice thereof, it is a Law of Nature. For whatsoever men are to take knowledge of for Law, not upon other mens words, but every one from his own reason, must be such as is agreeable to the reason of all men; which no Law can be, but the Law of Nature. The Lawes of Nature therefore need not any publishing, nor Proclamation; as being contained in this one Sentence, approved by all the world, *Do not that to another, which thou thinkest unreasonable to be done by another to thy selfe.*

[141]
Secondly, if it be a Law that obliges only some condition of men, or one particular man, and be not written, nor published by word, then also it is a Law of Nature; and known by the same arguments, and signs, that distinguish those in such a condition, from other Subjects. For whatsoever Law is not written, or some way published by him that makes it Law, can be known no way, but by the reason of him that is to obey it; and is therefore also a Law not only Civill, but Naturall. For Example, if the Soveraign employ a Publique Minister, without written Instructions what to doe; he is obliged to take for Instructions the Dictates of Reason; As if he make a Judge, The Judge is to take notice, that his Sentence ought to be according to the reason of his Soveraign, which being alwaies understood to be Equity, he is bound to it by the Law of Nature: Or if an Ambassador, he is (in all things not conteined in his written Instructions) to take for Instruction that which Reason dictates to be most conducing to his Soveraigns interest; and so of all other Ministers of the Soveraignty, publique and private. All which Instructions of naturall Reason may be comprehended under one name of *Fidelity;* which is a branch of naturall Justice.

The Law of Nature excepted, it belongeth to the essence of all other Lawes, to be made known, to every man that shall be obliged to obey them, either by word, or writing, or some other act, known to proceed from the Soveraign Authority. For the will of another, cannot be understood but by his own word, or act, or by conjecture taken from his scope and purpose; which in the person of the Commonwealth, is to be supposed alwaies consonant to Equity and Reason.

And in antient time, before letters were in common use, the Lawes were many times put into verse; that the rude people taking pleasure in singing, or reciting them, might the more easily reteine them in memory. And for the same reason *Solomon* adviseth a man, to bind the ten Commandements ★ upon his ten fingers. And for the Law which *Moses* gave to the people of *Israel* at the renewing of the Covenant, ★ he biddeth them to teach it their Children, by discoursing of it both at home, and upon the way; at going to bed, and at rising from bed; and to write it upon the posts, and dores of their houses; and ★ to assemble the people, man, woman, and child, to heare it read.

★ *Prov.*7.3.

★ *Deut.* 11.19.

★ *Deut.* 31.12.

Nor is it enough the Law be written, and published; but also that there be manifest signs, that it proceedeth from the will of the Soveraign. For private men, when they have, or think they have force enough to secure their unjust designes, and convoy them safely to their ambitious ends, may publish for Lawes what they please, without, or against the Legislative Authority. There is therefore requisite, not only a Declaration of the Law, but also sufficient signes of the Author, and Authority. The Author, or Legislator is supposed in every Common-wealth to be evident, because he is the Soveraign, who having been Constituted by the consent of every one, is supposed by every one to be sufficiently known. And though the ignorance, and security of men be such, for the most part, as that when the memory of the first Constitution of their Common-wealth is worn out, they doe not consider, by whose power they use to be defended against their enemies, and to have their industry protected, and to be righted when injury is done them; yet because no man that considers, can make question of it, no excuse can be derived from the ignorance of where the Soveraignty is placed. And it is a Dictate of Naturall Reason, and consequently an evident Law of Nature, that no man ought to weaken that power, the protection whereof he hath himself demanded, or wittingly received against others. Therefore of who is Soveraign, no man, but by his own fault, (whatsoever evill men suggest,) can make any doubt. The difficulty consisteth in the evidence of the Authority derived from him; The removing whereof, dependeth on the knowledge of the publique Registers, publique Counsels, publique Ministers, and publique Seales; by which all Lawes are sufficiently verified; Verifyed, I say, not Authorised: for the Verification, is but the Testimony and Record; not the Authority of the Law; which consisteth in the Command of the Soveraign only.

Nothing is Law where the Legislator cannot be known.

[142]

Difference between Verifying and Authorising.

The Law Verifyed by the subordinate Judge.

If therefore a man have a question of Injury, depending on the Law of Nature; that is to say, on common Equity; the Sentence of the Judge, that by Commission hath Authority to take cognisance of such causes, is a sufficient Verification of the Law of Nature in that individuall case. For though the advice of one that professeth the study of the Law, be useful for the avoyding of contention; yet it is but advice: tis the Judge must tell men what is Law, upon the hearing of the Controversy.

By the Publique Registers.

But when the question is of injury, or crime, upon a written Law; every man by recourse to the Registers, by himself, or others, may (if he will) be sufficiently enformed, before he doe such injury, or commit the crime, whither it be an injury or not: Nay he ought to doe so: For when a man doubts whether the act he goeth about, be just, or injust; and may informe himself, if he will; the doing is unlawfull. In like manner, he that supposeth himself injured, in a case determined by the written Law, which he may by himself, or others see and consider; if he complaine before he consults with the Law, he does unjustly, and bewrayeth a disposition rather to vex other men, than to demand his own right.

By Letters, Patent, and Publique Seale.

If the question be of Obedience to a publique Officer; To have seen his Commission, with the Publique Seale, and heard it read; or to have had the means to be informed of it, if a man would, is a sufficient Verification of his Authority. For every man is obliged to doe his best endeavour, to informe himself of all written Lawes, that may concerne his own future actions.

The Interpretation of the Law dependeth on the Soveraign Power.

[143]

The Legislator known; and the Lawes, either by writing, or by the light of Nature, sufficiently published; there wanteth yet another very materiall circumstance to make them obligatory. For it is not the Letter, but the Intendment, or Meaning; that is to say, the authentique Interpretation of the Law (which is the sense of the Legislator,) in which the nature of the Law consisteth; And therefore the Interpretation of all Lawes dependeth on the Authority Soveraign; and the Interpreters can be none but those, which the Soveraign, (to whom only the Subject oweth obedience) shall appoint. For else, by the craft of an Interpreter, the Law may be made to beare a sense, contrary to that of the Soveraign; by which means the Interpreter becomes the Legislator.

All Lawes need Interpretation.

All Laws, written, and unwritten, have need of Interpretation. The unwritten Law of Nature, though it be easy to such, as without partiality, and passion, make use of their naturall reason, and therefore leaves the violaters thereof without excuse; yet considering there be very few, perhaps none, that in some cases are not blinded by self love, or some other passion, it is now become of all Laws the most obscure; and has consequently the greatest need of able Interpreters. The written Laws, if they be short, are easily mis-interpreted, from the divers significations of a word, or two: if long, they be more obscure by the diverse significations of many words: in so much as no written Law, delivered in few, or many words, can be well understood, without a perfect understanding of the finall causes, for which the Law was made; the knowledge of which finall causes is in the Legislator. To him therefore there can not be any knot in the Law, insoluble; either by finding out the ends, to undoe it by; or else by making what ends he will, (as *Alexander* did with his sword in the Gordian knot,) by the Legislative power; which no other Interpreter can doe.

The Interpretation of the Lawes of Nature, in a Common-wealth, dependeth not on the books of Morall Philosophy. The Authority of writers, without the Authority of the Common-wealth, maketh not their opinions Law, be they never so true. That which I have written in this Treatise, concerning the Morall Vertues, and of their necessity, for the procuring, and maintaining peace, though it bee evident Truth, is not therefore presently Law; but because in all Commonwealths in the world, it is part of the Civill Law: For though it be naturally reasonable; yet it is by the Soveraigne Power that it is Law: Otherwise, it were a great errour, to call the Lawes of Nature unwritten Law; whereof wee see so many volumes *published by diverse authors,*[1] and in them so many contradictions of one another, and of themselves. *The Authenticall Interpretation of Law is not that of writers.*

The Interpretation of the Law of Nature, is the Sentence of the Judge constituted by the Soveraign Authority, to heare and determine such controversies, as depend thereon; and consisteth in the application of the Law to the present case. For in the act of Judicature, the Judge doth no more but consider, whither the demand of the party, be consonant to naturall reason, and Equity; and the Sentence he giveth, is therefore the Interpretation of the Law of Nature; which Interpretation is Authentique; not because it is his private Sentence; but *The Interpreter of the Law is the Judge giving sentence* vivâ voce *in every particular case.*

---

[1] *Syn.*: published,

because he giveth it by Authority of the Soveraign, whereby it becomes the Soveraigns Sentence; which is Law for that time, to the parties pleading.

The Sentence of a Judge, does not bind him, or another Judge to give like Sentence in like Cases ever after.

But because there is no Judge Subordinate, nor Soveraign, but may erre in a Judgement of Equity; if afterward in another like case he find it more consonant to Equity to give a contrary Sentence, he is obliged to doe it. No mans error becomes his own Law; nor obliges him to persist in it. Neither (for the same reason) becomes it a Law to other Judges, though sworn to follow it. For though a wrong Sentence given by authority of the Soveraign, if he know and allow it, in such Lawes as are mutable, be a constitution of a new Law, in cases, in which every little circumstance is the same; yet in Lawes immutable, such as are the Lawes of Nature, they are no Lawes to the same, or other Judges, in the like cases for ever after. Princes succeed one another; and one Judge passeth, another commeth; nay, Heaven and Earth shall passe; but not one title of the Law of Nature shall passe; for it is the Eternall Law of God. Therefore all the Sentences of precedent Judges that have ever been, cannot all together make a Law contrary to naturall Equity: Nor any Examples of former Judges, can warrant an unreasonable Sentence, or discharge the present Judge of the trouble of studying what is Equity (in the case he is to Judge,) from the principles of his own naturall reason. For example sake, 'Tis against the Law of Nature, *To punish the Innocent*; and Innocent is he that acquitteth himselfe Judicially, and is acknowledged for Innocent by the Judge. Put the case now, that a man is accused of a capitall crime, and seeing the power and malice of some enemy, and the frequent corruption and partiality of Judges, runneth away for feare of the event, and afterwards is taken, and brought to a legall triall, and maketh it sufficiently appear, he was not guilty of the crime, and being thereof acquitted, is neverthelesse condemned to lose his goods; this is a manifest condemnation of the Innocent. I say therefore, that there is no place in the world, which this can be an interpretation of a Law of Nature, or be made a Law by the Sentences of precedent Judges, that had done the same. For he that judged it first, judged unjustly; and no Injustice can be a pattern of Judgement to succeeding Judges. A written Law may forbid innocent men to fly, and they may be punished for flying: But that flying for feare of injury, should be taken *for a*[1] presumption of guilt, after a man is already absolved of the

---

[1] *Syn.*: for

crime Judicially, is contrary to the nature of a Presumption, which hath no place after Judgement given. Yet this is set down by a great Lawyer for the common Law of *England*.¹ *If a man* (saith he) *that is Innocent, be accused of Felony, and for feare flyeth for the same; albeit he judicially acquitteth himselfe of the Felony; yet if it be found that he fled for the Felony, he shall notwithstanding his Innocency, Forfeit all his goods, chattels, debts, and duties. For as to the Forfeiture of them, the Law will admit no proofe against the Presumption in Law, grounded upon his flight.* Here you see, *An Innocent man, Judicially acquitted, notwithstanding his Innocency,* (when no written Law forbad him to fly) after his acquittal, *upon a Presumption in Law,* condemned to lose all the goods he hath. If the Law ground upon his flight a Presumption of the fact, (which was Capitall,) the Sentence ought to have been Capitall: if the Presump- [145] tion were not of the Fact, for what then ought he to lose his goods? This therefore is no Law of *England*; nor is the condemnation grounded upon a Presumption of Law, but upon the Presumption of the Judges. It is also against Law, to say that no Proofe shall be admitted against a Presumption of Law. For all Judges, Soveraign and subordinate, if they refuse to heare Proofe, refuse to do Justice: for though the Sentence be Just, yet the Judges that condemn without hearing the Proofes offered, are Unjust Judges; and their Presumption is but Prejudice; which no man ought to bring with him to the Seat of Justice, whatsoever precedent judgements, or examples he shall pretend to follow. There be other things of this nature, wherein mens Judgements have been perverted, by trusting to Precedents: but this is enough to shew, that though the Sentence of the Judge, be a Law to the party pleading, yet it is no Law to any Judge, that shall succeed him in that Office.

In like manner, when question is of the Meaning of written Lawes, he is not the Interpreter of them, that writeth a Commentary upon them. For Commentaries are commonly more subject to cavill, than the Text; and therefore need other Commentaries; and so there will be no end of such Interpretation. And therefore unlesse there be an Interpreter authorised by the Soveraign, from which the subordinate Judges are not to recede, the Interpreter can be no other than the ordinary Judges, in the same manner, as they are in cases of the unwritten Law; and their Sentences are to be taken by them that

---

¹ i.e. Edward Coke (see biographical notes).

plead, for Lawes in that particular case; but not to bind other Judges, in like cases to give like judgements. For a Judge may erre in the Interpretation even of written Lawes; but no errour of a subordinate Judge, can change the Law, which is the generall Sentence of the Soveraigne.

The difference between the Letter and Sentence of the Law.

In written Lawes, men use to make a difference between the Letter, and the Sentence of the Law: And when by the Letter, is meant whatsoever can be gathered from the bare words, 'tis well distinguished. For the significations of almost all words, are either in themselves, or in the metaphoricall use of them, ambiguous; and may be drawn in argument, to make many senses; but there is onely one sense of the Law. But if by the Letter, be meant the literall sense, then the Letter, and the Sentence or intention of the Law, is all one. For the literall sense is that, which the Legislator intended, should by the letter of the Law be signified. Now the Intention of the Legislator is alwayes supposed to be Equity: For it were a great contumely for a Judge to think otherwise of the Soveraigne. He ought therefore, if the *Words*[1] of the Law doe not fully authorise a reasonable Sentence, to supply it with the Law of Nature; or if the case be difficult, to respit Judgement till he have received more ample authority. For Example, a written Law ordaineth, that he which is thrust out of his house by force, shall be restored by force: It happens that a man by negligence leaves his house empty, and returning is kept out by force, in which

[146]

case there is no speciall Law ordained. It is evident, that this case is contained in the same Law: for else there is no remedy for him at all; which is to be supposed against the Intention of the Legislator. Again, the word of the Law, commandeth to Judge according to the Evidence: A man is accused falsly of a fact, which the Judge saw himself done by another; and not by him that is accused. In this case neither shall the Letter of the Law be followed to the condemnation of the Innocent, nor shall the Judge give Sentence against the evidence of the Witnesses; because the Letter of the Law is to the contrary: but procure of the Soveraign that another be made Judge, and himself Witnesse. So that the incommodity that follows the bare words of a written Law, may lead him to the Intention of the Law, whereby to interpret the same the better; though no Incommodity can warrant a Sentence against the Law. For every Judge of Right, and

[1] *Syn.*: Word

Wrong, is not Judge of what is Commodious, or Incommodious to the Common-wealth.

The abilities required in a good Interpreter of the Law, that is to say, in a good Judge, are not the same with those of an Advocate; namely the study of the Lawes. For a Judge, as he ought to take notice of the Fact, from none but the Witnesses; so also he ought to take notice of the Law, from nothing but the Statutes, and Constitutions of the Soveraign, alledged in the pleading, or declared to him by some that have authority from the Soveraign Power to declare them; and need not take care before-hand, what hee shall Judge; for it shall bee given him what hee shall say concerning the Fact, by Witnesses; and what hee shall say in point of Law, from those that shall in their pleadings shew it, and by authority interpret it upon the place. The Lords of Parlament in *England* were Judges, and most difficult causes have been heard and determined by them; yet few of them were much versed in the study of the Lawes, and fewer had made profession of them: and though they consulted with Lawyers, that were appointed to be present there for that purpose; yet they alone had the authority of giving Sentence. In like manner, in the ordinary trialls of Right, Twelve men of the common People, are the Judges, and give Sentence, not onely of the Fact, but of the Right; and pronounce simply for the Complaynant, or for the Defendant; that is to say, are Judges not onely of the Fact, but also of the Right: and in a question of crime, not onely determine whether done, or not done; but also whether it be *Murder, Homicide, Felony, Assault,* and the like, which are determinations of Law: but because they are not supposed to know the Law of themselves, there is one that hath Authority to enforme them of it, in the particular case they are to Judge of. But yet if they judge not according to that he tells them, they are not subject thereby to any penalty; unlesse it be made appear, they did it against their consciences, or had been corrupted by reward.

The things that make a good Judge, or good Interpreter of the Lawes, are, first, *A right understanding* of that principall Law of Nature called *Equity;* which depending not on the reading of other mens Writings, but on the goodnesse of a mans own naturall Reason, and Meditation, is presumed to be in those most, that have had most leisure, and had the most inclination to meditate thereon. Secondly, *Contempt of unnecessary Riches,* and Preferments. Thirdly, *To be able in judgement to devest himselfe of all feare, anger, hatred, love,* and *com-*

The abilities required in a Judge.

[147]

195

passion. Fourthly, and lastly, *Patience to heare; diligent attention in hearing; and memory to retain, digest and apply what he hath heard.*

Divisions of Law.

The difference and division of the Lawes, has been made in divers manners, according to the different methods, of those men that have written of them. For it is a thing that dependeth not on Nature, but on the scope of the Writer; and is subservient to every mans proper method. In the Institutions of *Justinian*, we find seven sorts of Civill Lawes. 1. The *Edicts, Constitutions*, and *Epistles of the Prince*, that is, of the Emperour; because the whole power of the people was in him. Like these, are the Proclamations of the Kings of *England*.

2. *The Decrees of the whole people of Rome* (comprehending the Senate,) when they were put to the Question by the *Senate*. These were Lawes, at first, by the vertue of the Soveraign Power residing in the people; and such of them as by the Emperours were not abrogated, remained Lawes by the Authority Imperiall. For all Lawes, that bind, are understood to be Lawes by his authority that has power to repeale them. Somewhat like to these Lawes, are the Acts of Parliament in *England*.

3. *The Decrees of the Common people* (excluding the Senate,) when they were put to the question by the *Tribune* of the people. For such of them as were not abrogated by the Emperours, remained Lawes by the Authority Imperiall. Like to these, were the Orders of the House of Commons in *England*.

4. *Senatûs consulta*, the *Orders of the Senate*; because when the people of *Rome* grew so numerous, as it was inconvenient to assemble them; it was thought fit by the Emperour, that men should Consult the Senate, in stead of the people: And these have some resemblance with the Acts of Counsell.

5. *The Edicts of Praetors*, and (in some Cases) of the *Aediles*: such as are the Chiefe Justices in the Courts of *England*.

6. *Responsa Prudentum*; which were the Sentences, and Opinions of those Lawyers, to whom the Emperour gave Authority to interpret the Law, and to give answer to such as in matter of Law demanded their advice; which Answers, the Judges in giving Judgement were obliged by the Constitutions of the Emperour to observe: And should be like the Reports of Cases Judged, if other Judges be by the Law of *England* bound to observe them. For the Judges of the Common Law of *England*, are not properly Judges, but *Juris Consulti*; of whom the

Judges, who are either the Lords, or Twelve men of the Country, are in point of Law to ask advice.

7. Also, *Unwritten Customes*, (which in their own nature are an imitation of Law,) by the tacite consent of the Emperour, in case they be not contrary to the Law of Nature, are very Lawes.

Another division of Lawes, is into *Naturall* and *Positive*. *Naturall* are [148] those which have been Lawes from all Eternity; and are called not onely *Naturall*, but also *Morall* Lawes; consisting in the Morall Vertues, as Justice, Equity, and all habits of the mind that conduce to Peace, and Charity; of which I have already spoken in the fourteenth and fifteenth Chapters.

Positive, are those which have not been from Eternity; but have been made Lawes by the Will of those that have had the Soveraign Power over others; and are either written, or made known to men, by some other argument of the Will of their Legislator.

Again, of Positive Lawes some are *Humane*, some *Divine*: And of *Another* Humane positive lawes, some are *Distributive*, some *Penal*. *Distributive* *Division of* are those that determine the Rights of the Subjects, declaring to every *Law.* man what it is, by which he acquireth and holdeth a propriety in lands, or goods, and a right or liberty of action: and these speak to all the Subjects. *Penal* are those, which declare, what Penalty shall be inflicted on those that violate the Law; and speak to the Ministers and Officers ordained for execution. For though every one ought to be informed of the Punishments ordained beforehand for their transgression; neverthelesse the Command is not addressed to the Delinquent, (who cannot be supposed will faithfully punish himselfe,) but to publique Ministers appointed to see the Penalty executed. And these Penal Lawes are for the most part written together with the Lawes Distributive; and are sometimes called Judgements. For all Lawes are generall Judgements, or Sentences of the Legislator; as also every particular Judgement, is a Law to him, whose case is Judged.

Divine Positive Lawes (for Naturall Lawes being Eternall, and *Divine* Universall, are all Divine,) are those, which being the Commande- *Positive Law* ments of God, (not from all Eternity, nor universally addressed to all *how made* men, but onely to a certain people, or to certain persons,) are declared *Law.* for such, by those whom God hath authorised to declare them. But this Authority of man to declare what be these Positive Lawes of God, how can it be known? God may command a man by a supernaturall way, to deliver Lawes to other men. But because it is of the essence of Law, that he who is to be obliged, be assured of the Authority of him that declareth it, which we cannot naturally take notice to be from God, *How can a man without supernaturall Revelation be assured of the Revelation received by the declarer?* and *how can he be bound to obey them?* For the first question, how a man can be assured of the Revelation of another, without a Revelation particularly to himselfe, it is evidently impossible: For though a man may be induced to believe such Revelation, from the Miracles they see him doe, or from seeing the Extraordinary sanctity of his life, or from seeing the Extraordinary wisedome, or Extraordinary felicity of his Actions, all which are marks of God extraordinary favour; yet they are not assured evidences of speciall Revelation. Miracles are Marvellous workes: but that which is marvellous to one, may not be so to another. Sanctity may be feigned; and the visible felicities of this world, are most often the work of God by Naturall and ordinary causes. And therefore no man can infallibly know by naturall reason, that another has had a supernaturall revelation of Gods will; but only a beliefe; every one (as the signs thereof shall appear greater, or lesser) a firmer, or a weaker belief.

[149]

But for the second, how he can be bound to obey them; it is not so hard. For if the Law declared, be not against the Law of Nature (which is undoubtedly Gods Law) and he undertake to obey it, he is bound by his own act; bound I say to obey it, but not bound to believe it: for mens beliefe, and interiour cogitations, are not subject to the commands, but only to the operation of God, ordinary, or extraordinary. Faith of Supernaturall Law, is not a fulfilling, but only an assenting to the same; and not a duty that we exhibite to God, but a gift which God freely giveth to whom he pleaseth; as also Unbelief is not a breach of any of his Lawes; but a rejection of them all, except the Laws Naturall. But this that I say, will be made yet cleerer, by the Examples, and Testimonies concerning this point in holy Scripture. The Covenant God made with *Abraham* (in a Supernaturall manner) was thus, *This is the Covenant which thou shalt observe between Me and Thee and thy Seed after thee.* *Abrahams* Seed had not this revelation, nor were yet in being; yet they are a party to the Covenant, and bound to obey what *Abraham* should declare to them for Gods Law; which they could not be, but in vertue of the obedience they owed to their Parents; who (if they be Subject to no other earthly power, as here in

Gen. 17.10.

the case of *Abraham*) have Soveraign power over their children, and servants. Againe, where God saith to *Abraham, In thee shall all Nations of the earth be blessed: For I know thou wilt command thy children, and thy house after thee to keep the way of the Lord, and to observe Righteousnesse and Judgement,* it is manifest, the obedience of his Family, who had no Revelation, depended on their former obligation to obey their Soveraign. At Mount *Sinai Moses* only went up to God; the people were forbidden to approach on paine of death; yet were they bound to obey all that *Moses* declared to them for Gods Law. Upon what ground, but on this submission of their own, *Speak thou to us, and we will heare thee; but let not God speak to us, lest we dye?* By which two places it sufficiently appeareth, that in a Common-wealth, a subject that has no certain and assured Revelation particularly to himself concerning the Will of God, is to obey for such, the Command of the Common-wealth: for if men were at liberty, to take for Gods Commandements, their own dreams, and fancies, or the dreams and fancies of private men; scarce two men would agree upon what *are Gods Commandements;*[1] and yet in respect of them, every man would despise the Commandements of the Common-wealth. I conclude therefore, that in all things not contrary to the Morall Law, (that is to say, to the Law of Nature,) all Subjects are bound to obey that for divine Law, which is declared to be so, by the Lawes of the Common-wealth. Which also is evident to any mans reason; for whatsoever is not against the Law of Nature, may be made Law in the name of them that have the Soveraign power; and there is no reason men should be [150] the lesse obliged by it, when tis propounded in the name of God. Besides, there is no place in the world where men are permitted to pretend other Commandements of God, than are declared for such by the Common-wealth. Christian States punish those that revolt from Christian Religion, and all other States, those that set up any Religion by them forbidden. For in whatsoever is not regulated by the Common-wealth, tis Equity (which is the Law of Nature, and therefore an eternall Law of God) that every man equally enjoy his liberty.

There is also another distinction of Laws, into *Fundamentall*, and not *Fundamentall*: but I could never see in any Author, what a Fundamentall Law signifieth. Nevertheless one may very reasonably distinguish Laws in that manner.

Another division of Lawes.

---

[1] *Syn.*: is Gods Commandement;

A Funda-
mentall Law
what.

For a Fundamentall Law in every Common-wealth is that, which being taken away, the Common-wealth faileth, and is utterly dissolved; as a building whose Foundation is destroyed. And therefore a Fundamentall Law is that, by which Subjects are bound to uphold whatsoever power is given to the Soveraign, whether a Monarch, or a Soveraign Assembly, without which the Common-wealth cannot stand; such as is the power of War and Peace, of Judicature, of Election of Officers, and of doing whatsoever he shall think necessary for the Publique good. Not Fundamentall is that, the abrogating whereof, draweth not with it the dissolution of the Common-Wealth; such as are the Lawes concerning Controversies between subject and subject. Thus much of the Division of Lawes.

Difference
between Law
and Right:

I find the words *Lex Civilis*, and *Jus Civile*, that is to say, *Law* and *Right Civil*, promiscuously used for the same thing, even in the most learned Authors; which neverthelesse ought not to be so. For *Right* is *Liberty*, namely that Liberty which the Civil Law leaves us: But *Civill Law* is an *Obligation*; and takes from us the Liberty which the Law of Nature gave us. Nature gave a Right to every man to secure himselfe by his own strength, and to invade a suspected neighbour, by way of prevention: but the Civill Law takes away that Liberty, in all cases where the protection of the Law may be safely stayd for. Insomuch as *Lex* and *Jus*, are as different as *Obligation* and *Liberty*.

And between
a Law and a
Charter.

Likewise *Lawes* and *Charters* are taken promiscuously for the same thing. Yet Charters are Donations of the Soveraign; and not Lawes, but exemptions from Law. The phrase of a Law is *Jubeo, Injungo, I Command*, and *Enjoyn*: the phrase of a Charter is *Dedi, Concessi, I have Given, I have Granted*: but what is given or granted, to a man, is not forced upon him, by a Law. A Law may be made to bind All the Subjects of a Common-wealth: a Liberty, or Charter is only to One man, or some One part of the people. For to say all the people of a Common-wealth, have Liberty in any case whatsoever; is to say, that in such case, there hath been no Law made; or else having been made, is now abrogated.

CHAP. XXVII. [151]
Of CRIMES, EXCUSES, *and* EXTENUATIONS.

A *Sinne*, is not onely a Transgression of a Law, but also any Contempt   *Sinne what.*
of the Legislator. For such Contempt, is a breach of all his Lawes at
once. And therefore may consist, not onely in the *Commission* of a
Fact, or in the Speaking of Words by the Lawes forbidden, or in the
Omission of what the Law commandeth, but also in the *Intention*, or
purpose to transgresse. For the purpose to breake the Law, is some
degree of Contempt of him, to whom it belongeth to see it executed.
To be delighted in the Imagination onely, of being possessed of
another mans goods, servants, or wife, without any intention to take
them from him by force, or fraud, is no breach of the Law, that sayth,
Thou shalt not covet: nor is the pleasure a man may have in imagining,
or dreaming of the death of him, from whose life he expecteth nothing
but dammage, and displeasure, a Sinne; but the resolving to put some
Act in execution, that tendeth thereto. For to be pleased in the fiction
of that, which would please a man if it were reall, is a Passion so
adhaerent to the Nature both of man, and every other living creature,
as to make it a Sinne, were to make Sinne of being a man. The
consideration of this, has made me think them too severe, both to
themselves, and others, that maintain, that the First motions of the
mind, (though checked with the fear of God) be Sinnes. But I confesse it is safer to erre on that hand, than on the other.

A CRIME, is a sinne, consisting in the Committing (by Deed, or   *A Crime*
Word) of that which the Law forbiddeth, or the Omission of what it   *what.*
hath commanded. So that every Crime is a sinne; but not every sinne
a Crime. To intend to steale, or kill, is a sinne, though it never
appeare in Word, or Fact: for God that seeth the thoughts of man, can
lay it to his charge: but till it appear by some thing done, or said, by
which the intention may be argued by a humane Judge, it hath not the
name of Crime: which distinction the Greeks observed, in the word
ἁμάρτημα, and ἔγκλημα, or αἰτία; whereof the former, (which is

translated *Sinne*,) signifieth any swarving from the Law whatsoever; but the two later, (which are translated *Crime*,) signifie that sinne onely, whereof one man may accuse another. But of Intentions, which never appear by any outward act, there is no place for humane accusation. In like manner the Latines by *Peccatum*, which is *Sinne*, signifie all manner of deviation from the Law; but by *Crimen*, (which word they derive from *Cerno*, which signifies to perceive,) they mean onely such sinnes, as may be made appear before a Judge; and therfore are not meer Intentions.

Where no Civill Law is, there is no Crime.

[152]

From this relation of Sinne to the Law, and of Crime to the Civill Law, may be inferred, First, that where Law ceaseth, Sinne ceaseth. But because the Law of Nature is eternall, Violation of Covenants, Ingratitude, Arrogance, and all Facts contrary to any Morall vertue, can never cease to be Sinne. Secondly, that the Civill Law ceasing, Crimes cease: for there being no other Law remaining, but that of Nature, there is no place for Accusation; every man being his own Judge, and accused onely by his own Conscience, and cleared by the Uprightnesse of his own Intention. When therefore his Intention is Right, his fact is no Sinne: if otherwise, his fact is Sinne; but not Crime. Thirdly, That when the Soveraign Power ceaseth, Crime also ceaseth: for where there is no such Power, there is no protection to be had from the Law; and therefore every one may protect himself by his own power: for no man in the Institution of Soveraign Power can be supposed to give away the Right of preserving his own body; for the safety whereof all Soveraignty was ordained. But this is to be understood onely of those, that have not themselves contributed to the taking away of the Power that protected them: for that was a Crime from the beginning.

Ignorance of the Law of Nature excuseth no man.

The source of every Crime, is some defect of the Understanding; or some errour in Reasoning; or some sudden force of the Passions. Defect in the Understanding, is *Ignorance*; in Reasoning, *Erroneous Opinion*. Again, Ignorance is of three sorts; of the *Law*, and of the *Soveraign*, and of the *Penalty*. Ignorance of the Law of Nature Excuseth no man; because every man that hath attained to the use of Reason, is supposed to know, he ought not to do to another, what he would not have done to himselfe. Therefore into what place soever a man shall come, if he do any thing contrary to that Law, it is a Crime. If a man come from the *Indies* hither, and perswade men here to receive a new Religion or teach them any thing that tendeth to disobedience of the Lawes of this Country, though he be never so well perswaded of the truth of what he teacheth, he commits a Crime, and may be justly punished for the same, not onely because his doctrine is false, but also because he does that which he would not approve in another, namely, that comming from hence, he should endeavour to alter the Religion there. But ignorance of the Civill Law, shall Excuse a man in a strange Country, till it be declared to him; because, till then no Civill Law is binding.

In the like manner, if the Civill Law of a mans own Country, be not so sufficiently declared, as he may know it if he will; nor the Action against the Law of Nature; the Ignorance is a good Excuse: In other cases Ignorance of the Civill Law, Excuseth not. *Ignorance of the Civill Law excuseth sometimes.*

Ignorance of the Soveraign Power, in the place of a mans ordinary residence, Excuseth him not; because he ought to take notice of the Power, by which he hath been protected there. *Ignorance of the Soveraign excuseth not.*

Ignorance of the Penalty, where the Law is declared, Excuseth no man: For in breaking the Law, which without a fear of penalty to follow, were not a Law, but vain words, he undergoeth the penalty, though he know not what it is; because, whosoever voluntarily doth any action, accepteth all the known consequences of it; but Punishment is a known consequence of the violation of the Lawes, in every Common-wealth; which punishment, if it be determined already by the Law, he is subject to that; if not, then is he subject to Arbitrary punishment. For it is reason, that he which does Injury, without other limitation than that of his own Will, should suffer punishment without other limitation, than that of his Will whose Law is thereby violated. *Ignorance of the Penalty excuseth not.*

[153]

But when a penalty, is either annexed to the Crime in the Law it selfe, or hath been usually inflicted in the like cases; there the Delinquent is Excused from a greater penalty. For the punishment foreknown, *if it be*[1] not great enough to deterre men from the action, is an invitement to it: because when men compare the benefit of their Injustice, with the harm of their punishment, by necessity of Nature they choose that which appeareth best for themselves: and therefore when they are punished more than the Law had formerly determined, or more than others were punished for the same Crime; it is the Law that tempted, and deceiveth them. *Punishments declared before the Fact, excuse from greater punishments after it.*

No Law, made after a Fact done, can make it a Crime: because if the Fact be against the Law of Nature, the Law was before the Fact; and a Positive Law cannot be taken notice of, before it be made; and *Nothing can be made a Crime by a Law made after the Fact.*

¹ Syn.: if

203

therefore cannot be Obligatory. But when the Law that forbiddeth a Fact, is made before the Fact be done; yet he that doth the Fact, is lyable to the Penalty ordained after, in case no lesser Penalty were made known before, neither by Writing, nor by Example, for the reason immediatly before alledged.

False Principles of Right and Wrong causes of Crime.

From defect in Reasoning, (that is to say, from Errour,) men are prone to violate the Lawes, three wayes. First, by Presumption of false Principles: as when men from having observed how in all places, and in all ages, unjust Actions have been authorised, by the force, and victories of those who have committed them; and that potent men, breaking through the Cob-web Lawes of their Country, the weaker sort, and those that have failed in their Enterprises, have been esteemed the onely Criminals; have thereupon taken for Principles, and grounds of their Reasoning, *That Justice is but a vain word: That whatsoever a man can get by his own Industry, and hazard, is his own: That the Practice of all Nations cannot be unjust: That Examples of former times are good Arguments of doing the like again*; and many more of that kind: Which being granted, no Act in it selfe can be a Crime, but must be made so (not by the Law, but) by the successe of them that commit it; and the same Fact be vertuous, or vicious, as Fortune pleaseth; so that what *Marius* makes a Crime, *Sylla* shall make meritorious, and *Caesar* (the same Lawes standing) turn again into a Crime, to the perpetuall disturbance of the Peace of the Common-wealth.

False Teachers mis-interpreting the Law of Nature,

Secondly, by false Teachers, that either mis-interpret the Law of Nature, making it thereby repugnant to the Law Civill; or by teaching for Lawes, such Doctrines of their own, or Traditions of former times, as are inconsistent with the duty of a Subject.

Thirdly, by Erroneous Inferences from True Principles; which happens commonly to men that are hasty, and praecipitate in concluding, and resolving what to do; such as are they, that have both a great opinion of their own understanding, and believe that things of this nature require not time and study, but onely common experience, and a good naturall wit; whereof no man thinks himselfe unprovided: whereas the knowledge, of Right and Wrong, which is no lesse difficult, there is no man will pretend to, without great and long study. And of those defects in Reasoning, there is none that can Excuse (though some of them may Extenuate) a Crime, in any man, that pretendeth to the administration of his own private businesse; much lesse in them that undertake a publique charge; because they pretend

[154] And false Inferences from true Principles by Teachers.

to the Reason, upon the want whereof they would ground their Excuse.

Of the Passions that most frequently are the causes of Crime, one, is Vain-glory, or a foolish over-rating of their own worth; as if difference of worth, were an effect of their wit, or riches, or bloud, or some other naturall quality, not depending on the Will of those that have the Soveraign Authority. From whence proceedeth a Presumption that the punishments ordained by the Lawes, and extended generally to all Subjects, ought not to be inflicted on them, with the same rigour they are inflicted on poore, obscure, and simple men, comprehended under the name of *Vulgar*. *By their Passions;*

Therefore it happeneth commonly, that such as value themselves by the greatnesse of their wealth, adventure on Crimes, upon hope of escaping punishment, by corrupting publique Justice, or obtaining Pardon by Mony, or other rewards. *Presumption of Riches,*

And that such as have multitude of Potent Kindred; and popular men, that have gained reputation amongst the Multitude, take courage to violate the Lawes, from a hope of oppressing the Power, to whom it belongeth to put them in execution. *And Friends;*

And that such as have a great, and false opinion of their own Wisedome, take upon them to reprehend the actions, and call in question the Authority of them that govern, and so to unsettle the Lawes with their publique discourse, as that nothing shall be a Crime, but what their own designes require should be so. It happeneth also to the same men, to be prone to all such Crimes, as consist in Craft, and in deceiving of their Neighbours; because they think their designes are too subtile to be perceived. These I say are effects of a false presumption of their own Wisdome. For of them that are the first movers in the disturbance of Common-wealth, (which can never happen without a Civill Warre,) very few are left alive long enough, to see their new Designes established: so that the benefit of their Crimes, redoundeth to Posterity, and such as would least have wished it: which argues they were not so wise, as they thought they were. And those that deceive upon hope of not being observed, do commonly deceive themselves, (the darknesse in which they believe they lye hidden, being nothing else but their own blindnesse;) and are no wiser than Children, that think all hid, by hiding their own eyes. *Wisedome.*

And generally all vain-glorious men, (unlesse they be withall timorous), are subject to Anger; as being more prone than others to [155]

205

interpret for contempt, the ordinary liberty of conversation: And there are few Crimes that may not be produced by Anger.

Hatred, Lust, Ambition, Covetous-nesse, causes of Crime.

As for the Passions, of Hate, Lust, Ambition, and Covetousnesse, what Crimes they are apt to produce, is so obvious to every mans experience and understanding, as there needeth nothing to be said of them, saving that they are infirmities, so annexed to the nature, both of man, and all other living creatures, as that their effects cannot be hindred, but by extraordinary use of Reason, or a constant severity in punishing them. For in those things men hate, they find a continuall, and unavoydable molestation; whereby either a mans patience must be everlasting, or he must be eased by removing the power of that which molesteth him: The former is difficult; the later is many times impossible, without some violation of the Law. Ambition, and Covetousnesse are Passions also that are perpetually incumbent, and pressing; whereas Reason is not perpetually present, to resist them: and therefore whensoever the hope of impunity appears, their effects proceed. And for Lust, what it wants in the lasting, it hath in the vehemence, which sufficeth to weigh down the apprehension of all easie, or uncertain punishments.

Fear sometimes cause of Crime, as when the danger is neither present, nor corporeall.

Of all Passions, that which enclineth men least to break the Lawes, is Fear. Nay, (excepting some generous natures,) it is the onely thing, (when there is apparence of profit, or pleasure by breaking the Lawes,) that makes men keep them. And yet in many cases a Crime may be committed through Feare.

For not every Fear justifies the Action it produceth, but the fear onely of corporeall hurt, which we call *Bodily Fear*, and from which a man cannot see how to be delivered, but by the action. A man is assaulted, fears present death, from which he sees not how to escape, but by wounding him that assaulteth him; If he wound him to death, this is no Crime; because no man is supposed at the making of a Common-wealth, to have abandoned the defence of his life, or limbes, where the Law cannot arrive time enough to his assistance. But to kill a man, because from his actions, or his threatnings, I may argue he will kill me when he can, (seeing I have time, and means to demand protection, from the Soveraign Power,) is a Crime. Again, a man receives words of disgrace or some little injuries (for which they that made the Lawes, had assigned no punishment, nor thought it worthy of a man that hath the use of Reason, to take notice of,) and is afraid, unless he revenge it, he shall fall into contempt, and conse-

quently be obnoxious to the like injuries from others; and to avoyd
this breaks the Law, and protects himselfe for the future, by the
terrour of his private revenge. This is a Crime: For the hurt is not
Corporeall, but Phantasticall, and (though in this corner of the world,
made sensible by a custome not many years since begun, amongst
young and vain men,) so light, as a gallant man, and one that is
assured of his own courage, cannot take notice of. Also a man may
stand in fear of Spirits, either through his own superstition, or
through too much credit given to other men, that tell him of strange
Dreams and Visions; and thereby be made believe they will hurt him, [156]
for doing, or omitting divers things, which neverthelesse, to do, or
omit, is contrary to the Lawes; And that which is so done, or omitted,
is not to be Excused by this fear; but is a Crime. For (as I have shewn
before in the second Chapter) Dreams be naturally but the fancies
remaining in sleep, after the impressions our Senses had formerly
received waking; and when men are by any accident unassured they
have slept, seem to be reall Visions; and therefore he that presumes to
break the Law upon his own, or anothers Dream, or pretended
Vision, or upon other Fancy of the power of Invisible Spirits, than is
permitted by the Common-wealth, leaveth the Law of Nature, which
is a certain offence, and followeth the imagery of his own, or another
private mans brain, which he can never know whether it signifieth any
thing, or nothing, nor whether he that tells his Dream, say true, or lye;
which if every private man should have leave to do, (as they must by
the Law of Nature, if any one have it) there could no Law be made to
hold, and so all Common-wealth would be dissolved.

From these different sources of Crimes, it appeares already, that all   *Crimes not*
Crimes are not (as the Stoicks of old time maintained) of the same   *equall.*
allay. There is place, not only for EXCUSE, by which that which
seemed a Crime, is proved to be none at all; but also for EXTENUA-
TION, by which the Crime, that seemed great, is made lesse. For
though all Crimes doe equally deserve the name of Injustice, as all
deviation from a strait line is equally crookednesse, which the Stoicks
rightly observed; yet it does not follow that all Crimes are equally
unjust, no more than that all crooked lines are equally crooked; which
the Stoicks not observing, held it as great a Crime, to kill a Hen,
against the Law, as to kill ones Father.

That which totally Excuseth a Fact, and takes away from it the   *Totall*
nature of a Crime, can be none but that, which at the same time,   *Excuses.*

taketh away the obligation of the Law. For the fact committed once against the Law, if he that committed it be obliged to the Law, can be no other than a Crime.

The want of means to know the Law, totally Excuseth: For the Law whereof a man has no means to enforme himself, is not obligatory. But the want of diligence to enquire, shall not be considered as a want of means; Nor shall any man, that pretendeth to reason enough for the Government of his own affairs, be supposed to want means to know the Lawes of Nature; because they are known by the reason he pretends to: only Children, and Madmen are Excused from offences against the Law Naturall.

Where a man is captive, or in the power of the enemy, (and he is then in the power of the enemy, when his person, or his means of living, is so,) if it be without his own fault, the Obligation of the Law ceaseth; because he must obey the enemy, or dye; and consequently such obedience is no Crime: for no man is obliged (when the protection of the Law faileth,) not to protect himself, by the best means he can.

[157] If a man by the terrour of present death, be compelled to doe a fact against the Law, he is totally Excused; because no Law can oblige a man to abandon his own preservation. And supposing such a Law were obligatory; yet a man would reason thus, *If I doe it not, I die presently; if I doe it, I die afterwards; therefore by doing it, there is time of life gained*; Nature therefore compells him to the fact.

When a man is destitute of food, or other thing necessary for his life, and cannot preserve himselfe any other way, but by some fact against the Law; as if in a great famine he take the food by force, or stealth, which he cannot obtaine for mony nor charity; or in defence of his life, snatch away another mans Sword, he is totally Excused, for the reason next before alledged.

Excuses against the Author. Again, Facts done against the Law, by the authority of another, are by that authority Excused against the Author; because no man ought to accuse his own fact in another, that is but his instrument: but it is not Excused against a third person thereby injured; because in the violation of the Law, both the Author, and Actor are Criminalls. From hence it followeth that when that Man, or Assembly, that hath the Soveraign Power, commandeth a man to do that which is contrary to a former Law, the doing of it is totally Excused: For he ought not to condemn it himselfe, because he is the Author; and what cannot justly

208

be condemned by the Soveraign, cannot justly be punished by any other. Besides, when the Soveraign commandeth any thing to be done against his own former Law, the Command, as to that particular fact, is an abrogation of the Law.

If that Man, or Assembly, that hath the Soveraign Power, disclaime any Right essentiall to the Soveraignty, whereby there accrueth to the Subject, any liberty inconsistent with the Soveraign Power, that is to say, with the very being of a Common-wealth, if the Subject shall refuse to obey the Command in any thing, contrary to the liberty granted, this is neverthelesse a Sinne, and contrary to the duty of the Subject: for he ought to take notice of what is inconsistent with the Soveraignty, because it was erected by his own consent, and for his own defence; and that such liberty as is inconsistent with it, was granted through ignorance of the evill consequence thereof. But if he not onely disobey, but also resist a publique Minister in the execution of it, then it is a Crime; because he might have been righted, (without any breach of the Peace,) upon complaint.

The Degrees of Crime are taken on divers Scales, and measured, First, by the malignity of the Source, or Cause: Secondly, by the contagion of the Example: Thirdly, by the mischiefe of the Effect; and Fourthly, by the concurrence of Times, Places, and Persons.

The same Fact done against the Law, if it proceed from Presumption of strength, riches, or friends to resist those that are to execute the Law, is a greater Crime, than if it proceed from hope of not being discovered, or of escape by flight: For Presumption of impunity by force, is a Root, from whence springeth, at all times, and upon all temptations, a contempt of all Lawes; whereas in the later case, the apprehension of danger, that makes a man fly, renders him more obedient for the future. A Crime which we know to be so, is greater than the same Crime proceeding from a false perswasion that it is lawfull: For he that committeth it against his own conscience, presumeth on his force, or other power, which encourages him to commit the same again: but he that doth it by errour, after the errour shewn him, is conformable to the Law. *Presumption of Power aggravateth.*

[158]

Hee, whose errour proceeds from the authority of a Teacher, or an Interpreter of the Law publiquely authorised, is not so faulty, as he whose errour proceedeth from a peremptory pursute of his own principles, and reasoning: For what is taught by one that teacheth by publique Authority, the Common-wealth teacheth, and hath a resem- *Evill Teachers, Extenuate.*

blance of Law, till the same Authority controuleth it; and in all Crimes that contain not in them a denyall of the Soveraign Power, nor are against an evident *Law or authorised doctrine,*[1] Excuseth totally: whereas he that groundeth his actions, on his private Judgement, ought according to the rectitude, or errour thereof, to stand, or fall.

Examples of Impunity, Extenuate.

The same Fact, if it have been constantly punished in other men, is a greater Crime, than if there have been many precedent Examples of impunity. For those Examples, are so many hopes of Impunity, given by the Soveraign himselfe: And because he which furnishes a man with such a hope, and presumption of mercy, as encourageth him to offend, hath his part in the offence; he cannot reasonably charge the offender with the whole.

Prae-meditation, Aggravateth.

A Crime arising from a sudden Passion, is not so great, as when the same ariseth from long meditation: For in the former case there is a place for Extenuation, in the common infirmity of humane nature: but he that doth it with praemeditation, has used circumspection, and cast his eye, on the Law, on the punishment, and on the consequence thereof to humane society; all which in committing the Crime, hee hath contemned, and postposed to his own appetite. But there is no suddennesse of Passion sufficient for a totall Excuse: For all the time between the first knowing of the Law, and the Commission of the Fact, shall be taken for a time of deliberation; because he ought by meditation of the Law, to rectifie the irregularity of his *Passions continually.*[2]

When the Law is publiquely, and with assiduity, before all the people read, and interpreted; a fact done against it, is a greater Crime, than where men are left without such instruction, to enquire of it with difficulty, uncertainty, and interruption of their Callings, and be informed by private men: for in this case, part of the fault is discharged upon common infirmity; but in the former, there is apparent negligence, which is not without some contempt of the Soveraign Power.

Tacite approbation of the Soveraign, Extenuates.

Those facts which the Law expresly condemneth, but the Lawmaker by other manifest signes of his will tacitly approveth, are lesse Crimes, than the same facts, condemned both by the Law, and Lawmaker. For seeing the will of the Law-maker is a Law, there appear in

---

¹ *Syn.*: Law,   ² *Syn.*: Passions.

this case two contradictory Lawes; which would totally Excuse, if men [159] were bound to take notice of the Soveraigns approbation, by other arguments, than are expressed by his command. But because there are punishments consequent, not onely to the transgression of his Law, but also to the observing of it, he is in part a cause of the transgression, and therefore cannot reasonably impute the whole Crime to the Delinquent. For example, the Law condemneth Duells; the punishment is made capitall: On the contrary part, he that refuseth Duell, is subject to contempt and scorne, without remedy; and sometimes by the Soveraign himselfe thought unworthy to have any charge, or preferment in Warre: If thereupon he accept Duell, considering all men lawfully endeavour to obtain the good opinion of them that have the Soveraign Power, he ought not in reason to be rigorously punished; seeing part of the fault may be discharged on the punisher: which I say, not as wishing liberty of private revenges, or any other kind of disobedience; but a care in Governours, not to countenance any thing obliquely, which directly they forbid. The examples of Princes, to those that see them, are, and ever have been, more potent to govern their actions, than the Lawes themselves. And though it be our duty to do, not what they do, but what they say; yet will that duty never be performed, till it please God to give men an extraordinary, and supernaturall grace to follow that Precept.

Again, if we compare Crimes by the mischiefe of their Effects, First, the same fact, when it redounds to the dammage of many, is greater, than when it redounds to the hurt of few. And therefore, when a fact hurteth, not onely in the present, but also, (by example) in the future, it is a greater Crime, than if it hurt onely in the present: for the former, is a fertile Crime, and multiplyes to the hurt of many; the later is barren. To maintain doctrines contrary to the Religion established in the Common-wealth, is a greater fault, in an authorised Preacher, than in a private person: So also is it, to live prophanely, incontinently, or do any irreligious act whatsoever. Likewise in a Professor of the Law, to maintain any point, or do any act, that tendeth to the weakning of the Soveraign Power, is a greater Crime, than in another man: Also in a man that hath such reputation for wisedome, as that his counsells are followed, or his actions imitated by many, his fact against the Law, is a greater Crime, than the same fact in another: For such men not only commit Crime, but teach it for Law to all other men. And generally all Crimes are the greater, by the

Comparison of Crimes from their Effects.

scandall they give; that is to say, by becomming stumbling-blocks to the weak, that look not so much upon the way they go in, as upon the light that other men carry before them.

Laesa Majestas.

Also Facts of hostility against the present state of the Common-wealth, are greater Crimes, than the same acts done to private men: For the dammage extends it selfe to all: Such are the betraying of the strengths, or revealing of the secrets of the Common-wealth to an Enemy; also all attempts upon the Representative of the Common-wealth, be it a Monarch, or an Assembly; and all endeavours by word, or deed to diminish the Authority of the same, either in the present time, or in succession: which Crimes the Latines understand by *Crimina laesae Majestatis*, and consist in designe, or act, contrary to a Fundamentall Law.

[160]

Bribery and False testimony.

Likewise those Crimes, which render Judgements of no effect, are greater Crimes, than Injuries done to one, or a few persons; as to receive mony to give False judgement, or testimony, is a greater Crime, than otherwise to deceive a man of the like, or a greater summe; because not onely he has wrong, that falls by such judge-ments; but all Judgements are rendered uselesse, and occasion ministred to force, and private revenges.

Depeculation.

Also Robbery, and Depeculation of the Publique treasure, or Revenues, is a greater Crime, than the robbing, or defrauding of a Private man; because to robbe the publique, is to robbe many at once.

Counter-feiting Authority.

Also the Counterfeit usurpation of publique Ministery, the Coun-terfeiting of publique Seales, or publique Coine, than counterfeiting of a private mans person, or his seale; because the fraud thereof, extendeth to the dammage of many.

Crimes against private men compared.

Of facts against the Law, done to private men, the greater Crime, is that, where the dammage in the common opinion of men, is most sensible. And therefore

To kill against the Law, is a greater Crime, than any other injury, life preserved.

And to kill with Torment, greater, than simply to kill.

And Mutilation of a limbe, greater, than the spoyling a man of his goods.

And the spoyling a man of his goods, by Terrour of death, or wounds, than by clandestine surreption.

And by clandestine Surreption, than by consent fraudulently obtained.

And the violation of chastity by Force, greater, than by flattery.

And of a woman Married, than of a woman not married.

For all these things are commonly so valued; though some men are more, and some lesse sensible of the same offence. But the Law regardeth not the particular, but the generall inclination of mankind.

And therefore the offence men take, from contumely, in words, or gesture, when they produce no other harme, than the present griefe of him that is reproached, hath been neglected in the Lawes of the Greeks, Romans, and other both antient, and moderne Commonwealths; supposing the true cause of such griefe to consist, not in the contumely, (which takes no hold upon men conscious of their own vertue,) but in the Pusillanimity of him that is offended by it.

Also a Crime against a private man, is much aggravated by the person, time, and place. For to kill ones Parent, is a greater Crime, than to kill another: for the Parent ought to have the honour of a Soveraign, (though he have surrendred his Power to the Civill Law,) because he had it originally by Nature. And to Robbe a poore man, is [161] a greater Crime, than to robbe a rich man; because 'tis to the poore a more sensible dammage.

And a Crime committed in the Time, or Place appointed for Devotion, is greater, than if committed at another time or place: for it proceeds from a greater contempt of the Law.

Many other cases of Aggravation, and Extenuation might be added: but by these I have set down, it is obvious to every man, to take the altitude of any other Crime proposed.

Lastly, because in almost all Crimes there is an Injury done, not onely to some Private men, but also to the Common-wealth; the same Crime, when the accusation is in the name of the Common-wealth, is called *a *Publique Crime;**[1] and when in the name of a Private man, a **Private Crime;**[2] And the Pleas according thereunto called Publique, *Judicia Publica*, Pleas of the Crown; or Private Pleas. As in an Accusation of Murder, if the accuser be a Private man, the plea is a Private plea; if the accuser be the Soveraign, the plea is a Publique plea.

Publique Crimes what.

---

[1] *Syn.*: Publique Crime;   [2] *Syn.*: Private Crime;

CHAP. XXVIII.

Of PUNISHMENTS, *and* REWARDS.

The definition of Punishment.

A PUNISHMENT, *is an Evill inflicted by publique Authority, on him that hath done, or omitted that which is Judged by the same Authority to be a Transgression of the Law; to the end that the will of men may thereby the better be disposed to obedience.*

Right to Punish whence derived.

Before I inferre any thing from this definition, there is a question to be answered, of much importance; which is, by what door the Right, or Authority of Punishing in any case, came in. For by that which has been said before, no man is supposed bound by Covenant, not to resist violence; and consequently it cannot be intended, that he gave any right to another to lay violent hands upon his person. In the making of a Common-wealth, every man giveth away the right of defending another; but not of defending himselfe. Also he obligeth himselfe, to assist him that hath the Soveraignty, in the Punishing of another; but of himselfe not. But to covenant to assist the Soveraign, in doing hurt to another, unlesse he that so covenanteth have a right to doe it himselfe, is not to give him a Right to Punish. It is manifest therefore that the Right which the Common-wealth (that is, he, or they that represent it) hath to Punish, is not grounded on any concession, or gift of the Subjects. But I have also shewed formerly, that before the Institution of Common-wealth, every man had a right to every thing, and to do whatsoever he thought necessary to his own preservation; subduing, hurting, or killing any man in order thereunto. And this is the foundation of that right of Punishing, which is exercised in every Common-wealth. For the Subjects did not give the Soveraign that right; but onely in laying down theirs, strengthned him to use his own, as he should think fit, for the preservation of them all: so that it was not given, but left to him, and to him onely; and (excepting the limits set him by naturall Law) as entire, as in the condition of meer Nature, and of warre of every one against his neighbour.

[162]

Private injuries, and

From the definition of Punishment, I inferre, First, that neither private revenges, nor injuries of private men, can properly be stiled

Punishments[1]; because they proceed not from publique Authority.

Secondly, that to be neglected, and unpreferred by the publique favour, is not a Punishment; because no new evill is thereby on any man Inflicted; he is onely left in the estate he was in before.

Thirdly, that the evill inflicted by publique Authority, without precedent publique condemnation, is not to be stiled by the name of Punishment; but of an hostile act; because the fact for which a man is Punished, ought first to be Judged by publique Authority, to be a transgression of the Law.

Fourthly, that the evill inflicted by usurped power, and Judges without Authority from the Soveraign, is not Punishment; but an act of hostility; because the acts of power usurped, have not for Author, the person condemned; and therefore are not acts of publique Authority.

Fifthly, that all evill which is inflicted without intention, or possibility of disposing the Delinquent, or (by his example) other men, to obey the Lawes, is not Punishment; but an act of hostility; because without such an end, no hurt done is contained under that name.

Sixthly, whereas to certain actions, there be annexed by Nature, divers hurtfull consequences; as when a man in assaulting another, is himselfe slain, or wounded; or when he falleth into sicknesse by the doing of some unlawfull act; such hurt, though in respect of God, who is the author of Nature, it may be said to be inflicted, and therefore a Punishment divine; yet it is not contaned in the name of Punishment in respect of men, because it is not inflicted by the Authority of man.

Seventhly, If the harm inflicted be lesse than the benefit, or contentment that naturally followeth the crime committed, that harm is not within the definition; and is rather the Price, or Redemption, than the Punishment of a Crime: Because it is of the nature of Punishment, to have for end, the disposing of men to obey the Law; which end (if it be lesse than the benefit of the transgression) it attaineth not, but worketh a contrary effect.

Eighthly, If a Punishment be determined and prescribed in the Law it selfe, and after the crime committed, there be a greater Punishment inflicted, the excesse is not Punishment, but an act of hostility. For seeing the aym of Punishment is not a revenge, but

revenges no Punishments: Nor denyall of preferment:

Nor pain inflicted without publique hearing:

Nor pain inflicted by Usurped power:

Nor pain inflicted without respect to the future good.

Naturall evill consequences, no Punishments.

Hurt inflicted, if lesse than the benefit of transgressing, is not Punishment.

Where the Punishment is annexed to the Law, a greater hurt is not Punishment, but Hostility.

[1] *Syn.*: Punishment

terrour; and the terrour of a great Punishment unknown, is taken away by the declaration of a lesse, the unexpected addition is no part of the Punishment. But where there is no Punishment at all determined by the Law, there whatsoever is inflicted, hath the nature of Punishment. For he that goes about the violation of a Law, wherein no penalty is determined, expecteth an indeterminate, that is to say, an arbitrary Punishment.

[163]

Hurt inflicted for a fact done before the Law, no Punishment.

Ninthly, Harme inflicted for a Fact done before there was a Law that forbad it, is not Punishment, but an act of Hostility: For before the Law, there is no transgression of the Law: But Punishment supposeth a fact judged, to have been a transgression of the Law; Therefore Harme inflicted before the Law made, is not Punishment, but an act of Hostility.

The Representative of the Common-wealth Unpunishable.

Hurt to Revolted Subjects is done by right of War, not by way of Punishment.

Tenthly, Hurt inflicted on the Representative of the Common-wealth, is not Punishment, but an act of Hostility: Because it is of the nature of Punishment, to be inflicted by publique Authority, which is the Authority only of the Representative it self.

Lastly, Harme inflicted upon one that is a declared enemy, fals not under the name of Punishment: Because seeing they were either never subject to the Law, and therefore cannot transgresse it; or having been subject to it, and professing to be no longer so, by consequence deny they can transgresse it, all the Harmes that can be done them, must be taken as acts of Hostility. But in declared Hostility, all infliction of evill is lawfull. From whence it followeth, that if a subject shall by fact, or word, wittingly, and deliberatly deny the authority of the Representative of the Common-wealth, (whatsoever penalty hath been formerly ordained for Treason,) he may lawfully be made to suffer whatsoever the Representative will: For in denying subjection, he denyes such Punishment as by the Law hath been ordained; and therefore suffers as an enemy of the Common-wealth; that is, according to the will of the Representative. For the Punishments set down in the Law, are to Subjects, not to Enemies; such as are they, that having been by their own act Subjects, deliberately revolting, deny the Soveraign Power.

The first, and most generall distribution of Punishments, is into *Divine*, and *Humane*. Of the former I shall have occasion, to speak, in a more convenient place hereafter.

Humane, are those Punishments that be inflicted by the Com-

mandement of Man; and are either *Corporall*, or *Pecuniary*, or
Ignominy, or *Imprisonment*, or *Exile*, or mixt of these.

    Corporall Punishment is that, which is inflicted on the body directly,   *Punishments*
and according to the intention of him that inflicteth it: such as are   *Corporall.*
stripes, or wounds, or deprivation of such pleasures of the body, as
were before lawfully enjoyed.

    And of these, some be *Capitall*, some *Lesse* than *Capitall*. Capitall, is   *Capitall.*
the Infliction of Death; and that either simply, or with torment. Lesse
than Capitall, are Stripes, Wounds, Chains, and any other corporall
Paine, not in its own nature mortall. For if upon the Infliction of a
Punishment death follow not in the intention of the Inflicter, the
Punishment is not to bee esteemed Capitall, though the harme prove
mortall by an accident not to be foreseen; in which case death is not [164]
inflicted, but hastened.

    Pecuniary Punishment, is that which consisteth not only in the
deprivation of a Summe of Mony, but also of Lands, or any other
goods which are usually bought and sold for mony. And in case the
Law, that ordaineth such a punishment, be made with design to
gather mony, from such as shall transgresse the same, it is not properly a Punishment, but the Price of priviledge, and exemption from
the Law, which doth not absolutely forbid the fact, but only to those
that are not able to pay the mony: except where the Law is Naturall, or
part of Religion; for in that case it is not an exemption from the Law,
but a transgression of it. As where a Law exacteth a Pecuniary mulct,
of them that take the name of God in vaine, the payment of the mulct,
is not the price of a dispensation to sweare, but the Punishment of the
transgression of a Law undispensable. In like manner if the Law
impose a Summe of Mony to be payd, to him that has been Injured;
this is but a satisfaction for the hurt done him; and extinguisheth the
accusation of the party injured, not the crime of the offender.

    Ignominy, is the infliction of such Evill, as is made Dishonourable;   *Ignominy.*
or the deprivation of such Good, as is made Honourable by the
Common-wealth. For there be some things Honorable by Nature; as
the effects of Courage, Magnamity, Strength, Wisdome, and other
abilities of body and mind: Others made Honorable by the Common-
wealth; as Badges, Titles, Offices, or any other singular marke of the
Soveraigns favour. The former, (though they may faile by nature, or
accident,) cannot be taken away by a Law; and therefore the losse of

them is not Punishment. But the later, may be taken away by the publique authority that made them Honorable, and are properly Punishments: Such are degrading men condemned, of their Badges, Titles, and Offices; or declaring them uncapable of the like in time to come.

Imprisonment, is when a man is by publique Authority deprived of liberty; and may happen from two divers ends; whereof one is the safe custody of a man accused; the other is the inflicting of paine on a man condemned. The former is not Punishment; because no man is supposed to be Punisht, before he be Judicially heard, and declared guilty. And therefore whatsoever hurt a man is made to suffer by bonds, or restraint, before his cause be heard, over and above that which is necessary to assure his custody, is against the Law of Nature. But the later is Punishment, because Evill, and inflicted by publique Authority, for somewhat that has by the same Authority been Judged a Transgression of the Law. Under this word Imprisonment, I comprehend all restraint of motion, caused by an externall obstacle, be it a House, which is called by the general name of a Prison; or an Iland, as when men are said to be confined to it; or a place where men are set to worke, as in old time men have been condemned to Quarries, and in these times to Gallies; or be it a Chaine, or any other such impediment.

Exile, (Banishment) is when a man is for a crime, condemned to depart out of the dominion of the Common-wealth, or out of a certaine part thereof; and during a prefixed time, or for ever, not to return into it: and seemeth not in its own nature, without other circumstances, to be a Punishment; but rather an escape, or a publique commandement to avoid Punishment by flight. And *Cicero* sayes, there was never any such Punishment ordained in the City of *Rome*; but cals it a refuge of men in danger. For if a man banished, be neverthelesse permitted to enjoy his Goods, and the Revenue of his Lands, the meer change of ayr is no Punishment; nor does it tend to that benefit of the Common-wealth, for which all Punishments are ordained, (that is to say, to the forming of mens wils to the observation of the Law;) but many times to the dammage of the Common-wealth. For a Banished man, is a lawfull enemy of the Common-wealth that banished him; as being no more a Member of the same. But if he be withall deprived of his Lands, or Goods, then the Punishment lyeth not in the Exile, but is to be reckoned amongst Punishments Pecuniary.

All Punishments of Innocent subjects, be they great or little, are against the Law of Nature: For Punishment is only for Transgression of the Law, and therefore there can be no Punishment of the Inno- cent. It is therefore a violation, First, of that Law of Nature, which forbiddeth all men, in their Revenges, to look at any thing but some future good: For there can arrive no good to the Common-wealth, by Punishing the Innocent. Secondly, of that, which forbiddeth Ingratitude: For seeing all Soveraign Power, is originally given by the consent of every one of the Subjects, to the end they should as long as they are obedient, be protected thereby; the Punishment of the Inno- cent, is a rendring of Evill for Good. And thirdly, of the Law that commandeth Equity; that is to say, an equall distribution of Justice; which in Punishing the Innocent is not observed.

The Punishment of Innocent Subjects is contrary to the Law of Nature.

But the Infliction of what evill soever, on an Innocent man, that is not a Subject, if it be for the benefit of the Common-wealth, and without violation of any former Covenant, is no breach of the Law of Nature. For all men that are not Subjects, are either Enemies, or else they have ceased from being so, by some precedent covenants. But against Enemies, whom the Common-wealth judgeth capable to do them hurt, it is lawfull by the originall Right of Nature to make warre; wherein the Sword Judgeth not, nor doth the Victor make distinction of Nocent, and Innocent, as to the time past; nor has other respect of mercy, than as it conduceth to the good of his own People. And upon this ground it is, that also in Subjects, who deliberatly deny the Authority of the Common-wealth established, the vengeance is law- fully extended, not onely to the Fathers, but also to the third and fourth generation not yet in being, and consequently innocent of the fact, for which they are afflicted: because the nature of this offence, consisteth in the renouncing of subjection; which is a relapse into the condition of warre, commonly called Rebellion; and they that so offend, suffer not as Subjects, but as Enemies. For *Rebellion*, is but warre renewed.

But the Harme done to Innocents in War, not so:

Nor that which is done to declared Rebels.

[166]

REWARD, is either of *Gift*, or by *Contract*. When by Contract, it is called *Salary*, and *Wages*; which is benefit due for service performed, or promised. When of Gift, it is benefit proceeding from the *grace* of them that bestow it, to encourage, or enable men to do them service.

Reward is either Salary, or Grace.

And therefore when the Soveraign of a Common wealth appointeth a Salary to any publique Office, he that receiveth it, is bound in Justice to performe his office; otherwise, he is bound onely in honour, to acknowledgement, and an endeavour of requitall. For though men have no lawfull remedy, when they be commanded to quit their private businesse, to serve the publique, without Reward, or Salary; yet they are not bound thereto, by the Law of Nature, nor by the Institution of the Common-wealth, unlesse the service cannot otherwise be done; because it is supposed the Soveraign may make use of all their means, insomuch as the most common Souldier, may demand the wages of his warre-fare, as a debt.

Benefits bestowed for fear, are not Rewards. The benefits which a Soveraign bestoweth on a Subject, for fear of some power, and ability he hath to do hurt to the Common-wealth, are not properly Rewards; for they are not Salaryes; because there is in this case no contract supposed, every man being obliged already not to do the Common-wealth disservice: nor are they Graces; because they be extorted by fear, which ought not to be incident to the Soveraign Power: but are rather Sacrifices, which the Soveraign (considered in his naturall person, and not in the person of the Common-wealth) makes, for the appeasing the discontent of him he thinks more potent than himselfe; and encourage not to obedience, but on the contrary, to the continuance, and increasing of further extortion.

Salaries Certain and Casuall. And whereas some Salaries are certain, and proceed from the publique Treasure; and others uncertain, and casuall, proceeding from the execution of the Office for which the Salary is ordained; the later is in some cases hurtfull to the Common-wealth; as in the case of Judicature. For where the benefit of the Judges, and Ministers of a Court of Justice, ariseth for the multitude of Causes that are brought to their cognisance, there must needs follow two Inconveniences: One, is the nourishing of sutes; for the more sutes, the greater benefit: and another that depends on that, which is contention about Jurisdiction; each Court drawing to it selfe, as many Causes as it can. But in offices of Execution there are not those Inconveniences; because their employment cannot be encreased by any endeavour of their own. And thus much shall suffice for the nature of Punishment, and Reward; which are, as it were, the Nerves and Tendons, that move the limbes and joynts of a Common-wealth.

Hitherto I have set forth the nature of Man, (whose Pride and other Passions have compelled him to submit himselfe to Government;)

together with the great power of his Governour, whom I compared to *Leviathan*, taking that comparison out of the two last verses of the one and fortieth of *Job*; where God having set forth the great power of *Leviathan*, calleth him King of the Proud. *There is nothing*, saith he, *on* [167] *earth, to be compared with him. He is made so as not to be afraid. Hee seeth every high thing below him; and is King of all the children of pride.* But because he is mortall, and subject to decay, as all other Earthly creatures are; and because there is that in heaven, (though not on earth) that he should stand in fear of, and whose Lawes he ought to obey; I shall in the next following Chapters speak of his Diseases, and the causes of his Mortality; and of what Lawes of Nature he is bound to obey.

CHAP. XXIX.

Of those things that Weaken, or tend to the DISSOLUTION *of a Common-wealth.*

Though nothing can be immortall, which mortals make; yet, if men had the use of reason they pretend to, their Common-wealths might be secured, at least, from perishing by internall diseases. For by the nature of their Institution, they are designed to live, as long as Mankind, or as the Lawes of Nature, or as Justice it selfe, which gives them life. Therefore when they come to be dissolved, not by externall violence, but intestine disorder, the fault is not in men, as they are the *Matter*; but as they are the *Makers*, and orderers of them. For men, as they become at last weary of irregular justling, and hewing one another, and desire with all their hearts, to conforme themselves into one firme and lasting edifice; so for want, both of the art of making fit Lawes, to square their actions by, and also of humility, and patience, to suffer the rude and combersome points of their present greatnesse to be taken off, they cannot without the help of a very able Architect, be compiled, into any other than a crasie building, such as hardly lasting out their own time, must assuredly fall upon the heads of their posterity.

Dissolution of Common-wealths proceedeth from their Imperfect Institution.

    Amongst the *Infirmities* therefore of a Common-wealth, I will reckon in the first place, those that arise from an Imperfect Institution, and resemble the diseases of a naturall body, which proceed from a Defectuous Procreation.

Want of Absolute power.

Of which, this is one, *That a man to obtain a Kingdome, is sometimes content with lesse Power, than to the Peace, and defence of the Common-wealth is necessarily required.* From whence it commeth to passe, that when the exercise of the Power layd by, is for the publique safety to be resumed, it hath the resemblance of an unjust act; which disposeth great numbers of men (when occasion is presented) to rebell; In the same manner as the bodies of children, gotten by diseased parents, are subject either to untimely death, or to purge the ill quality, derived from their vicious conception, by breaking out into biles and scabbs. And when Kings deny themselves some such necessary Power, it is not alwayes (though sometimes) out of ignorance of what is necessary to the office they undertake; but many times out of a hope to recover

[168]

the same again at their pleasure: Wherein they reason not well; because such as will hold them to their promises, shall be maintained against them by forraign Common-wealths; who in order to the good of their own Subjects let slip few occasions to *weaken* the estate of their Neighbours. So was *Thomas Becket* Archbishop of *Canterbury*, supported against *Henry* the Second, by the Pope; the subjection of Ecclesiastiques to the Common-wealth, having been dispensed with by *William the Conquerour* at his reception, when he took an Oath, not to infringe the liberty of the Church. And so were the *Barons*, whose power was by *William Rufus* (to have their help in transferring the Succession from his Elder brother, to himselfe,) encreased to a degree, inconsistent with the Soveraign Power, maintained in their Rebellion against King *John*, by the French.

Nor does this happen in Monarchy onely. For whereas the stile of the antient Roman Common-wealth, was, *The Senate, and People of Rome*; neither Senate, nor People pretended to the whole Power; which first caused the seditions, of *Tiberius Gracchus, Caius Gracchus, Lucius Saturninus*, and others; and afterwards the warres between the Senate and the People, under *Marius* and *Sylla*; and again under *Pompey* and *Caesar*, to the Extinction of their Democraty, and the setting up of Monarchy.

The people of *Athens* bound themselves but from one onely Action; which was, that no man on pain of death should propound the renewing of the warre for the Island of *Salamis*; And yet thereby, if *Solon* had not caused to be given out he was mad, and afterwards in gesture and habit of a mad-man, and in verse, propounded it to the People that flocked about him, they had had an enemy perpetually in readinesse, even at the gates of their Citie; such dammage, or shifts, are all Common-wealths forced to, that have their Power never so little limited.

In the second place, I observe the *Diseases* of a Common-wealth, that proceed from the poyson of seditious doctrines; whereof one is, *That every private man is Judge of Good and Evill actions.* This is true in the condition of meer Nature, where there are no Civill Lawes; and also under Civill Government, in such cases as are not determined by the Law. But otherwise, it is manifest, that the measure of Good and Evill actions, is the Civill Law; and the Judge the Legislator, who is always *the Representative*[1] of the Common-wealth. From this false doctrine, men are disposed to debate with themselves, and dispute the commands of the Common-wealth; and afterwards to obey, or disobey them, as in their private judgements they shall think fit. Whereby the Common-wealth is distracted and *Weakened.* *Private Judgement of Good and Evill.*

Another doctrine repugnant to Civill Society, is, that *whatsoever a man does against his Conscience, is Sinne*; and it dependeth on the presumption of making himselfe judge of Good and Evill. For a mans Conscience, and his Judgement is the same thing; and as the Judgement, so also the Conscience may be erroneous. Therefore, though he that is subject to no Civill Law, sinneth in all he does against his Conscience, because he has no other rule to follow but his own reason; yet it is not so with him that lives in a Common-wealth; because the Law is the publique Conscience, by which he hath already undertaken to be guided. Otherwise in such diversity, as there is of private Consciences, which are but private opinions, the Common-wealth must needs be distracted, and no man dare to obey the Soveraign Power, farther than it shall seem good in his own eyes. *Erroneous conscience.* [169]

It hath been also commonly taught, *That Faith and Sanctity, are not to be attained by Study and Reason, but by supernaturall Inspiration, or Infusion.* Which granted, I see not why any man should render a reason of his Faith; or why every Christian should not be also a Prophet; or why any man should take the Law of his Country, rather than his own Inspiration, for the rule of his action. And thus wee fall *Pretence of Inspiration.*

---

[1] *Syn.*: Representative

again into the fault of taking upon us to Judge of Good and Evill; or to make Judges of it, such private men as pretend to be supernaturally Inspired, to the Dissolution of all Civill Government. Faith comes by hearing, and hearing by those accidents, which guide us into the presence of them that speak to us; which accidents are all contrived by God Almighty; and yet are not supernaturall, but onely, for the great number of them that concurre to every effect, unobservable. Faith, and Sanctity, are indeed not very frequent; but yet they are not Miracles, but brought to passe by education, discipline, correction, and other naturall wayes, by which God worketh them in his elect, at such times as he thinketh fit. And these three opinions, pernicious to Peace and Government, have in this part of the world, proceeded chiefly from the tongues, and pens of unlearned Divines; who joyning the words of Holy Scripture together, otherwise than is agreeable to reason, do what they can, to make men think, that Sanctity and Naturall Reason, cannot stand together.

Subjecting the Soveraign Power to Civill Lawes. A fourth opinion, repugnant to the nature of a Common-wealth, is this, *That he that hath the Soveraign Power, is subject to the Civill Lawes.* It is true, that Soveraigns are all subject to the Lawes of Nature; because such lawes be Divine, and cannot by any man, or Common-wealth be abrogated. But to those Lawes which the Soveraign him-selfe, that is, which the Common-wealth maketh, he is not subject. For to be subject to Lawes, is to be subject to the Common-wealth, that is to the Soveraign Representative, that is to himselfe; which is not subjection, but freedome from the Lawes. Which errour, because it setteth the Lawes above the Soveraign, setteth also a Judge above him, and a Power to punish him; which is to make a new Soveraign; and again for the same reason a third, to punish the second; and so continually without end, to the Confusion, and Dissolution of the Common-wealth.

Attributing of absolute Propriety to Subjects. A Fifth doctrine, that tendeth to the Dissolution of a Common-wealth, is, *That every private man has an absolute Propriety in his Goods; such, as excludeth the Right of the Soveraign.* Every man has indeed a Propriety that excludes the Right of every other Subject: And he has it only from the Soveraign Power; without the protection whereof,
[170] every other man should have equall Right to the same. But if the Right of the Soveraign also be excluded, he cannot performe the office they have put him into; which is, to defend them both from

forraign enemies, and from the injuries of one another; and consequently there is no longer a Common-wealth.

And if the Propriety of Subjects, exclude not the Right of the Soveraign Representative to their Goods; much lesse to their offices of Judicature, or Execution, in which they Represent the Soveraign himselfe.

There is a Sixth doctrine, plainly, and directly against the essence of a Common-wealth; and 'tis this, *That the Soveraign Power may be divided*. For what is it to divide the Power of a Common-wealth, but to Dissolve *it?*¹ for Powers divided mutually destroy each other. And for these doctrines, men are chiefly beholding to some of those, that making profession of the Lawes, endeavour to make them depend upon their own learning, and not upon the Legislative Power. *Dividing of the Soveraign Power.*

And as False Doctrine, so also often-times the Example of different Government in a neighbouring Nation, disposeth men to alteration of the forme already setled. So the people of the Jewes were stirred up to reject God, and to call upon the Prophet *Samuel*, for a King after the manner of the Nations: So also the lesser Cities of *Greece*, were continually disturbed, with seditions of the Aristocraticall, and Democraticall factions; one part of almost every Common-wealth, desiring to imitate the Lacedaemonians; the other, the Athenians. And I doubt not, but many men, have been contented to see the late troubles in *England*, out of an imitation of the Low Countries; supposing there needed no more to grow rich, than to change, as they had done, the forme of their Government. For the constitution of mans nature, is of it selfe subject to desire novelty: When therefore they are provoked to the same, by the neighbourhood also of those that have been enriched by it, it is almost impossible for them, not to be content with those that solicite them to change; and love the first beginnings, *(though they be grieved with the continuance)*² of disorder; like hot blouds, that having gotten the itch, tear themselves with their own nayles, till they can endure the smart no longer. *Imitation of Neighbour Nations.*

And as to Rebellion in particular against Monarchy; one of the most frequent causes of it, is the Reading of the books of Policy, and Histories of the antient Greeks, and Romans; from which, young men, and all others that are unprovided of the Antidote of solid Reason, *Imitation of the Greeks, and Romans.*

¹ *Syn.*: it;   ² *Syn.*: though they be grieved with the continuance

receiving a strong, and delightfull impression, of the great exploits of warre, atchieved by the Conductors of their Armies, receive withall a pleasing Idea, of all they have done besides; and imagine their great prosperity, not to have proceeded from the aemulation of particular men, but from the vertue of their popular forme of government: Not considering the frequent Seditions, and Civill warres, produced by the imperfection of their Policy. From the reading, I say, of such books, men have undertaken to kill their Kings, because the Greek and Latine writers, in their books, and discourses of Policy, make it law-full, and laudable, for any man so to do; provided before he do it, he call him Tyrant. For they say not *Regicide*, that is, killing of a King, but *Tyrannicide*, that is, killing of a Tyrant is lawfull. From the same books, they that live under a Monarch conceive an opinion, that the Subjects in a Popular Common-wealth enjoy Liberty; but that in a Monarchy they are all Slaves. I say, they that live under a Monarchy conceive such an opinion; not they that live under a Popular Government: for they find no such matter. In summe, I cannot imagine, how any thing can be more prejudiciall to a Monarchy, than the allowing of such books to be publikely read, without present applying such correctives of discreet Masters, as are fit to take away their Venime: Which Venime I will not doubt to compare to the biting of a mad Dogge, which is a disease the Physicians call *Hydrophobia*, or *fear of Water*. For as he that is so bitten, has a continuall torment of thirst, and yet abhorreth water; and is in such an estate, as if the poyson endeavoured to convert him into a Dogge: So when a Monarchy is once bitten to the quick, by those Democraticall writers, that continually snarle at that estate; it wanteth nothing more than a strong Monarch, which never-thelesse out of a certain *Tyrannophobia*, or feare of being strongly governed, when they have him, they abhorre.

As there have been Doctors, that hold there be three Soules in a man; so there be also that think there may be more Soules, (that is, more Soveraigns,) than one, in a Common-wealth; and set up a *Supremacy* against the *Soveraignty*; *Canons* against *Lawes*; and a *Ghostly Authority* against the *Civill*; working on mens minds, with words and distinctions, that of themselves signifie nothing, but bewray (by their obscurity) that there walketh (as some think invisibly) another King-dome, as it were a Kingdome of Fayries, in the dark. Now seeing it is manifest, that the Civill Power, and the Power of the Common-wealth is the same thing; and that Supremacy, and the Power of making

Canons, and granting Faculties, implyeth a Common-wealth; it followeth, that where one is Soveraign, another Supreme; where one can
make Lawes, and another make Canons; there must needs be two
Common-wealths, of one & the same Subjects; which is a Kingdome
divided in it selfe, and cannot stand. For notwithstanding the insignificant distinction of *Temporall*, and *Ghostly*, they are still two Kingdomes, and every Subject is subject to two Masters. For seeing the
Ghostly Power challengeth the Right to declare what is Sinne, it
challengeth by consequence to declare what is Law, (Sinne being
nothing but the transgression of the Law;) and again, the Civill Power
challenging to declare what is Law, every Subject must obey two
Masters, who both will have their Commands be observed as Law;
which is impossible. Or, if it be but one Kingdome, either the *Civill*,
which is the Power of the Common-wealth, must be subordinate to
the *Ghostly*, and then there is no Soveraignty but the *Ghostly*; or the
Ghostly must be subordinate to the *Temporall*, and then there is no
Supremacy but the *Temporall*. When therefore these two Powers
oppose one another, the Common-wealth cannot but be in great
danger of Civill warre, and Dissolution. For the *Civill* Authority being   [172]
more visible, and standing in the clearer light of naturall reason,
cannot choose but draw to it in all times a very considerable part of
the people: And the *Spirituall*, though it stand in the darknesse of
Schoole distinctions, and hard words; yet because the fear of
Darknesse, and Ghosts, is greater than other fears, cannot want a
party sufficient to Trouble, and sometimes to Destroy a Common-
wealth. And this is a Disease which not unfitly may be compared to
the Epilepsie, or Falling-sicknesse (which the Jewes took to be one
kind of possession by Spirits) in the Body Naturall. For as in this
Disease, there is an unnaturall spirit, or wind in the head that
obstructeth the roots of the Nerves, and moving them violently, taketh
away the motion which naturally they should have from the power of
the Soule in the Brain, and thereby causeth violent, and irregular
motions (which men call Convulsions) in the parts; insomuch as he
that is seized therewith, falleth down sometimes into the water, and
sometimes into the fire, as a man deprived of his senses; so also in the
Body Politique, when the Spirituall power, moveth the Members of a
Common-wealth, by the terrour of punishments, and hope of rewards
(which are the Nerves of it,) otherwise than by the Civill Power (which
is the Soule of the Common-wealth) they ought to be moved; and by

strange, and hard words suffocates their understanding, it must needs thereby Distract the people, and either Overwhelm the Common-wealth with Oppression, or cast it into the Fire of a Civill warre.

Sometimes also in the meerly Civill government, there be more than one Soule: As when the Power of levying mony, (which is the Nutritive faculty,) has depended on a general Assembly; the Power of conduct and command, (which is the Motive faculty,) on one man; and the Power of making Lawes, (which is the Rationall faculty,) on the accidentall consent, not onely of those two, but also of a third; This endangereth the Common-wealth, somtimes for want of consent to good Lawes; but most often for want of such Nourishment, as is necessary to Life, and Motion. For although few perceive, that such government, is not government, but division of the Common-wealth into three Factions, and call it mixt Monarchy; yet the truth is, that it is not one independent Common-wealth, but three independent Factions; nor one Representative Person, but three. In the Kingdome of God, there may be three Persons independent, without breach of unity in God that Reigneth; but where men Reigne, that be subject to diversity of opinions, it cannot be so. And therefore if the King bear the person of the People, and the generall Assembly bear also the person of the People, and another Assembly bear the person of a Part of the people, they are not one Person, nor one Soveraign, but three Persons, and three Soveraigns.

To what Disease in the Naturall Body of man, I may exactly compare this irregularity of a Common-wealth, I know not. But I have seen a man, that had another man growing out of his side, with an head, armes, breast, and stomach, of his own: If he had had another man growing out of his other side, the comparison might then have been exact.

Hitherto, I have named such Diseases of a Common-wealth, as are of the greatest, and most present danger. There be other, not so great; which neverthelesse are not unfit to be observed. As first, the difficulty of raising Mony, for the necessary uses of the Common-wealth; especially in the approach of warre. This difficulty ariseth from the opinion, that every Subject hath of a Propriety in his lands and goods, exclusive of the Soveraigns Right to the use of the same. From whence it commeth to passe, that the Soveraign Power, which foreseeth the necessities and dangers of the Common-wealth, (finding the passage of mony to the publique Treasure obstructed, by the tenacity of the people,) whereas it ought to extend it selfe, to encounter, and prevent such dangers in their beginnings, contracteth it selfe as long as it can, and when it cannot longer, struggles with the people by stratagems of Law, to obtain little summes, which not sufficing, he is fain at last violently to open the way for present supply, or Perish; and being put often to these extremities, at last reduceth the people to their due temper; or else the Common-wealth must perish. Insomuch as we may compare this Distemper very aptly to an Ague; wherein, the fleshy parts being congealed, or by venomous matter obstructed; the Veins which by their naturall course empty themselves into the Heart, are not (as they ought to be) supplyed from the Arteries, whereby there succeedeth at first a cold contraction, and trembling of the limbes; and afterwards a hot, and strong endeavour of the Heart, to force a passage for the Bloud; and before it can do that, contenteth it selfe with the small refreshments of such things as coole for a time, till (if Nature be strong enough) it break at last the contumacy of the parts obstructed, and dissipateth the venome into sweat; or (if Nature be too weak) the Patient dyeth.

Again, there is sometimes in a Common-wealth, a Disease, which resembleth the Pleurisie; and that is, when the Treasure of the Common-wealth, flowing out of its due course, is gathered together in too much abundance, in one, or a few private men, by Monopolies, or by Farmes of the Publique Revenues; in the same manner as the Blood in a Pleurisie, getting into the Membrane of the breast, breedeth there an Inflammation, accompanied with a Fever, and painfull stitches. *Monopolies and abuses of Publicans.*

Also, the Popularity of a potent Subject, (unlesse the Common-wealth have very good caution of his fidelity,) is a dangerous Disease; because the people (which should receive their motion from the Authority of the Soveraign,) by the flattery, and by the reputation of an ambitious man, are drawn away from their obedience to the Lawes, to follow a man, of whose vertues, and designes they have no knowledge. And this is commonly of more danger in a Popular Government, than in a Monarchy; because an Army is of so great force, and multitude, as it may easily be made believe, they are the People. By this means it was, that *Julius Caesar*, who was set up by the People against the Senate, having won to himselfe the affections of his Army, *Popular men.* [174]

229

made himselfe Master, both of Senate and People. And this proceeding of popular, and ambitious men, is plain Rebellion; and may be resembled to the effects of Witchcraft.

Excessive greatnesse of a *Town, or*[1] *multitude of Corporations.*

Another infirmity of a Common-wealth, is the immoderate greatnesse of a Town, when it is able to furnish out of its own Circuit, the number, and expence of a great Army: As also the great number of Corporations; which are as it were many lesser Common-wealths in the bowels of a greater, like wormes in the entrayles of a naturall man. To which may be added, the Liberty of Disputing against absolute Power, by pretenders to Politicall Prudence; which though bred for the most part in the Lees of the people; yet animated by False Doctrines, are perpetually medling with the Fundamentall Lawes, to the molestation of the Common-wealth; like the little Wormes, which Physicians call *Ascarides*.

Liberty of disputing against Soveraign Power.

We may further adde, the insatiable appetite, or *Bulimia*, of enlarging Dominion; with the incurable *Wounds* thereby many times received from the enemy; And the *Wens*, of ununited conquests, which are many times a burthen, and with lesse danger lost, than kept; As also the *Lethargy* of Ease, and *Consumption* of Riot and Vain Expence.

Dissolution of the Common-wealth.

Lastly, when in a warre (forraign, or intestine,) the enemies get a finall Victory; so as (the forces of the Common-wealth keeping the field no longer) there is no farther protection of Subjects in their loyalty; then is the Common-wealth DISSOLVED, and every man at liberty to protect himselfe by such courses as his own discretion shall suggest unto him. For the Soveraign, is the publique Soule, giving Life and Motion to the Common-wealth; which expiring, the Members are governed by it no more, than the Carcasse of a man, by his departed (though Immortall) Soule. For though the Right of a Soveraign Monarch cannot be extinguished by the act of another; yet the Obligation of the members may. For he that wants protection, may seek it any where; and when he hath it, is obliged (without fraudulent pretence of having submitted himselfe out of fear,) to protect his Protection as long as he is able. But when the Power of an Assembly is once suppressed, the Right of the same perisheth utterly; because the Assembly it selfe is extinct; and consequently, there is no possibility for the Soveraignty to re-enter.

[1] *Syn.: Town,*

CHAP. XXX. [175]

Of the Office *of the Soveraign Representative.*

The Office of the Soveraign, (be it a Monarch, or an Assembly,) consisteth in the end, for which he was trusted with the Soveraign Power, namely the procuration of *the safety of the people*; to which he is obliged by the Law of Nature, and to render an account thereof to God, the Author of that Law, and to none but him. But by Safety here, is not meant a bare Preservation, but also all other Contentments of life, which every man by lawfull Industry, without danger, or hurt to the Common-wealth, shall acquire to himselfe. *The Procuration of the Good of the People.*

And this is intended should be done, not by care applyed to Individualls, further than their protection from injuries, when they shall complain; but by a generall Providence, contained in publique Instruction, both of Doctrine, and Example; and in the making, and executing of good Lawes, to which individuall persons may apply their own cases. *By Instruction & Lawes.*

And because, if the essentiall Rights of Soveraignty (specified before in the eighteenth Chapter) be taken away, the Commonwealth is thereby dissolved, and every man returneth into the condition, and calamity of a warre with every other man, (which is the greatest evill that can happen in this life;) it is the Office of the Soveraign, to maintain those Rights entire; and consequently against his duty, First, to transferre to another, or to lay from himselfe any of them. For he that deserteth the Means, deserteth the Ends; and he deserteth the Means, that being the Soveraign, acknowledgeth himselfe subject to the Civill Lawes; and renounceth the Power of Supreme Judicature; or of making Warre, or Peace by his own Authority; or of Judging of the Necessities of the Common-wealth; or of levying Mony, and Souldiers, when, and as much as in his own conscience he shall judge necessary; or of making Officers, and Ministers both of Warre, and Peace; or of appointing Teachers, and examining what Doctrines are conformable, or contrary to the Defence, Peace, and Good of the people. Secondly, it is against his *Against the duty of a Soveraign to relinquish any Essentiall Right of Soveraignty:*

Or not to see the people taught the grounds of them. Duty, to let the people be ignorant, or mis-informed of the grounds, and reasons of those his essentiall Rights; because thereby men are easie to be seduced, and drawn to resist him, when the Common-wealth shall require their use and exercise.

And the grounds of these Rights, have the rather need to be diligently, and truly taught; because they cannot be maintained by any Civill Law, or terrour of legall punishment. For a Civill Law, that shall forbid Rebellion, (and such is all resistance to the essentiall Rights of Soveraignty,) is not (as a Civill Law) any obligation, but by vertue onely of the Law of Nature, that forbiddeth the violation of Faith; which naturall obligation if men know not, they cannot know the Right of any Law the Soveraign maketh. And for the Punishment, they take it but for an act of Hostility; which when they think they have strength enough, they will endeavour by acts of Hostility, to avoyd.

[176]

Objection of those that say there are no Principles of Reason for absolute Soveraignty. As I have heard some say, that Justice is but a word, without substance; and that whatsoever a man can by force, or art, acquire to himselfe, (not onely in the condition of warre, but also in a Common-wealth,) is his own, which I have already shewed to be false: So there be also that maintain, that there are no grounds, nor Principles of Reason, to sustain those essentiall Rights, which make Soveraignty absolute. For if there were, they would have been found out in some place, or other; whereas we see, there has not hitherto been any Common-wealth, where those Rights have been acknowledged, or challenged. Wherein they argue as ill, as if the Savage people of America, should deny there were any grounds, or Principles of Reason, so to build a house, as to last as long as the materials, because they never yet saw any so well built. Time, and Industry, produce every day new knowledge. And as the art of well building, is derived from Principles of Reason, observed by industrious men, that had long studied the nature of materials, and the divers effects of figure, and proportion, long after mankind began (though poorly) to build: So, long time after men have begun to constitute Common-wealths, imperfect, and apt to relapse into disorder, there may Principles of Reason be found out, by industrious meditation, to make their con-stitution (excepting by externall violence) everlasting. And such are those which I have in this discourse set forth: Which whether they come not into the sight of those that have Power to make use of them, or be neglected by them, or not, concerneth my particular interest, at this day, very little. But supposing that these of mine are not such Principles of Reason; yet I am sure they are Principles from Authority of Scripture; as I shall make it appear, when I shall come to speak of the Kingdome of God, (administred by *Moses*,) over the Jewes, his peculiar people by Covenant.

But they say again, that though the Principles be right, yet Common people are not of capacity enough to be made to understand them. I should be glad, that the Rich, and Potent Subjects of a Kingdome, or those that are accounted the most Learned, were no lesse incapable than they. But all men know, that the obstructions to this kind of doctrine, proceed not so much from the difficulty of the matter, as from the interest of them that are to learn. Potent men, digest hardly any thing that setteth up a Power to bridle their affections; and Learned men, any thing that discovereth their errours, and thereby lesseneth their Authority: whereas the Common-peoples minds, unlesse they be tainted with dependance on the Potent, or scribbled over with the opinions of their Doctors, are like clean paper, fit to receive whatsoever by Publique Authority shall be imprinted in them. Shall whole Nations be brought to *acquiesce* in the great Mysteries of Christian Religion, which are above Reason; and millions of men be made believe, that the same Body may be in innumerable places, at one and the same time, which is against Reason; and shall not men be able, by their teaching, and preaching, protected by the Law, to make that received, which is so consonant to Reason, that any unprejudicated man, needs no more to learn it, than to hear it? I conclude therefore, that in the instruction of the people in the Essentiall Rights (which are the Naturall, and Fundamental Lawes) of Soveraignty, there is no difficulty, (whilest a Soveraign has his Power entire,) but what proceeds from his own fault, or the fault of those whom he trusteth in the administration of the Common-wealth; and consequently, it is his Duty, to cause them so to be instructed; and not onely his Duty, but his Benefit also, and Security, against the danger that may arrive to himselfe in his naturall Person, from Rebellion.

Objection from the Incapacity of the vulgar.

[177]

And (to descend to particulars) the People are to be taught, First, that they ought not to be in love with any forme of Government they see in their neighbour Nations, more than with their own, nor (whatsoever present prosperity they behold in Nations that are otherwise governed than they,) to desire change. For the prosperity of a People ruled by an Aristocraticall, or Democraticall assembly, commeth not

Subjects are to be taught, not to affect change of Government:

from Aristocracy, nor from Democracy, but from the Obedience, and Concord of the Subjects: nor do the people flourish in a Monarchy, because one man has the right to rule them, but because they obey him. Take away in any kind of State, the Obedience, (and consequently the Concord of the People,) and they shall not onely not flourish, but in short time be dissolved. And they that go about by disobedience, to doe no more than reforme the Common-wealth, shall find they do thereby destroy it; like the foolish daughters of *Peleus* (in the fable;) which desiring to renew the youth of their decrepit Father, did by the Counsell of *Medea*, cut him in pieces, and boyle him, together with strange herbs, but made not of him a new man. This desire of change, is like the breach of the first of Gods Commandements: For there God sayes, *Non habebis Deos alienos*; Thou shalt not have the Gods of other Nations; and in another place concerning *Kings*, that they are *Gods*.

Nor adhere (against the Soveraign) to Popular men:
Secondly, they are to be taught, that they ought not to be led with admiration of the vertue of any of their fellow Subjects, how high soever he stand, nor how conspicuously soever he shine in the Common-wealth; nor of any Assembly, (except the Soveraign Assembly,) so as to deferre to them any obedience, or honour, appropriate to the Soveraign onely, whom (in their particular stations) they represent; nor to receive any influence from them, but such as is conveighed by them from the Soveraign Authority. For that Soveraign, cannot be imagined to love his People as he ought, that is not Jealous of them, but suffers them by the flattery of Popular men, to be seduced from their loyalty, as they have often been, not onely secretly, but openly, so as to proclaime Marriage with them *in facie Ecclesiae* by Preachers; and

[178]
by publishing the same in the open streets: which may fitly be compared to the violation of the second of the ten Commandements.

Nor to Dispute the Soveraign Power:
Thirdly, in consequence to this, they ought to be informed, how great a fault it is, to speak evill of the Soveraign Representative, (whether One man, or an Assembly of men;) or to argue and dispute his Power, or any way to use his Name irreverently, whereby he may be brought into Contempt with his People, and their Obedience (in which the safety of the Common-wealth consisteth) slackened. Which

And to have dayes set apart to learn their Duty:
doctrine the third Commandement by resemblance pointeth to.

Fourthly, seeing people cannot be taught this, nor when 'tis taught, remember it, nor after one generation past, so much as know in whom the Soveraign Power is placed, without setting a part from their ordinary labour, some certain times, in which they may attend those that are appointed to instruct them; It is necessary that some such times be determined, wherein they may assemble together, and (after prayers and praises given to God, the Soveraign of Soveraigns) hear those their Duties told them, and the Positive Lawes, such as generally concern them all, read and expounded, and be put in mind of the Authority that maketh them Lawes. To this end had the *Jewes* every seventh day, a *Sabbath*, in which the Law was read and expounded; and in the solemnity whereof they were put in mind, that their King was God; that having created the world in six dayes, he rested the seventh day; and by their resting on it from their labour, that that God was their King, which redeemed them from their servile, and painfull labour in *Egypt*, and gave them, a time, after they had rejoyced in God, to take joy also in themselves, by lawfull recreation. So that the first Table of the Commandements, is spent all, in setting down the summe of Gods absolute Power; not onely as God, but as King by pact, (in peculiar) of the Jewes; and may therefore give light, to those that have Soveraign Power conferred on them by the consent of men, to see what doctrine they Ought to teach their Subjects.

And because the first instruction of Children, dependeth on the care of their Parents; it is necessary that they should be obedient to them, whilest they are under their tuition; and not onely so, but that also afterwards (as gratitude requireth,) they acknowledge the benefit of their education, by externall signes of honour. To which end they are to be taught, that originally the Father of every man was also his Soveraign Lord, with power over him of life and death; and that the Fathers of families, when by instituting a Common-wealth, they resigned that absolute Power, yet it was never intended, they should lose the honour due unto them for their education. For to relinquish such right, was not necessary to the Institution of Soveraign Power; nor would there be any reason, why any man should desire to have children, or take the care to nourish and instruct them, if they were afterwards to have no other benefit from them, than from other men. And this accordeth with the fifth Commandement. *And to Honour their Parents.*

Again, every Soveraign Ought to cause Justice to be taught, which (consisting in taking from no man what is his) is as much as to say, to cause men to be taught not to deprive their Neighbours, by violence, or fraud, of any thing which by the Soveraign Authority is theirs. Of [179] *And to avoyd doing of Injury:*

235

things held in propriety, those that are dearest to a man are his own life, & limbs; and in the next degree, (in most men,) those that concern conjugall affection; and after them riches and means of living. Therefore the People are to be taught, to abstain from violence to one anothers person, by private revenges; from violation of conjugall honour; and from forcible rapine, and fraudulent surreption of one anothers goods. For which purpose also it is necessary they be shewed the evill consequences of false Judgement, by corruption either of Judges or Witnesses, whereby the distinction of propriety is taken away, and Justice becomes of no effect: all which things are intimated in the sixth, seventh, eighth, and ninth Commandements.

And to do all this sincerely from the heart.
Lastly, they are to be taught, that not onely the unjust facts, but the designes and intentions to do them, (though by accident hindred,) are Injustice; which consisteth in the pravity of the will, as well as in the irregularity of the act. And this is the intention of the tenth Commandement, and the summe of the second Table; which is reduced all to this one Commandement of mutuall Charity, *Thou shalt love thy neighbour as thy selfe*: as the summe of the first Table is reduced to *the love of God*; whom they had then newly received as their King.

The use of Universities.
As for the Means, and Conduits, by which the people may receive this Instruction, wee are to search, by what means so many Opinions, contrary to the peace of Man-kind, upon weak and false Principles, have neverthelesse been so deeply rooted in them. I mean those, which I have in the precedent Chapter specified: as That men shall Judge of what is lawfull and unlawfull, not by the Law it selfe, but by their own Consciences; that is to say, by their own private Judgements: That Subjects sinne in obeying the Commands of the Common-wealth, unlesse they themselves have first judged them to be lawfull: That their Propriety in their riches is such, as to exclude the Dominion, which the Common-wealth hath over the same: That it is lawfull for Subjects to kill such, as they call Tyrants: That the Soveraign Power may be divided, and the like; which come to be instilled into the People by this means. They whom necessity, or covetousnesse keepeth attent on their trades, and labour; and they, on the other side, whom superfluity, or sloth carrieth after their sensuall pleasures, (which two sorts of men take up the greatest part of Man-kind,) being diverted from the deep meditation, which the learning of truth, not onely in the matter of Naturall Justice, but also of all other

Sciences necessarily requireth, receive the Notions of their duty, chiefly from Divines in the Pulpit, and partly from such of their Neighbours, or familiar acquaintance, as having the Faculty of discoursing readily, and plausibly, seem wiser and better learned in cases of Law, and Conscience, than themselves. And the Divines, and such others as make shew of Learning, derive their knowledge from the [180] Universities, and from the Schooles of Law, or from the Books, which by men eminent in those Schooles, and Universities have been published. It is therefore manifest, that the Instruction of the people, dependeth wholly, on the right teaching of Youth in the Universities. But are not (may some man say) the Universities of *England* learned enough already to do that? or is it you will undertake to teach the Universities? Hard questions. Yet to the first, I doubt not to answer; that till towards the later end of *Henry the eighth*, the Power of the Pope, was alwayes upheld against the Power of the Common-wealth, principally by the Universities; and that the doctrines maintained by so many Preachers, against the Soveraign Power of the King, and by so many Lawyers, and others, that had their education there, is a sufficient argument, that though the Universities were not authors of those false doctrines, yet they knew not how to plant the true. For in such a contradiction of Opinions, it is most certain, that they have not been sufficiently instructed; and 'tis no wonder, if they yet retain a relish of that subtile liquor, wherever they were first seasoned, against the Civill Authority. But to the later question, it is not fit, not needfull for me to say either I, or No: for any man that sees what I am doing, may easily perceive what I think.

The safety of the People, requireth further, from him, or them that have the Soveraign Power, that Justice be equally administred to all degrees of People; that is, that as well the rich, and mighty, as poor and obscure persons, may be righted of the injuries done them; so as the great, may have no greater hope of impunity, when they doe violence, dishonour, or any Injury to the meaner sort, than when one of these, does the like to one of them: For in this consisteth Equity; to which, as being a Precept of the Law of Nature, a Soveraign is as much subject, as any of the meanest of his People. All breaches of the Law, are offences against the Common-wealth: but there be some, that are also against private Persons. Those that concern the Common-wealth onely, may without breach of Equity be pardoned; for every man may pardon what is done against himselfe, according to his own discretion. But an offence against a private man, cannot in Equity be pardoned, without the consent of him that is injured; or reasonable satisfaction.

The Inequality of Subjects, proceedeth from the Acts of Soveraign Power; and therefore has no more place in the presence of the Soveraign; that is to say, in a Court of Justice, then the Inequality between Kings, and their Subjects, in the presence of the King of Kings. The honour of great Persons, is to be valued for their benefi-cence, and the aydes they give to men of inferiour rank, or not at all. And the violences, oppressions, and injuries they do, are not extenu-ated, but aggravated by the greatnesse of their persons; because they have least need to commit them. The consequences of this partiality towards the great, proceed in this manner. Impunity maketh Insolence; Insolence Hatred; and Hatred, an Endeavour to pull down all oppressing and contumelious greatnesse, though with the ruine of the Common-wealth.

[181]
*Equall
Taxes.*
To Equall Justice, appertaineth also the Equall imposition of Taxes; the Equality whereof dependeth not on the Equality of riches, but on the Equality of the debt, that every man oweth to the Com-mon-wealth for his defence. It is not enough, for a man to labour for the maintenance of his life; but also to fight, (if need be,) for the securing of his labour. They must either do as the Jewes did after their return from captivity, in re-edifying the Temple, build with one hand, and hold the Sword in the other; or else they must hire others to fight for them. For the Impositions, that are layd on the People by the Soveraign Power, are nothing else but the Wages, due to them that hold the publique Sword, to defend private men in the exercise of *their severall*[1] Trades, and Callings. Seeing then the benefit that every one receiveth thereby, is the enjoyment of life, which is equally dear to poor, and rich; the debt which a poor man oweth them that defend his life, is the same which a rich man oweth for the defence of his; saving that the rich, who have the service of the poor, may be debtors not onely for their own persons, but for many more. Which considered, the Equality of Imposition, consisteth rather in the Equality of that which is consumed, that of the riches of the persons that consume the same. For what reason is there, that he which laboureth much, and sparing the fruits of his labour, consumeth little,

---

[1] *Syn.:* severall

should be more charged, then he that living idly, getteth little, and spendeth all he gets; seeing the one hath no more protection from the Common-wealth, then the other? But when the Impositions, are layd upon those things which men consume, every man payeth Equally for what he useth: Nor is the Common-wealth defrauded, by the luxurious waste of private men.

And whereas many men, by accident unevitable, become unable to maintain themselves by their labour; they ought not to be left to the Charity of private persons; but to be provided for, (as far-forth as the necessities of Nature require,) by the Lawes of the Common-wealth. For as it is Uncharitablenesse in any man, to neglect the impotent; so it is in the Soveraign of a Common-wealth, to expose them to the hazard of such uncertain Charity. *Publique Charity.*

But for such as have strong bodies, the case is otherwise: they are to be forced to work; and to avoyd the excuse of not finding employment, there ought to be such Lawes, as may encourage all manner of Arts; as Navigation, Agriculture, Fishing, and all manner of Manifacture that requires labour. The multitude of poor, and yet strong people still encreasing, they are to be transplanted into Countries not sufficiently inhabited: where neverthelesse, they are not to exterminate those they find there; but constrain them to inhabit closer together, and not range a great deal of ground, to snatch what they find; but to court each little Plot with art and labour, to give them their sustenance in due season. And when all the world is overchargd with Inhabitants, then the last remedy of all is Warre; which provideth for every man, by Victory, or Death. *Prevention of Idlenesse.*

To the care of the Soveraign, belongeth the making of Good Lawes. But what is a good Law? By a Good Law, I mean not a Just Law: for no Law can be Unjust. The Law is made by the Soveraign Power, and all that is done by such Power, is warranted, and owned by every one of the people; and that which every man will have so, no man can say is unjust. It is in the Lawes of a Common-wealth, as in the Lawes of Gaming: whatsoever the Gamesters all agree on, is Injustice to none of them. A good Law is that, which is *Needfull*, for the *Good of the People*, and withall *Perspicuous*. [182] *Good Lawes what.*

For the use of Lawes, (which are but Rules Authorised) is not to bind the People from all Voluntary actions; but to direct and keep them in such a motion, as not to hurt themselves by their own impetuous desires, rashnesse, or indiscretion; as Hedges are set, not *Such as are Necessary.*

to stop Travellers, but to keep them in the way. And therefore a Law that is not Needfull, having not the true End of a Law, is not Good. A Law may be conceived to be Good, when it is for the benefit of the Soveraign; though it be not Necessary for the People; but it is not so. For the good of the Soveraign and People, cannot be separated. It is a weak Soveraign, that has weak Subjects; and a weak People, whose Soveraign wanteth Power to rule them at his will. Unnecessary Lawes are not good Lawes; but trapps for Mony: which where the right of Soveraign Power is acknowledged, are superfluous; and where it is not acknowledged, unsufficient to defend the People.

Such as are Perspicuous. The Perspicuity, consisteth not so much in the words of the Law it selfe, as in a Declaration of the Causes, and Motives, for which it was made. That is it, that shewes us the meaning of the Legislator; and the meaning of the Legislator known, the Law is more easily understood by few, than many words. For all words, are subject to ambiguity; and therefore multiplication of words in the body of the Law, is multiplication of ambiguity: Besides it seems to imply, (by too much diligence,) that whosoever can evade the words, is without the compasse of the Law. And this is a cause of many unnecessary Processes. For when I consider how short were the Lawes of antient times; and how they grew by degrees still longer; me thinks I see a contention between the Penners, and Pleaders of the Law; the former seeking to circumscribe the later; and the later to evade their circumscriptions; and that the Pleaders have got the Victory. It belongeth therefore to the Office of a Legislator, (such as is in all Common-wealths the Supreme Representative, be it one Man, or an Assembly,) to make the reason Perspicuous, why the Law was made; and the Body of the Law it selfe, as short, but in as proper, and significant termes, as may be.

Punishments. It belongeth also to the Office of the Soveraign, to make a right application of Punishments, and Rewards. And seeing the end of punishing is not revenge, and discharge of choler; but correction, either of the offender, or of others by his example; the severest Punishments are to be inflicted for those Crimes, that are of most Danger to the Publique; such as are those which proceed from malice to the Government established; those that spring from contempt of Justice; those that provoke Indignation in the Multitude; and those, which unpunished, seem Authorised, as when they are committed by

[183]

Sonnes, Servants, or Favorites of men in Authority: For Indignation carrieth men, not onely against the Actors, and Authors of Injustice; but against all Power that is likely to protect them; as in the case of *Tarquin*; when for the Insolent act of one of his Sonnes, he was driven out of *Rome*, and the Monarchy it selfe dissolved. But Crimes of Infirmity; such as are those which proceed from great provocation, from great fear, great need, or from ignorance whether the Fact be a great Crime, or not, there is place many times for Lenity, without prejudice to the Common-wealth; and Lenity when there is such place for it, is required by the Law of Nature. The Punishment of the Leaders, and teachers in a Commotion; not the poore seduced People, when they are punished, can profit the Common-wealth by their example. To be severe to the People, is to punish that ignorance, which may in great part be imputed to the Soveraign, whose fault it was, they were no better instructed.

In like manner it belongeth to the Office, and Duty of the *Soveraign*, to apply his Rewards alwayes so, as there may arise from them benefit to the Common-wealth: wherein consisteth their Use, and End; and is then done, when they that have well served the Common-wealth, are with as little expence of the Common Treasure, as is possible, so well recompenced, as others thereby may be encouraged, both to serve the same as faithfully as they can, and to study the arts by which they may be enabled to do it better. To buy with Mony, or Preferment, from a Popular ambitious Subject, to be quiet, and desist from making ill impressions in the mindes of the People, has nothing of the nature of Reward; (which is ordained not for disservice, but for service past;) nor a signe of Gratitude, but of Fear: not does it tend to the Benefit, but to the Dammage of the Publique. It is a contention with Ambition, like that of *Hercules* with the Monster *Hydra*, which having many heads, for every one that was vanquished, there grew up three. For in like manner, when the stubbornnesse of one Popular man, is overcome with Reward, there arise many more (by the Example) that do the same Mischiefe, in hope of like Benefit: and as all sorts of Manifacture, so also Malice encreaseth by being vendible. And though sometimes a Civill warre, may be differed, by such wayes as that, yet the danger growes still the greater, and the Publique ruine more assured. It is therefore against the Duty of the Soveraign, to whom the Publique Safety is committed, to

Rewards.

Reward those that aspire to greatnesse by disturbing the Peace of their Country, and not rather to oppose the beginnings of such men, with a little danger, than after a longer time with greater.

Counsellours.   Another Businesse of the Soveraign, is to choose good Counsellours; I mean such, whose advice he is to take in the Government of the Common-wealth. For this word Counsell, *Consilium,* corrupted from *Considium,* is of a large signification, and comprehendeth all Assemblies of men that sit together, not onely to deliberate what is to be done hereafter, but also to judge of Facts past, and of Law for the present. I take it here in the first sense onely: And in this sense, there is no choyce of Counsell, neither in a Democracy, nor Aristocracy; because the persons Counselling are members of the person Counselled. The choyce of Counsellours therefore is proper to Monarchy; In which, the Soveraign that endeavoureth not to make choyce of those, that in every kind are the most able, dischargeth not his Office as he ought to do. The most able Counsellours, are they that have least hope of benefit by giving evill Counsell, and most knowledge of those things that conduce to the Peace, and Defence of the Common-wealth. It is a hard matter to know who expecteth benefit from publique troubles; but the signes that guide to a just suspicion, is the soothing of the people in their unreasonable, or irremediable grievances, by men whose estates are not sufficient to discharge their accustomed expences, and may easily be observed by any one whom it concerns to know it. But to know, who has most knowledge of the Publique affaires, is yet harder; and they that know them, need them a great deale the lesse. For to know, who knowes the Rules almost of any Art, is a great degree of the knowledge of the same Art; because no man can be assured of the truth of anothers Rules, but he that is first taught to understand them. But the best signes of Knowledge of any Art, are, much conversing in it, and constant good effects of it. Good Counsell comes not by Lot, nor by Inheritance; and therefore there is no more reason to expect good Advice from the rich, or noble, in matter of State, than in delineating the dimensions of a fortresse; unlesse we shall think there needs no method in the study of the Politiques, (as there does in the study of Geometry,) but onely to be lookers on; which is not so. For the Politiques is the harder study of the two. Whereas in these parts of *Europe,* it hath been taken for a Right of certain persons, to have place in the highest Councell of State by Inheritance; it is derived from the Conquests of the antient

[184]

Germans; wherein many absolute Lords joyning together to conquer other Nations, would not enter in to the Confederacy, without such Priviledges, as might be marks of difference in time following, between their Posterity, and the Posterity of their Subjects; which Priviledges being inconsistent with the Soveraign Power, by the favour of the Soveraign, they may seem to keep; but contending for them as their Right, they must needs by degrees let them go, and have at last no further honour, then adhaereth naturally to their abilities.

And how able soever be the Counsellours in any affaire, the benefit of their Counsell is greater, when they give every one his Advice, and the reasons of it apart, than when they do it in an Assembly, by way of Orations; and when they have praemeditated, than when they speak on the sudden; both because they have more time, to survey the consequences of action; and are lesse subject to be carried away to contradiction, through Envy, Emulation, or other Passions arising from the difference of opinion.

The best Counsell, in those things that concern not other Nations, but onely the ease, and benefit the Subjects may enjoy, by Lawes that [185] look onely inward, is to be taken from the generall informations, and complaints of the people of each Province, who are best acquainted with their own wants, and ought therefore, when they demand nothing in derogation of the essentiall Rights of Soveraignty, to be diligently taken notice of. For without those Essentiall Rights, (as I have often before said,) the Common-wealth cannot at all subsist.

A Commander of an Army in chiefe, if he be not Popular, shall not *Commanders.* be beloved, nor feared as he ought to be by his Army; and consequently cannot performe that office with good successe. He must therefore be Industrious, Valiant, Affable, Liberall and Fortunate, that he may gain an opinion both of sufficiency, and of loving his Souldiers. This is Popularity, and breeds in the Souldiers both desire, and courage, to recommend themselves to his favour; and protects the severity of the Generall, in punishing (when need is) the Mutinous, or negligent Souldiers. But this love of Souldiers, (if caution be not given of the Commanders fidelity,) is a dangerous thing to Soveraign Power; especially when it is in the hands of an Assembly not popular. It belongeth therefore to the safety of the People, both that they be good Conductors, and faithfull Subjects, to whom the Soveraign Commits his Armies.

But when the Soveraign himselfe is Popular; that is, reverenced and beloved of his People, there is no danger at all from the Popularity of a Subject. For Souldiers are never so generally unjust, as to side with their Captain; though they love him, against their Soveraign, when they love not onely his Person, but also his Cause. And therefore those, who by violence have at any time suppressed the Power of their lawfull Soveraign, before they could settle themselves in his place, have been alwayes put to the trouble of contriving their Titles, to save the People from the shame of receiving them. To have a known Right to Soveraign Power, is so popular a quality, as he that has it needs no more, for his own part, to turn the hearts of his Subjects to him, but that they see him able absolutely to govern his own Family: Nor, on the part of his enemies, but a disbanding of their Armies. For the greatest and most active part of Mankind, has never hetherto been well contented with the present.

Concerning the Offices of one Soveraign to another, which are comprehended in that Law, which is commonly called the *Law of Nations*, I need not say any thing in this place; because the Law of Nations, and the Law of Nature, is the same thing. And every Soveraign hath the same Right, in procuring the safety of his People, that any particular man can have, in procuring *his own safety.*[1] And the same Law, that dictateth to men that have no Civil Government, what they ought to do, and what to avoyd in regard of one another, dictateth the same to Common-wealths, that is, to the Consciences of Soveraign Princes, and Soveraign Assemblies; there being no Court of Naturall Justice, but in the Conscience onely; where not Man, but God raigneth; whose Lawes, (such of them as oblige all Mankind,) in respect of God, as he is the Author of Nature, are *Naturall*; and in respect of the same God, as he is King of Kings, are *Lawes*. But of the Kingdome of God, as King of Kings, and as King also of a peculiar People, I shall speak in the rest of this discourse.

[186]

---

[1] *Syn.*: the safety of his own Body.

CHAP. XXXI.
Of the KINGDOME OF GOD BY NATURE.

That the condition of meer Nature, that is to say, of absolute Liberty, such as is theirs, that neither are Soveraigns, nor Subjects, is Anarchy, and the condition of Warre: That the Praecepts, by which men are guided to avoyd that condition, are the Lawes of Nature: That a Common-wealth, without Soveraign Power, is but a word, without substance, and cannot stand: That Subjects owe to Soveraigns, simple Obedience, in all things, wherein their obedience is not repugnant to the Lawes of God, I have sufficiently proved, in that which I have already written. There wants onely, for the entire knowledge of Civill duty, to know what are those Lawes of God. For without that, a man knows not, when he is commanded any thing by the Civill Power, whether it be contrary to the Law of God, or not: and so, either by too much civill obedience, offends the Divine Majesty, or through feare of offending God, transgresses the commandements of the Common-wealth. To avoyd both these Rocks, it is necessary to know what are the Lawes Divine. And seeing the knowledge of all Law, dependeth on the knowledge of the Soveraign Power; I shall say something in that which followeth, of the KINGDOME OF GOD. *The scope of the following Chapters.*

God is King, let the Earth rejoyce, saith the Psalmist. And again, *God is King though the Nations be angry; and he that sitteth on the Cherubins, though the earth be moved.* Whether men will or not, they must be subject alwayes to the Divine Power. By denying the Existence, or Providence of God, men may shake off their Ease, but not their Yoke. But to call this Power of God, which extendeth it selfe not onely to Man, but also to Beasts, and Plants, and Bodies inanimate, by the name of Kingdome, is but a metaphoricall use of the word. For he onely is properly said to Raigne, that governs his Subjects, by his Word, and by promise of Rewards to those that obey it, and by threatning them with Punishment that obey it not. Subjects therefore in the Kingdome of God, are not Bodies Inanimate, nor creatures *Psal.*96.1. *Psal.*98.1. *Who are subjects in the kingdome of God.*

Irrationall; because they understand no Precepts as his: Nor Atheists; nor they that believe not that God has any care of the actions of mankind; because they acknowledge no Word for his, nor have hope of his rewards, or fear of his threatnings. They therefore that believe there is a God that governeth the world, and hath given Praecepts, and propounded Rewards, and Punishments to Mankind, are Gods Subjects; all the rest, are to be understood as Enemies.

A Threefold Word of God, Reason, Revelation, Prophecy.

To rule by Words, requires that such Words be manifestly made known; for else they are no Lawes: For to the nature of Lawes, belongeth a sufficient, and clear Promulgation, such as may take away the excuse of Ignorance; which in the Lawes of men is but of one onely kind, and that is, Proclamation, or Promulgation by the voyce of man. But God declareth his Lawes three ways; by the Dictates of *Naturall Reason*, by *Revelation*, and by the *Voyce* of some *man*, to whom by the operation of Miracles, he procureth credit with the rest. From hence there ariseth a triple Word of God, *Rational, Sensible,* and *Prophetique*: to which Correspondeth a triple Hearing; *Right Reason, Sense Supernaturall,* and *Faith*. As for Sense Supernaturall, which consisteth in Revelation, or Inspiration, there have not been any Universall Lawes so given, because God speaketh not in that manner, but to particular persons, and to divers men divers things.

A twofold Kingdome of God, Naturall and Prophetique.

From the difference between the other two kinds of Gods Word, *Rationall,* and *Prophetique*, there may be attributed to God, a twofold Kingdome, *Naturall,* and *Prophetique*: Naturall, wherein he governeth as many of Mankind as acknowledge his Providence, by the naturall Dictates of Right Reason; And Prophetique, wherein having chosen out one peculiar Nation (the Jewes) for his Subjects, he governed them, and none but them, not onely by naturall Reason, but by Positive Lawes, which he gave them by the mouths of his holy Prophets. Of the Naturall Kingdome of God I intend to speak in this Chapter.

The Right of Gods Soveraignty is derived from his Omnipotence.

The Right of Nature, whereby God reigneth over men, and punisheth those that break his Lawes, is to be derived, not from his Creating them as if he required obedience, as of Gratitude for his benefits; but from his *Irresistible Power*. I have formerly shewn, how the Soveraign Right ariseth from Pact: To shew how the same Right may arise from Nature, requires no more, but to shew in what case it is never taken away. Seeing all men by Nature had Right to All things, they had Right every one to reigne over all the rest. But because this

Right could not be obtained by force, it concerned the safety of every one, laying by that Right, to set up men (with Soveraign Authority) by common consent, to rule and defend them: whereas if there had been any man of Power Irresistible; there had been no reason, why he should not by that Power have ruled, and defended both himselfe, and them, according to his own discretion. To those therefore whose Power is irresistible, the dominion of all men adhaereth naturally by their excellence of Power; and consequently it is from that Power, that the Kingdome over men, and the Right of Afflicting men at his pleasure, belongeth Naturally to God Almighty; not as Creator, and Gracious; but as Omnipotent. And though Punishment be due for Sinne onely, because by that word is understood Affliction for Sinne; yet the Right of Afflicting, is not alwayes derived from mens Sinne, but from Gods Power.   [188]

This question, *Why Evill men often Prosper, and Good men suffer Adversity,* has been much disputed by the Antient, and is the same with this of ours, *by what Right God dispenseth the Prosperities and Adversities of this life*; and is of that difficulty, as it hath shaken the faith, not onely of the Vulgar, but of Philosophers, and which is more, of the Saints, concerning the Divine Providence. *How Good* (saith *David*) *is the God of Israel to those that are Upright in Heart; and yet my feet were almost gone, my treadings had well-nigh slipt; for I was grieved at the Wicked, when I saw the Ungodly in such Prosperity.* And *Job*, how earnestly does he expostulate with God, for the many Afflictions he suffered, notwithstanding his Righteousnesse? This question in the case of *Job*, is decided by God himselfe, not by arguments derived from *Job*'s Sinne, but his own Power. For whereas the friends of *Job* drew their arguments from his Affliction to his Sinne, and he defended himselfe by the conscience of his Innocence, God himselfe taketh up the matter, and having justified the Affliction by arguments drawn from his Power, such as this, *Where wast thou when I layd the foundations of the earth*, and the like, both approved *Job*'s Innocence, and reproved the Erroneous doctrine of his friends. Conformable to this doctrine is the sentence of our Saviour, concerning the man that was born Blind, in these words, *Neither hath this man sinned, nor his fathers; but that the works of God might be made manifest in him.* And though it be said, *That Death entred into the world by sinne*, (by which is meant that if *Adam* had never sinned, he had never dyed, that is, never suffered any separation of his soule from his body,) it follows not

Sinne not the cause of all Affliction.

*Psal.*72. *ver.*1,2,3.

Job 38.*v.*4.

thence, that God could not justly have Afflicted him, though he had not Sinned, as well as he afflicteth other living creatures, that cannot sinne.

Divine Lawes.

Having spoken of the Right of Gods Soveraignty, as grounded onely on Nature; we are to consider next, what are the Divine Lawes, or Dictates of Naturall Reason; which Lawes concern either the naturall Duties of one man to another, or the Honour naturally due to our Divine Soveraign. The first are the same Lawes of Nature, of which I have spoken already in the 14. and 15. Chapters of this Treatise; namely, Equity, Justice, Mercy, Humility, and the rest of the Morall Vertues. It remaineth therefore that we consider, what Prae-cepts are dictated to men, by their Naturall Reason onely, without other word of God, touching the Honour and Worship of the Divine Majesty.

Honour and Worship what.

Honour consisteth in the inward thought, and opinion of the Power, and Goodnesse of another: and therefore to Honour God, is to think as Highly of his Power and Goodnesse, as is possible. And of that opinion, the externall signes appearing in the Words, and Actions of men, are called *Worship*; which is one part of that which the Latines understand by the word *Cultus*: For *Cultus* signifieth properly, and constantly, that labour which a man bestowes on any thing, with a purpose to make benefit by it. Now those things whereof we make benefit, are either subject to us, and the profit they yeeld, followeth the labour we bestow upon them, as a naturall effect; or they are not subject to us, but answer our labour, according to their own Wills. In the first sense the labour bestowed on the Earth, is called *Culture*; and the education of Children a *Culture* of their mindes. In the second sense, where mens wills are to be wrought to our purpose, not by Force, but by Compleasance, it signifieth as much as Courting, that is, a winning of favour by good offices; as by praises, by acknowledging their Power, and by whatsoever is pleasing to them from whom we look for any benefit. And this is properly *Worship*: in which sense *Publicola*, is understood for a Worshipper of the People; and *Cultus Dei*, for the Worship of God.

[189]

Severall signes of Honour.

From internall Honour, consisting in the opinion of Power and Goodnesse, arise three Passions; *Love*, which hath reference to Goodnesse; and *Hope*, and *Fear*, that relate to Power: And three parts of externall worship; *Praise*, *Magnifying*, and *Blessing*: The subject of Praise, being Goodnesse; the subject of Magnifying, and Blessing, being Power, and the effect thereof of Felicity. Praise, and Magnifying are signified both by Words, and Actions: By Words, when we say a man is Good, or Great: By Actions, when we thank him for his Bounty, and obey his Power. The opinion of the Happinesse of another, can onely be expressed by words.

There be some signes of Honour, (both in Attributes and Actions,) that be Naturally so; as amongst Attributes, *Good, Just, Liberall*, and the like; and amongst Actions, *Prayers, Thanks*, and *Obedience*. Others are so by Institution, or Custome of men; and in some times and places are Honourable; in others Dishonourable; in others Indifferent: such as are the Gestures in Salutation, Prayer, and Thanksgiving, in different times and places, differently used. The former is *Naturall*; the later *Arbitrary* Worship. *Worship Naturall and Arbitrary.*

And of Arbitrary Worship, there bee two differences: For sometimes it is a *Commanded*, sometimes *a *Voluntary**[1] Worship: Commanded, when it is such as hee requireth, who is Worshipped: Free, when it is such as the Worshipper thinks fit. When it is Commanded, not the words, or gesture, but the obedience is the Worship. But when Free, the Worship consists in the opinion of the beholders: for if to them the words, or actions by which we intend honour, seem ridiculous, and tending to contumely; they are no Worship; because no signes of Honour; and no signes of Honour; because a signe is not a signe to him that giveth it, but to him to whom it is made; that is, to the spectator. *Worship Commanded and Free.*

Again, there is a *Publique*, and a *Private* Worship. Publique, is the Worship that a Common-wealth performeth, as one Person. Private, is that which a Private person exhibiteth. Publique, in respect of the whole Common-wealth, is Free; but in respect of Particular men it is not so. Private, is in secret Free; but in the sight of the multitude, it is never without some Restraint, either from the Lawes, or from the Opinion of men; which is contrary to the nature of Liberty. *Worship Publique and Private.*

The End of Worship amongst men, is Power. For where a man seeth another worshipped, he supposeth him powerfull, and is the readier to obey him; which makes his Power greater. But God has no Ends: the worship we do him, proceeds from our duty, and is directed according to our capacity, by those rules of Honour, that Reason dictateth to be done by the weak to the more potent men, in hope of *The End of Worship.* [190]

[1] Syn.: *Voluntary*

benefit, for fear of dammage, or in thankfulnesse for good already received from them.

That we may know what worship of God is taught us by the light of Nature, I will begin with his Attributes. Where, First, it is manifest, we ought to attribute to him *Existence*: For no man can have the will to honour that, which he thinks not to have any Beeing.

Secondly, that those Philosophers, who sayd the World, or the Soule of the World was God, spake unworthily of him; and denyed his Existence: For by God, is understood the cause of the World; and to say the World is God, is to say there is no cause of it, that is, no God.

Thirdly, to say the World was not Created, but Eternall, (seeing that which is Eternall has no cause,) is to deny there is a God.

Fourthly, that they who attributing (as they think) Ease to God, take from him the care of Man-kind; take from him his Honour: for it takes away mens love, and fear of him; which is the root of Honour.

Fifthly, in those things that signifie Greatnesse, and Power; to say he is *Finite*, is not to Honour him: For it is not a signe of the Will to Honour God, to attribute to him lesse than we can; and Finite, is lesse than we can; because to Finite, it is easie to adde more.

Therefore to attribute *Figure* to him, is not Honour; for all Figure is Finite:

Nor to say we conceive, and imagine, or have an *Idea* of him, in our mind: for whatsoever we conceive is Finite:

Nor to attribute to him *Parts*, or *Totality*; which are the Attributes onely of things Finite:

Nor to say he is in this, or that *Place*: for whatsoever is in Place, is bounded, and Finite:

Nor that he is *Moved*, or *Resteth*: for both these Attributes ascribe to him Place:

Nor that there be more Gods than one; because it implies them all Finite: for there cannot be more than one Infinite.

Nor to ascribe to him (unlesse Metaphorically, meaning not the Passion, but the Effect) Passions that partake of Griefe; as *Repentance, Anger, Mercy*: or of Want; as *Appetite, Hope, Desire*; or of any Passive faculty: For Passion, is Power limited by somewhat else.

And therefore when we ascribe to God a *Will*, it is not to be understood, as that of Man, for a *Rationall Appetite*; but as the Power, by which he effecteth every thing.

Likewise when we attribute to him *Sight*, and other acts of Sense;

as also *Knowledge*, and *Understanding*; which in us is nothing else, but a tumult of the mind, raised by externall things that presse the organicall parts of mans body: For there is no such thing in God; and being things that depend on naturall causes, cannot be attributed to him.

Hee that will attribute to God, nothing but what is warranted by [191] naturall Reason, must either use such Negative Attributes, as *Infinite*, *Eternall*, *Incomprehensible*; or Superlatives, as *Most High*, *most Great*, and the like; or Indefinite, as *Good*, *Just*, *Holy*, *Creator*; and in such sense, as if he meant not to declare what he is, (for that were to circumscribe him within the limits of our Fancy,) but how much wee admire him, and how ready we would be to obey him; which is a signe of Humility, and of a Will to honour him as much as we can: For there is but one Name to signifie our Conception of his Nature, and that is, I AM: and but one Name of his Relation to us, and that is *God*; in which is contained Father, King, and Lord.

Concerning the actions of Divine Worship, it is a most generall Precept of Reason, that they be signes of the Intention to Honour God; such as are, First, *Prayers*: For not the Carvers, when they made Images, were thought to make them Gods; but the People that *Prayed* to them. *Actions that are signes of Divine Honour.*

Secondly, *Thanksgiving*; which differeth from Prayer in Divine Worship, no otherwise, than that Prayers precede, and Thanks succeed the benefit; the end both of the one, and the other, being to acknowledge God, for Author of all benefits, as well past, as future.

Thirdly, *Gifts*; that is to say, *Sacrifices*, and *Oblations*, (if they be of the best,) are signes of Honour: for they are Thanksgivings.

Fourthly, *Not to Swear by any but God*, is naturally a signe of Honour: for it is a confession that God onely knoweth the heart; and that no mans wit, or strength can protect a man against Gods vengeance on the perjured.

Fifthly, it is a part of Rationall Worship, to speak Considerately of God; for it argues a Fear of him, and Fear, is a confession of his Power. Hence followeth, That the name of God is not to be used rashly, and to no purpose; for that is as much, as in Vain: And it is to no purpose, unlesse it be by way of Oath, and by order of the Common-wealth, to make Judgements certain; or between Commonwealths, to avoyd Warre. And that disputing of Gods nature is contrary to his Honour: For it is supposed, that in this naturall Kingdome of God, there is no other way to know any thing, but by naturall

Reason; that is, from the Principles of naturall Science; which are so farre from teaching us any thing of Gods nature, as they cannot teach us our own nature, nor the nature of the smallest creature living. And therefore, when men out of the Principles of naturall Reason, dispute of the Attributes of God, they but dishonour him: For in the Attributes which we give to God, we are not to consider the signification of Philosophicall Truth; but the signification of Pious Intention, to do him the greatest Honour we are able. From the want of which consideration, have proceeded the volumes of disputation about the Nature of God, that tend not to his Honour, but to the honour of our own wits, and learning; and are nothing else but inconsiderate, and vain abuses of his Sacred Name.

[192] Sixthly, in *Prayers, Thanksgiving, Offerings* and *Sacrifices*, it is a Dictate of naturall Reason, that they be every one in his kind the best, and most significant of Honour. As for example, that Prayers, and Thanksgiving, be made in Words and Phrases, not sudden, nor light, nor Plebeian; but beautifull, and well composed; For else we do not God as much honour as we can. And therefore the Heathens did absurdly, to worship Images for Gods: But their doing it in Verse, and with Musick, both of Voyce, and Instruments, was reasonable. Also that the Beasts they offered in sacrifice, and the Gifts they offered, and their actions in Worshipping, were full of submission, and commemorative of benefits received, was according to reason, as proceeding from an intention to honour him.-

Seventhly, Reason directeth not onely to worship God in Secret; but also, and especially, in Publique, and in the sight of men: For without that, (that which in honour is most acceptable) the procuring others to honour him, is lost.

Lastly, Obedience to his Lawes (that is, in this case to the Lawes of Nature,) is the greatest worship of all. For as Obedience is more acceptable to God than Sacrifice; so also to set light by his Commandements, is the greatest of all contumelies. And these are the Lawes of that Divine Worship, which naturall Reason dictateth to private men.

Publique Worship consisteth in Uniformity. But seeing a Common-wealth is but one Person, it ought also to exhibite to God but one Worship; which then it doth, when it commandeth it to be exhibited by Private men, Publiquely. And this is Publique Worship; the property whereof, is to be *Uniforme*: For those actions that are done differently, by different men, cannot be said to

252

be a Publique Worship. And therefore, where many sorts of Worship
be allowed, proceeding from the different Religions of Private men, it
cannot be said there is any Publique Worship, nor that the Common-
wealth is of any Religion at all.

And because words (and consequently the Attributes of God) have
their signification by agreement, and constitution of men; those
Attributes are to be held significative of Honour, that men intend
shall so be; and whatsoever may be done by the wills of particular
men, where there is no Law but Reason, may be done by the will of
the Common-wealth, by Lawes Civill. And because a Common-
wealth hath no Will, nor makes no Lawes, but those that are made by
the Will of him, or them that have the Soveraign Power; it followeth,
that those Attributes which the Soveraign ordaineth, in the Worship
of God, for signes of Honour, ought to be taken and used for such, by
private men in their publique Worship. *All Attributes depend on the Lawes Civill.*

But because not all Actions are signes by Constitution; but some
are Naturally signes of Honour, others of Contumely, these later
(which are those that men are ashamed to do in the sight of them they
reverence) cannot be made by humane power a part of Divine worship; nor the former (such as are decent, modest, humble Behaviour)
ever be separated from it. But whereas there be an infinite number of
Actions, and Gestures, of an indifferent nature; such of them as the
Common-wealth shall ordain to be Publiquely and Universally in use,
as signes of Honour, and part of Gods Worship, are to be taken and
used for such by the Subjects. And that which is said in the Scripture,
It is better to obey God than men, hath place in the kingdome of God by
Pact, and not by Nature. *Not all Actions.* [193]

Having thus briefly spoken of the Naturall Kingdome of God, and
his Naturall Lawes, I will adde onely to this Chapter a short declaration of his Naturall Punishments. There is no action of man in this
life, that is not the beginning of so long a chayn of Consequences, as
no *humans*[1] Providence, is high enough, to give a man a prospect to
the end. And in this Chayn, there are linked together both pleasing
and unpleasing events; in such manner, as he that will do any thing for
his pleasure, must engage himselfe to suffer all the pains annexed to
it; and these pains, are the Naturall Punishments of those actions,
which are the beginning of more Harme than Good. And hereby it *Naturall Punishments.*

[1] *Syn.*: humane

comes to passe, that Intemperance, is naturally punished with Diseases; Rashnesse, with Mischances; Injustice, with the Violence of Enemies; Pride, with Ruine; Cowardise, with Oppression; Negligent government of Princes, with Rebellion; and Rebellion, with Slaughter. For seeing Punishments are consequent to the breach of Lawes; Naturall Punishments must be naturally consequent to the breach of the Lawes of Nature; and therfore follow them as their naturall, not arbitrary effects.

The Conclusion of the Second Part. And thus farre concerning the Constitution, Nature, and Right of Soveraigns; and concerning the Duty of Subjects, derived from the Principles of Naturall Reason. And now, considering how different this Doctrine is, from the Practise of the greatest part of the world, especially of these Western parts, that have received their Morall learning from *Rome*, and *Athens*; and how much depth of Morall Philosophy is required, in them that have the Administration of the Soveraign Power; I am at the point of believing this my labour, as uselesse, as the Common-wealth of *Plato*; For he also is of opinion that it is impossible for the disorders of State, and change of Governments by Civill Warre, ever to be taken away, till Soveraigns be Philosophers. But when I consider again, that the Science of Naturall Justice, is the onely Science necessary for Soveraigns, and their principall Ministers; and that they need not be charged with the Sciences Mathematicall, (as by *Plato* they are,) further, than by good Lawes to encourage men to the study of them; and that neither *Plato*, nor any other Philosopher hitherto, hath put into order, and sufficiently, or probably proved all the Theoremes of Morall doctrine, that men may learn thereby, both how to govern, and how to obey; I recover some hope, that one time or other, this writing of mine, may fall into the hands of a Soveraign, who will consider it himselfe, (for it is short, and I think clear,) without the help of any interested, or envious Interpreter; and by the exercise of entire Soveraignty, in protecting the Publique teaching of it, convert this Truth of Speculation, into the Utility of Practice.

OF A CHRISTIAN COMMON-WEALTH

CHAP. XXXII.
Of the Principles of CHRISTIAN POLITIQUES.

I have derived the Rights of Soveraigne Power, and the duty of Subjects hitherto, from the Principles of Nature onely; such as Experience has found true, or Consent (concerning the use of words) has made so; that is to say, from the nature of Men, known to us by Experience, and from Definitions (of such words as are Essentiall to all Politicall reasoning) universally agreed on. But in that I am next to handle, which is the Nature and Rights of a CHRISTIAN COMMON-WEALTH, whereof there dependeth much upon Supernaturall Revelations of the Will of God; the ground of my Discourse must be, not only the Naturall Word of God, but also the Propheticall.

The Word of God delivered by Prophets is the main principle of Christian Politiques.

Neverthelesse, we are not to renounce our Senses, and Experience; nor (that which is the undoubted Word of God) our naturall Reason. For they are the talents which he hath put into our hands to negotiate, till the coming again of our blessed Saviour; and therefore not to be folded up in the Napkin of an Implicite Faith, but employed in the

Yet is not naturall Reason to be renounced.

255

purchase of Justice, Peace, and true Religion. For though there be many things in Gods Word above Reason; that is to say, which cannot by naturall reason be either demonstrated, or confuted; yet there is nothing contrary to it; but when it seemeth so, the fault is either in our unskilfull Interpretation, or erroneous Ratiocination.

Therefore, when any thing therein written is too hard for our examination, wee are bidden to captivate our understanding to the Words; and not to labour in sifting out a Philosophicall truth by Logick, of such mysteries as are not comprehensible, nor fall under any rule of naturall science. For it is with the mysteries of our Religion, as with wholsome pills for the sick, which swallowed whole, have the vertue to cure; but chewed, are for the most part cast up again without effect.

[196]
What it is to
captivate the
Under-
standing. But by the Captivity of our Understanding, is not meant a Submission of the Intellectuall faculty, to the Opinion of any other man; but of the Will to Obedience, where obedience is due. For Sense, Memory, Understanding, Reason, and Opinion are not in our power to change; but alwaies, and necessarily such, as the things we see, hear, and consider suggest unto us; and therefore are not effects of our Will, but our Will of them. We then Captivate our Understanding and Reason, when we forbear contradiction; when we so speak, as (by lawfull Authority) we are commanded; and when we live accordingly; which in sum, is Trust, and Faith reposed in him that speaketh, though the mind be incapable of any Notion at all from the words spoken.

How God
speaketh to
men. When God speaketh to man, it must be either immediately; or by mediation of another man, to whom he had formerly spoken by himself immediately. How God speaketh to a man immediately, may be understood by those well enough, to whom he hath so spoken; but how the same should be understood by another, is hard, if not impossible to know. For if a man pretend to me, that God hath spoken to him supernaturally, and immediately, and I make doubt of it, I cannot easily perceive what argument he can produce, to oblige me to beleeve it. It is true, that if he be my Soveraign, he may oblige me to obedience, so, as not by act or word to declare I beleeve him not; but not to think any otherwise then my reason perswades me. But if one that hath not such authority over me, shall pretend the same, there is nothing that exacteth either beleefe, or obedience.

For to say that God hath spoken to him in the Holy Scripture, is not to say God hath spoken to him immediately, but by mediation of the Prophets, or of the Apostles, or of the Church, in such manner as he speaks to all other Christian men. To say he hath spoken to him in a Dream, is no more then to say he *hath dreamt*[1] that God spake to him; which is not of force to win beleef from any man, that knows dreams are for the most part naturall, and may proceed from former thoughts; and such dreams as that, from selfe conceit, and foolish arrogance, and false opinion of a mans own godlinesse, or other vertue, by which he thinks he hath merited the favour of extraordinary Revelation. To say he hath seen a Vision, or heard a Voice, is to say, that he hath dreamed between sleeping and waking: for in such manner a man doth many times naturally take his dream for a vision, as not having well observed his own slumbering. To say he speaks by supernaturall Inspiration, is to say he finds an ardent desire to speak, or some strong opinion of himself, for which hee can alledge no naturall and sufficient reason. So that though God Almighty can speak to a man, by Dreams, Visions, Voice, and Inspiration; yet he obliges no man to beleeve he hath so done to him that pretends it; who (being a man) may erre, and (which is more) may lie.

How then can he, to whom God hath never revealed his Wil immediately (saving by the way of natural reason) know when he is to obey, or not to obey his Word, delivered by him, that sayes he is a Prophet. Of 400 Prophets, of whom the K. of *Israel* asked counsel, concerning the warre he made against *Ramoth Gilead*, only *Micaiah* was a true one. The Prophet that was sent to prophecy against the Altar set up by *Jeraboam*, though a true Prophet, and that by two miracles done in his presence appears to be a Prophet sent from God, was yet deceived by another old Prophet, that perswaded him as from the mouth of God, to eat and drink with him. If one Prophet deceive another, what certainty is there of knowing the will of God, by other way than that of Reason? To which I answer out of the Holy Scripture, that there be two marks, by which together, not asunder, a true Prophet is to be known. One is the doing of miracles; the other is the not teaching any other Religion than that which is already established. Asunder (I say) neither of these is sufficient. *If a Prophet rise amongst you, or a Dreamer of dreams, and shall pretend the doing of a miracle, and the miracle come to passe; if he say, Let us follow strange Gods, which thou*

By what marks Prophets are known.
1 Kings 22.
[197]
1 Kings 13.

Deut.13.v.1, 2,3,4,5.

---

[1] *Syn.*: dreamed

hast not known, thou shalt not hearken to him, & c. But that Prophet and Dreamer of dreams shall be put to death, because he hath spoken to you to Revolt from the Lord your God. In which words two things are to be observed; First, that God wil not have miracles alone serve for arguments, to approve the Prophets calling; but (as it is in the third verse) for an experiment of the constancy of our adherence to himself. For the works of the *Egyptian* Sorcerers, though not so great as those of *Moses*, yet were great miracles. Secondly, that how great soever the miracle be, yet if it tend to stir up revolt against the King, or him that governeth by the Kings authority, he that doth such miracle, is not to be considered otherwise than as sent to make triall of their allegiance. For these words, *revolt from the Lord your God*, are in this place equivalent to *revolt from your King*. For they had made God their King by pact at the foot of Mount *Sinai*; who ruled them by *Moses* only; for he only spake with God, and from time to time declared Gods Commandements to the people. In like manner, after our Saviour Christ had made his Disciples acknowledge him for the *Messiah*, (that is to say, for Gods anointed, whom the nation of the *Jews* daily expected for their King, but refused when he came,) he omitted not to advertise

Mat.24.24.   them of the danger of miracles. *There shall arise* (saith he) *false Christs, and false Prophets, and shall doe great wonders and miracles, even to the seducing (if it were possible) of the very Elect.* By which it appears, that false Prophets may have the power of miracles; yet are wee not to take

*Gal.*1.8.   their doctrin for Gods Word. St *Paul* says further to the *Galatians*, that *if himself, or an Angell from heaven preach another Gospel to them, than he had preached, let him be accursed.* That Gospel was, that Christ was King; so that all preaching against the power of the King received, in consequence to these words, is by St *Paul* accursed. For his speech is addressed to those, who by his preaching had already received *Jesus* for the *Christ*, that is to say, for King of the *Jews*.

    And as Miracles, without preaching that Doctrine which God hath established; so preaching the true Doctrine, without the doing of

[198]   Miracles, is an unsufficient argument of immediate Revelation. For if

The marks of   a man that teacheth not false Doctrine, should pretend to bee a
a Prophet in   Prophet without shewing any Miracle, he is never the more to bee
the old law,   regarded for his pretence, as is evident by *Deut.* 18.*v.*21,22. *If thou say*
Miracles, and   *in thy heart, How shall we know that the Word* (of the Prophet) *is not that*
Doctrine
conformable   *which the Lord hath spoken. When the Prophet shall have spoken in the*
to the law.   *name of the Lord, that which shall not come to passe, that's the word which*

the Lord hath not spoken, but the Prophet has spoken it out of the pride of his own heart, fear him not. But a man may here again ask, When the Prophet hath foretold a thing, how shal we know whether it will come to passe or not? For he may foretel it as a thing to arrive after a certain long time, longer than the time of mans life; or indefinitely, that it will come to passe one time or other: in which case this mark of a Prophet is unusefull; and therefore the miracles that oblige us to beleeve a Prophet, ought to be confirmed by an immediate, or a not long deferr'd event. So that it is manifest, that the teaching of the Religion which God hath established, and the shewing of a *present*[1] Miracle, joined together, were the only marks whereby the Scripture would have a true Prophet, that is to say, immediate Revelation to be acknowledged; neither of them being singly sufficient to oblige any other man to regard what he saith.

Seeing therefore Miracles now cease, we have no sign left, whereby to acknowledge the pretended Revelations, or Inspirations of any private man; nor obligation to give ear to any Doctrine, farther than it is conformable to the Holy Scriptures, which since the time of our Saviour, supply the place, and sufficiently recompense the want of all other Prophecy; and from which, by wise and learned interpretation, and carefull ratiocination, all rules and precepts necessary to the knowledge of our duty both to God and man, without Enthusiasme, or supernaturall Inspiration, may easily be deduced. And this Scripture is it, out of which I am to take the Principles of my Discourse, concerning the Rights of those that are the Supream Governors on earth, of Christian Common-wealths; and of the duty of Christian Subjects towards their Soveraigns. And to that end, I shall speak in the next Chapter, of the Books, Writers, Scope and Authority of the Bible.

Miracles ceasing, Prophets cease, and the Scripture supplies their place.

---

[1] *Syn.*: present

CHAP. XXXIII.

Of the Number, Antiquity, Scope, Authority, and Interpreters of the Books of Holy SCRIPTURE.

Of the Books of Holy Scripture. By the Books of Holy SCRIPTURE, are understood those, which ought to be the *Canon*, that is to say, the Rules of Christian life. And because all Rules of life, which men are in conscience bound to observe, are Laws; the question of the Scripture, is the question of what is Law throughout all Christendome, both Naturall, and Civill. For though it be not determined in Scripture, what Laws every Christian King shall constitute in his own Dominions; yet it is determined what laws he shall not constitute. Seeing therefore I have already proved, that Soveraigns in their own Dominions are the sole Legislators; those Books only are Canonicall, that is, Law, in every nation, which are established for such by the Soveraign Authority. It is true, that God is the Soveraign of all Soveraigns; and therefore, when he speaks to any Subject, he ought to be obeyed, whatsoever any earthly Potentate command to the contrary. But the question is not of obedience to God, but of *when*, and *what* God hath said; which to Subjects that have no supernaturall revelation, cannot be known, but by that naturall reason, which guided them, for the obtaining of Peace and Justice, to obey the authority of their severall Common-wealths; that is to say, of their lawfull Soveraigns. According to this obligation, I can acknowledge no other Books of the Old Testament, to be Holy Scripture, but those which have been commanded to be acknowledged for such, by the Authority of the Church of *England*. What Books these are, is sufficiently known, without a Catalogue of them here; and they are the same that are acknowledged by St. *Jerome*, who holdeth the rest, namely, the *Wisdome of Solomon, Ecclesiasticus, Judith, Tobias*, the first and the second of *Maccabees*, (though he had seen the first in *Hebrew*) and the third and fourth of *Esdras*, for *Apocrypha*. Of the Canonicall, *Josephus* a learned *Jew*, that wrote in the time of the Emperour *Domitian*, reckoneth *twenty two*, making the number agree with the *Hebrew* Alphabet. St. *Jerome* does the same, though they reckon them in different manner. For *Josephus* numbers *five* Books of *Moses, thirteen* of *Prophets*, that writ the History of their own times (which how it agrees with the Prophets writings contained in the Bible wee shall see hereafter), and *four* of *Hymnes* and Morall Precepts. But St. *Jerome* reckons *five* Books of *Moses, eight* of *Prophets*, and *nine* of other Holy writ, which he calls of *Hagiographa*. The *Septuagint*, who were 70. learned men of the *Jews*, sent for by *Ptolemy* King of *Egypt*, to translate the *Jewish* law, out of the *Hebrew* into the *Greek*, have left us   200] no other for holy Scripture in the *Greek* tongue, but the same that are received in the Church of *England*.

As for the Books of the New Testament, they are equally acknowledged for Canon by all Christian Churches, and by all Sects of Christians, that admit any Books at all for Canonicall.

Who were the originall writers of the severall Books of Holy Scripture, has not been made evident by any sufficient testimony of other History, (which is the only proof of matter of fact); nor can be by any arguments of naturall Reason: for Reason serves only to convince the truth (not of fact, but) of consequence. The light therefore that must guide us in this question, must be that which is held out unto us from the Bookes themselves: And this light, though it shew us not the writer of every book, yet it is not unusefull to give us knowledge of the time, wherein they were written. *Their Antiquity.*

And first, for the *Pentateuch*, it is not argument enough that they were written by *Moses*, because they are called the five Books of *Moses* no more than these titles, The Book of *Joshua*, the Book of *Judges*, the Book of *Ruth*, and the Books of the *Kings*, are arguments sufficient to prove, that they were written by *Joshua*, by the *Judges*, by *Ruth*, and by the *Kings*. For in titles of Books, the subject is marked, as often as the writer. The *History of Livy*, denotes the Writer; but the *History of *Alexander**[1], is denominated from the subject. We read in the last Chapter of *Deuteronomie*, ver. 6. concerning the sepulcher of *Moses*, *that no man knoweth of his sepulcher to this day*, that is, to the day wherein those words were written. It is therefore manifest, that those words were written after his interrement. For it were a strange interpretation, to say *Moses* spake of his own sepulcher (though by Prophecy), that it was not found to that day, wherein he was yet living. But it *The Pentateuch not written by Moses.*

---

[1] *Syn.: Scanderberg*

may perhaps be alledged, that the last Chapter only, not the whole *Pentateuch*, was written by some other man, but the rest not: Let us therefore consider that which we find in the Book of *Genesis, chap.* 12. *ver.* 6. *And* Abraham *passed through the land to the place of* Sichem, *unto the plain of* Moreh, *and the* Canaanite *was then in the land*; which must needs bee the words of one that wrote when the *Canaanite* was not in the land; and consequently, not of *Moses*, who dyed before he came into it. Likewise *Numbers* 21. *ver.* 14. the Writer citeth another more ancient Book, Entituled, *The Book of the Warres of the Lord*, wherein were registred the Acts of *Moses*, at the Red-sea, and at the brook of *Arnon*. It is therefore sufficiently evident, that the five Books of *Moses* were written after his time, though how long after it be not so manifest.

But though *Moses* did not compile those Books entirely, and in the form we have them; yet he wrote all that which hee is there said to have written: as for example, the Volume of the Law, which is contained, as it seemeth, in the 11 of *Deuteronomie*, and the following Chapters to the 27. which was commanded to be written on stones, in

Deut. 31.9.

[201]

their entry into the land of *Canaan*. And this also did *Moses* himself write, and deliver to the Priests and Elders of *Israel*, to be read every seventh year to all *Israel*, at their assembling in the feast of Tabernacles. And this is that Law which God commanded, that their Kings (when they should have established that form of Government)

Deut. 31.26.

should take a copy of from the Priests and Levites; and which *Moses* commanded the Priests and Levites to lay in the side of the Arke; and the same which having been lost, was long time after found again by

2 *King.* 22.8.
& 23.1,2,3.

Hilkiah, and sent to King *Josias*, who causing it to be read to the People, renewed the Covenant between God and them.

The Book of Joshua written after his time.

That the Book of *Joshua* was also written long after the time of *Joshua*, may be gathered out of many places of the Book it self. *Joshua* had set up twelve stones in the middest of *Jordan*, for a monument of

Josh. 4.9.

their passage; of which the Writer saith thus, *They are there unto this day*; for *unto this day*, is a phrase that signifieth a time past, beyond the

Josh. 5.9.

memory of man. In like manner, upon the saying of the Lord, that he had rolled off from the people the Reproach of *Egypt*, the Writer saith, *The place is called* Gilgal *unto this day*; which to have said in the time of

Josh. 7.26.

Joshua had been improper. So also the name of the Valley of *Achor*, from the trouble that *Achan* raised in the Camp, the Writer saith, *remaineth unto this day*; which must needs bee therefore long after the

time of *Joshua*. Arguments of this kind there be many other; as *Josh.*
8.29. 13.13. 14.14. 15.63.

The same is manifest by like arguments of the Book of *Judges*, chap.
1.21,26. 6.24. 10.4 15.19. 17.6. and *Ruth* 1.1. but especially *Judg.*
18.30. where it is said, that Jonathan *and his sonnes were Priests to the*
Tribe of Dan, *untill the day of the captivity of the land.*

The Booke of Judges and Ruth written long after the Captivity.

That the Books of *Samuel* were also written after his own time,
there ar? the like arguments, 1 *Sam.* 5.5. 7.13,15. 27.6. & 30.25.
where, after *David* had adjudged equall parts of the spoiles, to them
that guarded the Ammunition, with them that fought, the Writer
saith, *He made it a Statute and an Ordinance to* Israel *to this day.* Again,
when *David* (displeased, that the Lord had slain *Uzzah*, for putting
out his hand to sustain the Ark,) called the place *Perez-Uzzah*, the
Writer saith, it is called so *to this day*: the time therefore of the writing
of that Book, must be long after the time of the fact; that is, long after
the time of *David*.

The like of the Bookes of Samuel.

2 Sam. 6.4.

As for the two Books of the *Kings*, and the two Books of the
Chronicles, besides the places which mention such monuments, as the
Writer saith, remained till his own days; such as are 1 *Kings* 9.13.
9.21. 10.12. 12.19. 2 *Kings* 2.22. 8.22. 10.27. 14.7. 16.6. 17.23.
17.34. 17.41. 1 *Chron.* 4.41. 5.26. It is argument sufficient they were
written after the captivity in *Babylon*, that the History of them is
continued till that time. For the Facts Registred are alwaies more
ancient than the Register; and much more ancient than such Books as
make mention of, and quote the Register; as these Books doe in
divers places, referring the Reader to the Chronicles of the Kings of
Juda, to the Chronicles of the Kings of *Israel*, to the Books of the
Prophet *Samuel*, of the Prophet *Nathan*, of the Prophet *Ahijah*; to the
Vision of *Jehdo*, to the Books of the Prophet *Serveiah*, and of the
Prophet *Addo*.

The Books of the Kings, and the Chronicles.

The Books of *Esdras* and *Nehemiah* were written certainly after
their return from captivity; because their return, the re-edification of
the walls and houses of *Jerusalem*, the renovation of the Covenant, and
ordination of their policy are therein contained.

[202]

Ezra and Nehemiah.

The History of Queen *Esther* is of the time of the Captivity; and
therefore the Writer must have been of the same time, or after it.

Esther.

The Book of *Job* hath no mark in it of the time wherein it was
written: and though it appear sufficiently (*Ezekiel* 14.14. and *James*
5.11.) that he was no fained person; yet the Book it self seemeth not to

Job.

to be a History, but a Treatise concerning a question in ancient time much disputed, *why wicked men have often prospered in this world, and good men have been afflicted*; and it is the more probable, because from the beginning, to the third verse of the third chapter, where the complaint of *Job* beginneth, the *Hebrew* it (as St. *Jerome* testifies) in prose; and from thence to the sixt verse of the last chapter in Hexameter Verses; and the rest of that chapter again in prose. So that the dispute is all in verse; and the prose is added, but as a Preface in the beginning, and an Epilogue in the end. But Verse is no usuall stile of such, as either are themselves in great pain, as *Job*; or of such as come to comfort them, as his friends; but in Philosophy, especially morall Philosophy, in ancient time frequent.

The Psalter.

The *Psalmes* were written the most part by *David*, for the use of the Quire. To these are added some Songs of *Moses*, and other holy men; and some of them after the return from the Captivity, as the 137. and the 126. whereby it is manifest that the Psalter was compiled, and put into the form it now hath, after the return of the *Jews* from *Babylon*.

The Proverbs.

The *Proverbs*, being a Collection of wise and godly Sayings, partly of *Solomon*, partly of *Agur* the son of *Jakeh*, and partly of the Mother of King *Lemuel*, cannot probably be thought to have been collected by *Solomon*, rather then by *Agur*, or the Mother of *Lemuel*; and that, though the sentences be theirs, yet the collection or compiling them into this one Book, was the work of some other godly man, that lived after them all.

Ecclesiastes and the Canticles.

The Books of *Ecclesiastes* and the *Canticles* have nothing that was not *Solomons*, except it be the Titles, or Inscriptions. For *The Words of the Preacher, the Son of* David, *King in* Jerusalem; and, *The Song of Songs*, which is *Solomon*'s, seem to have been made for distinctions sake, then, when the Books of Scripture were gathered into one body of the Law; to the end, that not the Doctrine only, but the Authors also might be extant.

The Prophets.

Of the Prophets, the most ancient, are *Sophoniah, Jonas, Amos, Hosea, Isaiah* and *Michaiah*, who lived in the time of *Amaziah*, and *Azariah*, otherwise *Ozias*, Kings of *Judah*. But the Book of *Jonas* is not properly a Register of his Prophecy, (for that is contained in these few words, *Fourty dayes and* Ninivy *shall be destroyed*,) but a History or Narration of his frowardnesse and disputing Gods commandements; so that there is small probability he should be the Author, seeing he is the subject of it. But the Book of *Amos* is his Prophecy.

Jeremiah, Abdias, Nahum, and *Habakkuk* prophecyed in the time of [203] *Josiah.*

Ezekiel, Daniel, Aggeus, and *Zacharias,* in the Captivity.

When *Joel* and *Malachi* prophecyed, is not evident by their Writings. But considering the Inscriptions, or Titles of their Books, it is manifest enough, that the whole Scripture of the Old Testament, was set forth in the form we have it, after the return of the *Jews* from their Captivity in *Babylon,* and before the time of *Ptolemaus Philadelphus,* that caused it to bee translated into *Greek* by seventy men, which were sent him out of *Judea* for that purpose. And if the Books of *Apocrypha* (which are recommended to us by the Church, though not for Canonicall, yet for profitable Books for our instruction) may in this point be credited, the Scripture was set forth in the form wee have it in, by *Esdras;* as may appear by that which he himself saith, in the second book, chapt. 14. verse 21,22, &c. where speaking to God, he saith thus, *Thy law is burnt; therefore no man knoweth the things which thou hast done, or the works that are to begin. But if I have found Grace before thee, send down the holy Spirit into me, and I shall write all that hath been done in the world, since the beginning, which were written in thy Law, that men may find thy path, and that they which will live in the later days, may live.* And verse 45. *And it came to passe when the forty dayes were fulfilled, that the Highest spake, saying, The first that thou hast written, publish openly, that the worthy and unworthy may read it; but keep the seventy last, that thou mayst deliver them onely to such as be wise among the people.* And thus much concerning the time of the writing of the Bookes of the Old Testament.

The Writers of the New Testament lived all in lesse than an age *The New* after Christs Ascension, and had all of them seen our Saviour, or *Testament.* been his Disciples, except St. *Paul,* and St. *Luke;* and consequently whatsoever was written by them, is as ancient as the time of the Apostles. But the time wherein the Books of the New Testament were received, and acknowledged by the Church to be of their writing, is not altogether so ancient. For, as the Bookes of the Old Testament are derived to us, from no higher time then that of *Esdras,* who by the direction of Gods Spirit retrived them, when they were lost: Those of the New Testament, of which the copies were not many, nor could easily be all in any one private mans hand, cannot bee derived from a higher time, than that wherein the Governours of the Church collected, approved, and recommended them to us, as the writings of those Apostles and Disciples, under whose names they go. The first enumeration of all the Bookes, both of the Old, and New Testament, is in the Canons of the Apostles, supposed to be collected by *Clement* the *first*[1] Bishop of *Rome*. But because that is but supposed, and by many questioned, the Councell of *Laodicea* is the first we know, that recommended the Bible to the then Christian Churches, for the Writings of the Prophets and Apostles, and this Councell was held in the 364. yeer after Christ. *After*[2] which time, though ambition had so far prevailed on *some*[3] Doctors of the Church, as no more to esteem Emperours, though Christian, for the Shepherds of the people, but for Sheep; and Emperours not Christian, for Wolves; and endeavoured to passe their Doctrine, not for Counsell, and Information, as Preachers; but for Laws, as absolute Governours; and thought such frauds as tended to make the people the more obedient to Christian Doctrine, to be pious; yet I am perswaded they did not therefore falsifie the Scriptures, though the copies of the Books of the New Testament, were in the hands only of the Ecclesiasticks; because if they had had an intention so to doe, they would surely have made them more favorable to their power over Christian Princes, and Civill Soveraignty, than they are. I see not therefore any reason to doubt, but that the Old, and New Testament, as we have them now, are the true Registers of those things, which were done and said by the Prophets, and Apostles. And so perhaps are some of those Books which are called Apocrypha, if left out of the Canon, not for inconformity of Doctrine with the rest, but only because they are not found in the Hebrew. For after the conquest of Asia by Alexander the Great, there were few learned Jews, that were not perfect in the Greek tongue. For the seventy Interpreters that converted the Bible into Greek, were all of them Hebrews; and we have extant the works of *Philo* and *Josephus* both Jews, written by them eloquently in Greek. But it is not the Writer, but the authority of the Church, that maketh a Book Canonicall. And although these Books were written by divers men, yet it is manifest the Writers were all indued with one and the same Spirit, in that they conspire to one and the same end, which is the setting forth of the Rights of the Kingdome of *God*, the *Father*, *Son*, and *Holy Ghost*. For the Book of *Genesis*, deriveth the Genealogy of Gods people, from the creation of the World, to the going into

[204]

Their Scope.

---

[1] *Syn.*: first (after St. Peter)   [2] *Syn.*: At   [3] *Syn.*: the great

Egypt: the other four Books of *Moses*, contain the Election of God for their King, and the Laws which hee prescribed for their Government: The Books of *Joshua*, *Judges*, *Ruth*, and *Samuel*, to the time of *Saul*, describe the acts of Gods people, till the time they cast off Gods yoke, and called for a King, after the manner of their neighbour nations: The rest of the History of the Old Testament, derives the succession of the line of *David*, to the Captivity, out of which line was to spring the restorer of the Kingdome of God, even our blessed Saviour *God the Son*, whose coming was foretold in the Bookes of the Prophets, after whom the Evangelists writt his life, and actions, and his claim to the Kingdome, whilst he lived on earth: and lastly, the Acts, and Epistles of the Apostles, declare the coming of God, the *Holy Ghost*, and the Authority he left with them, and their successors, for the direction of the Jews, and for the invitation of the Gentiles. In summe, the Histories and the Prophecies of the old Testament, and the Gospels and Epistles of the New Testament, have had one and the same scope, to convert men to the obedience of God; 1. in *Moses*, and the Priests; 2. in the man *Christ*; and 3. in the *Apostles* and the successors to Apostolicall power. For these three at several times did represent the person of God: *Moses*, and his successors the High Priests, and Kings of Judah, in the Old Testament: *Christ* himself, in the time he lived on earth: and the *Apostles*, and their successors, from the day of Pentecost (when the *Holy Ghost* descended on them) to this day. [205]

    It is a question much disputed between the divers sects of Christian Religion, *From whence the Scriptures derive their Authority*; which question is also propounded sometimes in other terms, as, *How wee know them to be the Word of God*, or, *Why we beleeve them to be so*: And the difficulty of resolving it, ariseth chiefly from the impropernesse of the words wherein the question it self is couched. For it is beleeved on all hands, that the first and originall *Author* of them is God; and consequently the question disputed, is not that. Again, it is manifest, that none can know they are Gods Word, (though all true Christians beleeve it,) but those to whom God himself hath revealed it supernaturally; and therefore the question is not rightly moved, of our *Knowledge* of it. Lastly, when the question is propounded of our *Beleefe*; because some are moved to beleeve for one, and others for other reasons, there can be rendred no one generall answer for them all. The question truly stated is, *By what Authority they are made Law.*

The question of the Authority of the Scriptures stated.

267

As far as they differ not from the Laws of Nature, there is no doubt, but they are the Law of God, and carry their Authority with them, legible to all men that have the use of naturall reason: but this is no other Authority, then that of all other Morall Doctrine consonant to Reason; the Dictates whereof are Laws, not *made*, but *Eternall*.

If they be made Law by God himselfe, they are of the nature of written Law, which are Laws to them only to whom God hath so sufficiently published them, as no man can excuse himself, by saying, he knew not they were his.

He therefore, to whom God hath not supernaturally revealed, that they are his, nor that those that published them, were sent by him, is not obliged to obey them, by any Authority, but his, whose Commands have already the force of Laws; that is to say, by any other Authority, then that of the Common-wealth, residing in the Soveraign, who only has the Legislative power. Again, if it be not the Legislative Authority of the Common-wealth, that giveth them the force of Laws, it must bee some other Authority derived from God, either private, or publique: if private, it obliges onely him, to whom in particular God hath been pleased to reveale it. For if every man should be obliged, to take for Gods Law, what particular men, on pretence of private Inspiration, or Revelation, should obtrude upon him, (in such a number of men, that out of pride, and ignorance, take their own Dreams, and extravagant Fancies, and Madnesse, for testimonies of Gods Spirit; or out of ambition, pretend to such Divine testimonies, falsely, and contrary to their own consciences,) it were impossible that any Divine Law should be acknowledged. If publique, it is the Authority of the *Common-wealth*, or of the *Church*. But the Church, if it be one person, is the same thing with a Common-wealth of Christians; called a *Common-wealth*, because it consisteth of men united in one person, their Soveraign; and a *Church*, because it consisteth in Christian men, united in one Christian Soveraign. But if the Church be not one person, then it hath no authority at all; it can neither command, nor doe any action at all; nor is capable of having any power, or right to any thing; nor has any Will, Reason, nor Voice; for all these qualities are personall. Now if the whole number of Christians be not contained in one Common-wealth, they are not one person; nor is there an Universall Church that hath any authority over them; and therefore the Scriptures are not made Laws, by the Universall Church: or if it bee one Common-wealth, then all

Christian Monarchs, and States are private persons, and subject to bee judged, deposed, and punished by an Universall Soveraigne of all Christendome. So that the question of the Authority of the Scriptures, is reduced to this, *Whether Christian Kings, and the Soveraigne Assemblies in Christian Common-wealths, be absolute in their own Territories, immediately under God; or subject to one Vicar of Christ, constituted* *over*[1] *the Universall Church; to bee judged, condemned, deposed, and put to death, as hee shall think expedient, or necessary for the common good.*

Which question cannot bee resolved, without a more particular consideration of the Kingdome of God; from whence also, wee are to judge of the Authority of Interpreting the Scripture. For, whosoever hath a lawfull power over any Writing, to make it Law, hath the power also to approve, or disapprove the interpretation of the same.

CHAP. XXXIV.   [207]

Of the Signification of SPIRIT, ANGEL, *and* INSPIRATION *in the Books of Holy Scripture.*

Seeing the foundation of all true Ratiocination, is the constant Signification of words; which in the Doctrine following, dependeth not (as in naturall science) on the Will of the Writer, nor (as in common conversation) on vulgar use, but on the sense they carry in the Scripture; It is necessary, before I proceed any further, to determine, out of the Bible, the meaning of such words, as by their ambiguity, may render what I am to inferre upon them, obscure, or disputable. I will begin with the words BODY, and SPIRIT, which in the language of the Schools are termed, *Substances, Corporeall,* and *Incorporeall.*

Body and Spirit how taken in the Scripture.

The Word *Body,* in the most generall acceptation, signifieth that which filleth, or occupyeth some certain room, or imagined place; and dependeth not on the imagination, but is a reall part of that we call the *Universe.* For the *Universe,* being the Aggregate of all Bodies, there is no reall part thereof that is not also *Body*; nor any thing properly a

---

[1] *Syn.: of* [though corrected in the *Errata*].

269

Body, that is not also part of (that Aggregate of all *Bodies*) the *Universe*. The same also, because Bodies are subject to change, that is to say, to variety of apparence to the sense of living creatures, is called *Substance*, that is to say, *Subject*, to various accidents; as sometimes to be Moved, sometimes to stand Still; and to seem to our senses sometimes Hot, sometimes Cold, sometimes of one Colour, Smel, Tast, or Sound, somtimes of another. And this diversity of Seeming, (produced by the diversity of the operation of bodies, on the organs of our sense) we attribute to alterations of the Bodies that operate, & call them *Accidents* of those Bodies. And according to this acceptation of the word, *Substance* and *Body*, signifie the same thing; and therefore *Substance incorporeall* are words, which when they are joined together, destroy one another, as if a man should say, an *Incorporeall Body*.

But in the sense of common people, not all the Universe is called Body, but only such parts thereof as they can discern by the sense of Feeling, to resist their force, or by the sense of their Eyes, to hinder them from a farther prospect. Therefore in the common language of men, *Aire*, and *aeriall substances*, use not to be taken for *Bodies*, but (as often as men are sensible of their effects) are called *Wind*, or *Breath*, or (because the same are called in the Latine *Spiritus*) *Spirits*; as when they call that aeriall substance, which in the body of any living creature, gives it life and motion, *Vitall* and *Animall spirits*. But for those Idols of the brain, which represent Bodies to us, where they are not, as in a Looking-glasse, in a Dream, or to a Distempered brain waking, they are (as the Apostle saith generally of all Idols) nothing; Nothing at all, I say, there where they seem to bee; and in the brain it self, nothing but tumult, proceeding either from the action of the objects, or from the disorderly agitation of the Organs of our Sense. And men, that are otherwise imployed, then to search into their causes, know not of themselves, what to call them; and may therefore easily be perswaded, by those whose knowledge they much reverence, some to call them *Bodies*, and think them made of aire compacted by a power supernaturall, because the sight judges them corporeall; and some to call them *Spirits*, because the sense of Touch discerneth nothing in the place where they appear, to resist their fingers: So that the proper signification of *Spirit* in common speech, is either a subtile, fluid, and invisible Body, or a Ghost, or other Idol or Phantasme of the Imagination. But for metaphoricall significations, there be many:

[208]

for sometimes it is taken for Disposition or Inclination of the mind; as when for the disposition to controwl the sayings of other men, we say, *a spirit of contradiction*; For *a disposition to uncleannesse, an unclean spirit*; for *perversenesse, a froward spirit*; for *sullennesse, a dumb spirit*, and for *inclination to godlinesse, and Gods service, the Spirit of God*: sometimes for any eminent ability, or extraordinary passion, or disease of the mind; as when *great wisdome* is called the *spirit of wisdome*; and *mad men* are said to be *possessed with a spirit*.

Other signification of *Spirit* I find no where any; and where none of these can satisfie the sense of that word in Scripture, the place falleth not under humane Understandings; and our Faith therein consisteth not in our Opinion, but in our Submission; as in all places where God is said to be a *Spirit*; or where by the *Spirit of God*, is meant God himself. For the nature of God is incomprehensible; that is to say, we understand nothing of *what he is*, but only *that he is*; and therefore the Attributes we give him, are not to tell one another, *what he is*, nor to signifie our opinion of his Nature, but our desire to honor him with such names as we conceive most honorable amongst our selves.

Gen. 1.2. *The Spirit of God moved upon the face of the Waters.* Here if by the *Spirit of God* be meant God himself, then is *Motion* attributed to God, and consequently *Place*, which are intelligible only of Bodies, and not of substances incorporeall; and so the place is above our understanding, that can conceive nothing moved that changes not place, or that has not dimension; and whatsoever has dimension, is Body. But the meaning of those words is best understood by the like place, *Gen.*8.1. Where, when the earth was covered with Waters, as in the beginning, God intending to abate them, and again to discover the dry land, useth the like words, *I will bring my Spirit upon the Earth, and the waters shall be diminished*: in which place by *Spirit* is understood a Wind, (that is an Aire or *Spirit moved*,) which might be called (as in the former place) the *Spirit of God*, because it was Gods work. *The Spirit of God taken in the Scripture sometimes for a Wind, or Breath.*

*Gen.*41.38. *Pharaoh* calleth the *Wisdome* of *Joseph*, the *Spirit of God*. For *Joseph* having advised him to look out a wise and discreet man, and to set him over the land of Egypt, he saith thus, *Can we find such a man as this is, in whom is the Spirit of God?* And Exod. 28.3. *Thou shalt speak* (saith God) *to all that are wise hearted, whom I have filled with the Spirit of Wisdome, to make Aaron Garments, to consecrate him*. Where extraordinary Understanding, though but in making Garments, as [209] *Secondly, for extraordinary gifts of the Under-standing.*

271

being the *Gift* of God, is called the *Spirit* of God. The same is found again, *Exod.* 31.3,4,5,6. and 35.31. And *Isaiah* 11.2,3. *the*[1] Prophet speaking of the Messiah, saith, *The Spirit of the Lord shall abide upon him, the Spirit of wisdome and understanding, the Spirit of counsell, and fortitude; and the Spirit of the fear of the Lord.* Where manifestly is meant, not so many Ghosts, but so many eminent *graces* that God would give him.

Thirdly, for extraordinary Affections.   In the Book of *Judges*, an extraordinary Zeal, and Courage in the defence of Gods people, is called the *Spirit* of God; as when it excited Othoniel, Gideon, Jephtha, and Samson to deliver them from servitude, *Judg.* 3.10. 6.34. 11.29. 13.25. 14.6,19. And of *Saul*, upon the newes of the insolence of the Ammonites towards the men of Jabeth Gilead, it is said (1 *Sam.* 11.6) that *The Spirit of God came upon Saul, and his Anger* (or, as it is in the Latine, *his Fury*) *was kindled greatly.* Where it is not probable was meant a Ghost, but an extraordinary *Zeal* to punish the cruelty of the Ammonites. In like manner by the *Spirit* of God, that came upon Saul, when hee was amongst the Prophets that praised God in Songs, and Musick (1 *Sam.* 19.20.) is to be understood, not a Ghost, but an unexpected and sudden *Zeal* to join with them in their devotion.

Fourthly, for the gift of Prediction by Dreams and Visions.   The false Prophet *Zedekiah*, saith to *Micaiah* (1 *Kings* 22.24.) *Which way went the Spirit of the Lord from me to speak to thee?* Which cannot be understood of a Ghost; for *Micaiah* declared before the Kings of Israel and Judah, the event of the battle, as from a *Vision*, and not as from a *Spirit*, speaking in him.

In the same manner it appeareth, in the Books of the Prophets, that though they spake by the *Spirit* of God, that is to say, by a speciall grace of Prediction; yet their knowledge of the future, was not by a Ghost within them, but by some supernaturall *Dream* or *Vision*.

Fiftly, for Life.   *Gen.* 2.7. It is said, *God made man of the dust of the Earth, and breathed into his nostrills* (spiraculum vitae) *the breath of life, and man was made a living soul.* There the *breath of life* inspired by God, signifies no more, but that God gave him life; And (*Job* 27.3.) *as long as the Spirit of God is in my nostrils;* is no more then to say, *as long as I live.* So in *Ezek.* 1.20. *the Spirit of life was in the wheels,* is equivalent to, *the wheels were alive.* And (*Ezek.* 2.30.) *the Spirit entred into me, and set me on my feet,* that is, *I*

---

[1] *Syn.*: where the

recovered my vitall strength; not that any Ghost, or incorporeall substance entred into, and possessed his body.

In the 11 chap. of *Numbers*. verse 17. *I will take* (saith God) *of the Spirit, which is upon thee, and will put it upon them, and they shall bear the burthen of the people with thee*; that is, upon the seventy Elders: whereupon two of the seventy are said to prophecy in the campe; of whom some complained, and Joshua desired Moses to forbid them; which Moses would not doe. Whereby it appears; that Joshua knew not they had received authority so to do, and prophecyed according to the mind of Moses, that is to say, by a *Spirit*, or *Authority* subordinate to his own. *Sixtly, for a subordination to authority.* [210]

In the like sense we read (*Deut.* 34.9.) that *Joshua was full of the Spirit of wisdome, because Moses had laid his hands upon him*: that is, because he was *ordained* by Moses, to prosecute the work hee had himselfe begun, (namely, the bringing of Gods people into the promised land), but prevented by death, could not finish.

In the like sense it is said, (*Rom.*8.9.) *If any man have not the Spirit of Christ, he is none of his*: not meaning thereby the *Ghost* of Christ, but a *submission* to his Doctrine. As also (1 *John* 4.2.) *Hereby you shall know the Spirit of God; Every Spirit that confesseth that Jesus Christ is come in the flesh, is of God*; by which is meant the Spirit of unfained Christianity, or *submission* to that main Article of Christian faith, that Jesus is the Christ; which cannot be interpreted of a Ghost.

Likewise these words (*Luke* 4.1.) *And Jesus full of the Holy Ghost* (that is, as it is exprest, *Mat.*4.1. and *Mar.*1.12. *of the Holy Spirit*,) may be understood, for *Zeal* to doe the work for which hee was sent by God the Father: but to interpret it of a Ghost, is to say, that God himselfe (for so our Saviour was,) was filled with God; which is very unproper, and unsignificant. How we came to translate *Spirits*, by the word *Ghosts*, which signifieth nothing, neither in heaven, nor earth, but the Imaginary inhabitants of mans brain, I examine not: but this I say, the word *Spirit* in the text signifieth no such thing; but either properly a reall *substance*, or Metaphorically, some extraordinary *ability* or *affection* of the Mind, or of the Body.

The Disciples of Christ, seeing him walking upon the sea, (*Mat.*14.26. and *Marke* 6.49.) supposed him to be a *Spirit*, meaning thereby an Aeriall *Body*, and not a Phantasme: for it is said, they all saw him; which cannot be understood of the delusions of the brain, *Seventhly, for Aeriall Bodies.*

(which are not common to many at once, as visible Bodies are; but singular, because of the differences of Fancies), but of Bodies only. In like manner, where he was taken for a *Spirit*, by the same Apostles (*Luke* 24.3,7.): So also (*Acts* 12.15.) when St. *Peter* was delivered out of Prison, *and it*¹ would not be beleeved; but when the Maid said he was at the dore, they said it was his *Angel*; by which must be meant a corporeall substance, or we must say, the Disciples themselves did follow the common opinion *both of*² Jews and Gentiles, that *such*³ apparitions were not Imaginary, but Reall; and such as needed not the fancy of man for their Existence: These the Jews called *Spirits*, and *Angels*, Good or Bad; as the Greeks called the same by the name of *Daemons*. And some such apparitions may be reall, and substantiall; that is to say, subtile Bodies, which God can form by the same power, by which he formed all things, and make use of, as of Ministers, and Messengers (that is to say, Angels) to declare his will, and execute the same when he pleaseth, in extraordinary and supernaturall manner. But when hee hath so formed them they are Substances, endued with dimensions, and take up roome, and can be moved from place to place, which is peculiar to Bodies; and therefore are not Ghosts *incorporeall*, that is to say, Ghosts that are in *no place*; that is to say, that are *no where*; that is to say, that seeming to be *somewhat*, are *nothing*. But if Corporeall be taken in the most vulgar manner, for such Substances as are perceptible by our externall Senses; then is Substance Incorporeall, a thing not Imaginary, but Reall; namely, a thin Substance Invisible, but that hath the same dimensions that are in grosser Bodies.

Angel what.   By the name of ANGEL, is signified generally, a *Messenger*; and most often, a *Messenger of God*: And by a Messenger of God, is signified, any thing that makes known his extraordinary Presence; that is to say, the extraordinary manifestation of his power, especially by a Dream, or Vision.

    Concerning the creation of *Angels*, there is nothing delivered in the Scriptures. That they are Spirits, is often repeated: but by the name of Spirit, is signified both in Scripture, and vulgarly, both amongst Jews, and Gentiles, sometimes thin Bodies; as the Aire, the Wind, the Spirits Vitall, and Animall, of living creatures; and sometimes the Images that rise in the fancy in Dreams, and Visions; which are not

[211]

---

¹ *Syn.*: it   ² *Syn.*: of both   ³ *Syn.*: some such

reall Substances, nor last any longer then the Dream, or Vision they appear in; which Apparitions, though no reall Substances, but Accidents of the brain; yet when God raiseth them supernaturally, to signifie his Will, they are not unproperly termed Gods Messengers, that is to say, his *Angels.*

And as the Gentiles did vulgarly conceive the Imagery of the brain, for things really subsistent without them, and not dependent on the fancy; and out of them framed their opinions of *Daemons,* Good and Evill; which because they seemed to subsist really, they called *Substances*; and because they could not feel them with their hands, *Incorporeall*: so also the Jews upon the same ground, without any thing in the Old Testament that constrained them thereunto, had generally an opinion, (except the sect of the *Sadduces,*) that those apparitions (which it pleased God sometimes to produce in the fancie of men, for his own service, and therefore called them his *Angels*) were substances, not dependent on the fancy, but permanent creatures of God; whereof those which they thought were good to them, they esteemed the *Angels of God,* and those they thought would hurt them, they called *Evill Angels,* or Evill Spirits; such as was the Spirit of Python, and the Spirits of Mad-men, of Lunatiques, and Epileptiques: For they esteemed such as were troubled with such diseases, *Daemoniaques.*

But if we consider the places of the Old Testament where Angels are mentioned, we shall find, that in most of them, there can nothing else be understood by the word *Angel,* but some image raised [212] (supernaturally) in the fancy, to signifie the presence of God in the execution of some supernaturall work; and therefore in the rest, where their nature is not exprest, it may be understood in the same manner.

For we read *Gen.* 16. that the same apparition is called, not onely an *Angel,* but *God*; where that which (verse 7.) is called the *Angel* of the Lord, in the tenth verse, saith to Agar, *I will multiply thy seed exceedingly*; that is, speaketh in the person of God. Neither was this apparition a Fancy figured, but a Voice. By which it is manifest, that *Angel* signifieth there, nothing but *God* himself, that caused Agar supernaturally to apprehend a voice from heaven; or rather, nothing else but a Voice supernaturall, testifying Gods speciall presence there. Why therefore may not the Angels that appeared to Lot, and are called *Gen.* 19.13. *Men*; and to whom, though they were two, Lot speaketh (ver. 18.) as but to one, and that one, as God, (for the words

are, *Lot said unto them, Oh not so my Lord*) be understood of images of
men, supernaturally formed in the Fancy; as well as before by Angel
was understood a fancyed Voice? When the Angel called to Abraham
out of heaven, to stay his hand (*Gen.*22.11.) from slaying Isaac, there
was no Apparition, but a Voice; which neverthelesse was called properly enough a Messenger, or *Angel* of God, because it declared Gods
will supernaturally, and saves the labour of supposing any permanent
Ghosts. The Angels which Jacob saw on the Ladder of Heaven
(*Gen.*28.12.) were a Vision of his sleep; therefore onely Fancy, and a
Dream; yet being supernaturall, and signs of Gods speciall presence,
those apparitions are not improperly called *Angels.* The same is to be
understood (*Gen.*31.11.) where Jacob saith thus, *The Angel of the Lord
appeared to mee in my sleep.* For an apparition made to a man in his
sleep, is that which all men call a Dreame, whether such Dreame be
naturall, or supernaturall: and that which there Jacob calleth an *Angel,*
was God himselfe; for the same Angel saith (verse 13.) *I am the God of
Bethel.*

Also (*Exod.*14.9.) the Angel that went before the Army of Israel to
the Red Sea, and then came behind it, is (verse 19.) the Lord himself;
and he appeared not in the form of a beautifull man, but in form (by
day) of a *pillar of cloud,* and (by night) in form of a *pillar of fire;* and yet
this Pillar was all the apparition, and *Angel* promised to Moses
(*Exod.*14.9) for the Armies guide: For this cloudy pillar, is said, to
have descended, and stood at the dore of the Tabernacle, and to have
talked with Moses.

There you see Motion, and Speech, which are commonly
attributed to Angels, attributed to a Cloud, because the Cloud served
as a sign of Gods presence; and was no lesse an Angel, then if it had
had the form of a Man, or Child of never so great beauty; or *with
Wings,*[1] as usually they are painted, for the false instruction of
common people. For it is not the shape; but their use, that makes
them Angels. But their use is to be significations of Gods presence in
supernaturall operations; As when Moses (*Exod.* 33.14.) had desired
God to goe along with the Campe, (as he had done alwaies before the
making of the Golden Calfe,) God did not answer, *I will goe,* nor *I will
send an Angell in my stead;* but thus, *my presence shall goe with thee.*

To mention all the places of the Old Testament where the name of

[213]

---

[1] *Syn.*: Wings,

Angel is found, would be too long. Therefore to comprehend them all at once, I say, there is no text in that part of the Old Testament, which the Church of England holdeth for Canonicall; from which we can conclude, there is, or hath been created, any permanent thing (understood by the name of *Spirit* or *Angel*,) that hath not quantity; and that may not be, by the understanding divided; that is to say, considered by parts; so as one part may bee in one place, and the next part in the next place to it; and, in summe, which is not (taking Body for that, which is some what, or some where) Corporeall; but in every place, the sense will bear the interpretation of Angel, for Messenger; as John Baptist is called an Angel, and Christ the Angel of the Covenant; and as (according to the same Analogy) the Dove, and the Fiery Tongues, in that they were signes of Gods speciall presence, might also be called Angels. Though we find in Daniel two names of Angels, *Gabriel*, and *Michael*; yet it is cleer out of the text it selfe, (*Dan.* 12.1.) that by *Michael* is meant *Christ*, not as an Angel, but as a Prince: and that *Gabriel* (as the like apparitions made to other holy men in their sleep) was nothing but a supernaturall phantasme, by which it seemed to *Daniel*, in his dream, that two Saints being in talke, one of them said to the other, *Gabriel, let us make this man understand his Vision*: For God needeth not, to distinguish his Celestiall servants by names, which are usefull onely to the short memories of Mortalls. Nor in the New Testament is there any place, out of which it can be proved, that Angels (except when they are put for such men, as God hath made the Messengers, and Ministers of his word, or works) are things permanent, and withall incorporeall. That they are permanent, may bee gathered from the words of our Saviour himselfe, (*Mat.* 25.41.) where he saith, it shall be said to the wicked in the last day, *Go ye cursed into everlasting fire prepared for the Devil and his Angels*: which place is manifest for the permanence of Evill Angels, (unlesse wee might think the name of Devill and his Angels may be understood of the Churches Adversaries and their Ministers;) but then it is repugnant to their Immateriality; because Everlasting fire is no punishment to impatible substances, such as are all things Incorporeall. Angels therefore are not thence proved to be Incorporeall. In like manner where St. Paul sayes (1 *Cor.*6.3.) *Know ye not that wee shall judge the Angels?* And (2 *Pet.*2.4.) *For if God spared not the Angels that sinned, but cast them down into hell.* And (*Jude* 1, 6.) *And the Angels that kept not their first estate, but left their owne habitation, hee hath reserved in everlast-*

[214]

ing chaines under darknesse unto the Judgment of the last day; though it prove the Permanence of Angelicall nature, it confirmeth also their Materiality. And (*Mat.*22.30.) *In the resurrection men doe neither marry, nor give in marriage, but are as the Angels of God in heaven*: but in the resurrection men shall be Permanent, and not Incorporeall; so therefore also are the Angels.

There be divers other places out of which may be drawn the like conclusion. To men that understand the signification of these words, *Substance*, and *Incorporeall*; as *Incorporeall* is taken not for subtile body, but for *not Body*, they imply a contradiction: insomuch as to say, an Angel, or Spirit is (in that sense) an Incorporeall Substance, is to say in effect, there is no Angel nor Spirit at all. Considering therefore the signification of the word Angel in the Old Testament, and the nature of Dreams and Visions that happen to men by the ordinary way of Nature; I was enclined to this opinion, that Angels were nothing but supernaturall apparitions of the Fancy, raised by the speciall and extraordinary operation of God, thereby to make his presence and commandements known to mankind, and chiefly to his own people. But the many places of the New Testament, and our Saviours own words, and in such texts, wherein is no suspicion of corruption of the Scripture, have extorted from my feeble Reason, an acknowledgment, and beleef, that there be also Angels substantiall, and permanent. But to beleeve they be in no place, that is to say, no where, that is to say, nothing, as they (though indirectly) say, that will have them Incorporeall, cannot by Scripture bee evinced.

Inspiration what.

On the signification of the word *Spirit*, dependeth that of the word INSPIRATION; which must either be taken properly; and then it is nothing but the blowing into a man some thin and subtile aire, or wind, in such manner as a man filleth a bladder with his breath; or if Spirits be not corporeall, but have their existence only in the fancy, *then it*[1] is nothing but the blowing in of a Phantasme; which is improper to say, and impossible; for Phantasmes are not, but only seem to be somewhat. That word therefore is used in the Scripture metaphorically onely: As (*Gen.*2.7.) where it is said, that God *inspired* into man the breath of life, no more is meant, then that God gave unto him vitall motion. For we are not to think that God made first a living breath, and then blew it into Adam after he was made, whether that

---

[1] *Syn.*: it

breath were reall, or seeming; but only as it is (*Acts* 17.25.) *that he gave him life, and breath*; that is, made him a living creature. And where it is said (2 *Tim.*3.16.) *all Scripture is given by Inspiration from God*, speaking there of the Scripture of the Old Testament, it is an easie metaphor, to signifie, that God enclined the spirit or mind of those Writers, to write that which should be usefull, in teaching, reproving, correcting, and instructing men in the way of righteous living. But where St. Peter (2 *Pet.*1.21.) saith, that *Prophecy came not in old time by the will of man, but the holy men of God spake as they were moved by the Holy Spirit*, by the Holy Spirit, is meant the voice of God in a Dream, or Vision supernaturall, which is not *Inspiration*: Nor when our Saviour breathing on his Disciples, said, *Receive the Holy Spirit*, was that Breath the Spirit, but a sign of the spirituall graces he gave unto them. And though it be said of many, and of our Saviour himself, that he was full [215] of the Holy *Spirit*; yet that Fulnesse is not to be understood for *Infusion* of the substance of God, but for accumulation of his gifts, such as are the gift of sanctity of life, of tongues, and the like, whether attained supernaturally, or by study and industry; for in all cases they are the gifts of God. So likewise where God sayes (*Joel* 2.28.) *I will powre out my Spirit upon all flesh, and your Sons and your Daughters shall prophecy, your Old men shall dream Dreams, and your Young men shall see Visions*, wee are not to understand it in the proper sense, as if his *Spirit* were like water, subject to effusion, or infusion; but as if God had promised to give them Propheticall Dreams, and Visions. For the proper use of the word *infused*, in speaking of the graces of God, is an abuse of it; for those graces are Vertues, not Bodies to be carryed hither and thither, and to be powred into men, as into barrels.

In the same manner, to take *Inspiration* in the proper sense, or to say that Good *Spirits* entred into men to make them prophecy, or Evill *Spirits* into those that became Phrenetique, Lunatique, or Epileptique, is not to take the word in the sense of the Scripture; for the Spirit there is taken for the power of God, working by causes to us unknown. As also (*Acts* 2.2.) the wind, that is there said to fill the house wherein the Apostles were assembled on the day of Pentecost, is not to be understood for the Holy *Spirit*, which is the Deity it selfe; but for an Externall sign of Gods speciall working on their hearts, to effect in them the internall graces, and holy vertues hee thought requisite for the performance of their Apostleship.

CHAP. XXXV.

Of the Signification in Scripture of KINGDOME OF GOD, *of* HOLY, SACRED, *and* SACRAMENT.

The Kingdom of God taken by Divines Metaphorically, but in the Scriptures properly.

The *Kingdome of God* in the Writings of Divines, and specially in Sermons, and Treatises of Devotion, is taken most commonly for Eternall Felicity, after this life, in the Highest Heaven, which they also call the Kingdome of Glory; and sometimes for (the earnest of that felicity) Sanctification, which they terme the Kingdome of Grace; but never for the Monarchy, that is to say, the Soveraign Power of God over any Subjects acquired by their own consent, which is the proper signification of Kingdome.

To the contrary, I find the KINGDOME OF GOD, to signifie in most places of Scripture, a *Kingdome properly so named*, constituted by the Votes of the People of Israel in peculiar manner; wherein they chose God for their King by Covenant made with him, upon Gods promising them the possession of the land of Canaan; and but seldom metaphorically; and then it is taken for *Dominion over sinne*; (and only in the New Testament;) because such a Dominion as that, every Subject shall have in the Kingdome of God, and without prejudice to the Soveraign.

From the very Creation, God not only reigned over all men *naturally* by his might; but also had *peculiar* Subjects, whom he commanded by a Voice, as one man speaketh to another. In which manner he *reigned* over Adam, and gave him commandement to abstaine from the tree of cognizance of Good and Evill; which when he obeyed not, but tasting thereof, took upon him to be as God, judging between Good and Evill, not by his Creators commandement, but by his own sense, his punishment was a privation of the estate of Eternall life, wherein God had at first created him: And afterwards God punished his posterity, for their vices, all but eight persons, with an universall deluge; And in these eight did consist the then *Kingdom of God.*

The originall

After this, it pleased God to speak to Abraham, and (*Gen.* 17.7,8.) to

280

make a Covenant with him in these words, *I will establish my Covenant* *between me, and thee, and thy seed after thee in their generations, for an everlasting Covenant, to be a God to thee, and to thy seed after thee; And I will give unto thee, and to thy seed after thee, the land wherein thou art a stranger, all the land of Canaan for an everlasting possession.* In this Covenant *Abraham promiseth for himselfe and his posterity to obey as God, the Lord that spake to him: and God on his part promiseth to Abraham the land of Canaan for an everlasting possession.* And for a memoriall, and a [217] token of this Covenant, he ordaineth (verse 11.) the *Sacrament of Circumcision.* This is it which is called the *Old Covenant,* or *Testament*; and containeth a Contract between God and Abraham; by which Abraham obligeth himself, and his posterity, in a peculiar manner to be subject to Gods positive Law; for to the Law Morall he was obliged before, as by an Oath of Allegiance. And though the name of *King* be not yet given to God, nor of *Kingdome* to Abraham and his seed; yet the thing is the same; namely, an Institution by pact, of Gods peculiar Soveraignty over the seed of Abraham; which in the renewing of the same Covenant by Moses, at Mount Sinai, is expressely called a peculiar *Kingdome of God* over the Jews: and it is of Abraham (not of Moses) St. Paul saith (*Rom.4.11.*) that he is the *Father of the Faithfull*; that is, of those that are loyall, and doe not violate their Allegiance sworn to God, then by Circumcision, and afterwards in the *New Covenant* by Baptisme.

This Covenant, at the Foot of Mount Sinai, was renewed by Moses (*Exod.*19.5.) where the Lord commandeth Moses to speak to the people in this manner, *If you will obey my voice indeed, and keep my Covenant, then yee shall be a peculiar people to me, for all the Earth is mine; And yee shall be unto me a Sacerdotall Kingdome, and an holy Nation.* For a *Peculiar people*, the vulgar Latine hath, *Peculium de cunctis populis*: the English Translation made in the beginning of the Reign of King James, hath, a *Peculiar treasure unto me above all Nations*; and the Geneva French, *the most precious Jewel of all Nations.* But the truest Translation is the first, because it is confirmed by St. Paul himself (*Tit.*2.14.) where he saith, alluding to that place, that our blessed Saviour *gave himself for us, that he might purifie us to himselfe, a peculiar* (that is, an extraordinary) *people*: for the word is in the Greek περιούσιος, which is opposed commonly to the word ἐπιούσιος: and as this signifieth *ordinary, quotidian,* or (as in the Lords Prayer) *of daily use*; so the other signifieth that which is *overplus,* and *stored up,* and *enjoyed in a speciall manner,* which the Latines call *Peculium*: and this meaning of the place is confirmed by the reason God rendereth of it, which followeth immediately, in that he addeth, *For all the Earth is mine,* as if he should say, *All the Nations of the world are mine;* but it is not so that you are mine, but in a *speciall manner.* For they are all mine, by reason of my Power; but you shall be mine, by your own Consent, and Covenant; which is an addition to his ordinary title, to all nations.

The same is again confirmed in expresse words in the same text, *Yee shall be to me a Sacerdotall Kingdome, and an holy Nation.* The Vulgar Latine hath it, *Regnum Sacerdotale,* to which agreeth the Translation of that place (1 *Pet.*2.9.) *Sacerdotium Regale, a Regal Priest-hood;* as also the Institution it self, by which no man might enter into the *Sanctum Sanctorum,* that is to say, no man might enquire Gods will immediately of God himselfe, but onely the High Priest. The English Translation before mentioned, following that of Geneva, has, *a King-dom of Priests;* which is either meant of the succession of one High Priest after another, or else it accordeth not with St. Peter, nor with the exercise of the High priesthood: For there was never any but the High priest onely, that was to informe the People of Gods Will; nor any Convocation of Priests ever allowed to enter into the *Sanctum Sanctorum.*

Again, the title of a *Holy Nation* confirmes the same: For *Holy* signifies, that which is Gods by speciall, not by generall Right. All the Earth (as is said in the text) is Gods; but all the Earth is not called *Holy,* but that onely which is set apart for his especiall service, as was the Nation of the Jews. It is therefore manifest enough by this one place, that by the *Kingdome of God,* is properly meant a Common-wealth, instituted (by the consent of those which were to be subject thereto) for their Civill Government, and the regulating of their behaviour, not onely towards God their King, but also towards one another in point of justice, and towards other Nations both in peace and warre; which properly was a Kingdome, wherein God was King, and the High priest was to be (after the death of Moses) his sole Viceroy, or Lieutenant.

But there be many other places that clearly prove the same. As first (1 *Sam.*8.7.) when the Elders of Israel (grieved with the corruption of the Sons of Samuel) demanded a King, Samuel displeased therewith, prayed unto the Lord; and the Lord answering said unto him, *Hearken unto the voice of the People, for they have not rejected thee, but they have* *rejected me, that I should not reign over them.* Out of which it is evident, that God himself was then their King; and Samuel did not command the people, but only delivered to them that which God from time to time appointed him.

Again, (1 *Sam.*12.12.) where Samuel saith to the People, *When yee saw that Nahash King of the Children of Ammon came against you, ye said unto me, Nay, but a King shall reign over us, when the Lord your God was your King:* It is manifest that God was their King, and governed the Civill State of their Common-wealth.

And after the Israelites had rejected God, the Prophets did foretell his restitution; as (*Isaiah* 24.23.) *Then the Moon shall be confounded, and the Sun ashamed, when the Lord of Hosts shall reign in Mount Zion, and in Jerusalem*; where he speaketh expressely of his Reign in Zion, and Jerusalem; that is, on Earth. And (*Micah* 4.7.) *And the Lord shall reign over them in Mount Zion*: This Mount Zion is in Jerusalem upon the Earth. And (*Ezek.*20.33.) *As I live, saith the Lord God, surely with a mighty hand, and a stretched out arme, and with fury powred out, I wil rule over you*; and (verse 37.) *I will cause you to passe under the rod, and I will bring you into the bond of the Covenant*; that is, I will reign over you, and make you to stand to that Covenant which you made with me by Moses, and brake in your rebellion against me in the days of Samuel, and in your election of another King.

And in the New Testament, the Angel Gabriel saith of our Saviour (*Luke* 1.32,33.) *He shall be great, and be called the Son of the most High, and the Lord shall give him the throne of his Father David; and he shall* [219] *reign over the house of Jacob for ever; and of his Kingdome there shall be no end.* This is also a Kingdome upon Earth; for the claim whereof, as an enemy to Caesar, he was put to death; the title of his crosse, was, *Jesus of Nazareth, King of the Jews*; hee was crowned in scorn with a crown of Thornes; and for the proclaiming of him, it is said of the Disciples (*Acts* 17.7.) *That they did all of them contrary to the decrees of Caesar, saying there was another King, one Jesus.* The Kingdome therefore of God, is a reall, not a metaphoricall Kingdome; and so taken, not onely in the Old Testament, but the New; when we say, *For thine is the Kingdome, the Power, and Glory*, it is to be understood of Gods King-dome, by force of our Covenant, not by the Right of Gods Power; for such a Kingdome God alwaies hath; so that it were superfluous to say in our prayer, *Thy Kingdome come*, unlesse it be meant of the Restaura-tion of that Kingdome of God by Christ, which by revolt of the

Israelites had been interrupted in the election of Saul. Nor had it been proper to say, *The Kingdome of Heaven is at hand*; or to pray, *Thy Kingdome come*, if it had still continued.

There be so many other places that confirm this interpretation, that it were a wonder there is no greater notice taken of it, but that it gives too much light to Christian Kings to see their right of Ecclesiasticall Government. This they have observed, that in stead of a *Sacerdotall Kingdome*, translate, *a Kingdome of Priests*: for they may as well translate a *Royall Priesthood*, (as it is in St. Peter) into a *Priesthood of Kings*. And whereas, for a *peculiar people*, they put a *pretious jewel*, or *treasure*, a man might as well call the speciall Regiment, or Company of a Generall, the Generalls pretious Jewel, or his Treasure.

In short, the Kingdome of God is a Civill Kingdome; which consisted, first in the obligation of the people of Israel to those Laws, which Moses should bring unto them from Mount Sinai; and which afterwards the High Priest for the time being, should deliver to them from before the *Cherubins* in the *Sanctum Sanctorum*; and which Kingdome having been cast off, in the election of Saul, the Prophets foretold, should be restored by Christ; and the Restauration whereof we daily pray for, when we say in the Lords Prayer, *Thy Kingdome come*; and the Right whereof we acknowledge, when we adde, *For thine is the Kingdome, the Power, and Glory, for ever and ever, Amen*; and the Proclaiming whereof, was the Preaching of the Apostles; and to which men are prepared, by the Teachers of the Gospel; to embrace which Gospel, (that is to say, to promise obedience to Gods government) is, to bee in the *Kingdome of Grace*, because God hath *gratis* given to such the power to bee the Subjects (that is, Children) of God hereafter, when Christ shall come in Majesty to judge the world, and actually to govern his owne people, which is called *the Kingdome of Glory*. If the Kingdome of God (called also the Kingdome of Heaven, from the gloriousnesse, and admirable height of that throne) were not a King-dome which God by his Lieutenants, or Vicars, who deliver his Commandements to the people, did exercise on Earth; there would not have been so much contention, and warre, about who it is, by whom God speaketh to us; neither would many Priests have troubled themselves with Spirituall Jurisdiction, nor any King have denied it them.

Holy what. Out of this literall interpretation of the *Kingdome of God*, ariseth also the true interpretation of the word HOLY. For it is a word, which in Gods Kingdome answereth to that, which men in their Kingdomes use to call *Publique*, or the *Kings*.

The King of any Countrey is the *Publique* Person, or Representative of all his own Subjects. And God the King of Israel was the *Holy one* of Israel. The Nation which is subject to one earthly Soveraign, is the Nation of that Soveraign, that is, of the Publique Person. So the Jews, who were Gods Nation, were called (*Exod.* 19.6.) *a Holy Nation.* For by *Holy*, is alwaies understood, either God himselfe, or that which is Gods in propriety; as by Publique, is alwaies meant, either the Person of the Common-wealth it self, or something that is so the Common-wealths, as no private person can claim any propriety therein.

Therefore the Sabbath (Gods day) is a *Holy day*; the Temple, (Gods house) *a Holy house*; Sacrifices, Tithes, and Offerings (Gods tribute) *Holy duties*; Priests, Prophets, and anointed Kings, under Christ (Gods Ministers) *Holy men*; the Coelestiall ministring Spirits (Gods Messengers) *Holy Angels*; and the like: and wheresoever the word Holy is taken properly, there is still something signified of Propriety, gotten by consent. In saying *Hallowed be thy name*, we do but pray to God for grace to keep the first Commandement, of *having no other Gods but him.* Mankind is Gods Nation in propriety: but the Jews only were a *Holy Nation.* Why, but because they became his Propriety by covenant?

And the word *Profane*, is usually taken in the Scripture for the same with *Common*; and consequently their contraries, *Holy*, and *Proper*, in the Kingdome of God must be the same also. But figuratively, those men also are called *Holy*, that led such godly lives, as if they had forsaken all worldly designs, and wholly devoted, and given themselves to God. In the proper sense, that which is made *Holy* by Gods appropriating or separating it to his own use, is said to be *sanctified* by God, as the Seventh day in the fourth Commandement; and as the Elect in the New Testament were said to bee *sanctified*, when they were endued with the Spirit of godlinesse. And that which is made *Holy* by the dedication of men, and given to God, so as to be used *Sacred what.* onely in his publique service, is called also SACRED, and said to be consecrated, as Temples, and other Houses of Publique Prayer, and their Utensils, Priests, and Ministers, Victimes, Offerings, and the externall matter of Sacraments.

Degrees of
Sanctity.

    Of *Holinesse* there be degrees: for of those things that are set apart for the service of God, there may bee some set apart again, for a neerer and more especial service. The whole Nation of the Israelites were a people Holy to God; yet the tribe of Levi was amongst the Israelites a Holy tribe; and amongst the Levites, the Priests were yet more Holy; and amongst the Priests, the High Priest was the most Holy. So the Land of Judea was the Holy Land; but the Holy City wherein God was to be worshipped, was more Holy; and again, the Temple more Holy than the City; and the *Sanctum Sanctorum* more Holy than the rest of the Temple.

[221]

Sacrament.

    A S A C R A M E N T, is a separation of some visible thing from common use; and a consecration of it to Gods service, for a sign, either of our admission into the Kingdome of God, to be of the number of his peculiar people, or for a Commemoration of the same. In the Old Testament, the sign of Admission was *Circumcision*; in the New Testament, *Baptisme*. The Commemoration of it in the Old Testament, was the *Eating* (at a certaine time, which was Anniversary) of the *Paschall Lamb*; by which they were put in mind of the night wherein they were delivered out of their bondage in Egypt; and in the New Testament, the celebrating of the *Lords Supper*; by which, we are put in mind, of our deliverance from the bondage of sin, by our Blessed Saviours death upon the crosse. The Sacraments of *Admission*, are but once to be used, because there needs but one *Admission*; but because we have need of being often put in mind of our deliverance, and of our Alleagance, the Sacraments of *Commemoration* have need to be reiterated. And these are the principall Sacraments, and as it were the solemne oathes we make of our Alleageance. There be also other Consecrations, that may be called Sacraments, as the word implyeth onely Consecration to Gods service; but as it implies an oath, or promise of Alleageance to God, there were no other in the Old Testament, but *Circumcision*, and the *Passeover*; nor are there any other in the New Testament, but *Baptisme*, and the *Lords Supper*.

286

CHAP. XXXVI.
Of the WORD OF GOD, *and of*
PROPHETS.

When there is mention of the *Word of God*, or of *Man*, it doth not   *Word what.*
signifie a part of Speech, such as Grammarians call a Nown, or a
Verb, or any simple voice, without a contexture with other words to
make it significative; but a perfect Speech or Discourse, whereby the
speaker *affirmeth, denieth, commandeth, promiseth, threatneth, wisheth,* or
interrogateth. In which sense it is not *Vocabulum*, that signifieth a *Word*;
but *Sermo*, (in Greek λόγος) that is, some *Speech, Discourse,* or
Saying.

    Again, if we say the *Word* of *God*, or of *Man*, it may bee understood   *The words*
sometimes of the Speaker, (as the words that God hath spoken, or   *spoken by*
that a Man hath spoken: In which sense, when we say, the Gospel of   *God, and*
concerning
St. Matthew, we understand St. Matthew to be the Writer of it: and   *God, both*
sometimes of the Subject: In which sense, when we read in the Bible,   *are called*
The words of the days of the Kings of Israel, or Judah, 'tis meant, that the   *in Scripture.*
acts that were done in those days, were the Subject of those Words;
And in the Greek, which (in the Scripture) retaineth many
Hebraisms, by the Word of God is oftentimes meant, not that which
is spoken by God, but concerning God, and his government; that is
to say, the Doctrine of Religion: Insomuch, as it is all one, to say
λόγος θεοῦ, and *Theologia*; which is, that Doctrine which wee usually call *Divinity*, as is manifest by the places following [*Acts* 13.46.]
Then Paul and Barnabas waxed bold, and said, It was necessary that the
Word of God should first have been spoken to you, but seeing you put it from
you, and judge your selves unworthy of everlasting life, loe, we turn to the
Gentiles. That which is here called the Word of God, was the Doctrine of Christian Religion; as it appears evidently by that which goes
before. And [*Acts* 5.20.] where it is said to the Apostles by an Angel,
Go stand and speak in the Temple, all the Words of this life; by the Words
of this life, is meant, the Doctrine of the Gospel; as is evident by what
they did in the Temple, and is expressed in the last verse of the same
Chap. *Daily in the Temple, and in every house they ceased not to teach and*

preach Christ Jesus: In which place it is manifest, that Jesus Christ was the subject of this *Word of life*; or (which is all one) the subject of the *Words of this life eternall*, that our Saviour offered them. So [*Acts* 15.7.] the Word of God, is called *the Word of the Gospel*, because it containeth the Doctrine of the Kingdome of Christ; and the same Word [*Rom.* 10.8,9.] is called the *Word of Faith*; that is, as is there expressed, the Doctrine of Christ come, and raised from the dead. Also [*Mat.* 13.19.] *When any one heareth the Word of the Kingdome*; that is, the Doctrine of the Kingdome taught by Christ. Again, the same Word, is said [*Acts* 12.24.] *to grow and to be multiplyed*; which to understand of the Evangelicall Doctrine is easie, but of the Voice, or Speech of God, hard and strange. In the same sense the *Doctrine of Devils*, signifieth not the Words of any Devill, but the Doctrine of Heathen men concerning *Daemons*, and those Phantasms which they worshipped as Gods.

[223]

1 *Tim.*4.1.

Considering these two significations of the WORD OF GOD, as it is taken in Scripture, it is manifest in this later sense (where it is taken for the Doctrine of Christian Religion,) that the whole Scripture is the Word of God: but in the former sense not so. For example, though these words, *I am the Lord thy God*, &c. to the end of the Ten Commandements, were spoken by God to Moses; yet the Preface, *God spake these words and said*, is to be understood for the Words of him that wrote the holy History. The *Word of God*, as it is taken for that which he hath spoken, is understood sometimes *Properly*, sometimes *Metaphorically*. *Properly*, as the words, he hath spoken to his Prophets: *Metaphorically*, for his Wisdome, Power, and eternall Decree, in making the world; in which sense, those *Fiats*, *Let their be light, Let there be a firmament, Let us make man*, &c. [*Gen.*1.] are the Word of God. And in the same sense it is said [*John* 1.3.] *All things were made by it, and without it was nothing made that was made*: And [*Heb.*1.3.] *He upholdeth all things by the Word of his Power*, that is, by the Power of his Word; that is, by his Power: and [*Heb.*11.3.] *The worlds were framed by the Word of God*; and many other places to the same sense: As also amongst the Latines, the name of *Fate*, which signifieth properly *The Word spoken*, is taken in the same sense.

The Word of God metaphorically used, first, for the Decrees and Power of God.

Secondly, for the effect of his Word; that is to say, for the thing it self, which by his Word is Affirmed, Commanded, Threatned, or Promised; as [*Psalm* 105.19.] where Joseph is said to have been kept

Secondly, for the effect of his Word.

in prison, *till his Word was come*; that is, till that was come to passe which he had [*Gen.*40.13.] foretold to Pharaohs Butler, concerning his being restored to his office: for there by *his word was come*, is meant, the thing it self was come to passe. So also [1 *King.*18.36.] Elijah saith to God, *I have done all these thy Words*, in stead of *I have done all these things at thy Word*, or commandement: and [*Jer.*17.15.] *Where is the Word of the Lord*, is put for, *Where is the Evill he threatned*: And [*Ezek.*12.28.] *There shall none of my Words be prolonged any more*: by *words* are understood those *things*, which God promised to his people. And in the New Testament [*Mat.*24.35.] *heaven and earth shall pass away, but my Words shal not pass away*; that is, there is nothing that I have promised or foretold, that shall not come to passe. And in this sense it is, that St. John the Evangelist, and, I think, St. John onely calleth our Saviour himself as in the flesh *the Word of God* [as *Joh.*1.14.] *the Word was made Flesh*; that is to say, the Word, or Promise that Christ should come into the world; *who in the beginning was with God*; that is to say, it was in the purpose of God the Father, to [224] send God the Son into the world, to enlighten men in the way of Eternall life; but it was not till then put in execution, and actually incarnate; So that our Saviour is there called *the Word*, not because he was the promise, but the thing promised. They that taking occasion from this place, doe commonly call him the Verbe of God, do but render the text more obscure. They might as well term him the Nown of God: for as by *Nown*, so also by *Verbe*, men understand nothing but a part of speech, a voice, a sound, that neither affirms, nor denies, nor commands, nor promiseth, nor is any substance corporeall, or spirituall; and therefore it cannot be said to bee either God, or Man; whereas our Saviour is both. And this *Word* which St. *John* in his Gospel saith was with God, is [in his 1 Epistle, verse 1.] called the *Word of life*; and [verse 2.] *the Eternall life, which was with the Father*: so that he can be in no other sense called the *Word*, then in that, wherein he is called Eternall life; that is, *he that hath procured us Eternall life*, by his comming in the flesh. So also [*Apocalypse* 19.13.] the Apostle speaking of Christ, clothed in a garment dipt in bloud, saith; his name is *the Word of God*; which is to be understood, as if he had said his name had been, *He that was come according to the purpose of God from the beginning, and according to his Word and promises delivered by the Prophets.* So that there is nothing here of the Incarnation of a Word, but of the Incarnation of God the Son, therefore called *the Word*, because his Incarnation was the Performance of the Promise; In like manner as the Holy Ghost is called *the Promise*.

There are also places of the Scripture, where, by the *Word of God*, is signified such Words as are consonant to reason, and equity, though spoken sometimes neither by Prophet, nor by a holy man. For Pharaoh Necho was an Idolater; yet his Words to the good King Josiah, in which he advised him by Messengers, not to oppose him in his march against *Carchemish*, are said to have proceeded from the mouth of God; and that Josiah not hearkning to them, was slain in the battle; as is to be read 2 *Chron.*35.vers. 21,22,23. It is true, that as the same History is related in the first Book of Esdras, not Pharaoh, but Jeremiah spake these words to Josiah, from the mouth of the Lord. But wee are to give credit to the Canonicall Scripture, whatsoever be written in the Apocrypha.

The *Word of God*, is then also to be taken for the Dictates of reason, and equity, when the same is said in the Scriptures to bee written in mans heart; as *Psalm* 36.31. *Jerem.*31.33. *Deut.*30.11,14. and many other like places.

The name of PROPHET, signifieth in Scripture sometimes *Prolocutor*; that is, he that speaketh from God to Man, or from man to God: And sometimes *Praedictor*, or a foreteller of things to come: And sometimes one that speaketh incoherently, as men that are distracted. It is most frequently used in the sense of speaking from God to the People. *So Moses, Samuel, Elijah, Isaiah, Jeremiah*, and others were *Prophets*. And in this sense the High Priest was a *Prophet*, for he only went into the *Sanctum Sanctorum*, to enquire of God; and was to

declare his answer to the people. And therefore when Caiphas said, it was expedient that one man should die for the people, St. John saith [chap.11.51.] that *He spake not this of himselfe, but being High Priest that year, he prophesied that one man should dye for the nation.* Also they that in Christian Congregations taught the people [1 *Cor.*14.3.] are said to Prophecy. In the like sense it is, that God saith to *Moses* [*Exod.*4.16.] concerning *Aaron, He shall be thy Spokes-man to the People; and he shall be to thee a mouth, and thou shalt be to him in stead of God*: that which here is *Spokes-man*, is [chap.7.1.] interpreted Prophet; *See* (saith God) *I have made thee a God to Pharaoh, and Aaron thy Brother shall be thy Prophet.* In the sense of speaking from man to God, Abraham is called a Prophet [*Genes.*20.7.] where God in a Dream speaketh to

Abimelech in this manner, *Now therefore restore the man his wife, for he is a Prophet, and shall pray for thee*; whereby may be also gathered, that the name of Prophet may be given, not unproperly to them that in Christian Churches, have a Calling to say publique prayers for the Congregation. In the same sense, the Prophets that came down from the High place (or Hill of God) with a Psaltery, and a Tabret, and a Pipe, and a Harp [1 *Sam.* 10.5,6.] and [vers. 10.] Saul amongst them, are said to Prophecy, in that they praised God, in that manner publiquely. In the like sense, is Miriam [*Exod.* 15.20.] called a Prophetesse. So is it also to be taken [1 *Cor.* 11.4,5.] where St. Paul saith, *Every man that prayeth or prophecyeth with his head covered, &c. and every woman that prayeth or prophecyeth with her head uncovered*: For Prophecy in that place, signifieth no more, but praising God in Psalmes, and Holy Songs; which women might doe in the Church, though it were not lawfull for them to speak to the Congregation. And in this signification it is, that the Poets of the Heathen, that composed Hymnes and other sorts of Poems in the honor of their Gods, were called *Vates* (Prophets) as is well enough known by all that are versed in the Books of the Gentiles, and as is evident [*Tit.* 1.12.] where St. Paul saith of the Cretians, that a Prophet of their owne said, they were Liars; not that St. Paul held their Poets for Prophets, but acknowledgeth that the word Prophet was commonly used to signifie them that celebrated the honour of God in Verse.

When by Prophecy is meant Praediction, or foretelling of future Contigents; not only they were Prophets, who were Gods Spokesmen, and foretold those things to others, which God had foretold to them; but also all those Impostors, that pretend by the helpe of familiar spirits, or by superstitious divination of events past, from false causes, to foretell the like events in time to come: of which (as I have declared already in the 12. chapter of this Discourse) there be many kinds, who gain in the opinion of the common sort of men, a greater reputation of Prophecy, by one casuall event that may bee but wrested to their purpose, than can be lost again by never so many failings. Prophecy is not an Art, nor (when it is taken for Praediction) a constant Vocation; but an extraordinary, and temporary Employment from God, most often of Good men, but sometimes also of the Wicked. The woman of Endor, who is said to have had a familiar spirit, and thereby to have raised a Phantasme of Samuel, and foretold Saul his death, was not therefore a Prophetesse; for neither had she any science, whereby she

Prediction of future contingents, not alwaies Prophecy.

[226]

291

could raise such a Phantasme; nor does it appear that God commanded the raising of it; but onely guided that Imposture to be a means of Sauls terror and discouragement; and by consequent, of the discomfiture, by which he fell. And for Incoherent Speech, it was amongst the Gentiles taken for one sort of Prophecy, because the Prophets of their Oracles, intoxicated with a spirit, or vapor from the cave of the Pythian Oracle at Delphi, were for the time really mad, and spake like mad-men; of whose loose words a sense might be made to fit any event, in such sort, as all bodies are said to be made of *Materia prima*. In the Scripture I find it also so taken [1 *Sam*. 18.10] in these words, *And the Evill Spirit came upon Saul, and he Prophecyed in the midst of the house.*

*The manner how God hath spoken to the Prophets.*And although there be so many significations in Scripture of the word *Prophet*; yet is that the most frequent, in which it is taken for him, to whom God speaketh immediately, that which the Prophet is to say from him, to some other man, or to the people. And hereupon a question may be asked, in what manner God speaketh to such a Prophet. Can it (may some say) be properly said, that God hath voice and language, when it cannot be properly said, he hath a tongue, or other organs as a man? The Prophet David argueth thus, *Shall he that made the eye, not see? or he that made the ear, not hear?* But this may be spoken, not (as usually) to signifie Gods nature, but to signifie our intention to honor him. For to *see*, and *hear*, are Honorable Attributes, and may be given to God, to declare (as far as our capacity can conceive) his Almighty power. But if it were to be taken in the strict, and proper sense, one might argue from his making of all other parts of mans body, that he had also the same use of them which we have; which would be many of them so uncomely, as it would be the greatest contumely in the world to ascribe them to him. Therefore we are to interpret Gods speaking to men immediately, for that way (whatsoever it be), by which God makes them understand his will: And the wayes whereby he doth this, are many; and to be sought onely in the Holy Scripture: where though many times it be said, that God spake to this, and that person, without declaring in what manner; yet there be again many places, that deliver also the signes by which they were to acknowledge his presence, and commandement; and by these may be understood, how he spake to many of the rest.

*To the Extra-*In what manner God spake to *Adam*, and *Eve*, and *Cain*, and *Noah*, is not expressed; nor how he spake to *Abraham*, till such time as he came out of his own countrey to *Sichem* in the land of *Canaan*; and then [*Gen.*12.7.] God is said to have *appeared* to him. So there is one way, whereby God made his presence manifest; that is, by an *Appar-ition*, or *Vision*. And again, [*Gen.*15.1.] The Word of the Lord came to Abraham in a Vision; that is to say, somewhat, as a sign of Gods presence, appeared as Gods Messenger, to speak to him. Again, the Lord appeared to Abraham [*Gen.*18.1.] by an apparition of three Angels; and to Abimelech [*Gen.*20.3.] in a dream: To Lot [*Gen.*19.1.] by an apparition of two Angels: And to Hagar [*Gen.*21.17.] by the apparition of one Angel: And to Abraham again [*Gen.*22.11.] by the apparition of a voice from heaven: And [*Gen.*26.24.] to Isaac in the night; (that is, in his sleep, or by dream): And to Jacob [*Gen.*18.12.] in a dream; that is to say (as are the words of the text) *Jacob dreamed that he saw a ladder, &c.* And [*Gen.*32.1.] in a Vision of Angels: And to Moses [*Exod.*3.2.] in the apparition of a flame of fire out of the midst of a bush: And after the time of Moses, (where the manner how God spake immediately to man in the Old Testament, is expressed) hee spake alwaies by a Vision, or by a Dream; as to *Gideon, Samuel, Eliah, Elisha, Isaiah, Ezekiel,* and the rest of the Prophets; and often in the New Testament, as to *Joseph,* to St. *Peter,* to St. *Paul,* and to St. *John* the Evangelist in the Apocalypse.

ordinary Prophets of the Old Testament he spake by Dreams, or Visions.
[227]

Onely to Moses hee spake in a more extraordinary manner in Mount *Sinai,* and in the *Tabernacle*; and to the High Priest in the *Tabernacle,* and in the *Sanctum Sanctorum* of the Temple. But Moses, and after him the High Priests were Prophets of a more eminent place, and degree in Gods favour; And God himself in express words declareth, that to other Prophets hee spake in Dreams and Visions, but to his servant Moses, in such manner as a man speaketh to his friend. The words are these [*Numb.*12.6,7,8.] *If there be a Prophet among you, I the Lord will make my self known to him in a Vision, and will speak unto him in a Dream. My servant Moses is not so, who is faithfull in all my house; with him I will speak mouth to mouth, even apparently, not in dark speeches; and the similitude of the Lord shall he behold.* And [*Exod.*33.11.] *The Lord spake to Moses face to face, as a man speaketh to his friend.* And yet this speaking of God to Moses, was by mediation of an Angel, or Angels, as appears expressely, *Acts* 7.ver.35. and 53. and *Gal.*3.19. and was therefore a Vision, though a more cleer Vision than was given to other Prophets. And conformable hereunto, where God saith (*Deut.*13.1.) *If there arise amongst you a Prophet, or Dreamer of*

Dreams, the later word is but the interpretation of the former. And [*Joel* 2.28.] *Your sons and your daughters shall Prophecy; your old men shall dream Dreams, and your young men shall see Visions*: where again, the word *Prophecy* is expounded by *Dream*, and *Vision*. And in the same manner it was, that God spake to Solomon, promising him Wisdome, Riches, and Honor; for the text saith, [1 *Kings* 3.15.] *And Solomon awoak, and behold it was a Dream*: So that generally the Prophets extraordinary in the Old Testament took notice of the Word of God no otherwise, than from their Dreams, or Visions; that is to say, from the imaginations which they had in their sleep, or in an Extasie: which imaginations in every true Prophet were supernaturall; but in false Prophets were either naturall, or feigned.

[228]

The same Prophets were neverthelesse said to speak by the Spirit; as [*Zach.*7.12.] where the Prophet speaking of the Jewes, saith, *They made their hearts hard as Adamant, lest they should hear the law, and the words which the Lord of Hosts hath sent in his Spirit by the former Prophets*. By which it is manifest, that speaking by the *Spirit*, or *Inspiration*, was not a particular manner of Gods speaking, different from Vision, when they that were said to speak by the Spirit, were extraordinary Prophets, such as for every new message, were to have a particular Commission, or (which is all one) a new Dream, or Vision.

To Prophets of perpetuall Calling, and Supreme, God spake in the Old Testament from the Mercy Seat, in a manner not expressed in the Scripture. Of Prophets, that were so by a perpetuall Calling in the Old Testament, some were *supreme*, and some *subordinate*: Supreme were first Moses; and after him the High Priests, every one for his time, as long as the Priesthood was Royall; and after the people of the Jews, had rejected God, that he should no more reign over them, those Kings which submitted themselves to Gods government, were also his chief Prophets; and the High Priests office became Ministeriall. And when God was to be consulted, they put on the holy vestments, and enquired of the Lord, as the King commanded them, and were deprived of their office, when the King thought fit. For King Saul [1 *Sam.*13.9.] commanded the burnt offering to be brought, and [1 *Sam.*14.18.] he commands the Priest to bring the Ark neer him; and [ver.19] again to let it alone, because he saw an advantage upon his enemies. And in the same chapter Saul asketh counsell of God. In like manner King David, after his being anointed, though before he had possession of the Kingdome, is said to *enquire of the Lord* [1 *Sam.*23.2.] whether he should fight against the Philistines at *Keilah*; and [verse 10.] David commandeth the Priest to bring him the Ephod, to enquire whether he should stay in *Keilah*, or not. And King Solomon [1 *Kings* 2.27.] took the Priesthood from *Abiathar*, and gave it [verse 35.] to *Zadoc*. Therefore Moses, and the High Priests, and the pious Kings, who enquired of God on all extraordinary occasions, how they were to carry themselves, or what event they were to have, were all Soveraign Prophets. But in what manner God spake unto them, is not manifest. To say that when Moses went up to God in Mount *Sinai*, it was a Dream, or Vision, such as other Prophets had, is contrary to that distinction which God made between Moses, and other Prophets, *Numb.*12.6,7,8. To say God spake or appeared as he is in his own nature, is to deny his Infinitenesse, Invisibility, Incomprehensibility. To say he spake by Inspiration, or Infusion of the Holy Spirit, as the Holy Spirit signifieth the Deity, is to make Moses equall with Christ, in whom onely the Godhead [as St. Paul speaketh *Col.*2.9.] dwelleth bodily. And lastly, to say he spake by the Holy Spirit, as it signifieth the graces, or gifts of the Holy Spirit, is to attribute nothing to him supernaturall. For God disposeth men to Piety, Justice, Mercy, Truth, Faith, and all manner of Vertue, both Morall, and Intellectuall, by doctrine, example, and by severall occasions, naturall, and ordinary.

And as these ways cannot be applyed to God, in his speaking to Moses, at Mount *Sinai*; so also, they cannot be applyed to him, in his speaking to the High Priests, from the Mercy-Seat. Therefore in [229] what manner God spake to those Soveraign Prophets of the Old Testament, whose office it was to enquire of him, *as it is not declared, so also it is not intelligible, otherwise than by a voyce.*[1] In the time of the New Testament, there was no Soveraign Prophet, but our Saviour; who was both God that spake, and the Prophet to whom he spake.

To subordinate Prophets of perpetuall Calling, I find not any place that proveth God spake to them supernaturally; but onely in such manner, as naturally he inclineth men to Piety, to Beleef, to Righteousnesse, and to other vertues all other Christian men. Which way, though it consist in Constitution, Instruction, Education, and the occasions and invitements men have to Christian vertues; yet it is truly attributed to the operation of the Spirit of God, or Holy Spirit, (which we in our language call the Holy Ghost): For there is no good inclina-

To Prophets of perpetuall Calling, but subordinate, God spake by the Spirit.

[1] *Syn.*: is not intelligible.

tion, that is not of the operation of God. But these operations are not alwaies supernaturall. When therefore a Prophet is said to speak in the Spirit, or by the Spirit of God, we are to understand no more, but that he speaks according to Gods will, declared by the supreme Prophet. For the most common acceptation of the word Spirit, is in the signification of a mans intention, mind, or disposition.

In the time of Moses, there were seventy men besides himself, that *Prophecyed* in the Campe of the Israelites. In what manner God spake to them, is declared in the 11 of *Numbers*, verse 25. *The Lord came down in a cloud, and spake unto Moses, and took of the Spirit that was upon him, and gave it to the seventy Elders. And it came to passe, when the Spirit rested upon them, they Prophecyed, and did not cease.* By which it is manifest, first, that their Prophecying to the people, was subservient, and subordinate to the Prophecying of Moses; for that God took of the Spirit of Moses, to put upon them; so that they Prophecyed as Moses would have them: otherwise they had not been suffered to Prophecy at all. For there was [verse 27.] a complaint made against them to Moses; and Joshua would have *had Moses to forbid*[1] them; which he did not, but said to Joshua, Bee not jealous in my behalf. Secondly, that the Spirit of God in that place, signifieth nothing but the Mind and Disposition to obey, and assist Moses in the administration of the Government. For if it were meant they had the substantiall Spirit of God; that is, the Divine nature, inspired into them, then they had it in no lesse manner then Christ himself, in whom onely the Spirit of God dwelt bodily. It is meant therefore of the Gift and Grace of God, that guided them to co-operate with Moses; from whom their Spirit was derived. And it appeareth [verse 16.] that, they were such as Moses himself should appoint for Elders and Officers of the People: For the words are, *Gather unto me seventy men, whom thou knowest to be Elders and Officers of the people*: where, *thou knowest*, is the same with *thou appointest*, or *hast appointed to be such*. For we are told before [*Exod.*18.] that Moses following the counsell of Jethro his Father-in-law, did appoint Judges, and Officers over the people, such as feared God; and of these, were those Seventy, whom God by putting upon them Moses spirit, inclined to aid Moses in the Administration of the Kingdome: and in this sense the Spirit of God is said [1 *Sam.*16.13,14.] presently upon the anoint-

[230]

---

[1] *Syn.*: Moses to have forbidden

ing of David, to have come upon David, and left Saul; God giving his
graces to him he chose to govern his people, and taking them away
from him, he rejected. So that by the Spirit is meant Inclination to
Gods service; and not any supernaturall Revelation.

God spake also many times by the event of Lots; which were *God*
ordered by such as he had put in Authority over his people. So wee *sometimes*
read that God manifested by the Lots which Saul caused to be drawn *also spake by*
Lots.
[1 *Sam.*14.43.] the fault that Jonathan had committed, in eating a
honey-comb, contrary to the oath taken by the people. And
[*Josh.*18.10.] God divided the land of Canaan amongst the Israelite,
by the *lots that Joshua did cast before the Lord in Shiloh.* In the same
manner it seemeth to be, that God discovered [*Joshua* 7.16, *&c.*] the
crime of Achan. And these are the wayes whereby God declared his
Will in the Old Testament.

All which ways he used also in the New Testament. To the *Virgin*
Mary, by a Vision of an Angel: To *Joseph* in a Dream: again to *Paul* in
the way to Damascus in a Vision of our Saviour: and to *Peter* in the
Vision of a sheet let down from heaven, with divers sorts of flesh, of
clean, and unclean beasts; and in prison, by Vision of an Angel: And
to all the Apostles, and Writers of the New Testament, by the graces
of his Spirit; and to the Apostles again (at the choosing of Matthias in
the place of Judas Iscariot) by lot.

Seeing then all Prophecy supposeth Vision, or Dream, (which two, *Every man*
when they be naturall, are the same,) or some especiall gift of God, so *ought to*
examine the
rarely observed in mankind, as to be admired where observed; And *probability of*
seeing as well such gifts, as the most extraordinary Dreams, and *a pretended*
Visions, may proceed from God, not onely by his supernaturall, and *Prophets*
Calling.
immediate, but also by his naturall operation, and by mediation of
second causes; there is need of Reason and Judgment to discern
between naturall, and supernaturall Gifts, and between naturall, and
supernaturall Visions, or Dreams. And consequently men had need to
be very circumspect, and wary, in obeying the voice of man, that
pretending himself to be a Prophet, requires us to obey God in that
way, which he in Gods name telleth us to be the way to happinesse.
For he that pretends to teach men the way of so great felicity,
pretends to govern them; that is to say, to rule, and reign over them;
which is a thing, that all men naturally desire, and is therefore worthy
to be suspected of Ambition and Imposture; and consequently, ought
to be examined, and tryed by every man, before hee yeeld them

obedience; unlesse he have yeelded it them already, in the institution of a Common-wealth; as when the Prophet is the Civill Soveraign, or by the Civil Soveraign Authorized. And if this examination of Prophets, and Spirits, were not allowed to every one of the people, it had been to no purpose, to set out the marks, by which every man might be able, to distinguish between those, whom they ought, and those

[231] whom they ought not to follow. Seeing therefore such marks are set out [*Deut.* 13.1, &c.] to know a Prophet by; and [1 *John* 4.1. &c.] to know a Spirit by: and seeing there is so much Prophecying in the Old Testament; and so much Preaching in the New Testament against Prophets; and so much *a greater**[1] number ordinarily of false Prophets, then of true; every one is to beware of obeying their directions, at their own perill. And first, that there were many more false then true Prophets, appears by this, that when Ahab [1 *Kings* 12.] consulted four hundred Prophets, they were all false Imposters, but onely one Michaiah. And a little before the time of the Captivity, the Prophets were generally lyars. *The Prophets* (saith the Lord by *Jeremy*, cha. 14. verse 14.] *prophecy Lies in my name. I sent them not, neither have I commanded them, nor spake unto them, they prophecy to you a false Vision, a thing of naught; and the deceit of their heart.* In so much as God commanded the People by the mouth of the Prophet *Jeremiah* [chap.23.16.] not to obey them. *Thus saith the Lord of Hosts, hearken not unto the words of the Prophets, that prophecy to you. They make you vain, they speak a Vision of their own heart, and not out of the mouth of the Lord.*

All prophecy but of the Soveraign Prophet is to be examined by every Subject.

Seeing then there was in the time of the Old Testament, such quarrells amongst the Visionary Prophets, one contesting with another, and asking, When departed the Spirit from me, to go to thee? as between Michaiah, and the rest of the four hundred; and such giving of the Lye to one another, [as in *Jerem.* 14.14.] and such controversies in the New Testament at this day, amongst the Spirituall Prophets: Every man then was, and now is bound to make use of his Naturall Reason, to apply to all Prophecy those Rules which God hath given us, to discern the true from the false. Of which Rules, in the Old Testament, one was, conformable doctrine to that which Moses the Soveraign Prophet had taught them; and the other the miraculous power of foretelling what God would bring to passe, as I have already shewn out of *Deut.* 13.1. *&c.* And in the New Testament there was but

[1] Syn.: greater a

298

one onely mark; and that was the preaching of this Doctrine, *That Jesus is the Christ*, that is, the King of the Jews, promised in the Old Testament. Whosoever denyed that Article, he was a false Prophet, whatsoever miracles he might seem to work; and he that taught it was a true Prophet. For St. *John* [1 Epist. 4.2, &c.] speaking expressely of the means to examine Spirits, whether they be of God, or not; after he had told them that there would arise false Prophets, saith thus, *Hereby know ye the Spirit of God. Every Spirit that confesseth that Jesus Christ is come in the flesh, is of God*; that is, is approved and allowed as a Prophet of God: not that he is a godly man, or one of the Elect, for this, that he confesseth, professeth, or preacheth Jesus to be the Christ; but for that he is a Prophet avowed. For God sometimes speaketh by Prophets, whose persons he hath not accepted; as he did by Baalam; and as he foretold Saul of his death, by the Witch of Endor. Again in the next verse, *Every Spirit that confesseth not that Jesus Christ is come in the flesh, is not of Christ. And this is the Spirit of Antichrist.* So that the Rule is perfect on both sides; that he is a true Prophet, which preacheth the [232] Messiah already come, in the person of Jesus; and he a false one that denyeth him come, and looketh for him in some future Impostor, that shall take upon him that honour falsely, whom the Apostle there properly calleth Antichrist. Every man therefore ought to consider who is the Soveraign Prophet; that is to say, who it is, that is Gods Vicegerent on Earth; and hath next under God, the Authority of Governing Christian men; and to observe for a Rule, that Doctrine, which in the name of God, hee hath commanded to bee taught; and thereby to examine and try out the truth of those Doctrines, which pretended Prophets with miracle, or without, shall at any time advance: and if they find it contrary to that Rule, to doe as they did, that came to Moses, and complained that there were some that Prophecyed in the Campe, whose Authority so to doe they doubted of; and leave to the Soveraign, as they did to Moses to uphold, or to forbid them, as hee should see cause; and if hee disavow them, then no more to obey their voice; or if he approve them, then to obey them, as men to whom God hath given a part of the Spirit of their Soveraigne. For when Christian men, take not their Christian Soveraign, for Gods Prophet; they must either take their owne Dreames, for the Prophecy they mean to bee governed by, and the tumour of their own hearts for the Spirit of God; or they must suffer themselves to bee lead by some strange Prince; or by some of their fellow subjects, that can bewitch them, by slaunder of the government, into rebellion, without other miracle to confirm their calling, then sometimes an extraordinary successe, and Impunity; and by this means destroying all laws, both divine, and humane, reduce all Order, Government, and Society, to the first Chaos of Violence, and Civill warre.

[233]

CHAP. XXXVII.
Of MIRACLES, *and their Use.*

A Miracle is a work that causeth Admiration.

By *Miracles* are signified the Admirable works of God: & therefore they are also called *Wonders.* And because they are for the most part, done, for a signification of his commandement, in such occasions, as without them, men are apt to doubt, (following their private naturall reasoning,) what he hath commanded, and what not, they are commonly in Holy Scripture, called *Signes*, in the same sense, as they are called by the Latines, *Ostenta*, and *Portenta*, from shewing, and fore-signifying that, which the Almighty is about to bring to passe.

And must therefore be rare, and whereof there is no naturall cause known.

To understand therefore what is a Miracle, we must first understand what works they are, which men wonder at, and call Admirable. And there be but two things which make men wonder at any event: The one is, if it be strange, that is to say, such, as the like of it hath never, or very rarely been produced: The other is, if when it is produced, we cannot imagine it to have been done by naturall means, but onely by the immediate hand of God. But when wee see some possible, naturall cause of it, how rarely soever the like has been done; or if the like have been often done, how impossible soever it be to imagine a naturall means thereof, we no more wonder, nor esteem it for a Miracle.

Therefore, if a Horse, or Cow should speak, it were a Miracle; because both the thing is strange, & the naturall cause difficult to imagin: So also were it, to see a strange deviation of nature, in the production of some new shape of a living creature. But when a man, or other Animal, engenders his like, though we know no more how this is done, than the other; yet because 'tis usuall, it is no Miracle. In like manner, if a man be metamorphosed into a stone, or into a pillar, it is a Miracle; because strange: but if a peece of wood be so changed; because we see it often, it is no Miracle: and yet we know no more, by what operation of God, the one is brought to passe, than the other.

The first Rainbow that was seen in the world, was a Miracle, because the first; and consequently strange; and served for a sign from God, placed in heaven, to assure his people, there should be no more an universall destruction of the world by Water. But at this day, because they are frequent, they are not Miracles, neither to them that know their naturall causes, nor to them who know them not. Again, there be many rare works produced by the Art of man: yet when we know they are *so done;*[1] because thereby wee know also the means how they are done, we count them not for Miracles, because not wrought by the immediate hand of God, but by mediation of humane [234] Industry.

Furthermore, seeing Admiration and Wonder, is consequent to the knowledge and experience, wherewith men are endued, some more, some lesse; it followeth, that the same thing, may be a Miracle to one, and not to another. And thence it is, that ignorant, and superstitious men make great Wonders of those works, which other men, knowing to proceed from Nature, (which is not the immediate, but the ordinary work of God,) admire not at all: As when Ecclipses of the Sun and Moon have been taken for supernaturall works, by the common people; when neverthelesse, there were others, could from their naturall causes, have foretold the very hour they should arrive: Or, as when a man, by confederacy, and secret intelligence, getting knowledge of the private actions of an ignorant, unwary man, thereby tells him, what he has done in former time; it seems to him a Miraculous thing; but amongst wise, and cautelous men, such Miracles as those, cannot easily be done. *That which seemeth a Miracle to one man, may seem otherwise to another.*

Again, it belongeth to the nature of a Miracle, that it be wrought for the procuring of credit to Gods Messengers, Ministers, and Prophets, that thereby men may know, they are called, sent, and employed by God, and thereby be the better inclined to obey them. And therefore, though the creation of the world, and after that the destruction of all living creatures in the universall deluge, were admirable works; yet because they were not done to procure credit to any Prophet, or other Minister of God, they use not to be called Miracles. For how admir- *The End of Miracles.*

[1] *Syn.*: done;

able soever any work be, the Admiration consisteth not in that it could be done, because men naturally beleeve the Almighty can doe all things, but because he does it at the Prayer, or Word of a man. But the works of God in Egypt, by the hand of Moses, were properly Miracles; because they were done with intention to make the people of Israel beleeve, that Moses came unto them, not out of any design of his owne interest, but as sent from God. Therefore after God had commanded him to deliver the Israelites from the Egyptian bondage, when he said *They will not beleeve me, but will say, the Lord hath not appeared unto me*, God gave him power, to turn the Rod he had in his hand into a Serpent, and again to return it into a Rod; and by putting his hand into his bosome, to make it leprous; and again by pulling it out to make it whole, to make the Children of Israel beleeve (as it is verse 5.) that the God of their Fathers had appeared unto him: And if that were not enough, he gave him power to turn their waters into bloud. And when hee had done these Miracles before the people, it is said (verse 41.) that *they beleeved him.* Neverthelesse, for fear of Pharaoh, they durst not yet obey him. Therefore the other works which were done to plague Pharaoh, and the Egyptians, tended all to make the Israelites beleeve in Moses, and were properly Miracles. In like manner if we consider all the Miracles donè by the hand of Moses, and all the rest of the Prophets, till the Captivity; and those of our Saviour, and his Apostles afterward; we shall find, their end was alwaies to beget, or confirm beleefe, that they came not of their own motion, but were sent by God. Wee may further observe in Scripture, that the end of Miracles, was to beget beleef, not universally in all men, elect, and reprobate; but in the elect only; that is to say, in such as God had determined should become his Subjects. For those miraculous plagues of Egypt, had not for end, the conversion of Pharaoh; For God had told Moses before, that he would harden the heart of Pharaoh, that he should not let the people goe: And when he let them goe at last, not the Miracles perswaded him, but the plagues forced him to it. So also of our Saviour, it is written, (*Mat.*13.58.) that he wrought not many Miracles in his own countrey, because of their unbeleef; and (in *Marke* 6.5.) in stead of, *he wrought not many*, it is, *he could work none.* It was not because he wanted power; which to say, were blasphemy against God; nor that the end of Miracles was not to convert incredulous men to Christ; for the end of all the Miracles of Moses, of the Prophets, of our Saviour, and of his Apostles was to

*Exo.*4.1, *&c.*

[235]

adde men to the Church; but it was, because the end of their Miracles, was to adde to the Church (not all men, but) such as should be saved; that is to say, such as God had elected. Seeing therefore our Saviour was sent from his Father, hee could not use his power in the conversion of those, whom his Father had rejected. They that expounding this place of St. *Marke*, say, that this word, *Hee could not*, is put for, *He would not*, do it without example in the Greek tongue, (where *Would not*, is put sometimes for *Could not*, in things inanimate, that have no will; but *Could not*, for *Would not*, never,) and thereby lay a stumbling block before weak Christians; as if Christ could doe no Miracles, but amongst the credulous.

From that which I have here set down, of the nature, and use of a Miracle, we may define it thus, *A* MIRACLE, *is a work of God, (besides his operation by the way of Nature, ordained in the Creation,) done, for the making manifest to his elect, the mission of an extraordinary Minister for their salvation.* *The definition of a Miracle.*

And from this definition, we may inferre; First, that in all Miracles, the work done, is not the effect of any vertue in the Prophet; because it is the effect of the immediate hand of God; that is to say, God hath done it, without using the Prophet therein, as a subordinate cause.

Secondly, that no Devil, Angel, or other created Spirit, can do a Miracle. For it must either be by vertue of some naturall science, or by Incantation, that is, *by vertue*[1] of words. For if the Inchanters do it by their own power independent, there is some power that proceedeth not from God; which all men deny: and if they doe it by power given them, then is the work not from the immediate hand of God, but naturall, and consequently no Miracle.

There be some texts of Scripture, that seem to attribute the power of working wonders (equall to some of those immediate Miracles, wrought by God himself,) to certain Arts of Magick, and Incantation. As for example, when we read that after the Rod of Moses being cast on the ground became a Serpent, *the Magicians of Egypt did the like by their Enchantments*; and that after Moses had turned the waters of the Egyptian Streams, Rivers, Ponds, and Pooles of water into blood, *the Magicians of Egypt did so likewise, with their Enchantments*; and that after Moses had by the power of God brought frogs upon the land, *the Magicians also did so with their Enchantments, and brought up frogs upon* [236] *Exod.*7.11. *Exod.*7.22. *Exod.*8.7.

[1] *Syn.*: vertue

the land of Egypt; will not a man be apt to attribute Miracles to Enchantments; that is to say, to the efficacy of the sound of Words; and think the same very well proved out of this, and other such places? and yet there is no place of Scripture, that telleth us what an Enchantment is. If therefore Enchantment be not, as many think it, a working of strange effects by spells, and words; but Imposture, and delusion, wrought by ordinary means; and so far from supernaturall, as the Impostors need not the study so much as of naturall causes, but the ordinary ignorance, stupidity, and superstition of mankind, to doe them; those texts that seem to countenance the power of Magick, Witchcraft, and Enchantment, must needs have another sense, than at first sight they seem to bear.

That men are apt to be deceived by false Miracles.
For it is evident enough, that Words have no effect, but on those that understand them; and then they have no other, but to signifie the intentions, or passions of them that speak; and thereby produce, hope, fear, or other passions, or conceptions in the hearer. Therefore when a Rod seemeth a Serpent, or the Waters Bloud, or any other Miracle seemeth done by Enchantment; if it be not to the edification of Gods people, not the Rod, nor the Water, nor any other thing is enchanted; this is to say, wrought upon by the Words, but the Spectator. So that all the Miracle consisteth in this, that the Enchanter has deceived a man; which is no Miracle, but a very easie matter to doe.

For such is the ignorance, and aptitude to error generally of all men, but especially of them that have not much knowledge of naturall causes, and of the nature, and interests of men; as by innumerable and easie tricks to be abused. What opinion of miraculous power, before it was known there was a Science of the course of the Stars, might a man have gained, that should have told the people, This hour, or day the Sun should be darkned? A Juggler by the handling of his goblets, and other trinkets, if it were not now ordinarily practised, would be thought to do his wonders by the power at least of the Devil. A man that hath practised to speak by drawing in of his breath, (which kind of men in antient time were called *Ventriloqui*,) and so make the weaknesse of his voice seem to proceed, not from the weak impulsion of the organs of Speech, but from distance of place, is able to make very many men beleeve it is a voice from Heaven, whatsoever he please to tell them. And for a crafty man, that hath enquired into the secrets, and familiar confessions that one man ordinarily maketh to another of his actions and adventures past, to tell them him again is no hard matter; and yet there be many, that by such means as that, obtain the reputation of being Conjurers. But it is too long a businesse, to reckon up the several sorts of those men, which the Greeks called *Thaumaturgi*, that is to say, workers of things wonderfull; and yet these do all they do, by their own single dexterity. But if we looke upon the Impostures wrought by Confederacy, there is nothing how impossible soever to be done, that is impossible to bee beleeved. For two men conspiring, one to seem lame, the other to cure him with a charme, will deceive many: but many conspiring, one to seem lame, another so to cure him, and all the rest to bear witnesse; will deceive many more. [237]

In this aptitude of mankind, to give too hasty beleefe to pretended Miracles, there can be no better, nor I think any other caution, then that which God hath prescribed, first by Moses, (as I have said before in the precedent chapter,) in the beginning of the 13. and end of the 18. of *Deuteronomy*; That wee take not any for Prophets, that teach any other Religion, then that which Gods Lieutenant, (which at that time was Moses,) hath established; nor any, (though he teach the same Religion,) whose Praediction we doe not see come to passe. Moses therefore in his time, and Aaron, and his successors in their times, and the Soveraign Governour of Gods people, next under God himselfe, that is to say, the Head of the Church in all times, are to be consulted, what doctrine he hath established, before wee give credit to a pretended Miracle, or Prophet. And when that is done, the thing they pretend to be a Miracle, we must both see it done, and use all means possible to consider, whether it be really done; and not onely so, but whether it be such, as no man can do the like by his naturall power, but that it requires the immediate hand of God. And in this also we must have recourse to Gods Lieutenant; to whom in all doubtfull cases, wee have submitted our private judgments. For example; if a man pretend, that after certain words spoken over a peece of bread, that presently God hath made it not bread, but a God, or a man, or both, and neverthelesse it looketh still as like bread as ever it did; there is no reason for any man to think it really done; nor consequently to fear him, till he enquire of God, by his Vicar, or Lieutenant, whether it be done, or not. If he say not, then followeth that which Moses saith, (*Deut.* 18.22.) *he hath spoken it presumptuously, thou shalt not fear him.* If he say 'tis done, then he is not to contradict it. So also if wee see not, but onely hear tell of a Miracle, we are to

Cautions against the Imposture of Miracles.

consult the Lawful Church; that is to say, the lawful Head thereof, how far we are to give credit to the relators of it. And this is chiefly the case of men, that in these days live under Christian Soveraigns. For in these times, I do not know one man, that ever saw any such wondrous work, done by the charm, or at the word, or prayer of a man, that a man endued but with a mediocrity of reason, would think supernaturall: and the question is no more, whether what wee see done, be a Miracle; whether the Miracle we hear, or read of, were a reall work, and not the Act of a tongue, or pen; but in plain terms, whether the report be true, or a lye. In which question we are not every one, to make our own private Reason, or Conscience, but the Publique Reason, that is, the reason of Gods Supreme Lieutenant, Judge; and indeed we have made him Judge already, if wee have given him a Soveraign power, to doe all that is necessary for our peace and defence. A private man has alwaies the liberty, (because thought is free,) to beleeve, or not beleeve in his heart, those acts that have been given out for Miracles, according as he shall see, what benefit can accrew by mens belief, to those that pretend, or countenance them, and thereby conjecture, whether they be Miracles, or Lies. But when it comes to confession of that faith, the Private Reason must submit to the Publique, that is to say, to Gods Lieutenant. But who is this Lieutenant of God, and Head of the Church, shall be considered in its proper place hereafter.

CHAP. XXXVIII.

Of the Signification in Scripture of ETERNALL LIFE, HELL, SALVATION, THE WORLD TO COME, *and* REDEMPTION.

The maintenance of Civill Society, depending on Justice; and Justice on the power of Life and Death, and other lesse Rewards and Punishments, residing in them that have the Soveraignty of the Commonwealth; It is impossible a Common-wealth should stand, where any other than the Soveraign, hath a power of giving greater rewards than Life; and of inflicting greater punishments, than Death. Now seeing *Eternall life* is a greater reward, than the *life present*; and *Eternall torment* a greater punishment than the *death of Nature*; It is a thing worthy to be well considered, of all men that desire (by obeying Authority) to avoid the calamities of Confusion, and Civill war, what is meant in holy Scripture, by *Life Eternall*, and *Torment Eternall*; and for what offences, and against whom committed, men are to be *Eternally tormented*; and for what actions, they are to obtain *Eternall life*.

And first we find, that Adam was created in such a condition of life, as had he not broken the commandement of God, he had enjoyed it in the Paradise of Eden Everlastingly. For there was the *Tree of life*; whereof he was so long allowed to eat, as he should forbear to eat of the tree of Knowledge of Good and Evill; which was not allowed him. And therefore as soon as he had eaten of it, God thrust him out of Paradise, *lest he should put forth his hand, and take also of the tree of life, and live for ever*. By which it seemeth to me, (with submission neverthelesse both in this, and in all questions, whereof the determination dependeth on the Scriptures, to the interpretation of the Bible authorized by the Common-wealth, whose Subject I am,) that Adam if he had not sinned, had had an Eternall Life on Earth: and that Mortality entred upon himself, and his posterity, by his first Sin. Not that actuall Death then entred; for Adam then could never have had children; whereas he lived long after, and saw a numerous posterity ere he dyed. But where it is said, *In the day that thou eatest thereof, thou shalt surely die*, it must needs bee meant of his Mortality, and certitude of death. Seeing then Eternall life was lost by Adams forfeiture, in committing sin, he that should cancell that forfeiture was to recover thereby, that Life again. Now Jesus Christ hath satisfied for the sins of all that beleeve in him; and therefore recovered to all beleevers, that ETERNALL LIFE, which was lost by the sin of Adam. And in this sense it is, that the comparison of St. Paul holdeth (*Rom.* 5.18,19.) *As by the offence of one, Judgment came upon all men to condemnation, even so by the righteousnesse of one, the free gift came upon all men to Justification of Life*. Which is again (1 *Cor.* 15.21,22.) more perspicuously delivered in these words, *For since by man came death, by man came also the resurrection of the dead. For as in Adam all die, even so in Christ shall all be made alive.*

The place of Adams Eternity if he had not sinned, had been the terrestiall Paradise. Gen.3.22.

[239]

307

*Texts
concerning
the place of
Life Eternall,
for Beleevers.*

Concerning the place wherein men shall enjoy that Eternall Life, which Christ hath obtained for them, the texts next before alledged seem to make it on Earth. For if as in Adam, all die, that is, have forfeited Paradise, and Eternall Life on Earth, even so in Christ all shall bee made alive; then all men shall be made to live on Earth; for else the comparison were not proper. Hereunto seemeth to agree that of the Psalmist, (*Psal.*133.3.) *Upon Zion God commanded the blessing, even Life for evermore*: for Zion, is in Jerusalem, upon Earth: as also that of S. Joh. (*Rev.*2.7.) *To him that overcommeth I will give to eat of the tree of life, which is in the midst of the Paradise of God.* This was the tree of Adams Eternall life; but his life was to have been on Earth. The same seemeth to be confirmed again by St. Joh. (*Rev.*21.2.) where he saith, *I John saw the Holy City, New Jerusalem, coming down from God out of heaven, prepared as a Bride adorned for her husband*: and again v.10. to the same effect: As if he should say, the new Jerusalem, the Paradise of God, at the coming again of Christ, should come down to Gods people from Heaven, and not they goe up to it from Earth. And this differs nothing from that, which the two men in white clothing (that is, the two Angels) said to the Apostles, that were looking upon Christ ascending (*Acts* 1.11.) *This same Jesus, who is taken up from you into Heaven, shall so come, as you have seen him go up into Heaven.* Which soundeth as if they had said, he should come down to govern them under his Father, Eternally here; and not take them up to govern them in Heaven; and is conformable to the Restauration of the Kingdom of God, instituted under Moses; which was a Political government of the Jews on Earth. Again, that saying of our Saviour (*Mat.*22.30.) *that in the Resurrection they neither marry, nor are given in marriage, but are as the Angels of God in heaven,* is a description of an Eternall Life, resembling that which we lost in Adam in the point of Marriage. For seeing Adam, and Eve, if they had not sinned, had lived on Earth Eternally, in their individuall persons; it is manifest, they should not continually have procreated their kind. For if Immortals should have generated, as Mankind doth now; the Earth in a small time, would not have been able to afford them place to stand on. The Jews that asked our Saviour the question, whose wife the woman that had married many brothers, should be, in the resurrection, knew not what were the consequences of Life Eternall: and therefore our Saviour puts them in mind of this consequence of Immortality; that there shal be no Generation, and consequently no marriage, no more than there is Marriage, or generation among the Angels. The comparison between that Eternall life which Adam lost, and our Saviour by his Victory over death hath recovered; holdeth [240] also in this, that as Adam lost Eternall Life by his sin, and yet lived after it for a time, so the faithful Christian hath recovered Eternal Life by Christs passion, though he die a natural death, and remaine dead for a time; namely, till the Resurrection. For as Death is reckoned from the Condemnation of Adam, not from the Execution; so Life is reckoned from the Absolution, not from the Resurrection of them that are elected in Christ.

That the place wherein men are to live Eternally, after the Resurrection, is the Heavens, meaning by Heaven, those parts of the world, which are the most remote from Earth, as where the stars are, or above the stars, in another Higher Heaven, called *Coelum Empyreum*, (whereof there is no mention in Scripture, nor ground in Reason) is not easily to be drawn from any text that I can find. By the Kingdome of Heaven, is meant the Kingdom of the King that dwelleth in Heaven; and his Kingdome was the people of Israel, whom he *ruled on Earth*[1] by the Prophets his Lieutenants, first Moses, and after him Eleazar, and the Soveraign Priests, till in the days of Samuel they rebelled, and would have a mortall man for their King, after the manner of other Nations. And when our Saviour Christ, by the preaching of his Ministers, shall have perswaded the Jews to return, and called the Gentiles to his obedience, then shall there be a new Kingdom of Heaven; because our King shall then be God, whose *throne* is Heaven; without any necessity evident in the Scripture, that man shall ascend to his happinesse any higher than Gods *footstool* the Earth. On the contrary, we find written (*Joh.*3.13.) that *no man hath ascended into Heaven, but he that came down from Heaven, even the Son of man, that is in Heaven*. Where I observe by the way, that these words are not, as those which go immediately before, the words of our Saviour, but of St. John himself; for Christ was then not in Heaven, but upon the Earth. The like is said of David (*Acts* 2.34.) where St. Peter, to prove the Ascension of Christ, using the words of the Psalmist, (*Psal.*16.10.) *Thou wilt not leave my soule in Hell, not suffer thine Holy one to see corruption*, saith, they were spoken (not of David, but) of Christ; and to prove it, addeth this Reason, *For David is not*

Ascension into heaven.

---

[1] *Syn.*: ruled

ascended into Heaven. But to this a man may easily answer, and say, that though their bodies were not to ascend till the generall day of Judgment, yet their souls were in Heaven as soon as they were departed from their bodies; which also seemeth to be confirmed by the words of our Saviour (*Luke* 20.37,38.) who proving the Resurrection out of the words of Moses, saith thus, *That the dead are raised, even Moses shewed, at the bush, when he calleth the Lord, the God of Abraham, and the God of Isaac, and the God of Jacob. For he is not a God of the Dead, but of the Living; for they all live to him.* But if these words be to be understood only of the Immortality of the Soul, they prove not at all that which our Saviour intended to prove, which was the Resurrection of the Body, that is to say, the Immortality of the Man. Therefore our Saviour meaneth, that those Patriarchs were Immortall; not by a property consequent to the essence, and nature of mankind; but by the will of God, that was pleased of his mere grace, to bestow *Eternall* [241] *life* upon the faithfull. And though at that time the Patriarchs and many other faithfull men were *dead*, yet as it is in the text, they *lived to God*; that is, they were written in the Book of Life with them that were absolved of their sinnes, and ordained to Life eternall at the Resurrection. That the Soul of man is in its own nature Eternall, and a living Creature independent on the body; or that any meer man is Immortall, otherwise than by the Resurrection in the last day, (except *Enos* and *Elias*,) is a doctrine not apparent in Scripture. The whole 14. Chapter of *Job*, which is the speech not of his friends, but of himselfe, is a complaint of this Mortality of Nature; and yet no contradiction of the Immortality at the Resurrection. *There is hope of a tree* (saith hee verse 7.) *if it be cast down, Though the root thereof wax old, and the stock thereof die in the ground, yet when it senteth the water it will bud, and bring forth boughes like a Plant. But man dyeth, and wasteth away, yea, man giveth up the Ghost, and where is he?* and (verse 12.) *man lyeth down, and riseth not, till the heavens be no more.* But when is it, that the heavens shall be no more? St. Peter tells us, that it is at the generall Resurrection. For in his 2. Epistle, 3. Chapter, and 7 verse, he saith, that *the Heavens and the Earth that are now, are reserved unto fire against the day of Judgment, and perdition of ungodly men,* and (verse 12.) *looking for, and hasting to the comming of God, wherein the Heavens shall be on fire, and shall be dissolved, and the Elements shall melt with fervent heat. Neverthelesse, we according to the promise look for new Heavens, and a new Earth, wherein dwelleth righteousnesse.* Therefore where Job saith, man riseth not till the Heavens be no more; it is all one, as if he had said, the Immortall Life (and Soule and Life in the Scripture, do usually signifie the same thing) beginneth not in man, till the Resurrection, and day of Judgement; and hath for cause, not his specificall nature, and generation; but the Promise. For St. Peter *saies*[1] *Wee look for new heavens, and a new earth,* (*not from Nature,*[2]) but *from Promise.*

Lastly, seeing it hath been already proved out of divers evident places of Scripture, in the 35. chapter of this book, that the Kingdom of God is a Civil Common-wealth, where God himself is Soveraign, by vertue first of the *Old*, and since of the *New* Covenant, wherein he reigneth by his Vicar, or Lieutenant; the same places do therefore also prove, that after the comming again of our Saviour in his Majesty, and glory, to reign actually, and Eternally; the Kingdom of God is to be on Earth. But because this doctrine (though proved out of places of Scripture not few, nor obscure) will appear to most men a novelty; I doe but propound it; maintaining nothing in this, or any other paradox of Religion; but attending the end of that dispute of the sword, concerning the Authority, (not yet amongst my Countrey-men decided,) by which all sorts of doctrine are to bee approved, or rejected; and whose commands, both in speech, and writing, (whatsoever be the opinions of private men) must by all men, that mean to be protected by their Laws, be obeyed. For the points of doctrine concerning the Kingdome of God, have so great influence on the [242] Kingdome of Man, as not to be determined, but by them, that under God have the Soveraign Power.

As the Kingdome of God, and Eternall Life, so also Gods Enemies, and their Torments after Judgment, appear by the Scripture, to have their place on Earth. The name of the place, where all men remain till the Resurrection, that were either buryed, or swallowed up of the Earth, is usually called in Scripture, by words that signifie *under ground*; which the Latines read generally *Infernus*, and *Inferi*, and the Greeks ἅδης; that is to say, a place where men cannot see; and containeth as well the Grave, as any other deeper place. But for the place of the damned after the Resurrection, it is not determined, neither in the Old, nor New Testament, by any note of situation; but onely by the company: as that it shall bee, where such wicked men were, as God in former times in extraordinary, and miraculous

The place after Judgment, of those who were never in the Kingdome of God, or having been in, are cast out.

---

[1] *Syn.*: saies not   [2] *Syn.*: *from Nature,*

Tartarus.

manner, had destroyed from off the face of the Earth: As for example, that they are *in Inferno*, in *Tartarus*, or in the bottomlesse pit; because *Corah, Dathan,* and *Abirom,* were swallowed up alive into the earth. Not that the Writers of the Scripture would have us beleeve, there could be in the globe of the Earth, which is not only finite, but also (compared to the height of the Stars) of no considerable magnitude, a pit without a bottome; that is, a hole of infinite depth, such as the Greeks in their *Daemonologie* (that is to say, in their doctrine concerning *Daemons,*) and after them the Romans called *Tartarus*; of which Virgill sayes,

> *Bis patet in praeceps, tantum tendítque sub umbras,*
> *Quantus ad aethereum coeli suspectus Olympum:*

for that is a thing the proportion of Earth to Heaven cannot bear: but that wee should beleeve them there, indefinitely, where those men are, on whom God inflicted that Exemplary punnishment.

The congregation of Giants.

Again, because those mighty men of the Earth, that lived in the time of Noah, before the floud, (which the Greeks called *Heroes,* and the Scripture *Giants,* and both say, were begotten, by copulation of the children of God, with the children of men,) were for their wicked life destroyed by the generall deluge; the place of the Damned, is therefore also sometimes marked out, by the company of those deceased Giants; as *Proverbs* 21.16. *The man that wandreth out of the way of understanding, shall remain in the congregation of the Giants,* and Job 26.5. *Behold the Giants groan under water, and they that dwell with them.* Here the place of the Damned, is under the water. And *Isaiah* 14.9. *Hell is troubled how to meet thee,* (that is, the King of Babylon) *and will displace the Giants for thee*: and here again the place of the Damned, (if the sense be literall,) is to be under water.

Lake of Fire.

Thirdly, because the Cities of Sodom, and Gomorrah, by the extraordinary wrath of God, were consumed for their wickednesse with Fire and Brimstone, and together with them the countrey about made a stinking bituminous Lake: the place of the Damned is sometimes expressed by Fire, and a Fiery Lake: as in the *Apocalypse* ch.21.8. *But the timorous, incredulous, and abominable, and Murderers, and*

[243]

Whoremongers, and Sorcerers, and Idolaters, and all Lyars, shall have their part in the Lake that burneth with Fire, and Brimstone; which is the second Death. So that it is manifest, that Hell Fire which is here expressed by Metaphor, from the reall Fire, of Sodome, signifieth not any certain kind, or place of Torment; but is to be taken indefinitely, for Destruction, as it is in the 20. Chapter, at the 14. verse; where it is said, that *Death and Hell were cast into the Lake of Fire*; that is to say, were abolished, and destroyed; as if after the *second death,*[1] there shall be no more Dying, nor no more going into Hell; that is, no more going to *Hades* (from which word perhaps our word Hell is derived,) which is the same with no more Dying.

Fourthly, from the Plague of Darknesse inflicted on the Egyptians, of which it is written (*Exod.* 10.23.) *They saw not one another, neither rose any man from his place for three days; but all the Children of Israel had light in their dwellings*; the place of the wicked after Judgment, is called *Utter Darknesse*, or (as it is in the originall) *Darknesse without*. And so it is expressed (*Mat.* 22.13.) where the King commandeth his Servants, *to bind hand and foot the man that had not on his Wedding garment, and to cast him out*, εἰς τὸ σκότος τὸ ἐξώτερον, *Externall darknesse*, or *Darknesse without*: which though translated *Utter darknesse*, does not signifie *how great*, but *where* that darknesse is to be; namely, *without the habitation* of Gods Elect. *Utter Darknesse.*

Lastly, whereas there was a place neer Jerusalem, called the *Valley of the Children of Hinnon*; in a part whereof, called *Tophet*, the Jews had committed most grievous Idolatry, sacrificing their children to the Idol Moloch; and wherein also God had afflicted his enemies with most grievous punishments; and wherein Josias had burnt the Priests of Moloch upon their own Altars, as appeareth at large in the 2 of *Kings* chap. 23. the place served afterwards, to receive the filth, and garbage which was carried thither, out of the City; and there used to be fires made, from time to time, to purifie the aire, and take away the stench of Carrion. From this abominable place, the Jews used ever after to call the place of the Damned, by the name of *Gehenna*, or *Valley of Hinnon*. And this *Gehenna*, is that word, which is usually now translated HELL; and from the fires from time to time there burning, we have the notion of *Everlasting*, and *Unquenchable Fire*. *Gehenna, and Tophet.*

Seeing now there is none, that so interprets the Scripture, as that after the day of Judgment, the wicked are all Eternally to be punished in the Valley of Hinnon; or that they shall so rise again, as to be ever after under ground, or under water; or that after the Resurrection, they shall no more see one another; nor stir from one place to *Of the literall sense of the Scripture concerning Hell.*

[1] *Syn.*: day of Judgement,

313

another; it followeth, me thinks, very necessarily, that that which is thus said concerning Hell Fire, is spoken metaphorically; and that therefore there is a proper sense to bee enquired after, (for of all Metaphors there is some reall ground, that may be expressed in proper words) both of the *Place* of *Hell*, and the nature of *Hellish Torments*, and *Tormenters*.

[244]
Satan,
Devill, not
Proper
names, but
Appellatives.

And first for the Tormenters, wee have their nature, and properties, exactly and properly delivered by the names of, *The Enemy*, or *Satan*; *The Accuser*, or *Diabolus*; *The Destroyer*, or *Abaddon*. Which significant names, *Satan, Devill, Abaddon*, set not forth to us any Individuall person, as proper names use to doe; but onely an office, or quality; and are therefore Appellatives; which ought not to have been left untranslated, as they are, in the Latine, and Modern Bibles; because thereby they seem to be the proper names of *Daemons*; and men are the more easily seduced to beleeve the doctrine of Devills; which at that time was the Religion of the Gentiles, and contrary to that of Moses, and of Christ.

And because by the *Enemy*, the *Accuser*, and *Destroyer*, is meant, the Enemy of them that shall be in the Kingdome of God; therefore if the Kingdome of God after the Resurrection, bee upon the Earth, (as in the former Chapter I have shewn by Scripture it seems to be,) The Enemy, and his Kingdome must be on Earth also. For so also was it, in the time before the Jews had deposed God. For Gods Kingdome was in Palestine; and the Nations round about, were the Kingdomes of the Enemy; and consequently by *Satan*, is meant any Earthly Enemy of the Church.

Torments of
Hell.

The Torments of Hell, are expressed sometimes, by *weeping, and gnashing of teeth*, as *Mat.*8.12. Sometimes, by *the worm of Conscience*; as *Isa.*66.24. and *Mark* 9.44,46,48: sometimes, by *Fire*, as in the place now quoted, *where the worm dyeth not, and the fire is not quenched*, and many places beside: sometimes by *shame, and contempt*, as *Dan.*12.2. *And many of them that sleep in the dust of the Earth, shall awake; some to Everlasting life; and some to shame, and everlasting contempt*. All which places design metaphorically a grief, and discontent of mind, from the sight of that Eternall felicity in others, which they themselves through their own incredulity, and disobedience have lost. And because such felicity in others, is not sensible but by comparison with their own actuall miseries; it followeth that they are to suffer such bodily paines, and calamities, as are incident to those, who not onely live under evill

and cruell Governours, but have also for Enemy, the Eternall King of
the Saints, God Almighty. And amongst these bodily paines, is to be
reckoned also to every one of the wicked a second Death. For though
the Scripture bee clear for an universall Resurrection; yet wee do not
read, that to any of the Reprobate is promised an Eternall life. For
whereas St. *Paul* (1 *Cor.*15.42,43.) to the question concerning what
bodies men shall rise with again, saith, that *the body is sown in corrup-*
tion, and is raised in incorruption; It is sown in dishonour, it is raised in
glory; it is sown in weaknesse, it is raised in power; Glory and Power
cannot be applyed to the bodies of the wicked: Nor can the name of
Second Death, bee applyed to those that can never die but once: And
although in Metaphoricall Speech, a Calamitous life Everlasting, may
bee called an Everlasting Death; yet it cannot wel be understood of a
Second Death. The fire prepared for the wicked, is an Everlasting Fire: [245]
that is to say, the estate wherein no man can be without torture, both
of body and mind, after the Resurrection, shall endure *for ever,*[1]
and in that sense the Fire shall be unquenchable, and the torments
Everlasting: but it cannot thence be inferred, that hee who shall be
cast into that fire, or be tormented with those torments, shall endure,
and resist them so, as to be eternally burnt, and tortured; and yet
never be destroyed, nor die. And though there be many places that
affirm Everlasting Fire, and Torments (into which men may be cast
successively one after another *for ever;*[2]) yet I find none that affirm
there shall bee an Eternall Life therein of any individuall person; but
to the contrary, an Everlasting Death, which is the Second Death: *For*   *Apoc.*20.13,
after Death, and the Grave shall have delivered up the dead which were in   14.
them, and every man be judged according to his works; Death and the Grave
shall also be cast into the Lake of Fire. This is the Second Death. Whereby
it is evident, that there is to bee a Second Death of every one that shall
bee condemned at the day of Judgement, after which hee shall die no
more.

The joyes of Life Eternall, are in Scripture comprehended all   *The Joyes of*
under the name of SALVATION, or *being saved.* To be saved, is to be   *Life Eternall,*
secured, either respectively, against speciall Evills, or absolutely,   *and*
                                                                          Salvation the
against all Evill, comprehending Want, Sicknesse, and Death it self.   *same thing.*
And because man was created in a condition Immortall, not subject to   *Salvation*
corruption, and consequently to nothing that tendeth to the dissolu-   *from Sin,*
                                                                          and from
                                                                          Misery, all
[1] '25 Ornaments' and 'Bear' editions read: as long as the World stands;   *one.*
[2] '25 Ornaments' and 'Bear' editions read: as long as the World lasts,

tion of his nature; and fell from that happinesse by the sin of Adam; it followeth, that to be *saved* from Sin, is to be saved from all the Evill, and Calamities that Sinne hath brought upon us. And therefore in the Holy Scripture, Remission of Sinne, and Salvation from Death and Misery, is the same thing, as it appears by the words of our Saviour, who having cured a man sick of the Palsey, by saying, (*Mat*.9.2.) *Son be of good cheer, thy Sins be forgiven thee*; and knowing that the Scribes took for blasphemy, that a man should pretend to forgive Sins, asked them (v.5.) *whether it were easier to say, Thy Sinnes be forgiven thee, or, Arise and walk*; signifying thereby, that it was all one, as to the saving of the sick, to say, *Thy Sins are forgiven*, and *Arise and walk*; and that he used that form of speech, onely to shew he had power to forgive Sins. And it is besides evident in reason, that since Death and Misery, were the punishments of Sin, the discharge of Sinne, must also be a discharge of Death and Misery; that is to say, Salvation absolute, such as the faithfull are to enjoy after the day of Judgment, by the power, and favour of Jesus Christ, who for that cause is called our SAVIOUR.

Concerning Particular Salvations, such as are understood, 1 *Sam*.14.39. *as the Lord liveth that saveth Israel*, that is, from their temporary enemies, and 2 *Sam*.22.4. *Thou art my Saviour, thou savest me from violence*; and 2 *Kings* 13.5. *God gave the Israelites a Saviour, and so they were delivered from the hand of the Assyrians*, and the like, I need say nothing; there being neither difficulty, nor interest, to corrupt the interpretation of texts of that kind.

[246]

The Place of Eternall Salvation.

But concerning the Generall Salvation, because it must be in the Kingdome of Heaven, there is great difficulty concerning the Place. On one side, by *Kingdome* (which is an estate ordained by men for their perpetuall security against enemies, and want) it seemeth that this Salvation should be on Earth. For by Salvation is set forth unto us, a glorious Reign of our King, by Conquest; not a safety by Escape: and therefore there where we look for Salvation, we must look also for Triumph; and before Triumph, for Victory; and before Victory, for Battell; which cannot well be supposed, shall be in Heaven. But how good soever this reason may be, I will not trust to it, without very evident places of Scripture. The state of Salvation is described at large, *Isaiah* 33. ver.20,21,22,23,24.

Look upon Zion, the City of our solemnities; thine eyes shall see Jerusalem a quiet habitation, a tabernacle that shall not be taken down; not one of the stakes thereof shall ever be removed, neither shall any of the cords thereof be broken.

But there the glorious Lord will be unto us a place of broad rivers, and streams; wherein shall goe no Gally with oares; neither shall gallant ship passe thereby.

For the Lord is our Judge, the Lord is our Lawgiver, the Lord is our King, he will save us.

Thy tacklings are loosed; they could not well strengthen their mast; they could not spread the sail: then is the prey of a great spoil divided; the lame take the prey.

And the Inhabitant shall not say, I am sicke; the people that shall dwell therein shall be forgiven their Iniquity.

In which words wee have the place from whence Salvation is to proceed, *Jerusalem, a quiet habitation*; the Eternity of it, *a tabernacle that shall not be taken down, &c.* The Saviour of it, *the Lord, their Judge, their Lawgiver, their King, he will save us*; the Salvation, *the Lord shall be to them as a broad mote of swift waters, &c.* the condition of their Enemies, *their tacklings are loose, their masts weak, the lame shal take the spoil of them.* The condition of the Saved, *The Inhabitant shal not say, I am sick*: And lastly, all this is comprehended in Forgivenesse of sin, *The people that dwell therein shall be forgiven their iniquity.* By which It is evident, that Salvation shall be on Earth, then, when God shall reign, (at the coming again of Christ) in Jerusalem; and from Jerusalem shall proceed the Salvation of the Gentiles that shall be received into Gods Kingdome: as is also more expressely declared by the same Prophet, Chap.65.20,21. *And they* (that is, the Gentiles who had any Jew in bondage) *shall bring all your brethren, for an offering to the Lord, out of all nations, upon horses, and in charets, and in litters, and upon mules, and upon swift beasts, to my holy mountain, Jerusalem, saith the Lord, as the Children of Israel bring an offering in a clean vessell into the House of the Lord. And I will also take of them for Priests and for Levites, saith the Lord*: Whereby it is manifest, that the chief seat of Gods Kingdome (which is the Place, from whence the Salvation of us that were Gentiles, shall [247] proceed) shall be Jerusalem: And the same is also confirmed by our Saviour, in his discourse with the woman of Samaria, concerning the place of Gods worship; to whom he saith, *John* 4.22. that the Samaritans worshipped they knew not what, but the Jews worship what they knew, *For Salvation is of the Jews* (*ex Judaeis*, that is, begins at the Jews): as if he should say, you worship God, but know not by whom he wil save you, as we doe, that know it shall be by one of the tribe of Judah, a Jew, not a Samaritan. And therefore also the woman not impertinently answered him again, *We know the Messias shall come.* So that which our Saviour saith, *Salvation is from the Jews*, is the same that *St. Paul*[1] sayes (*Rom.* 1.16,17.) *The Gospel is the power of God to Salvation to every one that beleeveth: To the Jew first, and also to the Greek. For therein is the righteousnesse of God revealed from faith to faith*; from the faith of the Jew, to the faith of the Gentile. In the like sense the Prophet *Joel* describing the day of Judgment, (chap. 2.30,31.) that God would *shew wonders in heaven, and in earth, bloud, and fire, and pillars of smoak. The Sun should be turned to darknesse, and the Moon into bloud, before the great and terrible day of the Lord come*, he addeth verse 32. *and it shall come to passe, that whosoever shall call upon the name of the Lord, shall be saved. For in Mount Zion, and in Jerusalem shall be Salvation.* And *Obadiah* verse 17. saith the same, *Upon Mount Zion shall be Deliverance; and there shall be holinesse, and the house of Jacob shall possesse their possessions*, that is, the possessions of the *Heathen*, which *possessions* he expresseth more particularly in the following verses, by the *mount of Esau*, the *Land of the Philistines*, the *fields of Ephraim*, of *Samaria, Gilead*, and the *Cities of the South*, and concludes with these words, *the Kingdom shall be the Lords.* All these places are for Salvation, and the Kingdome of God (after the day of Judgement) upon Earth. On the other side, I have not found any text that can probably be drawn, to prove any Ascension of the Saints into Heaven; that is to say, into any *Coelum Empyreum*, or other aetheriall Region; saving that it is called the Kingdome of Heaven: which name it may have, because God, that was King of the Jews, governed them by his commands, sent to Moses by Angels from Heaven; and after their revolt, sent his Son from Heaven, to reduce them to their obedience; and shall send him thence again, to rule both them, and all other faithfull men, from the day of Judgment, Everlastingly: or from that, that the Throne of this our Great King is in Heaven; whereas the Earth is but his Footstoole. But that the Subjects of God should have any place as high as his Throne, or higher than his Footstoole, it seemeth not sutable to the dignity of a King, nor can I find any evident text for it in holy Scripture.

[1] *Syn.*: Paul

From this that hath been said of the Kingdom of God, and of Salvation, it is not hard to interpret what is meant by the WORLD TO COME. There are three worlds mentioned in Scripture, the *Old World*, the *Present World*, and the *World to come*. Of the first, St. Peter 2 *Pet*.2.5. speaks, *If God spared not the old World, but saved Noah the eighth person, a Preacher of righteousnesse, bringing the flood upon the world of the* [248] *ungodly, &c.* So the *first World*, was from Adam to the generall Flood. Of the present World, our Saviour speaks (*Iohn* 18.36.) *My Kingdome is not of this. World.* For he came onely to teach men the way of Salvation, and to renew the Kingdome of his Father, by his doctrine. Of the World to come, St. Peter speaks, *Neverthelesse we according to* 2 *Pet*.3.13. *his promise look for new Heavens, and a new Earth.* This is that WORLD, wherein Christ coming down from Heaven, in the clouds, with great power, and glory, shall send his Angels, and shall gather together his elect, from the four winds, and from the uttermost parts of the Earth, and thence forth reign over them, (under his Father) Everlastingly.

Salvation of a sinner, supposeth a precedent REDEMPTION; for he   *Redemption.* that is once guilty of Sin, is obnoxious to the Penalty of the same; and must pay (or some other for him) such Ransome, as he that is offended, and has him in his power, shall require. And seeing the person offended, is Almighty God, in whose power are all things; such Ransome is to be paid before Salvation can be acquired, as God hath been pleased to require. By this Ransome, is not intended a satisfaction for Sin, equivalent to the Offence; which no sinner for himselfe, nor righteous man can ever be able to make for another: The dammage a man does to another, he may make amends for by restitution, or recompence, but sin cannot be taken away by recompence; for that were to make the liberty to sin, a thing vendible. But sins may bee pardoned to the repentant, either *gratis*, or upon such penalty, as God is pleased to accept. That which God usually accepted in the Old Testament, was some Sacrifice, or Oblation. To forgive sin is not an act of Injustice, though the punishment have been threatned. Even amongst men, though the promise of Good, bind the *promisers;*[1] yet threats, that is to say, promises of Evill, bind them not; much lesse shall they bind God, who is infinitely more mercifull then men. Our Saviour Christ therefore to *Redeem* us, did not in that sense satisfie for the Sins of men, as that his Death, of its own vertue,

---

[1] *Syn.*: promiser;

could make it unjust in God to punish sinners with Eternall death; but did make that Sacrifice, and Oblation of himself, at his first coming, which God was pleased to require, for the Salvation at his second coming, of such as in the mean time should repent, and beleeve in him. And though this act of our *Redemption*, be not alwaies in Scripture called a *Sacrifice*, and *Oblation*, but sometimes a *Price*; yet by *Price* we are not to understand any thing, by the value whereof, he could claim right to a pardon for us, from his offended Father; but that Price which God the Father was pleased in mercy to demand.

CHAP. XXXIX.

Of the signification in Scripture of the word CHURCH.

Church the Lords house.

The word *Church*, (*Ecclesia*) signifieth in the Books of Holy Scripture divers things. Sometimes (though not often) it is taken for *Gods House*, that is to say, for a Temple, wherein Christians assemble to perform holy duties publiquely; as, 1 *Cor.* 14. ver. 34. *Let your women keep silence in the Churches*: but this is Metaphorically put, for the Congregation there assembled; and hath been since used for the Edifice it self, to distinguish between the Temples of Christians, and Idolaters. The Temple of Jerusalem was *Gods house*, and the House of Prayer; and so is any Edifice dedicated by Christians to the worship of Christ, *Christs house*: and therefore the Greek Fathers call it Κυριακὴ, *The Lords house*; and thence, in our language it came to be called *Kyrke*, and *Church*.

Ecclesia properly what.

Church (when not taken for a House) signifieth the same that *Ecclesia* signified in the Grecian Common-wealths; that is to say, a Congregation, or an Assembly of Citizens, called forth, to hear the Magistrate speak unto them; and which in the Common-wealth of Rome was called *Concio*, as he that spake was called *Ecclesiastes*, and *Concionator*. And when they were called forth by lawfull Authority, it *Acts* 19. 39. was *Ecclesia legitima*, a *Lawfull Church*, ἔννομος Ἐκκλησία. But when they were excited by tumultuous, and seditious clamor, then it was a confused Church, Ἐκκλησία συγκεχυμένη.

It is taken also sometimes for the men that have right to be of the Congregation, though not actually assembled; that is to say, for the whole multitude of Christian men, how far soever they be dispersed: as (*Act.* 8.3.) where it is said, that *Saul made havock of the Church*: And in this sense is *Christ* said to be Head of the Church. And sometimes for a certain part of Christians, as (*Col.* 4. 15.) *Salute the Church that is in his house*. Sometimes also for the Elect onely; as (*Ephes.* 5.27.) *A Glorious Church, without spot, or wrinkle, holy, and without blemish*; which is meant of the *Church triumphant*, or, *Church to come*. Sometimes, for a Congregation assembled, of professors of Christianity, whether their profession be true, or counterfeit, as it is understood, *Mat.* 18. 17. where it is said, *Tell it to the Church, and if hee neglect to hear the Church, let him be to thee as a Gentile, or Publican.*

And in this last sense only it is that the *Church* can be taken for one Person; that is to say, that is can be said to have power to will, to pronounce, to command, to be obeyed, to make laws, or to doe any other action whatsoever; For without authority from a lawfull Congregation, whatsoever act be done in a concourse of people, it is the particular act of every one of those that were present, and gave their aid to the performance of it; and not the act of them all in grosse, as of one body; much lesse the act of them that were absent, or that being present, were not willing it should be done. According to this sense, I define a CHURCH to be, *A company of men professing Christian Religion, united in the person of one Soveraign*; *at whose command they ought to assemble, and without whose authority they ought not to assemble.* And because in all Common-wealths, that Assembly, which is without warrant from the Civil Soveraign, is unlawful; that Church also, which is assembled in any Common-wealth, that hath forbidden them to assemble, is an unlawful Assembly.

It followeth also, that there is on Earth, no such universall Church, as all Christians are bound to obey; because there is no power on Earth, to which all other Common-wealths are subject: There are Christians, in the Dominions of severall Princes and States; but every one of them is subject to that Common-wealth, whereof he is himself a member; and consequently, cannot be subject to the commands of any other Person. And therefore a Church, such a one as is capable to Command, to Judge, Absolve, Condemn, or do any other act, is the same thing with a Civil Common-wealth, consisting of Christian men; and is called a *Civill State*, for that the subjects of it are *Men*; and a

In what sense the Church is one Person.

[248]

Church defined.

A Christian Common-wealth, and a Church all one.

321

Church, for that the subjects thereof are *Christians*. *Temporall* and *Spirituall* Government, are but two words brought into the world, to make men see double, and mistake their *Lawfull Soveraign*. It is true, that the bodies of the faithfull, after the Resurrection, shall be not onely Spirituall, but Eternall: but in this life they are grosse, and corruptible. There is therefore no other Government in this life, neither of State, nor Religion, but Temporall; nor teaching of any doctrine, lawfull to any Subject, which the Governour both of the State, and of the Religion, forbiddeth to be taught: And that Governor must be one; or else there must needs follow Faction, and Civil war in the Common-wealth, between the *Church* and *State*; between *Spiritualists*, and *Temporalists*; between the *Sword of Justice*, and the *Shield of Faith*; and (which is more) in every Christian mans own brest, between the *Christian*, and the *Man*. The Doctors of the Church, are called Pastors; so also are Civill Soveraignes: But if Pastors be not subordinate one to another, so as that there may bee one chief Pastor, men will be taught contrary Doctrines, whereof both may be, and one must be false. Who that one chief Pastor is, according to the law of Nature, hath been already shewn; namely, that it is the Civill Soveraign: And to whom the Scripture hath assigned that Office, we shall see in the Chapters following.

[249]

CHAP. XL.

Of the RIGHTS *of the Kingdome of God,* *in* Abraham, Moses, *the* High Priests; *and the* Kings of Judah.

The Soveraign Rights of Abraham.

The Father of the Faithfull, and first in the Kingdome of God by Covenant, was *Abraham*. For with him was the Covenant first made; wherein he obliged himself, and his seed after him, to acknowledge and obey the commands of God; not onely such, as he could take notice of, (as Morall Laws,) by the light of Nature; but also such, as God should in speciall manner deliver to him by Dreams, and

Visions. For as to the Morall law, they were already obliged, and needed not have been contracted withall, by promise of the Land of Canaan. Nor was there any Contract, that could adde to, or strengthen the Obligation, by which both they, and all men else were bound naturally to obey God Almighty: And therefore the Covenant which Abraham made with God, was to take for the Commandement of God, that which in the name of God was commanded him, in a Dream, or Vision; and to deliver it to his family, and cause them to observe the same.

In this Contract of God with Abraham, wee may observe three points of important consequence in the government of Gods people. First, that at the making of this Covenant, God spake onely to Abraham; and therefore contracted not with any of his family, or seed, otherwise then as their wills (which make the essence of all Covenants) were before the Contract involved in the will of Abraham; who was therefore supposed to have had a lawfull power, to make them perform all that he covenanted for them. According whereunto (*Gen.* 18. 18, 19.) God saith, *All the Nations of the Earth shall be blessed in him, For I know him that he will command his children and his houshold after him, and they shall keep the way of the Lord.* From whence may be concluded this first point, that they to whom God hath not spoken immediately, are to receive the positive commandements of God, from their Soveraign; as the family and seed of Abraham did from Abraham their Father, and Lord, and Civill Soveraign. And consequently in every Common-wealth, they who have no supernaturall Revelation to the contrary, ought to obey the laws of their own Soveraign, in the externall acts and profession of Religion. As for the inward *thought*, and *beleef* of men, which humane Governours can take no notice of, (for God onely knoweth the heart) they are not voluntary, nor the effect of the laws, but of the unrevealed will, and of the power of God; and consequently fall not under obligation.

Abraham had the sole power of ordering the Religion of his own people

[250]

From whence proceedeth another point, that it was not unlawfull for Abraham, when any of his Subjects should pretend Private Vision, or Spirit, or other Revelation from God, for the countenancing of any doctrine which Abraham should forbid, or when they followed, or adhered to any such pretender, to punish them; and consequently that it is lawfull now for the Soveraign to punish any man that shall oppose his Private Spirit against the Laws: For hee hath the same place in the Common-wealth, that Abraham had in his own Family.

No pretence of Private Spirit against the Religion of Abraham.

Abraham sole Judge, and Interpreter of what God spake. There ariseth also from the same, a third point; that as none but Abraham in his family, so none but the Soveraign in a Christian Common-wealth, can take notice what is, or what is not the Word of God. For God spake onely to Abraham; and it was he onely, that was able to know what God said, and to interpret the same to his family: And therefore also, they that have the place of Abraham in a Common-wealth, are the onely Interpreters of what God hath spoken.

The authority of Moses whereon grounded. The same Covenant was renewed with Isaac; and afterwards with Jacob; but afterwards no more, till the Israelites were freed from the Egyptians, and arrived at the Foot of Mount Sinai: and then it was renewed by Moses (as I have said before, chap. 35.) in such manner, as they became from that time forward the Peculiar Kingdome of God; whose Lieutenant was Moses, for his owne time: and the succession to that office was setled upon Aaron, and his heirs after him, to bee to God a Sacerdotall Kingdome for ever.

By this constitution, a Kingdome is acquired to God. But seeing Moses had no authority to govern the Israelites, as a successor to the right of Abraham, because he could not claim it by inheritance; it appeareth not as yet, that the people were obliged to take him for Gods Lieutenant, longer than they beleeved that God spake unto him. And therefore his authority (notwithstanding the Covenant they made with God) depended yet merely upon the opinion they had of his Sanctity, and of the reality of his Conferences with God, and the verity of his Miracles; which opinion coming to change, they were no more obliged to take any thing for the law of God, which he propounded to them in Gods name. We are therefore to consider, what other ground there was, of their obligation to obey him. For it could not be the commandement of God that could oblige them; because God spake not to them immediately, but by the mediation of Moses himself: And our Saviour saith of himself, *If I bear witnesse of my self, my witnesse is not true*; much lesse if Moses bear witnesse of himselfe, (especially in a claim of Kingly power over Gods people) ought his testimony to be received. His authority therefore, as the authority of all other Princes, must be grounded on the Consent of the People, and their Promise to obey him. And so it was: For *the people (Exod. 20.18.) when they saw the Thunderings, and the Lightnings, and the noyse of the Trumpet, and the mountaine smoaking, removed, and stood a far off. And they said unto Moses, speak thou with us, and we will hear, but let not God speak with us lest we die.* Here was their promise of obedience, and

John 5.31.

[251]

324

by this it was they obliged themselves to obey whatsoever he should deliver unto them for the Commandement of God.

And notwithstanding the Covenant constituteth a Sacerdotall Kingdome, that is to say, a Kingdome hereditary to Aaron; yet that is to be understood of the succession, after Moses should bee dead. For whosoever ordereth, and establisheth the Policy, as first founder of a Common-wealth (be it Monarchy, Aristocracy, or Democracy) must needs have Soveraign Power over the people all the while he is doing of it. And that Moses had that power all his own time, is evidently affirmed in the Scripture. First, in the text last before cited, because the people promised obedience, not to Aaron but to him. Secondly, (*Exod.* 24.1,2.) *And God said unto Moses, Come up unto the Lord, thou, and Aaron, Nadab and Abihu, and seventy of the Elders of Israel. And Moses alone shall come neer the Lord, but they shall not come nigh, neither shall the people goe up with him.* By which it is plain, that Moses who was alone called up to God, (and not Aaron, nor the other Priests, nor the Seventy Elders, nor the People who were forbidden to come up) was alone he, that represented to the Israelites the Person of God; that is to say, was their sole Soveraign under God. And though afterwards it be said (verse 9.) *Then went up Moses, and Aaron, Nadab, and Abihu, and seventy of the Elders of Israel, and they saw the God of Israel, and there was under his feet, as it were a paved work of a saphire stone, & c.* yet this was not till after Moses had been with God before, and had brought to the people the words which God had said to him. He onely went for the businesse of the people; the others, as the Nobles of his retinue, were admitted for honour to that speciall grace, which was not allowed to the people; which was, (as in the verse after appeareth) to see God and live. *God laid not his hand upon them, they saw God, and did eat and drink* (that is, did live), but did not carry any commandement from him to the people. Again, it is every where said, *The Lord spake unto Moses,* as in all other occasions of Government; so also in the ordering of the Ceremonies of Religion, contained in the 25, 26, 27, 28, 29, 30, and 31 Chapters of *Exodus,* and throughout *Leviticus:* to Aaron seldome. The Calfe that Aaron made, Moses threw into the fire. Lastly, the question of the Authority of Aaron, by occasion of his and Miriams mutiny against Moses, was (*Numbers* 12.) judged by God himself for Moses. So also in the question between Moses, and the People, who had the Right of Governing the People, when Corah, Dathan, and Abiram, and two hundred and fifty Princes

Moses was (under God) Soveraign of the Jews, all his own time, though Aaron had the Priesthood.

of the Assembly *gathered themselves together* (Numb. 16.3.) *against Moses, and against Aaron, and said unto them, Ye take too much upon you, seeing all the congregation are Holy, every one of them, and the Lord is amongst them, why lift you up your selves above the congregation of the Lord?* God caused the Earth to swallow Corah, Dathan, and Abiram with their wives and children alive, and consumed those two hundred and fifty Princes with fire. Therefore neither Aaron, nor the People, nor any Aristocracy of the chief Princes of the People, but Moses alone had next under God the Soveraignty over the Israelites: And that not onely in causes of Civill Policy, but also of Religion: For Moses onely spake with God, and therefore onely could tell the People, what it was that God required at their hands. No man upon pain of death might be so presumptuous as to approach the Mountain where God talked with Moses. *Thou shalt set bounds* (saith the Lord, Exod. 19.12.) *to the people round about, and say, Take heed to your selves that you goe not up into the Mount, or touch the border of it; whosoever toucheth the Mount shall surely be put to death.* And again (verse 21.) *Goe down, charge the people, lest they break through unto the Lord to gaze.* Out of which we may conclude, that whosoever in a Christian Common-wealth holdeth the place of Moses, is the sole Messenger of God, and Interpreter of his Commandements. And according hereunto, no man ought in the interpretation of the Scripture to proceed further then the bounds which are set by their severall Soveraigns. For the Scriptures since God now speaketh in them, are the Mount Sinai; the bounds whereof are the Laws of them that represent Gods Person on Earth. To look upon them, and therein to behold the wondrous works of God, and learn to fear him is allowed; but to interpret them; that is, to pry into what God saith to him whom he appointeth to govern under him, and make themselves Judges whether he govern as God commandeth him, or not, is to transgresse the bounds God hath set us, and to gaze upon God irreverently.

All spirits were subordinate to the spirit of Moses. There was no Prophet in the time of Moses, nor pretender to the Spirit of God, but such as Moses had approved, and Authorized. For there were in his time but Seventy men, that are said to Prophecy by the Spirit of God, and these were all of Moses his election; concerning whom God said to Moses (*Numb.* 11.16.) *Gather to mee Seventy of the Elders of Israel, whom thou knowest to be the Elders of the People.* To these God imparted his Spirit; but it was not a different Spirit from that of Moses; for it is said (verse 25.) *God came down in a cloud, and* took of the Spirit that was upon Moses, and gave it to the Seventy Elders. But as I have shewn before (chap. 36.) by *Spirit*, is understood the *Mind*; so that the sense of the place is no other than this, that God endued them with a mind conformable, and subordinate to that of Moses, that they might Prophecy, that is to say, speak to the people in Gods name, in such manner, as to set forward (as Ministers of Moses, and by his authority) such doctrine as was agreeable to Moses his doctrine. For they were but Ministers; and when two of them Prophecyed in the Camp, it was thought a new and unlawfull thing; and as it is in the 27. and 28. verses of the same Chapter, they were accused of it, and Joshua advised Moses to forbid them, as not knowing that it was by Moses his Spirit that they Prophecyed. By which it is manifest, that no Subject ought to pretend to Prophecy, or to the Spirit, in opposition to the doctrine established by him, whom God hath set in the place of Moses. [253]

Aaron being dead, and after him also Moses, the Kingdome, as being a Sacerdotall Kingdome, descended by vertue of the Covenant, to Aarons Son, Eleazar the High Priest: And God declared him (next under himself) for Soveraign, at the same time that he appointed Joshua for the Generall of their Army. For thus God saith expressely (*Numb.* 27.21.) concerning Joshua; *He shall stand before Eleazar the Priest, who shall ask counsell for him, before the Lord, at his word shall they goe out, and at his word they shall come in, both he, and all the Children of Israel with him*: Therefore the Supreme Power of making War and Peace, was in the Priest. The Supreme Power of Judicature belonged also to the High Priest: For the Book of the Law was in their keeping, and the Priests and Levites onely, were the subordinate Judges in causes Civill, as appears in *Deut.* 17.8,9,10. And for the manner of Gods worship, there was never doubt made, but that the High Priest till the time of Saul, had the Supreme Authority. Therefore the Civill and Ecclesiasticall Power were both joined together in one and the same person, the High Priest; and ought to bee so, in whosoever governeth by Divine Right; that is, by Authority immediate from God.

After Moses the Soveraignty was in the High Priest.

After the death of Joshua, till the time of Saul, the time between is noted frequently in the Book of *Judges by this,*[1] *that there was in those dayes no King in Israel*; and sometimes with this addition, that *every man did that which was right in his own eyes*. By which is to bee

Of the Soveraign power between the time of Joshua and of Saul.

[1] Syn.: Judges,

327

understood, that where it is said, *there was no King*, is meant, *there was no Soveraign Power* in Israel. And so it was, if we consider the Act, and Exercise of such power. For after the death of Joshua, & Eleazar, *there arose another generation* (Judges 2.10.) *that knew not the Lord, nor the works which he had done for Israel, but did evill in the sight of the Lord, and served Baalim.* And the Jews had that quality which St. Paul noteth, *to look for a sign*, not onely before they would submit themselves to the government of Moses, but also after they had obliged themselves by their submission. Whereas Signs, and Miracles had for End to procure Faith, not to keep men from violating it, when they have once given it; for to that men are obliged by the law of Nature. But if we consider not the Exercise, but the Right of Governing, the Soveraign power was still in the High Priest. Therefore whatsoever obedience was yeelded to any of the Judges (who were men chosen by God extraordinarily, to save his rebellious subjects out of the hands of the enemy,) it cannot bee drawn into argument against the Right the High Priest had to the Soveraign Power, in all matters, both of Policy and Religion. And neither the Judges, nor Samuel himselfe had an ordinary, but extraordinary calling to the Government; and were obeyed by the Israelites, not out of duty, but out of reverence to their favour with God, appearing in their wisdome, courage, or felicity. Hitherto therefore the Right of Regulating both the Policy, and the Religion, were inseparable.

[254]

Of the Rights of the Kings of Israel.

To the Judges, succeeded Kings: And whereas before, all authority, both in Religion, and Policy, was in the High Priest; so now it was all in the King. For the Soveraignty over the people, which was before, not onely by vertue of the Divine Power, but also by a particular pact of the Israelites in God, and next under him, in the High Priest, as his Vicegerent on earth, was cast off by the People, with the consent of God himselfe. For when they said to Samuel (1 *Sam.* 8. 5.) *make us a King to judge us, like all the Nations*, they signified that they would no more bee governed by the commands that should bee laid upon them by the Priest, in the name of God; but by one that should command them in the same manner that all other nations were commanded; and consequently in deposing the High Priest of Royall authority, they deposed that peculiar Government of God. And yet God consented to it, saying to Samuel (verse 7.) *Hearken unto the voice of the People, in all that they shall say unto thee; for they have not rejected thee, but they have rejected mee, that I should not reign over them.* Having therefore rejected God, in whose Right the Priests governed, there was no authority left to the Priests, but such as the King was pleased to allow them, which was more, or lesse, according as the Kings were good, or evill. And for the Government of Civill affaires, it is manifest, it was all in the hands of the King. For in the same Chapter, verse 20. They say they will be like all the Nations; that their King shall be their Judge, and goe before them, and fight their battells; that is, he shall have the whole authority, both in Peace and War. In which is contained also the ordering of Religion: for there was no other Word of God in that time, by which to regulate Religion, but the Law of Moses, which was their Civill Law. Besides, we read (1 *Kings* 2.27.) that Solomon *thrust out Abiathar from being Priest before the Lord*: He had therefore authority over the High Priest, as over any other Subject; which is a great mark of Supremacy in Religion. And we read also (1 *Kings* 8.) that hee dedicated the Temple; that he blessed the People; and that he himselfe in person made that excellent prayer, used in the Consecrations of all Churches, and houses of Prayer; which is another great mark of Supremacy in Religion. Again, we read (2 *Kings* 22.) that when there was question concerning the Book of the Law found in the Temple, the same was not decided by the High Priest, but Josiah sent both him, and others to enquire concerning it, of Hulda, the Prophetesse; which is another mark of the Supremacy in Religion. Lastly, wee read (1 *Chron.* 26.30.) that David made Hashabiah and his brethren, Hebronites, Officers of Israel among them Westward, *in all businesse of the Lord, and in the service of the King.* Likewise (verse 32.) that hee made other Hebronites, *rulers over the Reubenites, the Gadites, and the halfe tribe of Manasseh* (these were the rest of Israel that dwelt beyond Jordan) *for every matter pertaining to God, and affairs of the King.* Is not this full Power, both *temporall* and *spirituall*, as they call it, that would divide it? To conclude; from the first institution of Gods Kingdome, to the Captivity, the Supremacy of Religion, was in the same hand with that of the Civill Soveraignty; and the Priests office after the election of Saul, was not Magisteriall, but Ministeriall.

Nothwithstanding the government both in Policy and Religion, were joined, first in the High Priests, and afterwards in the Kings, so far forth as concerned the Right; yet it appeareth by the same Holy History, that the people understood it not; but there being amongst them a great part, and probably the greatest part, that no longer than

[255]

The practice of Supremacy in Religion, was not in the time of the Kings, according to the right thereof.

they saw great miracles, or (which is equivalent to a miracle) great abilities, or great felicity in the enterprises of their Governours, gave sufficient credit, either to the fame of Moses, or to the Colloquies between God and the Priests; they took occasion as oft as their Governours displeased them, by blaming sometimes the Policy, sometimes the Religion, to change the Government, or revolt from their Obedience at their pleasure: And from thence proceeded from time to time the civill troubles, divisions, and calamities of the Nation. As for example, after the death of Eleazar and Joshua, the next generation which had not seen the wonders of God, but were left to their own weak reason, not knowing themselves obliged by the Covenant of a Sacerdotall Kingdome, regarded no more the Commandement of the Priest, nor any law of Moses, but did every man that which was right in his own eyes; and obeyed in Civill affairs, such men, as from time to time they thought able to deliver them from the neighbour Nations that oppressed them; and consulted not with God (as they ought to doe), but with such men, or women, as they guessed to bee Prophets by their Praedictions of things to come; and though they had an Idol in their Chappel, yet if they had a Levite for their Chaplain, they made account they worshipped the God of Israel.

And afterwards when they demanded a King, after the manner of the nations; yet it was not with a design to depart from the worship of God their King; but despairing of the justice of the sons of Samuel, they would have a King to judg them in Civill actions; but not that they would allow their King to change the Religion which they thought was recommended to them by Moses. So that they alwaies kept in store a pretext, either of Justice, or Religion, to discharge themselves of their obedience, whensoever they had hope to prevaile. Samuel was displeased with the people, for that they desired a King, (for God was their King already, and Samuel had but an authority under him); yet did Samuel, when Saul observed not his counsell, in destroying Agag as God had commanded, anoint another King, namely, David, to take the succession from his heirs. Rehoboam was no Idolater; but when the people thought him an Oppressor; that Civil pretence carried from him ten Tribes to Jeroboam an Idolater. And generally through the whole History of the Kings, as well of Judah, as of Israel, there were Prophets that alwaies controlled the Kings, for transgressing the Religion; and sometimes also for Errours of State; as Jehosaphat was reproved by the Prophet Jehu, for aiding

2 Chro. 19.2.

the King of Israel against the Syrians; and Hezekiah, by Isaiah, for [256]
shewing his treasures to the Ambassadors of Babylon. By all which it
appeareth, that though the power both of State and Religion were in
the Kings; yet none of them were uncontrolled in the use of it, but
such as were gracious for their own naturall abilities, or felicities. So
that from the practise of those times, there can no argument be
drawn, that the Right of Supremacy in Religion was not in the Kings,
unlesse we place it in the Prophets; and conclude, that because
Hezekiah praying to the Lord before the Cherubins, was not
answered from thence, nor then, but afterwards by the Prophet
Isaiah, therefore Isaiah was supreme Head of the Church; or because
Josiah consulted Hulda the Prophetesse, concerning the Book of the
Law, that therefore neither he, nor the High Priest, but Hulda the
Prophetesse had the Supreme authority in matter of Religion; which I
thinke is not the opinion of any Doctor.

During the Captivity, the Jews had no Common-wealth at all: And
after their return, though they renewed their Covenant with God, yet
there was no promise made of obedience, neither to Esdras, nor to
any other: And presently after they became subjects to the Greeks
(from whose Customes, and Daemonology, and from the doctrine of
the Cabalists, their Religion became much corrupted): In such sort as
nothing can be gathered from their confusion, both in State and
Religion, concerning the Supremacy in either. And therefore so far
forth as concerneth the Old Testament, we may conclude, that
whosoever had the Soveraignty of the Common-wealth amongst the
Jews, the same had also the Supreme Authority in matter of Gods
externall worship; and represented Gods Person; that is the person of
God the Father; though he were not called by the name of Father, till
such time as he sent into the world his Son Jesus Christ, to redeem
mankind from their sins, and bring them into his Everlasting Kingdome, to be saved for evermore. Of which we are to speak in the
Chapter following.

*After the
Captivity the
Jews had no
settled
Common-
wealth.*

331

[261]

CHAP. XLI.
Of the OFFICE *of our* BLESSED SAVIOUR.

Three parts of the Office of Christ.

We find in Holy Scripture three parts of the *Office* of the *Messiah*: The first of a *Redeemer*, or *Saviour*. The second of a *Pastor, Counsellor,* or *Teacher*, that is, of a Prophet sent from God, to convert such as God hath elected to Salvation: The third of a *King*, an *eternall King*, but under his Father, as Moses and the High Priests were in their severall times. And to these three parts are correspondent three times. For our Redemption he *wrought it*[1] at his first coming, by the Sacrifice, wherein he offered up himself for our sinnes upon the Crosse: our Conversion he wrought partly then in his own Person; and partly worketh now by his Ministers; and will continue to work till his coming again. And after his coming again, shall begin that his glorious *Reign*[2] over his elect, which is to last eternally.

His Office as a Redeemer.

To the *Office* of a *Redeemer*, that is, of one that payeth the Ransome of Sin, (which Ransome is Death,) it appertaineth, that he was Sacrificed, and thereby bare upon his own head, and carryed away from us our iniquities, in such sort as God had required. Not that the death of one man, though without sinne, can satisfie for the offences of all men, in the rigour of Justice, but in the Mercy of God, that ordained such Sacrifices for sin, as he was pleased in his mercy to accept. In the Old Law (as we may read, *Leviticus* the 16.) the Lord required, that there should every year once, bee made an Atonement for the Sins of all Israel, both Priests, and others; for the doing whereof, Aaron alone was to sacrifice for himself and the Priests a young Bullock; and for the rest of the people, he was to receive from them two young Goates, of which he was to *sacrifice* one; but as for the other, which was the *Scape Goat*, he was to lay his hands on the head thereof, and by a confession of the iniquities of the people, to lay them all on that head, and then by some opportune man, to cause the Goat to be led into the

---

[1] *Syn.*: wrought   [2] *Syn.*: Reign

wildernesse, and there to *escape*, and carry away with him the iniquities of the people. As the Sacrifice of the one Goat was a sufficient (because an acceptable) price for the Ransome of all Israel; so the death of the Messiah, is a sufficient price, for the Sins of all mankind, because there was no more required. Our Saviour Christs sufferings seem to be here figured, as cleerly, as in the oblation of Isaac, or in any other type of him in the Old Testament: He was both the sacriced Goat, and the Scape Goat; *Hee was oppressed, and he was afflicted* (Esay 53. 7.); *he opened not his mouth; he is brought as a lamb to the slaughter, and as a sheep is dumbe before the shearer, so opened he not his* [262] *mouth:* Here he is the *sacrificed Goat. He hath born our Griefs*, (ver.4.) *and carried our sorrows:* And again, (ver. 6.) *the Lord hath laid upon him the iniquities of us all:* And so he is the *Scape Goat. He was cut off from the land of the living* (ver. 8.) *for the transgression of my People:* There again he is the *sacrificed Goat.* And again, (ver. 11.) *he shall bear their sins:* Hee is the *Scape Goat.* Thus is the Lamb of God equivalent to both those Goates; sacrificed, in that he dyed; and escaping, in his Resurrection; being raised opportunely by his Father, and removed from the habitation of men in his Ascension.

For as much therefore, as he that *redeemeth*, hath no title to the thing *redeemed*, before *the Redemption*, and Ransome paid; and this Ransome was the Death of the Redeemer; it is manifest, that our Saviour (as man) was not King of those that he Redeemed, before hee suffered death; that is, during that time hee conversed bodily on the Earth. I say, he was not then King in present, by vertue of the Pact, which the faithfull make with him in Baptisme: Neverthelesse, by the renewing of their Pact with God in Baptisme, they were obliged to obey him for King, (under his Father) whensoever he should be pleased to take the Kingdome upon him. According whereunto, our Saviour himself expressely saith, *(John* 18. 36.) *My Kingdome is not of this world.* Now seeing the Scripture maketh mention but of two *worlds since the Floud;*[1] this that is now, and shall remain to the day of Judgment, (which is therefore also called, *the last day;)* and that which shall bee after the day of Judgement, when there shall bee a new Heaven, and a new Earth; the Kingdome of Christ is not to begin till the generall Resurrection. And that is it which our Saviour saith, (*Mat.* 16. 27.) *The Son of man shall come in the glory of his Father, with*

Christs Kingdome not of this world.

---

[1] *Syn.:* worlds;

his Angels; and then he shall reward every man according to his works. To reward every man according to his works, is to execute the Office of a King; and this is not to be till he come in the glory of his Father, with his Angells. When our Saviour saith, (*Mat.* 23. 2.) *The Scribes and Pharisees sit in Moses seat; All therefore whatsoever they bid you doe, that observe and doe;* hee declareth plainly, that hee ascribeth Kingly Power, for that time, not to himselfe, but to them. And so hee doth also, where he saith, (*Luke* 12. 14.) *Who made mee a Judge, or Divider over you?* And (*John* 12.47.) *I came not to judge the world, but to save the world.* And yet our Saviour came into this world that hee might bee a King, and a Judge in the world to come: For hee was the Messiah, that is, the Christ, that is, the Anointed Priest, and the Soveraign Prophet of God; that is to say, he was to have all the power that was in Moses the Prophet, in the High Priests that succeeded Moses, and in the Kings that succeeded the Priests. And St. *John* saies expressely (chap. 5. ver. 22.) *The Father judgeth no man, but hath committed all judgment to the Son.* And this is not repugnant to that other place, *I*

[263]

came not to judge the world: for this is spoken of the world present, the other of the world to come; as also where it is said, that at the second coming of Christ, (*Mat.* 19. 28.) *Yee that have followed me in the Regeneration, when the Son of man shall sit in the throne of his Glory, yee shall also sit on twelve thrones, judging the twelve tribes of *Israel,* it is manifest his Kingdome was not begun then when he said it.*[1]

The End of Christs comming was to renew the Covenant of the Kingdome of God, and to perswade the Elect to imbrace it, which was the second part of his Office.

If then Christ whilest hee was on Earth, had no Kingdome in this world, to what end was his first coming? It was to restore unto God, by a new Covenant, the Kingdom, which being his by the Old Covenant, had been cut off by the rebellion of the Israelites in the election of Saul. Which to doe, he was to preach unto them, that he was the Messiah, that is, the King promised to them by the Prophets; and to offer himselfe in sacrifice for the sinnes of them that should by faith submit themselves thereto; and in case the nation generally should refuse him, to call to his obedience such as should beleeve in him amongst the Gentiles. So that there are two parts of our Saviours Office during his aboad upon the Earth: One to Proclaim himself the Christ; and another by Teaching, and by working of Miracles, to perswade, and prepare men to live so, as to be worthy of the Immortality Beleevers were to enjoy, at such time as he should come

[1] *Syn.: Israel.*

334

in majesty, to take possession of his Fathers Kingdome. And therefore it is, that the time of his preaching, is often by himself called the *Regeneration*; which is not properly a Kingdome, and thereby a warrant to deny obedience to the Magistrates that then were, (for hee commanded to obey those that sate then in Moses chaire, and to pay tribute to Caesar;) but onely an earnest of the Kingdome of God that was to come, to those to whom God had given the grace to be his disciples, and to beleeve in him; For which cause the Godly are said to bee already in the *Kingdome of Grace*, as naturalized in that heavenly Kingdome.

Hitherto therefore there is nothing done, or taught by Christ, that tendeth to the diminution of the Civill Right of the Jewes, or of Caesar. For as touching the Common-wealth which then was amongst the Jews, both they that bare rule amongst them, and they that were governed, did all expect the Messiah, and Kingdome of God; which they could not have done if their Laws had forbidden him (when he came) to manifest, and declare himself. Seeing therefore he did nothing, but by Preaching, and Miracles go about to prove himselfe to be that Messiah, hee did therein nothing against their laws. The Kingdome hee claimed was to bee in another world: He taught all men to obey in the mean time them that sate in Moses seat: He allowed them to give Caesar his tribute, and refused to take upon himselfe to be a Judg. How then could his words, or actions bee seditious, or tend to the overthrow of their then Civill Government? But God having determined his sacrifice, for the reduction of his elect to their former covenanted obedience, for the means, whereby he would bring the same to effect, made use of their malice, and ingratitude. Nor was it contrary to the laws of Caesar. For though Pilate himself (to gratifie the Jews) delivered him to be crucified; yet before he did so, he pronounced openly, that he found no fault in him: And put for title of his condemnation, not as the Jews required, *that he pretended to bee King*; but simply, *That hee was King of the Jews*; and notwithstanding their clamour, refused to alter it; saying, *What I have written, I have written*.

The preaching of Christ not contrary to the then law of the Jews, nor of Caesar.

[264]

As for the third part of his Office, which was to be *King*, I have already shewn that his Kingdome was not to begin till the Resurrection. But then he shall be King, not onely as God, in which sense he is King already, and ever shall be, of all the Earth, in vertue of his omnipotence; but also peculiarly of his own Elect, by vertue of the

The third part of his Office was to be King (under his Father) of the Elect.

pact they make with him in their Baptisme. And therefore it is, that our Saviour saith (*Mat.* 19. 28.) that his Apostles should sit upon twelve thrones, judging the twelve tribes of Israel, *When the Son of man shall sit in the throne of his glory*: whereby he signified that he should reign then in his humane nature; and (*Mat.* 16.27.) *The Son of man shall come in the glory of his Father, with his Angels, and then he shall reward every man according to his works.* The same we may read, *Marke* 13. 26. and 14.62. and more expressely for the time, *Luke* 22. 29, 30. *I appoint unto you a Kingdome, as my Father hath appointed to mee, that you may eat and drink at my table in my Kingdome, and sit on thrones judging the twelve tribes of Israel.* By which it is manifest, that the Kingdome of Christ appointed to him by his Father, is not to be before the Son of Man shall come in Glory, and make his Apostles Judges of the twelve tribes of Israel. But a man may here ask, seeing there is no marriage in the Kingdome of Heaven, whether men shall then eat, and drink; what eating therefore is meant in this place? This is expounded by our Saviour (*John* 6. 27.) where he saith, *Labour not for the meat which perisheth, but for that meat which endureth unto everlasting life, which the Son of man shall give you.* So that by eating at Christs table, is meant the eating of the Tree of Life; that is to say, the enjoying of Immortality, in the Kingdome of the Son of Man. By which places, and many more, it is evident, that our Saviours Kingdome is to bee exercised by him in his humane nature.

Christs authority in the Kingdome of God subordinate to that of his Father.

Again, he is to be King then, no otherwise than as subordinate, or Vicegerent of God the Father, as Moses was in the wildernesse; and as the High Priests were before the reign of Saul: and as the Kings were after it. For it is one of the Prophecies concerning Christ, that he should be like (in Office) to Moses: *I will raise them up a Prophet* (saith the Lord, *Deut.* 18. 18.) *from amongst their Brethren like unto thee, and will put my words into his mouth*, and this similitude with Moses, is also apparent in the actions of our Saviour himself, whilest he was conversant on Earth. For as Moses chose twelve Princes of the tribes, to govern under him; so did our Saviour choose twelve Apostles, who shall sit on twelve thrones, and judge the twelve tribes of Israel: And as Moses authorized Seventy Elders, to receive the Spirit of God, and to Prophecy to the people, that is, (as I have said before,) to speak unto them in the name of God; so our Saviour also ordained seventy Disciples, to preach his Kingdome, and Salvation to all Nations. And as when a complaint was made to Moses, against those of the Seventy

[265]

336

that prophecyed in the camp of Israel, he justified them in it, as being subservient therein to his government; so also our Saviour, when St. John complained to him of a certain man that cast out Devills in his name, justified him therein, saying, (*Luke* 9.50.) *Forbid him not, for hee that is not against us, is on our part.*

Again, our Saviour resembled Moses in the institution of *Sacraments*, both of *Admission* into the Kingdome of God, and of *Commemoration* of his deliverance of his Elect from their miserable condition. As the Children of Israel had for Sacrament of their Reception into the Kingdome of God, before the time of Moses, the rite of *Circumcision*, which rite having been omitted in the Wildernesse, was again restored as soon as they came into the land of Promise; so also the Jews, before the coming of our Saviour, had a rite of *Baptizing*, that is, of washing with water all those that being Gentiles, embraced the God of Israel. This rite St. John the Baptist used in the reception of all them that gave their names to the Christ, whom hee preached to bee already come into the world; and our Saviour instituted the same for a Sacrament to be taken by all that beleeved in him. From what cause the rite of Baptisme first proceeded, is not expressed formally in the Scripture; but it may be probably thought to be an imitation of the law of Moses, concerning Leprousie; wherein the Leprous man was commanded to be kept out of the campe of Israel for a certain time; after which time being judged by the Priest to be clean, hee was admitted into the campe after a solemne Washing. And this may therefore bee a type of the Washing in Baptisme; wherein such men as are cleansed of the Leprousie of Sin by Faith, are received into the Church with the solemnity of Baptisme. There is another conjecture drawn from the Ceremonies of the Gentiles, in a certain case that rarely happens; and that is, when a man that was thought dead, chanced to recover, other men made scruple to converse with him, as they would doe to converse with a Ghost, unlesse hee were received again into the number of men, by Washing, as Children new born were washed from the uncleannesse of their nativity, which was a kind of new birth. This ceremony of the Greeks, in the time that Judaea was under the Dominion of Alexander, and the Greeks his successors, may probably enough have crept into the Religion of the Jews. But seeing it is not likely our Saviour would countenance a Heathen rite, it is most likely it proceeded from the Legall Ceremony of Washing after Leprosie. And for the other

[266] Sacrament, of eating the *Paschall Lambe*, it is manifestly imitated in the Sacrament of the *Lords Supper*, in which the Breaking of the Bread, and the pouring out of the Wine, do keep in memory our deliverance from the Misery of Sin, by Christs Passion, as the eating of the Paschall Lambe, kept in memory the deliverance of the Jewes out of the Bondage of Egypt. Seeing therefore the authority of Moses was but subordinate, and hee but a Lieutenant to God; it followeth, that Christ, whose authority, as man, was to bee like that of Moses, was no more but subordinate to the authority of his Father. The same is more expressely signified, by that that hee teacheth us to pray, *Our Father, Let thy Kingdome come*; and, *For thine is the Kingdome, the Power, and the Glory*; and by that it is said, that *Hee shall come in the Glory of his Father*; and by that which St. Paul saith, (1 *Cor.* 15. 24.) *then commeth the end, when hee shall have delivered up the Kingdome to God, even the Father*; and by many other most expresse places.

One and the same God is the Person represented by Moses, and by Christ. Our Saviour therefore, both in Teaching, and Reigning, representeth (as Moses did) the Person of God; which God from that time forward, but not before, is called the Father; and being still one and the same substance, is one Person as represented by Moses, and another Person as represented by his Sonne the Christ. For *Person* being a relative to a *Representer*, it is consequent to plurality of Representers, that there bee a plurality of Persons, though of one and the same Substance.

[267]

CHAP. XLII.
Of POWER ECCLESIASTICALL.

For the understanding of POWER ECCLESIASTICALL, what, and in whom it is, we are to distinguish the time from the Ascension of our Saviour, into two parts; one before the Conversion of Kings, and men endued with Soveraign Civill Power; the other after their Conversion. For it was long after the Ascension, before any King, or Civill Soveraign embraced, and publiquely allowed the teaching of Christian Religion.

Of the Holy Spirit that And for the time between, it is manifest, that the *Power Ecclesiasticall*, was in the Apostles; and after them in such as were by them ordained to Preach the Gospell, and to convert men to Christianity, *fel on the* and to direct them that were converted in the way of Salvation; and *Apostles.* after these the Power was delivered again to others by these ordained, and this was done by Imposition of hands upon such as were ordained; by which was signified the giving of the Holy Spirit, or Spirit of God, to those whom they ordained Ministers of God, to advance his Kingdome. So that Imposition of hands, was nothing else but the Seal of their Commission to Preach Christ, and teach his Doctrine; and the giving of the Holy Ghost by that ceremony of Imposition of hands, was an imitation of that which Moses did. For Moses used the same ceremony to his Minister Joshua, as wee read *Deuteronomy* 34. ver. 9. *And Joshua the Son of Nun was full of the Spirit of Wisdome; for Moses had laid his hands upon him.* Our Saviour therefore between his Resurrection, and Ascension, gave his Spirit to the Apostles; first, by *Breathing on them, and saying,* (*John* 20.22.) *Receive yee the Holy Spirit*; and after his Ascension (*Acts* 2.2, 3.) by sending down upon them, a *mighty wind, and Cloven tongues of fire*; and not by Imposition of hands; as neither did God lay his hands on Moses: and his Apostles afterward, transmitted the same Spirit by Imposition of hands, as Moses did to Joshua. So that it is manifest hereby, in whom the Power Ecclesiasticall continually remained, in those first times, where there was not any Christian Common-wealth; namely, in them that received the same from the Apostles, by successive laying on of hands.

Here wee have the Person of God born now the third time. For as *Of the* Moses, and the High Priests, were Gods Representative in the Old *Trinity.* Testament; and our Saviour himselfe as Man, during his abode on earth: So the Holy Ghost, that is to say, the Apostles, and their successors, in the Office of Preaching, and Teaching, that had [268] received the Holy Spirit, have Represented him ever since. But a Person, (as I have shewn before, chapt. 13.) is he that is Represented, as often as hee is Represented; and therefore God, who has been Represented (that is, Personated) thrice, may properly enough be said to be three Persons; though neither the word *Person*, nor *Trinity* be ascribed to him in the Bible. St. *John* indeed (1 Epist. 5.7.) saith, *There be three that bear witnesse in heaven, the Father, the Word, and the Holy Spirit; and these Three are One*: But this disagreeth not, but accordeth fitly with three Persons in the proper signification of Persons; which is, that which is Represented by another. For so God the

Father, as Represented by Moses, is one Person; and as Represented by his Sonne, another Person; and as Represented by the Apostles, and by the Doctors that taught by authority from them derived, is a third Person; and yet every Person here, is the Person of one and the same God. But a man may here ask, what it was whereof these three bare witnesse. St. *John* therefore tells us (verse 11.) that they bear witnesse, that *God hath given us eternall life in his Son.* Again, if it should bee asked, wherein that testimony appeareth, the Answer is easie; for he hath testified the same by the miracles he wrought, first by Moses; secondly, by his Son himself; and lastly by his Apostles, that had received the Holy Spirit; all which in their times Represented the Person of God; and either prophecyed, or preached Jesus Christ. And as for the Apostles, it was the character of the Apostleship, in the twelve first and great Apostles, to bear Witnesse of his Resurrection; as appeareth expressely (*Acts* 1. ver. 21, 22.) where St. Peter, when a new Apostle was to be chosen in the place of Judas Iscariot, useth these words, *Of these men which have companied with us all the time that the Lord Jesus went in and out amongst us, beginning at the Baptisme of John, unto that same day that hee was taken up from us, must one bee ordained to be a Witnesse with us of his Resurrection*: which words interpret the *bearing of Witnesse*, mentioned by St. John. There is in the same place mentioned another Trinity of Witnesses in Earth. For (ver. 8.) he saith, *there are three that bear Witnesse in Earth, the Spirit, and the Water, and the Bloud; and these three agree in one*: that is to say, the graces of Gods Spirit, and the two Sacraments, Baptisme, and the Lords Supper, which all agree in one Testimony, to assure the consciences of beleevers, of eternall life; of which Testimony he saith (verse 10.) *He that beleeveth on the Son of man hath the Witnesse in himself.* In this Trinity on Earth, the Unity is not of the thing; for the Spirit, the Water, and the Bloud, are not the same substance, though they give the same testimony: But in the Trinity of Heaven, the Persons are the persons of one and the same God, though Represented in three different times and occasions. To conclude, the doctrine of the Trinity, as far as can be gathered directly from the Scripture, is in substance this; that God who is alwaies One and the same, was the Person Represented by Moses; the Person Represented by his Son Incarnate; and the Person Represented by the Apostles. As Represented by the Apostles, the Holy Spirit by which they spake, is God; As Represented by his Son (that was God and Man), the Son is

[269]

340

that God; As represented by Moses, and the High Priests, the Father, that is to say, the Father of our Lord Jesus Christ, is that God: From whence we may gather the reason why those names *Father, Son,* and *Holy Spirit* in the signification of the Godhead, are never used in the Old Testament: For they are Persons, that is, they have their names from Representing; which could not be, till divers men had Represented Gods Person in ruling, or in directing under him.

Thus wee see how the Power Ecclesiasticall was left by our Saviour to the Apostles; and how they were (to the end they might the better exercise that Power,) endued with the Holy Spirit, which is therefore called sometime in the New Testament *Paracletus* which signifieth an *Assister*, or one called to for helpe, though it bee commonly translated a *Comforter*. Let us now consider the Power it selfe, what it was, and over whom.

Cardinall Bellarmine in his third generall Controversie, hath handled a great many questions concerning the Ecclesiasticall Power of the Pope of Rome; and begins with this, Whether it ought to be Monarchicall, Aristocraticall, or Democraticall. All which sorts of Power, are Soveraign, and Coercive. If now it should appear, that there is no Coercive Power left them by our Saviour; but onely a Power to proclaim the Kingdom of Christ, and to perswade men to submit themselves thereunto; and by precepts and good counsell, to teach them that have submitted, what they are to do, that they may be received into the Kingdom of God when it comes; and that the Apostles, and other Ministers of the Gospel, are our Schoolmasters, and not our Commanders, and their Precepts not Laws, but wholesome Counsells; then were all that dispute in vain. *The Power Ecclesiasticall is but the power to teach.*

I have shewn already (in the last Chapter,) that the Kingdome of Christ is not of this world: therefore neither can his Ministers (unlesse they be Kings,) require obedience in his name. For if the Supreme King, have not his Regall Power in this world; by what authority can obedience be required to his Officers? As my Father sent me, (so saith our Saviour) I send you. But our Saviour was sent to perswade the Jews to return to, and to invite the Gentiles, to receive the Kingdome of his Father, and not to reign in Majesty, no not, as his Fathers Lieutenant, till the day of Judgment. *An argument thereof, *from the*[1] Power of Christ himself:*

The time between the Ascension, and the generall Resurrection, is *From the name of Regeneration:*

[1] *Syn.: the*

called, not a Reigning, but a Regeneration; that is, a Preparation of men for the second and glorious coming of Christ, at the day of Judgment; as appeareth by the words of our Saviour, *Mat.* 19.28. *You that have followed me in the Regeneration, when the Son of man shall sit in the throne of his glory, you shall also sit upon twelve Thrones*; And of St. Paul (*Ephes.* 6.15.) *Having your feet shod with the Preparation of the Gospell of Peace.*

And is compared by our Saviour, to Fishing; that is, to winning men to obedience, not by Coercion, and Punishing; but by Perswasion: and therefore he said not to his Apostles, hee would make them so many Nimrods, *Hunters of men; but Fishers of men.* It is compared also to Leaven; to Sowing of Seed, and to the Multiplication of a grain of Mustard-seed; by all which Compulsion is excluded; and consequently there can in that time be no actual Reigning. The work of Christs Ministers, is Evangelization; that is, a Proclamation of Christ, and a preparation for his second comming; as the Evangelization of John Baptist, was a preparation to his first coming.

Again, the Office of Christs Minister in this world, is to make men Beleeve, and have Faith in Christ. But Faith hath no relation to, nor dependence at all upon Compulsion, or Commandement; but onely upon certainty, or probability of Arguments drawn from Reason, or from something men beleeve already. Therefore the Ministers of Christ in this world, have no Power by that title, to Punish any man for not Beleeving, or for Contradicting what they say; they have I say no Power by that title of Christs Ministers, to Punish such: but if they have Soveraign Civill Power; by politick institution, then they may indeed lawfully Punish any Contradiction to their laws whatsoever: And St. Paul, of himselfe and other the then Preachers of the Gospell, saith in expresse words, *Wee have no Dominion over your Faith, but are Helpers of your Joy.*

Another Argument, that the Ministers of Christ in this present world have no right of Commanding, may be drawn from the lawfull Authority which Christ hath left to all Princes, as well Christians, as Infidels. St. Paul saith (*Col.* 3.20.) *Children obey your Parents in all things; for this is well pleasing to the Lord.* And ver. 22. *Servants obey in all things your Masters according to the flesh, not with eye-service, as men-pleasers, but in singlenesse of heart, as fearing the Lord*: This is spoken to them whose Masters were Infidells; and yet they are bidden to obey them *in all things.* And again, concerning obedience to Princes, (*Rom.*

From the comparison of it, with Fishing, Leaven, Seed.

From the nature of Faith.

2 *Cor.* 1.24.

From the Authority Christ hath left to Civill Princes.

[270]

342

13. the first 6. verses) exhorting *to be subject to the Higher Powers*, he saith, *that all Power is ordained of God*; and *that we ought to be subject to them, not onely for* fear of incurring their *wrath, but also for conscience sake*. And St. *Peter*, (1. Epist. chap. 2. ver. 13, 14, 15.) *Submit your selves to every Ordinance of Man, for the Lords sake, whether it bee to the King, as Supreme, or unto Governours, as to them that be sent by him for the punishment of evill doers, and for the praise of them that doe well; for so is the will of God*. And again St. Paul (*Tit.* 3.1.) *Put men in mind to be subject to Principalities, and Powers, and to obey Magistrates*. These Princes, and Powers, whereof St. Peter, and St. Paul here speak, were all Infidels: much more therefore we are to obey those Christians, [271] whom God hath ordained to have Soveraign Power over us. How then can wee be obliged to obey any Minister of Christ, if he should command us to doe any thing contrary to the Command of the King, or other Soveraign Representative of the Common-wealth, whereof we are members, and by whom we look to be protected? It is therefore manifest, that Christ hath not left to his Ministers in this world, unlesse they be also endued with Civill Authority, any authority to Command other men.

But what (may some object) if a King, or a Senate, or other Soveraign Person forbid us to beleeve in Christ? To this I answer, that such forbidding is of no effect; because Beleef, and Unbeleef never follow mens Commands. Faith is a gift of God, which Man can neither give, nor take away by promise of rewards, or menaces of torture. And if it be further asked, What if wee bee commanded by our lawfull Prince, to say with our tongue, *what wee*[1] beleeve not; must we obey such command? Profession with the tongue is but an externall thing, and no more then any other gesture whereby we signifie our obedience; and wherein a Christian, holding firmely in his heart the Faith of Christ, hath the same liberty which the Prophet Elisha allowed to Naaman the Syrian. Naaman was converted in his heart to the God of Israel; For hee saith (2 *Kings* 5.17.) *Thy servant will henceforth offer neither burnt offering, nor sacrifice unto other Gods but unto the Lord. In this thing the Lord pardon thy servant, that when my Master goeth into the house of Rimmon to worship there, and he leaneth on my hand, and I bow my selfe, in the house of Rimmon; when I bow my selfe in the house of Rimmon, the Lord pardon thy servant in this thing*. This the

What Christians may do to avoid persecution.

---

[1] *Syn.:* wee

343

Prophet approved, and bid him *Goe in peace*. Here Naaman beleeved in his heart; but by bowing before the Idol Rimmon, he denyed the true God in effect, as much as if he had done it with his lips. But then what shall we answer to our Saviours saying, *Whosoever denyeth me before men, I will deny him before my Father which is in Heaven?* This we may say, that whatsoever a Subject, as Naaman was, is compelled to in obedience to his Soveraign, and doth it not in order to his own mind, but in order to the laws of his country, that action is not his, but his Soveraigns; nor is it he that in this case denyeth Christ before men, but his Governour, and the law of his countrey. If any man shall accuse this doctrine, as repugnant to true, and unfeigned Christianity; I ask him, in case there should be a subject in any Christian Common-wealth, that should be inwardly in his heart of the Mahometan Religion, whether if his Soveraign command him to bee present at the divine service of the Christian Church, and that on pain of death, he think that Mahometan obliged in conscience to suffer death for that cause, rather than to obey that command of his lawfull Prince. If he say, he ought rather to suffer death, then he authorizeth all private men, to disobey their Princes, in maintenance of their Religion, true, or false: if he say, he ought to bee obedient, then he alloweth to himself, that which hee denyeth to another, contrary to the words of our Saviour, *Whatsoever you would that men should doe unto you, that doe yee unto them*; and contrary to the Law of Nature, (which is the indubitable everlasting Law of God) *Do not to another, that which thou wouldest not he should doe unto thee.*

[272]

Of Mar

But what then shall we say of all those Martyrs we read of in the History of the Church, that they have needlessely cast away their lives? For answer hereunto, we are to distinguish the persons that have been for that cause put to death; whereof some have received a Calling to preach, and professe the Kingdome of Christ openly; others have had no such Calling, nor more has been required of them than their owne faith. The former sort, if they have been put to death, for bearing witnesse to this point, that Jesus Christ is risen from the dead, were true Martyrs; For a *Martyr* is, (to give the true definition of the word) a Witnesse of the Resurrection of Jesus the Messiah; which none can be but those that conversed with him on earth, and saw him after he was risen: For a Witnesse must have seen what he testifieth, or else his testimony is not good. And that none but such, can properly be called Martyrs of Christ, is manifest out of the words of St.

344

Peter, *Act.* 1.21, 22. *Wherefore of these men which have companyed with us all the time that the Lord Jesus went in and out amongst us, beginning from the Baptisme of John unto that same day hee was taken up from us, must one be ordained to be a Martyr* (that is a Witnesse) *with us of his Resurrection*: Where we may observe, that he which is to bee a Witnesse of the truth of the Resurrection of Christ, that is to say, of the truth of this fundamentall article of Christian Religion, that Jesus was the Christ, must be some Disciple that conversed with him, and saw him before, and after his Resurrection; and consequently must be one of his originall Disciples: whereas they which were not so, can Witnesse no more, but that their antecessors said it, and are therefore but Witnesses of other mens testimony; and are but second Martyrs, or Martyrs of Christs Witnesses.

He, that to maintain every doctrine which he himself draweth out of the History of our Saviours life, and of the Acts, or Epistles of the Apostles; or which he beleeveth upon the authority of a private man, wil oppose the Laws and Authority of the Civill State, is very far from being a Martyr of Christ, or a Martyr of his Martyrs. 'Tis one Article onely, which to die for, meriteth so honorable a name; and that Article is this, that *Jesus is the Christ*; that is to say, He that hath redeemed us, and shall come again to give us salvation, and eternall life in his glorious Kingdome. To die for every tenet that serveth the ambition, or profit of the Clergy, is not required; nor is it the Death of the Witnesse, but the Testimony it self that makes the Martyr: for the word signifieth nothing else, but the man that beareth Witnesse, whether he be put to death for his testimony, or not.

Also he that is not sent to preach this fundamentall article, but taketh it upon him of his private authority, though he be a Witnesse, [273] and consequently a Martyr, either primary of Christ, or secundary of his Apostles, Disciples, or their Successors; yet is he not obliged to suffer death for that cause; because being not called thereto, tis not required at his hands; nor ought hee to complain, if he loseth the reward he expecteth from those that never set him on work. None therefore can be a Martyr, neither of the first, nor second degree, that have not a warrant to preach Christ come in the flesh; that is to say, none, but such as are sent to the conversion of Infidels. For no man is a Witnesse to him that already beleeveth, and therefore needs no Witnesse; but to them that deny, or doubt, or have not heard it. Christ sent his Apostles, and his Seventy Disciples, with authority to preach;

he sent not all that beleeved: And he sent them to unbeleevers; *I send you* (saith he) *as sheep amongst wolves*; not as sheep to other sheep.

Lastly, the points of their Commission, as they are expressely set down in the Gospel, contain none of them any authority over the Congregation.

We have first (*Mat.* 10.) that the twelve Apostles were sent *to the lost sheep of the house of Israel*, and commanded to Preach, *that the Kingdome of God was at hand.* Now Preaching in the originall, is that act, which a Crier, Herald, or other Officer useth to doe publiquely in Proclaiming of a King. But a Crier hath not right to Command any man. And (*Luke* 10.2.) the seventy Disciples are sent out, as *Labourers, not as Lords of the Harvest*; and are bidden (verse 9.) to say, *The Kingdome of God is come nigh unto you*; and by Kingdom here is meant, not the Kingdome of Grace, but the Kingdome of Glory; for they are bidden to denounce it (ver. 11.) to those Cities which shall not receive them, as a threatning, that it shall be more tolerable in that day for *Sodome*, than for such a City. And (*Mat.* 20.28.) our Saviour telleth his Disciples, that sought Priority of place, their Office was to minister, even as the Son of man came, not to be ministred unto, but to minister. Preachers therefore have not Magisteriall, but Ministeriall power: *Bee not called Masters*, (saith our Saviour, *Mat.* 23.10.) *for one is your Master, even Christ.*

Another point of their Commission, is, to *Teach all nations*; as it is in *Mat.* 28.19. or as in St. *Mark* 16.15. *Goe into all the world, and Preach the Gospel to every creature.* Teaching therefore, and Preaching is the same thing. For they that Proclaim the comming of a King, must withall make known by what right he commeth, if they mean men shall submit themselves unto him: As St. Paul did to the Jews of Thessalonica, when *three Sabbath dayes he reasoned with them out of the Scriptures, opening, and alledging that Christ must needs have suffered, and risen again from the dead, and that this Jesus is Christ.* But to teach out of the Old Testament that Jesus was Christ, (that is to say, King,) and risen from the dead, is not to say, that men are bound after they beleeve it, to obey those that tell them so, against the laws, and commands of their Soveraigns; but that they shall doe wisely, to expect the coming of Christ hereafter, in Patience, and Faith, with Obedience to their present Magistrates.

Another point of their Commission, is to *Baptize, in the name of the Father, and of the Son, and of the Holy Ghost.* What is Baptisme?

346

Dipping into water. But what is it to Dip a man into the water in the name of any thing? The meaning of these words of Baptisme is this. He that is Baptized, is Dipped or Washed, as a sign of becomming a new man, and a loyall subject to that God, whose Person was represented in old time by Moses, and the High Priests, when he reigned over the Jews; and to Jesus Christ, his Sonne, God, and Man, that hath redeemed us, and shall in his humane nature Represent his Fathers Person in his eternall Kingdome after the Resurrection; and to acknowledge the Doctrine of the Apostles, who assisted by the Spirit of the Father, and of the Son, were left for guides to bring us into that Kingdome, to be the onely, and assured way thereunto. This, being our promise in Baptisme; and the Authority of Earthly Soveraigns being not to be put down till the day of Judgment; (for that is expressely affirmed by S. Paul 1 *Cor.* 15.22, 23, 24, where he saith, *As in Adam all die, so in Christ all shall be made alive. But every man in his owne order. Christ the first fruits, afterward they that are Christs, as his comming; Then commeth the end, when he shall have delivered up the Kingdom to God, even the Father, when he shall have put down all Rule, and all Authority and Power*) it is manifest, that we do not in Baptisme constitute over us another authority, by which our externall actions are to bee governed in this life; but promise to take the doctrine of the Apostles for our direction in the way to life eternall.

The Power of *Remission, and Retention of Sinnes*, called also the Power of *Loosing*, and *Binding*, and sometimes the *Keyes of the Kingdome of Heaven*, is a consequence of the Authority to Baptize, or refuse to Baptize. For Baptisme is the Sacrament of Allegeance, of them that are to be received into the Kingdome of God; that is to say, into Eternall life; that is to say, to Remission of Sin: For as Eternall life was lost by the Committing, so it is recovered by the Remitting of mens Sins. The end of Baptisme is Remission of Sins: and therefore St. Peter, when they that were converted by his Sermon on the day of Pentecost, asked what they were to doe, advised them to *repent, and be Baptized in the name of Jesus, for the Remission of Sins.* And therefore seeing to Baptize is to declare the Reception of men into Gods Kingdome; and to refuse to Baptize is to declare their Exclusion; it followeth, that the Power to declare them Cast out, or Retained in it, was given to the same Apostles, and their Substitutes, and Successors. And therefore after our Saviour had breathed upon them, saying, (*John* 20.22.) *Receive the Holy Ghost,* hee addeth in the next

And to Forgive, and Retain Sinnes.

347

verse, *Whose soever Sins ye Remit, they are Remitted unto them; and whose soever Sins ye Retain, they are Retained.* By which words, is not granted an Authority to Forgive, or Retain Sins, simply and absolutely, as God Forgiveth or Retaineth them, who knoweth the Heart of man, and truth of his Penitence and Conversion; but conditionally, to the Penitent: And this Forgivenesse, or Absolution, in case the absolved have but a feigned Repentance, is thereby without other act, or sentence of the Absolvent, made void, and hath no effect at all to Salvation, but on the contrary, to the Aggravation of his Sin. Therefore the Apostles, and their Successors, are to follow but the outward marks of Repentance; which appearing, they have no Authority to deny Absolution; and if they appeare not, they have no authority to Absolve. The same also is to be observed in Baptisme: for to a converted Jew, or Gentile, the Apostles had not the Power to deny Baptisme; nor to grant it to the Un-penitent. But seeing no man is able to discern the truth of another mans Repentance, further than by externall marks, taken from his words, and actions, which are subject to hypocrisie; another question will arise, Who it is that is constituted Judge of those marks. And this question is decided by our Saviour himself; *If thy Brother* (saith he) *shal trespasse against thee, go and tell him his fault between thee, and him alone; if he shall hear thee, thou hast gained thy Brother. But if he will not hear thee, then take with thee one, or two more. And if he shall neglect to hear them, tell it unto the Church; but if he neglect to hear the Church, let him be unto thee as an Heathen man, and a Publican.* By which it is manifest, that the Judgment concerning the truth of Repentance, belonged not to any one Man, but to the Church, that is, to the Assembly of the Faithfull, or to them that have authority to bee their Representant. But besides the Judgment, there is necessary also the pronouncing of Sentence: And this belonged alwaies to the Apostle, or some Pastor of the Church, as Prolocutor; and of this our Saviour speaketh in the 18 verse, *Whatsoever ye shall bind on earth, shall be bound in heaven; and whatsoever ye shall loose on earth, shall be loosed in heaven.* And conformable hereunto was the practise of St. Paul (1 *Cor.* 5. 3, 4, & 5.) where he saith, *For I verily, as absent in body, but present in spirit, have determined already, as though I were present, concerning him that hath so done this deed; In the name of our Lord Jesus Christ when ye are gathered together, and my spirit, with the power of our Lord Jesus Christ, To deliver such a one to Satan;* that is to say, to cast him out of the Church, as a man whose Sins are not

[275]

Mat. 18.
15,16,17.

Forgiven. *St. Paul*[1] here pronounceth the Sentence; but the Assembly was first to hear the Cause, (for St. Paul was absent;) and by consequence to condemn him. But in the same chapter (ver.11,12.) the Judgment in such a case is more expressely attributed to the Assembly: *But now I have written unto you, not to keep company, if any man that is called a Brother be a Fornicator, &c. with such a one no not to eat. For what have I to do to judge them that are without? Do not ye judg them that are within?* The Sentence therefore by which a man was put out of the Church, was pronounced by the Apostle, or Pastor; but the Judgment concerning the merit of the cause, was in the Church; that is to say, (as the times were before the conversion of Kings, and men that had Soveraign Authority in the Commonwealth,) the Assembly of the Christians dwelling in the same City; as in Corinth, in the Assembly of the Christians of Corinth. [276]

This part of the Power of the Keyes, by which men were thrust out from the Kingdom of God, is that which is called *Excommunication*; and to *excommunicate*, is in the Originall, ἀποσυνάγωγον ποιεῖν, *to cast out of the Synagogue*; that is, out of the place of Divine service; a word drawn from the custome of the Jews, to cast out of their Synagogues, such as they thought in manners, or doctrine, contagious, as Lepers were by the Law of Moses separated from the congregation of Israel, till such time as they should be by the Priest pronounced clean. *Of Excommunication.*

The Use and Effect of Excommunication, whilest it was not yet strengthened with the Civill Power, was no more, than that they, who were not Excommunicate, were to avoid the company of them that were. It was not enough to repute them as Heathen, that never had been Christians; for with such they might eate, and drink; which with Excommunicate persons they might not do; as appeareth by the words of St. Paul, (1 *Cor.*5.ver.9, 10, *&c.*) where he telleth them, he had formerly forbidden them to *company with Fornicators*; but (because that could not bee without going out of the world,) he restraineth it to such Fornicators, and otherwise vicious persons, as were of the brethren; *with such a one* (he saith) they ought not to keep company, *no not to eat.* And this is no more than our Saviour saith (*Mat.*18. 17.) *Let him be to thee as a Heathen, and as a Publican.* For Publicans (which signifieth Farmers, and Receivers of the revenue of the Common-wealth) were so hated, and detested by the Jews that were to pay it, as that *Publican* *The use of Excommunication without Civill Power,*

---

[1] *Syn.*: Paul

and *Sinner* were taken amongst them for the same thing: Insomuch, as when our Saviour accepted the invitation of *Zacchaeus* a Publican; though it were to Convert him, yet it was objected to him as a Crime. And therefore, when our Saviour, to *Heathen*, added *Publican*, he did forbid them to eat with a man Excommunicate.

As for keeping them out of their Synagogues, or places of Assembly, they had no Power to do it, but that of the owner of the place, whether he were Christian, or Heathen. And because all places are by right, in the Dominion of the Common-wealth; as well hee that was Excommunicated, as hee that never was Baptized, might enter into *Acts 9.2.* them by Commission from the Civill Magistrate; as Paul before his conversion entred into their Synagogues at Damascus, to apprehend Christians, men and women, and to carry them bound to Jerusalem, by Commission from the High Priest.

Of no effect upon an Apostate. By which it appears, that upon a Christian, that should become an Apostate, in a place where the Civill Power did persecute, or not assist the Church, the effect of Excommunication had nothing in it, neither of dammage in this world, nor of terrour: Not of terrour, because of their unbeleef; nor of dammage, because they returned thereby into the favour of the world; and in the world to come, were to be in no worse estate, then they which never had beleeved. The dammage [277] redounded rather to the Church, by provocation of them they cast out, to a freer execution of their malice.

But upon the faithfull only. Excommunication therefore had its effect onely upon those, that beleeved that Jesus Christ was to come again in Glory, to reign over, and to judge both the quick, and the dead, and should therefore refuse entrance into his Kingdom, to those whose Sins were Retained; that is, to those that were Excommunicated by the Church. And thence it is that St. Paul calleth Excommunication, a delivery of the Excommunicate person to Satan. For without the Kingdom of Christ, all other Kingdomes after Judgment, are comprehended in the Kingdome of Satan. This is it that the faithfull stood in fear of, as long as they stood Excommunicate, that is to say, in an estate wherein their sins were not Forgiven. Whereby wee may understand, that Excommunication in the time that Christian Religion was not authorized by the Civill Power, was used onely for a correction of manners, not of errours in opinion: for it is a punishment, whereof none could be sensible but such as beleeved, and expected the coming again of our

Saviour to judge the world; and they who so beleeved, needed no
other opinion, but onely uprightnesse of life, to be saved.

There lyeth Excommunication for Injustice; as (*Mat.* 18.) If thy
Brother offend thee, tell it him privately; then with Witnesses; lastly,
tell the Church; and then if he obey not, *Let him be to thee as an
Heathen man, and a Publican.* And there lieth Excommunication for a
Scandalous Life, as (1 *Cor.*5.11.) *If any man that is called a Brother, be a
Fornicator, or Covetous, or an Idolater, or a Drunkard, or an Extortioner,
with such a one yee are not to eat.* But to Excommunicate a man that held
this foundation, that *Jesus was the Christ*, for difference of opinion in
other points, by which that Foundation was not destroyed, there
appeareth no authority in the Scripture, nor example in the Apostles.
There is indeed in St. Paul (*Titus* 3.10.) a text that seemeth to be to
the contrary. *A man that is an Haeretique, after the first and second
admonition, reject.* For an *Haeretique*, is he, that being a member of the
Church, teacheth neverthelesse some private opinion, which the
Church has forbidden: and such a one, S. Paul adviseth *Titus*, after
the first, and second admonition, to *Reject*. But to *Reject* (in this place)
is not to *Excommunicate* the Man; But to *give over admonishing him, to
let him alone, to set by disputing with him*, as one that is to be convinced
onely by himselfe. The same Apostle saith (2 *Tim.* 2. 23.) *Foolish and
unlearned questions avoid*: The word *Avoid* in this place, and *Reject* in
the former, is the same in the Originall, παραιτοῦ: but Foolish
questions may bee set by without Excommunication. And again,
(*Tit.*3.9.) *Avoid Foolish questions*, where the Originall περιΐστασο,
(*set them by*) is equivalent to the former word *Reject*. There is no other
place that can so much as colourably be drawn, to countenance the
Casting out of the Church faithfull men, such as beleeved the foundation, onely for a singular superstructure of their own, proceeding
perhaps from a good & pious conscience. But on the contrary, all such
places as command avoiding such disputes, are written for a Lesson to [278]
Pastors, (such as Timothy and Titus were) not to make new Articles
of Faith, by determining every small controversie, which oblige men
to a needlesse burthen of Conscience, or provoke them to break the
union of the Church. Which Lesson the Apostles themselves
observed well. S. Peter, and S. Paul, though their controversie were
great, (as we may read in *Gal.* 2. 11.) yet they did not cast one another
out of the Church. Neverthelesse, during the Apostles times, there

*For what
fault lyeth
Excommuni-
cation.*

were other Pastors that observed it not; As Diotrephes (*3 John 9. &c.*) who cast out of the Church, such as S. John himself thought fit to be received into it, out of a pride he took in Praeeminence; so early it was, that Vain-glory, and Ambition had found entrance into the Church of Christ.

Of persons liable to Excommunication. That a man be liable to Excommunication, there be many conditions requisite; as First, that he be a member of some Commonalty, that is to say, of some lawfull Assembly, that is to say, of some Christian Church, that hath power to judge of the cause for which hee is to bee Excommunicated. For where there is no Community, there can bee no Excommunication; nor where there is no power to Judge, can there bee any power to give Sentence.

From hence it followeth, that one Church cannot be Excommunicated by another: For either they have equall power to Excommunicate each other, in which case Excommunication is not Discipline, nor an act of Authority, but Schisme, and Dissolution of charity; or one is so subordinate to the other, as that they both have but one voice, and then they be but one Church; and the part Excommunicated, is no more a Church, but a dissolute number of individuall persons.

And because the sentence of Excommunication, importeth an advice, not to keep company, nor so much as to eat with him that is Excommunicate, if a Soveraign Prince, or Assembly bee Excommunicate, the sentence is of no effect. For all Subjects are bound to be in the company and presence of their own Soveraign (when he requireth it) by the law of Nature; nor can they lawfully either expell him from any place of his Dominion, whether profane or holy; nor go out of his Dominion, without his leave; much lesse (if he call them to that honour,) refuse to eat with him. And as to other Princes and States, because they are not parts of one and the same congregation, they need not any other sentence to keep them from keeping company with the State Excommunicate: for the very Institution, as it uniteth many men into one Community; so it dissociateth one Community from another: so that Excommunication is not needfull for keeping Kings and States asunder; nor has any further effect then is in the nature of Policy it selfe; unlesse it be to instigate Princes to warre upon one another.

Nor is the Excommunication of a Christian Subject, that obeyeth the laws of his own Soveraign, whether Christian, or Heathen, of any

effect. For if he beleeve that *Jesus is the Christ, he hath the Spirit of God,* [279]
(1 Joh. 4.1.) *and God dwelleth in him, and he in God,* (1 Joh. 4.15.) But
hee that hath the Spirit of God; hee that dwelleth in God; hee in
whom God dwelleth, can receive no harm by the Excommunication of
men. Therefore, he that beleeveth Jesus to be the Christ, is free from
all the dangers threatned to persons Excommunicate. He that
beleveeth it not, is no Christian. Therefore a true and unfeigned
Christian is not liable to Excommunication: Nor he also that is a
professed Christian, till his Hypocrisy appear in his Manners, that is,
till his behaviour bee contrary to the law of his Soveraign, which is the
rule of Manners, and which Christ and his Apostles have commanded
us to be subject to. For the Church cannot judge of Manners but by
externall Actions, which Actions can never bee unlawfull, but when
they are against the Law of the Commonwealth.

If a mans Father, or Mother, or Master bee Excommunicate, yet
are not the Children forbidden to keep them Company, not to Eat
with them; for that were (for the most part) to oblige them not to eat at
all, for want of means to get food; and to authorise them to disobey
their Parents, and Masters, contrary to the Precept of the Apostles.

In summe, the Power of Excommunication cannot be extended
further than to the end for which the Apostles and Pastors of the
Church have their Commission from our Saviour; which is not to rule
by Command and Coaction, but by Teaching and Direction of men in
the way of Salvation in the world to come. And as a Master in any
Science, may abandon his Scholar, when hee obstinately neglecteth
the practice of his rules; but not accuse him of Injustice, because he
was never bound to obey him: so a Teacher of Christian doctrine may
abandon his Disciples that obstinately continue in an unchristian life;
but he cannot say, they doe him wrong, because they are not obliged
to obey him: For to a Teacher that shall so complain, may be applyed
the Answer of God to Samuel in the like place, *They have not rejected
thee, but mee.* Excommunication therefore when it wanteth the 1 *Sam.* 8.
assistance of the Civill Power, as it doth, when a Christian State, or
Prince is Excommunicate by a forain Authority, is without effect; and
consequently ought to be without terrour. The name of *Fulmen
Excommunicationis* (that is, *the Thunderbolt of Excommunication*) proceeded from an imagination of the Bishop of Rome, which first used
it, that he was King of Kings, as the Heathen made Jupiter King of
the Gods; and assigned him in their Poems, and Pictures, a Thunder-

bolt, wherewith to subdue, and punish the Giants, that should dare to
deny his power: Which imagination was grounded on two errours;
one, that the Kingdome of Christ is of this world, contrary to our
Saviours owne words, *My Kingdome is not of this world*; the other, that
hee is Christs Vicar, not onely over his owne Subjects, but over all the
Christians of the World; whereof there is no ground in Scripture, and
the contrary shall bee proved in its due place.

St. Paul coming to *Thessalonica*, where was a Synagogue of the Jews,
(*Acts* 17.2,3.) *As his manner was, went in unto them, and three Sabbath
dayes reasoned with them out of the Scriptures, Opening and alledging, that
Christ must needs have suffered and risen again from the dead; and that this
Jesus whom he preached was the Christ.* The Scriptures here mentioned
were the Scriptures of the Jews, that is, the Old Testament. The men,
to whom he was to prove that Jesus was the Christ, and risen again
from the dead, were also Jews, and did beleeve already, that they were
the Word of God. Hereupon (as it is verse 4.) some of them beleeved,
and (as it is in the 5. ver.) some beleeved not. What was the reason,
when they all beleeved the Scripture, that they did not all beleeve
alike; but that some approved, others disapproved the Interpretation
of St. Paul that cited them; and every one Intepreted them to himself?
It was this; S. Paul came to them without any Legall Commission, and
in the manner of one that would not Command, but Perswade; which
he must needs do, either by Miracles, as Moses did to the Israelites in
Eygpt, that they might see his Authority in Gods works; or by Reasoning from the already received Scripture, that they might see the truth
of his doctrine in Gods Word. But whosoever perswadeth by reasoning from principles written, maketh him to whom hee speaketh Judge,
both of the meaning of those principles, and also of the force of his
inferences upon them. If these Jews of Thessalonica were not, who
else was the Judge of what S. Paul alledged out of Scripture? If S.
Paul, what needed he to quote any places to prove his doctrine? It had
been enough to have said, I find it so in Scripture, that is to say, in
your Laws, of which I am Interpreter, as sent by Christ. The Interpreter therefore of the Scripture, to whose Interpretation the Jews of
Thessalonica were bound to stand, could be none: every one might
beleeve, or not beleeve, according as the Allegations seemed to himselfe to be agreeable, or not agreeable to the meaning of the places
alledged. And generally in all cases of the world, hee that pretendeth
any proofe, maketh Judge of his proofe him to whom he addresseth

his speech. And as to the case of the Jews in particular, they were bound by expresse words (*Deut.* 17.) to receive the determination of all hard questions, from the Priests and Judges of Israel for the time being. But this is to bee understood of the Jews that were yet unconverted.

For the conversion of the Gentiles, there was no use of alledging the Scriptures, which they beleeved not. The Apostles therefore laboured by Reason to confute their Idolatry; and that done, to perswade them to the faith of Christ, by their testimony of his Life, and Resurrection. So that there could not yet bee any controversie concerning the authority to Interpret Scripture; seeing no man was obliged during his infidelity, to follow any mans Interpretation of any Scripture, except his Soveraigns Interpretation of the Laws of his countrey.

Let us now consider the Conversion it self, and see what there was [281] therein, that could be cause of such an obligation. Men were converted to no other thing then to the Beleef of that which the Apostles preached: And the Apostles preached nothing, but that Jesus was the Christ, that is to say, the King that was to save them, and reign over them eternally in the world to come; and consequently that hee was not dead, but risen again from the dead, and gone up into Heaven, and should come again one day to judg the world, (which also should rise again to be judged,) and reward every man according to his works. None of them preached that himselfe, or any other Apostle was such an Interpreter of the Scripture, as all that became Christians, ought to take their Interpretation for Law. For to Interpret the Laws, is part of the Administration of a present Kingdome; which the Apostles had not. They prayed then, and all other Pastors ever since, *Let thy Kingdome come*; and exhorted their Converts to obey their then Ethnique Princes. The New Testament was not yet published in one Body. Every of the Evangelists was Interpreter of his own Gospel; and every Apostle of his own Epistle; And of the Old Testament, our Saviour himselfe saith to the Jews (*John* 5.39.) *Search the Scriptures; for in them yee thinke to have eternall life, and they are they that testifie of me*. If hee had not meant they should Interpret them, hee would not have bidden them take thence the proof of his being the Christ: he would either have Interpreted them himselfe, or referred them to the Interpretation of the Priests.

When a difficulty arose, the Apostles and Elders of the Church assembled themselves together, and determined what should bee preached, and taught, and how they should Interpret the Scriptures to the People; but took not from the People the liberty to read, and Interpret them to themselves. The Apostles sent divers Letters to the Churches, and other Writings for their instruction; which had been in vain, if they had not allowed them to Interpret, that is, to consider the meaning of them. And as it was in the Apostles time, *so it*[1] must be till such time as there should be Pastors, that could authorise an Interpreter, whose Interpretation should generally be stood to: But that could not be till Kings were Pastors, or Pastors Kings.

Of the Power to make Scripture Law.   There be two senses, wherein a Writing may be said to be *Canonicall*; for *Canon*, signifieth a *Rule*; and a Rule is a Precept, by which a man is guided, and directed in any action whatsoever. Such Precepts, though given by a Teacher to his Disciple, or a Counsellor to his friend, without power to Compell him to observe them, are neverthelesse Canons; because they are Rules: But when they are given by one, whom he that receiveth them is bound to obey, then are those Canons, not onely Rules, but Laws: The question therefore here, is of the Power to make the Scriptures (which are the Rules of Christian Faith) Laws.

Of the Ten Commande-ments.

[282]   That part of the Scripture, which was first Law, was the Ten Commandements, written in two Tables of Stone, and delivered by God himselfe to Moses; and by Moses made known to the people. Before that time there was no written Law of God, who as yet having not chosen any people to bee his peculiar Kingdome, had given no Law to men, but the Law of Nature, that is to say, the Precepts of Naturall Reason, written in every mans own heart. Of these two Tables, the first containeth the law of Soveraignty; 1. That they should not obey, nor honour the Gods of other Nations, in these words, *Non habebis Deos alienos coram me*, that is, *Thou shalt not have for Gods the Gods that other Nations worship, but onely me*: whereby they were forbidden to obey, or honor, as their King and Governour, any other God, than him that spake unto them then by Moses, and afterwards by the High Priest. 2. That they *should not make any Image to represent him*; that is to say, they were not to choose to themselves, neither in heaven, nor in earth, any Representative of their own fancying, but obey Moses and Aaron, whom he had appointed to that

[1] Syn.: it

356

office. 3. That *they should not take the Name of God in vain*; that is, they should not speak rashly of their King, nor dispute his Right, nor the commissions of Moses and Aaron, his Lieutenants. 4. That *they should every Seventh day abstain from their ordinary labour*, and employ that time in doing him Publique Honor. The second Table containeth the Duty of one man towards another, as *To honor Parents; Not to kill; Not to Commit Adultery; Not to steale; Not to corrupt Judgment by false witnesse*; and finally, *Not so much as to designe in their heart the doing of any injury one to another*. The question now is, Who it was that gave to these written Tables the obligatory force of Lawes. There is no doubt but they were made Laws by God himselfe: But because a Law obliges not, nor is Law to any, but to them that acknowledge it to be the act of the Soveraign; how could the people of Israel that were forbidden to approach the Mountain to hear what God said to Moses, be obliged to obedience to all those laws which Moses propounded to them? Some of them were indeed the Laws of Nature, as all the Second Table; and therefore to be acknowledged for Gods Laws; not to the Israelites alone, but to all people: But of those that were peculiar to the Israelites, as those of the first Table, the question remains; saving that they had obliged themselves, presently after the propounding of them, to obey Moses, in these words (*Exod.* 20.19.) *Speak thou to us, and we will hear thee; but let not God speak to us, lest we dye.* It was therefore onely Moses then, and after him the High Priest, whom (by Moses) God declared should administer this his peculiar Kingdome, that had on Earth, the power to make this short Scripture of the Decalogue to bee Law in the Common-wealth of Israel. But Moses, and Aaron, and the succeeding High Priests were the Civill Soveraigns. Therefore hitherto, the Canonizing, or making of the Scripture Law, belonged to the Civill Soveraigne.

    The Judiciall Law, that is to say, the Laws that God prescribed to the Magistrates of Israel, for the rule of their administration of Justice, and of the Sentences, or Judgments they should pronounce, in Pleas between man and man; and the Leviticall Law, that is to say, the rule that God prescribed touching the Rites and Ceremonies of the Priests and Levites, were all delivered to them by Moses onely; and therefore also became Lawes, by vertue of the same promise of obedience to Moses. Whether these laws were then written, or not written, but dictated to the People by Moses (after his forty dayes being with God in the Mount) by word of mouth, is not expressed in

Of the Judiciall, and Leviticall Law.

[283]

the Text; but they were all positive Laws, and equivalent to holy Scripture, and made Canonicall by Moses the Civill Soveraign.

The Second Law. After the Israelites were come into the Plains of Moab over against Jericho, and ready to enter into the land of Promise, Moses to the former Laws added divers others; which therefore are called *Deuteronomy*; that is, *Second Laws*. And are (as it is written, *Deut.* 29.1.) *The words of a Covenant which the Lord commanded Moses to make with the Children of Israel, besides the Covenant which he made with them in Horeb.* For having explained those former Laws, in the beginning of the Book of *Deuteronomy*, he addeth others, that begin at the 12. Cha. and continue to the end of the 26. of the same Book. This Law (*Deut.* 27.1.) they were commanded to write upon great stones playstered over, at their passing over Jordan: This Law also was written by Moses himself in a Book; and delivered into the hands of the *Priests, and to the Elders of Israel,* (*Deut.* 31.9.) and commanded (ve. 26.) *to be put in the side of the Arke*; for in the Ark it selfe was nothing but the *Ten Commandements.* This was the Law, which Moses (*Deuteronomy* 17.18.) commanded the Kings of Israel should keep a copie of: And this is the Law, which having been long time lost, was found again in the Temple in the time of Josiah, and by his authority received for the Law of God. But both Moses at the writing, and Josiah at the recovery thereof, had both of them the Civill Soveraignty. Hitherto therefore the Power of making Scripture Canonicall, was in the Civill Soveraign.

Besides this Book of the Law, there was no other Book, from the time of Moses, till after the Captivity, received amongst the Jews for the Law of God. For the Prophets (except a few) lived in the time of the Captivity it selfe; and the rest lived but a little before it; and were so far from having their Prophecies generally received for Laws, as that their persons were persecuted, partly by false Prophets, and partly by the Kings which were seduced by them. And this Book it self, which was confirmed by Josiah for the Law of God, and with it all the History of the Works of God, was lost in the Captivity, and sack of the City of Jerusalem, as appears by that of 2 *Esdras* 14.21. *Thy Law is burnt; therefore no man knoweth the things that are done of thee, or the works that shall begin.* And before the Captivity, between the time when the Law was lost, (which is not mentioned in the Scripture, but may probably be thought to be the time of Rehoboam, when★ Shishak King of Egypt took the spoile of the Temple,) and the time of Josiah,

★1 *Kings* 14:26.

when it was found againe, they had no written Word of God, but [284]
ruled according to their own discretion, or by the direction of such, as
each of them esteemed Prophets.

From hence we may inferre, that the Scriptures of the Old Testa- *The Old*
ment, which we have at this day, were not Canonicall, nor a Law unto *Testament*
the Jews, till the renovation of their Covenant with God at their return *when made*
from the Captivity, and restauration of their Common-wealth under *Canonicall.*
Esdras. But from that time forward they were accounted the Law of
the Jews, and for such translated into Greek by Seventy Elders of
Judaea, and put into the Library of Ptolemy at Alexandria, and
approved for the Word of God. Now seeing Esdras was the High
Priest, and the High Priest was their Civill Soveraigne, it is manifest,
that the Scriptures were never made Laws, but by the Soveraign Civill
Power.

By the Writings of the Fathers that lived in the time before that *The New*
Christian Religion was received, and authorised by Constantine the *Testament*
Emperour, we may find, that the Books wee now have of the New *began to be*
Testament, were held by the Christians of that time (except a few, in *Canonicall*
respect of whose paucity the rest were called the Catholique Church, *under*
and others Haeretiques) for the dictates of the Holy Ghost; and *Christian*
consequently for the Canon, or Rule of Faith: such was the reverence *Soveraigns.*
and opinion they had of their Teachers; as generally the reverence
that the Disciples bear to their first Masters, in all manner of doctrine
they receive from them, is not small. Therefore there is no doubt, but
when S. Paul wrote to the Churches he had converted; or any another
Apostle, or Disciple of Christ, to those which had then embraced
Christ, they received those their Writings for the true Christian Doctrine. But in that time, when not the Power and Authority of the
Teacher, but the Faith of the Hearer caused them to receive it, it was
not the Apostles that made their own Writings Canonicall, but every
Convert made them so to himself.

But the question here, is not what any Christian made a Law, or
Canon to himself, (which he might again reject, by the same right he
received it;) but what was so made a Canon to them, as without
injustice they could not doe any thing contrary thereunto. That the
New Testament should in this sense be Canonicall, that is to say, a
Law in any place where the Law of the Common-wealth had not
made it so, is contrary to the nature of a Law. For a Law, (as hath
been already shewn) is the Commandement of that Man, or Assem-

bly, to whom we have given Soveraign Authority, to make such Rules for the direction of our actions, as hee shall think fit; and to punish us, when we doe any thing contrary to the same. When therefore any other man shall offer unto us any other Rules, which the Soveraign Ruler hath not prescribed, they are but Counsell, and Advice; which, whether good, or bad, hee that is counselled, may without injustice refuse to observe; and when contrary to the Laws already established, without injustice cannot observe, how good soever he conceiveth it to be. I say, he cannot in this case observe the same in his actions, nor in his dicourse with other men; though he may without blame beleeve his private Teachers, and wish he had the liberty to practise their advice; and that it were publiquely received for Law. For internall Faith is in its own nature invisible, and consequently exempted from all humane jurisdiction; whereas the words, and actions that proceed from it, as breaches of our Civill obedience, are injustice both before God and Man. Seeing then our Saviour hath denyed his Kingdome to be in this world, seeing he hath said, he came not to judge, but to save the world, he hath not subjected us to other Laws than those of the Common-wealth; that is, the Jews to the Law of Moses, (which he saith (*Mat.* 5.) he came not to destroy, but to fulfill,) and other Nations to the Laws of their severall Soveraigns, and all men to the Laws of Nature; the observing whereof, both he himselfe, and his Apostles have in their teaching recommended to us, as a necessary condition of being admitted by him in the last day into his eternall Kingdome, wherein shall be Protection, and Life everlasting. Seeing then our Saviour, and his Apostles, left not new Laws to oblige us in this world, but new Doctrine to prepare us for the next; the Books of the New Testament, which containe that Doctrine, untill obedience to them was commanded, by them that God had given power to on earth to be Legislators, were not obligatory Canons, that is, Laws, but onely good, and safe advice, for the direction of sinners in the way to salvation, which every man might take, and refuse at his owne perill, without injustice.

Again, our Saviour Christs Commission to his Apostles, and Disciples, was to Proclaim his Kingdome (not present, but) to come; and to Teach all Nations; and to Baptize them that should beleeve; and to enter into the houses of them that should receive them; and where they were not received, to shake off the dust of their feet against them; but not to call for fire from heaven to destroy them, nor to compell them to obedience by the Sword. In all which there is nothing of Power, but of Perswasion. He sent them out as Sheep unto Wolves, not as Kings to their Subjects. They had not in Commission to make Laws; but to obey, and teach obedience to Laws made; and consequently they could not make their Writings obligatory Canons, without the help of the Soveraign Civill Power. And therefore the Scripture of the New Testament is there only Law, where the lawfull Civill Power hath made it so. And there also the King, or Soveraign, maketh it a Law to himself; by which he subjecteth himselfe, not to the Doctor, or Apostle that converted him, but to God himself, and his Son Jesus Christ, as immediately as did the Apostles themselves.

That which may seem to give the New Testament, in respect of those that have embraced Christian Doctrine, the force of Laws, in the times, and places of persecution, is the decrees they made amongst themselves in their Synods. For we read (*Acts* 15.28.) the stile of the Councell of the Apostles, the Elders, and the whole Church, in this manner, *It seemed good to the Holy Ghost, and to us, to lay upon you no greater burthen than these necessary things, & c.* which is a stile that signifieth a Power to lay a burthen on them that had received their Doctrine. Now *to lay a burden on another*, seemeth the same that *to oblige*; and therefore the Acts of that Councell were Laws to the then Christians. Neverthelesse, they were no more Laws than are these other Precepts, *Repent; Be Baptized; Keep the Commandements; Beleeve the Gospel; Come unto me; Sell all that thou hast; Give it to the poor*; and, *Follow me*; which are not Commands, but Invitations, and Callings of men to Christianity, like that of *Esay* 55.1. *Ho, every man that thirsteth, come yee to the waters, come, and buy wine and milke without money*. For first, the Apostles power was no other than that of our Saviour, to invite men to embrace the Kingdome of God; which they themselves acknowledged for a Kingdome (not present, but) to come; and they that have no Kingdome, can make no Laws. And secondly, if their Acts of Councell, were Laws, they could not without sin be disobeyed. But we read not any where, that they who received not the Doctrine of Christ, did therein sin; but that they died in their sins; that is, that their sins against the Laws to which they owed obedience, were not pardoned. And those Laws were the Laws of Nature, and the Civill Laws of the State, whereto every Christian man had by pact submitted himself. And therefore by the Burthen, which the Apostles might lay on such as they had converted, are not to be understood

Of the Power of Councells to make the Scriptures Law.

[286]

Laws, but Conditions, proposed to those that sought Salvation; which they might accept, or refuse at their own perill, without a new sin, though not without the hazard of being condemned, and excluded out of the Kingdome of God for their sins past. And therefore of Infidels, S. John saith not, the wrath of God shall *come* upon them, but *the wrath of God remaineth upon them*; and not that they shall be condemned; but that *they are condemned already.* Nor can it be conceived, that the benefit of Faith, *is Remission of sins*, unlesse we conceive withall, that the dammage of Infidelity, is *the Retention of the same sins.*

John 3.36.
John 3.18.

But to what end is it (may some man aske), that the Apostles, and other Pastors of the Church, after their time, should meet together, to agree upon what Doctrine should be taught, both for Faith and Manners, if no man were obliged to observe their Decrees? To this may be answered, that the Apostles, and Elders of that Councell, were obliged even by their entrance into it, to teach the Doctrine therein concluded, and decreed to be taught, so far forth, as no precedent Law, to which they were obliged to yeeld obedience, was to the contrary; but not that all other Christians should be obliged to observe, what they taught. For though they might deliberate what each of them should teach; yet they could not deliberate what others should do, unless their Assembly had had a Legislative Power; which none could have but Civil Soveraigns. For though God be the Soveraign of all the world, we are not bound to take for his Law, whatsoever is propounded by every man in his name; nor anything contrary to the Civill Law, which God hath expressly commanded us to obey.

[287]

Seeing then the Acts of Councell of the Apostles, were then no Laws, but Counsells; much lesse are Laws the Acts of any other Doctors, or Councells since, if assembled without the Authority of the Civill Soveraign. And consequently, the Books of the New Testament, though most perfect Rules of Christian Doctrine, could not be made Laws by any other authority then that of Kings, or Soveraign Assemblies.

The first Councell, that made *the*[1] Scriptures we now have, Canon, is not extant: For that Collection of the Canons of the Apostles, attributed to *Clemens*, the first Bishop of Rome after S. Peter, is subject to question: For though the Canonicall books bee there reck-

---

[1] *Syn.*: of the [but corrected in the Errata]

oned up; yet these words, *Sint vobis omnibus Clerics & Laicis Libri venerandi, & c.* containe a distinction of Clergy, and Laity, that was not in use so neer St. Peters time. The first Councell for setling the Canonicall Scripture, that is extant, is that of Laodicea, *Can.* 59. which forbids the reading of other Books then those in the Churches; which is a Mandate that is not addressed to every Christian, but to those onely that had authority to read any thing publiquely in the Church; that is, to Ecclesiastiques onely.

Of Ecclesiasticall Officers in the time of the Apostles, some were Magisteriall, some Ministeriall. Magisteriall were the Offices of preaching of the Gospel of the Kingdom of God to Infidels; of administring the Sacraments, and Divine Service; and of teaching the Rules of Faith and Manners to those that were converted. Ministeriall was the Office of Deacons, that is, of them that were appointed to the administration of the secular necessities of the Church, at such time as they lived upon a common stock of mony, raised out of the voluntary contributions of the faithfull.

Of the Right of constituting Ecclesiasticall Officers in the time of the Apostles.

Amongst the Officers Magisteriall, the first, and principall were the Apostles; whereof there were at first but twelve; and these were chosen and constituted by our Saviour himselfe; and their Office was not onely to Preach, Teach, and Baptize, but also to be Martyrs, (Witnesses of our Saviours Resurrection.) This Testimony, was the specificall, and essentiall mark; whereby the Apostleship was distinguished from other Magistracy Ecclesiasticall; as being necessary for an Apostle, either to have seen our Saviour after his Resurrection, or to have conversed with him before, and seen his works, and other arguments of his Divinity, whereby they might be taken for sufficient Witnesses. And therefore at the election of a new Apostle in the place of Judas Iscariot, S. Peter saith (*Acts* 1.21, 22.) *Of these men that have companyed with us, all the time that the Lord Jesus went in and out among us, beginning from the Baptisme of John unto that same day that he was taken up from us,* must *one be ordained to be a* Witnesse *with us of his Resurrection*: where by this word *must*, is implyed a necessary property of an Apostle, to have companyed with the first and prime Apostles in the time that our Saviour manifested himself in the flesh.

[288]

The first Apostle, of those which were not constituted by Christ in the time he was upon the Earth, was *Matthias*, chosen in this manner: There were assembled together in Jerusalem about 120 Christians (*Acts* 1.15.) These appointed two, *Joseph* the *Just*, and *Matthias*, (ver.

Matthias made Apostle by the Congregation.

23.) and caused lots to be drawn; *and* (ver. 26.) *the Lot fell on Matthias, and he was numbred with the Apostles.* So that here we see the ordination of this Apostle, was the act of the Congregation, and not of St. Peter, nor of the eleven, otherwise then as Members of the Assembly.

Paul and Barnabas made Apostles by the Church of Antioch.

After him there was never any other Apostle ordained, but Paul and Barnabas; which was done (as we read (*Acts* 13.1, 2, 3.) in this manner. *There were in the Church that was at Antioch, certaine Prophets, and Teachers; as Barnabas, and Simeon that was called Niger, and Lucius of Cyrene, and Manaen; which had been brought up with Herod the Tetrarch, and Saul. As they ministred unto the Lord, and fasted, the Holy Ghost said, Separate mee Barnabas, and Saul for the worke whereunto I have called them. And when they had fasted, and prayed, and laid their hands on them, they sent them away.*

By which it is manifest, that though they were called by the Holy Ghost, their Calling was declared unto them, and their Mission authorized by the particular Church of Antioch. And that this their calling was to the Apostleship, is apparent by that, that they are both called (*Acts* 14.14.) Apostles: And that it was by vertue of this act of the Church of Antioch, that they were Apostles, S. Paul declareth plainly (*Rom.* 1.1.) in that hee useth the word, which the Holy Ghost used at his calling: For hee stileth himself, *An Apostle separated unto the Gospel of God*; alluding to the words of the Holy Ghost, *Separate me Barnabas and Saul, & c.* But seeing the work of an Apostle, was to be a Witnesse of the Resurrection of Christ, a man may here aske, how S. Paul, that conversed not with our Saviour before his passion, could know he was risen. To which is easily answered, that our Saviour himself appeared to him in the way to Damascus, from Heaven, after his Ascension; *and chose him for a vessell to bear his name before the Gentiles, and Kings, and Children of Israel*; and consequently (having seen the Lord after his passion) was a competent Witnesse of his Resurrection: And as for Barnabas, he was a Disciple before the Passion. It is therefore evident that Paul, and Barnabas were Apostles; and yet chosen, and authorized (not by the first Apostles alone, but) by the Church of Antioch; as Matthias was chosen, and authorized by the Church of Jerusalem.

What Offices in the Church are Magisteriall.

[289]

Bishop, a word formed in our language, out of the Greek *Episcopus*, signifieth an Overseer, or Superintendent of any businesse, and particularly a Pastor, or Shepherd; and thence by metaphor was taken, not only amongst the Jews that were originally Shepherds, but also amongst the Heathen, to signifie the Office of a King, or any other Ruler, or Guide of People, whether he ruled by Laws, or Doctrine. And so the Apostles were the first Christian Bishops, instituted by Christ himselfe: in which sense the Apostleship of Judas is called (*Acts* 1.20.) *his Bishoprick.* And afterwards, when there were constituted Elders in the Christian Churches, with charge to guide Christs flock by their doctrine, and advice; these Elders were also called Bishops. Timothy was an Elder (which word *Elder*, in the New Testament is a name of Office, as well as of Age;) yet he was also a Bishop. And Bishops were then content with the Title of Elders. Nay S. John himselfe, the Apostle beloved of our Lord, beginneth his Second Epistle with these words, *The Elder to the Elect Lady.* By which it is evident, that *Bishop, Pastor, Elder, Doctor,* that is to say, *Teacher,* were but so many divers names of the same Office in the time of the Apostles. For there was then no government by Coercion, but only by Doctrine, and Perswading. The Kingdome of God was yet to come, in a new world; so that there could be no authority to compell in any Church, till the Common-wealth had embraced the Christian Faith; and consequently no diversity of Authority, though there were diversity of Employments.

Besides these Magisteriall employments in the Church; namely, Apostles, Bishops, Elders, Pastors, and Doctors, whose calling was to proclaim Christ to the Jews, and Infidels, and to direct, and teach those that beleeved we read in the New Testament of no other. For by the names of *Evangelists* and *Prophets*, is not signified any Office, but severall Gifts, by which severall men were profitable to the Church: as Evangelists, by writing the life and acts of our Saviour; such as were S. *Matthew* and S. *John* Apostles, and S. *Marke* and S. *Luke* Disciples, and whosoever else wrote of that subject, (as S. *Thomas*, and S. *Barnabas* are said to have done, though the Church have not received the Books that have gone under their names:) and as Prophets, by the gift of interpreting the Old Testament; and sometimes by declaring their speciall Revelations to the Church. For neither these gifts, nor the gifts of Languages, nor the gift of Casting out Devils, or of Curing other diseases, nor any thing else did make an Officer in the Church, save onely the due calling and election to the charge of Teaching.

As the Apostles, Matthias, Paul, and Barnabas, were not made by our Saviour himself, but were elected by the Church, that is, by the Assembly of Christians; namely, Matthias by the Church of *Ordination of Teachers.*

Jerusalem, and Paul, and Barnabas by the Church of Antioch; so were also the *Presbyters*, and *Pastors* in other Cities, elected by the Churches of those Cities. For proof whereof, let us consider, first, how S. Paul proceeded in the Ordination of Presbyters, in the Cities where he had converted men to the Christian Faith, immediately after he and Barnabas had received their Apostleship. We read (*Acts* 14.23.) that

[290]

they ordained Elders in every Church; which at first sight may be taken for an Argument, that they themselves chose, and gave them their authority: But if we consider the Originall text, it will be manifest, that they were authorized, and chosen by the Assembly of the Christians of each City. For the words there are, χειροτονήσαντες αὐτοῖς πρεσβυτέρους κατ᾽ ἐκκλησίαν, that is, *When they had Ordained them Elders by the Holding up of Hands in every Congregation.* Now it is well enough known, that in all those Cities, the manner of choosing Magistrates, and Officers, was by plurality of suffrages; and (because the ordinary way of distinguishing the Affirmative Votes from the Negatives, was by Holding up of Hands) to ordain an Officer in any of the Cities, was no more but to bring the people together, to elect them by plurality of Votes, whether it were by plurality of elevated hands, or by plurality of voices, or plurality of balls, or beans, or small stones, of which every man cast in one, into a vessell marked for the Affirmative, or Negative; for divers Cities had divers customes in that point. It was therefore the Assembly that elected their own Elders: the Apostles were onely Presidents of the Assembly to call them together for such Election, and to pronounce them Elected, and to give them the benediction, which now is called Consecration. And for this cause they that were Presidents of the Assemblies, as (in the absence of the Apostles) the Elders were, were called προεστῶτες, and in Latin *Antistites*; which words signifie the Principall Person of the Assembly, whose office was to number the Votes, and to declare thereby who was chosen; and where the Votes were equall, to decide the matter in question, by adding his own; which is the Office of a President in Councell. And (because all the Churches had their Presbyters ordained in the same manner,) where the word is *Constitute*, (as *Titus* 1.5.) ἵνα καταστήσῃς κατὰ πόλιν πρεσβυτέρους, *For this cause left I thee in Crete, that thou shouldest constitute Elders in every City*, we are to understand the same thing; namely, that hee should call the faithfull together, and ordain them Presbyters by plurality of suffrages. It had been a strange thing, if in a Town, where men perhaps had never seen any Magistrate otherwise chosen then by an Assembly, those of the Town becomming Christians, should so much as have thought on any other way of Election of their Teachers, and Guides, that is to say, of their Presbyters, (otherwise called Bishops,) then this of plurality of suffrages, intimated by S. Paul (*Acts* 14.23.) in the word χειϱοτονήσαντες: Nor was there ever any choosing of Bishops, (before the Emperors found it necessary to regulate them in order to the keeping of the peace amongst them,) but by the Assemblies of the Christians in every severall Town.

The same is also confirmed by the continuall practise even to this day, in the Election of the Bishops of Rome. For if the Bishop of any place, had the right of choosing another, to the succession of the Pastorall Office, in any City, at such time as he went from thence, to plant the same in another place; much more had he had the Right, to appoint his successour in that place, in which he last resided and dyed: And we find not, that ever any Bishop of Rome appointed his [291] successor. For they were a long time chosen by the People, as we may see by the sedition raised about the Election, between *Damasus,* and *Ursicinus*; which Ammianus Marcellinus saith was so great, that *Juventius* the Praefect, unable to keep the peace between them, was forced to goe out of the City; and that there were above an hundred men found dead upon that occasion in the Church it self. And though they afterwards were chosen, first, by the whole Clergy of Rome, and afterwards by the Cardinalls; yet never any was appointed to the succession by his predecessor. If therefore they pretended no right to appoint their own successors, I think I may reasonably conclude, they had no right to appoint the successors of other Bishops, without receiving some new power; which none could take from the Church to bestow on them, but such as had a lawfull authority, not onely to Teach, but to Command the Church; which none could doe, but the Civill Soveraign.

The word *Minister* in the Originall Διάϰονος, signifieth one that voluntarily doth the businesse of another man; and differeth from a Servant onely in this, that Servants are obliged by their condition, to what is commanded them; whereas Ministers are obliged onely by their undertaking, and bound therefore to no more than that they have undertaken: So that both they that teach the Word of God, and they that administer the secular affairs of the Church, are both Ministers, but they are Ministers of different Persons. For the Pastors of

Ministers of the Church what:

367

the Church, called (*Acts* 6.4.) *The Ministers of the Word*, are Ministers of Christ, whose Word it is: But the Ministery of a *Deacon*, which is called (verse 2. of the same Chapter) *Serving of Tables*, is a service done to the Church, or Congregation: So that neither any one man, nor the whole Church, could ever of their Pastor say, he was their Minister; but of a Deacon, whether the charge he undertook were to serve tables, or distribute maintenance to the Christians, when they lived in each City on a common stock, or upon collections, as in the first times, or to take a care of the House of Prayer, or of the Revenue, or other worldly businesse of the Church, the whole Congregation might properly call him their Minister.

For their employment, as Deacons, was to serve the Congregation; though upon occasion they omitted not to Preach the Gospel, and maintain the Doctrine of Christ, every one according to his gifts, as S. Steven did; and both to Preach, and Baptize, as Philip did: For that Philip, which (*Act.* 8.5.) Preached the Gospell at Samaria, and (verse 38.) Baptized the Eunuch, was Philip the Deacon, not Philip the Apostle. For it is manifest (verse 1.) that when Philip preached in Samaria, the Apostles were at Jerusalem, and (verse 14.) *when they heard that Samaria had received the Word of God, sent Peter and John to them*; by imposition of whose hands, they that were Baptized, (verse 15.) received (which before by the Baptisme of Philip they had not received) the Holy Ghost. For it was necessary for the conferring of the Holy Ghost, that their Baptisme should be administred, or confirmed by a Minister of the Word, not by a Minister of the Church. And therefore to confirm the Baptisme of those that Philip the Deacon had Baptized, the Apostles sent out of their own number from Jerusalem to Samaria, Peter, and John; who conferred on them that before were but Baptized, those graces that were signs of the Holy Spirit, which at that time did accompany all true Beleevers; which what they were may be understood by that which S. *Marke* saith (chap. 16.17.) *These signes follow them that beleeve in my Name; they shall cast out Devills; they shall speak with new tongues; They shall take up Serpents, and if they drink any deadly thing, it shall not hurt them; They shall lay hands on the sick, and they shall recover.* This to doe, was it that Philip could not give; but the Apostles could, and (as appears by this place) effectually did to every man that truly beleeved, and was by a Minister of Christ himself Baptized: which power either Christs Ministers in

[292]

this age cannot conferre, or else there are very few true Beleevers, or Christ hath very few Ministers.

That the first Deacons were chosen, not by the Apostles, but by a Congregation of the Disciples; that is, of Christian men of all sorts, is manifest out of *Acts* 6. where we read that the *Twelve*, after the number of Disciples was multiplyed, called them together, and having told them, that it was not fit that the Apostles should leave the Word of God, and serve tables, said unto them (verse 3.) *Brethren looke you out among you seven men of honest report, full of the Holy Ghost, and of Wisdome, whom we may appoint over this businesse.* Here it is manifest, that though the Apostles declared them elected; yet the Congregation chose them; which also, (verse the fift) is more expressely said, where it is written, that *the saying pleased the multitude, and they chose seven, &c.*

And how chosen.

Under the Old Testament, the Tribe of Levi were onely capable of the Priesthood, and other inferiour Offices of the Church. The land was divided amongst the other Tribes (Levi excepted,) which by the subdivision of the Tribe of Joseph, into Ephraim and Manasses, were still twelve. To the Tribe of Levi were assigned certain Cities for their habitation, with the suburbs for their cattell: but for their portion, they were to have the tenth of the fruits of the land of their Brethren. Again, the Priests for their maintenance had the tenth of that tenth, together with part of the oblations, and sacrifices. For God had said to Aaron (*Numb.* 18.20.) *Thou shalt have no inheritance in their land, neither shalt thou have any part amongst them, I am thy part, and thine inheritance amongst the Children of Israel.* For God being then King, and having constituted the Tribe of Levi to be his Publique Ministers, he allowed them for their maintenance, the Publique revenue, that is to say, the part that God had reserved to himself; which were Tythes, and Offerings: and that is it which is meant, where God saith, I am thine inheritance. And therefore to the Levites might not unfitly be attributed the name of *Clergy* from Κλῆρος, which signifieth Lot, or Inheritance; not that they were heirs of the Kingdome of God, more than other; but that Gods inheritance, was their maintenance. Now seeing in this time God himself was their King, and Moses, Aaron, and the succeeding High Priests were his Lieutenants, it is manifest, that the Right of Tythes, and Offerings was constituted by the Civill Power.

Of Ecclesiasticall Revenue, under the Law of Moses.

[293]

After their rejection of God in the demanding of a King, they enjoyed still the same revenue; but the Right thereof was derived from that, that the Kings did never take it from them: for the Publique Revenue was at the disposing of him that was the Publique Person; and that (till the Captivity) was the King. And again, after the return from the Captivity, they paid their Tythes as before to the Priest. Hitherto therefore Church Livings were determined by the Civill Soveraign.

In our Saviours time, and after. Mat. 10.9, 10.
Of the maintenance of our Saviour, and his Apostles, we read onely they had a Purse, (which was carried by Judas Iscariot;) and, that of the Apostles, such as were Fisher-men, did sometimes use their trade; and that when our Saviour sent the Twelve Apostles to Preach, he forbad them *to carry Gold, and Silver, and Brasse in their purses, for that the workman is worthy of his hire:* By which it is probable, their ordinary maintenance was not unsuitable to their employment; for their employment was (ver. 8.) *freely to give, because they had freely received;* and their maintenance was the *free gift* of those that beleeved the good tyding they carryed about of the coming of the Messiah their Saviour. To which we may adde, that which was contributed out of gratitude; by such as our Saviour had healed of diseases; of which are mentioned *Certain women* (Luke 8.2, 3.) *which had been healed of evill spirits and infirmities; Mary Magdalen, out of whom went seven Devills; and Joanna the wife of Chuza, Herods Steward; and Susanna, and many others, which ministred unto him of their substance.*

*Acts 4.34.
After our Saviours Ascension, the Christians of every City lived in Common,* upon the mony which was made of the sale of their lands and possessions, and laid down at the feet of the Apostles, of good will, not of duty; for *whilest the Land remained* (saith S. Peter to Ananias *(Acts* 5.4.) *was it not thine? and after it was sold, was it not in thy power?* which sheweth he needed not have saved his land, nor his money by lying, as not being bound to contribute anything at all, unlesse he had pleased. And as in the time of the Apostles, so also all the time downward, till after Constantine the Great, we shall find, that the maintenance of the Bishops, and Pastors of the Christian Church, was nothing but the voluntary contribution of them that had embraced their Doctrine. There was yet no mention of Tythes: but such was in the time of Constantine, and his Sons, the affection of Christians to their Pastors, as Ammianus Marcellinus saith (describing the sedition of *Damasus* and *Ursicinus* about the Bishopricke,) that it was worth

their contention, in that the Bishops of those times by the liberality of
their flock, and especially of Matrons, lived splendidly, were carryed [294]
in Coaches, and were sumptuous in their fare and apparell.

But here may some ask, whether the Pastor were then bound to live *The*
upon voluntary contribution, as upon almes, *For who* (saith S. Paul 1 *Ministers of*
Cor. 9.7.) *goeth to war at his own charges? or who feedeth a flock, and eateth* *lived on the*
not of the milke of the flock? And again, *Doe ye not know that they which* *Benevolence*
minister about holy things, live of the things of the Temple; and they which *of their*
wait at the Altar, partake with the Altar; that is to say, have part of that *1 Cor. 9.13.*
which is offered at the Altar for their maintenance? And then he
concludeth, *Even so hath the Lord appointed, that they which preach the*
Gospel should live of the Gospel. From which place may be inferred
indeed, that the Pastors of the Church ought to be maintained by
their flocks; but not that the Pastors were to determine, either the
quantity, or the kind of their own allowance, and be (as it were) their
own Carvers. Their allowance must needs therefore be determined,
either by the gratitude, and liberality of every particular man of their
flock, or by the whole Congregation, By the whole Congregation it
could not be, because their Acts were then no Laws: Therefore the
maintenance of Pastors before Emperours and Civill Soveraigns had
made Laws to settle it, was nothing but Benevolence. They that
served at the Altar lived on what was offered. So may the Pastors also
take what is offered them by their flock; but not exact what is not
offered. In what Court should they sue for it, who had no Tribunalls?
Or if they had Arbitrators amongst themselves, who should execute
their Judgments, when they had no power to arme their Officers? It
remaineth therefore, that there could be no certaine maintenance
assigned to any Pastors of the Church, but by the whole Congregation; and then onely, when their Decrees should have the force (not
onely of *Canons*, but also) of *Laws*; which Laws could not be made,
but by Emperours, Kings, or other Civill Soveraignes. The Right of
Tythes in Moses Law, could not be applyed to the then Ministers of
the Gospell; because Moses and the High Priests were the Civill
Soveraigns of the people under God, whose Kingdom amongst the
Jews was present; whereas the Kingdome of God by Christ is yet to
come.

Hitherto hath been shewn what the Pastors of the Church are; what
are the points of their Commission (as that they were to Preach, to
Teach, to Baptize, to be Presidents in their severall Congregations;)

what is Ecclesiasticall Censure, *viz.* Excommunication, that is to say, in those places where Christanity was forbidden by the Civill Laws, a putting of themselves out of the company of the Excommunicate, and where Christianity was by the Civill Law commanded, a putting the Excommunicate out of the Congregations of Christians; who elected the Pastors and Ministers of the Church, (that it was, the Congregation); who consecrated and blessed them, (that it was the Pastor); what was their due revenue, (that it was none but their own possessions, and their own labour, and the voluntary contributions of devout and gratefull Christians). We are to consider now, what Office in the Church those persons have, who being Civill Soveraignes, have embraced also the Christian Faith.

[295]

That the Civill Soveraign being a Christian hath the Right of appointing Pastors.

And first, we are to remember, that the Right of Judging what Doctrines are fit for Peace, and to be taught the Subjects, is in all Common-wealths inseparably annexed (as hath been already proved cha. 18.) to the Soveraign Power Civill, whether it be in one Man, or in one Assembly of men. For it is evident to the meanest capacity, that mens actions are derived from the opinions they have of the Good, or Evill, which from those actions redound unto themselves; and consequently, men that are once possessed of an opinion, that their obedience to the Soveraign Power, will bee more hurtfull to them, that their disobedience, will disobey the Laws, and thereby overthrow the Common-wealth, and introduce confusion, and Civill war; for the avoiding whereof, all Civill Government was ordained. And therefore in all Common-wealths of the Heathen, the Soveraigns have had the name of Pastors of the People, because there was no Subject that could lawfully Teach the people, but by their permission and authority.

This Right of the Heathen Kings, cannot bee thought taken from them by their conversion to the Faith of Christ; who never ordained, that Kings for beleeving in him, should be deposed, that is, subjected to any but himself, or (which is all one) be deprived of the power necessary for the conservation of Peace amongst their Subjects, and for their defence against foraign Enemies. And therefore Christian Kings are still the Supreme Pastors of their people, and have power to ordain what Pastors they please, to teach the Church, that is, to teach the People committed to their charge.

Again, let the right of choosing them be (as before the conversion of Kings) in the Church, for so it was in the time of the Apostles themselves (as hath been shewn already in this chapter); even so also the Right will be in the Civill Soveraign, Christian. For in that he is a Christian, he allowes the Teaching; and in that he is the Soveraign (which is as much to say, the Church by Representation,) the Teachers hee elects, are elected by the Church. And when an Assembly of Christians choose their Pastor in a Christian Common-wealth, it is the Soveraign that electeth him, because tis done by his Authority; In the same manner, as when a Town choose their Maior, it is the act of him that hath the Soveraign Power: For every act done, is the act of him, without whose consent it is invalid. And therefore whatsoever examples may be drawn out of History, concerning the Election of Pastors, by the People, or by the Clergy, they are no arguments against the Right of any Civill Soveraign, because they that elected them did it by his Authority.

Seeing then in every Christian Common-wealth, the Civill Soveraign is the Supreme Pastor, to whose charge the whole flock of his Subjects is committed, and consequently that it is by his authority, [296] that all other Pastors are made, and have power to teach, and performe all other Pastorall offices; it followeth also, that it is from the Civill Soveraign, that all other Pastors derive their right of Teaching, Preaching, and other functions pertaining to that Office; and that they are but his Ministers; in the same manner as the Magistrates of Towns, Judges in Courts of Justice, and Commanders of Armies, are all but Ministers of him that is the Magistrate of the whole Common-wealth, Judge of all Causes, and Commander of the whole Militia, which is alwaies the Civill Soveraign. And the reason hereof, is not because they that Teach, but because they that are to Learn, are his Subjects. For let it be supposed, that a Christian King commit the Authority of Ordaining Pastors in his Dominions to another King, (as divers Christian Kings allow that power to the Pope;) he doth not thereby constitute a Pastor over himself, nor a Soveraign Pastor over his People; for that were to deprive himself of the Civill Power; which depending on the opinion men have of their Duty to him, and the fear they have of Punishment in another world, would depend also on the skill, and loyalty of Doctors, who are no lesse subject, not only to Ambition, but also to Ignorance, than any other sort of men. So that where a stranger hath authority to appoint Teachers, it is given him by the Soveraign in whose Dominions he teacheth. Christian Doctors are our Schoolmasters to Christianity; But Kings are Fathers of

Families, and may receive Schoolmasters for their Subjects from the recommendation of a stranger, but not from the command; especially when the ill teaching them shall redound to the great and manifest profit of him that recommends them: nor can they be obliged to retain them, longer than it is for the Publique good; the care of which they stand so long charged withall, as they retain any other essentiall Right of the Soveraignty.

The Pastorall Authority of Soveraigns only is de Jure Divino, that of other Pastors is Jure Civili.

If a man therefore should ask a Pastor, in the execution of his Office, as the chief Priests and Elders of the people (*Mat.* 21.23.) asked our Saviour, *By what authority dost thou these things, and who gave thee this authority*: he can make no other just Answer, but that he doth it by the Authority of the Common-wealth, given him by the King, or Assembly that representeth it. All Pastors, except the Supreme, execute their charges in the Right, that is by the Authority of the Civill Soveraign, that is, *Iure Civili.* But the King, and every other Soveraign, executeth his Office of Supreme Pastor, by immediate Authority from God, that is to say, *in Gods Right*, or *Iure Divino.* And therefore none but Kings can put into their Titles (a mark of their submission to God onely) *Dei gratiâ Rex, &c.* Bishops ought to say in the beginning of their Mandates, *By the favour of the Kings Majesty, Bishop of Such a Diocesse*; or as Civill Ministers, *In his Majesties Name.* For in saying, *Divinâ providentiâ*, which is the same with *Dei gratiâ*, though disguised, they deny to have received their authority from the Civill State; and sliely slip off the Collar of their Civill Subjection, contrary to the unity and defence of the Common-wealth.

[297]

Christian Kings have Power to execute all manner of Pastoral function.

But if every Christian Soveraign be the Supreme Pastor of his own Subjects, it seemeth that he hath also the Authority, not only to Preach (which perhaps no man will deny;) but also to Baptize, and to Administer the Sacrament of the Lords Supper; and to Consecrate both Temples, and Pastors to Gods service; which most men deny; partly because they use to do it; and partly because the Administration of Sacraments, and Consecration of Persons, and Places to holy uses, requireth the Imposition of such mens hands, as by the like Imposition successively from the time of the Apostles have been ordained to the like Ministery. For proof therefore that Christian Kings have power to Baptize, and to Consecrate, I am to render a reason, both why they use not to doe it, and how, without the ordinary ceremony of Imposition of hands, they are made capable of doing it, when they will.

There is no doubt but any King, in case he were skilfull in the Sciences, might by the same Right of his Office, read Lectures of them himself, by which he authorizeth others to read them in the Universities. Neverthelesse, because the care of the summe of the businesse of the Common-wealth taketh up his whole time, it were not convenient for him to apply himself in Person to that particular. A King may also if he please, sit in Judgment, to hear and determine all manner of Causes, as well as give others authority to doe it in his name; but that the charge that lyeth upon him of Command and Government, constrain him to bee continually at the Helm, and to commit the Ministeriall Offices to others under him. In the like manner our Saviour (who surely had power to Baptize) Baptized none⋆ himselfe, but sent his Apostles and Disciples to Baptize. So ⋆*John* 4.2. also S. Paul, by the necessity of Preaching in divers and far distant places, Baptized few: Amongst all the Corinthians he Baptized only⋆ ⋆1 *Cor.* *Crispus*, *Cajus*, and *Stephanus*; and the reason was, because his 1.14, 16. principall ⋆Charge was to Preach. Whereby it is manifest, that the ⋆1 *Cor.* greater Charge, (such as is the Government of the Church,) is a 1.17. dispensation for the lesse. The reason therefore why Christian Kings use not to Baptize, is evident, and the same, for which at this day there are few Baptized by Bishops, and by the Pope fewer.

And as concerning Imposition of Hands, whether it be needfull, for the authorizing of a King to Baptize, and Consecrate, we may consider thus.

Imposition of Hands, was a most ancient publique ceremony amongst the Jews, by which was designed, and made certain, the person, or other thing intended in a mans prayer, blessing, sacrifice, consecration, condemnation, or other speech. So Jacob in blessing the children of Joseph (*Gen.* 48.14.) *Laid his right Hand on Ephraim the younger, and his left Hand on Manasseh the first born*; and this he did [298] *wittingly* (though they were so presented to him by Joseph, as he was forced in doing it to stretch out his arms acrosse) to design to whom he intended the greater blessing. So also in the sacrificing of the Burnt offering, Aaron is commanded [*Exod.* 29.10.] *to Lay his Hands on the head of the bullock*; and [ver. 15.] *to Lay his Hand on the head of the ramme*. The same is also said again, *Levit.* 1.4. & 8.14. Likewise Moses when he ordained Joshua to be Captain of the Israelites, that is, consecrated him to Gods service, [*Numb.* 27.23.] *Laid his Hands upon him, and gave him his Charge*, designing, and rendring certain, who it was they were to obey in war. And in the consecration of the Levites [*Numb.* 8.10.] God commanded that *the Children of Israel should Put their Hands upon the Levites.* And in the condemnation of him that had blasphemed the Lord [*Levit.* 24.14.] God commanded that *all that heard him should Lay their Hands on his head, and that all the Congregation should stone him.* And why should they only that heard him, Lay their Hands upon him, and not rather a Priest, Levite, or other Minister of Justice, but that none else were able to design, and demonstrate to the eyes of the Congregation, who it was that had blasphemed, and ought to die? And to design a man, or any other thing, by the Hand to the Eye, is lesse subject to mistake, than when it is done to the Eare by a Name.

And so much was this ceremony observed, that in blessing the whole Congregation at once, which cannot be done by Laying on of Hands, yet *Aaron* [*Levit.* 9.22.] *did lift up his Hand towards the people when he blessed them.* And we read also of the like ceremony of Consecration of Temples amongst the Heathen, as that the Priest laid his Hands on some post of the Temple, all the while he was uttering the words of Consecration. So naturall it is to design any individuall thing, rather by the Hand, to assure the Eyes, than by Words to inform the Eare in matters of Gods Publique service.

This ceremony was not therefore new in our Saviours time. For Jairus [*Mark* 5.23.] whose daughter was sick, besought our Saviour (not to heal her, but) *to Lay his Hands upon her, that shee might bee healed.* And [*Matth.* 19.13.] *they brought unto him little children, that hee should Put his Hands on them, and Pray.*

According to this ancient Rite, the Apostles, and Presbyters, and the Presbytery it self, Laid Hands on them whom they ordained Pastors, and withall prayed for them that they might receive the Holy Ghost; and that not only once, but sometimes oftner, when a new occasion was presented: but the end was still the same, namely a punctuall, and religious designation of the person, ordained either to the Pastorall Charge in general, or to a particular Mission: so [*Act.* 6.6.] *The Apostles Prayed, and Laid their Hands* on the seven Deacons; which was done, not to give them the Holy Ghost, (for they were full of the Holy Ghost before they were chosen, as appeareth immediately before, verse 3.) but to design them to that Office. And after Philip the Deacon had converted certain persons in Samaria, Peter and John went down [*Act* 8.17.] *and Laid their Hands on them, and they received*

[299]

376

the Holy Ghost. And not only an Apostle, but a Presbyter had this power: For S. Paul adviseth Timothy [1 *Tim.* 5.22.] *Lay Hands suddenly on no man*; that is, designe no man rashly to the Office of a Pastor. The whole Presbytery Laid their Hands on Timothy, as we read 1 *Tim.* 4.14. but this is to be understood, as that some did it by the appointment of the Presbytery, and most likely their προεοτὼς, or Prolocutor, which it may be was St. Paul himself. For in his 2 Epist. to *Tim.* ver. 6. he saith to him, *Stirre up the gift of God which is in thee, by the Laying on of my Hands*: where note by the way, that by the Holy Ghost, is not meant the third Person in the Trinity, but the Gifts necessary to the Pastorall Office. We read also, that St. Paul had Imposition of Hands twice; once from Ananias at Damascus [*Acts* 9.17, 18.] at the time of his Baptisme; and again [*Acts* 13.3.] at Antioch, when he was first sent out to Preach. The use then of this ceremony considered in the Ordination of Pastors, was to design the Person to whom they gave such Power. But if there had been then any Christian, that had had the Power of Teaching before; the Baptizing of him, that is, the making him a Christian, had given him no new Power, but had onely caused him to preach true Doctrine, that is, to use his Power aright; and therefore the Imposition of Hands had been unnecessary; Baptisme it selfe had been sufficient. But every Soveraign, before Christianity, had the power of Teaching, and Ordaining Teachers; and therefore Christianity gave them no new Right, but only directed them in the way of teaching Truth; and consequently they needed no Imposition of Hands (besides that which is done in Baptisme) to authorize them to exercise any part of the Pastorall Function, as namely, to Baptize, and Consecrate. And in the Old Testament, though the Priest only had right to Consecrate, during the time that the Soveraignty was in the High Priest; yet it was not so when the Soveraignty was in the King: For we read [1 *Kings* 8.] That Solomon Blessed the People, Consecrated the Temple, and pronounced that Publique Prayer, which is the pattern now for Consecration of all Christian Churches, and Chappels: whereby it appears, he had not only the right of Ecclesiasticall Government; but also of exercising Ecclesiasticall Functions.

The Civill Soveraigne if a Christian, is head of the Church in his own Dominions.

From this consolidation of the Right Politique, and Ecclesiastique in Christian Soveraigns, it is evident, they have all manner of Power over their Subjects, that can be given to man, for the government of mens externall actions, both in Policy, and Religion; and may make such Laws, as themselves shall judge fittest, for the government of their own Subjects, both as they are the Common-wealth, and as they are the Church: for both State, and Church are the same men.

[300] If they please therefore, they may (as many Christian Kings now doe) commit the government of their Subjects in matters of Religion to the Pope; but then the Pope is in that point Subordinate to them, and exerciseth that Charge in anothers Dominion *Iure Civili*, in the Right of the Civill Soveraign; not *Iure Divino*, in Gods Right; and may therefore be discharged of that Office, when the Soveraign for the good of his Subjects shall think it necessary. They may also if they please, commit the care of Religion to one Supreme Pastor, or to an Assembly of Pastors; and give them what power over the Church, or one over another, they think most convenient; and what titles of honor, as of Bishops, Archbishops, Priests, or Presbyters, they will; and make such Laws for their maintenance, either by Tithes, or otherwise, as they please, so they doe it out of a sincere conscience, of which God onely is the Judge. It is the Civill Soveraign, that is to appoint Judges, and Interpreters of the Canonicall Scriptures; for it is he that maketh them Laws. It is he also that giveth strength to Excommunications; which but for such Laws and Punishments, as may humble obstinate Libertines, and reduce them to union with the Rest of the Church, would bee contemned. In summe, he hath the Supreme Power in all causes, as well Ecclesiasticall, as Civill, as far as concerneth actions, and words, for those onely are known, and may be accused; and of that which cannot be accused, there is no Judg at all, but God, that knoweth the heart. And these Rights are incident to all Soveraigns, whether Monarchs, or Assemblies: for they that are the Representants of a Christian People, are Representants of the Church: for a Church, and a Common-wealth of Christian People, are the same thing.

Cardinal Bellarmines Books De Summo Pontifice *considered.* Though this that I have here said, and in other places of this Book, seem cleer enough for the asserting of the Supreme Ecclesiasticall Power to Christian Soveraigns; yet because the Pope of Romes challenge to that Power universally, hath been maintained chiefly, and I think as strongly as is possible, by Cardinall Bellarmine, in his Controversie *De Summo Pontifice*; I have thought it necessary, as briefly as I can, to examine the grounds, and strength of his Discourse.

The first book. Of five Books he hath written of this subject, the first containeth three Questions: One, Which is simply the best government,

Monarchy, Aristocracy, or *Democracy*; and concludeth for neither, but for a government mixt of all three: Another, which of these is the best Government of the Church; and concludeth for the mixt, but which should most participate of Monarchy: The third, whether in this mixt Monarchy, St. Peter had the place of Monarch. Concerning his first Conclusion, I have already sufficiently proved (chapt. 18.) that all Governments, which men are bound to obey, are Simple, and Absolute. In Monarchy there is but One Man Supreme; and all other men that have any kind of Power in the State, have it by his Commission, during his pleasure; and execute it in his name: And in Aristocracy, and Democracy, but One Supreme Assembly, with the same Power that in Monarchy belongeth to the Monarch, which is not [301] a Mixt, but an Absolute Soveraignty. And of the three sorts, which is the best, is not to be disputed, where any one of them is already established; but the present ought alwaies to be preferred, maintained, and accounted best; because it is against both the Law of Nature, and the Divine postive Law, to doe any thing tending to the subversion thereof. Besides, it maketh nothing to the Power of any Pastor, (unlesse he have the Civill Soveraignty,) what kind of Government is the best; because their Calling is not to govern men by Commandement, but to teach them, and perswade them by Arguments, and leave it to them to consider, whether they shall embrace, or reject the Doctrine taught. For Monarchy, Aristocracy, and Democracy, do mark out unto us three sorts of Soveraigns, not of Pastors; or, as we may say, three sorts of Masters of Families, not three sorts of Schoolmasters for their children.

And therefore the second Conclusion, concerning the best form of Government of the Church, is nothing to the question of the Popes Power without his own Dominions: For in all other Common-wealths his Power (if hee have any at all) is that of the Schoolmaster onely, and not of the Master of the Family.

For the third Conclusion, which is, that St. Peter was Monarch of the Church, he bringeth for his chiefe argument the place of S. *Matth.* (chap. 16. 18, 19.) *Thou art Peter, And upon this rock I will build my Church, & c. And I will give thee the keyes of Heaven; whatsoever thou shalt bind on Earth, shalt be bound in Heaven, and whatsoever thou shalt loose on Earth, shall be loosed in Heaven.* Which place well considered, proveth no more, but that the Church of Christ hath for foundation one onely Article; namely, that which Peter in the name of all the

379

Apostles professing, gave occasion to our Saviour to speak the words here cited; which that wee may cleerly understand, we are to consider, that our Saviour preached by himself, by John Baptist, and by his Apostles, nothing but this Article of Faith, *that he was the Christ*; all other Articles requiring faith no otherwise, than as founded on that. John began first, (*Mat.* 3.2.) preaching only this, *The Kingdome of God is at hand.* Then our Saviour himself (*Mat.* 4.17.) preached the same: And to his Twelve Apostles, when he gave them their Commission (*Mat.* 10.7.) there is no mention of preaching any other Article but that. This was the fundamentall Article, that is the Foundation of the Churches Faith. Afterwards the Apostles being returned to him, he asketh them all, (*Mat.* 16.13.) not Peter onely, *Who men said he was*; and they answered, that *some said he was John the Baptist, some Elias, and other Jeremias, or one of the Prophets*: Then (ver. 15.) he asked them all again, (not Peter onely) *Whom say yee that I am?* Therefore S. Peter answered (for them all) *Thou art Christ, the Son of the Living God*; which I said is the Foundation of the Faith of the whole Church; from which our Saviour takes the occasion of saying, *Upon this stone I will build my Church*: By which it is manifest, that by the Foundation-Stone of the Church, was meant the Fundamentall Article of the Churches Faith. But why then (will some object) doth our Saviour interpose these words, *Thou art Peter?* If the originall of this text had been rigidly translated, the reason would easily have appeared: We are therefore to consider, that the Apostle Simon, was surnamed *Stone*, (which is the signification of the Syriacke word *Cephas*, and of the Greek word *Petrus*). Our Saviour therefore after the confession of that Funamentall Article, alluding to his name, said (as if it were in English) thus, Thou art *Stone*, and upon this Stone I will build my Church: which is as much as to say, this Article, that *I am the Christ*, is the Foundation of all the Faith I require in those that are to bee members of my Church: Neither is this allusion to a name, an unusuall thing in common speech: But it had been a strange, and obscure speech, if our Saviour intending to build his Church on the Person of S. Peter, had said, *thou art a Stone, and upon this Stone I will build my Church*, when it was so obvious without ambiguity to have said, *I will build my Church on thee*; and yet there had been still the same allusion to his name.

And for the following words, *I will give thee the Keyes of Heaven, & c.* it is no more than what our Saviour gave also to all the rest of his

[302]

Disciples [*Matth.* 18.18.] *Whatsoever yee shall bind on Earth, shall be bound in Heaven. And whatsoever ye shall loose on Earth, shall be loosed in Heaven.* But howsoever this be interpreted, there is no doubt but the Power here granted belongs to all Supreme Pastors; such as are all Christian Civill Soveraignes in their own Dominions. In so much, as if St. Peter, or our Saviour himself had converted any of them to beleeve him, and to acknowledge his Kingdome; yet because his Kingdome is not of this world, he had left the supreme care of converting his subjects to none but him; or else hee must have deprived him of the Soveraignty, to which the Right of Teaching is inseparably annexed. And thus much in refutation of his first Book, wherein hee would prove St. Peter to have been the Monarch Universall of the Church, that is to say, of all the Christians in the world.

The second Book hath two Conclusions: One, that S. Peter was Bishop of Rome, and there dyed: The other, that the Popes of Rome are his Successors. Both which have been disputed by others. But supposing them true; yet if by Bishop of Rome, bee understood either the Monarch of the Church, or the Supreme Pastor of it; not Silvester, but Constantine (who was the first Christian Emperour) was that Bishop; and as Constantine, so all other Christian Emperors were of Right supreme Bishops of the Roman Empire; I say of the Roman Empire, not of all Christendome: For other Christian Soveraigns had the same Right in their severall Territories, as to an Office essentially adhaerent to their Soveraignty. Which shall serve for answer to his second Book. *The second Book.*

In the third Book, he handleth the question whether the Pope be Antichrist. For my part, I see no argument that proves he is so, in that sense the Scripture useth the name: nor will I take any argument from the quality of Antichrist, to contradict the Authority he exerciseth, or hath heretofore exercised in the Dominions of any other Prince, or State. [303] *The third Book.*

It is evident that the Prophets of the Old Testament foretold, and the Jews expected a Messiah, that is, a Christ, that should re-establish amongst them the kingdom of God, which had been rejected by them in the time of Samuel, when they required a King after the manner of other Nations. This expectation of theirs, made them obnoxious to the Imposture of all such, as had both the ambition to attempt the attaining of the Kingdome, and the art to deceive the People by counterfeit miracles, by hypocriticall life, or by orations and doctrine plausible. Our Saviour therefore, and his Apostles forewarned men of False Prophets, and of False Christs. False Christs, are such as pretend to be the *Christ*, but are not, and are called properly *Antichrists*, in such sense, as when there happeneth a Schisme in the Church by the election of two Popes, the one calleth the other *Antipapa*, or the false Pope. And therefore Antichrist in the proper signification hath two essentiall marks; One, that he denyeth Jesus to be Christ; and another that he professeth himselfe to bee Christ. The first Mark is set down by S. *John* in his 1 Epist. 4. ch. 3. ver. *Every Spirit that confesseth not that Jesus Christ is come in the flesh, is not of God; And this is the Spirit of Antichrist.* The other Mark is expressed in the words of our Saviour, (*Mat.* 24.5.) *Many shall come in my name, saying, I am Christ*; and again, *If any man shall say unto you, Loe, here is Christ, there is Christ, beleeve it not.* And therefore Antichrist must be a False Christ, that is, some one of them that shall pretend themselves to be Christ. And out of these two Marks, *to deny Jesus to be the Christ*, and to *affirm himselfe to be the Christ*, it followeth, that he must also be an *Adversary of Jesus the true Christ*, which is another usuall signification of the word Antichrist. But of these many Antichrists, there is one speciall one, ὁ Ἀντίχριστος, *The Antichrist*, or *Antichrist*, definitely, as one certaine person; not indefinitely *an Antichrist*. Now seeing the Pope of Rome, neither pretendeth himself, nor denyeth Jesus to bee the Christ, I perceive not how he can be called Antichrist; by which word is not meant, one that falsely pretendeth to be *His* Lieutenant, or Vicar generall, but to be *Hee*. There is also some Mark of the time of this speciall Antichrist, as (*Mat.* 24.15.) when that abominable Destroyer, spoken of by Daniel, *shall stand in the Holy place, and such tribulation as was not since the beginning of the world, nor ever shall be again, insomuch as if it were to last long, (ver. 22.) *no flesh could be saved; but for the elects sake those days shall be shortened* (made fewer). But that tribulation is not yet come; for it is to be followed immediately (ver. 29.) by a darkening of the Sun and Moon, a falling of the Stars, a concussion of the Heavens, and the glorious coming again of our Saviour in the cloudes. And therefore *The Antichrist* is not yet come; whereas, many Popes are both come and gone. It is true, the Pope in taking upon him to give Laws to all Christian Kings, and Nations, usurpeth a Kingdome in this world, which Christ took not on him: but he doth it not *as Christ*, but as *for Christ*, wherein there is nothing of *The Antichrist*.

*Dan. 9.27.

[304]

In the fourth Book, to prove the Pope to be the supreme Judg in all questions of Faith and Manners, (*which is as much as to be the absolute Monarch of all Christians in the world,*) he bringeth three Propositions: The first, that his Judgments are Infallible: The second, that he can make very Laws, and punish those that observed them not: The third, that our Saviour conferred all Jurisdiction Ecclesiasticall on the Pope of Rome. *The fourth Book.*

For the Infallibility of his Judgments, he alledgeth the Scriptures: and first, that of *Luke* 22.31. *Simon, Simon, Satan hath desired you that hee may sift you as wheat; but I have prayed for thee, that thy faith faile not; and when thou art converted, strengthen thy thy Brethren.* This, according to Bellarmines expostion, is, that Christ gave here to Simon Peter two priviledges: one, that neither his Faith should fail, nor the Faith of any of his successors: the other, that neither he, nor any of his successors should ever define any point concerning Faith, or Manners erroneously, or contrary to the definition of a former Pope: Which is a strange, and very much strained interpretation. But he that with attention readeth that chapter, shall find there is no place in the whole Scripture, that maketh more against the Popes Authority, than this very place. The Priests and Scribes seeking to kill our Saviour at the Passeover, and Judas possessed with a resolution to betray him, and the day of killing the Passeover being come, our Saviour celebrated the same with his Apostles, which he said, till the Kingdome of God was come hee would doe no more; and withall told them, that one of them was to betray him: Hereupon they questioned, which of them it should be; and withall (seeing the next Passeover their Master would celebrate should be when he was King) entred into a contention, who should then be the greatest man. Our Saviour therefore told them, that the Kings of the Nations had Dominion over their Subjects, and are called by a name (in Hebrew) that signifies Bountifull; but I cannot be so to you, you must endeavour to serve one another; I ordain you a Kingdome, but it is such as my Father hath ordained mee; a Kingdome that I am now to purchase with my blood, and not to possesse till my second coming; then yee shall eat and drink at my Table, and sit on Thrones, judging the twelve Tribes of Israel: And then addressing himself to St. Peter, he saith, *Simon, Simon,* Satan seeks by suggesting a present domination, to weaken your faith of the future; but I have prayed for thee, that thy faith shall not fail; Thou therefore (Note this,) being converted, and understanding my King- *Texts for the Infallibility of the Popes Judgement in points of Faith.*

dome as of another world, confirm the same faith in thy Brethren: To which S. Peter answered (as one that no more expected any authority in this world) *Lord I am ready to goe with thee, not onely to Prison, but to Death*. Whereby it is manifest, S. Peter had not onely no jurisdiction given him in this world, but a charge to teach all the other Apostles, that they also should have none. And for the Infallibility of St. Peters sentence definitive in matter of Faith, there is no more to be attributed to it out of this Text, than that Peter should continue in the beleef of this point, namely, that Christ should come again, and possesse the Kingdome at the day of Judgement; which was not given by this Text to all his Successors; for wee see they claime it in the World that now is.

The second place is that of *Matth*. 16. *Thou art Peter, and upon this rocke I will build my Church, and the gates of Hell shall not prevail against it*. By which (as I have already shewn in this chapter) is proved no more, than that the gates of Hell shall not prevail against the confession of Peter, which gave occasion to that speech; namely this, that *Jesus is Christ the Sonne of God*.

The third Text is *John* 21. ver. 16, 17. *Feed my sheep*; which contains no more but a Commission of Teaching: And if we grant the rest of the Apostles to be contained in that name of *Sheep*; then it is the supreme Power of Teaching: but it was onely for the time that there were no Christian Soveraigns already possessed of that Supremacy. But I have already proved, that Christian Soveraignes are in their owne Dominions the supreme Pastors, and instituted thereto, by vertue of their being Baptized, though without other Imposition of Hands. For such Imposition being a Ceremony of designing the person, is needlesse, when hee is already designed to the Power of Teaching what Doctrine he will, by his institution to an Absolute Power over his Subjects. For as I have proved before, Soveraigns are supreme Teachers (in generall) by their Office; and therefore oblige themselves (by their Baptisme) to teach the Doctrine of Christ: And when they suffer others to teach their people, they doe it at the perill of their own souls; for it is at the hands of the Heads of Families that God will require the account of the instruction of his Children and Servants. It is of Abraham himself, not of a hireling, that God saith (*Gen*. 18.19.) *I know him that he will command his Children, and his houshold after him, that they keep the way of the Lord, and do justice and judgement*.

The fourth place is that of *Exod.* 28.30. *Thou shalt put in the Breast-plate of Judgment, the Urim and the Thummin*: which hee saith is interpreted by the Septuagint δήλωσιν καὶ ἀλήθειαν, that is, *Evidence* and *Truth*: And thence concludeth, God had given Evidence, and Truth, (which is almost Infallibility,) to the High Priest. But be it Evidence and Truth it selfe that was given; or be it but Admonition to the Priest to endeavour to inform himself cleerly, and give judgment uprightly; yet in that it was given to the High Priest, it was given to the Civill Soveraign: For such next under God was the High Priest in the Common-wealth of Israel; and is an argument for Evidence and [306] Truth, that is, for the Ecclesiasticall Supremacy of Civill Soveraigns over their own Subjects, against the pretended Power of the Pope. These are all the Texts hee bringeth for the Infallibility of the Judgement of the Pope, in point of Faith.

For the Infallibility of his Judgment concerning Manners, hee *Texts for the* bringeth one Text, which is that of *John* 16.13. *When the Spirit of truth* *same in point* *is come, hee will lead you into all truth*: where (saith he) by *all truth*, is *of Manners.* meant, as least, *all truth necessary to salvation.* But with this mitigation, he attributeth no more Infallibility to the Pope, than to any man that professeth Christianity, and is not to be damned: For if any man erre in any point, wherein not to erre is necessary to Salvation, it is impossible he should be saved; for that onely is necessary to Salvation, without which to be saved is impossible. What points these are, I shall declare out of the Scripture in the Chapter following. In this place I say no more, but that though it were granted, the Pope could not possibly teach any error at all, yet doth not this entitle him to any Jurisdiction in the Dominions of another Prince, unless we shall also say, a man is obliged in conscience to set on work upon all occasions the best workman, even then also when he hath formerly promised his work to another.

Besides the Text, he argueth from Reason, thus. If the Pope could erre in necessaries, then Christ hath not sufficiently provided for the Churches Salvation; because he hath commanded her to follow the Popes directions. But this Reason is invalid, unless he shew when, and where Christ commanded that, or took at all any notice of a Pope: Nay granting whatsoever was given to S. Peter, was given to the Pope; yet seeing there is in the Scripture no command to any man to obey St. Peter, no man can bee just, that obeyeth him, when his commands are contrary to those of his lawfull Soveraign.

Lastly, it hath not been declared by the Church, nor by the Pope himselfe, that he is the Civill Soveraign of all the Christians in the world; and therefore all Christians are not bound to acknowledge his Jurisdiction in point of Manners. For the Civill Soveraignty, and supreme Judicature in controversies of Manners, are the same thing: And the Makers of Civill Laws, are not onely Declarers, but also Makers of the justice, and injustice of actions; there being nothing in mens Manners that makes them righteous, or unrighteous, but their conformity with the Law of the Soveraign. And therefore when the Pope challengeth Supremacy in controversies of Manners, hee teacheth men to disobey the Civill Soveraign; which is an erroneous Doctrine, contrary to the many precepts of our Saviour and his Apostles, delivered to us in the Scripture.

To prove the Pope has Power to make Laws, he alledgeth many places; as first, *Deut.* 17.12. *The man that will doe presumptuously, and will not hearken unto the Priest, (that standeth to Minister there before the Lord thy God, or unto the Judge,) even that man shall die, and thou shalt put away the evill from Israel.* For answer whereunto, we are to remember that the High Priest (next and immediately under God) was the Civill Soveraign; and all Judges were to be constituted by him. The words alledged sound therefore thus. *The man that will presume to disobey the Civill Soveraign for the time being, or any of his Officers in the execution of their places, that man shall die, & c.* which is cleerly for the Civill Soveraignty, against the Universall power of the Pope.

Secondly, he alledgeth that of *Matth.* 16. *Whatsoever yee shall bind, & c.* and interpreteth it for such *binding* as is attributed (*Matth.* 23.4.) to the Scribes and Pharisees, *They bind heavy burthens, and grievous to be born, and lay them on mens shoulders*; by which is meant (he sayes) Making of Laws; and concludes thence, that the Pope can make Laws. But this also maketh onely for the Legislative power of Civill Soveraigns: For the Scribes, and Pharisees sat in Moses Chaire, but Moses next under God was Sovereign of the People of Israel: and therefore our Saviour commanded them to doe all that they should say, but not all that they should do. That is, to obey their Laws, but not follow their Example.

The third place, is *John* 21.16. *Feed my sheep*; which is not a Power to make Laws, but a command to Teach. Making Laws belongs to the Lord of the Family; who by his owne discretion choaseth his Chaplain, as also a Schoolmaster to Teach his children.

The fourth place *John* 20.21. is against him. The words are, *As my Father sent me, so send I you.* But our Saviour was sent to Redeem (by his Death) such as should Beleeve; and by his own, and his Apostles preaching to prepare them for their entrance into his Kingdome; which he himself saith, is not of this world, and hath taught us to pray for the coming of it hereafter, though hee refused (*Acts* 1.6, 7.) to tell his Apostles when it should come; and in which, when it comes, the twelve Apostles shall sit on twelve Thrones (every one perhaps as high as that of St. Peter) to judge the twelve tribes of Israel. Seeing then God the Father sent not our Saviour to make Laws in this present world, wee may conclude from the Text, that neither did our Saviour send S. Peter to make Laws here, but to perswade men to expect his second comming with a stedfast faith; and in the mean time, if Subjects, to obey their Princes; and if Princes, both to beleeve it themselves, and to do their best to make their Subjects doe the same; which is the Office of a Bishop. Therefore this place maketh most strongly for the joining of the Ecclesiasticall Supremacy to the Civill Soveraignty, contrary to that which Cardinall Bellarmine alledgeth it for.

The fift place is *Acts* 15.28. *It hath seemed good to the Holy Spirit, and to us, to lay upon you no greater burden, than these necessary things, that yee abstaine from meats offered to Idols, and from bloud, and from things strangled, and from fornication.* Here hee notes the word *Laying of burdens* for the Legislative Power. But who is there, that reading this [308] Text, can say, this stile of the Apostles may not as properly be used in giving Counsell, as in making Laws? The stile of a Law is, *We command*: But, *We think good*, is the ordinary stile of them, that but give Advice; and they lay a Burthen that give Advice, though it bee conditionall, that is, if they to whom they give it, will attain their ends: And such is the Burthen, of abstaining from things strangled, and from bloud; not absolute, but in case they will not erre. I have shewn before (chap. 25.) that Law, is distinguished from Counsell, in this, that the reason of a Law, is taken from the designe, and benefit of him that prescribeth it; but the reason of a Counsell, from the designe, and benefit of him, to whom the Counsell is given. But here, the Apostles aime onely at the benefit of the converted Gentiles, namely their Salvation; not at their own benefit; for having done their endeavour, they shall have their reward, whether they be obeyed, or not. And therefore the Acts of this Councell, were not Laws, but Counsells.

387

The sixt place is that of *Rom.* 13. *Let every Soul be subject to the Higher Powers, for there is no Power but of God*; which is meant, he saith not onely of Secular, but also of Ecclesiasticall Princes. To which I answer, first, that there are no Ecclesiasticall Princes but those that are also Civill Soveraignes; and their Principalities exceed not the compasse of their Civill Soveraignty; without those bounds though they may be received for Doctors, they cannot be acknowledged for Princes. For if the Apostle had meant, we should be subject both to our own Princes, and also to the Pope, he had taught us a doctrine, which Christ himself hath told us is impossible, namely, *to serve two Masters.* And though the Apostle say in another place, *I write these things being absent, lest being present I should use sharpnesse, according to the Power which the Lord hath given me*; it is not, that he challenged a Power either to put to death, imprison, banish, whip, or fine any of them, which are Punishments; but onely to Excommunicate, which (without the Civill Power) is no more but a leaving of their company, and having no more to doe with them, than with a Heathen man, or a Publican; which in many occasions might be a greater pain to the Excommunicant, than to the Excommunicate.

The seventh place is 1 *Cor.* 4.21. *Shall I come unto you with a Rod, or in love, and the spirit of lenity?* But here again, it is not the Power of a Magistrate to punish offenders, that is meant by a Rod; but onely the Power of Excommunication, which is not in its owne nature a Punishment, but onely a Denouncing of punishment, that Christ shall inflict, when he shall be in possession of his Kingdome, at the day of Judgment. Nor then also shall it bee properly a Punishment, as upon a Subject that hath broken the Law; but a Revenge, as upon an Enemy, or Revolter, that denyeth the Right of our Saviour to the Kingdome: And therefore this proveth not the Legislative Power of any Bishop, that has not also the Civill Power.

[309]   The eighth place is, *Timothy* 3.2. *A Bishop must be the husband but of one wife, vigilant, sober, &c.* which he saith was a Law. I thought that none could make a Law in the Church, but the Monarch of the Church, St. Peter. But suppose this Precept made by the authority of St. Peter; yet I see no reason why to call it a Law, rather than an Advice, seeing Timothy was not a Subject, but a Disciple of S. Paul; nor the flock under the charge of Timothy, his Subjects in the Kingdome, but his Scholars in the Schoole of Christ: If all the Precepts he giveth Timothy, be Laws, why is not this also a Law, *Drink no longer*

water, but use a little wine for thy healths sake? And why are not also the
Precepts of good Physitians, so many Laws? but that it is not the
Imperative manner of speaking, but an absolute Subjection to a Per-
son, that maketh his Precepts Laws.

In like manner, the ninth place, 1 *Tim.* 5.19. *Against an Elder receive
not an accusation, but before two or three Witnesses,* is a wise Precept, but
not a Law.

The tenth place is, *Luke* 10.16. *He that heareth you, heareth mee; and
he that despiseth you, despiseth me.* And there is no doubt, but he that
despiseth the Counsell of those that are sent by Christ, despiseth the
Counsell of Christ himself. But who are those now that are sent by
Christ, but such as are ordained Pastors by lawfull Authority? and
who are lawfully ordained, that are not ordained by the Soveraign
Pastor? and who is ordained by the Soveraign Pastor in a Christian
Common-wealth, that is not ordained by the authority of the
Soveraign thereof? Out of this place therefore it followeth, that he
which heareth his Soveraign being a Christian, heareth Christ; and
hee that despiseth the Doctrine which his King being a Christian,
authorizeth, despiseth the Doctrine of Christ (which is not that which
Bellarmine intendeth here to prove, but the contrary). But all this is
nothing to a Law. Nay more, a Christian King, as a Pastor, and
Teacher of his Subjects, makes not thereby his Doctrines Laws. He
cannot oblige men to beleeve; though as a Civill Soveraign he may
make Laws suitable to his Doctrine, which may oblige men to certain
actions, and sometimes to such as they would not otherwise do, and
which he ought not to command; and yet when they are commanded,
they are Laws; and the externall actions done in obedience to them,
without the inward approbation, are the actions of the Soveraign, and
not of the Subject, which is in that case but as an instrument, without
any motion of his owne at all; because God hath commanded to obey
them.

The eleventh, is every place, where the Apostle for Counsell, putteth some word, by which men use to signifie Command; or calleth
the following of his Counsell, by the name of Obedience. And therefore they are alledged out of 1 *Cor.* 11.2. *I commend you for keeping my
Precepts as I delivered them to you.* The Greek is, *I commend you for
keeping those things I delivered to you, as I delivered them.* Which is far
from signifying that they were Laws, or any thing else, but good [310]
Counsell. And that of 1 *Thess.* 4.2. *You know what commandements we*

gave you: where the Greek word is παραγγελίας ἐδώκαμεν, equivalent to παρεδώκαμεν, *what wee delivered to you*, as in the place next before alledged, which does not prove the Traditions of the Apostles, to be any more than Counsells; though as is said in the 8 verse, *he that despiseth them, despiseth not man, but God*: For our Saviour himself came not to Judge, that is, to be King in this world; but to Sacrifice himself for Sinners, and leave Doctors in his Church, to lead, not to drive men to Christ, who never accepteth forced actions, (which is all the Law produceth,) but the inward conversion of the heart; which is not the work of Laws, but of Counsell, and Doctrine.

And that of 2 *Thess.* 3.14. *If any man Obey not our word by this Epistle, note that man, and have no company with him, that he may bee ashamed*: where from the word *Obey*, he would inferre, that this Epistle was a Law to the Thessalonians. The Epistles of the Emperours were indeed Laws. If therefore the Epistle of S. Paul were also a Law, they were to obey two Masters. But the word *Obey*, as it is in the Greek ὑπακούει, signifieth *hearkning to*, or *putting in practice*, not onley that which is Commanded by him that has right to punish, but also that which is delivered in a way of Counsell for our good; and therefore St. Paul does not bid kill him that disobeys, nor beat, nor imprison, nor amerce him, which Legislators may all do; but avoid his company, that he may bee ashamed: whereby it is evident, it was not the Empire of an Apostle, but his Reputation amongst the Faithfull, which the Christians stood in awe of.

The last place is that of *Heb.* 13.17. *Obey your Leaders, and submit your selves to them, for they watch for your souls, as they that must give account*: And here also is intended by Obedience, a following of their Counsell: For the reason of our Obedience, is not drawn from the will and command of our Pastors, but from our own benefit, as being the Salvation of our Souls they watch for, and not for the Exaltation of their own Power, and Authority. If it were meant here, that all they teach were Laws, then not onely the Pope, but every Pastor in his Parish should have Legislative Power. Again, they that are bound to obey their Pastors, have no power to examine their commands. What then shall wee say to St. *John* who bids us (1 Epist. chap. 4. ver. 1.) *Not to beleeve every Spirit, but to try the Spirits whether they are of God, because many false Prophets are gone out into the world?* It is therefore manifest, that wee may dispute the Doctrine of our Pastors; but no man can dispute a Law. The Commands of Civill Soveraigns are on all sides granted to be Laws: if any else can make a Law besides himselfe, all Common-wealth, and consequently all Peace, and Justice must cease; which is contrary to all Laws, both Divine and Humane. Nothing therefore can be drawn from these, or any other places of Scripture, to prove the Decrees of the Pope, where he has not also the Civill Soveraignty, to be Laws.

The last point hee would prove, is this, *That our Saviour Christ has committed Ecclesiasticall Jurisdiction immediately to none but the Pope.* Wherein he handleth not the Question of Supremacy between the Pope and Christian Kings, but between the Pope and other Bishops. And first, he sayes it is agreed, that the Jurisdiction of Bishops, is at least in the generall *de Iure Divino*, that is, in the Right of God; for which he alledges S. Paul, *Ephes.* 4. 11. where hee sayes, that Christ after his Ascension into heaven, *gave gifts to men, some Apostles, some Prophets, and some Evangelists, and some Pastors, and some Teachers*: And thence inferres, they have indeed their Jurisdiction in Gods Right; but will not grant they have it immediately from God, but derived through the Pope. But if a man may be said to have his Jurisdiction *de Jure Divino*, and yet not immediately; what lawfull Jurisdiction, though but Civill, is there in a Christian Common-wealth, that is not also *de Jure Divino?* For Christian Kings have their Civill Power from God immediately; and the Magistrates under him exercise their severall charges in vertue of his Commission; wherein that which they doe, is no lesse *de Jure Divino mediato*, than that which the Bishops doe, in vertue of the Popes Ordination. All lawfull Power is of God, immediately in the Supreme Governour, and mediately in those that have Authority under him: So that either hee must grant every Constable in the State, to hold his Office in the Right of God; or he must not hold that any Bishop holds his so, besides the Pope himselfe.

But this whole Dispute, whether Christ left the Jurisdiction to the Pope onely, or to other Bishops also, if considered out of those places where the Pope has the Civill Soveraignty, is a contention *de lana Caprina*: For none of them (where they are not Soveraigns) has any Jurisdiction at all. For Jurisdiction is the Power of hearing and determining Causes between man and man; and can belong to none, but him that hath the Power to prescribe the Rules of Right and Wrong; that is, to make Laws; and with the Sword of Justice to

[311]

The question of Superiority between the Pope and other Bishops.

compell men to obey his Decisions, pronounced either by himself, or by the Judges he ordaineth thereunto; which none can lawfully do, but the Civill Soveraign.

Therefore when he alledgeth out of the 6 of *Luke*, that our Saviour called his Disciples together, and chose twelve of them which he named Apostles, he proveth that he Elected them *all, (except*¹ Matthias, Paul and Barnabas,) and gave them Power and Command to Preach, but not to Judge of Causes between man and man: for that is a Power which he refused to take upon himselfe, saying, *Who made me a Judge, or a Divider, amongst you?* and in another place, *My Kingdome is not of this world.* But hee that hath not the Power to hear, and determine Causes between man and man, cannot be said to have any Jurisdiction at all. And yet this hinders not, but that our Saviour gave them Power to Preach and Baptize in all parts of the world, supposing they were not by their own lawfull Soveraign forbidden: For to our own Soveraigns Christ himself, and his Apostles have in sundry places expressely commanded us in all things to be obedient.

The arguments by which he would prove, that Bishops receive their Jurisdiction from the Pope (seeing the Pope in the Dominions of other Princes hath no Jurisdiction himself,) are all in vain. Yet because they prove, on the contrary, that all Bishops receive Jurisdiction when they have it from their Civill Soveraigns, I will not omit the recitall of them.

The first, is from *Numbers* 11. where Moses not being able alone to undergoe the whole burthen of administring the affairs of the People of Israel, God commanded him to choose Seventy Elders, and took part of the spirit of Moses, to put it upon those Seventy Elders: by which is understood, not that God weakened the spirit of Moses, for that had not eased him at all; but that they had all of them their authority from him; wherein he doth truly, and ingenuously interpret that place. But seeing Moses had the entire Soveraignty in the Common-wealth of the Jews, it is manifest, that it is thereby signified, that they had their Authority from the Civill Soveraign: and therefore that place proveth, that Bishops in every Christian Common-wealth have their Authority from the Civill Soveraign; and from the Pope in his own Territories only, and not in the Territories of any other State.

The second argument, is from the nature of Monarchy; wherein all

[312]

---

¹ *Syn.*: (all, except

Authority is in one Man, and in others by derivation from him: But the Government of the Church, he says, is Monarchicall. This also makes for Christian Monarchs. For they are really Monarchs of their own people; that is, of their own Church (for the Church is the same thing with a Christian people;) whereas the Power of the Pope, though hee were S. Peter, is neither Monarchy, nor hath any thing of *Archicall*, nor *Craticall*, but onely of *Didacticall*; For God accepteth not a forced, but a willing obedience.

The third, is, from that the *Sea* of S. Peter is called by S. Cyprian, the *Head*, the *Source*, the *Roote*, the *Sun*, from whence the Authority of Bishops is derived. But by the Law of Nature (which is a better Principle of Right and Wrong, than the word of any Doctor that is but a man) the Civill Soveraign in every Common-wealth, is the *Head*, the *Source*, the *Root*, and the *Sun*, from which all Jurisdiction is derived. And therefore the Jurisdiction of Bishops, is derived from the Civill Soveraign.

The fourth, is taken from the Inequality of their Jurisdictions: For if God (saith he) had given it them immediately, he had given aswell Equality of Jurisdiction, as of Order: But wee see, some are Bishops but of own Town, some of a hundred Towns, and some of many whole Provinces; which differences were not determined by the command of God; their Jurisdiction therefore is not of God, but of Man; and one has a greater, another a lesse, as it pleaseth the Prince of the Church. Which argument, if he had proved before, that the Pope had had an Universall Jurisdiction over all Christians, had been for his [313] purpose. But seeing that hath not been proved, and that it is notoriously known, the large Jurisdiction of the Pope was given him by those that had it, that is, by the Emperours of Rome, (for the Patriarch of Constantinople, upon the same title, namely, of being Bishop of the Capitall City of the Empire, and Seat of the Emperour, claimed to be equall to him,) it followeth, that all other Bishops have their Jurisdiction from the Soveraigns of the place wherein they exercise the same: And as for that cause they have not their Authority *de Iure Divino*; so neither hath the Pope his *de Iure Divino*, except onely where hee is also the Civill Soveraign

His fift argument is this, *If Bishops have their Jurisdiction immediately from God, the Pope could not take it from them, for he can doe nothing contrary to Gods ordination*; And this consequence is good, and well proved. *But* (saith he) *the Pope can do this, and has done it*. This also is granted, so he doe it in his own Dominions, or in the Dominions of any other Prince that hath given him that Power; but not universally, in Right of the Popedome: For that power belongeth to every Christian Soveraign, within the bounds of his owne Empire, and is inseparable from the Soveraignty. Before the People of Israel had (by the commandment of God to Samuel) set over themselves a King, after the manner of other Nations, the High Priest had the Civill Government; and none but he could make, nor depose an inferiour Priest: But that Power was afterwards in the King, as may be proved by this same argument of Bellarmine; For if the Priest (be he the High Priest or any other) had his Jurisdiction immediately from God, then the King could not take it from him; *for he could doe nothing contrary to Gods ordinance*: But it is certain, that King Solomon (1 *Kings* 2.26.) deprived Abiathar the High Priest of his Office, and placed Zadok (verse 35.) in his room. Kings therefore may in the like manner Ordaine, and Deprive Bishops, as they shall thinke fit, for the well governing of their Subjects.

His sixth argument is this, If Bishops have their Jurisdiction *de Iure Divino* (that is, *immediately from God,*) they that maintaine it, should bring some Word of God to prove it: But they can bring none. The argument is good; I have therefore nothing to say against it. But it is an argument no lesse good, to prove the Pope himself to have no Jurisdiction in the Dominion of any other Prince.

Lastly, hee bringeth for argument, the testimony of two Popes, *Innocent*, and *Leo*; and I doubt not but hee might have alledged, with as good reason, the testimonies of all the Popes almost since S. Peter: For considering the love of Power naturally implanted in mankind, whosoever were made Pope, he would be tempted to uphold the same opinion. Neverthelesse, they should therein but doe, as *Innocent*, and *Leo* did, bear witnesse of themselves, and therefore their witnesse should not be good.

[314]
*Of the Popes
Temporall
Power.*
    In the fift Book he hath four Conclusions. The first is, *That the Pope is not Lord of all the world*: the second, *That the Pope is not Lord of all the Christian world*: The third, *That the Pope* (without his owne Territory) *has not any Temporall Jurisdiction DIRECTLY*: These three Conclusions are easily granted. The fourth is, *That the Pope has* (in the Dominions of other Princes) the Supreme *Temporall Power INDIRECTLY*: which is denied; unlesse hee mean by *Indirectly*, that he has gotten it by Indirect means; then is that also granted. But I

understand, that when he saith he hath it *Indirectly*, he means, that such Temporall Jurisdiction belongeth to him of Right, but that this Right is but a Consequence of his Pastorall Authority, the which he could not exercise, unlesse he have the other with it: And therefore to the Pastorall Power (which he calls Spirituall) the Supreme Power Civill is necessarily annexed; and that thereby hee hath a Right to change Kingdomes, giving them to one, and taking them from another, when he shall think it conduces to the Salvation of Souls.

Before I come to consider the Arguments by which hee would prove this Doctrine, it will not bee amisse to lay open the Consequences of it; that Princes, and States, that have the Civill Soveraignty in their severall Common-wealths, may bethink themselves, whether it bee convenient for them, and conducing to the good of their Subjects, of whom they are to give an account at the day of Judgment, to admit the same.

When it is said, the Pope hath not (in the Territories of other States) the Supreme Civill Power *Directly*; we are to understand, he doth not challenge it, as other Civill Soveraigns doe, from the originall submission thereto of those that are to be governed. For it is evident, and has already been sufficiently in this Treatise demonstrated, that the Right of all Soveraigns, is derived orginally from the consent of every one of those that are to bee governed; whether they that choose him, doe it for their common defence against an Enemy, as when they agree amongst themselves to appoint a Man, or an Assembly of men to protect them; or whether they doe it, to save their lives, by submission to a conquering Enemy. The Pope therefore, when he disclaimeth the Supreme Civill Power over other States *Directly*, denyeth no more, but that his Right cometh to him by that way; He ceaseth not for all that, to claime it another way; and that is, (without the consent of them that are to be governed) by a Right given him by God, (which hee calleth *Indirectly*,) in his Assumption to the Papacy. But by what way soever he pretend, the Power is the same; and he may (if it bee granted to be his Right) depose Princes and States, as often as it is for the Salvation of Soules, that is, as often as he will; for he claimeth also the Sole Power to Judge, whether it be to the Salvation of mens Souls, or not. And this is the Doctrine, not onely that Bellarmine here, and many other Doctors teach in their Sermons and Books, but also that some Councells have decreed, and the Popes have accordingly, when the occasion hath served them, put [315] in practise. For the fourth Councell of Lateran held under Pope *Innocent* the third, (in the third Chap. *De Haereticis*,) hath this Canon. *If a King at the Popes admonition, doe not purge his Kingdome of Haeretiques, and being Excommunicate for the same, make not satisfaction within a yeer, his Subjects are absolved of their Obedience.* And the practise hereof hath been seen on divers occasions; as in the Deposing of *Chilperique*, King of France; in the Translation of the Roman Empire to *Charlemaine*; in the Oppression of *John* King of England; in Transferring the Kingdome of *Navarre*; and of late years, in the League against *Henry* the third of France, and in many more occurrences. I think there be few Princes that consider not this as Injust, and Inconvenient; but I wish they would all resolve to be Kings, or Subjects. Men cannot serve two Masters: They ought therefore to ease them, either by holding the Reins of Government wholly in their own hands; or by wholly delivering them into the hands of the Pope; that such men as are willing to be obedient, may be protected in their obedience. For this distinction of Temporall, and Spirituall Power is but words. Power is as really divided, and as dangerously to all purposes, by sharing with another *an *Indirect* Power, as a*[1] *Direct* one. But to come now to his Arguments.

The first is this, *The Civill Power is subject to the Spirituall: Therefore he that hath the Supreme Power Spirituall, hath right to command Temporall Princes, and dispose of their Temporalls in order to the Spirituall.* As for the distinction of Temporall, and Spirituall, *let*[2] us consider in what sense it may be said intelligibly, that the Temporall, or Civill Power is subject to the Spirituall. There be but two ways that those words can be made sense. For when wee say, one Power is subject to another Power, the meaning either is, that he which hath the one, is subject to him that hath the other; or that the one Power is to the other, as the means to the end. For wee cannot understand, that one Power hath Power over another Power; or that one Power can have Right or Command over another: For Subjection, Command, Right, and Power are accidents, not of Powers, but of Persons: One Power may be subordinate to another, as the art of a Sadler, to the art of a Rider. If then it bee granted, that the Civill Government be ordained as a means to bring us to a Spirituall felicity; yet it does not follow,

---

[1] *Syn.: Indirect* Power, as with a

[2] Scribal MS had: I intend to examine it in another place, therefore passing it over for the present, let . . . This was deleted by Hobbes himself.

that if a King have the Civill Power, and the Pope the Spirituall, that therefore the King is bound to obey the Pope, more then every Sadler is bound to obey every Rider. Therefore as from Subordination of an Art, cannot be inferred the Subjection of the Professor; so from the Subordination of a Government, cannot be inferred the Subjection of the Governor. When therefore he saith, the Civill Power is Subject to the Spirituall, his meaning is, that the Civill Soveraign, is Subject to the Spirituall Soveraign. And the Argument stands thus, *The Civil Soveraign, is subject to the Spirituall; Therefore the Spirituall Prince may command Temporall Princes.* Where the Conclusion is the same, with the Antecedent he should have proved. But to prove it, he alledgeth [316] first, this reason, *Kings and Popes, Clergy and Laity make but one Common-wealth; that is to say, but one Church: And in all Bodies the Members depend one upon another: But things Spirituall depend not of things Temporall: Therefore Temporall depend on Spirituall. And therefore are Subject to them.* In which Argumentation there be two grosse errours: one is, that all Christian Kings, Popes, Clergy, and all other Christian men, make but one Common-wealth: For it is evident that France is one Common-wealth, Spain another, and Venice a third, &c. And these consist of Christians; and therefore also are severall Bodies of Christians; that is to say, severall Churches: And their severall Soveraigns Represent them, whereby they are capable of command-ing and obeying, of doing and suffering, as a naturall man; which no Generall or Universall Church is, till it have a Representant; which it hath not on Earth: for if it had, there is no doubt but that all Christendome were one Common-wealth, whose Soveraign were that Representant, both in things Spirituall and Temporall: And the Pope, to make himself this Representant, wanteth three things that our Saviour hath not given him, to *Command*, and to *Judge*, and to *Punish*, otherwise than (by Excommunication) to run from those that will not Learn of him: For though the Pope were Christs onely Vicar, yet he cannot exercise his government, till our Saviours second coming: And then also it is not the Pope, but St. Peter himselfe, with the other Apostles, that are to be Judges of the world.

The other errour in this his first Argument is, that he sayes, the Members of every Common-wealth, as of a naturall Body, depend one of another: It is true, they cohaere together; but they depend onely on the Soveraign, which is the Soul of the Common-wealth; which failing, the Common-wealth is dissolved into a Civill war, no one man so much as cohaering to another, for want of a common Dependance on a known Soveraign; Just as the Members of the naturall Body dissolve into Earth, for want of a Soul to hold them together. Therefore there is nothing in this similitude, from whence to inferre a dependance of the Laity on the Clergy, or of the Temporall Officers on the Spirituall; but of both on the Civill Soveraign; which ought indeed to direct his Civill commands to the Salvation of Souls; but is not therefore subject to any but *to God*[1] himselfe. And thus you see the laboured fallacy of the first Argument, to deceive such men as distinguish not between the Subordination of Actions in the way to the End; and the Subjection of Persons one to another in the administration of the Means. For to every. End, the Means are determined by Nature, or by God himselfe supernaturally: but the Power to make men use the Means, is in every nation resigned (by the Law of Nature, which forbiddeth men to violate their Faith given) to the Civill Soveraign.

[317]   His second Argument is this, *Every Common-wealth, (because it is supposed to be perfect and sufficient in it self,) may command any other Common-wealth, not subject to it, and force it to change the administration of the Government; nay depose the Prince, and set another in his room, if it cannot otherwise defend it selfe against the injuries he goes about to doe them: much more may a Spirituall Common-wealth command a Temporall one to change the administration of their Government, and may depose Princes, and institute others, when they cannot otherwise defend the Spirituall Good.*

That a Common-wealth, to defend it selfe against injuries, may lawfully doe all that he hath here said, is very true; and hath already in that which hath gone before been sufficiently demonstrated. And if it were also true, that there is now in this world a Spirituall Common-wealth, distinct from a Civill Common-wealth, then might the Prince thereof, upon injury done him, or upon want of caution that injury be not done him in time to come, repaire, and secure himself by Warre; which is in summe, deposing, killing, or subduing, or doing any act of Hostility. But by the same reason, it would be no lesse lawfull for a Civill Soveraign, upon the like injuries done, or feared, to make warre upon the Spirituall Soveraign; which I beleeve is more than Cardinall Bellarmine would have inferred from his own proposition.

But Spirituall Common-wealth there is none in this world: for it is

---

[1] *Syn.*: God

the same thing with the Kingdome of Christ; which he himselfe saith, is not of this world; but shall be in the next world, at the Resurrection, when they that have lived justly, and beleeved that he was the Christ, shall (though they died *Naturall* bodies) rise *Spirituall* bodies; and then it is, that our Saviour shall judge the world, and conquer his Adversaries, and make a Spirituall Common-wealth. In the mean time, seeing there are no men on earth, whose bodies are Spirituall; there can be no Spirituall Common-wealth amongst men that are yet in the flesh; unlesse wee call Preachers, that have Commission to Teach, and prepare men for their reception into the Kingdome of Christ at the Resurrection, a Common-wealth; which I have proved already to bee none.

The third Argument is this; *It is not lawfull for Christians to tolerate an Infidel, or Haereticall King, in case he endeavour to draw them to his Haeresie, or Infidelity. But to judge whether a King draw his subjects to Haeresie, or not, belongeth to the Pope. Therefore hath the Pope Right, to determine whether the Prince be to be deposed, or not deposed.*

To this I answer, that both these assertions are false. For Christians, (or men of what Religion soever,) if they tolerate not their King, whatsoever law hee maketh, though it bee concerning Religion, doe violate their faith, contrary to the Divine Law, both *Naturall* and *Positive*: Nor is there any Judge of Haeresie amongst Subjects, but their owne Civill Soveraign: For *Haeresie is nothing else, but a private opinion, obstinately maintained, contrary to the opinion which the Publique* [318] *Person* (that is to say, the Representant of the Common-wealth) *hath commanded to bee taught.* By which it is manifest, that an opinion publiquely appointed to bee taught, cannot be Haeresie; nor the Soveraign Princes that authorize them, Haeretiques. For Haeretiques are none but private men, that stubbornly defend some Doctrine, prohibited by their lawfull Soveraigns.

But to prove that Christians are not to tolerate Infidell, or Haereticall Kings, he alledgeth a place in *Deut.* 17. where God forbiddeth the Jews, when they shall set a King over themselves, to choose a stranger: And from thence inferreth, that it is unlawfull for a Christian, to choose a King, that is not a Christian. And 'tis true, that he that is a Christian, that is, hee that hath already obliged himself to receive our Saviour when he shall come, for his King, shal tempt God too much in choosing for King in this world, one that hee knoweth will endeavour, both by terrour, and perswasion to make him violate

his faith. But, it is (saith hee) the same danger, to choose one that is
not a Christian, for King, and not to depose him, when hee is chosen.
To this I say, the question is not of the danger of not deposing; but of
the Justice of deposing him. To choose him, may in some cases bee
unjust; but to depose him, when he is chosen, is in no case Just. For it
is *alwaies a*[1] violation of faith, and consequently against the Law of
Nature, which is the eternall Law of God. Nor doe wee read, that any
such Doctrine was accounted Christian in the time of the Apostles;
nor in the time of the Romane Emperours, till the Popes had the
Civill Soveraignty of Rome. But to this he hath replyed, that the
Christians of old, deposed not *Nero*, nor *Dioclesian*, nor *Julian*, nor
Valens an Arrian, for this cause onely, that they wanted Temporall
forces. Perhaps so. But did our Saviour, who for calling for, might
have had twelve Legions of immortall, invulnerable Angels to assist
him, want forces to depose *Caesar*, or at least *Pilate*, that unjustly,
without finding fault in him, delivered him to the Jews to bee crucified? Or if the Apostles wanted Temporall forces to depose *Nero*, was
it therefore necessary for them in their Epistles to the new made
Christians, to teach them (as they did) to obey the Powers constituted
over them, (whereof *Nero* in that time was one,) and that they ought to
obey them, not for fear of their wrath, but for conscience sake? Shall
we say they did not onely obey, but also teach what they meant not, for
want of strength? It is not therefore for want of strength, but for
conscience sake, that Christians are to tolerate their Heathen Princes,
or Princes (for I cannot call any one whose Doctrine is the Publique
Doctrine, an Haeretique) that authorize the teaching of an Errour.
And whereas for the Temporall Power of the Pope, he alledgeth
further, that St. Paul (1 *Cor.* 6.) appointed Judges under the Heathen
Princes of those times, such as were not ordained by those Princes; it
is not true. For St. Paul does but advise them, to take some of their
Brethren to compound their differences, as Arbitrators, rather than to
goe to law one with another before the Heathen Judges; which is a
wholsome Precept, and full of Charity, fit to bee practised also in the
best Christian Common-wealths. And for the danger that may arise to
Religion, by the Subjects tolerating of an Heathen, or an Erring
Prince, it is a point, of which a Subject is no competent Judge; or if
hee bee, the Popes Temporall Subjects may judge also of the Popes

[319]

---

[1] *Syn.*: alwaies

Doctrine. For every Christian Prince, as I have formerly proved, is no lesse Supreme Pastor of his own Subjects, than the Pope of his.

The fourth Argument, is taken from the Baptisme of Kings; wherein, that they may be made Christians they submit their Scepters to Christ; and promise to keep, and defend the Christian Faith. This is true; for Christian Kings are no more but Christs Subjects: but they may, for all that, bee the Popes Fellowes; for they are Supreme Pastors of their own Subjects; and the Pope is no more but King, and Pastor, even in Rome it selfe.

The fifth Argument, is drawn from the words spoken by our Saviour, *Feed my sheep*; by which was given all Power necessary for a Pastor; as the Power to chase away Wolves, such as are Haeretiques; the Power to shut up Rammes, if they be mad, or push at the other Sheep with their Hornes, such as are Evill (though Christian) Kings; and Power to give the Flock convenient food: From whence hee inferreth, that St. Peter had these three Powers given him by Christ. To which I answer, that the last of these Powers, is no more than the Power, or rather Command to Teach. For the first, which is to chase away Wolves, that is, Haeretiques, the place hee quoteth is (*Matth.* 7.15.) *Beware of false Prophets which come to you in Sheeps clothing, but inwardly are ravening Wolves.* But neither are Haeretiques false Prophets, or at all Prophets: nor (admitting Haeretiques for the Wolves there meant,) were the Apostles commanded to kill them, or if they were Kings, to depose them; but to beware of, fly, and avoid them: nor was it to St. Peter, nor to any of the Apostles, but to the multitude of the Jews that followed him into the mountain, men for the most part not yet converted, that hee gave this Counsell, to Beware of false Prophets: which therefore if it conferre a Power of chasing away Kings, was given, not onely to private men; but to men that were not at all Christians. And as to the Power of Separating, and Shutting up of furious Rammes, (by which hee meaneth Christian Kings that refuse to submit themselves to the Roman Pastor,) our Saviour refused to take upon him that Power in this world himself, but advised to let the Corn and Tares grow up together till the day of Judgment: much lesse did hee give it to St. Peter, or can S. Peter give it to the Popes. St. Peter, and all other Pastors, are bidden to esteem those Christians that disobey the Church, that is, (that disobey the Christian Soveraigne) as Heathen men, and as Publicans. Seeing then [320] men challenge to the Pope no authority over Heathen Princes, they ought to challenge none over those that are to bee esteemed as Heathen.

But from the Power to Teach onely, hee inferreth also a Coercive Power in the Pope, over Kings. The Pastor (saith he) must give his flock convenient food: Therefore the Pope may, and ought to compell Kings to doe their duty. Out of which it followeth, that the Pope, as Pastor of Christian men, is King of Kings: which all Christian Kings ought indeed either to Confesse, or else they ought to take upon themselves the Supreme Pastorall Charge, every one in his own Dominion.

His sixth, and last Argument, is from Examples. To which I answer, first, that Examples prove nothing: Secondly, that the Examples he alledgeth make not so much as a probability of Right. The fact of Jehoiada, in Killing Athaliah (2 *Kings* 11.) was either by the Authority of King Joash, or it was a horrible Crime in the High Priest, which (ever after the election of King Saul) was a mere Subject. The fact of St. Ambrose, in Excommunicating Theodosius the Emperour, (if it were true hee did so,) was a Capitall Crime. And for the Popes, Gregory 1. Greg. 2. Zachary, and Leo 3. their Judgments are void, as given in their own Cause; and the Acts done by them conformably to this Doctrine, are the greatest Crimes (especially that of Zachary) that are incident to Humane Nature. And thus much of *Power Ecclesiasticall*; wherein I had been more briefe, forbearing to examine these Arguments of Bellarmine, if they had been his, as a Private man, and not as the Champion of the Papacy, against all other Christian Princes, and States.

[321]

CHAP. XLIII.

Of what is NECESSARY *for a Mans Reception into the Kingdome of Heaven.*

The difficulty of obeying God and Man both at once, The most frequent praetext of Sedition, and Civill Warre, in Christian Common-wealths hath a long time proceeded from a difficulty, not yet sufficiently resolved, of obeying at once, both God, and Man, then when their Commandements are one contrary to the other.

It is manifest enough, that when a man receiveth two contrary Commands, and knows that one of them is Gods, he ought to obey that, and not the other, though it be the command even of his lawfull Soveraign (whether a Monarch, or a soveraign Assembly,) or the command of his Father. The difficulty therefore consisteth in this, that men when they are commanded in the name of God, know not in divers Cases, whether the command be from God, or whether he that commandeth, doe but abuse Gods name for some private ends of his own. For as there were in the Church of the Jews, many false Prophets, that sought reputation with the people, by feigned Dreams, and Visions; so there have been in all times in the Church of Christ, false Teachers, that seek reputation with the people, by phantasticall and false Doctrines; and by such reputation (as is the nature of Ambition,) to govern them for their private benefit.

But this difficulty of obeying both God, and the Civill Soveraign on earth, to those that can distinguish between what is *Necessary*, and what is not *Necessary* for their *Reception* into the *Kingdome of God*, is of no moment. For if the command of the Civill Soveraign bee such, as that it may be obeyed, without the forfeiture of life Eternall; not to obey it is unjust; and the precept of the Apostle takes place; *Servants obey your Masters in all things*; and, *Children obey your Parents in all things*; and the precept of our Saviour, *The Scribes and Pharisees sit in Moses Chaire, All therefore they shall say, that observe, and doe.* But if the command be such, as cannot be obeyed, without being damned to Eternall Death, then it were madnesse to obey it, and the Counsell of our Saviour takes place, (*Mat.* 10.28.) *Fear not those that kill the body, but cannot kill the soule.* All men therefore that would avoid, both the punishments that are to be in this world inflicted, for disobedience to their earthly Soveraign, and those that shall be inflicted in the world to come for disobedience to God, have need be taught to distinguish well between what is, and what is not Necessary to Eternall Salvation.

All that is NECESSARY *to Salvation*, is contained in two Vertues, *Faith in Christ*, and *Obedience to Laws*. The latter of these, if it were perfect, were enough to us. But because wee are all guilty of disobedience to Gods Law, not onely originally in Adam, but also actually by our own transgressions, there is required at our hands now, not onely *Obedience* for the rest of our time, but also a *Remission* of sins for the time past; which Remission is the reward of our Faith in Christ. That nothing else is Necessarily required to Salvation, is manifest

Is none to them that distinguish between what is, and what is not Necessary to Salvation.

[322]
All that is Necessary to Salvation is contained in Faith and Obedience.

from this, that the Kingdome of Heaven is shut to none but to Sinners; that is to say, to the disobedient, or transgressors of the Law; nor to them, in case they Repent, and Beleeve all the Articles of Christian Faith, Necessary to Salvation.

What Obedience is Necessary;

The Obedience required at our hands by God, that accepteth in all our actions the Will for the Deed, is a serious Endeavour to Obey him; and is called also by all such names as signifie that Endeavour. And therefore Obedience, is sometimes called by the names of *Charity*, and *Love*, because they imply a Will to Obey; and our Saviour himself maketh our Love to God, and to one another, a Fulfilling of the whole Law: and sometimes by the name of *Righteousnesse*; for Righteousnesse is but the will to give to every one his owne, that is to say, the will to obey the Laws: and sometimes by the name of *Repentance*; because to Repent, implyeth a turning away from sinne, which is the same, with the return of the will to Obedience. Whosoever therefore unfeignedly desireth to fulfill the Commandements of God, or repenteth him truely of his transgressions, or that loveth God with all his heart, and his neighbor as himself, hath all the Obedience Necessary to his Reception into the Kingdom of God: For if God should require perfect Innocence, there could no flesh be saved.

And to what Laws.

But what Commandements are those that God hath given us? Are all those Laws which were given to the Jews by the hand of Moses, the Commandements of God? If they bee, why are not Christians taught to Obey them? If they be not, what others are so, besides the Law of Nature? For our Saviour Christ hath not given us new Laws, but Counsell to observe those wee are subject to; that is to say, the Laws of Nature, and the Laws of our severall Soveraigns: Nor did he make any new Law to the Jews in his Sermon on the Mount, but onely expounded the Laws of Moses, to which they were subject before. The Laws of God therefore are none but the Laws of Nature, whereof the principall is, that we should not violate our Faith, that is, a commandement to obey our Civill Soveraigns, which wee constituted over us, by mutuall pact one with another. And this Law of God, that commandeth Obedience to the Law Civill, commandeth by consequence Obedience to all the Precepts of the Bible; which (as I have proved in the precedent Chapter) is there onely Law, where the Civill Soveraign hath made it so; and in other places but Counsell; which a man at his own perill, may without injustice refuse to obey.

Knowing now what is the Obedience Necessary to Salvation, and to whom it is due; we are to consider next concerning Faith, whom, and why we beleeve; and what are the Articles, or Points necessarily to be beleeved by them that shall be saved. And first, for the Person whom we beleeve, because it is impossible to beleeve any Person, before we know what he saith, it is necessary he be one that wee have heard speak. The Person therefore, whom Abraham, Isaac, Jacob, Moses and the Prophets beleeved, was God himself, that spake unto them supernaturally: And the Person, whom the Apostles and Disciples that conversed with Christ beleeved, was our Saviour himself. But of them, to whom neither God the Father, nor our Saviour ever spake, it cannot be said, that the Person whom they beleeved, was God. They beleeved the Apostles, and after them the Pastors and Doctors of the Church, that recommended to their faith the History of the Old and New Testament: so that the Faith of Christians ever since our Saviours time, hath had for foundation, first, the reputation of their Pastors, and afterward, the authority of those that made the Old and New Testament to be received for the Rule of Faith; which none could do but Christian Soveraignes; who are therefore the Supreme Pastors, and the onely Persons, whom Christians now hear speak from God; except such as God speaketh to, in these days supernaturally. But because there be many false Prophets *gone out into the world*, *men*[1] are to examine such Spirits (as St. *John* adviseth us, 1 Epistle, Chap. 4. ver. 1.) *whether they be of God, or not.* And therefore, seeing the Examination of Doctrines belongeth to the Supreme Pastor, the Person which all they that have no speciall revelation are to beleeve, is (in every Common-wealth) the Supreme Pastor, that is to say, the Civill Soveraigne.

The causes why men beleeve any Christian Doctrine, are various: For Faith is the gift of God; and he worketh it in each severall man, by such wayes, as it seemeth good unto himself. The most ordinary immediate cause of our beleef, concerning any point of Christian Faith, is, that wee beleeve the Bible to be the Word of God. But why wee beleeve the Bible to be the Word of God, is much disputed, as all questions must needs bee, that are not well stated. For they make not the question to be, *Why we Beleeve it*, but, *How wee Know it*; as if

Marginal notes:
[323]
In the Faith of a Christian, who is the Person beleeved.

The causes of Christian Faith.

---

[1] *Syn.:* other men

Beleeving and *Knowing* were all one. And thence while one side ground their Knowledge upon the Infallibility of the Church, and the other side, on the Testimony of the Private Spirit, neither side concludeth what it pretends. For how shall a man know the Infallibility of the Church, but by knowing first the Infallibility of the Scripture? Or how shall a man know his own Private spirit to be other than a beleef, grounded upon the Authority, and Arguments of his Teachers; or upon a Presumption of his own Gifts? Besides, there is nothing in the Scripture, from which can be inferred the Infallibility of the Church; much lesse, of any particular Church; and least of all, the Infallibility of any particular man.

[324]
Faith comes by Hearing.
    It is manifest therefore, that Christian men doe not know, but onely beleeve the Scripture to be the Word of God; and that the means of making them beleeve which God is pleased to afford men ordinarily, is according to the way of Nature, that is to say, from their Teachers. It is the Doctrine of St. Paul concerning Christian Faith in generall, (*Rom.* 10.17.) *Faith cometh by Hearing*, that is, by Hearing our lawfull Pastors. He saith also (ver. 14, 15. of the same Chapter) *How shall they beleeve in him of whom they have not heard? and how shall they hear without a Preacher? and how shall they Preach, except they be sent?* Whereby it is evident, that the ordinary cause of beleeving that the Scriptures are the Word of God, is the same with the cause of the beleeving of all other Articles of our Faith, namely, the Hearing of those that are by the Law allowed and appointed to Teach us, as our Parents in their Houses, and our Pastors in the Churches: Which also is made more manifest by experience. For what other cause can there bee assigned, why in Christian Common-wealths all men either beleeve, or at least professe the Scripture to bee the Word of God, and in other Common-wealths scarce any; but that in Christian Common-wealths they are taught it from their infancy; and in other places they are taught otherwise?

    But if Teaching be the cause of Faith, why doe not all beleeve? It is certain therefore that Faith is the gift of God, and hee giveth it to whom he will. Nevertheless, because to them to whom he giveth it, he giveth it by the means of Teachers, the immediate cause of Faith is Hearing. In a School, where many are taught, and some profit, others profit not, the cause of learning in them that profit, is the Master; yet it cannot be thence inferred, that learning is not the gift of God. All good things proceed from God; yet cannot all that have them, say they are Inspired; for that implies a gift supernaturall, and the immediate hand of God; which he that pretends to, pretends to be a Prophet, and is subject to the examination of the Church.

But whether men *Know*, or *Beleeve*, or *Grant* the Scriptures to be the Word of God; if out of such places of them, as are without obscurity, I shall shew what Articles of Faith are necessary, and onely necessary for Salvation, those men must needs *Know*, *Beleeve*, or *Grant* the same.

The (*Unum Necessarium*) Onely Article of Faith, which the Scripture maketh simply Necessary to Salvation, is this, that J E S U S I S T H E C H R I S T. By the name of *Christ*, is understood the King, which God had before promised by the Prophets of the Old Testament, to send into the world, to reign (over the Jews, and over such of other nations as should beleeve in him) under himself eternally; and to give them that eternall life, which was lost by the sin of Adam. Which when I have proved out of Scripture, I will further shew when, and in what sense some other Articles may bee also called *Necessary*. *The onely Necessary Article of Christian Faith;*

For Proof that the Beleef of this Article, *Jesus is the Christ*, is all the Faith required to Salvation, my first Argument shall bee from the Scope of the Evangelists; which was by the description of the life of our Saviour, to establish that one Article, *Jesus is the Christ*. The summe of St. Matthews Gospell is this, That Jesus was of the stock of David; Born of a Virgin; which are the Marks of the true Christ: That the *Magi* came to worship him as King of the Jews: That Herod for the same cause sought to kill him: That John Baptist proclaimed him: That he preached by himselfe, and his Apostles that he was that King: That he taught the Law, not as a Scribe, but as a man of Authority: That he cured diseases by his Word onely, and did many other Miracles, which were foretold the Christ should doe: That he was saluted King when hee entred into Jerusalem: That he fore-warned them to beware of all others that should pretend to be Christ: That he was taken, accused, and put to death, for saying, hee was King: That the cause of his condemnation written on the Crosse, was J E S U S O F N A Z A R E T H, T H E K I N G O F T H E J E W E S. All which tend to no other end than this, that men should beleeve, that *Jesus is the Christ*. Such therefore was the Scope of St. Matthews Gospel. But the Scope of all the Evangelists (as may appear by reading them) was the same. Therefore the Scope of the whole Gospell, was the establishing of that onely Article. And St. John expressely makes it his conclusion, *[325] Proved from the Scope of the Evangelists:*

John 20.31. *These things are written, that you may know that Jesus is the Christ, the Son of the living God.*

From the Sermons of the Apostles:

My second Argument is taken from the Subject of the Sermons of the Apostles, both whilest our Saviour lived on earth, and after his Ascension. The Apostles in our Saviours time were sent, *Luke* 9.2. to Preach the Kingdome of God: For neither there, nor *Mat.* 10.7. giveth he any Commission to them, other than this, *As ye go, Preach, saying, the Kingdome of Heaven is at hand*; that is, that *Jesus* is the *Messiah*, the *Christ*, the *King* which was to come. That their Preaching also after his ascension was the same, is manifest out of *Acts* 17.6. *They drew* (saith St. Luke) *Jason and certain Brethren unto the Rulers of the City, crying, These that have turned the world upside down are come hither also, whom Jason hath received. And these all do contrary to the Decrees of Caesar, saying, that there is another King, one Jesus*: And out of the 2. & 3. verses of the same Chapter, where it is said, that St. *Paul as his manner was, went in unto them; and three Sabbath dayes reasoned with them out of the Scriptures; opening and alledging, that Christ must needs have suffered, and risen againe from the dead, and that this Jesus (whom hee preached) is Christ.*

From the Easinesse of the Doctrine:

The third Argument is, from those places of Scripture, by which all the Faith required to Salvation is declared to be Easie. For if an inward assent of the mind to all the Doctrines concerning Christian Faith now taught, (whereof the greatest part are disputed,) were necessary to Salvation, there would be nothing in the world so hard, as to be a Christian. The Thief upon the Crosse though repenting, could not have been saved for saying, *Lord remember me when thou commest into thy Kingdome*; by which he testified no beleefe of any other Article, but this, *That Jesus was the King*. Nor could it bee said (as it is *Mat.* 11.30.) that *Christs yoke is Easy, and his burthen Light*: Nor that *Little Children beleeve in him*, as it is *Matth.* 18.6. Nor could St. Paul have said (1 *Cor.* 1.21.) *It pleased God by the Foolishnesse of preaching, to save them that beleeve*: Nor could St. Paul himself have been saved, much lesse have been so great a Doctor of the Church so suddenly, that never perhaps thought of Transubtantiation, nor Purgatory, nor many other Articles now obtruded.

[326]

From formall and cleer texts.

The fourth Argument is taken from places expresse, and such as receive no controversie of Interpretation; as first, *John* 5.39. *Search the Scriptures, for in them yee thinke yee have eternall life; and they are they that testifie of mee.* Our Saviour here speaketh of the Scriptures only of the Old Testament; for the Jews at that time could not search the

Scriptures of the New Testament, which were not written. But the Old Testament hath nothing of Christ, but the Markes by which men might know him when hee came; as that he should descend from David, be born at Bethlem, and of a Virgin; doe great Miracles, and the like. Therefore to beleeve that this Jesus was He, was sufficient to eternall life: but more than sufficient is not Necessary; and consequently no other Article is required. Again, (*John* 11.26.) *Whosoever liveth and beleeveth in mee, shall not die eternally,* Therefore to beleeve in Christ, is faith sufficient to eternall life; and consequently no more faith than that is Necessary, But to beleeve in Jesus, and to beleeve that Jesus is the Christ, is all one, as appeareth in the verses immediately following. For when our Saviour (verse 26.) had said to Martha, *Beleevest thou this?* she answereth (verse 27.) *Yea Lord, I beleeve that thou art the Christ, the Son of God, which should come into the world*: Therefore this Article alone is faith sufficient to life eternall; and more than sufficient is not Necessary. Thirdly, *John* 20.31. *These things are written that yee might beleeve, that Jesus is the Christ, the Son of God, and that beleeving yee might have life through his name.* There, to beleeve that *Jesus is the Christ,* is faith sufficient to the obtaining of life; and therefore no other Article if Necessary. Fourthly, 1 *John* 4.2. *Every spirit that confesseth that Jesus Christ is come in the flesh, is of God.* And 1 *Joh.* 5.1. *Whosoever beleeveth that Jesus is the Christ, is born of God.* And verse 5. *Who is hee that overcommeth the world, but he that beleeveth that Jesus is the Son of God?* Fiftly, *Act.* 8. ver. 36, 37. *See* (saith the Eunuch) *here is water, what doth hinder me to be baptized? And Philip said, If thou beleevest with all thy heart thou mayst. And hee answered and said, I beleeve that Jesus Christ is the Son of God.* Therefore this Article beleeved, *Jesus is the Christ,* is sufficient to Baptisme, that is to say, to our Reception into the Kingdome of God, and by consequence, onely Necessary. And generally in all places where our Saviour saith to any man, *Thy faith hath saved thee,* the cause he saith it, is some Confession, which directly, or by consequence, implyeth a beleef, that *Jesus is the Christ.* [327]

The last Argument is from the places, where this Article is made the Foundation of Faith: For he that holdeth the Foundation shall bee saved. Which places are first, *Mat.* 24.23. *If any man shall say unto you, Loe, here is Christ, or there, beleeve it not, for there shall arise false Christs, and false Prophets, and shall shew great signes and wonders, &c.* Here wee see, this Article *Jesus is the Christ,* must bee held, though hee that shall

From that it is the Foundation of all other Articles.

teach the contrary should doe great miracles. The second place is, *Gal.* 1.8. *Though we, or an Angell from Heaven preach any other Gospell unto you, than that wee have preached unto you, let him bee accursed.* But the Gospell which Paul, and the other Apostles, preached, was onely this Article, that *Jesus is the Christ:* Therefore for the Beleef of this Article, we are to reject the Authority of an Angell from heaven; much more of any mortall man, if he teach the contrary. This is therefore the Fundamentall Article of Christian Faith. A third place is, 1 *Joh.* 4.1. *Beloved, beleeve not every spirit. Hereby yee shall know the Spirit of God; every spirit that confesseth that Jesus Christ is come in the flesh, is of God.* By which it is evident, that this Article, is the measure, and rule, by which to estimate, and examine all other Articles; and is therefore onely Fundamentall. A fourth is, *Matt.* 16.18. where after St. Peter had professed this Article, saying to our Saviour, *Thou art Christ the Son of the living God,* Our Saviour answered, *Thou art Peter, and upon this Rock I will build my Church:* from whence I inferre, that this Article is that, on which all other Doctrines of the Church are built, as on their Foundation. A fift is (1 *Cor.* 3. ver. 11, 12, & c.) *Other Foundation can no man lay, than that which is laid, Jesus is the Christ. Now if any man build upon this Foundation, Gold, Silver, pretious Stones, Wood, Hay, Stubble; Every mans work shall be made manifest; For the Day shall declare it, because it shall be revealed by fire, and the fire shall try every mans work, of what sort it is. If any mans work abide, which he hath built thereupon, he shall receive a reward: If any mans work shall bee burnt, he shall suffer losse; but he himself shall be saved, yet so as by fire.* Which words, being partly plain and easie to understand, and partly allegoricall and diffi-cult; out of that which is plain, may be inferred, that Pastors that teach this Foundation, that *Jesus is the Christ,* though they draw from it false consequences, (which all men are sometimes subject to,) they may neverthelesse bee saved; much more that they may bee saved, who being no Pastors, but Hearers, beleeve that which is by their lawfull Pastors taught them. Therefore the beleef of this Article is sufficient; and by consequence, there is no other Article of Faith Necessarily required to Salvation.

[328]   Now for the part which is Allegoricall, as *That the fire shall try every mans work,* and that *They shall be saved, but so as by fire,* or *through fire,* (for the originall is διὰ πυρὸς,) it maketh nothing against this con-clusion which I have drawn from the other words, that are plain. Neverthelesse, because upon this place there hath been an argument

taken, to prove the fire of Purgatory, I will also here offer you my conjecture concerning the meaning of this triall of Doctrines, and saving of men as by Fire. The Apostle here seemeth to allude to the words of the Prophet Zachary, Ch. 13.8, 9. who speaking of the Restauration of the Kingdome of God, saith thus, *Two parts therein shall be cut off, and die, but the third shall be left therein; And I will bring the third part through the Fire, and will refine them as Silver is refined, and will try them as Gold is tryed; they shall call on the name of the Lord, and I will hear them.* The day of Judgment, is the day of the Restauration of the Kingdome of God; and at that day it is, that St. Peter tells us ★ shall be the Conflagration of the world, wherein the wicked shall perish; but the remnant which God will save, shall passe through that Fire, unhurt, and be therein (as Silver and Gold are refined by the fire from their drosse) tryed, and refined from their Idolatry, and be made to call upon the name of the true God. Alluding whereto St. Paul here saith, That *the Day* (that is, the Day of Judgment, the Great Day of our Saviours comming to restore the Kingdome of God in Israel) shall try every mans doctrine, by Judging, which are Gold, Silver, Pretious Stones, Wood, Hay, Stubble; And then they that have built false Consequences on the true Foundation, shall see their Doctrines condemned; neverthelesse they themselves shall be saved, and passe unhurt through this universall Fire, and live eternally, to call upon the name of the true and onely God. In which sense there is nothing that accordeth not with the rest of Holy Scripture, or any glimpse of the fire of Purgatory.

★2 Pet. 3 v 7, 10, 12.

But a man may here aske, whether it bee not as necessary to Salvation, to beleeve, that God is Omnipotent; Creator of the world; that Jesus Christ is risen; and that all men else shall rise again from the dead at the last day; as to beleeve, that *Jesus is the Christ.* To which I answer, they are; and so are many more Articles: but they are such, as are contained in this one, and may be deduced from it, with more, or lesse difficulty. For who is there that does not see, that they who beleeve Jesus to be the Son of the God of Israel, and that the Israelites had for God the Omnipotent Creator of all things, doe therein also beleeve, that God is the Omnipotent Creator of all things? Or how can a man beleeve, that Jesus is the King that shall reign eternally, unlesse hee beleeve him also risen again from the dead? For a dead man cannot exercise the Office of a King. In summe, he that holdeth this Foundation, *Jesus is the Christ,* holdeth Expressely all that hee

In what sense other Articles may be called Necessary.

[329]

seeth rightly deduced from it, and Implicitely all that is consequent thereunto, though he have not skill enough to discern the consequence. And therefore it holdeth still good, that the beleef of this one Article is sufficient faith to obtaine remission of sinnes to the *Penitent*, and consequently to bring them into the Kingdome of Heaven.

That Faith, and Obedience are both of them Necessary to Salvation.

Now that I have shewn, that all the Obedience required to Salvation, consisteth in the will to obey the Law of God, that is to say, in Repentance; and all the Faith required to the same, is comprehended in the beleef of this Article *Jesus is the Christ*; I will further alledge those places of the Gospell, that prove, that all that is Necessary to Salvation is contained in both these joined together. The men to whom St. Peter preached on the day of Pentecost, next after the Ascension of our Saviour, asked him, and the rest of the Apostles, saying, (*Act.* 2.37.) *Men and Brethren what shall we doe?* To whom St. Peter answered (in the next verse) *Repent, and be Baptized every one of you, for the remission of sins, and ye shall receive the gift of the Holy Ghost.* Therefore Repentance, and Baptisme, that is, beleeving that *Jesus is the Christ*, is all that is Necessary to Salvation. Again, our Saviour being asked by a certain Ruler, (*Luke* 18. 18.) *What shall I doe to inherite eternall life?* Answered (verse 20.) *Thou knowest the Commandements, Doe not commit Adultery, Doe not Kill, Doe not Steal, Doe not bear false witnesse, Honor thy Father, and thy Mother*: which when he said he had observed, our Saviour added, *Sell all thou hast, give it to the Poor, and come and follow me*: which was as much as to say, Relye on me that am the King: Therefore to fulfill the Law, and to beleeve that Jesus is the King, is all that is required to bring a man to eternall life. Thirdly, St. Paul saith (*Rom.* 1. 17.) *The Just shall live by Faith*; not every one, but the *Just*; therefore *Faith* and *Justice* (that is, the *will to be Just*, or *Repentance*) are all that is Neccessary to life eternall. And (*Mark* 1.15.) our Saviour preached, saying, *The Time is fulfilled, and the Kingdom of God is at hand, Repent and Beleeve the Evangile*, that is, the Good news that the Christ was come. Therefore to Repent, and to Beleeve that Jesus is the Christ, is all that is required to Salvation.

What each them contributes thereunto.

Seeing then it is Necessary that Faith, and Obedience (implyed in the world Repentance) do both concurre to our Salvation; the question by which of the two we are Justified, is impertinently disputed. Nevertheless, it will not be impertinent, to make manifest in what manner each of them contributes thereunto; and in what sense it is said, that we are to be Justified by the one, and by the other. And first,

if by Righteousnesse be understood the Justice of the Works themselves, there is no man that can be saved; for there is none that hath
not transgressed the Law of God. And therefore when wee are said to
be Justified by Works, it is to be understood of the Will, which God
doth alwaies accept for the Work it selfe, as well in good, as in evill
men. And in this sense onely it is, that a man is called *Just*, or *Unjust*;
and that his Justice Justifies him, that is, gives him the title, in Gods
acceptation, of *Just*; and renders him capable of *living by his Faith*,
which before he was not. So that Justice Justifies in that sense, in [330]
which to *Justifie*, is the same that to *Denominate a man Just*; and not in
the signification of discharging the Law; whereby the punishment of
his sins should be unjust.

But a man is then also said to be Justified, when his Plea, though in
it selfe unsufficient, is accepted; as when we Plead our Will, our
Endeavour to fulfill the Law, and Repent us of our failings, and God
accepteth it for the Performance is selfe: And because God accepteth
not the Will for the Deed, but onely in the Faithfull; it is therefore
Faith that makes good our Plea; and in this sense it is, that Faith onely
Justifies: So that *Faith* and *Obedience* are both Necessary to Salvation;
yet in severall senses each of them is said to Justifie.

Having thus shewn what is Necessary to Salvation; it is not hard to
reconcile our Obedience to God, with our Obedience to the Civill
Soveraign; who is either Christian, or Infidel. If he bee a Christian, he
alloweth the beleefe of this Article, that *Jesus is the Christ*; and of all
the Articles that are contained in, or are by evident consequence
deduced from it: which is all the Faith Necessary to Salvation. And
because he is a Soveraign, he requireth Obedience to all his owne,
that is, to all the Civill Laws; in which also are contained all the Laws
of Nature, that is, all the Laws of God: for besides the Laws of
Nature, and the Laws of the Church, which are part of the Civill Law,
(for the Church that can make Laws is the Common-wealth,) there
bee no other Laws Divine. Whosoever therefore obeyeth his
Christian Soveraign, is not thereby hindred, neither from beleeving,
nor from obeying God. But suppose that a Christian King should
from this Foundation *Jesus is the Christ*, draw some false consequences, that is to say, make some superstructions of Hay, or Stubble,
and command the teaching of the same; yet seeing St. Paul says, he
shal be saved; much more shall he be saved, that teacheth them by his
command; and much more yet, he that teaches not, but onely beleeves

Obedience to
God and to
the Civill
Soveraign
not
inconsistent,
whether
Christian,

413

his lawfull Teacher. And in case a Subject be forbidden by the Civill Soveraign to professe some of those his opinions, upon what just ground can he disobey? Christian Kings may erre in deducing a Consequence, but who shall Judge? Shall a private man Judge, when the question is of his own obedience? or shall any man Judg but he that is appointed thereto by the Church, that is, by the Civill Soveraign that representeth it? or if the Pope, or an Apostle Judge, may he not erre in deducing of a consequence? did not one of the two, St. Peter, or St. Paul erre in a superstructure, when St. Paul withstood St. Peter to his face? There can therefore be no contradiction between the Laws of God, and the Laws of a Christian Common-wealth.

Or Infidel.　　And when the Civill Soveraign is an Infidel, every one of his own Subjects that resisteth him, sinneth against the Laws of God (for such are the Laws of Nature,) and rejecteth the counsell of the Apostles, that admonisheth all Christians to obey their Princes, and all Children and Servants to obey their Parents, and Masters, in all things. And for their *Faith*, it is internall, and invisible; They have the licence that Naaman had, and need not put themselves into danger for it. But if they do, they ought to expect their reward in Heaven, and not complain of their Lawfull Soveraign; much lesse make warre upon him. For he that is not glad of any just occasion of Martyrdome, has not the faith he professeth, but pretends it onely, to set some colour upon his own contumacy. But what Infidel King is so unreasonable, as knowing he has a Subject, that waiteth for the second comming of Christ, after the present world shall bee burnt, and intendeth then to obey him (which is the intent of beleeving that Jesus is the Christ,) and in the mean time thinketh himself bound to obey the Laws of that Infidel King, (which all Christians are obliged in conscience to doe,) to put to death, or to persecute such a Subject?

And thus much shall suffice, concerning the Kingdome of God, and Policy Ecclesiasticall. Wherein I pretend not to advance any Position of my own, but onely to shew what are the Consequences that seem to me deducible fron the Principles of Christian Politiques, (which are the holy Scriptures,) in confirmation of the Power of Civill Soveraigns, and the Duty of their Subjects. And in the allegation of Scripture, I have endeavoured to avoid such texts as are of obscure, or controverted Interpretations; and to alledge none, but in such sense as is most plain, and agreeable to the harmony and scope of the whole

[331]

Bible; which was written for the re-establishment of the Kingdome of God in Christ. For it is not the bare Words, but the Scope of the writer that giveth the true light, by which any writing is to bee interpreted; and they that insist upon single Texts, without considering the main Designe, can derive no thing from them cleerly; but rather by casting atomes of Scripture, as dust before mens eyes, make every thing more obscure than it is; an ordinary artifice of those that seek not the truth, but their own advantage.

OF THE KINGDOME OF DARKNESSE.

CHAP. XLIV.
Of Spirituall Darknesse from MISINTERPRETATION *of Scripture.*

The Kingdom of Darknesse what.

Besides these Soveraign Powers, *Divine,* and *Humane,* of which I have hitherto discoursed, there is mention in Scripture of another Power, namely, ★that of *the Rulers of the Darknesse of this world,* ★ *the Kingdome of Satan,* and ★ *the Principality of Beelzebub over Daemons,* that is to say, over Phantasmes that appear in the Air: For which cause Satan is also called ★ *the Prince of the Power of the Air,* and (because he ruleth in the darknesse of this world) ★ *The Prince of this world*: And in consequence hereunto, they who are under his Dominion, in opposition to the faithfull (who are the *Children of the Light*) are called the *Children of Darknesse.* For seeing Beelzebub is Prince of Phantasmes, Inhabitants of his Dominion of Air and Darknesse, the Children of Darknesse, and these Daemons, Phantasmes, or Spirits of Illusion, signifie allegorically the same thing. This considered, the Kingdome of Darknesse, as it is set forth in these, and other places of the Scripture, is nothing else but a *Confederacy of Deceivers, that to obtain dominion*

★*Eph.*6. 12.
★*Mat.*12.26.
★*Mat.*9. 34.
★*Eph.*2. 2.
★*Jeh.*16.11.

417

over men in this present world, endeavour by dark, and erroneous Doctrines, to extinguish in them the Light, both of Nature, and of the Gospell; and so to dis-prepare them for the Kingdome of God to come.

[334]
The Church not yet fully freed of Darknesse.

As men that are utterly deprived from their Nativity, of the light of the bodily Eye, have no Idea at all, of any such light; and no man conceives in his imagination any greater light, than he hath at some time, or other, perceived by his outward Senses: so also is it of the light of the Gospel, and of the light of the Understanding, that no man can conceive there is any greater degree of it, than that which he hath already attained unto. And from hence it comes to passe, that men have no other means to acknowledge their owne Darknesse, but onely by reasoning from the un-foreseen mischances, that befall them in their ways; The Darkest part of the Kingdom of Satan, is that which is without the Church of God; that is to say, amongst them that beleeve not in Jesus Christ. But we cannot say, that therefore the Church enjoyeth (as the land of Goshen) all the light, which to the performance of the work enjoined us by God, is necessary. Whence comes it, that in Christendome there has been, almost from the time of the Apostles, such justling of one another out of their places, both by forraign, and Civill war? such stumbling at every little asperity of their own fortune, and every little eminence of that of other men? and such diversity of ways in running to the same mark, *Felicity*, if it be not Night amongst us, or at least a Mist? wee are therefore yet in the Dark.

Four Causes of Spirituall Darknesse.

The Enemy has been here in the Night of our naturall Ignorance, and sown the tares of Spirituall Errors; and that, First, by abusing, and putting out the light of the Scriptures: For we erre, not knowing the Scriptures. Secondly, by introducing the Daemonology of the Heathen Poets, that is to say, their fabulous Doctrine concerning Daemons, which are but Idols, or Phantasms of the braine, without any reall nature of their own, distinct from humane fancy; such as are dead mens Ghosts, and Fairies, and other matter of old Wives tales. Thirdly, by mixing with the Scripture divers reliques of the Religion, and much of the vain and erroneous Philosophy of the Greeks, especially of Aristotle. Fourthly, by mingling with both these, false, or uncertain Traditions, and fained, or uncertain History. And so we come to erre, by *giving heed to seducing Spirits*, and the Daemonology of such *as speak lies in Hypocrisie*, (or as it is in the Originall, 1 *Tim*.4. 1, 2. *of those that play the part of lyars*) *with a seared conscience*, that is, contrary to their own knowledge. Concerning the first of these, which is the Seducing of men by abuse of Scripture, I intend to speak briefly in this Chapter.

The greatest, and main abuse of Scripture, and to which almost all the rest are either consequent, or subservient, is the wresting of it, to prove that the Kingdome of God, mentioned so often in the Scripture, is the present Church, or multitude of Christian men now living, or that being dead, are to rise again at the last day: whereas the Kingdome of God was first instituted by the Ministery of Moses, over the Jews onely; who were therefore called his Peculiar People; and ceased afterwards, in the election of Saul, when they refused to be governed by God any more, and demanded a King after the manner of the nations; which God himself consented unto, as I have more at large proved before, in the 35. Chapter. After that time, there was no other Kingdome of God in the world, by any Pact, or otherwise, than he ever was, is, and shall be King, of all men, and of all creatures, as governing according to his Will, by his infinite Power. Neverthelesse, he promised by his Prophets to restore this his Government to them again, when the time he hath in his secret counsell appointed for it shall bee fully come, and when they shall turn unto him by repentance, and amendment of life: and not onely so, but he invited also the Gentiles to come in, and enjoy the happinesse of his Reign, on the same conditions of conversion and repentance; and hee promised also to send his Son into the world, to expiate the sins of them all by his death, and to prepare them by his Doctrine, to receive him at his second coming: Which second coming not yet being, the Kingdome of God is not yet come, and wee are not now under any other Kings by Pact, but our Civill Soveraigns; saving onely, that Christian men are already in the Kingdome of Grace, in as much as they have already the Promise of being received at his comming againe.

Consequent to this Errour, that the present Church is Christs Kingdome, there ought to be some one Man, or Assembly, by whose mouth our Saviour (now in heaven) speaketh, *and giveth*[1] law, and which representeth his Person to all Christians, or divers Men, or divers Assemblies that doe the same to divers parts of Christendome. This power Regal under Christ, being challenged, universally by the Pope, and in particular Common-wealths by Assemblies of the

Errors from misinterpreting the Scriptures, concerning the Kingdome of God.

[335]

As that the Kingdome of God is the present Church:

[1] *Syn.*: giveth

Pastors of the place, (when the Scripture gives it to none but to Civill Soveraigns,) comes to be so passionately disputed, that it putteth out the Light of Nature, and causeth so great a Darknesse in mens understanding, that they see not who it is to whom they have engaged their obedience.

And that the Pope is his Vicar generall:

Consequent to this claim of the Pope to *be vicar*[1] Generall of Christ in the present Church, (supposed to be that Kingdom of his, to which we are addressed in the Gospel,) is the Doctrine, that it is necessary for a Christian King, to receive his Crown by a Bishop; as if it were from that Ceremony, that he derives the clause of *Dei gratiâ* in his title; and that then onely he is made King by the *favour*[2] of God, when he is crowned by the authority of Gods universall Vicegerent on earth; and that every Bishop whosoever be his Soveraign, taketh at his Consecration an oath of absolute Obedience to the Pope. Consequent to the same, is the Doctrine of the fourth Councell of Lateran, held under Pope *Innocent* the third, (Chap. 3.*de Haereticis.*) *That if a King at the Popes admonition, doe not purge his Kingdome of Haeresies, and being excommunicate for the same, doe not give satisfaction within a year, his Subjects are absolved of the bond of their obedience.* Where, by Haeresies are understood all opinions which the Church of Rome hath forbidden to be maintained. And by this means, as often as there is any repugnancy between the Politicall designes of the Pope, and other Christian Princes, as there is very often, there ariseth such a Mist amongst their Subjects, that they know not a stranger that thrusteth himself into the throne of their lawfull Prince, from him whom they had themselves placed there; and in this Darknesse of mind, are made to fight one against another, without discerning their enemies from their friends, under the conduct of another mans ambition.

Vide Pontific Greg. 13. fol[3]

[336]

And that the Pastors are the Clergy.

From the same opinion, that the present Church is the Kingdome of God, it proceeds that Pastours, Deacons, and all other Ministers of the Church, take the name to themselves of the *Clergy*; giving to other Christians the name of *Laity*, that is, simply *People*. For Clergy signifies those, whose maintenance is that Revenue, which God having reserved to himselfe during his Reigne over the Israelites, assigned to the tribe of Levi (who were to be his publique Ministers, and had no portion of land set them out to live on, as their brethren) to be their

---

[1] *Syn.*: Vicar   [2] *Syn.*: favour
[3] Marginal note inserted by Hobbes in MS. See biographical note on Pope Gregory IX.

inheritance. The Pope therefore, (pretending the present Church to be, as the Realme of Israel, the Kingdome of God) challenging to himselfe and his subordinate Ministers, the like revenue, as the Inheritance of God, the name of Clergy was sutable to that claime. And thence it is, that Tithes, and other tributes paid to the Levites, as *in Gods*[1] Right, amongst the Israelites, have a long time been demanded, and taken of Christians, by Ecclesiastiques, *Iure divino*, that is, in Gods Right. By which meanes, the people every where were obliged to a double tribute; one to the State, another to the Clergy; whereof, that to the Clergy, being the tenth of their revenue, is double to that which a King of Athens (and esteemed a Tyrant) exacted of his subjects for the defraying of all publique charges: For he demanded no more but the twentieth part; and yet abundantly maintained therewith the Commonwealth. And in the Kingdome of the Jewes, during the Sacerdotall Reigne of God, the Tithes and Offerings were the whole Publique Revenue.

From the same mistaking of the present Church for the Kingdom of God, came in the distinction betweene the *Civill* and the *Canon* Laws: The Civil Law being the Acts of *Soveraigns* in their own Dominions, and the Canon Law being the Acts of the *Pope* in the same Dominions. Which Canons, though they were but Canons, that is, *Rules Propounded*, and but voluntarily received by Christian Princes, till the translation of the Empire to *Charlemain*; yet afterwards, as the power of the Pope encreased, became *Rules Commanded*, and the Emperours themselves (to avoyd greater mischiefes, which the people blinded might be led into) were forced to let them passe for Laws.

From hence it is, that in all Dominions, where the Popes Ecclesiasticall power is entirely received, Jewes, Turkes, and Gentiles, are in the Roman Church tolerated in their Religion, as farre forth, as in the exercise and profession thereof they offend not against the civill power: whereas in a Christian, though a stranger, not to be of the Roman Religion, is Capitall; because the Pope pretendeth that all Christians are his Subjects. For otherwise it were as much against [337] the law of Nations, to persecute a Christian stranger, for professing the Religion of his owne country, as an Infidell; or rather more, in as much as they that are not against Christ, are with him.

From the same it is, that in every Christian State there are certaine

[1] Syn.: Gods

men, that are exempt, by Ecclesiasticall liberty, from the tributes, and from the tribunals of the Civil State; for so are the secular Clergy, besides Monks and Friars, which in many places, bear so great a proportion to the common people, as if need were, there might be raised out of them alone, an Army, sufficient for any warre the Church militant should imploy them in, against their owne, or other Princes.

Error from mistaking Consecration for Conjuration. A second generall abuse of Scripture, is the turning of Consecration into Conjuration, or Enchantment. To *Consecrate*, is in Scripture, to Offer, Give, or Dedicate, in pious and decent language and gesture, a man, or any other thing to God, by separating of it from common use; that is to say, to Sanctifie, or make its Gods, and to be used only by those, whom God hath appointed to be his Publike Ministers, (as I have already proved at large in the 35. Chapter;) and thereby to change, not the thing Consecrated, but onely the use of it, from being Profane and common, to be Holy, and peculiar to Gods service. But when by such words, the nature or qualitie of the thing it selfe, is pretended to be changed, it is not Consecration, but either an extraordinary worke of God, or a vaine and impious Conjuration. But *(seeing for the frequency of pretending the change of Nature in their Consecrations, it cannot be esteemed a work extraordinary,)*[1] it is no other than a *Conjuration* or *Incantation*, whereby they would have men to beleeve an alteration of Nature that is not, contrary to the testimony of mans Sight, and of all the rest of his Senses. As for example, when the Priest, in stead of Consecrating Bread and Wine to Gods peculiar service in the Sacrament of the Lords Supper, (which is but a separation of it from the common use, to signifie, that is, to put men in mind of their Redemption, by the Passion of Christ, whose body was broken, and blood shed upon the Crosse for our transgressions,) pretends, that by saying of the words of our Saviour, *This is my Body*, and *This is my Blood*, the nature of Bread is no more there, but his very Body; notwithstanding there appeareth not to the Sight, or other Sense of the Receiver, any thing that appeared not before the Consecration. The Egyptian Conjurers, that are said to have turned their Rods to Serpents, and the Water into Bloud, are thought but to have deluded the senses of the Spectators by a false shew of things, yet are esteemed Enchanters: But what should wee have thought of them, if

---

[1.] *Syn.*: seeing (for the frequency of pretending the change of Nature in their Consecrations,) it cannot be esteemed a work extraordinary,

there had appeared in their Rods nothing like a Serpent, and in the Water enchanted, nothing like Bloud, nor like any thing else but Water, but that they had faced down the King, that they were Serpents that looked like Rods, and that it was Bloud that seemed Water? That had been both Enchantment, and Lying. And yet in this daily act of the Priest, they doe the very same, by turning the holy [338] words into the manner of a Charme, which produceth nothing new to the Sense; but they face us down, that it hath turned the Bread into a Man; nay more; into a God; and require men to worship it, as if it were our Saviour himself present God and Man, and thereby to commit most grosse Idolatry. For if it bee enough to excuse it of Idolatry, to say it is no more Bread, but God; why should not the same excuse serve the Egyptians, in case they had the faces to say, the Leeks, and Onyons they worshipped, were not very Leeks, and Onyons, but a Divinity under their *species*, or likenesse. The words, *This is my Body*, are aequivalent to these, *This signifies, or represents my Body*; and it is an ordinary figure of Speech: but to take it literally, is an abuse; nor though so taken, can it extend any further, than to the Bread which Christ himself with his own hands Consecrated. For hee never said, that of what Bread soever, any Priest whatsoever, should say, *This is my Body*, or, *This is Christs Body*, the same should presently be transubstantiated. Nor did the Church of Rome ever establish this Transubstantiation, till the time of *Innocent* the third; which was not above 500. years agoe, when the Power of Popes was at the Highest, and the Darknesse of the time grown so great, as men discerned not the Bread that was given them to eat, especially when it was stamped with the figure of Christ upon the Crosse, as if they would have men beleeve it were Transubstantiated, not only into the Body of Christ, but also into the Wood of his Crosse, and that they did eat both together in the Sacrament.

The like Incantation, in stead of Consecration, is used also in the *Incantation in the Ceremonies of Baptisme.* Sacrament of Baptisme: Where the abuse of Gods name in each severall Person, and in the whole Trinity, with the sign of the Crosse at each name, maketh up the Charm: As first, when they make the Holy water, the Priest saith, *I Conjure thee, thou Creature of Water, in the name of God the Father Almighty, and in the name of Jesus Christ his onely Son our Lord, and in vertue of the Holy Ghost, that thou become Conjured water, to drive away all the Powers of the Enemy, and to eradicate, and supplant the Enemy, &c.* And the same in the Benediction of the

Salt to be mingled with it; *That thou become Conjured Salt, that all Phantasmes, and Knavery of the Devills fraud may fly and depart from the place wherein thou are sprinkled; and every unclean Spirit bee Conjured by Him that shall come to judg the quicke and the dead.* The same in the Benediction of the Oyle, *That all the Power of the Enemy, all the Host of the Devill, all Assaults and Phantasmes of Satan, may be driven away by this Creature of Oyle.* And for the Infant that is to be Baptized, he is subject to many Charms: First, at the Church dore the Priest blows thrice in the Childs face, and sayes, *Goe out of him unclean Spirit, and give place to the Holy Ghost the Comforter.* As if all Children, till blown on by the Priest were Daemoniaques: Again, before his entrance into the Church, he saith as before, *I Conjure thee, &c. to goe out, and depart*

[339] *from this Servant of God*: And again the same Exorcisme is repeated once more before he be Baptized. These, and some other Incantations, are those that are used in stead of Benedictions, and Consecrations, in administration of the Sacraments of Baptisme, and the Lords Supper; wherein every thing that serveth to those holy uses (except the unhallowed Spittle of the Priest) hath some set form of Exorcisme.

And in Marriage, in Visitation of the Sick, and in Consecration of Places.   Nor are the other rites, as of Marriage, of Extreme Unction, of Visitation of the Sick, of Consecrating Churches, and Church-yards, and the like, exempt from Charms; in as much as there is in them the use of Enchanted Oyle, and Water, with the abuse of the Crosse and of the holy word of David, *Asperges me Domine Hyssopo*, as things of efficacy to drive away Phantasmes, and Imaginary Spirits.

Errors from mistaking Eternall Life, and Everlasting Death: Another generall Error, is from the Misinterpretation of the words *Eternall Life, Everlasting Death*, and the *Second Death*. For though we read plainly in holy Scripture, that God created Adam in an estate of Living for Ever, which was conditionall, that is to say, if he disobeyed not his Commandement; which was not essentiall to Humane Nature, but consequent to the vertue of the Tree of Life; whereof hee had liberty to eat, as long as hee had not sinned; and that hee was thrust out of Paradise after he had sinned, lest hee should eate thereof, and live for ever; and that Christs Passion is a Discharge of sin to all that beleeve on him; and by consequence, a restitution of Eternall Life, to all the Faithfull, and to them onely: yet the Doctrine is now, and hath been a long time far otherwise; namely, that every man hath Eternity of Life by Nature, in as much as his Soul is Immortall: So that the flaming Sword at the entrance of Paradise, though it hinder a man from coming to the Tree of Life, hinders him not from the Immortality which God took from him for his Sin; nor makes him to need the sacrificing of Christ, for the recovering of the same; and consequently, not onely the faithfull and righteous, but also the wicked, and the Heathen, shall enjoy Eternall Life, without any Death at all; much lesse a Second, and Everlasting Death. To salve this, it is said, that by *Second*, and *Everlasting Death*, is meant a Second, and Everlasting Life, but in Torments; a Figure never used, but in this very Case.

All which Doctrine is founded onely on some of the obscurer places of the New Testament; which neverthelesse, the whole scope of the Scripture considered, are cleer enough in a different sense, and *is unnecessary*¹ to the Christian Faith. For supposing that when a man dies, there remaineth nothing of him but his carkasse; cannot God that raised inanimated dust and clay into a living creature by his Word, *easily*² raise a dead carkasse to life again, and continue him alive for Ever, or make him die again, by another Word? the *Soule* in Scripture, signifieth alwaies, either the Life, or the Living Creature; and the Body and Soule jointly, the *Body alive*. In the fift day of the [340] Creation, God said, Let the waters produce *Reptile animae viventis*, the creeping thing that hath in it a Living Soule; the English translate it, *that hath Life*: And again, God created Whales, *& omnem animam viventem*; which in the English is, *every Living Creature*: And likewise of Man, God made him of the dust of the earth, and breathed in his face the breath of Life, *& factus est Homo in animam viventem*, that is, *and Man was made a Living Creature*: And after *Noah* came out of the Arke, God saith, hee will no more smite *omnem animam viventem*, that is, *every Living Creature*: And Deut. 12. 23. *Eate not the Bloud, for the Bloud is the Soule*, that is, *the Life*. From which places, if by *Soule* were meant a *Substance Incorporeall*, which an existence separated from the Body, it might as well be inferred of any other living Creature, as of Man. But that the Souls of the Faithfull, are not of their own Nature, but by Gods speciall Grace, to remaine in their Bodies, from the Resurrection to all Eternity, I have already I think sufficiently proved out of the Scriptures, in the 38. Chapter. And for the places of the

---

¹ *Syn.*: unnecessary   ³ *Syn.*: as easily

New Testament, where it is said that any man shall be cast Body and Soul into Hell fire, it is no more than Body and Life; that is to say, they shall be cast alive into the perpetuall fire of Gehenna.

As the Doctrine of Purgatory, and Exorcismes, and Invocation of Saints.

This window it is, that gives entrance to the Dark Doctrine, first, of Eternall Torments; and afterwards of Purgatory, and consequently of the walking abroad, especially in places Consecrated, Solitary, or Dark, of the Ghosts of men deceased; and thereby to the pretences of Exorcisme and Conjuration of Phantasmes; as also of Invocation of men dead; and to the Doctrine of Indulgences; that is to say, of exemption for a time, or for ever, from the fire of Purgatory, wherein these Incorporeall Substances are pretended by burning to be cleansed, and made fit for Heaven. For men being generally possessed before the time of our Saviour, by contagion of the Daemonology of the Greeks, of an opinion, that the Souls of men were substances distinct from their Bodies, and therefore that when the Body was dead, the Soule of every man, whether godly, or wicked, must subsist somewhere by vertue of its own nature, without acknowledging therein any supernaturall gift of *God;**¹ the Doctors of the Church doubted a long time, what was the place, which they were to abide in, till they should be re-united to their Bodies in the Resurrection; supposing for a while, they lay under the Altars: but afterward the Church of Rome found it more profitable, to build for them this place of Purgatory; which by some other Churches in this later age, has

The Texts alledged for the Doctrines aforementioned have been answered before.

[341]

been demolished.

Let us now consider, what texts of Scripture seem most to confirm these three generall Errors, I have here touched. As for those which Cardinall Bellarmine hath alledged, for the present Kingdome of God administred by the Pope, (than which there are none that make a better shew of proof,) I have already answered them; and made it evident, that the Kingdome of God, instituted by Moses, ended in the election of Saul: After which time the Priest of his own authority never deposed any King. That which the High Priest did to Athaliah, was not done in his owne right, but in the right of the young King Joash her Son: But Solomon in his own right deposed the High Priest Abiathar, and set up another in his place. The most difficult place to answer, of all those that can be brought, to prove the Kingdome of God by Christ is already in this world, is alledged, not by Bellarmine,

---

¹ *Syn.*: Gods;

nor any other of the Church of Rome; but by Beza; that will have it to begin from the Resurrection of Christ. But whether hee intend thereby, to entitle the Presbytery to the Supreme Power Ecclesiasticall in the Common-wealth of Geneva, (and consequently to every Presbytery in every other Common-wealth,) or to Princes, and other Civill Soveraigns, I doe not know. For the Presbytery hath challenged the power to Excommunicate their owne Kings, and to bee the Supreme Moderators in Religion, in the places where they have that form of Church government, no lesse than the Pope challengeth it universally.

The words are *Marke 9.1.*[1] *Verily I say unto you, that there be some of them that stand here, which shall not tast of death, till they have seene the Kingdome of God come with power.* Which words, if taken grammatically, make it certaine, that either some of those men that stood by Christ at that time, are yet alive; or else, that the Kingdome of God must be now in this present world. And then there is another place more difficult: For when the Apostles after our Saviours Resurrection, and immediately before his Ascension, asked our Saviour, saying, (Acts 1.6.) *Wilt thou at this time restore again the Kingdome to Israel,* he answered them, *It is not for you to know the times and the seasons, which the Father hath put in his own power; But ye shall receive power by the comming of the Holy Ghost upon you, and yee shall be my (Martyrs) witnesses both in Jerusalem, & in all Judea, and in Samaria, and unto the uttermost part of the Earth*: Which is as much as to say, My Kingdome is not yet come, nor shall you foreknow when it shall come; for it shall come as a theefe in the night; But I will send you the Holy Ghost, and by him you shall have power to beare witnesse to all the world (by your preaching) of my Resurrection, and the workes I have done, and the doctrine I have taught, that they may beleeve in me, and expect eternall life, at my comming againe: How does this agree with the comming of Christs Kingdome at the Resurrection? And that which St. *Paul* saies (1 *Thessal.*1.9,10.) *That they turned from Idols, to serve the living and true God, and to waite for his Sonne from Heaven*; Where to waite for his Sonne from Heaven, is to wait for his comming to be King in power; which were not necessary, if his Kingdome had beene then present. Againe, if the Kingdome of God began (as *Beza* on that place (*Mark* 9.1.) would have it) at the Resurrection; what reason is

Answer to the text on which Beza inferreth that the Kingdome of Christ began at the Resurrection.

---

[1] *Syn.*: (Marke 9.1.)

there for Christians ever since the Resurrection to say in their prayers, *Let thy Kingdome Come?* It is therefore manifest, that the words of St. *Mark* are not so to be interpreted. There be some of them that stand here (saith our Saviour) that shall not tast of death till they have seen the Kingdome of God come in power. If then this Kingdome were to come at the Resurrection of Christ, why is it said, *some of them*, rather than *all?* For they all lived till after Christ was risen.

Explication of the Place in Mark 9. 1.

But they that require an exact interpretation of this text, let them interpret first the like words of our Saviour to St. *Peter* concerning St. John, (chap.21.22.) *If I will that he tarry till I come, what is that to thee?* upon which was grounded a report that hee should not dye: Neverthelesse the truth of that report was neither confirmed, as well grounded; nor refuted, as ill grounded on those words; but left as a saying not understood. The same difficulty is also in the place of St. Marke. And if it be lawfull to conjecture at their meaning, by that which immediately followes, both here, and in St. Luke, where the same is againe repeated, it is not unprobable, to say they have relation to the Transfiguration, which is described in the verses immediately following; where it is said, that *After six dayes Jesus taketh with him Peter, and James, and John* (not all, but some of his Disciples) *and leadeth them up into an high mountaine apart by themselves, and was transfigured before them. And his rayment became shining, exceeding white as snow; so as no Fuller on earth can white them: And there appeared unto them Elias with Moses, and they were talking with Jesus, &c.* So that they saw Christ in Glory and Majestie, as he is to come; insomuch as *They were sore afraid.* And thus the promise of our Saviour was accomplished by way of *Vision*: For it was a Vision, as may probably bee inferred out of St. Luke, that reciteth the same story (ch.9.ve.28.) and saith, that Peter and they that were with him, were heavy with sleep: But most certainly out of Matth. 17.9. (where the same is again related;) for our Saviour charged them, saying, *Tell no man the Vision untill the Son of man be Risen from the dead.* Howsoever it be, yet there can from thence be taken no argument, to prove that the Kingdome of God taketh beginning till the day of Judgement.

Abuse of some other texts in defence of the Power of the Pope.

As for some other texts, to prove the Popes Power over civill Soveraignes (besides those of *Bellarmine*;) as that the two Swords that Christ and his Apostles had amongst them, were the Spirituall and the Temporall Sword, which they say St. Peter had given him by

Christ: And, that of the two Luminaries, the greater signifies the Pope, and the lesser the King; One might as well inferre out of the first verse of the Bible, that by Heaven is meant the Pope, and by Earth the King: Which is not arguing from Scripture, but a wanton insulting over Princes, *which*[1] came in fashion after the time the Popes were growne so secure of their greatnesse, as to contemne all Christian Kings; and Treading on the necks of Emperours, to mocke both them, and the Scripture, in the words of the 91.Psalm, *Thou shalt Tread upon the Lion and the Adder, the young Lion and the Dragon thou shalt Trample under thy feet.*

As for the rites of Consecration, though they depend for the most part upon the discretion and judgement of the governors of the Church, and not upon the Scriptures; yet those governors are obliged to such direction, as the nature of the action it selfe requireth; as that the ceremonies, words, and gestures, be both decent, and significant, or at least conformable to the action. When Moses consecrated the Tabernacle, the Altar, and the Vessels belonging to them, (*Exod.* 40.) he anointed them with the Oyle which God had commanded to bee made for that purpose; and they were holy: There was nothing Exorcized, to drive away Phantasmes. The same Moses (the civill Soveraigne of Israel) when he consecrated Aaron (the High Priest,) and his Sons, did wash them with Water, (not Exorcized water,) put their Garments upon them, and anointed them with Oyle; and they were sanctified, to minister unto the Lord in the Priests office; which was a simple and decent cleansing, and adorning them, before hee presented them to God, to be his servants. When King *Solomon*, (the civill Soveraigne of Israel) consecrated the Temple hee had built, (2 *Kings* 8.) he stood before all the Congregation of Israel; and having blessed them, he gave thankes to God, for putting into the heart of his father, to build it; and for giving to himselfe the grace to accomplish the same; and then prayed unto him, first, to accept that House, though it were not sutable to his infinite Greatnesse; and to hear the prayers of his Servants that should pray therein, or (if they were absent,) towards it; and lastly, he offered a sacrifice of Peace-offering, and the House was dedicated. Here was no Procession; the King stood still in his first place; no Exorcised Water; no *Asperges me*, nor other impertinent application of words spoken upon another occa-

The manner of Consecrations in the Scripture, was without Exorcisms. [343]

---

[1] *Syn.*: that

sion; but a decent, and rationall speech, and such as in making to God a present of his new built House, was most conformable to the occasion.

We read not that St. John did Exorcize the Water of Jordan; nor Philip the Water of the river wherein he baptized the Eunuch; nor that any Pastor in the time of the Apostles, did take his spittle, and put it to the nose of the person to be Baptized, and say, *In odorem suavitatis,* that is, *for a sweet favour unto the Lord*; wherein neither the Ceremony of Spittle, for the uncleannesse; nor the application of that Scripture for the levity, can by any authority of man be justified.

The immortality of mans Soule, not proved by Scripture to be of Nature, but of Grace. To prove that the Soule separated from the Body, liveth eternally, not onely the Soules of the Elect, by especiall grace, and restauration of the Eternall Life which Adam lost by Sinne, and our Saviour restored *(by the sacrifice of himself,)*[1] to the Faithfull; but also the Soules of Reprobates, as a property naturally consequent to the essence of mankind, without other grace of God, but that which is universally given to all mankind; there are divers places, which at the first sight seem sufficiently to serve the turn: but such, as when I compare them with that which I have before (Chapter 38.) alledged out of the 14 of *Job*, seem to mee much more subject to a divers interpretation, than the words of *Job*.

And first there are the words of Solomon (*Ecclesiastes* 12. 7.) *Then shall the Dust return to Dust, as it was, and the Spirit shall return to God that gave it.* Which may bear well enough (if there be no other text directly against it) this interpretation, that God onely knows, (but Man not,) what becomes of a mans spirit, when he expireth; and the same Solomon, in the same Book, (Chap. 3. ver.20,21.) delivereth the same sentence in the sense I have given it: His words are, *All goe* (man and beast) *to the same place; all are of the dust, and all turn to dust again; who knoweth that the spirit of Man goeth upward, and that the spirit of the Beast goeth downward to the earth?* That is, none knows but God; Nor is it an unusuall phrase to say of things we understand not, *God Knows what,* and *God Knows where.* That of *Gen.* 5. 24. *Enoch walked with God, and he was not; for God took him*; which is expounded Heb. *ii.*[2] 5. *He was translated, that he should not die; and was not found, because God had translated him. For before his Translation, he had this testimony, that he pleased God,* making as much for the Immortality of the Body, as of the

[344]

---

[1] *Syn.*: by the Sacrifice of himself   [2] *Syn.*: 13.

430

Soule, proveth, that this his translation was peculiar to them that please God; not common to them with the wicked; and depending on Grace, not on Nature. But on the contrary, what interpretation shall we give, besides the literall sense of the words of Solomon (*Eccles.* 3.19.) *That which befalleth the Sons of Men, befalleth Beasts, even one thing befalleth them; as the one dyeth, so doth the other, yea, they have all one breath* (one spirit;) *so that a Man hath no praeeminence above a Beast, for all is vanity.* By the literal sense, here is no Naturall Immortality of the Soule; nor yet any repugnancy with the Life Eternall, which the Elect shall enjoy by Grace. And (chap 4. ver.3.) *Better is he that hath not yet been, than both they;* that is, than they that live, or have lived; which, if the Soule of all them that have lived, were Immortall, were a hard saying; for then to have an Immortall Soule, were worse than to have no Soule at all. And againe, (Chap. 9. 5.) *The living know they shall die, but the dead know not any thing;* that is, Naturally, and before the resurrection of the body.

Another place which seems to make for a Naturall Immortality of the Soule, is that, where our Saviour saith, that Abraham, Isaac, and Jacob are living: but this is spoken of the promise of God, and of their certitude to rise again, not of a Life then actuall; and in the same sense that God said to Adam, that on the day hee should eate of the forbidden fruit, he should certainly die; from that time forward he was a dead man by sentence; but not by execution, till almost a thousand years after. So Abraham, Isaac, and Jacob were alive by promise, then, when Christ spake; but are not actually till the Resurrection. And the History of Dives and Lazarus, make nothing against this, if wee take it (as it is) for a Parable.

But there be other places of the New Testament, where an Immortality seemeth to be directly attributed to the wicked. For it is evident, that they shall all rise to Judgement. And it is said besides in many places, that they shall goe into *Everlasting fire, Everlasting torments, Everlasting punishments; and that the worm of conscience never* [345] *dyeth;* and all this is comprehended in the word *Everlasting Death,* which is ordinarily interpreted *Everlasting Life in torments*: And yet I can find no where that any man shall live in torments Everlastingly. Also, it seemeth hard, to say, that God who is the Father of Mercies, that doth in Heaven and Earth all that hee will; that hath the hearts of all men in his disposing; that worketh in men both to doe, and to will; and without whose free gift a man hath neither inclination to good, nor repentance of evill, should punish mens transgressions without any end of time, and with all the extremity of torture, that men can imagine, and more. We are therefore to consider, what the meaning is, of *Everlasting Fire*, and other the like phrases of Scripture.

I have shewed already, that the Kingdome of God by Christ beginneth at the day of Judgment: That in that day, the Faithfull shall rise again, with glorious, and spirituall Bodies, and bee his Subjects in that his Kingdome, which shall be Eternall: That they shall neither marry, nor be given in marriage, nor eate and drink, as they did in their naturall bodies; but live for ever in their individuall persons, without the specificall eternity of generation: And that the Reprobates also shall rise again, to receive punishments for their sins: As also, that those of the Elect, which shall be alive in their earthly bodies at that day, shall have their bodies suddenly changed, and made spirituall, and Immortall. But that the bodies of the Reprobate, who make the Kingdome of Satan, shall also be glorious, or spirituall bodies, or that they shall bee as the Angels of God, neither eating, nor drinking, nor engendring; or that their life shall be Eternall in their individuall persons, as the life of every faithfull man is, or as the life of Adam had been if hee had not sinned, there is no place of Scripture to prove it; save onely these places concerning Eternall Torments; which may otherwise be interpreted.

From whence may be inferred, that as the Elect after the Resurrection shall be restored to the estate, wherein Adam was before he had sinned; so the Reprobate shall be in the estate, that Adam, and his posterity were in after the sin committed; saving that God promised a Redeemer to Adam, and such of his seed as should trust in him, and repent; but not to them that should die in their sins, as do the Reprobate.

Eternall Torments what. These things considered, the texts that mention *Eternall Fire, Eternall Torments, or the Worm that never dieth*, contradict not the Doctrine of a Second, and Everlasting Death, in the proper and naturall sense of the word *Death*. The Fire, or Torments prepared for the wicked in *Gehenna, Tophet*, or in what place soever, may continue *for ever;*[1] and there may never want wicked men to be tormented in them; though not every, nor any one Eternally.* For the wicked being left in the estate they were in after Adams sin, may at the Resurrection

---

[1] "25 Ornaments" and "Bear" editions read: to the end of this World;

live as they did, marry, and give in marriage, and have grosse and
corruptible bodies, as all mankind now have; and consequently may [346]
engender perpetually, after the Resurrection, as they did before: For
there is no place of Scripture to the contrary.*[1] For St. Paul, speaking
of the Resurrection (1 *Cor.*15.) understandeth it onely of the Resurrection to Life Eternall; and not the Resurrection to Punishment. And
of the first, he saith that the Body is *Sown in Corruption, raised in
Incorruption; sown in Dishonour, raised in Honour; sown in Weaknesse,
raised in Power; sown a Naturall body, raised a Spirituall body*: There is
no such thing can be said of the bodies of them that rise to Punishment. So also our Saviour, when hee speaketh of the Nature of Man
after the Resurrection, meaneth, the Resurrection to Life Eternall,
not to Punishment. The text is *Luke* 20. verses 34, 35, 36. a fertile
text. *The Children of this world marry, and are given in marriage; but they
that shall be counted worthy to obtaine that world, and the Resurrection from
the dead, neither marry, nor are given in marriage: Neither can they die any
more; for they are equall to the Angells, and are the Children of God, being
the Children of the Resurrection*: The Children of this world, that are in
the estate which Adam left them in, shall marry, and be given in
marriage; that is, corrupt, and generate successively; which is an
Immortality of the Kind, but not of the Persons of men: They are not
worthy to be counted amongst them that shall obtain the next world,
and an absolute Resurrection from the dead; but onely a short time,
as inmates of that world; and to the end onely to receive condign
punishment for their contumacy. The Elect are the onely children of
the Resurrection; that is to say, the sole heirs of Eternall Life: they
only can die no more: it is they that are equall to the Angels, and that
are the children of God; and not the Reprobate. To the Reprobate
there remaineth after the Resurrection, a *Second*, and *Eternall* Death:
between which Resurrection, and their Second, and Eternall death, is
but a time of Punishment and Torment; and to last by succession of
sinners thereunto, as long as the kind of Man by propagation shall
endure; which is Eternally.

    Upon this Doctrine of the Naturall Eternity of separated Soules, is   *Answer of*
founded (as I said) the Doctrine of Purgatory. For supposing Eternall   *the Texts*
Life by Grace onely, there is no Life, but the Life of the Body; and no   *alledged for*
Immortality till the Resurrection. The texts for Purgatory alledged by   *Purgatory.*

---

[1] This sentence is omitted in the "25 Ornaments" and "Bear" editions

Bellarmine out of the Canonicall Scripture of the old Testament, are first, the Fasting of *David* for *Saul* and *Jonathan*, mentioned (2 *Kings*,1.12.); and againe, (2 *Sam*.3.35.) for the death of *Abner*. This Fasting of *David*, he saith, was for the obtaining of something for them at Gods hands, after their death; because after he had Fasted to procure the recovery of his owne child, assoone as he knew it was dead, he called for meate. Seeing then the Soule hath an existence separate from the Body, and nothing can be obtained by mens Fasting for the Soules that are already either in Heaven, or Hell, it followeth that there be some Soules of dead men, that are neither in Heaven, nor in Hell; and therefore they must bee in some third place, which must be Purgatory. And thus with hard straining, hee has wrested those places to the proofe of a Purgatory: whereas it is manifest, that the ceremonies of Mourning, and Fasting, when they are used for the death of men, whose life was not profitable to the Mourners, they are used for honours sake to their persons; and when tis done for the death of them by whose life the Mourners had benefit, it proceeds from their particular dammage: And so *David* honoured *Saul*, and *Abner*, with his Fasting; and in the death of his owne child, recomforted himselfe, by receiving his ordinary food.

[347]

In the other places, which he alledgeth out of the old Testament, there is not so much as any shew, or colour of proofe. He brings in every text wherein there is the word *Anger*, or *Fire*, or *Burning*, or *Purging*, or *Clensing*, in case any of the Fathers have but in a Sermon rhetorically applied it to the Doctrine of Purgatory, already beleeved. The first verse of Psalme,37. *O Lord rebuke me not in thy wrath, nor chasten me in thy hot displeasure*: What were this to Purgatory, if Augustine had not applied the *Wrath* to the fire of Hell, and the *Displeasure* to that of Purgatory? And what is it to Purgatory, that of *Psalme*, 66.12. *Wee went through fire and water, and thou broughtest us to a moist place*; and other the like texts, (with which the Doctors of those times entended to adorne, or extend their Sermons, or Commentaries) haled to their purposes by force of wit?

Places of the New Testament for Purgatory answered. But he alledgeth other places of the New Testament, that are not so easie to be answered: And first that of *Matth.* 12. 32. *Whosoever speaketh a word against the Sonne of man, it shall be forgiven him; but whosoever speaketh against the Holy Ghost, it shall not bee forgiven him neither in this world, nor in the world to come*: Where he will have Purgatory to be the World to come, wherein some sinnes may be forgiven, which in this World were not forgiven: notwithstanding that it is manifest, there are but three Worlds; one from the Creation to the Flood, which was destroyed by Water, and is called in Scripture *the Old World*; another from the Flood, to the day of Judgement, which is *the Present World*, and shall bee destroyed by Fire; and the third, which shall bee from the day of Judgement forward, everlasting, which is called *the World to come*; and in which it is agreed by all, there shall be no Purgatory: And therefore the World to come, and Purgatory, are inconsistent. But what then can bee the meaning of those our Saviours words? I confesse they are very hardly to bee reconciled with all the Doctrines now unanimously received: Nor is it any shame, to confesse the profoundnesse of the Scripture, to bee too great to be sounded by the shortnesse of humane understanding. Neverthelesse, I may propound such things to the consideration of more learned Divines, as the text it selfe suggesteth. And first, seeing to speake against the Holy Ghost, as being the third Person of the Trinity, is to speake against the Church, in which the Holy Ghost resideth; it seemeth the comparison is made, betweene the Easinesse of our Saviour, in bearing with offences done to him while hee himselfe taught the world, that is, when he was on earth, and the Severity of the Pastors after him, against those which should deny their authority, which was from the Holy Ghost: As if he should say, You that deny my Power; nay you that shall crucifie me, shall be [348] pardoned by mee, as often as you turne unto mee by Repentance: But if you deny the Power of them that teach you hereafter, by vertue of the Holy Ghost, they shall be inexorable, and shall not forgive you, but persecute you in this World, and leave you without absolution, (though you turn to me, unlesse you turn also to them,) to the punishments (as much as lies in them) of the World to come: And so the words may be taken as a Prophecy, or Praediction concerning the times, as they have *long*[1] been in the Christian Church: Or if this be not the meaning, (for I am not peremptory in such difficult places,) perhaps there may be place left after the Resurrection for the Repentance of some sinners: And there is also another place, that seemeth to agree therewith. For considering the words of St. Paul (1 *Cor.* 15. 29.) *What shall they doe which are Baptized for the dead, if the dead rise not at all? why also are they Baptized for the dead?* a man may probably inferre,

---

[1] *Syn.*: along

435

as some have done, that in St. Pauls time, there was a custome by receiving Baptisme for the dead, (as men that now beleeve, are Sureties and Undertakers for the Faith of Infants, that are not capable of beleeving,) to undertake for the persons of their deceased friends, that they should be ready to obey, and receive our Saviour for their King, at his coming again; and then the forgivenesse of sins in the world to come, has no need of a Purgatory. But in both these interpretations, there is so much of paradox, that I trust not to them; but propound them to those that are throughly versed in the Scripture, to inquire if there be no clearer place that contradicts them. Onely of thus much, I see evident Scripture, to perwade me, that there is neither the word, nor the thing of Purgatory, neither in this, nor any other text; nor any thing that can prove a necessity of a place for the Soule without the Body; neither for the Soule of Lazarus during the four days he was dead; nor for the Soules of them which the Romane Church pretend to be tormented now in Purgatory. For God, that could give a life to a peece of clay, hath the same power to give life again to a dead man, and renew his inanimate, and rotten Carkasse, into a glorious, spirituall, and immortall Body.

Another place is that of 1 *Cor. 3.* where it is said, that they which built Stubble, Hay, &c. on the true Foundation, their work shall perish; but *they themselves shall be saved; but as through Fire:* This Fire, he will have to be the Fire of Purgatory. The words, as I have said before, are an allusion to those of *Zach.* 13. 9. where he saith, *I will bring the third part through the Fire, and refine them as Silver is refined, and will try them as Gold is tryed:* Whis is spoken of the comming of the Messiah in Power and Glory; that is, at the day of Judgment, and Conflagration of the present world; wherein the Elect shall not be consumed, but be refined; that is, depose their erroneous Doctrines, and Traditions, and have them as it were sindged off; and shall afterwards call upon the name of the true God. In like manner, the Apostle saith of them, that holding this Foundation *Jesus is the Christ,* shall build thereon some other Doctrines that be erroneous, that they shall not be consumed in that fire which reneweth the world, but shall passe through it to Salvation; but so, as to see, and relinquish their former Errours. The Builders, are the *Pastors;* the Foundation, that *Jesus is the Christ;* the Stubble and Hay, *False Consequences drawn from it through Ignorance, or Frailty;* the Gold, Silver, and pretious Stones, are their *True Doctrines;* and their Refining or Purging, the *Relinquish-*

[349]

436

ing of their Errors. In all which there is no colour at all for the burning of Incorporeall, that is to say, Impatible Souls.

A third place is that of 1 *Cor.* 15. before mentioned, concerning Baptisme for the Dead: out of which he concludeth, first, that Prayers for the Dead are not unprofitable; and out of that, that there is a Fire of Purgatory: But neither of them rightly. For of many interpretations of the word Baptisme, he approveth this in the first place, that by Baptisme is meant (metaphorically) a Baptisme of Penance; and that men are in this sense Baptized, when they Fast, and Pray, and give Almes: And so Baptisme for the Dead, and Prayer for the Dead, is the same thing. But this is a Metaphor, of which there is no example, neither in the Scripture, nor in any other use of language, and which is also discordant to the harmony, and scope of the Scripture. The word Baptisme is used (*Mar.*10.38.&*Luke.*12.50.) for being Dipped in ones own bloud, as Christ was upon the Cross, and as most of the Apostles were, for giving testimony of him. But it is hard to say, that Prayer, Fasting, and Almes, have any similitude with Dipping. The same is used also *Mat.* 3. 11. (which seemeth to make somewhat for Purgatory) for a Purging with Fire. But it is evident the Fire and Purging here mentioned, is the same whereof the Prophet *Zachary* speaketh (chap, 13.v.9.) *I will bring the third part through the Fire, and will Refine them, &c.* And St. Peter after him (1 Epist. 1. 7.) *That the triall of your Faith, which is much more precious than of Gold that perisheth, though it be tryed with Fire, might be found unto praise, and honour, and glory at the Appearing of Jesus Christ;* And St. Paul (1 *Cor.* 3.13.) *The Fire shall trie every mans work of what sort it is.* But St. Peter, and St. Paul speak of the Fire that shall be at the Second Appearing of Christ; and the Prophet Zachary of the Day of Judgment: And therefore this place of S. Mat. may be interpreted of the same; and then there will be no necessity of the Fire of Purgatory.

Another interpretation of Baptisme for the Dead, is that which I have before mentioned, which he preferreth to the second place of probability: And thence also he inferreth the utility of Prayer for the Dead. For if after the Resurrection, such as have not heard of Christ, or not beleeved in him, may be received into Christs Kingdome; it is not in vain, after their death, that their friends should pray for them, till they should be risen. But granting that God, at the prayers of the faithfull, may convert unto him some of those that have not heard Christ preached, and consequently cannot have rejected Christ, and

Baptisme for the Dead, how understood.

that the charity of men in that point, cannot be blamed; yet this concludeth nothing for Purgatory, because to rise from Death to Life, is one thing; to rise from Purgatory to Life is another; as being a rising from Life to Life, from a Life in torments to a Life in joy.

A fourth place is that of *Mat.* 5.25. *Agree with thine Adversary quickly, whilest thou art in the way with him, lest at any time the Adversary deliver thee to the Judge, and the Judge deliver thee to the Officer, and thou be cast into prison. Verily I say unto thee, thou shalt by no means come out thence, till thou hast paid the uttermost farthing.* In which Allegory, the Offender is the *Sinner*, both the Adversary and the Judge is *God*; the Way is this *Life*; the Prison is the *Grave*; the Officer, *Death*; from which, the sinner shall not rise again to life eternall, but to a second Death, till he have paid the utmost farthing, or Christ pay it for him by his Passion, which is a full Ransome for all manner of sin, as well lesser sins, as greater crimes; both being made by the passion of Christ equally veniall.

The fift place, is that of *Matth.* 5.22. *Whosoever is angry with his Brother without a cause, shall be guilty in Judgment. And whosoever shall say to his Brother, RACHA, shall be guilty in the Councel. But whosoever shall say, Thou Foole, shall be guilty to hell fire.* From which words he inferreth three sorts of Sins, and three sorts of Punishments; and that none of those sins, but the last, shall be punished with hell fire; and consequently, that after this life, there is punishment of lesser sins in Purgatory. Of which inference, there is no colour in any interpretation that hath yet been given of them: Shall there be a distinction after this life of Courts of Justice, as there was amongst the Jews in our Saviours time, to hear, and determine divers sorts of Crimes; as the Judges, and the Councell? Shall not all Judicature appertain to Christ, and his Apostles? To understand therefore this text, we are not to consider it solitarily, but jointly with the words precedent, and subsequent. Our Saviour in this Chapter interpreteth the Law of Moses; which the Jews thought was then fulfilled, when they had not transgressed the Grammaticall sense thereof, howsoever they had transgressed against the sentence, or meaning of the Legislator. Therefore whereas they thought the Sixth Commandement was not broken, but by Killing a man; nor the Seventh, but when a man lay with a woman, not his wife; our Saviour tells them, the inward Anger of a man against his brother, if it be without just cause, is Homicide: You have heard (saith hee) the Law of Moses, *Thou shalt not Kill*, and that

Whosoever shall Kill, shall bee condemned before the Judges, or before the Session of the Seventy: But I say unto you, to be Angry with ones Brother without cause; or to say unto him *Racha,* or *Foole,* is Homicide, and shall be punished at the day of Judgment, and Session of Christ, and his Apostles, with Hell fire: so that those words were not used to distinguish between divers Crimes, and divers Courts of Justice, and divers Punishments; but to taxe the distinction between sin, and sin, which the Jews drew not from the difference of the Will in Obeying God, but from the difference of their Temporall Courts of [351] Justice; and to shew them that he that had the Will to hurt his Brother, though the effect appear but in Reviling, or not at all, shall be cast into hell fire, by the Judges, and by the Session, which shall be the same, not different Courts at the day of Judgment. This considered, what can be drawn from this text, to maintain Purgatory, I cannot imagine.

The sixth place is *Luke* 16.9. *Make yee friends of the unrighteous Mammon, that when yee faile, they may receive you into Everlasting Tabernacles.* This he alledges to prove Invocation of Saints departed. But the sense is plain, That we should make friends with our Riches, of the Poore; and thereby obtain their Prayers whilest they live. *He that giveth to the Poore, lendeth to the Lord.*

The seventh is *Luke* 23. 42. *Lord remember me when thou commest into thy Kingdome:* Therefore, saith hee, there is Remission of sins after this life. But the consequence is not good. Our Saviour then forgave him; and at his comming againe in Glory, will remember to raise him againe to Life Eternall.

The Eight is *Acts* 2. 24. where St. Peter saith of Christ, *that God had raised him up, and loosed the Paines of Death, because it was not possible he should be holden of it:* Which hee interprets to bee a descent of Christ into Purgatory, to loose some Soules there from their torments: whereas it is manifest, that it was Christ that was loosed; it was hee that could not bee holden of Death, or the Grave; and not the Souls in Purgatory. But if that which Beza sayes in his notes on this place be well observed, there is none that will not see, that in stead of *Paynes,* it should be *Bands*; and then there is no further cause to seek for Purgatory in this Text.

CHAP. XLV.

Of Daemonology, *and other Reliques of the Religion of the Gentiles.*

The Originall of Daemonology.

The impression made on the organs of Sight, by lucide Bodies, either in one direct line, or in many lines, reflected from Opaque, or refracted in the passage through Diaphanous Bodies, produceth in living Creatures, in whom God hath placed such Organs, an Imagination of the Object, from whence the Impression proceedeth; which Imagination is called *Sight*; and seemeth not to bee a meer Imagination, but the Body it selfe without us; in the same manner, as when a man violently presseth his eye, there appears to him a light without, and before him, which no man perceiveth but himselfe; because there is indeed no such thing without him, but onely a motion in the interiour organs, pressing by resistance outward, that makes him think so. And the motion made by this pressure, continuing after the object which caused it is removed, is that we call *Imagination*, and *Memory*, and (in sleep, and sometimes in great distemper of the organs by Sicknesse, or Violence) a *Dream*: of which things I have already spoken briefly, in the second and third Chapters.

This nature of Sight having never been discovered by the ancient pretenders to Naturall Knowledge; much lesse by *those that consider not things so remote (as that Knowledge is) from their present use; it was hard for men to conceive of those Images in the Fancy, and in the Sense, otherwise, than of things really without us:*[1] Which some (because they vanish away, they know not whither, nor how,) will have to be absolutely Incorporeall, that is to say Immateriall*,*[2] Formes without Matter; Colour and Figure, without any coloured or figured Body; and that they can put on Aiery bodies (as a garment) to make them Visible when they will to our bodily Eyes; and others say,

---

[1] Scribal MS reads: other men that busie in the pursuit of power, honor and the meanes to satisfy and secure their animal appetites, have eyther no leasure, or no will to looke after any so remote a cause of that they looke for, as this of knowing the nature of theyr owne Phancye, is the cause that all nations have conceaved that those Images, which are made by sense, are thinges really existent without us.

[2] *Syn.*: , or

are Bodies, and living Creatures, but made of Air, or other more subtile and aethereall Matter, which is, *(then, when they will be seen,)*[1] condensed. But Both of them agree on one generall appellation of them, DAEMONS. As if the Dead of whom they Dreamed, were not Inhabitants of their own Brain, but of the Air, or of Heaven, or Hell; not Phantasmes, but Ghosts; with just as much reason, as if one should say, he saw his own Ghost in a Looking-Glasse, or the Ghosts of the Stars in a River; or call the ordinary apparition of the Sun, of the quantity of about a foot, the *Daemon*, or Ghost of that great Sun that enlighteneth the whole visible world: And by that means have feared them, as things of an unknown, that is, of an unlimited power to doe them good, or harme; and consequently, given occasion to the Governours of the Heathen Common-wealths [353] to regulate this their fear, by establishing that DAEMONOLOGY (in which the Poets, as Principall Priests of the Heathen Religion, were specially employed, or reverenced) to the Publique Peace, and to the Obedience of Subjects necessary thereunto; and to make some of them Good *Daemons*, and others Evill; the one as a Spurre to the Observance, the other, as Reines to withhold them from the *Violation*[2] of the Laws.

What kind of things they were, to whom they attributed the name of *Daemons*, appeareth partly in the Genealogie of their Gods, written by Hesiod, one of the most ancient Poets of the Graecians; and partly in other Histories; of which I have observed some few before, in the 12. Chapter of this discourse. *What were the Daemons of the Ancients.*

The Graecians, by their Colonies and Conquests, communicated their Language and Writings into Asia, Egypt, and Italy; and therein, by necessary consequence their *Daemonology*, or (as St. *Paul* calles it) *their Doctrines of Devils*: And by that meanes, the contagion was derived also to the Jewes, both of *Judaea*, and *Alexandria*, and other parts, whereinto they were dispersed. But the name of *Daemon* they did not (as the Graecians) attribute to Spirits both Good, and Evill; but to the Evill onely: And to the Good *Daemons* they gave the name of the Spirit of God; and esteemed those into whose bodies they entred to be Prophets. In summe, all singularity if Good, they attributed to the Spirit of God; and if Evill, to some *Daemon*, but a κακοδαίμων, an Evill *Daemon*, that is, a *Devill*. And therefore, they called *Daemoniaques*, that is, *possessed by the Devill*, such as we call *How that Doctrine was spread.* *How far received by the Jews.*

1 Syn.: then, when they will be seen,   *2 Syn.*: Violation.

Mad-men or Lunatiques; or such as had the Falling Sicknesse; or that spoke any thing, which they for want of understanding, thought absurd: As also of an Unclean person in a notorious degree, they used to say he had an Unclean Spirit; of a Dumbe man, that he had a Dumbe Devill; and of *John Baptist* (*Math*. 11.18.) for the singularity of his fasting, that he had a Devill; and of our Saviour, because he said,

John 8.52. hee that keepeth his sayings should not see Death *in aeternum, Now we know thou hast a Devil; Abraham is dead, and the Prophets are dead:* And again, because he said (*John* 7.20.) *They went about to kill him,* the people answered, *Thou hast a Devill, who goeth about to kill thee?* Whereby it is manifest, that the Jewes had the same *opinion with the Greekes*[1] concerning Phantasmes, namely, that they were not Phantasmes, that is, Idols of the braine, but things reall, and independent on the Fancy.

Why our Saviour controlled it not. Which doctrine if it be not true, why (may some say) did not our Saviour contradict it, and teach the contrary? nay why does he use on diverse occasions, such forms of speech as seem to confirm it? To this I answer, that first, where Christ saith, *A spirit hath not flesh and bone,* though hee shew that there be Spirits, yet hee denies not that they are Bodies: And where St. *Paul* saies, *We shall rise spirituall Bodies,* he acknowledgeth the nature of Spirits, but that they are Bodily Spirits; which is not difficult to understand. For Air and many other things are Bodies, though not Flesh and Bone, or any other grosse body, to

[354] bee discerned by the eye. But when our Saviour speaketh to the Devill, and commandeth him to go out of a man, if by the Devill, be meant a Disease, as Phrenesy, or Lunacy, or a corporeal Spirit, is not the speech improper? can Diseases heare? or can there be a corporeall Spirit in a Body of Flesh and Bone, full already of vitall and animall Spirits? Are there not therefore Spirits, that neither have Bodies, nor are meer Imaginations? To the first I answer, that the addressing of our Saviours command to the Madnesse, or Lunacy he cureth, is no more improper, than was his rebuking of the Fever, or of the Wind, and Sea; for neither do these hear: Or than was the command of God, to the Light, to the Firmament, to the Sunne, and Starres, when he commanded them to bee: for they could not heare before they had a beeing. But those speeches are not improper, because they signifie the power of Gods Word: no more therefore is it improper, to com-

---

[1] *Syn.*: opinion.

mand Madnesse, or Lunacy (under the appellation of Devils, by which they were then commonly understood,) to depart out of a mans body. To the second, concerning their being Incorporeall, I have not yet observed any place of Scripture, from whence it can be gathered, that any man was ever possessed with any other Corporeall Spirit, but that of his owne, by which his body is naturally moved.

Our Saviour, immediately after the Holy Ghost descended upon him in the form of a Dove, is said by St. *Matthew* (Chapt.4.1.) to have been *led up by the Spirit into the Wildernesse*; and the same is recited (*Luke* 4.1.) in these words, *Jesus being full of the Holy Ghost, was led in the Spirit into the Wildernesse*: Whereby it is evident, that by *Spirit* there, is meant the Holy Ghost. This cannot be interpreted for a Possession: For Christ, and the Holy Ghost, are but one and the same substance; which is no possession of one substance, or body, by another. And whereas in the verses following, he is said *to have been taken up by the Devill into the Holy City, and set upon a pinnacle of the Temple*, shall we conclude thence that hee was possessed of the Devill, or carryed thither by violence? And again, *carryed thence by the Devill into an exceeding high mountain, who shewed him thence all the Kingdomes of the world*: Wherein, wee are not to beleeve he was either possessed, or forced by the Devill; nor that any Mountaine is high enough, (according to the literall sense,) to shew him one whole Hemisphere. What then can be the meaning of this place, other than that he went of himself into the Wildernesse; and that this carrying of him up and down, from the Wildernesse to the City, and from thence into a Mountain, was a Vision? Conformable whereunto, is also the phrase of St. Luke, that hee was led into the Wildernesse, not *by*, but *in* the Spirit: whereas concerning His being Taken up into the Mountaine, and unto the Pinnacle of the Temple, hee speaketh as St. Matthew doth. Which suiteth with the nature of a Vision.

The Scriptures doe not teach that Spirits are Incorporeall.

Again, where St. Luke sayes of Judas Iscariot, that *Satan entred into him, and thereupon that he went and communed with the Chief Priests, and Captaines, how he might betray Christ unto them*: it may be answered, that by the Entring of *Satan* (that is the *Enemy*) into him, is meant, the hostile and traiterous intention of selling his Lord and Master. For as by the Holy Ghost, is frequently in Scripture understood, the Graces and good Inclinations given by the Holy Ghost; so by the Entring of Satan, may bee understood the wicked Cogitations, and Designes of the Adversaries of Christ, and his Disciples. For as it is hard to say,

[355]

443

that the Devill was entred into Judas, before he had any such hostile designe; so it is impertinent to say, he was first Christs Enemy in his heart, and that the Devill entred into him afterwards. Therefore the Entring of Satan, and his Wicked Purpose, was one and the same thing.

But if there be no Immateriall Spirit, nor any Possession of mens bodies by any Spirit Corporeall, it may again be asked, why our Saviour and his Apostles did not teach the People so; and in such cleer words, as they might no more doubt thereof. But such questions as these, are more curious, than necessary for a Christian mans Salvation. Men may as well aske, why Christ that could have given to all men Faith, Piety, and all manner of morall Vertues, gave it to some onely, and not to all: and why he left the search of naturall Causes, and Sciences, to the naturall Reason and Industry of men, and did not reveal it to all, or any man supernaturally; and many other such questions: Of which neverthelesse there may be alledged probable and pious reasons. For as God, when he brought the Israelites into the Land of Promise, did not secure them therein, by subduing all the Nations round about them; but left many of them, as thornes in their sides, to awaken from time to time their Piety and Industry: so our Saviour, in conducting us toward his heavenly Kingdome, did not destroy all the difficulties of Naturall Questions; but left them to exercise our Industry, and Reason; the Scope of his preaching, being onely to shew us this plain and direct way to Salvation, namely, the beleef of this Article, *that he was the Christ, the Son of the living God, sent into the world to sacrifice himselfe for our Sins, and at his comming again, gloriously to reign over his Elect, and to save them from their Enemies eternally*: To which, the opinion of Possession by Spirits, or Phantasmes, are no impediment in the way; though it be to some an occasion of going out of the way, and to follow their own Inventions. If wee require of the Scripture an account of all questions, which may be raised to trouble us in the performance of Gods commands; we may as well complaine of Moses for not having set downe the time of the creation of such Spirits, as well as of the Creation of the Earth, and Sea, and of Men, and Beasts. To conclude, I find in Scripture that there be Angels, and Spirits, good and evill; but not that they are Incorporeall, as are the Apparitions men see in the Dark, or in a Dream, or Vision; which the Latines call *Spectra*, and took for *Daemons*. And I find that there are Spirits Corporeall, (though subtile and Invisible;) but not that any mans body was possessed, or inhabited by them; And that the Bodies of the Saints shall be such, namely, Spirituall Bodies, as St. Paul calls them.

    Neverthelesse, the contrary Doctrine, namely, that there be Incorporeall Spirits, hath hitherto so prevailed in the Church, that the use of Exorcisme, (that is to say, of ejection of Devills by Conjuration) is thereupon built; and (though rarely and faintly practised) is not yet totally given over. That there were many Daemoniaques in the Primitive Church, and few Mad-men, and other such singular diseases; whereas in these times we hear of, and see many Mad-men, and few Daemoniaques, proceeds not from the change of Nature; but of Names. But how it comes to passe, that whereas heretofore the Apostles, and after them for a time, the Pastors of the Church, did cure those singular Diseases, which now they are not seen to doe; as likewise, why it is not in the power of every true Beleever now, to doe all that the Faithfull did then, that is to say, as we read (*Mark* 16.17.) *In Christs name to cast out Devills, to speak with new Tongues, to take up Serpents, to drink deadly Poison without harm taking, and to cure the Sick by the laying on of their hands*, and all this without other words, but *in the Name of Jesus*, is another question. And it is probable, that those extraordinary gifts were given to the Church, for no longer a time, than men trusted wholly to Christ, and looked for their felicity onely in his Kingdome to come; and consequently, that when they sought Authority, and Riches, and trusted to their own Subtilty for a Kingdome of this world, these supernaturall gifts of God were again taken from them.

    Another relique of Gentilisme, is the *Worship of Images*, neither instituted by Moses in the Old, nor by Christ in the New Testament; nor yet brought in from the Gentiles; but left amongst them, after they had given their names to Christ. Before our Saviour preached, it was the generall Religion of the Gentiles, to worship for Gods, those Apparences that remain in the Brain from the impression of externall Bodies upon the organs of their Senses, which are commonly called *Ideas, Idols, Phantasmes, Conceits,* as being Representations of those externall Bodies, which cause them, and have nothing in them of reality, no more than there is in the things that seem to stand before us in a Dream: And this is the reason why St. Paul says, *Wee know that an Idol is Nothing*: Not that he thought that an Image of Metall, Stone, or Wood, was nothing; but that the thing which they honored, or

The Power of Casting out Devills, not the same it was in the Primitive Church.

Another relique of Gentilisme, Worshipping of Images, left in the Church, not brought into it.

445

feared in the Image, and held for a God, was a meer Figment, without place, habitation, motion, or existence, but in the motions of the Brain. And the worship of these with Divine Honour, is that which is in the Scripture called Idolatry, and Rebellion against God. For God being King of the Jews, and his Lieutenant being first Moses, and afterward the High Priest; if the people had been permitted to worship, and pray to Images, (which are Representations of their own Fancies,) they had had no farther dependence on the true God, of whom their can be no similitude; nor on his prime Ministers, Moses, and the High Priests; but every man had governed himself according to his own appetite, to the utter eversion of the Common-wealth, and their own destruction for want of Union. And therefore the first Law of God was, *They should not take for Gods,* A L I E N O S D E O S, *that is, the Gods of other nations, but that onely true God, who vouchsafed to commune with Moses, and by him to give them laws and directions, for their peace, and for their salvation from their enemies.* And the second was, that *they should not make to themselves any Image to Worship, of their own Invention.* For it is the same deposing of a King, to submit to another King, whether he be set up by a neighbour nation, or by our selves.

Answer to certain seeming texts for Images.

The places of Scripture pretended to countenance the setting up of Images, to worship them; or to set them up at all in the places where God is worshipped, are First, two Examples; one of the Cherubins over the Ark of God; the other of the Brazen Serpent: Secondly, some texts whereby we are commanded to worship certain Creatures for their relation to God; as to worship his Footstool: and lastly, some other texts, by which is authorized, a religious honoring of Holy things. But before I examine the force of those places, to prove that which is pretended, I must first explain what is to be understood by *Worshipping,* and what by *Images,* and *Idols.*

What is Worship.

I have already shewn in the 20 Chapter of this Discourse, that to Honor, is to value highly the Power of any person: and that such value is measured, by our comparing him with others. But because there is nothing to be compared with God in Power; we Honor him not, but Dishonour him by any Value lesse than Infinite. And thus Honor is properly of its own nature, secret, and internall in the heart. But the inward thoughts of men, which appear outwardly in their words and actions, are the signes of our Honoring, and these goe by the name of W O R S H I P, in Latine C U L T U S. Therefore, to Pray to, to Swear by, to Obey, to bee Diligent, and Officious in Serving: in summe, all

[357]

words and actions that betoken Fear to Offend, or Desire to Please, is *Worship*, whether those words and actions be sincere, or feigned: and because they appear as signes of Honoring, are ordinarily also called *Honor*.

The Worship we exhibite to those we esteem to be but men, as to Kings, and men in Authority, is *Civill Worship*: But the worship we exhibite to that which we think to bee God, whatsoever the words, ceremonies, gestures, or other actions be, is *Divine Worship*. To fall prostrate before a King, in him that thinks him but a Man, is but Civill Worship: And he that but putteth off his hat in the Church, for this cause, that he thinketh it the House of God, worshippeth with Divine Worship. They that seek the distinction of Divine and Civill Worship, not in the intention of the Worshipper, but in the Words δουλεία, and λατρεία, deceive themselves. For whereas there be two sorts of Servants; that sort, which is of those that are absolutely in the power of their Masters, as Slaves taken in war, and their Issue, whose bodies are not in their own power, (their lives depending on the Will of their Masters, in such manner as to forfeit them upon the least dis-obedience,) and that are brought and sold as Beasts, were called Δοῦλοι, that is properly, Slaves, and their Service Δουλεία: The other, which is of those that serve (for hire, or in hope of benefit from their Masters) voluntarily; are called Θῆτες, that is, Domestique Servants; to whose service the Masters have no further right, than is contained in the Covenants made betwixt them. These two kinds of Servants have thus much common to them both, that their labour is appointed them by another: And the word Λάτρις, is the generall name of both, signifying him that worketh for another, whether, as a Slave, or a voluntary Servant: So that Λατρεία signifieth generally all Service; but Δουλεία the service of Bondmen onely, and the condition of Slavery: And both are used in Scripture (to signifie our Service of God) promiscuously. Δουλεία, because we are Gods Slaves; Λατρεία, because wee Serve him: and in all kinds of Service is contained, not onely Obedience, but also Worship; that is, such actions, gestures, and words, as signifie Honor.

An IMAGE (in the most strict signification of the word) is the Resemblance of some thing visible: In which sense the Phantasticall Formes, Apparitions, or Seemings of visible Bodies to the Sight, are onely *Images*; such as are the Shew of a man, or other thing in the Water, by Reflexion, or Refraction; or of the Sun, or Stars by Direct

Distinction between Divine and Civill Worship.

[358]

An Image what. Phantasmes.

Vision in the Air; which are nothing reall in the things seen, nor in the place where they seem to bee; nor are their magnitudes and figures the same with that of the object; but changeable, by the variation of the organs of Sight, or by glasses; and are present oftentimes in our Imagination, and in our Dreams, when the object is absent; or changed into other colours, and shapes, as things that depend onely upon the Fancy. And these are the Images which are originally and most properly called *Ideas*, and IDOLS, and derived from the language of the Graecians, with whom the word *Εἴδω* signifieth to *See*. They are also called PHANTASMES, which is in the same language, *Apparitions*. And from these Images it is that one of the faculties of mans Nature, is called the *Imagination*. And from hence it is manifest, that there neither is, nor can bee any Image made of a thing Invisible.

It is also evident, that there can be no Image of a thing Infinite: for all the Images, and Phantasmes that are made by the Impression of things visible, are figured: but Figure is a quantity every way determined: And therefore there can bee no Image of God; nor of the Soule of Man; nor of Spirits; but onely of Bodies Visible, that is, Bodies that have light in themselves, or are by such enlightened.

Fictions.

[359]
*Materiall
Images.*

And whereas a man can fancy Shapes he never saw; making up a Figure out of the parts of divers creatures; as the Poets make their Centaures, Chimaeras, and other Monsters never seen: So can he also give Matter to those Shapes, and make them in Wood, Clay or Metall. And these are also called Images, not for the resemblance of any corporeall thing, but for the resemblance of some Phantasticall Inhabitants of the Brain of the Maker. But in these Idols, as they are originally in the Brain, and as they are painted, carved, moulded, or moulten in matter, there is a similitude of the one to the other, for which the Materiall Body made by Art, may be said to be the Image of the Phantasticall Idoll made by Nature.

But in a larger use of the word Image, is contained also, any Representation of one thing by another. So an earthly Soveraign may be called the Image of God: And an inferiour Magistrate the Image of an earthly Soveraign. And many times in the Idolatry of the Gentiles there was little regard to the similitude of their Materiall Idol to the Idol in their fancy, and yet it was called the Image of it. For a Stone unhewn has been set up for Neptune, and divers other shapes far different from the shapes they conceived of their Gods. And at this day we see many Images of the Virgin Mary, and other Saints, unlike one another, and without correspondence to any one mans Fancy; and yet serve well enough for the purpose they were erected for; which was no more but by the Names onely, to represent the Persons mentioned in the History; to which every man applyeth a Mentall Image of his owne making, or none at all. And thus an Image in the largest sense, is either the Resemblance, or the Representation of some thing Visible; or both together, as it happeneth for the most part.

But the name of Idoll is extended yet further in Scripture, to signifie also the Sunne, or a Starre, or any other Creature, visible or invisible, when they are worshipped for Gods.

Having shewn what is *Worship*, and what an *Image*; I will now put them together, and examine what that IDOLATRY is, which is forbidden in the Second Commandement, and other places of the Scripture. *Idolatry what.*

To worship an Image, is voluntarily to doe those externall acts, which are signes of honoring either the matter of the Image, which is Wood, Stone, Metall, or some other visible creature; or the Phantasme of the brain, for the resemblance, or representation whereof, the matter was formed and figured; or both together, as one animate Body, composed of the Matter and the Phantasme, as of a Body and Soule.

To be uncovered, before a man of Power and Authority, or before the Throne of a Prince, or in such other places as hee ordaineth to that purpose in his absence, is to Worship that man, or Prince with Civill Worship; as being a signe, not of honoring the stoole, or place, but the Person; and is not Idolatry. But if hee that doth it, should suppose the Soule of the Prince to be in the Stool, or should present a Petition to the Stool, it were Divine Worship, and Idolatry.

To pray to a King for such things, as hee is able to doe for us, though we prostrate our selves before him, is but Civill Worship; because we acknowledge no other power in him, but humane: But voluntarily to pray unto him for fair weather, or for any thing which God onely can doe for us, is Divine Worship, and Idolatry. On the other side, if a King compell a man to it by the terrour of Death, or other great corporall punishment, it is not Idolatry: For the Worship which the Soveraign commandeth to bee done unto himself by the terrour of his Laws, is not a sign that he that obeyeth him, does inwardly honour him as a God, but that he is desirous to save himselfe [360] from death, or from a miserable life; and that which is not a sign of internall honor, is no Worship; and therefore no Idolatry. Neither can it bee said, that hee that does it, scandalizeth, or layeth any stumbling block before his Brother; because how wise, or learned soever he be that worshippeth in that manner, another man cannot from thence argue, that he approveth it; but that he doth it for fear; and that it is not his act, but the act of his Soveraign.

To worship God, in some peculiar Place, or turning a mans face towards an Image, or determinate Place, is not to worship, or honor the Place, or Image; but to acknowledge it Holy, that is to say, to acknowledge the Image, or the Place to be set apart from common use: for that is the meaning of the word *Holy*; which implies no new quality in the Place, or Image; but onely a new Relation by Appropriation to God; and therefore is not Idolatry; no more than it was Idolatry to worship God before the Brazen Serpent; or for the Jews when they were out of their owne countrey, to turn their faces (when they prayed) toward the Temple of Jerusalem; or for Moses to put off his Shoes when he was before the Flaming Bush, the ground appertaining to Mount Sinai; which place God had chosen to appear in, and to give his Laws to the People of Israel, and was therefore Holy ground, not by inhaerent sanctity, but by separation to Gods use; or for Christians to worship in the Churches, which are once solemnly dedicated to God for that purpose, by the Authority of the King, or other true Representant of the Church. But to worship God, as inanimating, or inhabiting, such Image, or place; that is to say, an infinite substance in a finite place, is Idolatry: for such finite Gods, are but Idols of the brain, nothing reall; and are commonly called in the Scripture by the names of *Vanity*, and *Lyes*, and *Nothing*. Also to worship God, not as inanimating, or present in the place, or Image; but to the end to be put in mind of him, or of some works of his, in case the Place, or Image be dedicated, or set up by private authority, and not by the authority of them that are our Soveraign Pastors, is Idolatry. For the Commandement is, *Thou shalt not make to thy selfe any graven Image*. God commanded Moses to set up the Brazen Serpent; hee did not make it to himselfe; it was not therefore against the Commandement. But the making of the Golden Calfe by Aaron, and the People, as being done without authority from God, was Idolatry; not onely because they held it for God, but also because they

[361]

450

made it for a Religious use, without warrant either from God their Soveraign, or from Moses, that was his Lieutenant.

The Gentiles worshipped for Gods, Jupiter, and others; that living, were men perhaps that had done great and glorious Acts; and for the Children of God, divers men and women, supposing them gotten between an Immortall Deity, and a mortall man. This was Idolatry, because they made them so to themselves, having no authority from God, neither in his eternall Law of Reason, nor in his positive and revealed Will. But though our Saviour was a man, whom wee also beleeve to bee God Immortall, and the Son of God; yet this is no Idolatry; because wee build not that beleef upon our own fancy, or judgment, but upon the Word of God revealed in the Scriptures. And for the adoration of the Eucharist, if the words of Christ, *This is my Body*, signifie, *that he himselfe, and the seeming bread in his hand; and not onely so, but that all the seeming morsells of bread that have ever since been, and any time hereafter shall bee consecrated by Priests, bee so many Christs bodies, and yet all of them but one body*, then is that no Idolatry, because it is authorized by our Saviour: but if that text doe not signifie that, (for there is no other that can be alledged for it,) then, because it is a worship of humane institution, it is Idolatry. For it is not enough to say, God can transubstantiate the Bread into Christs Body: For the Gentiles also held God to be Omnipotent; and might upon that ground no lesse excuse their Idolatry, by pretending, as well as others, a transubstantiation of their Wood, and Stone into God Almighty.

Whereas there be, that pretend Divine Inspiration, to be a supernaturall entring of the Holy Ghost into a man, and not an acquisition of Gods graces, by doctrine, and study; I think they are in a very dangerous Dilemma. For if they worship not the men whom they beleeve to be so inspired, they fall into Impiety; as not adoring Gods supernaturall Presence. And again, if they worship them, they commit Idolatry; for the Apostles would never permit themselves to be so worshipped. Therefore the safest way is to beleeve, that by the Descending of the Dove upon the Apostles; and by Christs Breathing on them, when hee gave them the Holy Ghost; and by the giving of it by Imposition of Hands, are understood the signes which God hath been pleased to use, or ordain to bee used, of his promise to assist those persons in their study to Preach his Kingdome, and in their Conversation, that it might not be Scandalous, but Edifying to others.

Scandalous
worship of
Images.

[362]

Besides the Idolatrous Worship of Images, there is also a Scandalous Worship of them; which is also a sin; but not Idolatry. For *Idolatry* is to worship by signes of an internall, and reall honour: but *Scandalous Worship*, is but Seeming Worship; and may sometimes bee joined with an inward, and hearty detestation, both of the Image, and of the Phantasticall *Daemon*, or Idol, to which it is dedicated; and proceed onely from the fear of death, or other grievous punishment; and is neverthelesse a sin in them that so worship, in case they be men whose actions are looked at by others, as lights to guide them by; because following their ways, they cannot but stumble, and fall in the way of Religion: Whereas the example of those we regard not, works not on us at all, but leaves us to our own diligence and caution; and consequently are no causes of our falling.

If therefore a Pastor lawfully called to teach and direct others, or any other, of whose knowledge there is a great opinion, doe externall honor to an Idol for fear; unlesse he make his feare, and unwillingnesse to it, as evident as the worship; he Scandalizeth his Brother, by seeming to approve Idolatry. For his Brother arguing from the action of his teacher, or of him whose knowledge he esteemeth great, concludes it to bee lawfull in it selfe. And this Scandall, is Sin, and a *Scandall given*. But if one being no Pastor, nor of eminent reputation for knowledge in Christian Doctrine, doe the same, and another follow him; this is no Scandall given; for he had no cause to follow such example: but is a pretence of Scandall which hee taketh of himselfe for an excuse before men: For an unlearned man, that is in the power of an Idolatrous King, or State, if commanded on pain of death to worship before an Idoll, hee detesteth the Idoll in his heart, hee doth well; though if he had the fortitude to suffer death, rather than worship it, he should doe better. But if a Pastor, who as Christs Messenger, has undertaken to teach Christs Doctrine to all nations, should doe the same, it were not onely a sinfull Scandall, in respect of other Christian mens consciences, but a perfidious forsaking of his charge.

The summe of that which I have said hitherto, concerning the Worship of Images, is this, that he that worshippeth in an Image, or any Creature, either the Matter thereof, or any Fancy of his own, which he thinketh to dwell in it; or both together; or beleeveth that such things hear his Prayers, or see his Devotions, without Ears, or Eyes, committeth Idolatry: and he that counterfeiteth such Worship for fear of punishment, if he bee a man whose example hath power amongst his Brethren, committeth a sin: But he that worshippeth the Creator of the world before such an Image, or in such a place as he hath not made, or chosen of himselfe, but taken from the commandement of Gods Word, as the Jewes did in worshipping God before the Cherubins, and before the Brazen Serpent for a time, and in, or towards the Temple of Jerusalem, which was also but for a time, committeth not Idolatry.

Now for the Worship of Saints, and Images, and Reliques, and other things at this day practised in the Church of Rome, I say they are not allowed by the Word of God, nor brought into the Church of Rome, from the Doctrine there taught; but partly left in it at the first [363] conversion of the Gentiles; and afterwards countenanced, and confirmed, and augmented by the Bishops of Rome.

As for the proofs alledged out of Scripture, namely, those examples of Images appointed by God to bee set up; They were not set up for the people, or any man to worship; but that they should worship God himselfe before them; as before the Cherubins over the Ark, and *before the*[1] Brazen Serpent. For we read not, that the Priest, or any other did worship the Cherubins; but contrarily wee read (2 *Kings* 18.4.) that Hezekiah brake in pieces the Brazen Serpent which Moses had set up, because the People burnt incense to it. Besides, those examples are not put for our Imitation, that we also should set up Images, under pretence of worshipping God before them; because the words of the second Commandement, *Thou shalt not make to thy selfe any graven Image, &c.* distinguish between the Images that God commanded to be set up, and those which wee set up to our selves. And therefore from the Cherubins, or Brazen Serpent, to the Images of mans devising; and from the Worship commanded by God, to the Will-Worship of men, the argument is not good. This also is to bee considered, that as Hezekiah brake in pieces the Brazen Serpent, because the Jews did worship it, to the end they should doe so no more; so also Christian Soveraigns ought to break down the Images which their Subjects have been accustomed to worship; that there be no more occasion of such Idolatry. For at this day, the ignorant People, where Images are worshipped, doe really beleeve there is a Divine Power in the Images; and are told by their Pastors, that some

Answer to the Argument from the Cherubins, and Brazen Serpent.

---

[1] *Syn.*: the

453

of them have spoken; and have bled; and that miracles have been done by them; which they apprehend as done by the Saint, which they think either is the Image it self, or in it. The Israelites, when they worshipped the Calfe, did think they worshipped the God that brought them out of Egypt; and yet it was Idolatry, because they thought the Calfe either was that God, or had him in his belly. And though some man may think it impossible for people to be so stupid, as to think the Image to be God, or a Saint; or to worship it in that notion; yet it is manifest in Scripture to the contrary; where when the Golden Calfe was made, the people said, ★ *These are thy Gods O Israel*; and where the Images of Laban ★ are called his Gods. And wee see daily by experience in all sorts of People, that such men as study nothing but their food and ease, are content to beleeve any absurdity, rather than to trouble themselves to examine it; holding their faith as it were by entaile unalienable, except by an expresse and new Law.

★ Exod.32.2.

★ Gen.31. 30.

But they inferre from some other places, that it is lawfull to paint Angels, and also God himselfe: as from Gods walking in the Garden; from Jacobs seeing God at the top of the ladder; and from other Visions, and Dreams. But Visions, and Dreams, whether naturall or supernaturall, are but Phantasmes: and he that painteth an Image of any of them, maketh not an Image of God, but of his own Phantasm, which is, making of an Idol. I say not, that to draw a Picture after a fancy, is a Sin; but when it is drawn, to hold it for a Representation of God, is against the second Commandement; and can be of no use, but to worship. And the same may be said of the Images of Angels, and of men dead; unlesse as Monuments of friends, or of men worthy remembrance: For such use of an Image, is not Worship of the Image, but a civill honoring of the Person, not that is, but that was: But when it is done to the Image which we make of a Saint, for no other reason, but that we think he heareth our prayers, and is pleased with the honour wee doe him, when dead, and without sense, wee attribute to him more than humane power; and therefore it is Idolatry.

Painting of Fancies no Idolatry: but abusing them to Religious Worship is.

[364]

Seeing therefore there is no authority, neither in the Law of Moses, nor in the Gospel, for the religious Worship of Images, or other Representations of God, which men set up to themselves; or for the Worship of the Image of any Creature in Heaven, or Earth, or under the Earth: And whereas Christian Kings, who are living Representants of God, are not to be worshipped by their Subjects, by any act, that signifieth a greater esteem of his power, than the nature of mortall man is capable of; It cannot be imagined, that the Religious Worship now in use, was brought into the Church, by misunderstanding of the Scripture. It resteth therefore, that it was left in it, by not destroying the Images themselves, in the conversion of the Gentiles that worshipped them.

The cause whereof, was the immoderate esteem, and prices set upon the workmanship of them, which made the owners (though converted, from worshipping them as they had done Religiously for Daemons) to retain them still in their houses, upon pretence of doing it in the honor of *Christ*, of the *Virgin Mary*, and of the *Apostles*, and other the Pastors of the Primitive Church; as being easie, by giving them new names, to make that an Image of the *Virgin Mary*, and of her *Sonne* our Saviour, which before perhaps was called the Image of *Venus*, and *Cupid*; and so of a *Jupiter* to make a *Barnabas*, and of *Mercury* a *Paul*, and the like. And as worldly ambition creeping by degrees into the Pastors, drew them to an endeavour of pleasing the new made Christians; and also to a liking of this kind of honour, which they also might hope for after their decease, as well as those that had already gained it: so the worshipping of the Images of Christ and his Apostles, grew more and more Idolatrous; save that somewhat after the time of Constantine, divers Emperors, and Bishops, and generall Councells observed, and opposed the unlawfulnesse thereof; but too late, or too weakly. *How Idolatry was left in the Church.*

The *Canonizing of Saints*, is another Relique of Gentilisme: It is neither a misunderstanding of Scripture, nor a new invention of the Roman Church, but a custome as ancient as the Common-wealth of *Rome* it self. The first that ever was canonized at Rome, was *Romulus*, and that upon the narration of *Julius Proculus*, that swore before the Senate, he spake with him after his death, and was assured by him, he dwelt in Heaven, and was there called *Quirinus*, and would be propitious to the State of their new City: And thereupon the Senate gave *publique testimony* of his Sanctity. *Julius Caesar*, and other Emperors after him, had the like *testimony*; that is, were Canonized for Saints; for by such testimony is CANONIZATION, now defined; and is the same with the Ἀποθέωσις of the Heathen. *Canonizing of Saints.* [365]

It is also from the Roman Heathen, that the Popes have received the name, and power of PONTIFEX MAXIMUS. This was the name of him that in the ancient Common-wealth of Rome, had the Supreme Authority under the Senate and People, of regulating all Ceremonies, *The name of Pontifex.*

and Doctrines concerning their Religion: And when *Augustus Caesar* changed the State into a Monarchy, he took to himselfe no more but this office, and that of Tribune of the People, (that is to say, the Supreme Power both in State, and Religion;) and the succeeding Emperors enjoyed the same. But when the Emperour Constantine lived, who was the first that professed and authorized Christian Religion, it was consonant to his profession, to cause Religion to be regulated (under his authority) by the Bishop of Rome: Though it doe not appear they had so soon the name of *Pontifex*; but rather, that the succeeding Bishops took it of themselves, to countenance the power they exercised over the Bishops of the Roman Provinces. For it is not any Priviledge of St. Peter, but the Priviledge of the City of Rome, which the Emperors were alwaies willing to uphold, that gave them such authority over other Bishops; as may be evidently seen by that, that the Bishop of Constantinople, when the Emperour made that City the Seat of the Empire, pretended to bee equall to the Bishop of Rome; though at last, not without contention, the Pope carryed it, and became the *Pontifex Maximus*; but in right onely of the Emperour; and not without the bounds of the Empire; nor any where, after the Emperour had lost his power in Rome; though it were the Pope himself that took his power from him. From whence wee may by the way observe, that there is no place for the superiority of the Pope over other Bishops, except in the territories whereof he is himself the Civill Soveraign; and where the Emperour having Soveraign Power Civill, hath expressely chosen the Pope for the chief Pastor under himselfe, of his Christian Subjects.

Procession of Images.   The carrying about of Images in *Procession*, is another Relique of the Religion of the Greeks, and Romans: For they also carried their Idols from place to place, in a kind of Chariot, which was peculiarly dedicated to that use, which the Latines called *Thensa*, and *Vehiculum Deorum*; and the Image was placed in a frame, or Shrine, which they called *Ferculum*: And that which they called *Pompa*, is the same that now is named *Procession*: According whereunto, amongst the Divine Honors which were given to *Julius Caesar* by the Senate, this was one, that in the Pompe (or Procession) at the Circaean games, he should have *Thensam & Ferculum*, a sacred Chariot, and a Shrine; which was as much, as to be carried up and down as a God: Just as at this day the Popes are carried by Switzers under a Canopie.

To these Processions also belonged the bearing of burning Torches, and Candles, before the Images of the Gods, both amongst the Greeks, and Romans. For afterwards the Emperors of Rome received the same honor; as we read of *Caligula*, that at his reception to the Empire, he was carried from *Misenum* to *Rome*, in the midst of a throng of People, the wayes beset with Altars, and Beasts for Sacrifice, and burning *Torches*: And of *Caracalla* that was received into *Alexandria* with Incense, and with casting of Flowers, and δαδουχίαις, that is, with Torches; for Δαδοῦχοι were they that amongst the Greeks carried Torches lighted in the Processions of their Gods: And in processe of time, the devout, but ignorant People, did many times honor their Bishops with the like pompe of Wax Candles, and the Images of our Saviour, and the Saints, constantly, in the Church it selfe. And thus came in the use of Wax Candles; and was also established by some of the ancient Councells.

[366]
Wax Candles, and Torches lighted.

The Heathens had also their *Aqua Lustralis*, that is to say, *Holy Water*. The Church of Rome imitates them also in their *Holy Dayes*. They had their *Bacchanalia*; and we have our *Wakes*, answering to them: They their *Saturnalia*, and we our *Carnevalls*, and Shrovetuesdays liberty of Servants: They their Procession of *Priapus*; wee our fetching in, erection, and dancing about *May-poles*; and Dancing is one kind of Worship: They had their Procession called *Ambarvalia*; and we our Procession about the fields in the *Rogation week*. Nor do I think that these are all the Ceremonies that have been left in the Church, from the first conversion of the Gentiles: but they are all that I can for the present call to mind; and if a man would wel observe that which is delivered in the Histories, concerning the Religious Rites of the Greeks and Romanes, I doubt not but he might find many more of these old empty Bottles of Gentilisme, which the Doctors of the Romane Church, either by Negligence, or Ambition, have filled up again with the new Wine of Christianity, that will not faile in time to break them.

CHAP. XLVI.

Of DARKNESSE *from* VAIN PHILOSOPHY, *and* FABULOUS TRADITIONS.

What Philosophy is.

By PHILOSOPHY, is understood *the Knowledge acquired by Reasoning, from the Manner of the Generation of any thing, to the Properties; or from the Properties, to some possible Way of Generation of the same; to the end to bee able to produce, as far as matter, and humane force permit, such Effects, as humane life requireth.* So the Geometrician, from the Construction of Figures, findeth out many Properties thereof; and from the Properties, new Ways of their Construction, by Reasoning; to the end to be able to measure Land, and Water; and for infinite other uses. So the Astronomer, from the Rising, Setting, and Moving of the Sun, and Starres, in divers parts of the Heavens, findeth out the Causes of Day, and Night, and of the different Seasons of the Year; whereby he keepeth an account of Time: And the like of other Sciences.

Prudence no part of Philosophy.

By which Definition it is evident, that we are not to account as any part thereof, that originall knowledge called Experience, in which consisteth Prudence: Because it is not attained by Reasoning, but found as well in Brute Beasts, as in Man; and is but a Memory of successions of events in times past, wherein the omission of every little circumstance altering the effect, frustrateth the expectation of the most Prudent: whereas nothing is produced by Reasoning aright, but generall, eternall, and immutable Truth.

No false Doctrine is part of Philosophy: No more is Revelation supernaturall:

Nor are we therefore to give that name to any false Conclusions: For he that Reasoneth aright in words he understandeth, can never conclude an Error:

Nor to that which any man knows by supernaturall Revelation; because it is not acquired by Reasoning:

Nor *to that*[1] which is gotten by Reasoning from the Authority of

---

[1] *Syn.:* that

Books; because it is not by Reasoning from the Cause to the Effect, nor from the Effect to the Cause; and is not Knowledg, but Faith. *Nor learning taken upon credit of Authors.*

The faculty of Reasoning being consequent to the use of Speech, it was not possible, but that there should have been some generall Truthes found out by Reasoning, as ancient almost as Language it selfe. The Savages of America, are not without some good Morall Sentences; also they have a little Arithmetick, to adde, and divide in Numbers not too great: but they are not therefore Philosophers. For as there were Plants of Corn and Wine in small quantity dispersed in the Fields and Woods, before men knew their vertue, or made use of them for their nourishment, or planted them apart in Fields, and Vineyards; in which time they fed on Akorns, and drank Water: so also there have been divers true, generall, and profitable Speculations from the beginning; as being the naturall plants of humane Reason: But they were at first but few in number; men lived upon grosse Experience; there was no Method; that is to say, no Sowing, nor Planting of Knowledge by it self, apart from the Weeds, and common Plants of Errour and Conjecture: And the cause of it being the want of leisure from procuring the necessities of life, and defending themselves against their neighbors, it was impossible, till the erecting of great Common-wealths, it should be otherwise. *Leasure* is the mother of *Philosophy*; and *Common-wealth*, the mother of *Peace*, and *Leasure*. Where first were great and flourishing *Cities*, there was first the study of *Philosophy*. The *Gymnosophists* of *India*, the *Magi* of *Persia*, and the *Priests* of *Chaldaea* and *Egypt*, are counted the most ancient Philosophers; and those Countreys were the most ancient of Kingdomes. *Philosophy* was not risen to the *Graecians*, and other people of the West, whose *Common-wealths* (no greater perhaps than *Lucca*, or *Geneva*) had never *Peace*, but when their fears of one another were equall; nor the *Leasure* to observe any thing but one another. At length, when Warre had united many of these *Graecian* lesser Cities, into fewer, and greater; then began *Seven men*, of severall parts of *Greece*, to get the reputation of being *Wise*; some of them for *Morall* and *Politique* Sentences; and others for the learning of the *Chaldaeans* and *Egyptians*, which was *Astronomy*, and *Geometry*. But we hear not yet of any *Schools of Philosophy*. *Of the Beginnings and Progresse of Philosophy.* [368]

After the *Athenians* by the overthrow of the *Persian* Armies, had gotten the Dominion of the Sea; and thereby, of all the Islands, and Maritime Cities of the *Archipelago*, as well of *Asia* as *Europe*; and were *Of the Schools of Philosophy amongst the Athenians.*

grown wealthy; they that had no employment, neither at home, nor abroad, had little else to employ themselves in, but either (as St. *Luke* says, *Acts* 17.21.) *in telling and hearing news*, or in discoursing of *Philosophy* publiquely to the youth of the City. Every Master took some place for that purpose. *Plato* in certain publique Walks called *Academia*, from one *Academus*: *Aristotle* in the Walk of the Temple of *Pan*, called *Lycaeum*: others in the *Stoa*, or covered Walk, wherein the Merchants Goods were brought to land: others in other places; where they spent the time of their Leasure, in teaching or in disputing of their Opinions: and some in any place, where they could get the *youth*[*1] together to hear them talk. And this was it which *Carneades* also did at *Rome*, when he was Ambassadour: which caused *Cato* to advise the Senate to dispatch him quickly, for feare of corrupting the manners of the young men that delighted to hear him speak (as they thought) fine things.

From this it was, that the place where any of them taught, and disputed, was called *Schola*, which in their Tongue signifieth Leasure;
[369] and their Disputations, *Diatribae*, that is to say, *Passing of the time*. Also the Philosophers themselves had the name of their Sects, some of them from these their Schools: For they that followed *Plato*'s Doctrine, were called *Academiques*; The followers of *Aristotle*, *Peripatetiques*, from the Walk hee taught in; and those that *Zeno* taught, *Stoiques*, from the *Stoa*: as if we should denominate men from *More-fields*, from *Pauls-Church*, and from the *Exchange*, because they meet there often, to prate and loyter.

Neverthelesse, men were so much taken with this custome, that in time it spread it selfe over all Europe, and the best part of Afrique; so as there were Schools publiquely erected, and maintained for Lectures, and Disputations, almost in every Common-wealth.

Of the Schools of the Jews. There were also Schools, anciently, both before, and after the time of our Saviour, amongst the *Jews*: but they were Schools of their Law. For though they were called *Synagogues*, that is to say, Congregations of the People; yet in as much as the Law was every Sabbath day read, expounded, and disputed in them, they differed not in nature, but in name onely from Publique Schools; and were not onely in Jerusalem, but in every City of the Gentiles, where the Jews inhabited. There was such a Schoole at *Damascus*, whereinto *Paul* entred, to persecute.

[1] *Syn*.: youth of the City

There were others at *Antioch*, *Iconium* and *Thessalonica*, whereinto he entred, to dispute: And such was the Synagogue of the *Libertines*, *Cyrenians*, *Alexandrians*, *Cilicians*, and those of *Asia*; this is to say, the Schoole of *Libertines*, and of *Jewes*, that were strangers in *Jerusalem*: And of this Schoole they were that disputed (*Act.*6.9.) with *Saint Steven*.

But what has been the Utility of those Schools? what Science is there at this day acquired by their Readings and Disputings? That wee have of Geometry, which is the Mother of all Naturall Science, wee are not indebted for it to the Schools. *Plato* that was the best Philosopher of the Greeks, forbad entrance into his Schoole, to all that were not already in some measure Geometricians. There were many that studied that Science to the great advantage of mankind: but there is no mention of their Schools; nor was there any Sect of Geometricians; nor did they then passe under the name of Philosophers. The naturall Philosophy of those Schools, was rather a Dream than Science, and set forth in senselesse and insignificant Language; which cannot be avoided by those that will teach Philosophy, without having first attained great knowledge in Geometry: For Nature worketh by Motion; the Wayes, and Degrees whereof cannot. be known, without the knowledge of the Proportions and Properties of Lines, and Figures. Their Morall Philosophy is but a description of their own Passions. For the rule of Manners, without Civill Government, is the Law of Nature; and in it, the Law Civill; that determineth what is *Honest*, and *Dishonest*; what is *Just*, and *Unjust*; and generally what is *Good*, and *Evill*: whereas they make the Rules of *Good*, and *Bad*, by their own *Liking*, and *Disliking*: By which means, in so great diversity of *tastes,*[1] there is nothing generally agreed on; but every one doth (as far as he dares) whatsoever seemeth good in his owne eyes, to the subversion of Common-wealth. Their *Logique* which should bee the Method of Reasoning, is nothing else but Captions of Words, and Inventions how to puzzle such as should goe about to pose them. To conclude, there is nothing so absurd, that the old Philosophers (as *Cicero* saith, who was one of them) have not some of them maintained. And I beleeve that scarce any thing can be more absurdly said in naturall Philosophy, than that which now is called *Aristotles Metaphysiques*; nor more repugnant to Government,

The Schoole of the Graecians unprofitable.

[370]

---

[1] *Syn.*: taste,

than much of that hee hath said in his *Politiques*; nor more ignorantly, than a great part of his *Ethiques*.

The Schools of the Jews unprofitable. The Schoole of the Jews, was originally a Schoole of the Law of Moses; who commanded (*Deut.*31.10.) that at the end of every seventh year, at the Feast of the Tabernacles, it should be read to all the people, that they might hear, and learn it: Therefore the reading of the Law (which was in use after the Captivity) every Sabbath day, ought to have had no other end, but the acquainting of the people with the Commandements which they were to obey, and to expound unto them the writings of the Prophets. But it is manifest, by the many reprehensions of them by our Saviour, that they corrupted the Text of the Law with their false Commentaries, and vain Traditions; and so little understood the Prophets, that they did neither acknowledge Christ, nor the works he did; of which the Prophets prophecyed. So that by their Lectures and Disputations in their Synagogues, they turned the Doctrine of their Law into a Phantasticall kind of Philosophy, concerning the incomprehensible nature of God, and of Spirits; which they compounded of the Vain Philosophy and Theology of the Graecians, mingled with their own fancies, drawn from the obscurer places of the Scripture, and which might most easily bee wrested to their purpose; and from the Fabulous Traditions of their Ancestors.

University what it is. That which is now called an *University*, is a Joyning together, and an Incorporation under one Government of many Publique Schools, in one and the same Town or City. In which, the principall Schools were ordained for the three Professions, that is to say, of the Romane Religion, of the Romane Law, and of the Art of Medicine. And for the study of Philosophy it hath no otherwise place, then as a hand-maid to the Romane Religion: And since the Authority of Aristotle is onely current there, that study is not properly Philosophy, (the nature whereof dependeth not on Authors,) but Aristotelity. And for Geometry, till of very late times it had no place at all; as being subservient to nothing but rigide Truth. And if any man by the ingenuity of his owne nature, had attained to any degree of perfection therein, hee was commonly thought a Magician, and his Art Diabolicall.

[371] *Errors brought into Religion from* Now to descend to the particular Tenets of Vain Philosophy, derived to the Universities, and thence into the Church, partly from Aristotle, partly from Blindnesse of understanding; I shall first con-

sider *these*[1] Principles. There is a certain *Philosophia prima*, on which all other Philosophy ought to depend; and consisteth principally, in right limiting of the significations of such Appellations, or Names, as are of all others the most Universall: Which Limitations serve to avoid ambiguity, and aequivocation in Reasoning; and are commonly called Definitions; such as are the Definitions of Body, Time, Place, Matter, Forme, Essence, Subject, Substance, Accident, Power, Act, Finite, Infinite, Quantity, Quality, Motion, Action, Passion, and divers others, necessary to the explaining of a mans Conceptions concerning the Nature and Generation of Bodies. The Explication (that is, the setling of the meaning) of which, and the like Terms, is commonly in the Schools called *Metaphysiques*; as being a part of the Philosophy of Aristotle, which hath that for title: but it is in another sense; for there it signifieth as much, as *Books written, or placed after his naturall Philosophy*: But the Schools take them for *Books of supernaturall Philosophy*: for the word *Metaphysiques* will bear both these senses. And indeed that which is there written, is for the most part so far from the possibility of being understood, and so repugnant to naturall Reason, that whosoever thinketh there is any thing to bee understood by it, must needs think it supernaturall.

Aristotles Meta-physiques.

From these Metaphysiques, which are mingled with the Scripture to make Schoole Divinity, wee are told, there be in the world certaine Essences separated from Bodies, which they call *Abstract Essences, and Substantiall Formes*: For the Interpreting of which *Jargon*, there is need of somewhat more than ordinary attention in this place. Also I ask pardon of those that are not used to this kind of Discourse, for applying my selfe to those that are. The World, (I mean not the Earth onely, that denominates the Lovers of it *Worldly men*, but the *Universe*, that is, the whole masse of all things that are) is Corporeall, that is to say, Body; and hath the dimensions of Magnitude, namely, Length, Bredth, and Depth: also every part of Body, is likewise Body, and hath the like dimensions; and consequently every part of the Universe, is Body; and that which is not Body, is no part of the Universe: And because the Universe is All, that which is no part of it, is *Nothing*; and consequently *no where*. Nor does it follow from hence, that Spirits are *nothing*: for they have dimensions, and are therefore really *Bodies*; though that name in common Speech be given to such Bodies onely,

Errors concerning Abstract Essences.

---

[1] *Syn.*: their

as are visible, or palpable; that is, that have some degree of Opacity: But for Spirits, they call them Incorporeall; which is a name of more honour, and may therefore with more piety bee attributed to God himselfe; in whom wee consider not what Attribute expresseth best his Nature, which is Incomprehensible; but what best expresseth our desire to honour Him.

[372]

To know now upon what grounds they say there be *Essences Abstract*, or *Substantiall Formes*, wee are to consider what those words do properly signifie. The use of Words, is to register to our selves, and make manifest to others the Thoughts and Conceptions of our Minds. Of which Words, some are the names of the Things con-ceived; as the names of all sorts of Bodies, that work upon the Senses, and leave an Impression in the Imagination: Others are the names of the Imaginations themselves; that is to say, of those Ideas, or mentall Images we have of all things wee see, or remember: And others againe are names of Names; or of different sorts of Speech: As *Universall, Plurall, Singular*, are the names of Names; and *Definition, Affirmation, Negation, True, False, Syllogisme, Interrogation, Promise, Covenant*, are the names of certain Forms of Speech. Others serve to shew the Consequence, or Repugnance of one name to another; as when one saith, *A Man is a Body*, hee intendeth that the name of *Body* is necessarily consequent to the name of *Man*; as being but severalll names of the same thing, *Man*; which *Consequence is signified by coupling them together with the word *Is*.*[1] And as wee use the Verbe *Is*; so the Latines use their Verbe *Est*, and the Greeks their Ἐστι through all its Declinations. Whether all other Nations of the world have in their severall languages a word that answereth to it, or not, I cannot tell; but I am sure they have not need of it: For the placing of two names in order may serve to signifie their Consequence, if it were the custome, (for Custome is it, that gives words their force,) as well as the words *Is*, or *Bee*, or *Are*, and the like.

And if it were so, that there were a Language without any Verb answerable to *Est*, or *Is*, or *Bee*; yet the men that used it would bee not a jot the lesse capable of Inferring, Concluding, and of all kind of Reasoning, than were the Greeks, and Latines. But what then would become of these Terms, of *Entity, Essence, Essentiall, Essentiality*, that

---

[1] Scribal MS reads: consequence signified by coupling them with the word *Is* (which word is not the name of any thing, but) signifyes the consequence of the later name *Body*, to the former name *Man*.

are derived from it, and of many more that depend on these, applyed as most commonly they are? They are therefore no Names of Things; but Signes, by which wee make known, that wee conceive the Consequence of one name or Attribute to another: as when we say, *a Man, is, a living Body*, wee mean not that the *Man* is one thing, the *Living Body* another, and the *Is*, or *Beeing* a third: but that the *Man*, and the *Living Body*, is the same thing; because the Consequence, *If hee bee a Man, hee is a living Body*, is a true Consequence, signified by that word *Is*. Therefore, *to bee a Body, to Walke, to bee Speaking, to Live, to See*, and the like Infinitives, also *Corporeity, Walking, Speaking, Life, Sight*, and the like, that signifie just the same, are the names of *Nothing*; as I have elsewhere more amply expressed.

But to what purpose (may some man say) is such subtilty in a work of this nature, where I pretend to nothing but what is necessary to the doctrine of Government and Obedience? It is to this purpose, that men may no longer suffer themselves to be abused, by them, that by [373] this doctrine of *Separated Essences*, built on the Vain Philosophy of Aristotle, would fright them from Obeying the Laws of their Countrey, with empty names; as men fright Birds from the Corn with an empty doublet, a hat, and a crooked stick. For it is upon this ground, that when a Man is dead and buried, they say his Soule (that is his Life) can walk separated from his Body, and is seen by night amongst the graves. Upon the same ground they say, that the Figure, and Colour, and Tast of a peece of Bread, has a being, there, where they say there is no Bread: And upon the same ground they say, that Faith, and Wisdome, and other Vertues are sometimes *powred* into a man, sometimes *blown* into him from Heaven; as if the Vertuous, and their Vertues could be asunder; and a great many other things that serve to lessen the dependance of Subjects on the Soveraign Power of their Countrey. For who will endeavour to obey the Laws, if he expect Obedience to be Powred or Blown into him? Or who will not obey a Priest, that can make God, rather than his Soveraign; nay than God himselfe? Or who, that is in fear of Ghosts, will not bear great respect to those that can make the Holy Water, that drives them from him? And this shall suffice for an example of the Errors, which are brought into the Church, from the *Entities*, and *Essences* of Aristotle: which it may be he knew to be false Philosophy; but writ it as a thing consonant to, and corroborative of their Religion; and fearing the fate of Socrates.

465

Being once fallen into this Error of *Separated Essences*, they are thereby necessarily involved in many other absurdities that follow it. For seeing they will have these Forms to be reall, they are obliged to assign them *some place*. But because they hold them Incorporeall, without all dimension of Quantity, and all men know that Place is Dimension, and not to be filled, but by that which is corporeall; they are driven to uphold their credit with a distinction, that they are not indeed any where *Circumscriptivè*, but *Definitivè*: Which Terms being meer Words, and in this occasion insignificant, passe onely in Latine, that the vanity of them may bee concealed. For the Circumscription of a thing, is nothing else but the Determination, or Defining of its Place; and so both the Terms of the Distinction are the same. And in particular, of the Essence of a Man, which (they say) is his Soule, they affirm it, to be All of it in his little Finger, and All of it in every other Part (how small soever) of his Body; and yet no more Soule in the Whole Body, than in any one of those Parts. Can any man think that God is served with such absurdities? And yet all this is necessary to beleeve, to those that will beleeve the Existence of an Incorporeall Soule, Separated from the Body.

And when they come to give account, how an Incorporeall Substance can be capable of Pain, and be tormented in the fire of Hell, or Purgatory, they have nothing at all to answer, but that it cannot be known how fire can burn Soules.

[374] Again, whereas Motion is change of Place, and Incorporeall Substances are not capable of Place, they are troubled to make it seem possible, how a Soule can goe hence, without the Body to Heaven, Hell, or Purgatory; and how the Ghosts of men (and I may adde of their clothes which they appear in) can walk by night in Churches, Church-yards, and other places of Sepulture. To which I know not what they can answer, unlesse they will say, they walke *definitivè*, not *circumscriptivè*, or *spiritually*, not *temporally*: for such egregious distinctions are equally applicable to any difficulty whatsoever.

Nunc-stans. For the meaning of *Eternity*, they will not have it to be an Endlesse Succession of Time; for then they should not be able to render a reason how Gods Will, and Praeordaining of things to come, should not be before his Praescience of the same, as the Efficient Cause before the Effect, or Agent before the Action; nor of many other their bold opinions concerning the Incomprehensible Nature of God. But they will teach us, that Eternity is the Standing still of the Present

466

Time, a *Nunc-stans* (as the Schools call it;) which neither they, nor any else understand, no more than they would a *Hic-stans* for an Infinite greatnesse of Place.

And whereas men divide a Body in their thought, by numbring parts of it, and in numbring those parts, number also the parts of the Place it filled; it cannot be, but in making many parts, wee make also many places of those parts; whereby there cannot bee conceived in the mind of any man, more, or fewer parts, than there are places for: yet they will have us beleeve, that by the Almighty power of God, one body may be at one and the same time in many places; and many bodies at one and the same time in one place; as if it were an acknowledgement of the Divine Power, to say, that which is, is not; or that which has been, has not been. And these are but a small part of the Incongruities they are forced to, from their disputing Philosophically, in stead of admiring, and adoring of the Divine and Incomprehensible Nature; whose Attributes cannot signifie what he is, but ought to signifie our desire to honour him, with the best Appellations we can think on. But they that venture to reason of his Nature, from these Attributes of Honour, losing their understanding in the very first attempt, fall from one Inconvenience into another, without end, and without number; in the same manner, as when a man ignorant of the Ceremonies of Court, comming into the presence of a greater Person than he is used to speak to, and stumbling at his entrance, to save himselfe from falling, lets slip his Cloake; to recover his Cloake, lets fall his Hat; and with one disorder after another, discovers his astonishment and rusticity.

One Body in many places, and many Bodies in one place at once.

Then for *Physiques*, that is, the knowledge of the subordinate, and secundary causes of naturall events; they render none at all, but empty words. If you desire to know why some kind of bodies sink naturally downwards towards the Earth, and others goe naturally from it; The Schools will tell you out of Aristotle, that the bodies that sink downwards, are *Heavy*; and that this Heavinesse is it that causes them to descend: But if you ask what they mean by *Heavinesse*, they will define it to bee an endeavour to goe to the center of the Earth: so that the cause why things sink downward, is an Endeavour to be below: which is as much as to say, that bodies descend, or ascend, because they doe. Or they will tell you the center of the Earth is the place of Rest, and Conservation for Heavy things; and therefore they endeavour to be there: As if Stones, and Metalls had a desire, or could discern the

Absurdities in naturall Philosophy, as Gravity the Cause of Heavinesse.
[375]

place they would bee at, as Man does; or loved Rest, as Man does not; or that a peece of Glasse were lesse safe in the Window, than falling into the Street.

Quantity put into Body already made.
If we would know why the same Body seems greater (without adding to it) one time, than another; they say, when it seems lesse, it is *Condensed*; when greater, *Rarefied*. What is that *Condensed*, and *Rarefied?* Condensed, is when there is in the very same Matter, lesse Quantity than before; and Rarefied, when more. As if there could be Matter, that had not some determined Quantity; when Quantity is nothing else but the Determination of Matter; that is to say of Body, by which we say one Body is greater, or lesser than another, by thus, or thus much. Or as if a Body were made without any Quantity at all, and that afterwards more, or lesse were put into it, according as it is intended the Body should be more, or lesse Dense.

Powring in of Soules.
For the cause of the Soule of Man, they say, *Creatur Infundendo*, and *Creando Infunditur*: that is, *It is Created by Powring it in*, and *Powred in by Creation*.

Ubiquity of Apparition.
For the Cause of Sense, an ubiquity of *Species*; that is, of the *Shews* or *Apparitions* of objects; which when they be Apparitions to the Eye, is *Sight*; when to the Eare, *Hearing*; to the Palate, *Tast*; to the Nostrill, *Smelling*; and to the rest of the Body, *Feeling*.

Will, the Cause of Willing.
For cause of the Will, to doe any particular action, which is called *Volitio*, they assign the Faculty, that is to say, the Capacity in generall, that men have, to will sometimes one thing, sometimes another, which is called *Voluntas*; making the *Power* the cause of the *Act*: As if one should assign for cause of the good or evill Acts of men, their Ability to doe them.

*Sympathy, antipathy and other occult qualityes.*1
And in many occasions they put for cause of Naturall events, their own Ignorance; but disguised in other words: As when they say, Fortune is the cause of things contingent; that is, of things whereof they know no cause: And as when they attribute many Effects to *occult qualities*; that is, qualities not known to them; and therefore also (as they thinke) to no Man else. And to *Sympathy, Antipathy, Antiperistasis, Specificall Qualities*, and other like Termes, which signifie neither the Agent that produceth them, nor the Operation by which they are produced.

[376]
If such *Metaphysiques*, and *Physiques* as this, be not *Vain Philosophy*, there was never any; nor needed St. Paul to give us warning to avoid it.

1 Syn.: Ignorance an occult Cause.

And for their Morall, and Civill Philosophy, it hath the same, or greater absurdities. If a man doe an action of Injustice, that is to say, an action contrary to the Law, God they say is the prime cause of the Law, and also the prime cause of that, and all other Actions; but no cause at all of the Injustice; which is the Inconformity of the Action to the Law. This is Vain Philosophy. A man might as well say, that one man maketh both a streight line, and a crooked, and another maketh their Incongruity. And such is the Philosophy of all men that resolve of their Conclusions, before they know their Premises; pretending to comprehend, that which is Incomprehensible; and of Attributes of Honour to make Attributes of Nature; as this distinction was made to maintain the Doctrine of Free-Will, that is, of a Will of man, not subject to the Will of God. **And that one makes the things incongruent, and another the Incongruity.*1*

Aristotle, and other Heathen Philosophers define Good, and Evill, by the Appetite of men; and well enough, as long as we consider them governed every one by his own Law: For in the condition of men that have no other Law but their own Appetites, there can be no generall Rule of Good, and Evill Actions. But in a Common-wealth this measure is false: Not the Appetite of Private men, but the Law, which is the Will and Appetite of the State is the measure. And yet is this Doctrine still practised; and men judge the Goodnesse, or Wickednesse of their own, and of other mens actions, and of the actions of the Common-wealth it selfe, by their own Passions; and no man calleth Good or Evill, but that which is so in his own eyes, without any regard at all to the Publique Laws; except onely Monks, and Friers, that are bound by Vow to that simple obedience to their Superiour, to which every Subject ought to think himself bound by the Law of Nature to the Civill Soveraign. And this private measure of Good, is a Doctrine, not onely Vain, but also Pernicious to the Publique State. **And that private Appetite [is] the rule of publique good and evil;*2*

It is also Vain and false Philosophy, to say the work of Marriage is repugnant to Chastity, or Continence, and by consequence to make* it Morall Vice;*3 as they doe, that pretend Chastity, and Continence, for the ground of denying Marriage to the Clergy. For they confesse it is no more, but a Constitution of the Church, that requireth in those holy Orders that continually attend the Altar, and administration of the Eucharist, a continuall Abstinence from women, under the name *And that lawfull Marriage* is incontinence:*4*

---

1 Syn.: One makes the things incongruent, another the Incongruity.
2 Syn.: Private Appetite the rule of Publique good:
3 Syn.: them Moral Vices;   *4 Syn.: is Unchastity.*

of continuall Chastity, Continence, and Purity. Therefore they call the lawfull use of Wives, want of Chastity, and Continence; and so make Marriage a Sin, or at least a thing so impure, and unclean, as to render a man unfit for the Altar. If the Law were made because the use of Wives is Incontinence, and contrary to Chastity, then all Marriage is vice: If because it is a thing too impure, and unclean for a man consecrated to God; much more should other naturall, necessary, and daily works which all men doe, render men unworthy to bee Priests, because they are more unclean.

[377]

But the secret foundation of this prohibition of Marriage of Priests, is not likely to have been laid so slightly, as upon such errours in Morall Philosophy; nor yet upon the preference of single life, to the estate of Matrimony; which proceeded from the wisdome of St. Paul, who perceived how inconvenient a thing it was, for those that in those times of persecution were Preachers of the Gospel, and forced to fly from one countrey to another, to be clogged with the care of wife and children; but upon the designe of the Popes, and Priests of aftertimes, to make themselves the Clergy, that is to say, sole Heirs of the Kingdome of God in this world; to which it was necessary to take from them the use of Marriage, because our Saviour saith, that at the coming of his Kingdome the Children of God *shall neither Marry, nor bee given in Marriage, but shall bee as the Angels in heaven*; that is to say, Spirituall. Seeing then they had taken on them the name of Spirituall, to have allowed themselves (when there was no need) the propriety of Wives, had been an Incongruity.

And that all Government but Popular, is Tyranny:

From Aristotles Civill Philosophy, they have learned, to call all manner of Common-wealths but the Popular, (such as was at that time the state of Athens,) *Tyranny*. All Kings they called Tyrants; and the Aristocracy of the thirty Governours set up there by the Lacedemonians that subdued them, the thirty Tyrants: As also to call the condition of the people under the Democracy, *Liberty*. A *Tyrant* originally signified no more simply, but a *Monarch*: But when afterwards in most parts of Greece that kind of government was abolished, the name began to signifie, not onely the thing it did before, but with it, the hatred which the Popular States bare towards it: As also the name of King became odious after the deposing of the Kings in Rome, as being a thing naturall to all men, to conceive some great Fault to be signified in any Attribute, that is given in despight, and to a great Enemy. And when the same men shall be displeased with those that have the administration of the Democracy, or Aristocracy, they are not to seek for disgracefull names to expresse their anger in; but call readily the one *Anarchy*, and the other, *Oligarchy*, or the *Tyranny of a Few*. And that which offendeth the People, is no other thing, but that they are governed, not as every one of them would himselfe, but as the Publique Representant, be it one Man, or an Assembly of men thinks fit; that is, by an Arbitrary government: for which they give evill names to their Superiors; never knowing (till perhaps a little after a Civill warre) that without such Arbitrary government, such Warre must be perpetuall; and that it is Men, and Arms, not Words, and Promises, that make the Force and Power of the Laws.

And therefore this is another Errour of Aristotles Politiques, that in a wel ordered Common-wealth, not Men should govern, but the Laws. What man, that has his naturall Senses, though he can neither write nor read, does not find himself governed by them he fears, and beleeves can kill or hurt him when he obeyeth not? or that beleeves the Law can hurt him; that is, Words, and Paper, without the Hands, and Swords of men? And this is of the number of pernicious Errors: for they induce men, as oft as they like not their Governours, to adhaere to those that call them Tyrants, and to think it lawfull to raise warre against them: And yet they are many times cherished from the Pulpit, by the Clergy.

There is another Errour in their Civill Philosophy (which they never learned of Aristotle, nor Cicero, nor any other of the Heathen,) to extend the power of the Law, which is the Rule of Actions onely, to the very Thoughts, and Consciences of men, by Examination, and *Inquisition* of what they Hold, notwithstanding the Conformity of their Speech and Actions: By which, men are either punished for answering the truth of their thoughts, or constrained to answer an untruth for fear of punishment. It is true, that the Civill Magistrate, intending to employ a Minister in the charge of Teaching, may enquire of him, if hee bee content to Preach such, and such Doctrines; and in case of refusall, may deny him the employment: But to force him to accuse himselfe of Opinions, when his Actions are not by Law forbidden, is against the Law of Nature; and especially in them, who teach, that a man shall bee damned to Eternall and extream torments, if he die in a false opinion concerning an Article of the Christian Faith. For who is

That not Men, but Law governs. [378]

*That lawes may [illegible] *to the conscience.*1*

---

[1] *Syn.: Laws over the Conscience.*

there, that knowing there is so great danger in an error, whom the naturall care of himself, compelleth not to hazard his Soule upon his own judgement, rather than that of any other man that is unconcerned in his damnation?

For a Private man, without the Authority of the Common-wealth, that is to say, without permission from the Representant thereof, to Interpret the Law by his own Spirit, is another Error in the Politiques; but not drawn from Aristotle, nor from any other of the Heathen Philosophers. For none of them deny, but that in the Power of making Laws, is comprehended also the Power of Explaining them when there is need. And are not the Scriptures, in all places where they are Law, made Law by the Authority of the Common-wealth, and consequently, a part of the Civill Law?

Of the same kind it is also, when any but the Soveraign restraineth in any man that power which the Common-wealth hath not restrained; as they do, that impropriate the Preaching of the Gospell to one certain Order of men, where the Laws have left it free. If the State give me leave to preach, or teach; that is, if it forbid me not, no man can forbid me. If I find my selfe amongst the Idolaters of America, shall I that am a Christian, though not in Orders, think it a sin to preach Jesus Christ, till I have received Orders from Rome? or when I have preached, shall not I answer their doubts, and expound the Scriptures to them; that is, shall I not Teach? But for this may some say, as also for administring to them the Sacraments, the necessity shall be esteemed for a sufficient Mission; which is true: But this is true also, that for whatsoever, a dispensation is due for the necessity, for the same there needs no dispensation, when there is no Law that forbids it. Therefore to deny these functions to those, to whom the Civill Soveraigne hath not denyed them, is a taking away of a lawfull Liberty, which is contrary to the Doctrine of Civill Government.

[379]

More examples of Vain Philosophy, brought into Religion by the Doctors of Schoole-Divinity, might be produced; but other men may if they please observe them of themselves. I shall only adde this, that *Language of Schoole-Divines,* the Writings of Schoole-Divines, are nothing else for the most part, but insignificant Traines of strange and barbarous words, or words otherwise used, then in the common use of the Latine tongue; such as

---

¹ *Syn.: Private Interpretation of Law.*

would pose Cicero, and Varro, and all the Grammarians of ancient Rome. Which if any man would see proved, let him (as I have said once before) see whether he can translate any Schoole-Divine into any of the Modern tongues, as French, English, or any other copious language: for that which cannot in most of these be made Intelligible, is not Intelligible in the Latine. Which Insignificancy of language, though I cannot note it for false Philosophy; yet it hath a quality, not onely to hide the Truth, but also to make men think they have it, and desist from further search.

Lastly, for the Errors brought in from false, or uncertain History, what is all the Legend of fictitious Miracles, in the lives of the Saints; and all the Histories of Apparitions, and Ghosts, alledged by the Doctors of the Romane Church, to make good their Doctrines of Hell, and Purgatory, the power of Exorcisme, and other Doctrines which have no warrant, neither in Reason, nor Scripture; as also all those Traditions which they call the unwritten Word of God; but old Wives Fables? Whereof, though they find dispersed somewhat in the Writings of the ancient Fathers; yet those Fathers were men, that might too easily beleeve false reports; and the producing of their opinions for testimony of the truth of what they beleeved, hath no other force with them that (according to the Counsell of St. *John* 1 Epist. chap. 4. verse 1.) examine Spirits, than in all things that concern the power of the Romane Church, (the abuse whereof either they suspected not, or had benefit by it,) to discredit their testimony, in respect of too rash beleef of reports; which the most sincere men, without great knowledge of naturall causes, (such as the Fathers were) are commonly the most subject to: For naturally, the best men are the least suspicious of fraudulent purposes. Gregory the Pope, and S. Bernard have somewhat of Apparitions of Ghosts, that said they were in Purgatory; and so has our Beda: but no where, I beleeve, but by report from others. But if they, or any other, relate any such stories of their own knowledge, they shall not thereby confirm the more such vain reports; but discover their own Infirmity, or Fraud.

With the Introduction of False, we may joyn also the suppression of True Philosophy, by such men, as neither by lawfull authority, nor sufficient study, are competent Judges of the truth. Our own Navigations make manifest, and all men learned in humane Sciences, now acknowledge there are Antipodes: And every day it appeareth more and more, that Years, and Dayes are determined by Motions of the

Errors from Tradition.

[380]
Suppression of Reason.

473

Earth. Neverthelesse, men that have in their Writings but supposed such Doctrine, as an occasion to lay open the reasons for, and against it, have been punished for it by Authority Ecclesiasticall. But what reason is there for it? Is it because such opinions are contrary to true Religion? that cannot be, if they be true. Let therefore the truth be first examined by competent Judges, or confuted by them that pretend to know the contrary. Is it because they be contrary to the Religion established? Let them be silenced by the Laws of those, to whom the Teachers of them are subject; that is, by the Laws Civill: For dis-obedience may lawfully be punished in them, that against the Laws teach even true Philosophy. Is it because they tend to disorder in Government, as countenancing Rebellion, or Sedition? then let them be silenced, and the Teachers punished by vertue of his Power to whom the care of the Publique quiet is committed; which is the Authority Civill. For whatsoever Power Ecclesiastiques take upon themselves (in any place where they are subject to the State) in their own Right, though they call it Gods Right, is but Usurpation.

CHAP. XLVII.

Of the BENEFIT *that proceedeth from such Darknesse, and to whom it accreweth.*

He that receiveth Benefit by a Fact, is presumed to be the Author.

Cicero maketh honorable mention of one of the *Cassii*, a severe Judge amongst the Romans, for a custome he had, in Criminall causes, (when the testimony of the witnesses was not sufficient,) to ask the Accusers, *Cui bono*; that is to say, what Profit, Honor, or other Con-tentment, the accused obtained, or expected by the Fact. For amongst Praesumptions, there is none that so evidently declareth the Author, as doth the BENEFIT of the Action. By the same rule I intend in this place to examine, who they may be, that have possessed the People so long in this part of Christendome, with these Doctrines, contrary to the Peaceable Societies of Mankind.

That the Church Militant is the

And first, to this Error, *that the present Church now Militant on Earth, is the Kingdome of God*, (that is, the Kingdome of Glory, or the Land of Promise; not the Kingdome of Grace, which is but a Promise of the

Land,) are annexed these worldly Benefits; First, that the Pastors, and Teachers of the Church, are entitled thereby, as Gods Publique Ministers, to a Right of Governing the Church; and consequently (because the Church, and Common-wealth are the same Persons) to be Rectors, and Governours of the Commonwealth. By this title it is, that the Pope prevailed with the subjects of all Christian Princes, to beleeve, that to disobey him, was to disobey Christ himselfe; and in all differences between him and other Princes, (charmed with the word *Power Spirituall*,) to abandon their lawful Soveraigns; which is in effect an universall Monarchy over all Christendome. For though they were first invested in the right of being Supreme Teachers of Christian Doctrine, by, and under Christian Emperors, within the limits of the Romane Empire (as is acknowledged by themselves) by the title of *Pontifex Maximus*, who was an Officer subject to the Civill State; yet after the Empire was divided, and dissolved, it was not hard to obtrude upon the people already subject to them, another Title, namely, the Right of St. Peter; not onely to save entire their pretended Power; but also to extend the same over the same Christian Provinces, though no more united in the Empire of Rome. This Benefit of an Universall Monarchy, (considering the desire of men to bear Rule) is a sufficient Presumption, that the Popes that pretended to it, and for a long time enjoyed it, were the Authors of the Doctrine, by which it was obtained; namely, that the Church now on Earth, is the Kingdome of Christ. For that granted, it must be understood, that Christ hath some Lieutenant amongst us, by whom we are to be told what are his Commandements.

Kingdome of God, was first taught by the Church of Rome.

After that certain Churches had renounced this universall Power of the Pope, one would expect in reason, that the Civill Soveraigns in all those Churches, should have recovered so much of it, as (before they had unadvisedly let it goe) was their own Right, and in their own hands. And in England it was so in effect; saving that they, by whom the Kings administred the Government of Religion, by maintaining their imployment to be in Gods Right, seemed to usurp, if not a Supremacy, yet an Independency on the Civill Power: and they but seemed to usurpe it, in as much as they acknowledged a Right in the King, to deprive them of the Exercise of their Functions at his pleasure.

[382]

But in those places where the Presbytery took that Office, though many other Doctrines of the Church of Rome were forbidden to be

And maintained also by the Presbytery.

taught; yet this Doctrine, that the Kingdome of Christ is already come, and that it began at the Resurrection of our Saviour, was still retained. But *cui bono?* What Profit did they expect from it? The same which the Popes expected: to have a Soveraign Power over the People. For what is it for men to excommunicate their lawful King, but to keep him from all places of Gods publique Service in his own Kingdome? and with force to resist him, when he with force endeavoureth to correct them? Or what is it, without Authority from the Civill Soveraign, to excommunicate any person, but to take from him his Lawfull Liberty, that is, to usurpe an unlawfull Power over their Brethren? The Authors therefore of this Darknesse in Religion, are the Romane, and the Presbyterian Clergy.

Infallibility.　　To this head, I referre also all those Doctrines, that serve them to keep the possession of this spirituall Soveraignty after it is gotten. As first, that the *Pope in his publique capacity cannot erre.* For who is there, that beleeving this to be true, will not readily obey him in whatsoever he commands?

Subjection of Bishops.　　Secondly, that all other Bishops, in what Common-wealth soever, have not their Right, neither immediately from God, nor mediately from their Civill Soveraigns, but from the Pope, is a Doctrine, by which there comes to be in every Christian Common-wealth many potent men, (for so are Bishops,) that have their dependance on the Pope, and owe obedience to him, though he be a forraign Prince; by which means he is able, (as he hath done many times) to raise a Civill War against the State that submits not it self to be governed according to his pleasure and Interest.

Exemptions of the Clergy.　　Thirdly, the exemption of these, and of all other Priests, and of all Monkes, and Fryers, from the Power of the Civill Laws. For by this means, there is a great part of every Common-wealth, that enjoy the benefit of the Laws, and are protected by the Power of the Civill State, which neverthelesse pay no part of the Publique expence; nor are lyable to the penalties, as other Subjects, due to their crimes; and consequently, stand not in fear of any man, but the Pope; and adhere to him onely, to uphold his universall Monarchy.

The names of Sacerdotes, and Sacrifices.
[383]　　Fourthly, the giving to their Priests (which is no more in the New Testament but Presbyters, that is, Elders) the name of *Sacerdotes*, that is, Sacrificers, which was the title of the Civill Soveraign, and his publique Ministers, amongst the Jews, whilest God was their King. Also, the making the Lords Supper a Sacrifice, serveth to make the

People beleeve the Pope hath the same power over all Christians, that Moses and Aaron had over the Jews; that is to say, all Power, both Civill and Ecclesiasticall, as the High Priest then had.

Fiftly, the teaching that Matrimony is a Sacrament, giveth to the Clergy the Judging of the lawfulnesse of Marriages; and thereby, of what Children are Legitimate; and consequently, of the Right of Succession to haereditary Kingdomes. *The Sacramentation of Marriage.*

Sixtly, the Deniall of Marriage to Priests, serveth to assure this Power of the Pope over Kings. For if a King be a Priest, he cannot Marry, and transmit his Kingdome to his Posterity; If he be not a Priest then the Pope pretendeth this Authority Ecclesiasticall over him, and over his people. *The single life of Priests.*

Seventhly, from Auricular Confession, they obtain, for the assurance of their Power, better intelligence of the designs of Princes, and great persons in the Civill State, than these can have of the designs of the State Ecclesiasticall. *Auricular Confession.*

Eighthly, by the Canonization of Saints, and declaring who are Martyrs, they assure their Power, in that they induce simple men into an obstinacy against the Laws and Commands of their Civill Soveraigns even to death, if by the Popes excommunication, they be declared Heretiques or Enemies to the Church; that is, (as they interpret it,) to the Pope. *Canonization of Saints, and declaring of Martyrs.*

Ninthly, they assure the same, by the Power they ascribe to every Priest, of making Christ; and by the Power of ordaining Pennance; and of Remitting, and Retaining of sins. *Transubstantiation, Pennance, Absolution.*

Tenthly, by the Doctrine of Purgatory, of Justification by externall works, and of Indulgences, the Clergy is enriched. *Purgatory, Indulgences, Externall works.*

Eleventhly, by their Daemonology, and the use of Exorcisme, and other things appertaining thereto, they keep (or thinke they keep) the People more in awe of their Power. *Daemonology and Exorcism.*

Lastly, the Metaphysiques, Ethiques, and Politiques of Aristotle, the frivolous Distinctions, barbarous Terms, and obscure Language of the Schoolmen, taught in the Universities, (which have been all erected and regulated by the Popes Authority,) serve them to keep these Errors from being detected, and to make men mistake the *Ignis fatuus* of Vain Philosophy, for the Light of the Gospell. *School-Divinity.*

To these, if they sufficed not, might be added other of their dark Doctrines, the profit whereof redoundeth manifestly, to the setting up of an unlawfull Power over the lawfull Soveraigns of Christian *The Authors of spirituall Darknesse, who they be.*

People; or for the sustaining of the same, when it is set up; or to the worldly Riches, Honour, and Authority of those that sustain it. And therefore by the aforesaid rule, of *Cui bono*, we may justly pronounce for the Authors of all this Spirituall Darknesse, the Pope, and Roman Clergy, and all those besides that endeavour to settle in the mindes of men this erroneous Doctrine, that the Church now on Earth, is that Kingdome of God mentioned in the Old and New Testament.

[384]
But the Emperours, and other Christian Soveraigns, under whose Government these Errours, and the like encroachments of Ecclesiastiques upon their Office, at first crept in, to the disturbance of their possessions, and of the tranquillity of their Subjects, though they suffered the same for want of foresight of the Sequel, and of insight into the designs of their Teachers, may neverthelesse bee esteemed accessaries to their own, and the Publique dammage: For without their Authority there could at first no seditious Doctrine have been publiquely preached. I say they might have hindred the same in the beginning: But when the people were once possessed by those spirituall men, there was no humane remedy to be applyed, that any man could invent: And for the remedies that God should provide, who never faileth in his good time to destroy all the Machinations of men against the Truth, wee are to attend his good pleasure, that suffereth many times the prosperity of his enemies, together with their ambition, to grow to such a height, as the violence thereof openeth the eyes, which the warinesse of their predecessours had before sealed up, and makes men by too much grasping let goe all, as Peters net was broken, by the struggling of too great a multitude of Fishes; whereas the Impatience of those, that strive to resist such encroachment, before their Subjects eyes were opened, did but encrease the power they resisted. I doe not therefore blame the Emperour Frederick for holding the stirrop to our countryman Pope Adrian; for such was the disposition of his subjects then, as if hee had not done it, hee was not likely to have succeeded in the Empire: But I blame those, that in the beginning, when their power was entire, by suffering such Doctrines to be forged in the Universities of their own Dominions, have holden the Stirrop to all the succeeding Popes, whilest they mounted into the Thrones of all Christian Soveraigns, to ride, and tire, both them, and their people, at their pleasure.

But as the Inventions of men are woven, so also are they ravelled out; the way is the same, but the order is inverted: The web begins at the first Elements of Power, which are Wisdom, Humility, Sincerity, and other vertues of the Apostles, whom the people converted, obeyed, out of Reverence, not by Obligation: Their Consciences were free, and their Words and Actions subject to none but the Civill Power. Afterwards the Presbyters (as the Flocks of Christ encreased) assembling to consider what they should teach, and thereby obliging themselves to teach nothing against the Decrees of their Assemblies, made it to be thought the people were thereby obliged to follow their Doctrine, and when they refused, refused to keep them company, (that was then called Excommunication,) not as being Infidels, but as being disobedient: And this was the first knot upon their Liberty. And the number of Presbyters encreasing, the Presbyters of the chief City *of a*[1] Province, got themselves an authority over the Parochiall Presbyters, and appropriated to themselves the names of Bishops: And this was a second knot on Christian Liberty. Lastly, the Bishop [385] of Rome, in regard of the Imperiall City, took upon him an Authority (partly by the wills of the Emperours themselves, and by the title of *Pontifex Maximus*, and at last when the Emperours were grown weak, by the priviledges of St. Peter) over all other Bishops of the Empire: Which was the third and last knot, and the whole *Synthesis* and *Construction* of the Pontificiall Power.

And therefore the *Analysis*, or *Resolution* is by the same way; but beginneth with the knot that was last tyed; as wee may see in the dissolution of the praeterpoliticall Church Government in England. First, the Power of the Popes was dissolved totally by Queen Elizabeth; and the Bishops, who before exercised their Functions in Right of the Pope, did afterwards exercise the same in Right of the Queen and her Successours; though by retaining the phrase of *Iure Divino*, they were thought to demand it by immediate Right from God: And so was untyed the first knot. After this, the Presbyterians lately in England obtained the putting down of Episcopacy: And so was the second knot dissolved: And almost at the same time, the Power was taken also from the Presbyterians: And so we are reduced to the Independency of the Primitive Christians to follow Paul, or Cephas, or Apollos, every man as he liketh best: Which, if it be without contention, and without measuring the Doctrine of Christ, by our affection to the Person of his Minister, (the fault which the

[1] *Syn.*: or

479

Apostle reprehended in the Corinthians,) is perhaps the best: First, because there ought to be no Power over the Consciences of men, but of the Word it selfe, working Faith in every one, not always according to the purpose of them that Plant and Water, but of God himself, that giveth the Increase: and secondly, because it is unreasonable in them, who teach there is such danger in every little Errour, to require of a man endued with Reason of his own, to follow the Reason of any other man, or of the most voices of many other men; Which is little better, then to venture his Salvation at crosse and pile. Nor ought those Teachers to be displeased with this losse of their antient Authority: For there is none should know better then they, that power is preserved by the same Vertues by which it is acquired; that is to say, by Wisdome, Humility, Clearnesse of Doctrine, and sincerity of Conservation; and not by suppression of the Naturall Sciences, and of the Morality of Naturall Reason; nor by obscure Language; nor by Arrogating to themselves more Knowledge than they make appear; nor by Pious Frauds; nor by such other faults, as in the Pastors of Gods Church are not only Faults, but also scandalls, apt to make men stumble one time or other upon the suppression of their Authority.

Comparison of the Papacy with the Kingdome of Fayries.

[386]

But after this Doctrine, *that the Church now Militant, is the Kingdome of God spoken of in the Old and New Testament*, was received in the World; the ambition, and canvasing for the Offices that belong thereunto, and especially for that great Office of being Christs Lieutenant, and the Pompe of them that obtained therein the principall Publique Charges, became by degrees so evident, that they lost the inward Reverence due to the Pastorall Function: in so much as the Wisest men, of them that had any power in the Civill State, needed nothing but the authority of their Princes, to deny them any further Obedience. For, from the time that the Bishop of Rome had gotten to be acknowledged for Bishop Universall, by pretence of Succession to St. Peter, their whole Hierarchy, or Kingdome of Darknesse, may be compared not unfitly to the *Kingdome of Fairies*; that is, to the old wives *Fables* in England, concerning *Ghosts* and *Spirits*, and the feats they play in the night. And if a man consider the originall of this great Ecclesiasticall Dominion, he will easily perceive, that the *Papacy*, is no other, than the *Ghost* of the deceased *Romane Empire*, sitting crowned upon the grave thereof: For so did the Papacy start up on a Sudden out of the Ruines of that Heathen Power.

The *Language* also, which they use, both in the Churches, and in their Publique Acts, being *Latine,* which is not commonly used by any Nation now in the world, what is it but the *Ghost* of the Old *Romane Language?*

The *Fairies* in what Nation soever they converse, have but one Universall King, which some Poets of ours call King *Oberon*; but the Scripture calls *Beelzebub,* Prince of *Daemons.* The *Ecclesiastiques* likewise, in whose Dominions soever they be found, acknowledge but one Universall King, the *Pope.*

The *Ecclesiastiques* are *Spirituall* men, and *Ghostly* Fathers. The Fairies are *Spirits,* and *Ghosts. Fairies* and *Ghosts* inhabite Darknesse, Solitudes, and Graves. The *Ecclesiastiques* walke in Obscurity of Doctrine, in Monasteries, Churches, and Church-yards.

The *Ecclesastiques* have their Cathedrall Churches; which, in what Towne soever they be erected, by vertue of Holy Water, and certain Charmes called Exorcismes, have the power to make those Townes, Cities, that is to say, Seats of Empire. The *Fairies* also have their enchanted Castles, and certain Gigantique Ghosts, that domineer over the Regions round about them.

The *Fairies* are not to be seized on; and brought to answer for the hurt they do. So also the *Ecclesiastiques* vanish away from the Tribunals of Civill Justice.

The *Ecclesiastiques* take from young men, the use of Reason, by certain Charms compounded of Metaphysiques, and Miracles, and Traditions, and Abused Scripture, whereby they are good for nothing else, but to execute what they command them. The *Fairies* likewise are said to take young Children out of their Cradles, and to change them into Naturall Fools, which Common people do therefore call *Elves,* and are apt to mischief.

In what Shop, or Operatory the Fairies make their Enchantment, the old Wives have not determined. But the Operatories of the *Clergy,* are well enough known to be the Universities, that received their Discipline from Authority Pontificiall.

When the *Fairies* are displeased with any body, they are said to send [387] their Elves, to pinch them. The *Ecclesiastiques,* when they are displeased with any Civill State, make also their Elves, that is, Superstitious, Enchanted Subjects, to pinch their Princes, by preaching Sedition; or one Prince enchanted with promises, to pinch another.

The *Fairies* marry not; but there be amongst them *Incubi,* that have copulation with flesh and bloud. The *Priests* also marry not.

The *Ecclesiastiques* take the Cream of the Land, by Donations of ignorant men, that stand in aw of them, and by Tythes: So also it is in the Fable of *Fairies*, that they enter into the Dairies, and Feast upon the Cream, which they skim from the Milk.

What kind of Money is currant in the Kingdome of *Fairies*, is not recorded in the Story. But the *Ecclesiastiques* in their Receipts accept of the same Money that we doe; though when they are to make any Payment, it is in Canonizations, Indulgences, and Masses.

To this, and such like resemblances between the *Papacy*, and the Kingdome of *Fairies*, may be added this, that as the *Fairies* have no existence, but in the Fancies of ignorant people, rising from the Traditions of old Wives, or old Poets: so the Spirituall Power of the *Pope* (without the bounds of his own Civill Dominion) consisteth onely in the Fear that Seduced people stand in, of their *Excommunication;*[1] upon hearing of false Miracles, false Traditions, and false Interpretations of the Scripture.

It was not therefore a very difficult matter, for Henry 8. by his Exorcisme; nor for Qu. Elizabeth by hers, to cast them out. But who knows that this Spirit of Rome, now gone out, and walking by Missions through the dry places of China, Japan, and the Indies, that yeeld him little fruit, may not return, or rather an Assembly of Spirits worse than he, enter, and inhabite this clean swept house, and make the End thereof worse than the Beginning? For it is not the Romane Clergy onely, that pretends the Kingdome of God to be of this World, and thereby to have a Power therein, distinct from that of the Civill State. And this is all I had a design to say, concerning the Doctrine of the POLITIQUES. Which when I have reviewed, I shall willingly expose it to the censure of my Countrey.

[1] *Syn.*: Excommunications;

A *REVIEW*, and *CONCLUSION*.

From the contrariety of some of the Naturall Faculties of the Mind, one to another, as also of one Passion to another, and from their reference to Conversation, there has been an argument taken, to inferre an impossibility that any one man should be sufficiently disposed to all sorts of Civill duty. The Severity of Judgment, they say, makes men Censorious, and unapt to pardon the Errours and Infirmities of other men: and on the other side, Celerity of Fancy, makes the thoughts lesse steddy than is necessary, to discern exactly between Right and Wrong. Again, in all Deliberations, and in all Pleadings, the faculty of solid Reasoning, is necessary: for without it, the Resolutions of men are rash, and their Sentences unjust: and yet if there be not powerfull Eloquence, which procureth attention and Consent, the effect of Reason will be little. But these are contrary Faculties; the former being grounded upon principles of Truth; the other upon Opinions already received, true, or false; and upon the Passions and Interests of men, which are different, and mutable.

And amongst the Passions, *Courage*, (by which I mean the Contempt of Wounds, and violent Death) enclineth men to private Revenges, and sometimes to endeavour the unsetling of the Publique Peace: And *Timorousnesse*, many times disposeth to the desertion of the Publique Defence. Both these they say cannot stand together in the same person.

And to consider the contrariety of mens Opinions, and Manners in generall, It is they say, impossible to enterain a constant Civill Amity with all those, with whom the Businesse of the world constrains us to converse: Which Businesse, consisteth almost in nothing else but a perpetuall contention for Honor, Riches, and Authority.

To which I answer, that these are indeed great difficulties, but not Impossibilities: For by Education, and Discipline, they may bee, and are sometimes reconciled. Judgment, and Fancy may have place in the same man; but by turnes; as the end which he aimeth at requireth. As the Israelites in Egypt, were sometimes fastened to their labour of making Bricks, and other times were ranging abroad to gather Straw: So also may the Judgement sometimes be fixed upon one certain Consideration, and the Fancy at another time wandring about the world. So also Reason, and Eloquence, (though not perhaps in the

483

[390]

Naturall Sciences, yet in the Morall) may stand very well together. For wheresoever there is place for adorning and preferring of Errour, there is much more place for adorning and preferring of Truth, if they have it to adorn. Nor is there any repugnancy between fearing the Laws, and not fearing a publique Enemy; nor between abstaining from Injury, and pardoning it in others. There is therefore no such Inconsistence of Humane Nature, with Civill Duties, as some think. I have known cleernesse of Judgment, and largenesse of Fancy; strength of Reason, and gracefull Elocution; a Courage for the Warre, and a Fear for the Laws, and all eminently in one man; and that was my most noble and honored friend Mr. *Sidney Godolphin*; who hating no man, nor hated of any, was unfortunately slain in the beginning of the late Civill warre, in the Publique quarrell, by an undiscerned, and an undiscerning hand.

To the Laws of Nature, declared in the 15. Chapter, I would have this added, *That every man is bound by Nature, as much as in him lieth, to protect in Warre, the Authority, by which he is himself protected in time of Peace.* For he that pretendeth a Right of Nature to preserve his owne body, cannot pretend a Right of Nature to destroy him, by whose strength he is preserved: It is a manifest contradiction of himselfe. And though this Law may bee drawn by consequence, from some of those that are there already mentioned; yet the Times require to have it inculcated, and remembered.

And because I find by divers English Books lately printed, that the Civill warres have not yet sufficiently taught men, in what point of time it is, that a Subject becomes obliged to the Conquerour; nor what is Conquest; nor how it comes about, that it obliges men to obey his Laws: Therefore for farther satisfaction of men therein, I say, the point of time, wherein a man becomes subject to a Conquerour, is that point, wherein having liberty to submit to him, he consenteth, either by expresse words, or by other sufficient sign, to be his Subject. When it is that a man hath the liberty to submit, I have shewed before in the end of the 21. Chapter; namely, that for him that hath no obligation to his former Soveraign but that of an ordinary Subject, it is then, when the means of his life is within the Guards and Garrisons of the Enemy; for it is then, that he hath no longer Protection from him, but is protected by the adverse party for his Contribution. Seeing therefore such contribution is every where, as a thing inevitable, (not withstanding it be an assistance to the Enemy,) esteemed lawfull; a totall Submission, which is but an assistance to the Enemy, cannot be esteemed unlawful. Besides, if a man consider that they who submit, assist the Enemy but with part of their estates, whereas they that refuse, assist him with the whole, there is no reason to call their Submission, or Composition an Assistance; but rather a Detriment to the Enemy. But if a man, besides the obligation of a Subject, hath taken upon him a new obligation of a Souldier, then he hath not the liberty to submit to a new Power, as long as the old one keeps the field, and giveth him means of subsistence, either in his Armies, or Garrisons: for in this case, he cannot complain of want of Protection, and means to live as a Souldier: But when that also failes, a Souldier [391] also may seek his Protection wheresoever he has most hope to have it; and may lawfully submit himself to his new Master. And so much for the Time when he may do it lawfully, if hee will. If therefore he doe it, he is undoubtedly bound to be a true Subject: For a Contract lawfully made, cannot lawfully be broken.

By this also a man may understand, when it is, that men may be said to be Conquered; and in what the nature of Conquest, and the Right of a Conquerour consisteth: For this Submission is *it that*[1] implyeth them all. Conquest, is not the Victory it self; but the Acquisition by Victory, of a Right, over the persons of men. He therefore that is slain, is Overcome, but not Conquered: He that is taken, and put into prison, or chaines, is not Conquered, though Overcome; for he is still an Enemy, and may save himself if hee can: But he that upon promise of Obedience, hath his Life and Liberty allowed him, is then Conquered, and a Subject; and not before. The Romanes used to say, that their Generall had *Pacified* such a *Province*, that is to say, in English, *Conquered* it; and that the Countrey was *Pacified* by Victory, when the people of it had promised *Imperata facere*, that is, *To doe what the Romane People commanded them*: this was to be Conquered. But this promise may be either expresse, or tacite: Expresse, by Promise: Tacite, by other signes. As for example, a man that hath not been called to make such an expresse Promise, (because he is one whose power perhaps is not considerable;) yet if he live under their Protection openly, hee is understood to submit himselfe to the Government: But if he live there secretly, he is lyable to any thing that may bee done to a Spie, and Enemy of the State. I say not, hee does any Injustice,

---

¹ Syn.: it

(for acts of open Hostility bear not that name); but that he may be justly put to death. Likewise, if a man, when his Country is conquered, be out of it, he is not Conquered, nor Subject: but if at his return, he submit to the Government, he is bound to obey it. So that *Conquest* (to define it) is the Acquiring of the Right of Soveraignty by Victory. Which Right, is acquired, in the peoples Submission, by which they contract with the Victor, promising Obedience, for Life and Liberty.

In the 29.Chapter I have set down for one of the causes of the Dissolutions of Common-wealths, their Imperfect Generation, consisting in the want of an Absolute and Arbitrary Legislative Power; for want whereof, the Civill Soveraign is fain to handle the Sword of Justice unconstantly, and as if it were too hot for him to hold: One reason whereof (which I have not there mentioned) is this, That they will all of them justifie the War, by which their Power was at first gotten, and whereon (as they think) their Right dependeth, and not on the Possession. As if, for example, the Right of the Kings of England did depend on the goodnesse of the cause of *William* the Conquerour, and upon their lineall, and directest Descent from him; by which means, there would perhaps be no tie of the Subjects obedience to their Soveraign at this day in all the world: wherein whilest they needlessely think to justifie themselves, they justifie all the successefull Rebellions that Ambition shall at any *time after*[1] raise against them, and their Successors. Therefore I put down for one of the most effectuall seeds of the Death of any State, that the Conquerors require not onely a Submission of mens actions to them for the future, but also an Approbation of all their actions past; when there is scarce a Common-wealth in the world, whose beginnings can in conscience be justified.

And because the name of Tyranny, signifieth nothing more, nor lesse, than the name of Soveraignty, be it in one, or many men, saving that they that use the former word, are understood to bee angry with them they call Tyrants; I think the toleration of a professed hatred of Tyranny, is a Toleration of hatred to Common-wealth in generall, and another evill seed, not differing much from the former. For to the Justification of the Cause of a Conqueror, the Reproach of the Cause of the Conquered, is for the most part necessary: but neither of them

---

[1] *Syn.*: time

necessary for the Obligation of the Conquered. And thus much I have thought fit to say upon the Review of the first and second part of this Discourse.

In the 35. Chapter, I have sufficiently declared out of the Scripture, that in the Common-wealth of the Jewes, God himselfe was made the Soveraign, by Pact with the People; who were therefore called his *Peculiar People*, to distinguish them from the rest of the world, over whom God reigned not by their Consent, but by his own Power: And that in this Kingdome Moses was Gods Lieutenant on Earth; and that it was he that told them what Laws God appointed them to be ruled by. But I have omitted to set down who were the Officers appointed to doe Execution; especially in Capitall Punishments; not then thinking it a matter of so necessary consideration, as I find it since. Wee know that generally in all Common-wealths, the Execution of Corporeall Punishments, was either put upon the Guards, or other Souldiers of the Soveraign Power; or given to those, in whom want of means, contempt of honour, and hardnesse of heart, concurred, to make them sue for such an Office. But amongst the Israelites it was a Positive Law of God their Soveraign, that he that was convicted of a capitall Crime, should be stoned to death by the People; and that the Witnesses should cast the first Stone, and after the Witnesses, then the rest of the People. This was a Law that designed who were to be the Executioners; but not that any one should throw a Stone at him before Conviction and Sentence, where the Congregation was Judge. The Witnesses were neverthelesse to be heard before they proceeded to Execution, unlesse the Fact were committed in the presence of the Congregation it self, or in sight of the lawfull Judges; for then there needed no other Witnesses but the Judges themselves. Neverthelesse, this manner of proceeding being not throughly understood, hath given occasion to a dangerous opinion, that any man may kill another, in some cases, by a Right of Zeal; as if the Executions done upon Offenders in the Kingdome of God in old time, proceeded not from the Soveraign Command, but from the Authority of Private Zeal: [393] which, if we consider the texts that seem to favour it, is quite contrary.

First, where the Levites fell upon the People, that had made and worshipped the Golden Calfe, and slew three thousand of them; it was by the Commandement of Moses, from the mouth of God; as is manifest, *Exod.* 32. 27. And when the Son of a woman of Israel had blasphemed God, they that heard it, did not kill him, but brought him before Moses, who put him under custody, till God should give Sentence against him; as appears, *Levit.*25. 11, 12. Again, (*Numbers* 25. 6,7.) when Phinehas killed Zimri and Cosbi, it was not by right of Private Zeale: Their Crime was committed in the sight of the Assembly; there needed no Witnesse; the Law was known, and he the heir apparent to the Soveraignty; and which is the principall point, the Lawfulnesse of his Act depended wholly upon a subsequent Ratification by Moses, whereof he had no cause to doubt. And this Presumption of a future Ratification, is sometimes necessary to the safety of a Common-wealth; as in a sudden Rebellion, any man that can suppresse it by his own Power in the Countrey where it begins, without expresse Law or Commission, may lawfully doe it, and provide to have it Ratified, or Pardoned, whilest it is in doing, or after it is done. Also *Numb.* 35. 30. it is expressely said, *Whosoever shall kill the Murtherer, shall kill him upon the word of Witnesses*: but Witnesses suppose a formall Judicature, and consequently condemn that pretence of *Ius Zelotarum.* The Law of Moses concerning him that enticeth to Idolatry, (that is to say, in the Kingdome of God to a renouncing of his Allegiance (*Deut.* 13. 8.) forbids to conceal him, and commands the Accuser to cause him to be put to death, and to cast the first stone at him; but not to kill him before he be Condemned. And (*Deut.* 17. ver. 4, 5, 6.) the Processe against Idolatry is exactly set down: For God there speaketh to the People, as Judge, and commandeth them, when a man is Accused of Idolatry, to Enquire diligently of the Fact, and finding it true, then to Stone him; but still the hand of the Witnesse throweth the first stone. This is not Private Zeale, but Publique Condemnation. In like manner when a Father hath a rebellious Son, the Law is (*Deut.* 21. 18.) that he shall bring him before the Judges of the Town, and all the people of the Town shall Stone him. Lastly, by pretence of these Laws it was, that St. Steven was Stoned, and not by pretence of Private Zeal: for before hee was carried away to Execution, he had Pleaded his Cause before the High Priest. There is nothing in all this, nor in any other part of the Bible, to countenance Executions by Private Zeal; which being oftentimes but a conjunction of Ignorance and Passion, is against both the Justice and *the Peace*[1] of a Common-wealth.

In the 36. Chapter I have said, that it is not declared in what

[1] *Syn.*: Peace

manner God spake supernaturally to Moses: Not that he spake not to him sometimes by Dreams and Visions, and by a supernaturall Voice, as to other Prophets: For the manner how he spake unto him from the Mercy-Seat, is expressely set down *Numbers* 7. 89. in these words, [394] *From that time forward, when Moses entred into the Tabernacle of the Congregation to speak with God, he heard a Voice which spake unto him from over the Mercy-Seate, which is over the Arke of the Testimony, from between the Cherubins he spake unto him.* But it is not declared in what consisted the praeeminence of the manner of Gods speaking to Moses, above that of his speaking to other Prophets, as to Samuel, and to Abraham, to whom he also spake by a Voice, (that is, by Vision) Unlesse the difference consist in the cleernesse of the Vision. For *Face to Face,* and *Mouth to Mouth,* cannot be literally understood of the Infinitenesse, and Incomprehensibility of the Divine Nature.

And as to the whole Doctrine, I see not yet, but the Principles of it are true and proper; and the Ratiocination solid. For I ground the Civill Right of Soveraigns, and both the Duty and Liberty of Subjects, upon the known naturall Inclinations of Mankind, and upon the Articles of the Law of Nature; of which no man, that pretends but reason enough to govern his private family, ought to be ignorant. And for the Power Ecclesiasticall of the same Soveraigns, I ground it on such Texts, as are both evident in themselves, and consonant to the Scope of the whole Scripture. And therefore am perswaded, that he that shall read it with a purpose onely to be informed, shall be informed by it. But for those that by Writing, or Publique Discourse, or by their eminent actions, have already engaged themselves to the maintaining of contrary opinions, they will not bee so easily satisfied. For in such cases, it is naturall for men, at one and the same time, both to proceed in reading, and to lose their attention, in the search of objections to that they had read before: Of which, in a time wherein the interests of men are changed (seeing much of that Doctrine, which serveth to the establishing of a new Government, must needs be contrary to that which conduced to the dissolution of the old,) there cannot choose but be very many.

In that part which treateth of a Christian Common-wealth, there are some new Doctrines, which, it may be, in a State where the contrary were already fully determined, were a fault for a Subject without leave to divulge, as being an usurpation of the place of a Teacher. But in this time, that men call not onely for Peace, but also for Truth, to offer such

Doctrine[1] as I think True, and that manifestly tend to Peace and Loyalty, to the consideration of those that are yet in deliberation, is no more, but to offer New Wine, to bee put into New Cask, that both may be preserved together. And I suppose, that then, when Novelty can breed no trouble, nor disorder in a State, men are not generally so much inclined to the reverence of Antiquity, as to preferre Ancient Errors, before New and well proved Truth.

There is nothing I distrust more than my Elocution; which neverthelesse I am confident (excepting the Mischances of the Presse) is not obscure. That I have neglected the Ornament of quoting ancient Poets, Orators, and Philosophers, contrary to the custome of late time, (whether I have done well or ill in it,) proceedeth from my judgment, grounded on many reasons. For first, all Truth of Doctrine dependeth either upon *Reason*, or upon *Scripture*; both which give credit to many, but never receive it from any Writer. Secondly, the matters in question are not of *Fact*, but of *Right*, wherein there is no place for *Witnesses*. There is scarce any of those old Writers, that contradicteth not sometimes both himself, and others; which makes their Testimonies insufficient. Fourthly, such Opinions as are taken onely upon Credit of Antiquity, are not intrinsecally the Judgment of those that cite them, but Words that passe (like gaping) from mouth to mouth. Fiftly, it is many times with a fraudulent Designe that men stick their corrupt Doctrine with the Cloves of other mens Wit. Sixtly, I find not that the Ancients they cite, took it for an Ornament, to doe the like with those that wrote before them. Seventhly, it is an argument of Indigestion, when Greek and Latine Sentences unchewed come up again, as they use to doe, unchanged. Lastly, though I reverence those men of Ancient time, that either have written Truth perspicuously, or set us in a better way to find it out our selves; yet to the Antiquity it self I think nothing due: For if we will reverence the Age, the Present is the Oldest. If the Antiquity of the Writer, I am not sure, that generally they to whom such honor is given, were more Ancient when they wrote, than I am that am Writing: But if it bee well considered, the praise of Ancient Authors, proceeds not from the reverence of the Dead, but from the competition, and mutuall envy of the Living.

To conclude, there is nothing in this whole Discourse, nor in that I

[395]

---

[1] *Syn.*: Doctrines

writ before of the same Subject in Latine, as far as I can perceive, contrary either to the Word of God, or to good Manners; or *tending to*¹ the disturbance of the Publique Tranquillity. Therefore I think it may be profitably printed, and more profitably taught in the Universities, in case they also think so, to whom the judgment of the same belongeth. For seeing the Universities are the Fountains of Civill, and Morall Doctrine, from whence the Preachers, and the Gentry, drawing such water as they find, use to sprinkle the same (both from the Pulpit, and in their Conversation) upon the People, there ought certainly to be great care taken, to have it pure, both from the Venime of Heathen Politicians, and from the Incantation of Deceiving Spirits. And by that means the most men, knowing their Duties, will be the less subject to serve the Ambition of a few discontented persons, in their purposes against the State; and be the lesse grieved with the Contributions necessary for their Peace, and Defence; and the Governours themselves have the lesse cause, to maintain at the Common charge any greater Army, than is necessary to make good the Publique Liberty, against the Invasions and Encroachments of forraign Enemies.

And thus I have brought to an end my Discourse of Civill and Ecclesiasticall Government, occasioned by the disorders of the present time, without partiality, without application, and without other designe, than to set before mens eyes the mutuall Relation between Protection and Obedience; of which the condition of [396] Humane Nature, and the Laws Divine, (both Naturall and Positive) require an inviolable observation. And though in the revolution of States, there can be no very good Constellation for Truths of this nature to be born under, (as having an angry aspect from the dissolvers of an old Government, and seeing but the backs of them that erect a new;) yet I cannot think it will be condemned at this time, either by the Publique Judge of Doctrine, or by any that desires the continuance of Publique Peace. And in this hope I return to my interrupted Speculation of Bodies Naturall; wherein, (if God give me health to finish it,) I hope the Novelty will as much please, as in the Doctrine of this Artificiall Body it useth to offend. For such Truth, as opposeth no mans profit, nor pleasure, is to all men welcome.

FINIS.

¹ *Syn.:* to

491

1. Index of subjects

(Certain subjects, such as Sovereign and Common-wealth, occur on virtually every page of *Leviathan*; in such cases, the entries below refer only to the passages in which there is some extended discussion on the subject.)

2. Index of proper names

(This index does not include names in the section on Further Reading.)

3. Index of place names

Abdera (Greek city), 56
Adrianople, battle of, xci
Africa, 78
Albania, lxxxix
Amalek, lxvi
America, 89, 158, 459
Anglican Church, *see* England
Antioch, 364, 366, 377, 461
Arnon, brook of, 262
Athens, lxvii, lxxvii, 148, 149, 150, 222–3, 225, 254; Schools of Philosophy, 459–60

Babel, tower of, 25
Babylon, lxxiii, lxxiv, lxxxv, 264, 265, 312
Bersabee, 85
Burgundy, lxix

Canaan, lxv, 262, 280–1, 293, 297
Canterbury, lxviii, 222
Chaldaea, 459
Champagne (France), lxix
Chatsworth, Derbyshire, lvii, lix
China, 482
Constantinople, lxxxix, 149
Cornwall, lxxv

Damascus, lxxxvi, 350, 377, 460
Devon, lxxv
Dunbar, Battle of, xi, liv

Egypt, lxxxvii, 235, 262, 286, 454, 459, 484; Joseph in, lxi, 271; Moses

leads Jews out of, lxiv, 85, 302, 303–4; plague of darkness, 313; sorcerers, 258
England, 396; Anglican Church, ix, xl–xlv, lxxiv, 260, 261, 277; and the Church of Rome, 85–6, 482; Civil War, xi, lii; Norman, xci, 173; power of Barons, 222; Presbyterians in, xl, xliv, liv; rights of kings of, 486; rulers and representation in, xxx, xxxvii; under Elizabeth I, lxxiv; under Henry II, lxxvi; under Henry VIII, lxxvi–lxxviii, 237; under James I, lxxviii; under William I, xci, 173; under William II, xci; union with Scotland, 138

Florence, lviii
France, x, xix, xliii, lvii, lix, 396, 397; Paris, x, xix–xx, xliii, xlviii, lix, xix–xx; philosophers in, xix–xx; under Henry III, lxxvi

Geneva, xiii, lviii
Germany: coats of arms, 67–8; Upper, lxxiii
Gomorrah, 312
Greece, ancient, lxvii–lxviii, 1, 67, 149, 164, 225, 274, 305, 312, 337; fits of madness in, 56; law, 213; and philosophy, 459–60, 461–2; procession of images, 456–7; tyranny, 470; *see also* Athens

Hardwick Hall, Derbyshire, xiii, lvii, lix

4. A concordance with earlier editions

This concordance is designed to enable the reader to locate in the Cambridge edition any page references from the three editions most commonly cited by scholars, those of Macpherson (Penguin), Oakeshott (Blackwell) and Molesworth (Hobbes's *English Works*, Vol. III)

Cambridge	Macpherson	Oakeshott	Molesworth
3	75, 76	2	v, vi
4	76	2	vi
5	77	3	vii
6	78, 79	3, 4	vii, viii
7	79	4	viii
9	81, 82	5	ix, x
10	82, 83	5, 6	x, xi
11	83	6	xi
13	85	7	1, 2
14	85, 86, 87	7, 8	2, 3
15	87, 88	8, 9	3, 4, 5
16	88, 89, 90	9, 10	5, 6
17	90, 91	10, 11	6, 7, 8
18	91, 92	11, 12	8, 9
19	92, 93, 94	12, 13	9, 10, 11
20	94, 95	13, 14	11, 12
21	95, 96	14, 15	12, 13, 14
22	96, 97, 98	15, 16	14, 15
23	98, 99	16, 17	15, 16, 17
24	99, 100	17, 18	17, 18, 19
25	100, 101, 102	18, 19	19, 20
26	102, 103	19, 20	20, 21, 22
27	103, 104, 105	20, 21	22, 23
28	105, 106	21, 22	23, 24, 25
29	106, 107	22, 23	26, 27, 28
30	107, 108, 109	23, 24	26, 27, 28
31	109, 110	24, 25	28, 29
32	110, 111	25, 26	29, 30, 31
33	111, 112, 113	26, 27	31, 32

Cambridge	Macpherson	Oakeshott	Molesworth
34	113, 114	27, 28	32, 33, 34
35	114, 115	28, 29	34, 35
36	115, 116, 117	29, 30	35, 36, 37
37	117, 118	30, 31	37, 38
38	118, 119	31, 32	38, 39, 40
39	119, 120, 121	32, 33	40, 41
40	121, 122	33, 34	41, 42, 43
41	122, 123, 124	34, 35	43, 44
42	124, 125	35, 36	44, 45, 46
43	125, 126	36, 37	46, 47
44	126, 127, 128	37, 38	47, 48
45	128, 129	38, 39	49, 50
46	129, 130	39	50, 51
47	130, 131	40	51, 52, 53
48	131, 132, 133	40, 41	53, 54
49	133, 134	41, 42	54, 55
50	134, 135	42, 43	56, 57
51	135, 136	43, 44	57, 58
52	137, 138	44, 45	58, 59, 60
53	138, 139	45, 46	60, 61
54	139, 140	46, 47	61, 62, 63
55	140, 141, 142	47, 48	63, 64
56	142, 143	48, 49	64, 65, 66
57	143, 144, 145	49, 50	66, 67, 68
58	145, 146	50, 51	68, 69
59	146, 147	51, 52	69, 70
60	147, 148	53	71
61	149	54, 55	72, 73
62	150, 151	56	74, 75
63	151, 152	56, 57	75, 76
64	152, 153	57, 58	76, 77
65	153, 154, 155	58, 59	78, 79
66	155, 156	59, 60	79, 80
67	156, 157, 158	60, 61	80, 81, 82
68	158, 159	61, 62	82, 83
69	159, 160	62, 63	83, 84, 85
70	160, 161, 162	63, 64	85, 86
71	162, 163	64, 65	86, 87, 88
72	163, 164	65, 66	88, 89, 90
73	164, 165	66, 67	90, 91
74	165, 166, 167	67, 68	91, 92, 93
75	167, 168	68, 69	93, 94
76	168, 169, 170	69, 70	94, 95
77	170, 171	70, 71	95, 96, 97
78	171, 172	71, 72	97, 98
79	172, 173, 174	72, 73	98, 99, 100
80	174, 175	73, 74	100, 101
81	175, 176	74, 75	101, 102, 103
82	176, 177, 178	75, 76	103, 104
83	178, 179	76, 77	104, 105
84	179, 180	77, 78	105, 106, 107

Cambridge	Macpherson	Oakeshott	Molesworth
85	180, 181, 182	78, 79	107, 108
86	182, 183	79, 80	108, 109, 110
87	183, 184	80, 81	110, 111
88	184, 185, 186	81, 82	111, 112, 113
89	186, 187	82, 83	113, 114
90	187, 188	83, 84	114, 115, 116
91	189, 190	84, 85	116, 117
92	190, 191	85, 86	117, 118, 119
93	191, 192	86, 87	119, 120
94	192, 193, 194	87, 88	120, 121, 122
95	194, 195	88, 89	122, 123
96	195, 196	89, 90	123, 124, 125
97	196, 197, 198	90, 91	125, 126
98	198, 199	91, 92	126, 127, 128
99	199, 200, 201	92, 93	128, 129, 130
100	201, 202	93, 94	130, 131
101	202, 203	94, 95	131, 132
102	203, 204, 205	95, 96	132, 133, 134
103	205, 206	96, 97	134, 135
104	206, 207, 208	97, 98	135, 136, 137
105	208, 209	98, 99	137, 138
106	209, 210	99, 100	138, 139, 140
107	210, 211, 212	100, 101	140, 141
108	212, 213	101, 102	141, 142, 143
109	213, 214	102, 103	143, 144
110	214, 215, 216	103, 104	144, 145, 146
111	216, 217	104, 105	146, 147
112	217, 218	105, 106	147, 148, 149
113	218, 219, 220	106, 107	149, 150
114	220, 221	107, 108	150, 151, 152
115	221, 222	108	152
117	223	109	153, 154
118	223, 224, 225	109, 110	154, 155
119	225, 226	110, 111	155, 156, 157
120	226, 227	111, 112	157, 158
121	227, 228, 229	112, 113	158, 159, 160
122	229, 230	113, 114	160, 161
123	230, 231, 232	114, 115	161, 162, 163
124	232, 233	115, 116	163, 164
125	233, 234	116, 117	164, 165, 166
126	234, 235, 236	117, 118	166, 167
127	236, 237	118, 119	167, 168
128	237, 238	119, 120	168, 169, 170
129	238, 239, 240	120, 121	170, 171
130	240, 241	121, 122	171, 172, 173
131	241, 242	122, 123	173, 174
132	242, 243, 244	123, 124	174, 175, 176
133	244, 245	124, 125	176, 177, 178
134	245, 246	125, 126	178, 179
135	246, 247, 248	126, 127	179, 180, 181
136	248, 249	127, 128	181, 182

Cambridge	Macpherson	Oakeshott	Molesworth
137	249, 250, 251	128, 129	182, 183, 184
138	251, 252	129, 130	184, 185
139	252, 253	130, 131	185, 186, 187
140	253, 254, 255	131, 132	187, 188
141	255, 256	132, 133	188, 189, 190
142	256, 257	132, 133	190, 191
143	257, 258, 259	134, 135	191, 192, 193
144	259, 260	135, 136	193, 194, 195
145	260, 261, 262	136, 137	195, 196
146	262, 263	137, 138	196, 197, 198
147	263, 264	138, 139	198, 199
148	264, 265, 266	139	199, 200, 201
149	266, 267	140	201, 202
150	267, 268	141, 142	202, 203, 204
151	268, 269, 270	142, 143	204, 205
152	270, 271	143, 144	205, 206, 207
153	271, 272	144, 145	207, 208
154	272, 273, 274	145	208, 209
155	274, 275	146	210, 211
156	275, 276	146, 147	211, 212
157	276, 277, 278	148, 149	212, 213, 214
158	278, 279	149	214, 215
159	279, 280	149, 150	215, 216, 217
160	280, 281, 282	150, 151	217, 218
161	282, 283	151, 152	218, 219, 220
162	283, 284, 285	152, 153	220, 221
163	285, 286	153, 154	221, 222, 223
164	286, 287	154, 155	223, 224
165	287, 288	155, 156	224, 225
166	289, 290	156, 157	226, 227
167	290, 291	157, 158	227, 228
168	291, 292	158, 159	228, 229, 230
169	292, 293, 294	159, 160	230, 231
170	294, 295	160, 161	231, 232
171	295, 296	161, 162	232, 233, 234
172	296, 297, 298	162, 163	234, 235
173	298, 299	163, 164	235, 236, 237
174	299, 300	164	237, 238
175	300, 301, 302	164, 165	238, 239, 240
176	302, 303	165, 166	240, 241
177	303, 304	166, 167	241, 242, 243
178	304, 305, 306	167, 168	243, 244
179	306, 307	168, 169	244, 245, 246
180	307, 308	169, 170	246, 247
181	308, 309, 310	170, 171	247, 248, 249
182	310, 311	171, 172	249, 250
183	311, 312	172, 173	250, 251
184	312, 313, 314	173, 174	251, 252, 253
185	314, 315	174, 175	253, 254
186	315, 316	175, 176	254, 255, 256
187	316, 317, 318	176, 177	256, 257

Cambridge	Macpherson	Oakeshott	Molesworth
188	318, 319	177, 178	257, 258, 259
189	319, 320	178, 179	259, 260
190	320, 321, 322	179, 180	259, 260
191	322, 323	180, 181	262, 263
192	323, 324	181, 182	263, 264, 265
193	324, 325, 326	182, 183	265, 266
194	326, 327	183, 184	266, 267, 268
195	327, 328	184	268, 269
196	328, 329, 330	184, 185	269, 270, 271
197	330, 331	185, 186	271, 272
198	331, 332, 333	186, 187	272, 273, 274
199	333, 334	187, 188	274, 275
200	334, 335	188, 189	275, 276, 277
201	335, 336	189, 190	277, 278
202	336, 337, 338	190, 191	278, 279, 280
203	338, 339	191, 192	280, 281
204	339, 340, 341	192, 193	281, 282, 283
205	341, 342	193, 194	283, 284
206	342, 343	194, 195	284, 285, 286
207	343, 344, 345	195, 196	286, 287
208	345, 346	196, 197	287, 288, 289
209	346, 347, 348	197, 198	289, 290
210	348, 349	198, 199	290, 291, 292
211	349, 350	199, 200	292, 293
212	350, 351, 352	200, 201	293, 294, 295
213	352, 353	201, 202	295, 296
214	353, 354	202, 203	297, 298
215	354, 355	203, 204	298, 299
216	355, 356, 357	204, 205	299, 300, 301
217	357, 358	205, 206	301, 302
218	358, 359	206, 207	302, 303, 304
219	359, 360, 361	207, 208	304, 305
220	361, 362	208, 209	305, 306, 307
221	362, 363	209, 210	307, 308
222	363, 364, 365	210, 211	308, 309, 310
223	365, 366	211, 212	310, 311
224	366, 367, 368	212, 213	311, 312, 313
225	368, 369	213, 214	313, 314
226	369, 370	214, 215	314, 315, 316
227	370, 371, 372	215, 216	316, 317
228	372, 373	216, 217	318, 319
229	373, 374	217	319, 320
230	374, 375, 376	217, 218	320, 321, 322
231	376, 377	219	322, 323
232	377, 378	220, 221	323, 324, 325
233	378, 379, 380	221	325, 326
234	380, 381	221, 222	326, 327, 328
235	381, 382	222, 223	328, 329
236	382, 383, 384	223, 224	329, 330, 331
237	384, 385	224, 225	331, 332
238	385, 386, 387	225, 226	332, 333, 334

Cambridge	Macpherson	Oakeshott	Molesworth
239	387, 388	226, 227	334, 335
240	388, 389	227, 228	335, 336, 337
241	389, 390, 391	228, 229	337, 338
242	391, 392	229, 230	338, 339, 340
243	392, 393	230, 231	340, 341
244	393, 394	231, 232	341, 342, 343
245	395, 396	232, 233	343, 344
246	396, 397	233, 234	344, 345, 346
247	397, 398	234, 235	346, 347
248	398, 399, 400	235, 236	347, 348, 349
249	400, 401	236, 237	349, 350
250	401, 402, 403	237, 238	350, 351, 352
251	403, 404	238, 239	352, 353, 354
252	404, 405	239, 240	354, 355
253	405, 406, 407	240, 241	355, 356
254	407, 408	241	356, 357, 358
255	409	242	359, 360
256	409, 410, 411	243	360, 361
257	411, 412	243, 244	361, 362, 363
258	412, 413, 414	244, 245	363, 364
259	414, 415	245, 246	364, 365
260	415, 416	246, 247	366, 367
261	416, 417	247, 248	367, 368
262	417, 418, 419	248, 249	368, 369, 370
263	419, 420	249, 250	370, 371, 372
264	420, 421	250, 251	372, 373
265	421, 422, 423	251, 252	373, 374, 375
266	423, 424	252, 253	375, 376
267	424, 425	253, 254	376, 377, 378
268	425, 426, 427	254, 255	378, 379
269	427, 428	255, 256	379, 380, 381
270	428, 429, 430	256, 257	381, 382
271	430, 431	257, 258	382, 383, 384
272	431, 432	258, 259	384, 385
273	432, 433, 434	259, 260	385, 386, 387
274	434, 435	260, 261	387, 388
275	435, 436	261, 262	388, 389, 390
276	436, 437, 438	262	390, 391
277	438, 439	262, 263	391, 392, 393
278	439, 440	263, 264	393, 394
279	440, 441, 442	264, 265	394, 395, 396
280	442, 443	266	396, 397
281	443, 444	266, 267	397, 398, 399
282	444, 445, 446	267, 268	399, 400
283	446, 447	268, 269	400, 401, 402
284	447, 448, 449	269, 270	402, 403, 404
285	449, 450	270, 271	404, 405
286	450, 451	271, 272	405, 406
287	451, 452	272, 273	407, 408
288	452, 453, 454	273, 274	408, 409, 410
289	454, 455	274, 275	410, 411

Cambridge	Macpherson	Oakeshott	Molesworth
290	455, 456	275, 276	411, 412, 413
291	456, 457, 458	276, 277	413, 414
292	458, 459	277, 278	414, 415, 416
293	459, 460, 461	278, 279	416, 417, 418
294	461, 462	279, 280	418, 419
295	462, 463	280, 281	419, 420, 421
296	463, 464, 465	281, 282	421, 422
297	465, 466	282, 283	422, 423, 424
298	466, 467	283, 284	424, 425
299	467, 468, 469	284, 285	425, 426, 427
300	469, 470	285, 286	427, 428
301	470, 471, 472	286, 287	428, 429, 430
302	472, 473	287, 288	430, 431
303	473, 474	288, 289	431, 432, 433
304	474, 475, 476	289	433, 434
305	476, 477	289, 290	434, 435, 436
306	477, 478	290, 291	436, 437
307	478, 479, 480	291, 292	437, 438, 439
308	480, 481	292, 293	439, 440
309	481, 482	293, 294	440, 441, 442
310	482, 483, 484	294, 295	442, 443
311	484, 485	295, 296	443, 444, 445
312	485, 486	296, 297	445, 446
313	486, 487, 488	297, 298	446, 447, 448
314	488, 489	298, 299	448, 449
315	489, 490	299, 300	449, 450, 451
316	490, 491, 492	300, 301	451, 452, 453
317	492, 493	301, 302	453, 454
318	493, 494	302, 303	454, 455, 456
319	494, 495, 496	303, 304	456, 457
320	496, 497	304, 305	457, 458
321	497, 498	305, 306	458, 459, 460
322	498, 499, 500	306, 307	460, 461
323	500, 501	307, 308	461, 462, 463
324	501, 502	308, 309	463, 464
325	502, 503, 504	309, 310	464, 465, 466
326	504, 505	310, 311	466, 467, 468
327	505, 506	311, 312	468, 469
328	506, 507, 508	312, 313	469, 470, 471
329	508, 509	313, 314	471, 472
330	509, 510, 511	314, 315	472, 473, 474
331	511, 512	315	474, 475
332	512, 513	316	475, 476
333	513, 514	316, 317	476, 477, 478
334	514, 515, 516	317, 318	478, 479
335	516, 517	318, 319	479, 480, 481
336	517, 518	319, 320	481, 482, 483
337.	518, 519, 520	320, 321	483, 484
338	520, 521	321, 322	484, 485
339	521, 522	322, 323	485, 486, 487
340	522, 523, 524	323, 324	487, 488, 489

Cambridge	Macpherson	Oakeshott	Molesworth
341	524, 525	324, 325	489, 490
342	525, 526, 527	325, 326	490, 491, 492
343	527, 528	326, 327	492, 493
344	528, 529	327, 328	493, 494, 495
345	529, 530, 531	328, 329	495, 496
346	531, 532	329, 330	496, 497, 498
347	532, 533	330, 331	498, 499
348	533, 534, 535	331, 332	499, 500, 501
349	535, 536	332, 333	501, 502, 503
350	536, 537, 538	333, 334	503, 504
351	538, 539	334, 335	504, 505, 506
352	539, 540	335, 336	506, 507
353	540, 541, 542	336, 337	507, 508, 509
354	542, 543	337, 338	509, 510
355	543, 544	338, 339	510, 511, 512
356	544, 545, 546	339, 340	512, 513
357	546, 547	340, 341	513, 514, 515
358	547, 548, 549	341, 342	515, 516
359	549, 550	342, 343	516, 517, 518
360	550, 551	343	518, 519
361	551, 552, 553	343, 344	519, 520, 521
362	553, 554	344, 345	521, 522
363	554, 555, 556	345, 346	522, 523, 524
364	556, 557	346, 347	524, 525, 526
365	557, 558	347, 348	526, 527
366	558, 559, 560	348, 349	527, 528, 529
367	560, 561	349, 350	529, 530
368	561, 562, 563	350, 351	530, 531, 532
369	563, 564	351, 352	532, 533
370	564, 565	352, 353	533, 534, 535
371	565, 566, 567	353, 354	535, 536, 537
372	567, 568	354, 355	537, 538
373	568, 569	355, 356	538, 539, 540
374	569, 570, 571	356, 357	540, 541
375	571, 572	357, 358	541, 542, 543
376	572, 573	358, 359	543, 544
377	573, 574, 575	359, 360	544, 545, 546
378	575, 576	360, 361	546, 547
379	576, 577, 578	361, 362	547, 548, 549
380	578, 579	362, 363	549, 550
381	579, 580	363, 364	550, 551, 552
382	580, 581, 582	364, 365	552, 553, 554
383	582, 583	365, 366	554, 555
384	583, 584, 585	366, 367	555, 556, 557
385	585, 586	367, 368	557, 558
386	586, 587	368, 369	558, 559, 560
387	587, 588, 589	369, 370	560, 561
388	589, 590	370, 371	561, 562, 563
389	590, 591	371, 372	563, 564, 565
390	591, 592, 593	372, 373	565, 566
391	593, 594	373, 374	566, 567, 568

Cambridge	Macpherson	Oakeshott	Molesworth
392	594, 595, 596	374	568, 569
393	596, 597	374, 375	569, 570, 571
394	597, 598	375, 376	571, 572
395	598, 599, 600	376, 377	572, 573, 574
396	600, 601	377, 378	574, 575
397	601, 602	378, 379	575, 576, 577
398	602, 603, 604	379, 380	577, 578
399	604, 605	380, 381	578, 579, 580
400	605, 606	381, 382	580, 581
401	606, 607, 608	382, 383	581, 582, 583
402	608, 609	383, 384	583, 584
403	609, 610, 611	384, 385	584, 585, 586
404	611, 612	385, 386	586, 587
405	612, 613	386, 387	587, 588
406	613, 614, 615	387, 388	588, 589, 590
407	615, 616	388, 389	590, 591
408	616, 617	389, 390	591, 592, 593
409	617, 618, 619	390, 391	593, 594, 595
410	619, 620	391, 392	595, 596
411	620, 621, 622	392, 393	596, 597, 598
412	622, 623	393, 394	598, 599
413	623, 624	394, 395	599, 600, 601
414	624, 625, 626	395, 396	601, 602
415	626	396	602
417	627	397	603, 604
418	628, 629	397, 398	604, 605
419	629, 630	398, 399	605, 606, 607
420	630, 631	399, 400	607, 608
421	632, 633	400, 401	608, 609
422	633, 634	401, 402	609, 610, 611
423	634, 635	402, 403	611, 612
424	636, 637	403, 404	612, 613, 614
425	637, 638	404, 405	614, 615
426	638, 639	405, 406	615, 616, 617
427	639, 640, 641	406, 407	617, 618
428	641, 642	407, 408	618, 619, 620
429	642, 643	408, 409	620, 621
430	643, 644, 645	409	621, 622, 623
431	645, 646	409, 410	623, 624, 625
432	646, 647	410, 411	625, 626
433	647, 648, 649	411, 412	626, 627
434	649, 650	412, 413	627, 628, 629
435	650, 651, 652	413, 414	629, 630
436	652, 653	414, 415	630, 631, 632
437	653, 654	415, 416	632, 633, 634
438	654, 655, 656	416, 417	634, 635
439	656, 657	417, 418	635, 636
440	657, 658	418, 419	637, 638
441	658, 659, 660	419, 420	638, 639
442	660, 661	420, 421	639, 640, 641
443	661, 662	421, 422	641, 642

Cambridge	Macpherson	Oakeshott	Molesworth
444	662, 663, 664	422, 423	642, 643, 644
445	664, 665	423, 424	644, 645
446	665, 666	424, 425	645, 646, 647
447	666, 667, 668	425, 426	647, 648
448	668, 669	426, 427	648, 649, 650
449	669, 670, 671	427	650, 651
450	671, 672	427, 428	651, 652, 653
451	672, 673	428, 429	653, 654, 655
452	673, 674, 675	429, 430	655, 656
453	675, 676	430, 431	656, 657, 658
454	676, 677, 678	431, 432	658, 659
455	678, 679	432, 433	659, 660, 661
456	679, 680	433, 434	661, 662
457	680, 681	434, 435	662, 663
458	682, 683	435, 436	664, 665
459	683, 684	436, 437	665, 666
460	684, 685	437, 438	666, 667, 668
461	685, 686, 687	438, 439	668, 669
462	687, 688	439, 440	669, 670, 671
463	688, 689	440, 441	671, 672
464	689, 690, 691	441	672, 673, 674
465	691, 692	441, 442	674, 675
466	692, 693	442, 443	675, 676, 677
467	693, 694, 695	443, 444	677, 678
468	695, 696	444, 445	678, 679, 680
469	696, 697	445, 446	680, 681
470	697, 698, 699	446, 447	681, 682, 683
471	699, 700	447, 448	683, 684
472	700, 701, 702	448, 449	684, 685, 686
473	702, 703	449, 450	686, 687
474	703, 704	450, 451	687, 688, 689
475	704, 705	451, 452	689, 690
476	705, 706, 707	452, 453	690, 691, 692
477	707, 708	453, 454	692, 693
478	708, 709, 710	454, 455	693, 694, 695
479	710, 711	455, 456	695, 696
480	711, 712	456, 457	696, 697, 698
481	712, 713, 714	457, 458	698, 699
482	714, 715	458, 459	699, 700
483	717, 718	460	701, 702
484	718, 719	460, 461	702, 703
485	719, 720	461, 462	703, 704, 705
486	720, 721, 722	462, 463	705, 706
487	722, 723	463, 464	706, 707, 708
488	723, 724	464, 465	708, 709
489	724, 725, 726	465, 466	709, 710, 711
490	726, 727	466, 467	711, 712
491	727, 728	467, 468	712, 713
492	728, 728	468	714

Cambridge Texts in the History of Political Thought

Titles published in the series thus far

Aristotle *The Politics and The Constitution of Athens* (edited by Stephen Everson)
  0 521 48400 6 paperback
Arnold *Culture and Anarchy and other writings* (edited by Stefan Collini)
  0 521 37796 x paperback
Astell *Political Writings* (edited by Patricia Springborg)
  0 521 42845 9 paperback
Augustine *The City of God against the Pagans* (edited by R.W. Dyson)
  0 521 46843 4 paperback
Austin *The Province of Jurisprudence Determined* (edited by Wilfrid E. Rumble)
  0 521 44756 9 paperback
Bacon *The History of the Reign of King Henry VII* (edited by Brian Vickers)
  0 521 58663 1 paperback
Bakunin *Statism and Anarchy* (edited by Marshall Shatz)
  0 521 36973 8 paperback
Baxter *Holy Commonwealth* (edited by William Lamont)
  0 521 40580 7 paperback
Bayle *Political Writings* (edited by Sally L. Jenkinson)
  0 521 47677 1 paperback
Beccaria *On Crimes and Punishments and other writings* (edited by Richard Bellamy)
  0 521 47982 7 paperback
Bentham *Fragment on Government* (introduction by Ross Harrison)
  0 521 35929 5 paperback
Bernstein *The Preconditions of Socialism* (edited by Henry Tudor)
  0 521 39808 8 paperback
Bodin *On Sovereignty* (edited by Julian H. Franklin)
  0 521 34992 3 paperback
Bolingbroke *Political Writings* (edited by David Armitage)
  0 521 58697 6 paperback
Bossuet *Politics Drawn from the Very Words of Holy Scripture* (edited by Patrick Riley)
  0 521 36807 3 paperback
The British Idealists (edited by David Boucher)
  0 521 45951 6 paperback
Burke *Pre-Revolutionary Writings* (edited by Ian Harris)
  0 521 36800 6 paperback
Christine De Pizan *The Book of the Body Politic* (edited by Kate Langdon Forhan)
  0 521 42259 0 paperback
Cicero *On Duties* (edited by M. T. Griffin and E. M. Atkins)
  0 521 34835 8 paperback
Cicero *On the Commonwealth and On the Laws* (edited by James E. G. Zetzel)
  0 521 45959 1 paperback
Comte *Early Political Writings* (edited by H. S. Jones)
  0 521 46923 6 paperback
Conciliarism and Papalism (edited by J. H. Burns and Thomas M. Izbicki)
  0 521 47674 7 paperback
Constant *Political Writings* (edited by Biancamaria Fontana)
  0 521 31632 4 paperback
Dante *Monarchy* (edited by Prue Shaw)
  0 521 56781 5 paperback
Diderot *Political Writings* (edited by John Hope Mason and Robert Wokler)
  0 521 36911 8 paperback
The Dutch Revolt (edited by Martin van Gelderen)
  0 521 39809 6 paperback
Early Greek Political Thought from Homer to the Sophists (edited by Michael Gagarin and Paul Woodruff)
  0 521 43768 7 paperback
The Early Political Writings of the German Romantics (edited by Frederick C. Beiser)
  0 521 44951 0 paperback
The English Levellers (edited by Andrew Sharp)
  0 521 62511 4 paperback
Erasmus *The Education of a Christian Prince* (edited by Lisa Jardine)
  0 521 58811 1 paperback
Fenelon *Telemachus* (edited by Patrick Riley)
  0 521 45662 2 paperback

Ferguson *An Essay on the History of Civil Society* (edited by Fania Oz-Salzberger)
   0 521 44736 4 paperback
Filmer *Patriarcha and Other Writings* (edited by Johann P. Sommerville)
   0 521 39903 3 paperback
Fletcher *Political Works* (edited by John Robertson)
   0 521 43994 9 paperback
Sir John Fortescue *On the Laws and Governance of England* (edited by Shelley Lockwood)
   0 521 58996 7 paperback
Fourier *The Theory of the Four Movements* (edited by Gareth Stedman Jones and Ian Patterson)
   0 521 35693 8 paperback
Gramsci *Pre-Prison Writings* (edited by Richard Bellamy)
   0 521 42307 4 paperback
Guicciardini *Dialogue on the Government of Florence* (edited by Alison Brown)
   0 521 45623 1 paperback
Harrington *The Commonwealth of Oceana* and *A System of Politics* (edited by J. G. A. Pocock)
   0 521 42329 5 paperback
Hegel *Elements of the Philosophy of Right* (edited by Allen W. Wood and H. B. Nisbet)
   0 521 34888 9 paperback
Hegel *Political Writings* (edited by Laurence Dickey and H. B. Nisbet)
   0 521 45979 3 paperback
Hobbes *On the Citizen* (edited by Michael Silverthorne and Richard Tuck)
   0 521 43780 6 paperback
Hobbes *Leviathan* (edited by Richard Tuck)
   0 521 56797 1 paperback
Hobhouse *Liberalism and Other Writings* (edited by James Meadowcroft)
   0 521 43726 1 paperback
Hooker *Of the Laws of Ecclesiastical Polity* (edited by A. S. McGrade)
   0 521 37908 3 paperback
Hume *Political Essays* (edited by Knud Haakonssen)
   0 521 46639 3 paperback
King James VI and I *Political Writings* (edited by Johann P. Sommerville)
   0 521 44729 1 paperback
Jefferson *Political Writings* (edited by Joyce Appleby and Terence Ball)
   0 521 64841 6 paperback
John of Salisbury *Policraticus* (edited by Cary Nederman)
   0 521 36701 8 paperback
Kant *Political Writings* (edited by H. S. Reiss and H. B. Nisbet)
   0 521 39837 1 paperback
Knox *On Rebellion* (edited by Roger A. Mason)
   0 521 39988 2 paperback
Kropotkin *The Conquest of Bread and other writings* (edited by Marshall Shatz)
   0 521 45990 7 paperback
Lawson *Politica sacra et civilis* (edited by Conal Condren)
   0 521 39248 9 paperback
Leibniz *Political Writings* (edited by Patrick Riley)
   0 521 35899 X paperback
The Levellers (edited by Andrew Sharp)
   0 521 62511 4 paperback
Locke *Political Essays* (edited by Mark Goldie)
   0 521 47861 8 paperback
Locke *Two Treatises of Government* (edited by Peter Laslett)
   0 521 35730 6 paperback
Loyseau *A Treatise of Orders and Plain Dignities* (edited by Howell A. Lloyd)
   0 521 45624 X paperback
Luther and Calvin on Secular Authority (edited by Harro Höpfl)
   0 521 34986 9 paperback
Machiavelli *The Prince* (edited by Quentin Skinner and Russell Price)
   0 521 34993 1 paperback
de Maistre *Considerations on France* (edited by Isaiah Berlin and Richard Lebrun)
   0 521 46628 8 paperback
Malthus *An Essay on the Principle of Population* (edited by Donald Winch)
   0 521 42972 2 paperback
Marsiglio of Padua *Defensor minor* and *De translatione Imperii* (edited by Cary Nederman)
   0 521 40846 6 paperback
Marx *Early Political Writings* (edited by Joseph O'Malley)
   0 521 34994 X paperback
Marx *Later Political Writings* (edited by Terrell Carver)
   0 521 36739 5 paperback

James Mill *Political Writings* (edited by Terence Ball)

    0 521 38748 5 paperback

J. S. Mill *On Liberty*, with *The Subjection of Women* and *Chapters on Socialism* (edited by Stefan Collini)

    0 521 37917 2 paperback

Milton *Political Writings* (edited by Martin Dzelzainis)

    0 521 34866 8 paperback

Montesquieu *The Spirit of the Laws* (edited by Anne M. Cohler, Basia Carolyn Miller and Harold Samuel Stone)

    0 521 36974 6 paperback

More *Utopia* (edited by George M. Logan and Robert M. Adams)

    0 521 40318 9 paperback

Morris *News from Nowhere* (edited by Krishan Kumar)

    0 521 42233 7 paperback

Nicholas of Cusa *The Catholic Concordance* (edited by Paul E. Sigmund)

    0 521 56773 4 paperback

Nietzsche *On the Genealogy of Morality* (edited by Keith Ansell-Pearson)

    0 521 40610 2 paperback

Paine *Political Writings* (edited by Bruce Kuklick)

    0 521 66799 2 paperback

Plato *The Republic* (edited by G. R. F. Ferrari and Tom Griffith)

    0 521 48443 X paperback

Plato *Statesman* (edited by Julia Annas and Robin Waterfield)

    0 521 44778 X paperback

Price *Political Writings* (edited by D. O. Thomas)

    0 521 40969 1 paperback

Priestley *Political Writings* (edited by Peter Miller)

    0 521 42561 1 paperback

Proudhon *What is Property?* (edited by Donald R. Kelley and Bonnie G. Smith)

    0 521 40556 4 paperback

Pufendorf *On the Duty of Man and Citizen according to Natural Law* (edited by James Tully)

    0 521 35980 5 paperback

The Radical Reformation (edited by Michael G. Baylor)

    0 521 37948 2 paperback

Rousseau *The Discourses and other early political writings* (edited by Victor Gourevitch)

    0 521 42445 3 paperback

Rousseau *The Social Contract and other later political writings* (edited by Victor Gourevitch)

    0 521 42446 1 paperback

Seneca *Moral and Political Essays* (edited by John Cooper and John Procope)

    0 521 34818 8 paperback

Sidney *Court Maxims* (edited by Hans W. Blom, Eco Haitsma Mulier and Ronald Janse)

    0 521 46736 5 paperback

Sorel *Reflections on Violence* (edited by Jeremy Jennings)

    0 521 55910 3 paperback

Spencer *The Man versus the State* and *The Proper Sphere of Government* (edited by John Offer)

    0 521 43740 7 paperback

Stirner *The Ego and Its Own* (edited by David Leopold)

    0 521 45647 9 paperback

Thoreau *Political Writings* (edited by Nancy Rosenblum)

    0 521 47675 5 paperback

Utopias of the British Enlightenment (edited by Gregory Claeys)

    0 521 45590 1 paperback

Vitoria *Political Writings* (edited by Anthony Pagden and Jeremy Lawrance)

    0 521 36714 X paperback

Voltaire *Political Writings* (edited by David Williams)

    0 521 43727 X paperback

Weber *Political Writings* (edited by Peter Lassman and Ronald Speirs)

    0 521 39719 7 paperback

William of Ockham *A Short Discourse on Tyrannical Government* (edited by A. S. McGrade and John Kilcullen)

    0 521 35803 5 paperback

William of Ockham *A Letter to the Friars Minor and other writings* (edited by A. S. McGrade and John Kilcullen)

    0 521 35804 3 paperback

Wollstonecraft *A Vindication of the Rights of Men* and *A Vindication of the Rights of Woman* (edited by Sylvana Tomaselli)

    0 521 43633 8 paperback